SKELETON
KEYS

SKELETON KEYS

AN INTRODUCTION TO HUMAN SKELETAL MORPHOLOGY, DEVELOPMENT, AND ANALYSIS

Jeffrey H. Schwartz

New York   Oxford
OXFORD UNIVERSITY PRESS
1995

Oxford University Press

Oxford   New York
Athens   Auckland   Bangkok   Bombay
Calcutta   Cape Town   Dar es Salaam   Delhi
Florence   Hong Kong   Istanbul   Karachi
Kuala Lumpur   Madras   Madrid   Melbourne
Mexico City   Nairobi   Paris   Singapore
Taipei   Tokyo   Toronto

and associated companies in
Berlin   Ibadan

Published by Oxford University Press, Inc.,
198 Madison Avenue, New York, New York 10016

Oxford is a registered trademark of Oxford University Press

Library of Congress Cataloging-in-Publication Data
Schwartz, Jeffrey H.
Skeleton keys : an introduction to human skeletal morphology,
development, and analysis / Jeffrey H. Schwartz.
p. cm.   Includes bibliographical references and index.
ISBN 0-19-505638-8
1. Human skeleton.   2. Forensic osteology.   I. Title.
QM101.S38   1995
611'.71—dc20   94-49420

3 5 7 9 8 6 4 2

Printed in the United States of America
on acid-free paper

Preface

This book was conceived with the idea of bringing some originality to the study of human osteology while also adhering to the format typical of these texts. However, the end product does not fit the mold. There is much more basic morphology than usual: somewhat like a *Gray's Anatomy* of bones. But rather than base the descriptions on only one or two specimens, I used at least eight and often as many as fourteen specimens of the same bone in conjunction with illustrations and descriptions available in the literature. Thus the descriptions provided here incorporate variation as a normal facet of morphology. I have attempted to put morphology into a developmental and ultimately, systematic context.

Much of the approach used in this book comes from a developmental perspective. Thus, for example, some items that typically are included in a pathology chapter are here introduced in the first chapter, which deals with normal and abnormal aspects of bone growth. The topic of nonmetric variation is also discussed in terms of development. In another break with tradition, the subject of sexing the human skeleton is included in the chapter on nonmetric variation as a subset of the latter. Together, these topics are discussed in the last chapter as "differentially expressed morphological character states." As the last chapter, it emphasizes (for me, anyway) the reason for studying human skeletal morphology in the first place: trying to figure out the systematics of *Homo sapiens* at, below, and above the species level. The appendices at the end of the book are meant to provide information—definitions, terminology, synonomies, and anthropometric formulae—that will help guide most, if not all, students through this as well as most other osteological publications. The comparative osteology appendix is meant to illustrate basic similarities and differences between the human skeleton and some common mammalian skeletal remains which—especially if fragmentary—might initially be mistaken because of their size to be human. Perhaps these renderings might inspire curious osteologists to broaden their background and become more conversant in comparative mammalian osteology.

There is, however, a limit on just how much can be usefully provided in any text. For those interested in trace element and stable isotope analysis, I recommend the contributions by, respectively, Sandford (1992) and Katzenberg (1992), as well as the volume edited by Price (1989). The article by Hancock et al. (1989) is a useful review of some of the problems resulting from bone diagenesis. On a forensic note, the volume edited by İşcan and Helmer (1993) is the most recent compendium on craniofacial reconstruction.

Essentially, then, this book is an inquiry into why we should study and practice human osteology. For example, how can we think about the topics often presented in cookbook fashion—sexing, aging, nonmetric variation, anthropometry—in, perhaps, a broader context? To be sure, it would be counterproductive to reject or choose to exclude the approaches or techniques that have become commonplace and, thus, expected in a textbook. But it also would seem to be the responsibility of the textbook author to raise questions, point out errors, propose alternative ways of thinking about and interpreting things, and suggest possible avenues of future research. Although not typical of traditional textbooks, I think the latter steps certainly represent the spirit of intellectual inquiry—which is what a textbook ultimately should stimulate. I hope that I have at least made some progress in reaching that goal.

Inasmuch as I am not the same individual who years ago proposed doing this textbook, I owe some of this change to the many students in my osteology classes who, over the years, have asked those kinds of questions that often demand a rethinking of what is taken for granted. I thank them all for contributing to the formulation of this book. Although I had pursued human skeletal studies for decades, much of the way in which I think about, first, development came from early on working with Andrew Lumsden (Guy's Hospital, London) and, second, systematics—especially below the species level—was inspired by my collaborations with Ian Tattersall (American Museum of Natural History, New York). Questions raised in this book and alternative ways of thinking about human skeletal analysis also derive from a broad study on *Homo sapiens* that I began while a Kalbfleisch Fellow in the Department of Anthropology, American Museum of Natural History. I thank Jaymie Brauer and Penny Gordon for their help in collecting data for this latter project and Linda Winkler, Joan Kimmel, David Hyland, Laurie Corwin, and Andrea Peffley for reading and commenting on earlier versions of various chapters. More specifically, my father, Jack J. Schwartz, and Joan Kimmel helped clarify some of the more confusing aspects of pathology, Linda Winkler and Gen Suwa offered helpful criticisms on aspects of sexing, Owen Lovejoy talked me through the determination of skeletal age using his multifactorial approach, and Frank Houghton provided valuable discussion of Harris lines. David Hyland assisted in the compilation of some the appendices.

Several textbooks are now available in which individual bones and teeth are illustrated photographically. Each type of illustrative representation has its good and bad points. I have chosen to illustrate most items in this book in the form of drawings or diagrams. Photography is used primarily to illustrate types of pathology. I thank John Anderton for the drawings of adult skeletal morphology, Diana Salles for the drawings of the fetal postcranium and the comparative osteology appendix, and Tim D. Smith for all other hand-rendered illustrations. Tim Smith and Annie Burrows labeled all illustrations. David Burr generously provided photographs of bone histology and Betsy Dumont those on tooth microstructure. All other photographs were taken by the author. Special thanks go to Ian Tattersall (American Museum of Natural History), Herbert Langdon (University of Pittsurgh Dental School), and Ronald Michaels (California State College, PA) for access to specimens illustrated here.

Bill Curtis (formerly of Oxford University Press) took the initial gamble on this book and Kirk Jensen, the editor who inherited the good and the bad, valiantly picked up the loose ends and allowed the project to come to completion. I am certain that Kirk and his colleagues at Oxford University Press are relieved to see closure on this effort, but probably no one is as relieved as my wife.

Pittsburgh   J.H.S.
December 1994

Contents

SKELETON
KEYS

An Introduction to the Skeleton and Bone

In this chapter we begin with the large-scale view of the skeleton and the terminology of anatomical direction. This will allow the osteologist to orient an isolated whole bone or bone fragment in its proper anatomical position. Throughout this book, the positions of specific anatomical features and landmarks, as well as the positions of anatomical features relative to one another, are described in the text rather than being left to the reader to decipher from the accompanying drawings alone. The goal is to provide as many opportunities as possible for gaining a working knowledge of each bone so that, when confronted with a small bone (e.g. a carpal or wrist bone) or a small fragment of bone, the student will be able to identify it accurately and thus to incorporate it into the appropriate analysis. From the broader picture, we narrow our focus to the finer details: to the anatomy of a bone, its organic and nonorganic constituents, its cellular development, and its growth, both normal and abnormal. Ontogenetic changes in the shapes and sizes of individual bones are dealt with in the specific chapters on these bones.

The Terminology of Anatomical Position

In principle, one should be able to refer to the different sides of an animal's body simply by using such terms as "front," "back," "up," "down." More complicated forms of reference could be "toward the middle of the body" and "away from the middle of the body." Unfortunately, since such forms of reference are seen as unscientific, a lexicon of terms has been devised to refer to the different anatomical planes and directions. The situation is made even more complicated by the fact that humans walk upright and bipedally; thus, their vertebral columns and long bones are held vertically and the skull sits atop the vertebral column. In contrast, most other mammals are quadrupedal and, on the same principle as a suspension bridge, have a horizontal vertebral column that lies at a right angle to the vertically oriented limbs; the skull, while facing forward, as in humans, typically articulates with the vertebral column from behind. A consequence of these differences between humans and other mammals is that the sides of the same bone would be identified differently in each because the bone is oriented differently in each. Although throughout the book I use the terminology relevant to humans, the contrasts between humans and other mammals are presented here.

Terminology and simple definitions that are applicable to all vertebrates, not just to mammals, include the following (see Figures 1–1 to 1–3): **anterior** (toward the front of the body; in the direction of the eyes); **posterior** (toward the rear of the body; in the direction away from the eyes); **cranial** (toward the head); **caudal** (toward the tail); **superior** (toward the highest or uppermost part of a bone); **inferior** (toward the lower or underside of a bone); **proximal** (toward the point of attachment of a bone); **distal** (away from the point of attachment or articulation of a bone); **dorsal** (toward the vertebral column);

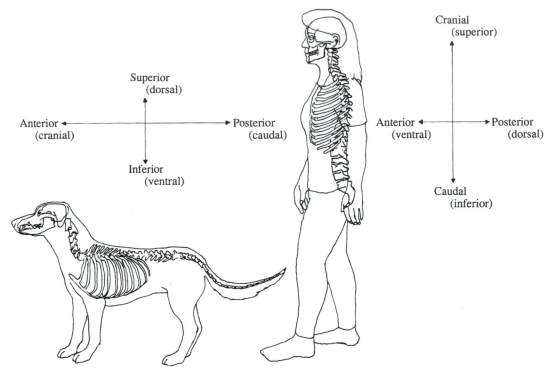

Figure 1–1   Terms used for defining anatomical position in the axial skeleton of a quadruped *(left)* and biped *(right)*.

ventral (toward the belly); **medial** (toward the midline of the body); **lateral** (away from the midline of the body). Because humans are upright, bipedal animals, some of these terms become interchangeable (Figures 1–1 to 1–3).

In humans, "anterior" is the same direction as "ventral" while "posterior" is equivalent to "dorsal." I follow convention throughout most of the text, in using "anterior" and "posterior"—but, on occasion, when it seems to make the point better, I use "dorsal" or "ventral." For example, it is perhaps more meaningful to refer to the relevant sides of the human sternum (breastbone), the scapula (shoulder blade), or the os coxae (pelvis or hipbone) as dorsal and ventral rather than anterior and posterior. "Anterior" and "posterior" are preferred when referring, for example, to the long bones of the arm or leg. This would be the terminology used for these bones in quadrupeds.

In a quadrupedal animal, "cranial" and "caudal" denote the same directions as "anterior" and "posterior," respectively, in a human. In humans, the terms "cranial," "superior," and (in most cases) "proximal" are equivalent,

as are "caudal," "inferior," and (in most cases) "distal." The terms "cranial" and "caudal" are used most appropriately, for example, in referring to opposite ends of a vertebra; one end points toward the head and the other toward the tail, regardless of whether the animal is a biped or a quadruped. As defined above, "proximal" refers to the point of attachment of a bone to the body, or the end of the bone that, by linkage, attaches to the body. Thus the upper end of the humerus is the proximal end of that bone because it attaches to the body via the shoulder joint, and the upper end of the radius is its proximal end because it attaches to the body via the humerus and shoulder joint. "Distal" refers to the other end of a bone for which a proximal end can be defined.

Units of the Skeleton and Their Articular Relations

The skeleton typically is subdivided in two different ways. One subdivision distinguishes the head region—the **cranial skeleton**—from the

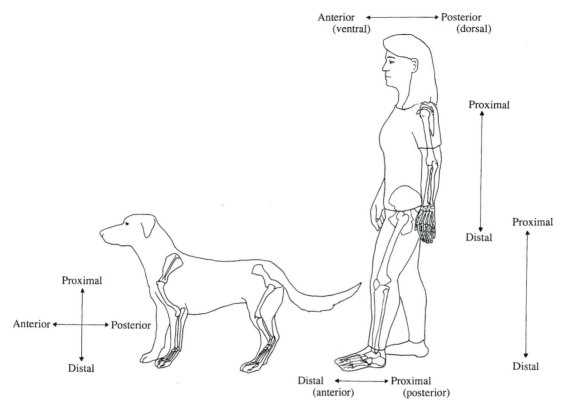

Figure 1–2 Terms used for defining anatomical position in the appendicular skeleton of a quadruped *(left)* and biped *(right)*.

rest of the skeleton, the **postcranial skeleton**; the term "postcranial" applies most literally to quadrupedal animals in which the bulk of the skeleton, indeed, does lie posterior to the skull. The other major subdivision delineates an **axial** from an **appendicular skeleton**. The axial skeleton consists of the skull, the vertebral column, the sternum, and the ribs. The limbs and the bones that link the limbs with the axial skeleton (the scapula and clavicle and the os coxae) make up the appendicular skeleton.

The region at which two or more bones contact one another is referred to as a **joint**. However, in contrast to the general notion of free motion implied by the word "joint," there are different categories of joints, each defined by certain ranges of motion and tissue components. The three major categories of joints, proceeding from the most to least mobile, are **synovial**, **cartilaginous**, and **fibrous**.

In general, a **synovial joint** [obsolete terminology, diarthrosis (pl. -es)] is a freely movable joint; it is characterized by the presence of lu-

bricated articular cartilage on the opposing bony surfaces and an articular cavity that is bound by a fibrous joint capsule lined with a fluid-secreting synovial membrane. The categories of synovial joints are **plane, hinge, pivot, ellipsoidal, saddle,** and **ball-and-socket**. Plane, hinge, and pivot joints are *monaxial joints* (i.e. motion is confined to a single axis); ellipsoidal and saddle joints are *biaxial;* and ball-and-socket joints are *multiaxial*. Some joints are referred to as *composite* because they incorporate features of more than one joint type (e.g. the knee, which is typically identified as a hinge joint, it is more accurately classified as a sliding hinge joint). Definitions of terms of movement may be found in Appendix C.

In a **plane joint** (also called a *gliding* or *sliding joint*), the opposing bones can slide across one another because their articular surfaces are flat or nearly flat. Movement across a plane joint is limited, however: e.g. in the acromioclavicular (shoulder blade-collarbone), sacroiliacal (posterior pelvic), proximal tibiofibular,

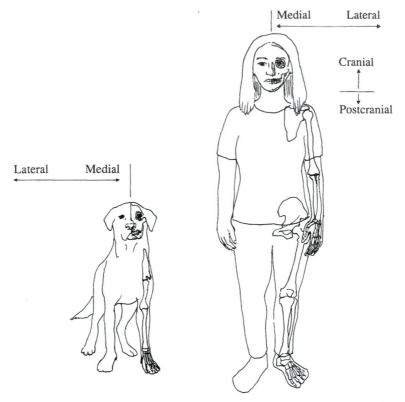

Figure 1–3   Terms used for defining anatomical position in the appendicular skeleton of a quadruped *(left)* and biped *(right)*.

intercarpal (wrist), carpometacarpal (wrist-palm, except that of the pollex), and inter-metacarpal (palm) joints and the corresponding joints of the foot. In a **hinge joint** (also called a *ginglymus)*, the motions of flexion and extension of the opposing bones rotate around an axis that is at a right angle to the long axis of the opposing bones [e.g. tibiofemoral (knee), ta-locrural (ankle), humeroulnar (elbow), and inter-phalangeal joints]. A **pivot joint** (also called a *trochoidal joint)* is characterized by rotatory movement around the long axis of the opposing bone [e.g. the atlantoaxial joint (between the first and second cervical vertebrae) and proximal and distal radioulnar joints].

An **ellipsoidal joint** (also called a *condyloid joint)* allows movement in two axes that are at right angles to one another. The shapes of the articular surfaces of opposing bones are ellipsoidal when viewed on end. One bone's articular surface is mildly convex in two dimensions, but the curvature is unequal along the two axes

that define the ellipse; the opposing bone's articular surface is a concave mirror image of the former. The unequal curvature of these articular surfaces limits rotation. However, flexion, extension, abduction (movement away from the midline of the body), adduction (movement toward the midline of the body), as well as the composite movement of circumduction (pivotal rotation at the joint with the end that is away from the joint transcribing a circle) are all possible. Examples of ellipsoidal joints are the metacarpophalangeal (palm-finger), metatarsophalangeal (midfoot-toe), and radiocarpal (wrist) joints.

There is only one **saddle joint** (also called a *sellar joint)* in the human skeleton: the carpometacarpal joint of the pollex (i.e. the joint at the base of the thumb). The articular surfaces of the opposing bones are reciprocally concavoconvex and resemble two horses' saddles. These opposite surfaces fit snugly together because one surface is rotated 90° relative to the other. This type of joint is capable not only of all the motions of an ellipsoidal joint but of some rotation as well.

A **ball-and-socket joint** [also called an *enarthrosis* (pl. -es)] or *spheroidal joint*] has the widest range of motion: flexion, extension, abduction, adduction, circumduction, and medial and lateral rotation are all possible. The articular surface of one bone is ball-shaped and is received by the cup-shaped articular surface of the opposing bone [e.g. the glenohumeral (shoulder), coxofemoral (hip), and incudostapedial (inner ear bone) joints].

A **cartilaginous joint** [obsolete terminology, amphiarthrosis (pl. -es)] or synchondrosis is formed when bones are connected by either *hyaline cartilage* or *fibrocartilage*. In a **synchondrosis** (also called *primary* or *hyaline cartilaginous joint*), bones are connected by a plate of hyaline cartilage, which permits little or no movement between contiguous bones. A synchondrosis may be *temporary* [as with the epiphyseal plate between the diaphysis (shaft) and the epiphysis (end) of a growing bone] or *permanent* (as with the costal cartilage that connects the first rib to the manubrium of the sternum, or in the juncture of the sphenoid and occipital bones). In a **symphysis** (pl. -es) (also *secondary cartilaginous* or *fibrocartilaginous joint),* the articular surfaces of the opposing bones are covered by a thin layer of hyaline cartilage, but the connection between opposing bones is via a plate of fibrocartilage: a small amount of movement is possible. Symphyseal joints occur between vertebrae (intervertebral joints), the manubrium and body of the sternum (manubriosternal joint), the xiphoid process and the body of the sternum (xiphisternal joint), and right and left pubic bones (pubic symphysis).

Fibrous joints (obsolete terminology, synarthrosis, pl. -es) occur when elements are connected to one another by bands of fibrous tissue. There are three kinds of fibrous joints: **sutures**, **syndesmoses**, and **gomphoses**. A **suture** is characterized by having the least amount of fibrous tissue and, therefore, the greatest amount of movement possible between bones. The joints between the flat bones of the skull are sutures. Sutures may fuse or close over completely (e.g. as some cranial sutures do with increasing age),

and, in doing so, transform a fibrous joint into a bony joint, i.e. a **synostosis**. A **syndesmosis** (pl. -es) is characterized by the presence of an abundance of fibrous connective tissue that may take the form of a *ligament* or an *interosseous membrane*. A syndesmosis permits slight-to-moderate movement between bones (e.g. as in the distal tibiofibular joint and the radioulnar and tibiofibular interosseous membranes). The fibrous connection between the root of a tooth and its alveolus is called a **gomphosis** (pl. -es); movement is limited.

Gross Anatomy of Bone

A cross section through any part of the skeleton will reveal that the bone that has been laid down is not uniform in its characteristics. In adult or **mature** bone, the outer layer of bone (**cortex** or **cortical bone**) is hard and denser than the bone it encases; cortical bone is also referred to as **compact bone** (Figure 1–4). An articular region can be distinguished from other parts of a bone because its compact bone is typically smoother and more finely granular in quality. In the dried state, the bone encased by compact bone is characterized by a network of thin bony plates (s. **trabecula**, pl. -ae) that surround variably small air cells; in living bone, these cells are filled with **collagen**, a soft, fibrous connective tissue. This pneumaticized bone is called **spongy** or **cancellous** bone (Figure 1–4); in cranial bones, it is referred to as **diploë** (Figure 1–5). Spongy bone transfers stresses to the walls of the bone itself. In cranial bones, a layer of spongy bone is sandwiched between an outer and an inner layer or table of compact bone.

Technically, the spongy bone of postcranial bones is **secondary spongiosa**, which overlies and is a continuation of **primary spongiosa**, which, in turn, is a continuation of the cartilaginous matrix that precedes the deposition of bone (see below). The degree to which spongy bone, in general, is compactly or spaciously distributed depends, for instance, on the specific region of the bone itself and the age of the individual. With increasing age, compact bone thins and cancellous bone, in general, becomes even more vacuous; in the case of long bones, cancellous bone becomes less extensively dis-

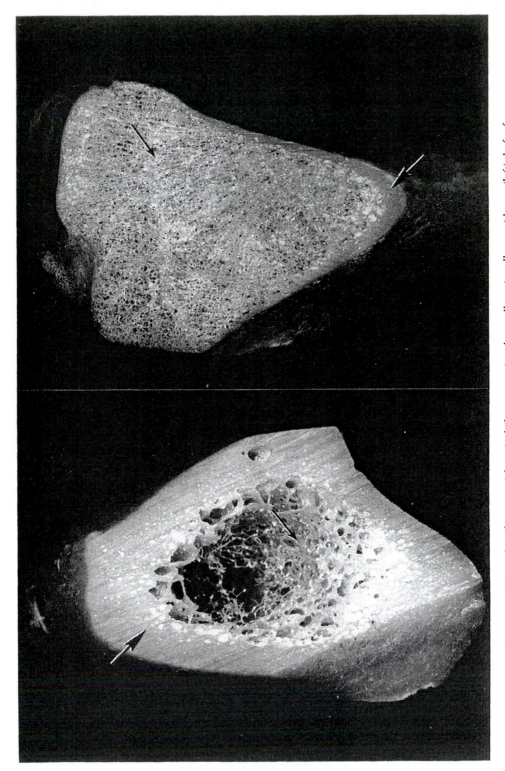

Figure 1–4 Examples of postcranial cortical (*large arrow*) and cancellous (*small arrow*) bone: (*left*) shaft of tibia also illustrating medullary cavity and nutrient foramen (*asterisk*); (*right*) proximal tibia.

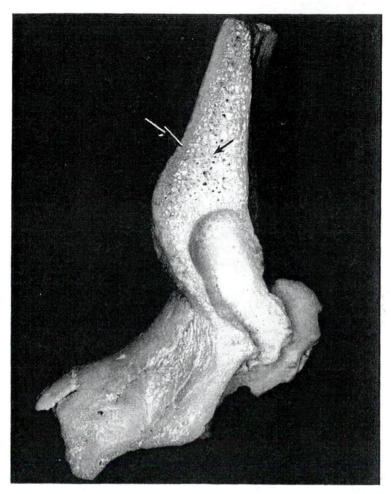

Figure 1–5 Example of cranial cortical bone *(large arrow)* and diploë *(small arrow):* parasagittal section of frontal bone (with frontal sinus and crista galli behind it), left nasal bone, and frontal process of left maxilla.

tributed along the shaft of the bone. Many post-cranial bones develop a **medullary cavity** (Figure 1–4) within the core, which enlarges as bone marrow is laid down. In addition to marrow, nutrient arteries arborize within the medullary cavity and send finer capillary branches into the walls of the bone itself. As an individual ages, the medullary cavity becomes more pervasive through the shaft of a long bone as the spongy bone retreats toward the two ends of the bone.

Many bones of the postcranial skeleton can be characterized as being longer than they are wide and as having two identifiable ends. This description is most applicable to the long bones but can also encompass the fingers and toes (the phalanges) as well as the bones of the palm (metacarpals) and midportion of the foot (metatarsals). The long, somewhat tubular portion of a long bone is the shaft or **diaphysis,** and each end is an **epiphysis** (pl. -es) (Figure 1–6). An epiphysis is delineated from the diaphysis because, developmentally, it and the diaphysis each arise as separate elements that eventually fuse. Complete union of the epiphysis and diaphysis along the perimeter is indicated by a thin, indented **epiphyseal line,** which, in advanced age, may be filled in and obliterated. The terminal portion of an isolated diaphysis—to which an epiphysis would fuse—is identified as the **metaphysis.** In determining the age of juveniles and young adults from skeletal remains, one can use the relative times at which epiphyses fuse to their respective diaphyses (see Chapters 4, 5, and 7). Obviously, in young individ-

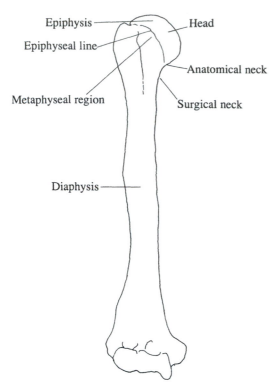

Epiphysis ——
Epiphyseal line —
—— Head
—— Anatomical neck
Metaphyseal region
Surgical neck
Diaphysis ——

Figure 1–6   Gross anatomy of a long bone.

uals in whom epiphyseal fusion has not or has only minimally begun, epiphyses and their diaphyses can become dissociated as the corpse progresses through stages of decay and disarticulation.

The upper or proximal epiphysis of a long bone is referred to as the **head** (which, as in the femur and humerus, may be rounded). However, the round head of a metatarsal or metacarpal is at the distal end of the bone and only in the second to fifth metatarsals and metacarpals is the head a true epiphysis. The head of a rib is the end that articulates with the vertebral column (the other end of a rib is its sternal end); the right and left heads of the mandible are those projections that articulate with the skull; the head of the scapula articulates with the head of the humerus. All of these osteological heads are true epiphyses. A bone may have two ends, but each may not be an epiphysis. In bones for which a head can be defined, the region immediately adjacent to it is often identified as the **neck** (which may be different from the **surgical neck**).

A bone is ensheathed completely in a connective tissue called **periosteum** (see below). The outer layer of periosteum functions in the attachment of tendons and also carries blood cells, lymphatics, and nerves. **Endosteum** lines the bone marrow cavities as well as the trabeculae of spongy bone and the vascular canals of compact bone. The inner layer of cells of both periosteum and endosteum is capable of producing bone cells that participate in growth as well as in fracture repair (see below). Endosteum, like the marrow it surrounds, also can contribute to the production of blood cells (i.e. it has *hemopoietic* properties).

Blood is supplied to a bone via vascular systems or units that correspond to different functional or developmental units of the bone. **Periosteal arteries** (within the periosteum) encase the bone in a continuous vascular network; in long bones, the network of vascularity is least dense toward the center of the diaphysis, but it increases markedly (with the proliferation of hundreds of small vessels) toward the metaphyseal ends. Each epiphysis is supplied separately, usually by one to three **epiphyseal arteries**. A **nutrient artery** supplies the interior of a bone. In a long bone, the single nutrient artery penetrates the diaphysis obliquely, typically somewhere within the middle third of the shaft; in the long bones of the arm, the direction of penetration is toward the elbow joint, whereas in the long bones of the leg, the direction of penetration is away from the knee. Once within a bone, the nutrient artery arborizes in all directions (into ascending and descending branches) and ultimately sends branches into the endosteum as well as into the inner walls of the bone itself. Toward the metaphyseal region of the diaphysis, periosteal arterial branches penetrate the bone and form connections or *anastamose* with nutrient arterial branches within the bone. The metaphyseal regions of a dried long bone are riddled with variably small canals and holes (*foramina*; singular, *foramen*) that attest to this anastamosis. In young individuals, in whom longitudinal bone growth is still taking place and in whom a plate of cartilage still separates the epiphysis from the diaphysis, the cartilaginous epiphyseal plate is itself also supplied by perforating epiphyseal metaphyseal arteries as well as by superficial epiphyseal arteries.

Osteogenesis: The Formation of Bone

Bone is a highly specialized type of connective tissue that is distinguished by its being mineralized and thus hard. Bone formation (**osteogenesis**), broadly defined, refers to the creation of both *"new"* and *"mature"* bone. "New" bone is laid down either at the beginning of **skeletogenesis** (the formation of the skeleton) or in the process of healing a break or wound. "Mature" bone replaces "new" bone. This particular, organlike property of renewal distinguishes bone from tooth enamel, another mineralized tissue. But although the formation of bone does differ to some extent from the formation of other hard tissues in the body—such as cementum and enamel, which contribute to the anatomy of a tooth—there are certain elements that all hard tissues have in common (Ten Cate and Osborn, 1976).

A primary feature of all hard tissues is the modification of an **organic matrix**. This transformation requires a specialized type of cell, the differentiation of which is correlated with areas of concentrated vascularization. These cells are themselves characterized by having higher concentrations of RNA and higher levels of enzyme activity involved in oxygen and water uptake. These specialized cells both synthesize and secrete material, including proteins that form a *fibrous, extracellular component* of the organic matrix (i.e. **extracellular matrix**) as well as a substance (the *ground substance*) that accumulates between these fibers. The conversion of the extracellular organic matrix into a hard substance is achieved by the deposition, or accretion, of calcium and phosphate ions. These ions accumulate in localized areas—in vesicles that bud off from the extracellular matrix—in concentrations higher than those normally occurring throughout the body.

In bone, the specialized cells are **osteoblasts** and **osteocytes** and the fibrous protein of the extracellular matrix is **collagen** (Parfitt, 1983). *Type I collagen* is found in bone as well as in teeth, skin, ligaments, and tendons. In its unmineralized state, the extracellular organic matrix is identified as **osteoid**, which achieves its hardness through the deposition of **calcium phosphate**. Coincident with the onset of mineralization is the appearance of **osteonectin** and **osteocalcin**, which belong to a group of molecules called **phosphoproteins** that are specific to bone.

Bone may arise in one of two ways: either by direct development or by the replacement of cartilage, a precursor connective tissue. Bone that develops directly is referred to as **intramembranous** or **membrane bone**. Bone that replaces a cartilaginous predecessor is called **replacement, intracartilaginous, enchondral,** or **endochondral bone;** (the root "chond-" refers to cartilage). **Intramembranous bone** formation (as commonly described) is restricted primarily to the head region, giving rise to the flat bones of the cranial vault and some of the facial skeleton; specifically, these are the frontals, the parietals, the squamous portions of the temporals and he occipitals, the nasal bones, and the vomer as well as some portion of the sphenoid, palatines, and mandible. The clavicle also arises as membrane bone. **Endochondral bone** formation characterizes the development of the postcranial skeleton and also contributes to the development of the petrosal portions of the temporals, the basilar portions of the occipitals, as well as some of the sphenoid, palatines, and mandible. The development of the shaft of a long bone as well as the ongoing processes of bone growth and resorption, rebuilding and remodeling, may be seen however more accurately as occurring via an intramembranous mechanism—in the sense that bone deposition and formation immediately beneath the periosteum is actually direct and not by a mode of replacement (see below).

Bone deposition occurs in essentially the same way in membrane and endochondral bone (Parfitt, 1983). The transformation of cartilage into bone-forming cells, however, may occur in several possible ways. There can apparently be a direct transformation of cartilage cells (**chondroblasts** and **chondrocytes**) into bone cells (osteoblasts and osteocytes), as has been found to be the case in the ribs, mandible, and articular areas of the mouse's pelvis. Alternatively, the cellular membrane surrounding the cartilaginous precursor (the **perichondrium**) may cease to produce cartilage cells and, instead, produces bone cells, which, in turn, replace the cells of the cartilaginous precursor as these precursor cells deteriorate; the transformed, bone-producing cellular membrane would no longer be identified as perichondrium but rather as **perios-**

teum. Lastly, bone cells may be transported into the cartilaginous precursor by way of the vascular system, coincident with the spread of vascularization throughout the territory of the cartilaginous precursor (Hall, 1988).

Although it was long believed that cartilage and bone arose from the mesodermal germ layer of the developing embryo (with the *ectoderm* forming, for instance, the nervous system and skin, and the *endoderm*, for instance, the gut), it appears that only the postcranial skeleton is ultimately derived from the *mesoderm*. Cranial bone—whether membrane or endochondral bone—takes its origin from cells that migrate into the embryonically presumptive head region from the developing neural tube, which, in turn, develops into the presumptive spinal cord and brain (Gans and Northcutt, 1983; Hall, 1988). These migrating cells (called **neural crest cells**) differentiate along the infold-

ing edges of the neural plate and are "released" as the neural plate completely closes over to form the neural tube, which is then overlaid by the epithelium that will become skin (Figure 1–7). Having invaded different areas of the embryo, these neural crest cells, which may now be referred to as **mesenchyme** (or **ectomesenchyme**), interact with epithelial cells; then and only then do they acquire the specificity to become bone cells. Until the migrating neural crest cells enter into this relatively prolonged period of epithelial interaction, their role—at least as bone cells—is not defined. (It also may be that, en route to their final locations in the embryonic head, migrating neural crest cells interact with epithelial cells as well as with extracellular matrix, and that these interactions contribute to defining their role in the production of cartilage.)

Coincident with the initiation of bone min-

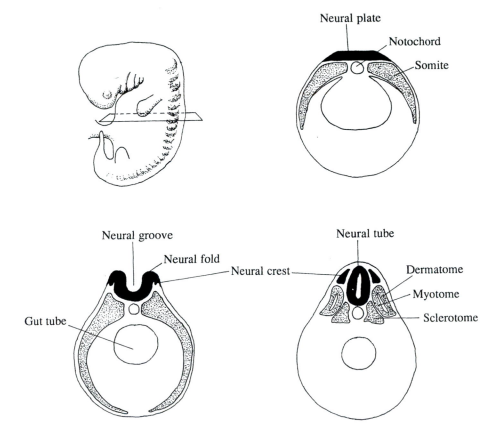

Figure 1–7   Diagram of development of the neural crest and tube and derivatives of the somite in a mammalian embryo. The plane of the section is indicated in the diagram of the embryo *(upper left)*. Neural crest cells originating in the head region migrate into the presumptive jaws and face to contribute to the formation of teeth and bone.

eralization is an increase in vascularization of the mesenchyme and the transformation of mesenchymal cells into **osteoblasts** (the bone-forming cells). As suggested above, an osteoblast produces the ground substance and presumptive collagen (**procollagen**) that eventually contributes to the formation of osteoid surrounding the cell itself, in which mineralization occurs. Mineralization begins within budlike extensions that the osteoblast sends out into the osteoid. Further mineralization via crystal growth eventually surrounds the osteoblast, at which time the cell is no longer identified as an osteoblast but is called an **osteocyte**. In addition to its being captured in a bony space or lacuna, an osteocyte can be identified further histologically by its extensions or **dendritic processes**, which are contained within bony tubes or **canaliculi**.

"New" bone is laid down rapidly as plates or **trabeculae** that eventually come to surround collagenous connective tissue and blood vessels. Given its appearance, this initial, **embryonic bone** is also referred to as **coarse-fibered woven bone**. After this network of embryonic bone is laid down, bone is deposited as fine-fibered sheets or **lamellae** on the inner walls of the trabeculae. Lamellae are deposited as a series of concentric rings that eventually replace the soft connective tissue and come to surround a core region through which the blood vessels course. (When viewed in polarized light, these lamellae have a vague resemblance to tree rings.) This "unit," consisting of concentric lamellae that capture a core of soft connective tissue and vasculature, is referred to as a **primary osteon** (Figure 1–8). During circumferential bone growth—wherein the girth of a bone is enlarged—longitudinal blood vessels within the periosteum may be captured and encased in lamellae. This, too, creates a primary osteon. (As will become clearer, a primary osteon can be distinguished histologically from what will later develop and be identified as a secondary osteon by virtue of the fact that it has a poorly defined perimeter and lacks cement lines that accrue when bone deposition is interrupted.)

"Mature" bone develops as a natural outcome of bone remodeling, which begins with the resorption of primary osteons and embryonic bone (Parfitt, 1983). Resorption of bone is accomplished by another type of bone cell called an **osteoclast**. An osteoclast can be recognized histologically as a giant cell with a variably large number of nuclei and some number of extending processes. As an osteoclast resorbs bone, dense, collagen-free connective tissue comes to line the surface of the tunnel or depression created by the resorptive cell. The action of multiple osteoclasts gives the margin of the region undergoing bone resorption a scalloped or irregular contour. When, eventually, bone is laid down in the resorbed region—as a series of lamellae that eventually come to capture blood vessels, lymphatics, nerves, and connective tissue—a distinct line of demarcation (**cement line**) comes to delineate the newly formed outer lamella from the unresorbed bone around it. Thus a **secondary osteon** is distinguished from a primary osteon by its irregular but more clearly defined perimeter (Figure 1–8). Sometimes, during the formation of a secondary osteon, deposition of bony lamellae is interrupted. When this happens, a new cement line (also called an **arrest line**), but one with a smooth perimeter, will form. Thus, a secondary osteon can be distinguished further from a primary osteon by the presence of a series of smooth-bordered, concentric layers of lamellae within a clearly defined but scallop-shaped perimeter.

The canal of a secondary osteon is referred to as a **haversian canal**; it and its contents constitute a **haversian system**. A primary osteon is referred to as a **non-haversian system**. Continued resorption of bone may occur by way of osteoclasts that arise in haversian systems or in the walls of transverse canals (called **Volkmann's canals**) that connect haversian canals and allow for vascularization laterally. As osteoclasts burrow to create a tunnel of resorption, they destroy previously formed osteons. Thus, with increasing age, the frequency of primary osteons decreases and the number of osteon fragments increases.

The initial site of mineralization is called an **ossification center**. In the development of intramembranous as well as endochondral bones, one or more centers of ossification may have contributed to the formation of what, in the adult skeleton, is a single bone. Discussion of typical and variant numbers of ossification centers will be introduced elsewhere in the text in the appropriate section for each bone. With

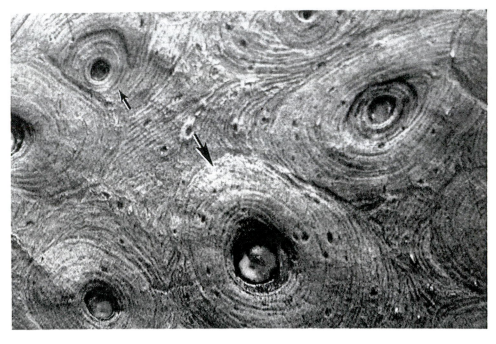

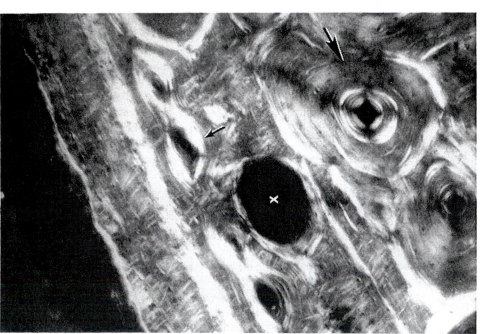

Figure 1-8 Haversian and nonhaversian systems. *(Left)* Old World monkey (*Macaca arctoides*; photomicrograph taken in polarized light). *(From bottom right to top left)*: Secondary osteons (harversian systems) (e.g. *see large arrow*), region of remodeling (x), primary osteons (non-haversian systems) (e.g. *see small arrow*), and layer of primary lamellar bone being apposed to surface of periosteum. *(Right)* fossil hominid [Kabwe ("Broken Hill") skull, photomicrograph taken using reflected light with Nomarski optics]: secondary osteons (e.g. *see large arrow*), osteon fragments (e.g. *see small arrow*), and interstitial lamellae (between whole and fragmentary osteons). *(Photomicrographs courtesy of D. Burr.)*

particular regard to bones with epiphyses, however, it is the rule that each diaphysis as well as each epiphysis arises from a single center of ossification. The center of ossification that leads to the formation of the diaphysis is called the **primary center** of ossification, whereas the center of ossification of each epiphysis is referred to as a **secondary center** of ossification. The centers of ossification that give rise to structures that, like epiphyses, eventually fuse to the diaphysis are also identified as secondary centers of ossification (e.g. see discussion below on the origin of the greater and lesser tubercles of the proximal humerus or of the iliac crest).

It may be relatively easy to envision the intramembranous development of platelike bones as an ever-expanding sheet of crystallizing minerals, or the broadening of the girth of a shaft of bone by the accretion of successive generations of lamellae encased in a more compact bony sheath. However, the somewhat more complicated course of longitudinal bone growth may be more difficult to understand at first.

With the onset of the replacement of cartilage—which is heralded by the appearance of primary and secondary centers of ossification—the basic bony units have been defined. If we take a simple case of one primary center of ossification (for the diaphysis) and two secondary centers of ossification (for a proximal and a distal epiphysis), there would come a time when all cartilage—at least theoretically—would be replaced by bone. Bone girth could continue to expand as outlined above, but bone length would have to be achieved by adding to the ends of epiphyses in such a way that the shape of the epiphysis was not deformed or functionally deficient. However, a mechanism that permits longitudinal bone growth as well as growth of the epiphyses and the diaphysis as individual structures does exist.

An epiphysis and its associated diaphysis eventually become well mineralized; however, as long as growth is taking place, mineralization proceeds only to the point that a **cartilaginous disc** (the **epiphyseal disc** or **plate**) remains between the two structures (McLean and Urist, 1964). The epiphyseal surface of this cartilaginous disc is typically covered by a layer of bone, whereas the surface facing the diaphysis remains totally cartilaginous. Elongation of the diaphysis occurs by the ongoing process of proliferating cartilage from the epiphyseal surface of the disc and the replacement of cartilage by bone at the metaphyseal region of the diaphysis. This process also keeps the cartilaginous epiphyseal disc at a relatively constant thickness. The cartilage cells in the zone of proliferation are arranged in columns; columns of cells are separated by longitudinal bands of extracellular matrix, whereas individual cells are separated from one another by transverse slips of matrix. As the epiphyses and diaphyses increase in girth, so does the epiphyseal plate. When reduction of growth hormone secretion (see below) signals the cessation of growth, the epiphyseal plate ceases to generate cartilage. Ossification in the metaphyseal region continues until it eventually replaces the the perimeter of the epiphyseal plate and begins to coalesce with the perimeter of the epiphysis. A much reduced cartilaginous epiphyseal plate thus becomes "captured" between the epiphysis and the metaphysis. Mineralization of the longitudinal and transverse bands of extracellular matrix produces a dense region of calcified tissue that persists as the **epiphyseal line** or **scar** that in the adult delineates the epiphysis from the diaphysis. Obviously, the epiphyseal line represents the ultimate **growth arrest line** (Harris, 1926, 1931).

At times prior to the onset of union between epiphysis and diaphysis, the growth process may be interrupted or delayed long enough for mineralization of the longitudinal and transverse bands of extracellular matrix at the more rapidly growing ends of long bones to occur—at least sufficiently to be recorded radiographically and histologically. These radio-opaque bands of mineralization are variably referred to as **growth arrest lines** (Harris, 1926, 1931), **transverse lines** (e.g. Hunt and Hatch, 1981), and **Harris lines**. The most commonly cited causes of growth arrest or Harris lines are illness/infection and malnutrition. For this reason, the radiographic assessment of Harris lines is often included in paleoepidemiological and paleopathological studies, and attempts (e.g. McHenry and Schulz, 1976) are sometimes made to correlate these skeletal recordings of bodily insult with those that may be found reflected dentally, in linear enamel hypoplasias (see Chapter 6 for discussion of enamel hypoplasias). The presence of several or more Harris lines in the same bone has been interpreted as representing recurrent or seasonal conditions (e.g. nutritionally difficult times of year).

The bone most frequently scrutinized for Harris lines is the tibia, especially the distal end. The reason for this is that the zone of proliferating cartilage is particularly well defined in this region. This zone is also well defined in the proximal end of the tibia and femur and distal ends of the humerus, radius, and ulna but less so in the other ends of these bones. The absence of detectable Harris lines does not, however, necessarily testify to the absence of temporary growth-arresting phenomena. Harris lines are as subject to osteoclastic activity and remodeling as any other bony formation. Thus, even though the most tenacious Harris lines appear to be those formed early in childhood (Garn et al., 1968), they begin to disappear relatively soon after they have formed.

Regulation of and Abnormalities in Bone Growth

The epiphyseal plate (as mentioned above) receives its vascularization from various epiphyseal and metaphyseal arteries. If blood supply from the epiphyseal arteries is interrupted, cartilage formation in the epiphyseal plate will be curtailed, as will bone formation and, ultimately, growth. If metaphyseal arterial supply is cut off, the metaphyseal portion of the epiphyseal plate will not mineralize and growth will cease. Interference with the growth of cartilage—regardless of the source—results in a condition referred to as **dyschondroplasia** (McLean and Urist, 1964). This may be hereditarily based (**Ollier's disease**) or brought about by chemical or metabolic alterations (e.g. **rickets**, which results from vitamin D and phosphate deficiencies).

General body size and weight, as well as longitudinal bone growth, are maintained by **growth (somatotrophic) hormone** produced in the **anterior lobe** of the **pituitary gland** or **hypophysis**. Under normal circumstances and normal production of growth hormone, bone growth continues until proliferation of cartilage in the epiphyseal plate ceases and concomitant mineralization causes a coalescence of the epiphysis and diaphysis around a much reduced epiphyseal plate (Ortner and Putschar, 1981).

If the hypophysis is obliterated prematurely (most often because of the development of a tumor), proliferation of cartilage in the epiphyseal plate will cease, as will bone growth, and fusion of epiphysis to diaphysis will occur; although smaller in size, the coalesced epiphysis and diaphysis will encase a reduced epiphyseal plate—in fact, this will be a miniature of the normal adult configuration. When growth is curtailed and the result is the proportioned miniaturization of the individual, the condition is referred to as **midgetism** (also called **hypopituitarism**). Reduction in or lack of sufficient growth hormone production will result in **pituitary dwarfism**, in which the body proportions remain those of an infant, the appearance of secondary centers of ossification is retarded, and closure or fusion (respectively, for example, of sutures and epiphyses) does not occur until late in life.

If growth hormone continues to be produced beyond the age at which bone growth normally slows down and ceases or a new surge of growth hormone production occurs at that age, bone formation and growth will continue, resulting in **gigantism** (**hyperpituitarism**). Activation of growth hormone production after epiphyses have joined diaphyses and after longitudinal bone growth has ceased will create a condition known as **acromegaly**, in which renewed bone growth causes bones to thicken or expand. Particularly affected first are the bones of the hands and feet. Bone enlargement is also common in the region of the middle and upper face (e.g. broadening of the cheekbone regions) and mandible (creating the so-called lantern jaw). Acromegalic features may be superimposed on those of gigantism.

Thyroid hormone (**thyroxin**) secretion also affects proper bone growth, primarily by having a feedback effect on the hypophysis to secrete growth hormone (McLean and Urist, 1964). Lack of proper thyroxin secretion results in overall stunting of bone growth and development and the retention (or nonreplacement) of cartilage and primary spongiosa. **Cretinism**, which has long been recognized historically, is a type of **hypothyroidism** that is characterized by dwarfism and mental deficiency; it is expressed during fetal development either through the nondevelopment of the thyroid gland or inhibition of the fetal thyroid as a result of the mother herself being hypothyroid. In the case of fetal thyroid absence (**sporadic cretinism**), the effects of dwarfism are more dramatic; whereas in the maternal/fetal case (**endemic cretinism**), the impact on the developing fetus is related to the degree of hypothyroidism expressed in the mother.

Experimentally induced **hyperthyroidism** can cause early fusion of epiphyses and thus cessation of growth. Hyperthyroidism in young individuals is often expressed as retardation in the growth of long bones. In adults, the effects of hyperthyroidism may be mild, only advancing the rate of resorption leading to a more friable and porous *(osteoporotic* or *porotic)* condition.

Gonad-stimulating and **gonad-produced** hormones also have an effect on proper bone growth. Gonad-stimulating hormones or **chorionic gonadotropins** are produced primarily by the placenta and have an effect on the fetus similar to that of somatotrophic hormone produced by the anterior lobe of the pituitary gland. An insufficiency in gonad-produced hormones (**estrogen** in the female and **androgen** in the male, with the most extreme cases resulting from castration, e.g. as in a eunuch) can result in a retardation of the appearance of secondary centers of ossification, truncation of cortical bone deposition, and a delay in epiphyseal closure—all of which leads to thin-boned, typically longer-legged (and also longer lower-jawed) individuals (features typical, e.g. of eunuchs). Complete failure in or incompleteness of development of the ovaries can lead to dwarfism, the characteristics of which are otherwise of the sort produced by hypopituitarism. Cessation of estrogen (e.g. menopause) or androgen production after the individual reaches adulthood leads to general porosity *(osteoporosis)* of the postcranial axial skeleton.

Of the various steroidal hormones produced by the cortex of the adrenal gland (**adrenal corticosteroids**), some—most notably, the glucocorticoids **hydrocortisone** and **cortisone**—have demonstrable although nonspecific effects on the growth of the skeleton (McLean and Urist, 1964). The action of these steroids is controlled ultimately by way of a feedback mechanism with the anterior lobe of the pituitary gland (hypophysis), which secretes **adrenocorticotropic hormone** (**corticotropin** or **ACTH**); ablation of the hypophysis leads to the reduction of adrenal corticosteroid secretion. Overproduction of ACTH or one of the glucocorticoids suppresses osteoblast activity and thus leads to retardation in both the growth of young individuals and the mending of fractures. Hypersecretion of cortisone (**hypercortisonism** or **Cushing's syndrome**), which may be caused by more than one agency (e.g. basophil adenoma of the hypophysis, primary hyperplasia, a tumor of the adrenal cortex), results in severe overall osteoporosis of the ribs and vertebrae (possibly leading to their subsequent collapse) as well as internal osteoporosis of the long bones.

Vitamin A is critical for the proper growth and regulation of bone (McLean and Urist, 1964). It is necessary for growth of endochondrally- and periosteally-derived bone as well as for the ongoing process of bone remodeling. Vitamin A deficiency (**avitaminosis A**) will result in bones becoming misshaped and foramina failing to keep pace with the increasing size of the nerves or neurovascular bundles that course through them; the latter leads, ultimately, to the death *(necrosis)* of these neurovascular structures. The intake of too much vitamin A (**hypervitaminosis A**) results in increased osteoclastic activity, which has the effect not only of increasing bone destruction (**osteolysis**) but also of increasing bone cell turnover. Together, this can lead to inconsistencies in mineralization and in the development of compact cortical bone as well as to overall bone fragility.

Vitamin C (ascorbic acid) plays a major role in the proper formation and maintenance of the collagenous extracellular matrices of bone, cartilage, and other connective tissue as well as in the formation and maintenance of the dentin of teeth (Ortner and Putschar, 1981). With vitamin C deficiency (**scurvy**), collagen formation is either suppressed or the collagen that is produced cannot mineralize. The effects of scurvy are most deleterious in infants and children but decrease in severity as bone growth itself slows down. **Infantile scurvy** (**Möller-Barlow's disease**) is characterized by subperiosteal hemorrhaging with induced reactive bone formation and fractures or separations of fast-growing metaphyseal regions. Not uncommon in infantile scurvy is a sinking inward of the sternum (breastbone), which creates the so-called the *scorbutic rosary*. Infantile scurvy typically is expressed by the end of the first year of life. In adults, scurvy most often affects the rib cage, which leads to separation within or fracture of the region where bone and cartilage join one another. Since vitamin C is a water-soluble vitamin that is not stored in the body, resumed intake can correct the effects of scurvy, especially in adults.

Vitamin D also is needed for proper bone growth in that it plays a role in the absorption of calcium and thus the mineralization of bone; it can also influence the demineralization of bone (Ortner and Putschar, 1981). Although vitamin D is vital for overall systemic calcium metabolism and mineralization, it does not act alone in this process. The efficacy and impact of vitamin D is mediated by a hormone secreted by the **parathyroid glands (parathormone)**, which acts to maintain a proper level of calcium in the blood plasma. Although parathormone, in the process of regulating calcium ion concentration, can cause the release of calcium from the skeleton, it apparently does not play a role in the process of mineralization. Parathormone also acts on the renal tubules of the kidney; increased secretion of this hormone results in increased excretion of phosphate in the urine.

In contrast to vitamin C or A, little vitamin D comes from diet. Instead, vitamin D is synthesized in the skin under the influence of ultraviolet light. Although indigenous populations of tropical and subtropical regions tend to have a higher incidence of vitamin D deficiency than those in other locales, this is more likely due to dietary deficiencies in calcium than to a deleteriously high rate of ultraviolet light absorbed by the melanin in skin.

Vitamin D deficiency, which is not life-threatening, can affect infants and children (**rickets**) as well as adults (**osteomalacia**); most cases of rickets occur in children 4 years of age or below. Since the most important stages of bone formation and growth occur during infancy and childhood, vitamin D deficiency during this period will have the most profound consequences; in older individuals, in whom growth has ceased, the effects will be somewhat different. However, in both afflictions, the collagenous extracellular matrix does not become mineralized.

Rickets is similar to scurvy in that its effects are most notable in areas of rapid bone growth (e.g. junctures of ribs, metaphyseal regions).

The result is that unmineralized matrix accumulates next to growth plates (e.g. in ribs and long bones) or comes to replace bone during intramembranous bone growth. In cranial bone, this can lead to a thickening of the bone(s) involved; the smooth, compact-boned outer table also becomes transformed in that it acquires an incised appearance. Postcranial bones become thick-walled along the shaft and expanded at the metaphyseal regions. Ribs and their attendant cartilage can become swollen at their sternal ends, creating the so-called *rachitic rosary*. Extreme porosity and fragility of bone would indicate that the individual not only had been *rachitic* but also had suffered from malnutrition. Bones of the cranial vault appear porotic; in individuals with prolonged vitamin D deficiency, portions of cranial bones may become completely porous, from the inner to the outer surface. In vitamin D–deficient rickets, postcranial bones become thin-walled with expanded medullary cavities and thus become increasingly susceptible to stress fractures and bending. Rickets alone (i.e. uncomplicated by malnutrition) is referred to as **hyperplastic**, as opposed to **porotic**.

Since **osteomalacia** affects mature bone that is maintaining stasis in resorption and reconstitution, the result is a decrease in ossified material; the effects of vitamin D deficiency are most notable in bones that are predominantly spongy bone and in which bone turnover is rapid (e.g. ribs, vertebrae). Over time, the increase in unmineralized tissue creates vacuities, which make desiccated bone feel light and papery; the surface of the bone may also become porous. In severe cases—when bone becomes excessively fragile and malleable—a bone may become deformed or may fracture. Loss of calcium during pregnancy or lactation can put a vitamin D–deficient female at further risk of osteomalacia; indeed, the incidence of osteomalacia is greater in women between 20 and 40 years of age.

Large doses of vitamin D—creating **hypervitaminosis D** (**rickets**)—leads to increased resorption of bone and an increase in poorly calcified spongy bone because of the increased production of an unmineralizable extracellular matrix. Such affected bone also tends to become porotic.

Since parathyroid hormone (parathormone) is involved in maintaining calcium levels in the blood, **hypoparathyroidism** leads to a lowering and **hyperparathyroidism** to an elevation of calcium levels. It appears that parathormone stimulates osteoclastic action, resulting in liberation of calcium; increased secretion of parathormone also seems to convert vitamin D to an inactive state, after which it is eliminated in the bile.

Hypoparathyroidism, resulting from absence of or interference with the parathyroid glands, occurs infrequently in human populations. Because hypoparathyroidism leads to a decreased stimulation of osteoclastic activity, compact and spongy bone builds up, creating thickened bone walls and densely packed trabecular bone. Lowered levels of calcium also often produce painful muscle spasms *(tetany).*

Oversecretion of parathormone (leading to hyperparathyroidism) may result directly from overactivity of the parathyroid glands (**primary hyperparathyroidism**) or as a consequence of the parathyroid glands responding to kidney disease, which, in turn, can interfere with proper phosphate levels and cause loss of calcium via the kidneys (**secondary hyperparathyroidism**).

In general, hyperparathyroidism is characterized by increasing osteoporosis, which results from the release of calcium due to increased osteoclast activity. Particularly affected in primary hyperparathyroidism are the surfaces of phalanges, alveoli (root sockets for teeth), and cranial vault bones; vertebral bodies may become depressed as trabecular resorption and thus porosity become pronounced. The contin-

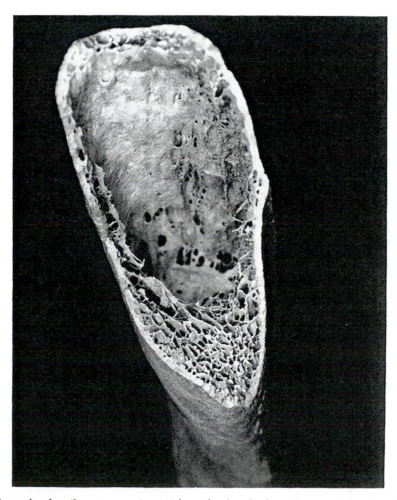

Figure 1–9 Example of senile osteoporosis: note loss of trabecular bone, increased size of medullary cavity, and thinned cortical bone (left tibia, prehistoric, Pennsylvania).

ually demineralizing skeleton becomes increasingly susceptible to fracture and hemorrhage. Bones—especially the mandible, long bones, metatarsals, metacarpals, phalanges, and os coxae—can also become brittle through the development of pockets of unmineralized matrix that become encased in a thin bony wall; in dried bone, these pockets present themselves as air pockets. The accumulation of unmineralized matrix may also cause bone to expand. The effects of secondary hyperparathyroidism in children are compounded by symptoms similar to those of rickets and hypopituitarism; in fact, hyperparathyroidism can affect joints in a manner similar to rickets. In adults, hyperparathyroidism may be accompanied by symptoms of osteomalacia. In both young and old, hyperparathyroidism can also cause calcium to build up around the joints. Obviously, diagnosis of hyperparathyroidism can be difficult, because the development of porosity, which can result from any number of causes, may be the only clue. Hyperthyroidism may also be confused with hyperparathyroidism.

Other Pathological Aspects of Bone Growth and Physiology

Although the term "osteoporotic" was used above in the description of various effects of abnormal bone growth, the process of osteoporosis—which is *a systemic rather than localized increase in soft tissue at the expense of mineralized tissue*—should be recognized as an abnormality in itself. In general, osteoporosis is an affliction of the aged (although it can occur in younger individuals) that affects the spongy bone, first and especially, of the ribs, vertebrae, os coxae, and femoral neck. With advancing age, the bones of the extremities can become involved. Cortical bone thickness and density of trabeculae and transverse plates become reduced (Figure 1–9). Affected bone continues to lose calcium and phosphate in spite of the fact that diet, as well as vitamin and mineral intake and serum levels, may be normal. Hypercortisonism is known to cause osteoporosis. Other specific causes are less clearly delineated, although diets deficient in calcium, nutrition- or

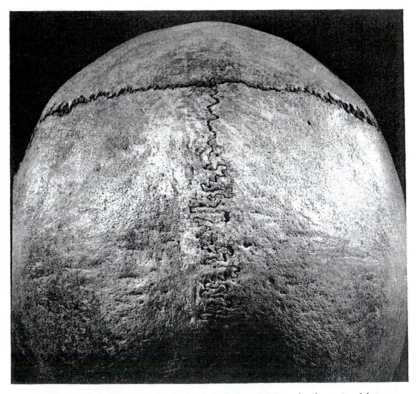

Figure 1–10 Extensive cribra crania (porotic hyperostosis) on both parietal bones as well as the frontal bone of an adult (prehistoric, Pennsylvania).

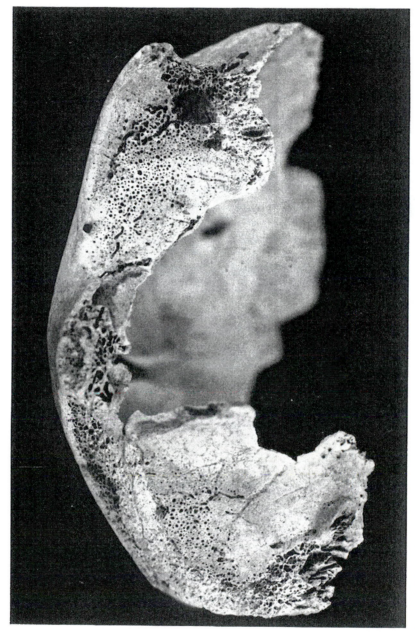

Figure 1–11   Cribra orbitalia in a 12- to 14-year-old (frontal fragment, Vandal or Byzantine period, Tunisia).

disease-related weight loss, castration, and hyperthyroidism appear to exacerbate extant osteoporosis.

A pathologic condition, which begins as localized phenomena (perhaps because of disruptions in capillary circulation) but which can eventually affect much of the skeleton, is **Paget's disease** (**osteitis deformans**) (Ortner and Putschar, 1981). The disease manifests itself as an acceleration and distortion of osteoclastic and osteoblastic changes that spread along the bone from the point of origin, thickening cortical bone and creating a coarser and more interwoven trabecular pattern along the way. As the disease spreads, large numbers of osteoclasts resorb osteons, leaving behind vacuous and distorted haversian systems. Redeposited cortical bone is characterized by a mosaic pattern of these deformed haversian systems amid mineralized lamellae bounded by thick and irregularly configured cement lines. As the disease progresses, bone thickens and hardens (i.e. becomes *sclerotic)* periosteally and endosteally, and trabecular bone as well as the medullary cavities of long bones become diminished. A general descriptor of the bone formed as a result of Paget's disease is *pumice bone. Secondary kyphosis* (kyphosis being an exaggeration of the outward curvature of the thoracic region of the vertebral column), in which vertebrae collapse and become wedge-shaped, can result as a consequence of Paget's disease as well as of hyperparathyroidism, osteomalacia, and osteoporosis.

Anemias, which are either *hereditarily hemolytic* (causing the destruction of red blood cells) or due to *iron deficiency,* may lead to conditions in which cranial cortical bone presents itself at the same time as being both thickened (hyperostotic) as well as perforated by a series of quite visible pinholes (porotic) (e.g. Stuart-Macadam, 1989). It appears that this condition—referred to generally as **porotic hyperostosis**—is the result of a bony response to an increased production of red blood cells from bone marrow. Iron-deficiency anemia can result from blood loss (e.g. from parasitic infection or menstruation) and/or dietary factors (e.g. prolonged reliance on iron-poor foods or intake of substances that can decrease the availability or utility of iron); the latter are thought to have had more of an impact on prehistoric populations (Klepinger, 1992). It has also recently been suggested that porotic hyperostosis can reflect anemia that was induced by perspiring with subsequent water loss but without cooling. This would be the case in humid coastal environments (Steinberg, 1994). When affecting the bones of the cranial vault, porotic hyperostosis is referred to as **cribra crania** (although some osteologists simply identify it as porotic hyperostosis) (Figure 1–10). When localized in the orbital roofs, the lesions are often specified as **cribra orbitalia** (Figure 1–11). Cribra orbitalia typically occurs in younger individuals.

The Skull

The **skull** comprises the **braincase** or **cranium** and the **lower jaw** or **mandible**; often, the **hyoid bone** is included (see below). The points of articulation of the mandible with the skull are the only areas of significant movement between bones of the skull. Otherwise, the numerous bones of various sizes that make up the cranium become relatively or completely immovable along their sutural zones of contact.

A convenient way in which to think of the skull is in terms of its major functions. The cranium, as its synonym suggests, protects the brain. Thus, the braincase is basically a container and the bones that contribute to it are, on at least three sides, platelike; the basilar region, in particular, is pervaded by holes or passageways for the exit of various nerves emanating from the brain (the cranial nerves) as well as for the entrance and exit of blood vessels that serve the brain and its attendant structures. The face is dominated by the bony accommodation of the sense organs and other structures associated with sensation. Right and left sockets or *orbits* protect the eyes. Between and below the orbits lies the *nasal aperture,* which opens into the *nasal cavity.* The upper jaw bears teeth. Although teeth are used for gathering and processing food, they were probably derived evolutionarily from the sensory dermal scales seen in fish—which is in part betrayed by the fact that teeth are innervated by sensory nerves. The lower jaw or mandible also serves to anchor teeth, which are innervated by a branch of the same sensory nerve (ultimately, a branch of the fifth cranial nerve, the trigeminal nerve) that innervates the upper teeth.

As is detailed in this chapter, the number of bones in the adult is actually considerably less than the number of centers of ossification and even the number of bony units in the neonate. Thus, although it may be practical to learn cranial anatomy by studying the adult first, one should bear in mind that this is the last stage of development. As such, the ontogeny of individual bones is also discussed.

Certain analyses require the skull to be oriented in a standard position. To do so, align the bottom or inferior edge of the orbit with the top or superior margin of the opening of the bony "ear hole" (the tubular *external auditory* or *acoustic meatus* at the side of the skull) and align this plane parallel to the ground. The vertical axis of the skull should be at a right angle to this horizontal plane. Positioned thus, the skull will be in the *Frankfort plane* or *horizontal.* With the skull in the Frankfort horizontal, one can study it properly from the front (i.e. in *norma facialis* or *frontalis*), from behind (*norma occipitalis*), from the side (*norma lateralis*), from below (*norma basilaris*), or from above (*norma verticalis*). It is also when the skull is oriented in the Frankfort horizontal that standardized measurements, from standardized anthropometric landmarks, can be taken with accuracy and thus be comparable with measurements taken by other osteologists.

External Morphology

Cranium

The cranium (Figure 2–1) can be subdivided into two units: the **calvaria** (sometimes the word "calvarium" is used, but this is based on

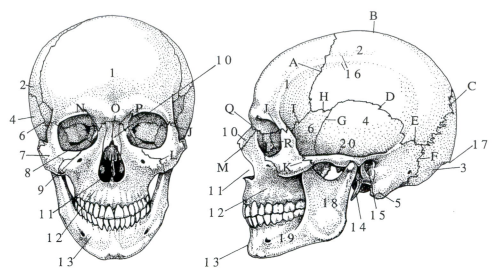

Figure 2-1 Articulated skull and mandible: *(left)* anterior and *(right)* lateral views. Major features/bones: (1) frontal, (2) parietal, (3) occipital, (4) temporal, (5) mastoid process (temporal bone), (6) greater wing of sphenoid, (7) zygoma, (8) ethmoid, (9) lacrimal, (10) nasal, (11) nasal aperture, (12) maxilla, (13) mandible, (14) styloid process, (15) external acoustic meatus, (16) temporal lines, (17) mental protuberance, (18) ascending ramus, (19) body of mandible, (20) temporal fossal. Sutures: (A) coronal, (B) sagittal, (C) lambdoid, (D) squamosal, (E) parietomastoid, (F) occipitomastoid, (G) sphenotemporal, (H) sphenoparietal, (I) sphenofrontal, (J) zygomaticofrontal, (K) zygomaticotemporal, (L) zygomaticomaxillary, (M) nasomaxillary, (N) frontomaxillary, (O) nasal, (P) frontonasal, (Q) frontolacrimal, (R) ethmolacrimal.

the misconception that "calvaria" is, in Latin, the neuter plural and not the feminine singular) and the **facial skeleton** or face; at times, "calvaria" and "braincase" are used interchangeably.

The calvaria is composed of eight major bones: the **ethmoid, frontal, occipital, parietal, sphenoid,** and **temporal.** In the adult, the ethmoid, frontal, occipital, and sphenoid bones are single bones, whereas the parietal and temporal bones are paired (right and left) bones. For the most part, the frontal and occipital bones and especially the parietal bones are platelike in configuration. The temporal bone contains the bony contributions to the **ear region** and thus houses the minuscule **inner ear bones**—the **incus, malleus,** and **stapes**—which are also paired bones.

The **frontal bone,** as its name suggests, lies at the front of the braincase. Essentially, it constitutes the forehead and anterior region of the top of the skull. The frontal bone also contributes to the orbital regions—to the orbital roof, the superior orbital rim, and the posterior wall of the orbit—and somewhat so to the sides of the

cranium superiorly. The frontal bone contacts the paired nasal bones, which lie between the orbits. One of the major muscles of mastication courses from the mandible superiorly, spreading over much of the lateral wall of the cranium. As it does so, this muscle—the *temporal muscle*—rides up behind the frontal bone's contribution to the posterior wall of the orbit and arcs superiorly and posteriorly over the side of that bone. Features on the frontal bone itself reflect the presence of the muscle: the portion of bone immediately behind the lateral and superior "corner" of the orbit is thickened into a ridge (the *temporal ridge*), which bounds the temporal muscle anteriorly; this ridge, which is variably developed among different individuals (and thus may be 1 cm or more long and differentially ridgelike), eventually appears to bifurcate into two low-lying, somewhat parallel lines called the *temporal lines*. These lines represent the attachment scars left by the temporal muscle, and thus they reflect the course of the muscle over the cranium.

At approximately the same height as or a little below the most superior extent of the temporal lines themselves, the frontal bone may be swollen variably into two rounded, perhaps bossed regions, one above each orbit. These swellings are the *frontal eminences*. They are more pronounced in young individuals. Among adults, they typically remain more distinct in females than in males.

The anthropometric landmark *frontotemporale* (see Appendix F) is located on the temporal ridge, at its most medial point. (The delineation of anthropometric landmarks is not only useful for taking standardized measurements but also provides a shorthand for referring to a point on the skull.) Another landmark is defined on the frontal bone at the midline of the skull, above the nasal region and between the orbits, parallel with the highest extent of the superior rims of the orbits. This landmark is *glabella*, which sometimes constitutes the most anterior point on the frontal bone.

The bulk of the sides and top of the skull is formed by the **parietal bones**, which sit behind or posterior to the frontal bone, and which meet along the midsagittal plane of the skull. In many individuals, particularly in females, each parietal bone bulges and bears a bossed region that is located approximately halfway along the bone's length and away from the midline of the skull laterally. In some individuals, this region is quite prominent and swollen, giving the skull the appearance of having a blunt corner. This feature is called the *parietal eminence*. Right and left parietal eminences are often coincident with the points that give the cranium its greatest width or breadth. In general, and regardless of where it is located, the anthropometric landmark on the skull from which one measures the greatest cranial width or breadth is called *euryon*.

The **occipital bone** abuts the parietal bones posteriorly and extends inferiorly and basally; this bone contains the opening (the *foramen magnum*) through which the spinal cord exits the skull. The occipital bone presents itself posteriorly as comprising two morphologically distinguishable moieties: a relatively smooth-boned superior component, the *planum occipitale*, and a rougher, muscle-scarred inferior portion, the *planum nuchale*; the neck or nuchal muscles attach on the planum nuchale. The two regions typically are delineated from one another by the roughly undulating *superior nuchal line*, which increases in size and thickness as it approaches the midline of the skull, at which point it is often elevated variably as a blunt to peaked and distended feature called the *external occipital protuberance*. Sometimes, the external occipital protuberance is coincident with the anthropometric landmark called *inion*, which is located at the midline of the superior nuchal line. The most posterior point on the skull, which is usually on the planum occipitale, is identified as another anthropometric landmark, *opisthocranion*. In some primates, including various fossil hominids, inion and opisthocranion coincide. Basally, additional anthropometric landmarks are identified on the foramen magnum. Posteriorly, *opisthion* is located in the midline, just on the margin of the foramen magnum. On the anterior border of the foramen, again in the midline, is *basion*.

The **temporal bone**, which lies below the parietal bone and in front of the occipital bone, contributes to the lower portion of the lateral wall of the cranium. It appears platelike from the side but is actually quite thick and bulky as it protrudes inward or medially to form part of the basilar region of the skull. The platelike portion of the temporal bone is called the *squama* or *squamous portion of the temporal*; ("squamous" means "flat" or "scalelike"). The thick, bulky, basilar extension is called the *petrous portion of the temporal bone* or just the *petrosal bone*. A variably gracile bony strut—the *zygomatic process of the temporal bone*—emanates from the side of the squamous portion of the temporal bone, just in front of the external opening of the bony tube or meatus of the ear region, and projects anteriorly, ultimately contributing to the formation of the cheekbone or *zygomatic arch*. The "space" above the horizontal plane of the zygomatic arch is the *temporal fossa* and that below is the *infratemporal fossa*; sometimes the "space" between the zygomatic arch and the lateral wall of the cranium is also referred to as the *infratemporal fossa*.

Behind the external auditory meatus, the temporal bone is enlarged. It extends posteriorly along its contact with the parietal bone as a rather horizontal ledge and swells inferiorly into a variably pointed and distended projection (the *mastoid process*). The horizontal posterior extension of the temporal bone forms a noticeably sharp angle—called the *parietal notch*—

with the squamous portion of the temporal, into which a "corner" of the parietal bone nests firmly.

The midpoint of the superior margin of the external auditory meatus—which is used in determining the Frankfort horizontal—is identified as the anthropometric landmark called *porion*. A vertical line projected upward from an imaginary line connecting right and left porions (and also at a right angle to the Frankfort horizontal) will terminate superiorly at the landmark *apex*, which frequently is the highest point on the skull. ("Apex" can be measured directly from a coronal radiograph. When measured on the cranium, the end of the arm of the osteometer is placed on porion, the stem of the osteometer is held vertically and at a right angle to the Frankfort horizontal, and the other arm of the osteometer is extended over the top of the skull and brought down on the skull. The point of contact will be "apex.") The tip of the mastoid process is referred to as *mastoidale*.

Intervening between the temporal bone anteriorly and the frontal bone is an extension of the **sphenoid bone**—the *greater wing of the sphenoid*—which completes the braincase laterally. Right and left greater wings spread out from the body of the sphenoid, the bulk of which lies in the midregion of the cranium, contributing to the base of the skull as well as to the walls of the orbits. The greater and the much smaller *lesser wings of the sphenoid* are visible within the orbits. The greater wing forms much of the inferior and posterior portion of the lateral orbital wall, while the lesser wing constitutes the most posterior and most minor contribution to the medial orbital wall as well as to the orbit's roof. The greater wing is separated inferiorly from the floor of the orbit by a deep "gash"—the *inferior orbital fissure*—which communicates primarily with the infratemporal fossa but also with the *pterygopalatine fossa* (see discussion of palatine bones, below). The inferior orbital fissure "originates" laterally from the posterior edge of the zygomatic bone (see below) and courses medially and posteriorly to the back of the funnel-shaped orbit. At its "terminus," another fissure—the *superior orbital fissure*—takes origin, coursing upward and arcing somewhat laterally to intervene between the lesser and greater wings of the sphenoid. (The oculomotor, trochlear, and ab-

ducent nerves and the terminal branches of the ophthalmic nerve as well as of the ophthalmic veins course through the superior orbital fissure.) The superior orbital fissure communicates with the interior of the cranium, specifically, the middle cranial fossa (see below). The deepest part or *apex* of the orbit lies just medial to the superior orbital fissure.

The inferior orbital fissure transmits the maxillary nerve, which continues as the infraorbital nerve through the maxilla superiorly, just under the floor of the orbit in the *infraorbital canal*, and eventually exits upon the face through a hole just below the inferior orbital rim, the *infraorbital foramen*. Just before this nerve becomes totally encased in a bony canal, it first lies in a short, superiorly open groove—the *infraorbital groove*—which creates a variably distinct notch in the anterior margin of the inferior orbital fissure. Just medial to the superior orbital fissure (and the apex of the orbit) lies the *optic foramen*, through which the optic nerve and ophthalmic artery course as they proceed from the anterior cranial fossa, through the sphenoid, and into the orbit.

The sphenoid also extends inferiorly from the greater wing, onto the basilar side of the cranium, where it comes to lie adjacent to the anterior border of the petrous portion of the temporal. The "tip" of the petrosal, which is directed anteriorly and medially, in conjunction with the body of the sphenoid, subtends a large, jagged-edged hole—the *foramen lacerum*—which in life is plugged with cartilage. The tip of the petrosal opens upon the foramen lacerum as the *carotid canal*. From the general region of each foramen lacerum, the sphenoid descends to the level of the palate as two stout but narrow platelike wings that are joined anteriorly and thereby bracket on either side a shallow but elongate depression. These two winglike sphenoidal structures are the *medial* and *lateral pterygoid plates* or *laminae* and the depression they subtend is the *pterygoid fossa*.

The **ethmoid**, which lies in front of the sphenoid, is contained largely within the nasal cavity. The paper-thin lateral sides of the ethmoid are exposed in, and are thus components of, the medial walls of the orbits; an ethmoid exposure in the medial orbital wall is sometimes referred to as the *os planum*. Humans and the two African apes—the chimpanzee and gorilla—apparently are the only extant primates in which the ethmoid is internally subdivided into air cells or chambers. The African apes develop only a few large air cells, whereas humans are distinguished by an abundance of ethmoidal air cells. Indeed, in many human skulls, the lateral wall (or os planum) of the ethmoid is sufficiently thin and translucent that one can see the pattern of the air cells within.

All of the aforementioned bones—the ethmoid included—contribute to the interior surface of the braincase and bear evidence of association with soft tissue structures attendant to or emanating from the brain.

The juncture between the frontal bone and the parietal bones is identified as the *coronal suture*. This suture courses from side to side across the skull. The coronal suture is formed by an edge-to-edge contact of the bones involved and presents itself externally as three segments, of which the middle segment is the most denticulate and severely undulating. An imaginary plane (at a right angle to the ground) passing through the body via the coronal suture is referred to as the *coronal plane*. The coronal suture terminates inferiorly at the superior extent of the greater wing of the sphenoid, which is roughly at the same level as the highest point of the superior margin of the orbit.

Coursing posteriorly from the coronal suture along the midline of the cranium is the *sagittal suture*, which is formed by an edge-to-edge contact of the two parietal bones; posteriorly, the sagittal suture terminates at the occipital bone. An imaginary plane (at a right angle to the ground) passing through the sagittal suture is referred to as the *sagittal plane*. The vaguely "T"-shaped juncture between the sagittal suture and the coronal suture is identified as the anthropometric landmark *bregma*. The sagittal suture is variably oscillating along its length: proceeding posteriorly from bregma, it is low and mildly undulating for approximately one-third of its length, then high and peaked for a short burst, very low and quiet for a short distance, and then quite excited again for the remainder. The contact between the parietal bone and the greater wing of the sphenoid is referred to as the *sphenoparietal suture*. This suture marks the general area (not specific point) of the anthropometric landmark *pterion*. The contact between the frontal bone and the greater wing

of the sphenoid can be referred to as the *sphenofrontal suture*.

Sometimes small islands of bone may form within segments of the sagittal suture. Such intrusive, supernumerary bony elements are referred to interchangeably as *ossicles* or *intrasutural*, *accessory*, or *wormian bones*. If found in the sagittal suture, they can be identified as, for example, *sagittal ossicles* or *wormian bones in the sagittal suture*. A wormian bone located at bregma is called a *bregmatic bone* or *ossicle*, or an *ossicle at bregma*. An ossicle at pterion is identified as an *epipteric bone*, and one in the region of the parietal notch is a *parietal notch bone*.

The suture between the parietal and the occipital bones—the *lambdoid suture*—courses down to the lateral part of the abutment between the occipital bone and the mastoid region of the temporal bone. The juncture between the lambdoid and sagittal sutures represents the anthropometric landmark *lambda*. (An extremely large ossicle at lambda—wherein a substantial portion of the occipital bone appears as if it has been cut off superiorly from the rest of the bone by a horizontal suture—is identified as an *Inca* or *interparietal bone*.) The continuation of the occipital bone alongside and inferiorly around the posterior edge of the mastoid region of the temporal bone is referred to as the *occipitomastoid suture*. Variation with regard to the *mastoid foramen*, which is usually located in the occipitomastoid suture just behind the mastoid process, is noted when it lies outside of the suture (or is *exsutural*), penetrating the mastoid process; there may also be smaller, accessory mastoid foramina, and these are usually exsutural. The tripartite juncture of the occipital, parietal, and temporal bones is the anthropometric landmark *asterion*; it is vaguely star-shaped in appearance.

Basally (Figure 2–2) and somewhat centrally, the spit of the occipital bone that protrudes anteriorly from the region of the foramen magnum—the *basilar portion of the occipital bone* or the *basiocciput*—meets the *basilar portion of the sphenoid* or the *basisphenoid*. The plane of contact between these two bones is the *sphenooccipital synchondrosis* (sometimes also referred to as the *basilar suture*). Eventually the basiocciput and the basisphenoid coalesce. The side of the basiocciput is bordered by the thick

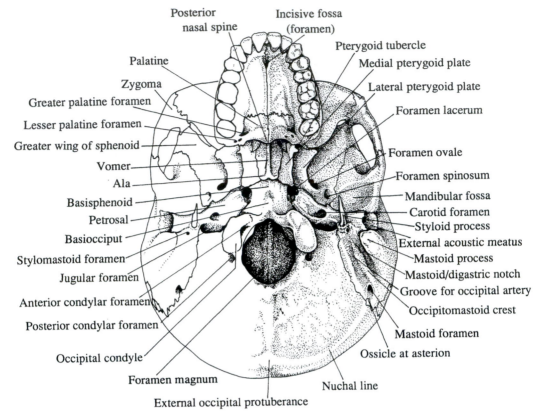

Figure 2–2 Basal view of skull.

and craggy petrous portion of the temporal bone, but these two sections of bone never coalesce. Basally and posteriorly, the sides of the basiocciput and the petrosal bone are concave and, together, contribute to the formation of a moderately large hole, the *jugular foramen*, through which the jugular vein courses as it proceeds away from the brain. Anterior to the jugular foramen, the basiocciput and the petrosal bone become associated more intimately, but they remain individual entities, being separated by the *petro-occipital fissure*.

The platelike squamous portion of the temporal bone forms an arcuate suture primarily with the parietal bone, which it overlaps rather than abuts. This suture is identified as the *squamosal suture*. Thin striations often radiate out from the squamosal suture over the external surface of the parietal bone. The contact between the temporal bone and the greater wing of the sphenoid is the *sphenotemporal suture*. The zone of contact between the mastoid region

of the temporal bone and the parietal bone is referred to specifically as the *parietomastoid suture*.

Facial Skeleton

The facial skeleton (Figure 2–1) proper is typically represented as being composed of 12 major bones: the **maxillary, nasal, zygomatic** or **malar, lacrimal,** and **palatine bones,** the **inferior nasal conchae,** and the **vomer,** all of which are paired bones. With the **mandible,** the number of bones increases to 13. Another bone, the **hyoid,** is often included in discussions of the skull because it derives embryologically from the second and third branchial arches and thus belongs to the cartilaginous branchial arch skeleton, as do the **incus,** the **malleus,** and (part of) the mandible. In the adult, the hyoid bone is a single, "U"-shaped bone that is distinguished by its being the only bone in the body that does not make contact with any other bone; rather, it is suspended in the throat region, below the mandible, by ligaments that attach to processes on the base of the skull.

A point of debate over the years has been whether or not humans possess a **premaxilla**, as do other mammals (see review by Schwartz, 1982). A premaxillary bone, as its name suggests, lies anterior to, or in front of, the maxilla; it also contributes inferiorly to the nasal aperture. The best evidence for the existence of a premaxilla in humans comes from studies of fetal development and, osteologically, from investigation of the facial regions of young individuals; this topic is discussed elsewhere in the text. With the mandible and hyoid bone being single elements in the adult, whereas the premaxillae are paired, the total number of bones in the adult facial skeleton—in the expanded sense—is 16. For the purposes of the general description that follows, though (and following tradition), the term "maxilla" will be used to embrace both the maxilla and the premaxilla.

The **nasal bones** lie in the midsagittal plane of the face, articulating with the frontal bone above. They are typically short bones that broaden inferiorly. They form the superior margin of the nasal aperture superiorly. Among primates, the nasal bones project outward and protrude somewhat from the facial plane only in humans and various other species of the genus *Homo*. On either side of each nasal bone lies a projection—the *frontal process*—of the maxilla (also the frontal process of the premaxilla), which also makes contact with the frontal bone.

Lateral and inferior to the maxillary frontal process, the maxilla contributes to the formation of the *inferior border (rim, margin) of the orbit.* It is folded or creased in this region. A posteriorly tapering tongue of maxilla extending from this flexure contributes to the formation of the floor of the orbit. This maxillary component maintains contact medially with the inferior border of the ethmoidal contribution to the medial orbital wall. However, it does not contribute to the lateral orbital wall, as it is separated from the greater wing of the sphenoid to the lateral orbital wall by the inferior orbital fissure. The bulk of the maxilla lies below the inferior rim of the orbit, spreading out to contribute to the *cheekbone,* or *zygomatic* or *malar*

region, below which the maxilla becomes truncated or "waisted" as it approaches the border in which the teeth are anchored. The nasal aperture, which is taller than it is wide and typically broader at its base than superiorly, is subtended primarily by the maxilla. The shape of the nasal aperture is technically trapezoidal but can also be described as broadly piriform or pear-shaped. At the midline of the inferior margin of the nasal aperture, the abutting right and left maxillae may be distended anteriorly into a small/blunt to large/spikelike, sometimes bifid projection called the *anterior nasal spine.* The reason this spine may be bifid is that the apparently single structure results from the appression or coalescence of what ontogenetically arise as two spikelike projections; the suture between right and left anterior nasal spines often persists into the adult. The maxillary contribution to the floor of the nasal cavity is typically smooth and planar. The teeth sit in a raised peripheral portion of the maxilla—the *alveolar process, margin* or *border*—medial to which the palatal region is variably vaulted. At the midline of the palate and approximately 1 to 2 cm posterior to the alveolar margin, the two maxillae contribute to the formation of a single, relatively large opening in the palate, the *incisive foramen* or *fossa.*

In the medial wall of the orbit and sandwiched between the frontal process of the maxilla and the orbital exposure of the ethmoid is the small **lacrimal bone.** (Although the lacrimal bone in other mammals, including other primates, may extend partially outside the inferior orbital rim—onto the face—the lacrimal bone in humans lies entirely within the medial orbital wall.) The lacrimal bone in humans is dominated by its large *lacrimal fossa, groove,* or *sulcus,* which is bordered posteriorly by the *posterior lacrimal crest,* lying on the lacrimal bone itself. The posterior lacrimal crest can be crestlike, but it can also be a minimal swelling or a distended sheet of bone. An *anterior lacrimal crest* also exists, but it lies on the frontal process of the premaxilla (maxilla), at the edge of the orbit. This crest is more consistently configured as a blunt rise. The anterior and posterior lacrimal crests bound the broad and variably deep lacrimal fossa.

The maxilla also contacts the **zygomatic** or

malar bone, which contributes laterally to the inferior orbital rim and constitutes the major component of the lateral portion of the orbital rim. The zygomatic also projects upward to contact a short extension of the frontal bone (the *zygomatic process of the frontal bone*). Together, these two extensions form a barlike structure that lies lateral and slightly posterior to the orbit. More or less at the same level as the inferior rim of the orbit, a short extension of the zygomatic—the *zygomatic process of the zygomatic bone*—projects posteriorly. This zygomatic process of the zygomatic bone contacts the anteriorly directed zygomatic process of the temporal bone.

The **palatine bones** lie posterior to the maxilla on its oral cavity side and constitute the posteriormost extension of the hard palate. A palatine bone is much wider (mediolaterally) than it is long (anteroposteriorly). At the midline of their posterior border, the abutting palatine bones are distended in concert into a single but variably roundedly blunt, to peaked, to squared *posterior nasal spine*. On the lateral side, each palatine bone contributes to the formation of a large, somewhat ovoid or elliptical foramen, the *greater palatine foramen*. The lateral wall of this foramen may be formed by the maxilla. Posterolaterally, each palatine bone is bounded by the inferiormost portion of the region at which the medial and lateral pterygoid plates become confluent. Just in front of the wall created by the medial and lateral pterygoid plates, there may be a small *lesser palatine foramen* and/or an *accessory lesser palatine foramen*. The "space" posterior to the palatine bones and pterygoid plates (i.e. the border created by the palatine bones and the pterygoid plates on one side and the basiocciput on the other) is referred to as the *pterygopalatine fossa*, through which various structures pass, including branches of the maxillary, mandibular, nasopalatine, and greater palatine nerves and their attendant arteries. The pterygopalatine fossa is also confluent with the inferior orbital fissure [however, the confluence between the pterygopalatine and infratemporal fossae is greater (see discussion above of the inferior orbital fissure)].

The remaining bones of the face—the **vomer** and the **inferior nasal conchae**—are visible only when one is looking directly through the nasal aperture into the *nasal cavity*. The **vomer** is a thin, vertical sheet of bone in the midline that rises up from the floor of the nasal cavity to contact an equally thin, sheetlike bony extension of the ethmoid bone, the *perpendicular plate of the ethmoid*. Together, these contiguous, vertical plates of bone bisect the nasal cavity. The vomer spans the distance between the anterior and posterior nasal spines and thus overlaps both the maxilla and the palatine bones. Extending down from the lateral walls of the nasal cavity and protruding in toward, but not touching, the vomer are the **inferior nasal conchae**. Each concha takes origin as a relatively thin and smooth-boned, winglike structure that is expanded medially and inferiorly into a more rugose ledge.

The **mandible** consists of a somewhat horizontally oriented *body* and a fairly vertical *ascending ramus* on each side. The body of the mandible contains teeth (which are anchored in the *alveolar process* or *margin* of the mandible) and its general contour mirrors the arc of the *dental arcade* of the upper jaw. The general region of the "corner" formed by the ascending ramus and the mandibular body is the *goneal region*. The angle that can be measured between the inferior margin of the body and the posterior margin of the ascending ramus is the *goneal* or *mandibular angle*; an alternative is to measure this angle at the intersection of the imaginary long axes of the body and ascending ramus. Often, in males, the external surface of the goneal region is more markedly muscle-scarred and lipped around its edge than in females. The mandibular angle in young to middle-aged adult males tends to approach 90°, whereas it is more obtuse in females of similar age. In young and very old individuals of either sex, however, the mandibular angle is universally more obtuse: in the former case, adult features have not yet been established, while in the latter, the bone has become thinned and remodeled as a result of resorption that normally occurs with age and/or dental/periodontal disease.

Superiorly, the ascending ramus bifurcates broadly and shallowly into a thin anterior projection (which comes to lie within the infratemporal fossa when the upper and lower jaws are in occlusion) and a posterior, wider, barlike end (which articulates directly with the skull). The thin projection is called the *coronoid process,* and from it emanates a large muscle of mastication—the *temporal muscle*—that passes up between the zygomatic arch and the lateral wall of the skull and then fans out over the sidewall of the braincase. The perimeter of this muscle leaves a set of roughly parallel muscle scars, the *superior* and *inferior temporal lines.* These lines (1) course up behind the orbit and along the posterior orbital wall; (2) arc superiorly at their peak just behind the coronal suture and then arc inferiorly toward the lambdoid suture; (3) curve inward beyond asterion as they proceed anteriorly and in parallel with the zygomatic process of the temporal bone; and then (4) fade out. Separate superior and inferior muscle scars are most distinct as they proceed away from the temporal ridge (of the posterior orbital region of the frontal bone) and until the point at which they begin their descent toward asterion.

The part of the ascending ramus that articulates with the base of the skull has been called the *head of the mandible,* the *mandibular condyle,* or the *condyloid* or *condylar process of the mandible.* When the upper and lower jaws are in occlusion, the mandibular condyle sits in a typically shallow but variably ovoid to elliptical depression that lies in front of the external auditory meatus, inferior and medial to the root of the zygomatic process of the temporal bone. This depression—the *glenoid, articular,* or *mandibular fossa*—is wider (mediolaterally) than it is long (anteroposteriorly).

The contact between the frontal bone and the nasal bones is identified as the *frontonasal suture;* between the frontal bone and the maxilla, the contact is called the *frontomaxillary suture;* between the frontal and the zygomatic bone it is the *frontozygomatic suture;* and between the frontal and the lacrimal bones it is the *frontolacrimal suture.* The midline suture between the two nasal bones is called the *nasal, internasal,* or *nasonasal suture.* The suture between a nasal bone and the maxilla is the *nasomaxillary suture.* The course of the edge of the frontal bone that contributes to the formation of sutures with the nasal bones, the frontal process of the maxilla, and the lacrimal bones will be variably arcuate, depending especially on the degree to which the nasal bones extend beyond the superior margins of the maxillary frontal pro-

cesses. The contact between the lacrimal bone and the maxilla is identified as the *lacrimomaxillary suture* and that between the lacrimal and the ethmoid is the *ethmolacrimal suture.*

The facial skeleton bears a profusion of anthropometric landmarks. Sometimes coincident with the frontozygomatic suture is the landmark called *ectoconchion,* which is defined as the most lateral extent of the orbital wall. The juncture of the internasal and frontonasal sutures is called *nasion.* Somewhat lateral to nasion is *maxillofrontale,* or the *anterior lacrimal point,* which is identified as the juncture of the anterior lacrimal crest and the frontomaxillary suture. Just lateral to maxillofrontale is *dacryon*—the point at which the frontomaxillary, frontolacrimal, and maxillolacrimal sutures meet; some authorities (e.g. Vallois, 1965) consider the term "dacryon" to be obsolete and use only "maxillofrontale" when they take measurements involving the orbital region. The juncture between the posterior lacrimal crest and the frontolacrimal suture constitutes the anthropometric landmark called *lacrimale.*

Various anthropometric landmarks are located in the median sagittal plane of the facial skeleton. For example, *nasospinale,* which is usually found at the base of the anterior nasal spine, is defined as the midpoint of a line connecting the lowest extents of the inferior margins of the right and left sides of the nasal aperture (technically, the lowest point of the right or left side of the inferior margin of the nasal aperture is called *nariale*). Below nasospinale lies the region of *prosthion,* which used to be subdivided into two landmarks, *hypoprosthion* and *exoprosthion.* Hypoprosthion was defined as the most inferior bony extension (of the alveolar bone or margin) between the upper central incisors. Nowadays, the locus of hypoprosthion is almost exclusively referred to as *alveolare.* Exoprosthion, which would be situated slightly superior to hypoprosthion, was defined as the most anterior point or extension of the alveolar margin. The landmark "prosthion" is now taken as being the same as "exoprosthion." Regardless of the terms used, the distinction between two different landmarks in the medial sagittal plane of the alveolar region is warranted because, in fact, the two may be quite separated from one another. "Prosthion" is used for measuring longitudinal diameters and "alveolare" for vertical measurements (see Vallois, 1965).

On the mandible, the anterior and superior extent of the alveolar bone between the lower central incisors is identified as the landmark *infradentale*. Farther inferiorly, *pogonion* represents the anteriormost point on the chin, below which is *gnathion*, which is located at the most anterior and inferior point on the mandible. On the palatal side of the maxilla, the point where the medial sagittal plane is crossed by a line connecting the most posterior borders of the sockets of the central incisors is identified as *orale*. Much farther back is *staphylion*, which is defined as the most posterior extent of the hard palate along the medial sagittal plane; this is usually the same point as the posterior nasal spine. Just in front of, or sometimes coincident with, staphylion is *alveolon*, which is the intersection between the medial sagittal plane and a line drawn between the most posterior extents of the right and left alveolar processes.

Anthropometric landmarks for determining maxillary and mandibular widths are, respectively, *endomolare* and *ectomolare*, and *gonion*. Endomolare is the most medial point of the medial margin of the alveolar bone surrounding the second upper molar. Ectomolare is the most lateral point on the lateral alveolar border of the tooth. Gonion is located externally on the goneal region of the mandible; it is the most lateral point of the goneal or angular region of the mandible.

Well back within the orbit and visible only when one peers obliquely into the orbit to study the medial orbital wall, lies the short and vertically oriented *sphenoethmoidal suture*. Superiorly, this suture contributes to a tripartite juncture with the *frontoethmoidal* and *sphenofrontal sutures*. The frontoethmoidal suture courses more or less horizontally posteriorly along the medial orbital wall. The sphenofrontal suture can be located by looking directly into the orbit (when the skull is in norma frontalis). It courses laterally and anteriorly from the tripartite sutural juncture noted above and meanders along the short exposure into the orbit of the lesser wing of the sphenoid, over the superior flexure of the superior orbital fissure, and across the orbital contribution of the greater wing of the sphenoid until it becomes confluent with the frontozygomatic suture. The "juncture" between the sphenofrontal and frontozygomatic sutures is delineated by the termination superiorly of the rather vertically oriented, variably undulating, *sphenozygomatic suture*, which descends to the slight upward invagination of the anterior end of the inferior orbital fissure.

Variation is noted in the development of an *exsutural anterior ethmoid foramen* (i.e. lying in the medial orbital wall in the frontal alone, rather than being captured in the suture between the frontal and the ethmoid) and a *posterior ethmoid foramen*. The sphenoid and maxilla meet along the *sphenomaxillary suture* and the sphenoid and the zygomatic bone create the *sphenozygomatic suture*.

Internal Morphology

Skull Cap

(Discussion of such an artificial "unit" as the skull cap (Figure 2–3) is necessary in light of the preparation and the availability of typical study specimens. However, it is important to learn the association of different parts of the cranium— whether it be skull cap or base of the skull— since paleontologically, archeologically, and/or forensically recovered cranial fragments more often come in the form of parts of bones connected along sutural lines than as pristine, isolated bones.)

In order to expose the interior of the cranium, it is necessary to remove some portion of its surrounding vaultlike structure. Typically, the part of the top of the cranium—the skull cap—that is removed consists of portions of the frontal, parietal, and occipital bones; the superior extent of the squamous region of the temporal bone is not included in the detached skull cap. With the skull cap removed, one can also study cranial bone in cross section and thus gain appreciation of differences in thickness within the same bone as well as between adjacent bones. (For example, the parietal bones are more consistently thinner than the frontal and occipital bones; the occipital bone is the thickest and is expanded further toward its midline; the frontal bone bears a prominent crest along its midline.)

Most clearly noted in the region of the frontal and occipital bones is the three-layered mor-

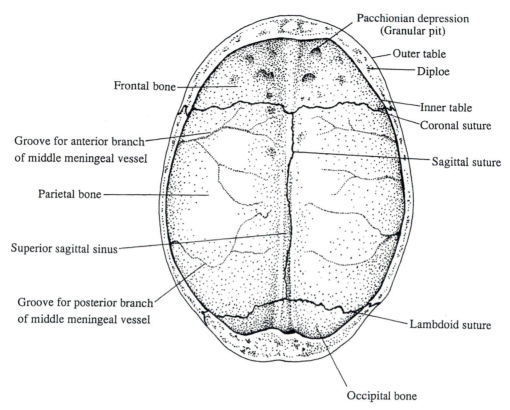

Pacchionian depression
(Granular pit)

Outer table

Diploe

Frontal bone

Inner table

Coronal suture

Groove for anterior branch
of middle meningeal vessel

Sagittal suture

Parietal bone

Superior sagittal sinus

Groove for posterior branch
of middle meningeal vessel

Lambdoid suture

Occipital bone

Figure 2–3   Internal morphology of skullcap.

phology typical of many cranial bones. There is an *outer table* of bone and an *inner table,* both of which are compact bone, and an intervening layer of spongy bone, the *diploë.* In regions where the bone is not very thick (e.g. much of the length of the parietal bones, the posterior extents of the frontal bone), the diploic layer may not be noticeably expressed. The bone thus appears to be continuously solid.

Among the dominant features of the interior of the skull cap, especially of younger individuals, are the *coronal, sagittal,* and *lambdoid* sutures. Sutural distinctiveness tends to diminish with increasing age as the sutures themselves coalesce and fuse. In general, sutures close from the inside out (*endocranially* to *ectocranially*), with the endocranial sequence usually being coronal → sagittal → lambdoid and the ectocranial sequence being sagittal and lambdoid sutures at about the same time and well before the coronal suture. Endocranially, the lambdoid suture represents the most variable degree of completeness of closure (e.g. it may be minimally

fused even in some of the most senile individuals). In contrast, the coronal suture is almost always completely closed by 30 years of age and the sagittal suture is completely fused in 67% of individuals 70 years of age or older.

Persistent throughout the adult life of an individual are the impressions left by the *meningeal vessels,* which attend the meninges of the brain. The network of grooves left by the meningeal vessels is confined primarily to the inner table of the parietal bones. However, a few meningeal branches may cross onto the frontal bone, as well as, but less frequently so, onto the occipital bone. Anteriorly on the parietal bone, and coursing more or less in parallel with the coronal suture, is the *anterior division* or *branch of the middle meningeal vessel.* This meningeal branch divides into a variable number of smaller branches, the majority of which typically lie posterior to the primary trunk. Posterior to the anterior branch of the middle meningeal vessel and its divisions—approximately halfway along the parietal bone—are the *pos-*

terior divisions of the middle meningeal vessels, which, like the anterior complex, arborize superiorly and posteriorly. Two characteristic features of the internal surface of the parietal bone, therefore, are that (1) there are fewer grooves for the middle meningeal vessels along the inferior portion of the bone and (2) these grooves, reflecting the pattern of the vessels, ramify and fan out in a posterosuperior direction. Thus, in addition to the configuration of the sutures that delineate the parietal bone, the branching pattern of the middle meningeal vessels provides a major clue to determining the side of the body from which a given parietal bone or fragment of a parietal bone comes.

Coursing along the internal aspect of the sagittal suture one finds a relatively broad and generally shallow groove—the *sagittal sulcus*—which is the impression made upon the inner table of bone by the superior sagittal sinus, which is a conduit of venous drainage associated with the brain and its meninges. The sagittal sulcus is most clearly expressed along the posterior portion of the sutural region itself, but traces of it often are found anteriorly on the frontal bone. Within the trough and along the perimeter of the sulcus there are often pits of small to medium size that are formed by *arachnoid granulations* of *Pacchionian bodies* (from the arachnoid meningeal layer), which protrude into the bone. These *granular pits* (granular foveolae) become deeper and wider and increase in number with increasing age. In older individuals, the large pits are referred to as *Pacchionian depressions*.

The **frontal bone** (superiorly) is noted for its relative lack of morphological adornment. In the middle of it, in the median sagittal plane, the sharp and prominent *frontal crest* protrudes. This crest serves as a site of attachment for the falx cerebri, which tethers the brain anteriorly to the interior of the skull. The impression of the sulcus of the superior sagittal sinus is usually visible at the "base" (i.e. the superiormost portion) of the frontal crest.

The **occipital bone**—what little of it is captured in the creation of a skull cap—also tends to be relatively free of morphological adornment. However, the bone does tend to bulge along the median sagittal plane (providing a site of attachment for the falx cerebri), and the sulcus for the superior sagittal sinus may be visible

veering off to one side or the other of this low "crest." Typically, in humans, the sulcus for the superior sagittal sinus takes a course to the right side of the median "bulge" of the occipital bone (see Falk and Conroy, 1983; Tobias, 1967; and references therein).

Base of the Skull

Given the gross external configuration of the brain, it is understandable that anatomists have subdivided the interior of the base of the skull (Figure 2–4) into three major paired "units" or depressions that receive (from front to back) the paired frontal, temporal, and occipital lobes of the cerebrum. These depressions, respectively, are the right and left portions of the **anterior, middle,** and **posterior cranial fossae** (a fossa is a depression, concavity, or pit). The surface of the anterior cranial fossa is the most irregular topographically due to impressions left by the gyri (i.e. raised areas) of the brain; the clarity and profusion of these gyral impressions varies in accordance with the extent to which the meninges mask the surface of the brain. The middle cranial fossa may bear some gyral impressions.

The **anterior cranial fossa** is confined anteriorly and laterally by a platelike portion of the frontal bone. It is bounded inferiorly by the orbital portion of the frontal bone as well as by parts of the ethmoid and sphenoid. The ethmoid lies in front of the sphenoid. It intervenes midsagittally between the rugose and upwardly bulging frontal contributions to the *orbital plate*. In line with the frontal crest is the relatively narrow and anteroposteriorly elongate *crista galli* ("crest of a chicken" or cock's comb) of the ethmoid (which is reminiscent of the comb of a rooster protruding from the orbital plate). The crista galli achieves its greatest height and breadth anteriorly. From there, it descends and tapers posteriorly; it may also slope quite markedly. Anteriorly and inferiorly, the crista galli spreads out like a winged mantle, forming a sutural contact with the surrounding frontal bone, into which it appears to protrude. The wings or *alae* (also *ethmoidal alae*) of this mantle appear to embrace on either side the crest of the frontal bone (the frontal crest). A small foramen lies between the "mantle" of the crista galli and the base of the frontal crest. This

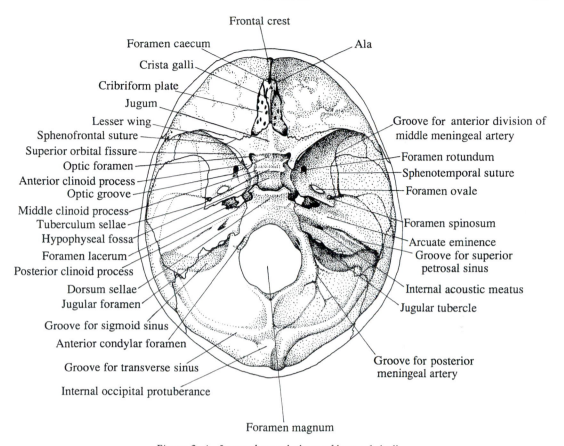

Figure 2–4 Internal morphology of base of skull.

small foramen is called the *foramen caecum* (a cecum is a blind pouch or cul-de-sac) and typically opens only on the floor of the anterior cranial fossa; sometimes, however, the foramen caecum does transmit a vein from the superior sagittal sinus.

On either side of the crista galli, and often extending around it posteriorly, is a narrow expanse of thin, perforated bone, the *cribriform plate of the ethmoid*. The cribriform plate forms a shallow trough around the crista galli and thus isolates it (1) on its sides from the frontal portion of the orbital plate and (2) posteriorly from the body of the sphenoid. The cribriform plate forms the thin roof of the nasal cavity; tiny branches of the olfactory nerve course from the mucous membrane of the nasal cavity, through the perforations or foramina of the cribriform plate, to the olfactory bulbs. The cribriform plate lies well below the level of the frontal contributions to the orbital plate.

The sphenoid contributes to the posterior

margin of the anterior cranial fossa: i.e. the laterally tapering lesser wings of the sphenoid embrace from behind the frontal contribution to the orbital plate. Posterior to the cribriform plate, the midsagittal portion between the lesser wings is broad, deep, smooth, and relatively flat; it is referred to as the *jugum* (jugal region). In younger individuals, the suture between the lesser wings of the sphenoid and the orbital plate of the frontal is visible; one can also often delineate the region where the jugum overlaps the ethmoid. Posteriorly, in the macerated skull, the winglikeness of the lesser wings is emphasized further by blunt to pointed projections that jut out into "open space" from either side of the jugum. These projections are the *anterior clinoid processes*, which overlie the right and left superior orbital fissures. The *optic foramen* lies medially and anteriorly at the base of each anterior clinoid process.

Whereas the surfaces of the right and left anterior cranial fossae are convex (bulging somewhat on either side of the midline), the two parts of the **middle cranial fossa** are concave: i.e. two deep concavities expand outward from a narrow, "saddle-shaped" midsagittal depression in the sphenoid. The saddle-shaped structure is identified as the *sella turcica* because of its resemblance to a saddle.

The sella turcica is bounded superolaterally by the anterior clinoid processes and superiorly across the midline by a variably distinct groove, the *optic groove*. This groove courses between the optic foramina and is bordered anteriorly and posteriorly by variably distinct ridges. The anterior wall of the sella turcica, which descends from the optic groove, is called the *tuberculum sellae* and the concavity upon which it terminates is the *hypophyseal fossa*, in which the cerebral hypophysis sits. Occasionally and below the level of the optic groove, the superior part of the tuberculum sellae may bear small, lateral protrusions, which are identified as the *middle* or *medial clinoid processes*. The sella turcica is confined posteriorly by an anteriorly sloping plate of bone—the *dorsum sellae*—which is distended either upward or laterally at its superolateral "corners" into the *posterior clinoid processes*. Midsagittally, the superior margin of the dorsum sellae is variably excavated or carved out. The posterior end of the base of the dorsum sellae contacts the basiocciput. The sides of the base of the sella turcica are indented. These indentations constitute the sphenoidal contributions to the right and left *foramina lacera* (singular is "foramen lacerum"). The right and left temporal lobes of the cerebrum sit like saddlebags on either side of the sella turcica; each temporal lobe is held in a shallow, depressed area, the *lateral part of the middle cranial fossa*.

The middle cranial fossa is broad anteriorly but tapers posteriorly, being truncated obliquely along its medial margin. Anteriorly and anteroinferiorly, the fossa is bounded by the interior surface of the greater wing of the sphenoid and the anterior part of the squamous portion of the temporal bone. The fossa is subtended laterally and, in part, lateroinferiorly, by the squamous portion of the temporal. The petrous portion of the temporal bounds the lateral part of the middle cranial fossa medially and medioinferiorly.

Anteriorly, medially, and somewhat superi-

orly, the arcuate superior orbital fissure connects the lateral part of the middle cranial fossa with the orbit. A series of foramina continues the arcuate trajectory of the superior orbital fissure. Situated below and slightly lateral to the inferiormost extent of the superior orbital fissure is the (essentially round) *foramen rotundum*. This foramen is unique in that its orientation through the greater wing of the sphenoid is (essentially) parallel to the Frankfort horizontal (i.e. the foramen rotundum is "pointed forward"). A bristle passed through the foramen rotundum from the middle cranial fossa demonstrates that it opens onto the posterior pole of the maxilla via the pterygopalatine fossa. The maxillary nerve (mentioned earlier in this chapter with regard to the sensory innervation of the upper teeth) courses from the trigeminal ganglion at the base of the brain through the foramen rotundum to the maxillary region, wherein it sends branches to teeth and then (identified as the infraorbital nerve) continues anteriorly along the floor of the orbit to exit upon the face from the infraorbital foramen.

Below and somewhat lateral to the foramen rotundum is the larger, oval-shaped *foramen ovale*. The long axis of this foramen is typically oriented obliquely, in an anteromedial to posterolateral direction. The foramen ovale is easily located externally, at the base and just to the lateral side of the lateral pterygoid plate. The mandibular nerve, which penetrates the mandible on its medial side (via the mandibular foramen) and then innervates lower dentition, exits the cranial base through the foramen ovale.

Completing the arcuate arrangement of foramina in the middle cranial fossa is the *foramen spinosum*, which is the smallest of the foramina. It is located behind and lateral to the posterolateral end of the foramen ovale, just medial to the sphenosquamosal suture. Although variation exists in the development of accessory foramina ovale, or septa that subdivide the primary foramen ovale, it appears that variability in the expression of the foramen spinosum is more common, resulting in, for example, this foramen's incomplete separation from the foramen ovale posteriorly or its continuity with the thin fissure that separates the petrous portion of the temporal anteromedially from the neighboring sphenoid. (The middle meningeal artery courses through the foramen spinosum. This artery parallels the middle meningeal veins in arborizing laterally across the squamous portion of the temporal bone.)

Medial and also sometimes slightly anterior to the foramen ovale, a tiny foramen—the *emissary sphenoidal foramen*—is often found, usually bilaterally (this foramen, therefore, lies outside the arcuate distribution of major foramina discussed above). Apparently quite infrequently, as well as unilaterally, the emissary sphenoidal foramen may not be closed off completely by bone and thus will open as a notch upon the foramen lacerum. This small emissary foramen may also be associated with a variably shallow depression or demonstrable groove that occasionally extends as far as the inferior border of the superior orbital fissure. Occasionally, and unilaterally, a small accessory foramen may lie just below the inferior border of the fissure; if this small accessory foramen is present, the shallow depression/groove will terminate at it.

The rest of the lateral part of the middle cranial fossa is relatively unremarkable. It is traversed by sutures and grooves for middle meningeal vessels and is slightly and variably corrugated by impressions of cerebral gyri; midway along the length of the petrous portion of the temporal lies a small mound, the *arcuate eminence*. At a variable distance laterally away from the foramen spinosum, the groove for the middle meningeal vessel bifurcates into anterior and posterior divisions or branches. The posterior division courses up and usually posteriorly along the squamous portion of the temporal and may cross the squamosal suture prior to establishing its branching pattern.

Depending on how far up the squamous portion of the temporal bone the groove for the middle meningeal vessel ascends before bifurcating, there may also be a relatively long anterior division of the middle meningeal vessel coursing upward and anteriorly, roughly paralleling the sphenosquamosal suture. This anterior division may then cross the sphenosquamosal suture to ascend the superiormost portion of the greater wing of the sphenoid; or, a short anterior branch of this primary anterior division may course across the sphenosquamosal suture and then the superior part of the greater wing of the sphenoid. In either case, the primary anterior division continues up the lateral wall of the middle cranial fossa and eventually along the parietal bone. In addition to these variant patterns, the anterior division may sometimes be enclosed in a bony canal a few centimeters in length that takes origin beneath the lateralmost extent of the lesser wing of the sphenoid—and/or this primary anterior division also may bifurcate, with its secondary branch arcing toward the lateral margin of the superior orbital fissure.

The **posterior cranial fossa** dominates the interior of the cranium. From above, the shape of the posterior cranial fossa is bluntly triangular anteriorly and swollen or bulbous posteriorly. It is narrowest anteriorly, being delimited by the dorsum sellae and the basisphenoid. The fossa then broadens laterally and posteriorly in concert with the crisp superomedial margins of the petrosal portions of the temporal bones, beneath which the fossa is even slightly more expansive. The uppermost lateral portion of the posterior cranial fossa is defined by the part of the parietal bone that contributes to the region of the parietal notch and asterion. Much of the base and posterior part of the posterior cranial fossa is bound—actually "cupped"—by the occipital bone.

In specific detail, the apex of the triangular portion of the posterior cranial fossa is formed by the confluence of the basisphenoid and basiocciput, which together create a slightly concave and somewhat vertical wall. Below the contact with the anterior part of the petrosal, this wall broadens inferiorly and thickens bilaterally into the *jugular tubercles* and then continues to form the anterior border of the *foramen magnum*. The anterior border of the foramen magnum is deep or thick—because of the verticality of the basioccipital region itself and the near confluence of the jugular tubercles with the anterior border of the foramen—whereas the posterior margin of the foramen is relatively thin and more edgelike. Each of a pair of *occipital condyles* is located on the anterolateral margin of the foramen magnum; the innermost edge of an occipital condyle may extend a bit more medially than the margin of the foramen magnum and thus be visible from within the cranial base.

In addition to the foramen magnum, the posterior cranial fossa contains other major cranial foramina. Bilaterally and lateral to the jugular tubercle is a moderately large and variably shaped foramen—the *jugular foramen*—through which the jugular vein exits. The paired jugular veins represent the conduits through which blood drains from the meningeal sinuses. The jugular foramen is bounded above by the inferior margin of the petrosal portion of the temporal and, below, by the occipital bone. In its most complex configurations, a jugular foramen actually appears as a series of variably deep pockets (Schwartz, unpublished data).

In terms of impressions left on bone, the descending superior sagittal sinus bifurcates at the raised *internal occipital protuberance* into right and left grooves; the groove veering to the right is often the more dominant (see above). From the internal occipital protuberance to the landmark asterion, these right and left grooves are oriented fairly horizontally. Each is identified as a *groove for the transverse sinus*. The grooves for the transverse sinuses form the border between the fossae for the cerebellar hemispheres (below) and the fossae for the cerebral occipital lobes (above). Beyond asterion, each transverse groove swings under the petrous portion of the temporal and then arcs anteriorly to become confluent with the jugular foramen. The curved part of this sinus drainage system is called the *groove for the sigmoid sinus*. In accordance with the right transverse and sigmoid sinuses typically being more pronounced than the left, the right jugular foramen tends to be the larger and/or more vacuous and pocketed.

Sometimes, just on the internal side of the occipital margin of the jugular foramen, there is a smaller foramen that courses posteroinferiorly, penetrating the thickened rim of the foramen magnum. This foramen is interpreted as a nonmetric *variant* and usually is not present bilaterally. However, a "normally occurring" foramen in the same region is located below the thickening of the jugular tubercle, on the superior and inferior surface of the occipital condyle. This foramen—the *anterior condylar foramen*—perforates the superior portion of the occipital condyle, exiting the posterior cranial fossa above the raised, lateral margin of the condyle. On occasion, one may also find an *accessory anterior condylar foramen*, which is the internal opening of a *posterior condylar foramen*. The posterior condylar foramen typically manifests itself as a variably deep, nonpatent pit

behind and lateral to the posterior margin of the occipital condyle. When this foramen is patent, it opens externally, slightly lateral to the posterior margin of the occipital condyle. In anatomy texts, the anterior condylar foramen may be identified as the *hypoglossal canal* (the "canalis hypoglossi" of the *Nomina Anatomica*) and the posterior condylar foramen as the *condyloid foramen* or *canal* ("canalis condylaris").

Above the jugular foramen the *internal acoustic (auditory) meatus* emerges from the petrous portion of the temporal bone. The internal acoustic meatus lies (more or less) in a horizontal plane and opens upon the posterior cranial fossa obliquely, being oriented anteriorly and medially. The apparent simplicity of this opening (which, for all intents and purposes, looks like a foramen) belies the fact that, internally, the petrosal is quite complex, housing, for example, the cochlear region of the inner ear. The auditory nerve, both roots of the facial nerve, and the auditory vessels course through the internal acoustic meatus.

The last penetration of the posterior cranial fossa to be discussed is the *mastoid foramen*, which was mentioned earlier in the description of the external morphology of the skull. The point was made then that the "normal" position of the mastoid foramen is sutural; the exsutural condition is the variant. Internally, however, this foramen typically is contained entirely in the squamous portion of the temporal bone. The mastoid foramen is oriented horizontally, faces straight forward, and opens upon the downwardly coursing portion of the sigmoid sinus.

Surface topography in the posterior cranial fossa (in addition to the internal occipital protuberance, the grooves for sinuses, and the cerebellar and cerebral fossae described above) is limited essentially to *posterior meningeal grooves* and to a variably impressed *groove for the superior petrosal sinus*. The latter groove courses along the superior and medial edge of the petrous portion of the temporal bone.

Nasal Cavity

Not uncommonly, cranial fragments recovered in paleontological, archeological, and forensic contexts retain elements that contribute to the nasal cavity (Figure 2–5). Thus, although indi-

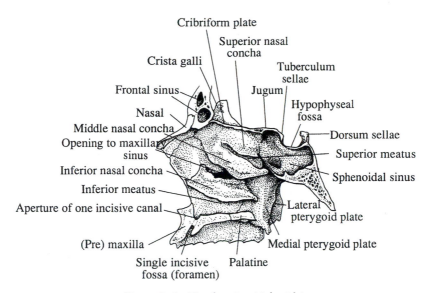

Figure 2–5 Nasal cavity *(right side).*

vidual bones are discussed elsewhere, some discussion of the general region is also necessary.

Typically construed as constituting elements of the nasal cavity are the *vomer*, the *ethmoid* and its extensions, the *maxillary* and *palatine* contributions to the "floor" of the nasal cavity, and the *nasal*, *frontal*, *sphenoidal*, and *inferior nasal conchal* contributions to the "roof" and/or "walls" of the cavity. Critical to understanding the nature of the nasal cavity is the recognition that some of these bones, in addition to confining and delineating the space, house the *paranasal sinuses,* which are confluent with or open upon the nasal cavity via variably sized orifices.

Somewhat within the nasal aperture, the *vomer* (below) and the *perpendicular plate of the ethmoid* (above) form a vertical bony plate that bifurcates the nasal cavity (in life, a cartilaginous septum continues the bifurcation farther anteriorly). The separateness of right and left nasal cavity chambers persists posteriorly.

In adult humans, the *floor of the nasal cavity* is typically smooth and relatively flat. In younger individuals, especially those in whom the successional anterior teeth are forming and still unerupted, the floor of the nasal cavity anteriorly may be swollen and raised. Just behind that portion of the vomer where its anterior "root" swells (from which point the anterior nasal spine appears to take origin), and on either side of the vomer, variably small to moderate foramina penetrate the floor of the nasal cavity. These foramina persist for awhile as separate canals—the *incisive canals* or *foramina of Stenson*—before opening within and becoming confluent with the large, single *incisive fossa* (also referred to as the *incisive foramen*) that emerges anteriorly, on the oral cavity side of the maxilla. At times, the incisive canals are located on the right and left sides of the maxillomaxillary suture, while at others one canal (corresponding to the left canal) lies anterior to the other. Some branches of the (sensory) nasopalatine (sphenopalatine) nerve and artery, which course anteriorly along the floor of the nasal cavity, are transmitted toward the oral cavity via the incisive canals, through which also pass branches of the greater palatine nerve and artery as they course from the oral cavity toward the nasal cavity. Especially in younger individuals, a fine sutural line may extend laterally from the aperture on the floor of the nasal cavity of each incisive canal. When present, this suture represents the contact between the premaxilla and maxilla. Sometimes these fine sutures continue for a short distance up the lateral wall of the nasal cavity, delineating, internally, the boundary of the frontal process of the premaxilla. More consistently observable into adulthood is the palatomaxillary suture.

Although the bony palate is relatively thick

and, because of this, is often preserved after interment, much of the remaining contributions to the nasal cavity are thin and friable and often do not survive. (This fact can be appreciated, for example, by noting the sorry state of preservation of the vomer, perpendicular plate, and/or inferior nasal conchae among skulls in any laboratory or museum osteology collection.)

Superiorly and superolaterally, the nasal cavity is bounded by elements of the ethmoid. The perpendicular plate terminates superiorly in the lacelike cribriform plate. On either side of the perpendicular plate lie the variably inflated and thinly waferlike *superior* and *middle conchae*, which emanate from the medial surfaces of the ethmoid. Farther posteriorly and superiorly, where the vomer splays out into the wings or *alae* that embrace the sphenoid from below, the sphenoid is pervaded by two relatively large sinus chambers. The bulk of the left *sphenoidal sinus* lies directly above the alae of the vomer, whereas the right sphenoidal sinus extends under the jugum and hypophyseal fossa. The lateral wall of the nasal cavity is formed primarily by the thin medial wall of the maxilla, whose surface is perforated by a variably moderate to large opening through which the *maxillary sinus* communicates with the nasal cavity. The maxillary sinus pervades the maxilla laterally as well as throughout the bone's length.

Often the lower facial skeleton is found dissociated from the rest of the skull. Appreciation of the nature of the contributions to the nasal cavity and to these contributions' exposure elsewhere in the skull makes this understandable. The lacrimal and ethmoid bones are extremely thin, not only in their contribution to the nasal cavity but also within the orbit. The bone surrounding the sphenoidal sinuses is thin. The zygomatic bone maintains a meager contact with the zygomatic process of the temporal bone. Aside from a strutlike abutment with the zygomatic process of the frontal, the zygomatic bone makes only a thin sutural contact with the greater wing of the sphenoid. The remaining sutural attachments of the nasal bones and the frontal process of the premaxilla with the frontal are insufficient by themselves to hold the lower facial skeleton to the rest of the skull. In addition, the region of glabella is lightened internally by the pervasion of the *frontal sinuses*, which develop via pneumatization of the frontal

bone by the anteriormost cell of the ethmoidal sinus complex. The specific location within the ethmoidal sinus complex from which the frontal sinuses (there is a right and left) originate is variable. As mentioned above, all sinuses open upon the nasal cavity either directly (i.e. the sphenoidal, ethmoidal, or maxillary sinuses) or via other sinuses (i.e. the frontal via the ethmoid).

Individual Bones of the Skull

Individual bones of the skull will be discussed because students may have the opportunity to study them in the laboratory and they are sometimes preserved separately and intact, particularly in the case of individuals in whom fusion has not yet occurred. Of particular importance is the morphology and orientation of bony features and landmarks—foramina, vascular grooves, and sutures. When studying individual bones, the student should also become familiar with changes in the cross-sectional thickness and shape of each bone. Knowledge of the combination of all these attributes is essential in being able to identify and then use in reconstruction the more commonly preserved osteological fragments (i.e. a piece of a bone that is also broken at or along a suture, or parts of two or more bones fused together along their zone of sutural contact). Since, in many cases, a certain amount of detail pertaining to each bone has already been presented, repetition here is kept to a minimum. In order to gain further appreciation of the morphological similarities between bones of the juvenile and the adult, the development of each bone is discussed. This provides a context for understanding age-related features as well as the etiology of many "nonmetric variants" and "pathologies." Figures 2–6 to 2–11 of fetal and postnatal crania illustrate overall as well as detailed growth-related changes that are discussed below for individual bones.

Mandible

MORPHOLOGY. Additional features on the external surface of the mandible (Figure 2–12) include the *oblique line* and the *incisive fossa*. An incisive fossa occurs on each side of the mental protuberance; muscles of the lower lip and

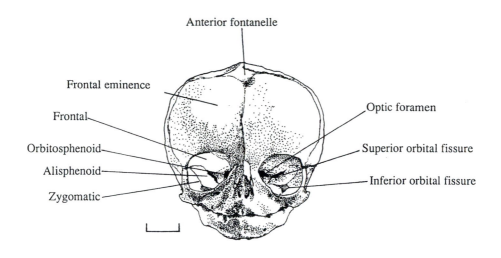

Anterior fontanelle

Frontal eminence

Frontal

Orbitosphenoid

Alisphenoid

Zygomatic

Optic foramen

Superior orbital fissure

Inferior orbital fissure

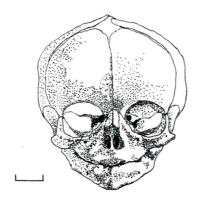

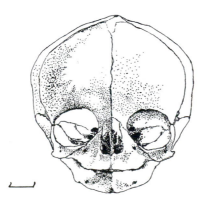

Figure 2–6   Anterior view of fetal skulls *(from top to bottom):* 6, 7, and 8 months (scale = 1 cm).

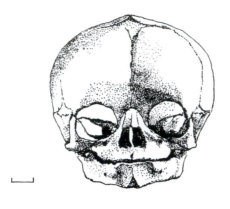

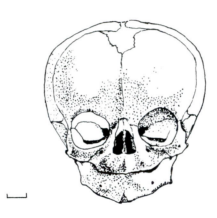

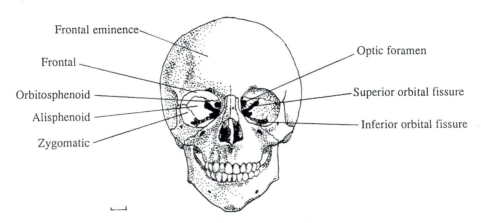

Figure 2–7 Anterior view of postnatal skulls *(from top to bottom):* neonate, 3 months, and 5 years (scale = 1 cm).

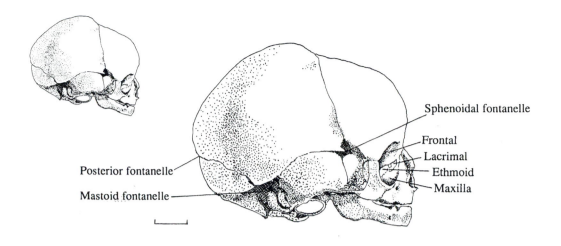

Sphenoidal fontanelle

Frontal
Lacrimal
Ethmoid
Maxilla

Posterior fontanelle

Mastoid fontanelle

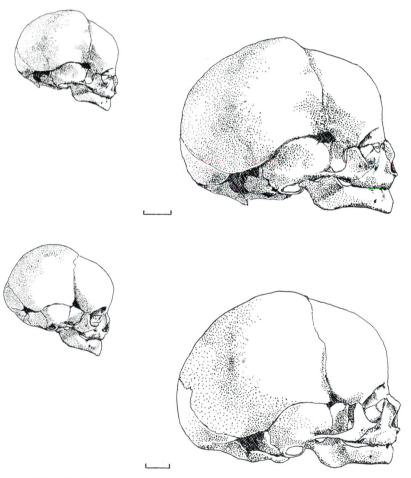

Figure 2–8 Lateral view of fetal skulls (from top to bottom): 6, 7, and 8 months; the smaller image to the left of each skull is that skull oriented in the Frankfort horizontal (scale = 1 cm).

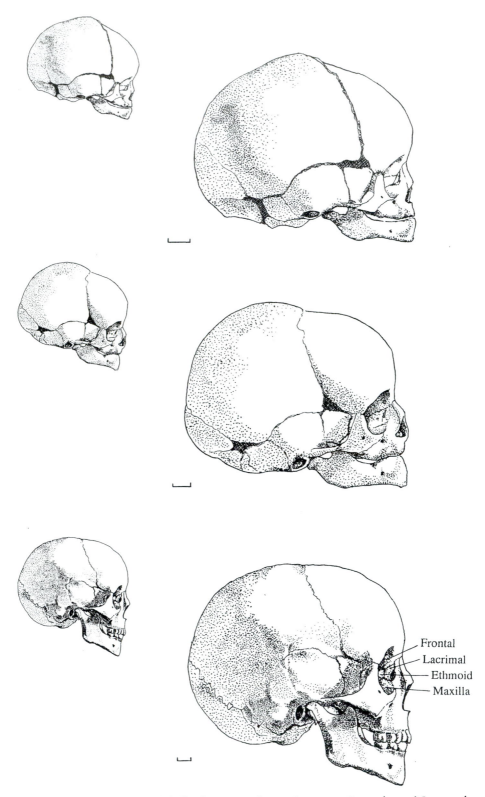

Frontal
Lacrimal
Ethmoid
Maxilla

Figure 2–9 Lateral view of postnatal skulls *(from top to bottom)*: neonate, 3 months, and 5 years; the smaller image to the left of each skull is that skull oriented in the Frankfort horizontal (scale = 1 cm).

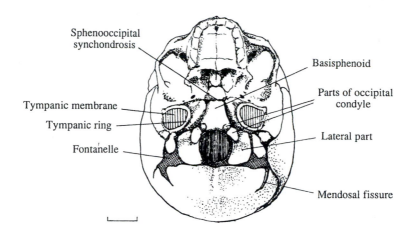

Sphenooccipital
synchondrosis

Basisphenoid

Tympanic membrane

Parts of occipital
condyle

Tympanic ring

Fontanelle

Lateral part

Mendosal fissure

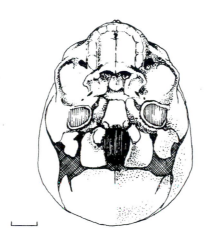

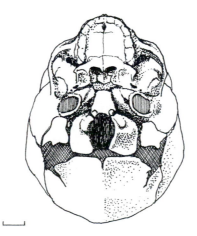

Figure 2–10 Basal view of fetal skulls *(from top to bottom):* 6, 7, and 8 months (scale = 1 cm).

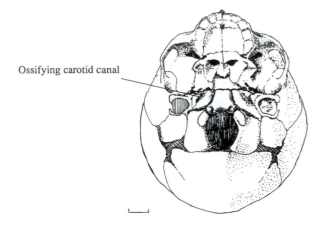

Ossifying carotid canal

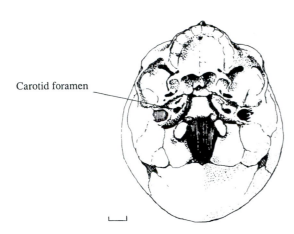

Carotid foramen

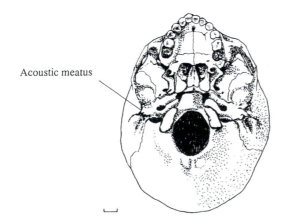

Acoustic meatus

mouth take origin there. The oblique line is a variably developed ridge that courses somewhat arcuately between the mental tubercle and the inferior portion of the anterior border of the ascending ramus; depressor muscles of the lower lip and the mouth attach anteriorly to the oblique line.

On the internal surface of the mandible, proceeding from front to back and up the ascending ramus, are various telltale mandibular features. On either side of the midline of the mandible, and typically somewhat closer to the rounded *inferior border* of the mandible than to the alveolar margin, are the variably distended and pointed *mental spines* (sometimes also referred to as the *genial tubercles*). Muscles of the tongue attach to the mental spines, which are usually larger in males than in females. A muscle that courses between the hyoid bone and mandible attaches on the internal surface beneath the mental spines; the (unnamed) scar this muscle leaves may take the form of elevations below each mental spine or a ridge in the midline of the mandible, below and between the mental spines. Lateral to each mental spine is a shallow, ovoid depression (longer than it is high) which is the *fossa for the sublingual gland*. Below each sublingual fossa, almost on the inferior border of the mandible itself, is the roughened, variably ovoid *digastric fossa*, to which the anterior belly of the digastric muscle attaches (the posterior belly of the digastric muscle courses through the digastric or mastoid notch that lies medial to the mastoid process and attaches behind the mastoid process). Proceeding toward the general region of the sublingual fossa and the mental spine is a variably rugose line or thin ridge, which appears to originate below and slightly behind the third molar. This, the *mylohyoid line,* may diminish in intensity anteriorly, or it may retain its character throughout its entire length. The mylohyoid line may course above the sublingual fossa and terminate at the mental spine, or it may end at the lateral border of the fossa. Beneath the mylohyoid line, and perhaps intervening slightly between the sublingual and digastric fossae, is the elongate but shallow *submandibular fossa*.

Figure 2–11 Basal view of postnatal skulls *(from top to bottom)*: neonate, 3 months, and 5 years (scale = 1 cm).

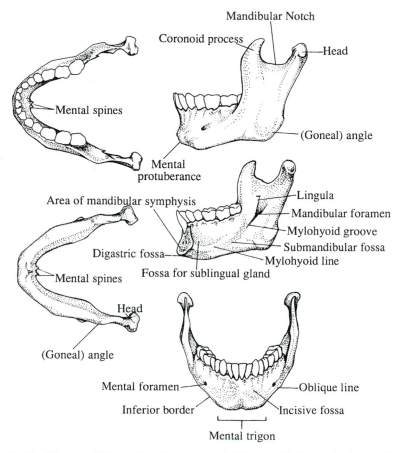

Figure 2–12 The mandible: *(left top)* occlusal, *(left bottom)* inferior, *(right top)* lateral, *(right middle)* internal, and *(right bottom)* anterior views.

The ascending ramus of the mandible is adorned internally by the *mylohyoid groove*, which courses inferiorly and somewhat anteriorly from the inferior margin of the mandibular foramen. Anterior to the mandibular foramen is a tonguelike, variably superiorly projecting slip of bone—called the *lingula*—to which attaches a ligament that assists in tethering the mandible to the base of the skull.

Overall, the mandible of a male is usually larger, bulkier, and more rugose than that of a female. Typically more pronounced in males are muscle scarring and/or distension of the coronoid process, the lingula, the mylohyoid line, the digastric fossae, the mental spines, and, in particular, the goneal region (i.e. the inferior margin of the mandibular angle); the mental region and especially the mental tubercles; the distance from infradentale to pogonion; and the verticality of the ascending ramus.

DEVELOPMENT AND OSSIFICATION. The mandible is derived from the cartilaginous branchial arch skeleton (Figure 2–13). Specifically, ossification begins during the the sixth to seventh fetal weeks as two laminae on either side (internally and externally) of Meckel's cartilage (i.e. the first arch), which eventually disintegrates. The two laminae come to fuse inferiorly, forming a troughlike structure in which the lower primary teeth and their accompanying alveolar bone develop. Growth of the mandible is rapid. By the middle of the third gestational month, it has attained a recognizable shape.

During ossification, the mandible envelopes a large portion of a branch of the mandibular nerve, which is called the inferior alveolar (dental) nerve. The hole through which this nerve enters the mandible is identified as the *mandibular foramen*. The inferior alveolar nerve extends to the front of the jaw and the canal in

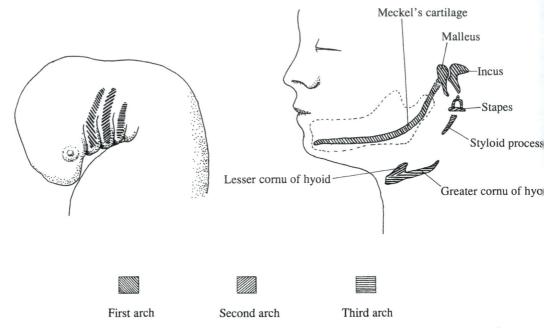

First arch   Second arch   Third arch

Figure 2–13   (Left) embryo with *(from left to right)* first, second, and third branchial arches emphasized; *(right)* child with branchial arch derivatives delineated (first arch = Meckel's cartilage, incus, and malleus; second = stapes and parts of styloid process and hyoid; third = remainder of hyoid bone). *(After Moore, 1974.)*

which it is housed within the mandible is called the *mandibular canal.* Anteriorly, a branch of the inferior alveolar nerve is not captured by bone but is instead "free" and courses on the external side of the mandible; this branch is referred to as the mental nerve. The point at which the mental nerve exits the mandibular body is called the *mental foramen; variation,* bilaterally as well as asymmetrically, is sometimes noted in the presence of an accessory mental foramen. The body of the mandible becomes distended anteriorly into the *mental protuberance*—the chin—which is further distended on each side inferiorly and slightly lateral to the midline by a *mental tubercle.* When viewed from the front, the mental region is variably triangular (with the two tubercles forming the angles of the bas) and thus is referred to as the *mental trigon* or *triangle.* Mental tubercles are typically developed more prominently in males than in females.

Sometime after the tenth fetal week, accessory cartilaginous nuclei form in the regions of the condylar and coronoid processes as well as the angle of the mandible; they are subsequently replaced by surrounding membranous bone. Cartilaginous nuclei also appear in the presumptive alveolar region (for discussion of

tooth development, see Chapter 6). By the time of birth, growth and ossification have proceeded along the pattern laid down during the first trimester; the primary antemolar teeth have calcified to varying degrees of completeness. Of particular interest in following the course of development of the mandible is that, at birth, the *ascending ramus* is shorter relative to mandibular body size than in the adult and is oriented at approximately a 45° angle, thereby creating an exceedingly obtuse mandibular angle. The *head of the mandible (condylar process)* does not usually rise above the highest level of the body of the mandible, whereas the large *coronoid process* does. The right and left mandibles are not fused across the midline—across the *mandibular* or *mental symphysis*—but instead are held together by fibrous mesenchymal tissue. Mineralization in the mandibular symphysis begins with the appearance of one to four centers of ossification, which fuse together by the fifth to sixth month after birth; during the first to second year, these islands of ossification fuse with the mandible.

Other changes in the mandible after birth include (1) a lengthening of the mandibular body, especially posteriorly, to accommodate the proliferating molar class teeth; (2) a deepening of the mandibular body in conjunction with the development of the primary and then (and especially) the successional teeth, their roots, and attendant alveolar bone; (3) an increase in length as well as in elevation of the ascending ramus with, concomitantly, a decrease in the obtuseness of the mandibular angle so that, in the adult, the ascending ramus approaches the vertical; and (4) a deepening of the *mandibular notch* between the coronoid and condylar processes, caused, at least in part, by an elongation of these two processes. With increasing age and on into old age, resorptive processes can reverse the growth profile of the mandible. Most striking is the thinning and overall remodeling of mandibular bone, in which the mandibular body and ascending ramus become more gracile and the mandibular angle increases in obtuseness. Such remodeling also causes a narrowing anteroposteriorly of the coronoid process and condylar neck as well as an increased deepening of the mandibular notch. If tooth loss occurs with aging, resorption of the alveolar bone will ensue and the affected portion of the mandibular body will become extremely thin.

Maxilla

MORPHOLOGY. (Because most of the relevant features of the "maxilla" (Figure 2–14), as the term is used for the adult, are discussed elsewhere in this chapter, review here is kept to a minimum.)

It is important to remember that the maxilla contributes to the wall and floor of the nasal cavity, to the floor of the orbit, to the roof of the oral cavity, and to the dental arcade; it also circumscribes the nasal aperture. The maxilla is thus an interesting bone because it is not uniform in thickness or overall appearance. For example, the bone associated with the margin of the nasal aperture, the floor of the orbit, the wall of the nasal cavity, and the facial region below the infraorbital canal is quite thin (the latter three surfaces form the walls of the maxillary sinus). The *frontal process* itself and its continuation (in part via the *anterior lacrimal crest)* into the inferior orbital margin is thicker, while the bone of the palate and of the alveolar process is quite thick.

The sutural zones of the maxilla are also notable. The region of the *frontomaxillary suture* is slightly thicker than the portion of the frontal process below it. This short suture typically is deeply invaginated and densely packed with tall, fingerlike projections that interdigitate with their counterparts on the frontal bone. The *zygomaticomaxillary suture* has distinct internal as well as external characteristics. Externally, the edge of the suture courses downward from the inferior margin of the orbit. In fact, the external edge of the zygomaticomaxillary suture is convexly arcuate downward to approximately the same degree that the margin of the orbit (i.e. the lateral margin of the frontal process) is concavely arcuate upward. The internal aspect of the zygomaticomaxillary suture follows the plane of the floor of the orbit itself. This disparity in height and orientation between the inner and outer aspects of the zygomaticomaxillary suture creates (1) a denticulate and craggy, anteriorly facing articular surface (descending from the internal aspect) that leads (2) to a denticulated furrow or receptacle (bound by the external edge of the zygomaticomaxillary suture) in which the zygomatic bone nestles.

The *intermaxillary suture* is also distinctive: it presents itself as two components of somewhat differing morphology separated by the *incisive canals* and *foramen.* In cross section, the maxillary palate is relatively thick posteriorly (where it abuts the palatine bone) and increases in thickness or depth anteriorly toward the incisive canals and foramen. Anterior to the region of the incisive canals and foramen, the palate is distended markedly and steeply downward. The bone lining the incisive canals is smooth. Behind the canals, the surface of the intermaxillary suture is pervaded by a network of thin, more or less vertical, and relatively closely spaced "plates " of bone separated by lacunae or spaces; right and left intermaxillary sutural ridges interdigitate. This ridge pattern extends (inferiorly) from the floor of the nasal cavity and terminates at the solid, unridged layer of bone that forms the roof of the oral cavity. This solid layer of bone is thickest in the midregion of this portion of the maxillary palate; it becomes thinner posteriorly (toward the palatine bone) as well as anteriorly (toward the incisive canals). The posterior part of the intermaxillary suture is solid, compact bone. The part of the intermaxillary suture that lies anterior to the incisive canal also is adorned with ridges, but the plates of each ridge are longer,

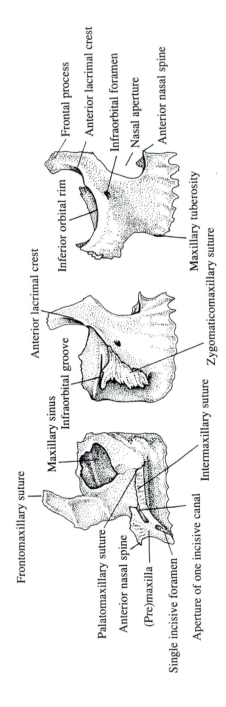

Figure 2–14 Right maxilla: *(left)* internal, *(middle)* lateral, and *(right)* anterior views.

Frontal process

Anterior lacrimal crest

Infraorbital foramen

Nasal aperture

Anterior nasal spine

Inferior orbital rim

Maxillary tuberosity

Zygomaticomaxillary suture

Anterior lacrimal crest

Maxillary sinus

Infraorbital groove

Intermaxillary suture

Frontomaxillary suture

Palatomaxillary suture

Anterior nasal spine

(Pre)maxilla

Single incisive foramen

Aperture of one incisive canal

individually more distinct, and separated from one another by longer, deeper grooves. Only toward the neck of the central incisor might the bone become solid and compact.

The maxilla's contribution to the *palatomaxillary suture* is varied. Along the hard palate itself, the sutural surface is essentially a variably thickened and smooth to roughened wall of compact bone against which the thinner palatine bone abuts. Contact between the maxilla and the palatine bone becomes less intimate as the palatomaxillary suture "rounds the corner" at the base of the alveolar process and courses toward and eventually beyond the *greater palatine foramen*. In the region of the *maxillary tuberosity,* the palatine bone (more specifically, that portion of the palatine bone that overlaps and caps inferiorly the lateral pterygoid plate of the sphenoid) is merely and variably appressed to the smooth surface of the maxilla.

DEVELOPMENT AND OSSIFICATION. The *maxilla* develops from the upper portion of the first branchial arch, which is created when the arch folds in half. It ossifies as membranous bone derived from the first pharyngeal arch. By the sixth to seventh fetal week, two to three ossification centers appear (i.e., one or two in the *maxillary prominence* and one in the *median nasal prominence*). The posterior one or two centers of ossification coalesce into the presumptive maxilla while the anteriormost center represents the presumptive *premaxilla*. By the fourth fetal month, the presumptive maxilla and premaxilla are partially united. The details of the union of maxilla and premaxilla are still debated.

The traditional interpretation has been that two separate bones fuse together along a plane of contact. However, detailed embryological and histochemical studies (Andersen and Matthiessen, 1967) reveal that the presumptive human maxilla and premaxilla become united via ossification of a bridge—the *maxillary isthmus*—that maintains mesenchymal continuity between the maxillary and median nasal prominences from the onset of facial development. The floor of the infraorbital canal and foramen represents the region of the embryonic maxillary isthmus. A *premaxillary-maxillary suture,* formed between contributions of equal size from the premaxilla and maxilla (and which

may persist into the young adult), may bisect the superior margin of the infraorbital foramen vertically. *Variation* does exist, however, in the extent to which the maxillary contribution to the superior margin of the infraorbital foramen (1) extends to the midline of the foramen, (2) forms the entire superior margin of the foramen, or (3) expands beyond the superior margin of the foramen to contact the frontal process of the premaxilla (Schwartz, 1982). Evidence of a premaxillary-maxillary suture may persist along the oral cavity side of the palate, with right and left sutural components emanating laterally from the incisive foramen and coursing to the general regions of the canines. As early ossification of the premaxilla creates a sheet of woven bone that extends down from the nasal bone to overlie the developing tooth germs (Schwartz and Langdon, unpublished data), and ossification in its palatal region is confined to thin septa growing between and lingually around tooth germs, it could very well be that the bone of the premaxilla palatally is alveolar bone in origin (also see argument in Schwartz, 1982). Given the above, it is obvious why the premaxillary-maxillary suture in humans is not as clearly or as continuously expressed as in other mammals.

The *hard palate* of the maxilla begins embryonically with the appearance of ossification centers in the palatine processes, which are initially vertically oriented downward. With hydration and under proper developmental conditions, these processes become elevated and meet in the midline of the presumptive palate. The embryonically distinct dental ridge is "sandwiched" between the median nasal and maxillary prominences and the palatine process (e.g. Andersen and Matthiessen, 1967; Nery, Kraus, and Croup, 1970). By the end of the third trimester, the "maxilla, " plus the premaxilla, dental arcade, and palate, are sufficiently joined (or gomphosed) along their zones of contact that they appear to represent a single bony unit. The *inferior orbital rim*, which lies close to the presumptive alveolar margin, dominates this "maxilla" (as the word is used for the adult). During the third month after birth, the *maxillary sinus*, which was previously a groove along the wall of the nasal cavity, begins to become more vacuous and, at about the fourth month after birth, the alveolar process begins to enlarge; both events are apparently correlated with the development of the dentition. With increasing age, the maxilla deepens and lengthens, especially posteriorly, in concert with the development, growth, and eruption of the primary and successional teeth. With senescence, bone resorption reduces the bulk of the maxilla. If tooth loss also occurs with increasing age, maxillary depth will be reduced severely as a result of concomitant resorption of alveolar bone.

The Palatine Bone

The palatine bone comprises both a *horizontal* and a *perpendicular plate*; the former contributes to the hard palate and the latter projects into the nasal cavity.

MORPHOLOGY. The *horizontal plate* of the palatine bone (Figure 2–15) is a relatively thin, medially projecting sheet of bone. The sister palatine bones thicken markedly at their juncture along the *median palatine suture*. This sutural zone is also elevated, in correspondence with an arcuate elevation of the floor of the nasal cavity. The median palatine sutural surface itself is an irregular swirl and/or layering of thin, sheer ridges separated by variably deep spaces. In contrast, the edge of the palatine bone that contributes to the *palatomaxillary suture* (i.e. the anterior and lateral margins of the bone) may present a more regularly layered appearance. The points of contact (usually one large area as well as one or more accessory areas) that the pyramidal process maintains with the maxillary tuberosity are variably thickened and rugose.

The morphologically more complicated *per-perpendicular plate* extends anteriorly and superiorly. It forms an arcuate "corner" laterally with the horizontal plate. Anteriorly and slightly above the floor of the nasal cavity, the *maxillary process* is overlapped medially by the maxilla; these two bones together form the broadly "V"-shaped, inferiorly pointed margin of the opening of the maxillary sinus. At the approximate level at which the maxilla overlaps the maxillary process of the palatine bone, the band- or ridgelike *conchal crest*, with which the *inferior nasal concha* articulates, courses horizontally across the medial surface of the palatine bone. The conchal crest and the inferior nasal concha delineate below them the *inferior meatus*. The *middle meatus* is defined as the region between the conchal crest and the *ethmoidal crest*. This region is represented by a vertical sheet of bone above the conchal crest that is exceedingly thin and gently concave. The ethmoidal crest is located at the point where this sheet of bone thickens and flares somewhat medially. The *middle nasal concha* articulates with the ethmoidal crest. Together, the middle nasal concha and the superior portion of the perpendicular plate of the palatine bone form the *superior meatus*. The *sphenopalatine foramen* lies below and sometimes even behind the posterior end of the ethmoidal crest.

The superiormost part of the perpendicular plate—the *orbital process*—articulates anteriorly with the maxilla, posteriorly with the sphenoid, and medially with the ethmoidal labyrinth. The orbital process also presents a *lateral surface*, which lies obliquely under the border of the inferior orbital fissure. This lateral surface, however, is actually the region of flex-

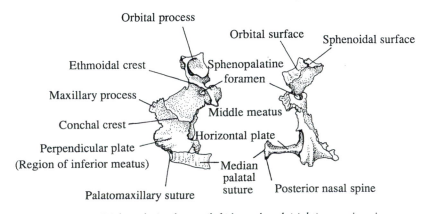

Figure 2–15   Right palatine bone: *(left)* lateral and *(right)* posterior views.

ure that serves to delineate the *orbital surface,* which constitutes the posteriormost contribution to the orbital floor.

DEVELOPMENT AND OSSIFICATION. During (approximately) the eighth fetal week, a single center of ossification appears intramembranously in the angle of what will develop into the horizontal and perpendicular plates. First, ossification spreads medially into the horizontal plate as well as laterally and inferiorly into the presumptive *pyramidal process.* The pyramidal process will eventually wrap itself partially around the maxillary tuberosity posteriorly and come to embrace the inferior extent of the lateral pterygoid plate. It is in the region of the "neck" of the pyramidal process that the *lesser palatine foramen* (or foramina) forms. A thinly triangular, concave or furrowed slip of bone extends superiorly from the pyramidal process. This slip of bone separates the *medial* and *lateral pterygoid plates* inferiorly and thus contributes to the *pterygoid fossa,* which intervenes between the two plates. Within 2 weeks of its onset, ossification has proceeded vertically, into the presumptive perpendicular plate and its *orbital* and *sphenoidal processes.* In the adult, the height of the perpendicular plate is approximately twice the width (mediolaterally) of the horizontal plate. At birth, however, the two plates are subequal in these dimensions.

Nasal Bone

MORPHOLOGY. In cross section, a nasal bone (Figure 2–16) is thickest superiorly (at its con-

tribution to the frontonasal suture). It tapers and thins quite drastically toward its inferior edge. At the midline but on the internal surface of a nasal bone is the *nasal crest,* lateral to which the bone is gently concave; the external surface of the bone is concomitantly convex. Again internally, but on or about the midline of each nasal bone, a groove—the *ethmoidal sulcus*—courses prominently for most of the length of the bone; this groove marks the path of the external nasal branch of the anterior ethmoidal nerve. Within the nasal cavity, the superior portion of the nasal bone is overlapped slightly by the ethmoid.

The *internasal suture* lies in the median sagittal plane and is essentially straight. The internasal sutural surface is variably roughened along its length but is most corrugated superiorly, in the region of the frontonasal suture. The contribution to the *frontonasal suture* is incised by variably (but often very) deep, thin grooves or pits, which create the fingerlike projections on the nasal bone's portion of the frontonasal suture, which, in turn, interdigitate with the corresponding fingerlike projections of the frontal bone's contribution to the frontonasal suture. The surface of the *nasomaxillary suture* is much less severely adorned with sutural interdigitation.

DEVELOPMENT AND OSSIFICATION. During the eighth to ninth fetal week, the single ossification center that gives rise to each nasal bone appears intramembranously. The paired nasal bones together are broader inferiorly than superiorly and, in the adult, form an odd hourglass shape,

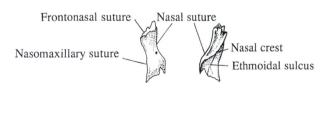

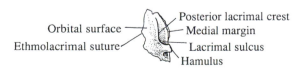

Figure 2–16 (Top left) anterior and *(top right)* posterior (internal) views of right nasal bone; *(bottom)* right lacrimal bone, lateral view.

being somewhat "pinched" or "waisted" near the midpoint of their length. In the newborn, however, the sides of the nasal bones are relatively straight and thus the pair of bones presents a more trapezoidal configuration. The nasal bones also appear squatter and straighter across the superior border of the nasal aperture in the newborn, but, with increasing age, they become more elongated and variably distended inferolaterally.

Lacrimal Bone

The ossification center for the lacrimal bone (Figure 2–16) appears during the 12th fetal week in the membrane surrounding the cartilaginous nasal capsule. The lacrimal bone contributes to the *medial orbital wall* and is the smallest bone of the facial skeleton. This bone is characterized by the relatively shallow and (for the bone itself) relatively broad groove— the *lacrimal sulcus*—that courses for the entire superoinferior length of the bone. This groove is oriented slightly obliquely (facing somewhat anteriorly and laterally). Thus the thin medial margin is situated just anterior to the more robust *posterior lacrimal crest*, which forms the lateral border of the sulcus (recall that the *anterior lacrimal crest* actually lies on the *frontal process of the maxilla*). The thin medial margin of the lacrimal sulcus overlaps the edge of the frontal process of the maxilla along the lacrimomaxillary suture; on the frontal process, an indentation marks the region in which the thin medial margin of the lacrimal sulcus rests. The posterior lacrimal crest terminates in a variably small, hooklike, anteriorly facing projection that nestles into the maxilla along the floor of the orbit and which, in part, circumscribes further the inferior border of the lacrimal sulcus. This projection is called the *lacrimal hamulus* ("hamulus" meaning a "hooklike process"). On occasion, the lacrimal hamulus may arise from its own center of ossification and then fuse to the lacrimal bone.

The region of the lacrimal groove represents the thickest portion of the lacrimal bone. Beyond the groove, the lateral surface of the lacrimal bone (that which faces upon the medial orbital wall) and its medial surface (that which faces upon the middle meatus of the nasal cavity and which also complements the ethmoidal air cells) taper as they converge posteriorly, with the result that the edge of contact between the lacrimal and the ethmoid behind it (i.e. the *ethmolacrimal suture*) is relatively thin. The orbital surface of the lacrimal bone is slightly concave and smooth, whereas the medial surface is topographically diverse, even to the extent of bearing a furrow that mirrors the lacrimal crest. By identifying the sulcus and the hamulus and orienting the thinnest part of the bone posteriorly, one should be able to distinguish the right from the left lacrimal bone.

Frontal Bone

MORPHOLOGY. Following convention, the *orbital portion* of the frontal bone (Figures 2–17 and 2–18) is defined as that part which contributes to the roofs of the orbits and the nasal cavity. The *squama* constitutes everything else. The squama, therefore, begins with the superior or *supraorbital margins* of the orbits and proceeds upward. The contour of the supraorbital margin is typically more arcuate and its edge crisper and sharper to the touch in females than in males; in the latter, the edge of the supraorbital margin is usually thicker and blunter and its midsection may be straighter.

Features of note associated with the supraorbital margin are the *supraorbital notch* and the *supraorbital foramen,* the former incompletely capturing the supraorbital vessels and nerve, which otherwise would course through the foramen. The notch and foramen usually lie medial to the midline of the supraorbital margin. In most populations studied in terms of the development of one or the other of these character states, the presence of the supraorbital notch (i.e. the incomplete foramen) was by far the most prevalent, even though the notched condition was considered the nonmetric variant (Berry, 1968). Additional variation can be noted in the degree to which (1) the notch is bounded by a spit or converging spits of bone, (2) the condition observed is bilateral, and (3) there are accessory notches or foramina.

Often confused with a supraorbital foramen is the *frontal foramen* (or, if multiple, frontal foramina), which may be variably small to moderate in size and which usually is found lateral to the supraorbital notch or foramen. Frontal foramina lie closer to the midline of the su-

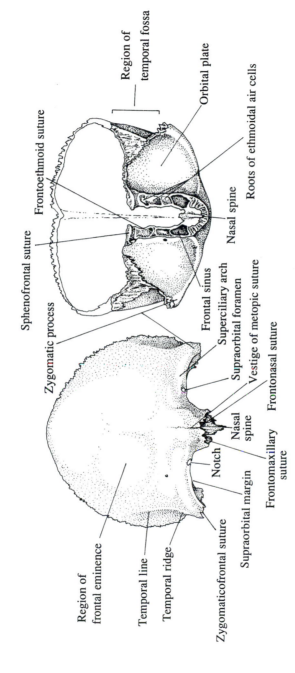

Figure 2–17 Frontal bone: *(left)* anterior (external) and *(right)* inferior views.

Region of
frontal eminence

Temporal line

Temporal ridge

Zygomaticofrontal suture

Supraorbital margin

Frontomaxillary
suture

Notch

Nasal
spine

Frontonasal suture

Vestige of metopic suture

Supraorbital foramen

Superciliary arch

Frontal sinus

Zygomatic process

Sphenofrontal suture

Frontoethmoid suture

Region of
temporal fossa

Orbital plate

Roots of ethmoidal air cells

Nasal spine

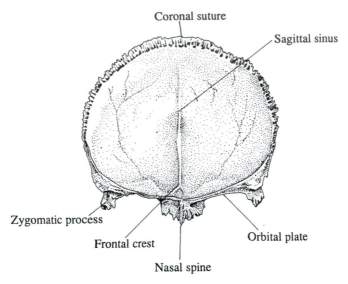

Figure 2–18   Internal morphology of frontal bone.

praorbital margin than do supraorbital foramina. One also can define a frontal foramen as a foramen that is located well above the supraorbital margin (e.g. 0.25 to 0.50 cm above the margin), in contrast to a supraorbital foramen, which lies at the edge of the margin. On occasion, a frontal foramen may be present in the form of a deeply invaginated notch. Frontal foramina may be single or multiple, and/or uni- or bilaterally expressed and may occur in 45% of the population under study.

Slightly above the supraorbital margin and arcing upward and outward from the region of glabella is a variably prominent swelling, the *superciliary arch,* which, if excessively developed (as it is in various fossil hominids, apes, and monkeys) is referred to as the *supraorbital torus* (otherwise known as the browridge). In modern humans, right and left superciliary arches swell as they proceed laterally away from the region of glabella; they peak in both height and distension over the area of the supraorbital notch/foramen; and then they tend to fade out as they proceed laterally and down toward the supraorbital margin, often becoming indistinct at or just lateral to the midline of the supraorbital margin. Lateral to the midline of the supraorbital margin, the bone of the margin is flatter and more platelike, and it also is slanted posteriorly. The dimorphic configuration of the human supraorbital region has been characterized as bipartite (e.g. Stringer et al., 1984). Differ-

ences between males and females in the degree to which glabella is swollen (stereotypically male) or flat (stereotypically female) also characterize sexually dimorphic expressions of the superciliary arch. However, the degrees to which glabella and the superciliary arch are "male" or "female" do not appear to be correlated.

Proceeding farther up the frontal bone one encounters the two *frontal eminences,* each of which lies approximately 3 cm above the supraorbital margins and above and slightly lateral to the peaked elevations of the superciliary arches. The frontal eminence is typically more pronounced in females than in males. As discussed earlier, the frontal eminences in females may be so prominent that they appear to create "corners" on the bone. In males, the typically more backwardly sloping frontal bone usually bears only faintly developed frontal eminences.

The isolated frontal bone is distinguished (1) inferiorly by the semicupped and winglike *orbital plates* that bound on either side the long, narrow "space" in which the superior portion of the ethmoid is lodged, (2) by the spikiness of much of the parietal border (i.e. the surface contributing to the *coronal suture*), and (3) by the sweep of the *temporal ridge* as it rises up from the strutlike zygomatic process and arcs back over the postorbital constriction that contributes to the formation of the temporal fossa.

Throughout most of the frontal bone's parietal border, the sutural digitations of the inner table of bone are longer than those of the outer table. Thus, for much of its length, the frontal's contribution to the coronal suture is oblique, the bone's inner table being overlain by the long digitations of the parietal bone's outer table. Within a few centimeters of bregma, the sutural digitations of the inner and outer tables are more equal in length and tend to be much shorter than elsewhere along the suture. At bregma itself, and perhaps for approximately 1 cm on either side of it, the sutural digitations of the outer table may be longer than those of the inner table, although the digitations in both cases are quite truncated. (Recall that the coronal suture is minimally undulating within a few centimeters of bregma, whereas the most jagged region of the articulated coronal suture is that which crosses the temporal line.)

Although it represents a small portion of the entire frontal bone, the region delineated by the temporal ridge/line (superiorly), by the zygomatic process (anteriorly), and by the coronal suture (posteriorly) is particularly distinctive, not only because of the features just cited but also because of the uniqueness of its contribution to the sphenofrontal suture. Where the frontal sits atop the greater wing of the sphenoid, the contact is essentially triangular and its surface is riddled by such a profusion of spikelike projections that it is reminiscent of the roof of a cave adorned with a myriad of closely packed, pointed but short stalactites. From the anterior corner of this triangular surface, a thin edge of bone extends forward and laterally and then swells into the area of sutural contact between the zygomatic process of the frontal bone and the zygomatic bone itself. This stubby contribution to the frontozygomatic suture is distended inferiorly but irregularly and is adorned with platelike sutural digitations. Extending inward from the apex of the triangular contact with the greater wing of the sphenoid, the surface of the frontal bone that contributes to the *sphenofrontal suture* is relatively thin and its edge finely jagged. This region represents the contact between the posterior border of the orbital plate and the anterior margin of the lesser wing of the sphenoid. In the area where the jugum of the sphenoid protrudes anteriorly into the cribriform plate, the orbital plate is distended into a thin, platelike, severely angled "corner" that overlaps the sphenoid. The surface of this portion of the frontal bone's contribution to the sphenofrontal suture is roughened and irregularly configured.

The *frontoethmoid suture* courses anteriorly beyond the severely angled medial corner of the orbital plate. This zone of frontoethmoid contact is distinguished by its thin medial and lateral edges, which are (1) distended somewhat inferiorly and (2) form walls that subtend a longitudinal furrow. This furrow is subdivided unevenly by thin bony septa that represent the roofs of air cells contained primarily in the ethmoid. The anteriormost of the air cells that lie along the frontoethmoid suture is the largest and constitutes the *frontal sinus*, which invades the region of glabella and extends above the variably semilunar to semicircular contact between the frontal bone and the frontal process of the maxilla and nasal bones. The contact between the lacrimal and the edge of the frontal bone that subtends the frontal sinus is thin. The frontal bone's contribution to the *frontomaxillary* and *frontonasal sutures* is a much broader surface. It is variably deeply but finely pitted with fine digitations that mesh with the frontal process of the maxilla as well as with the nasal bones.

DEVELOPMENT AND OSSIFICATION. By the end of the second fetal month, ossification of the frontal bone has begun, radiating out from the intramembranous center that appears at or near the midline of the (presumptive) *superior orbital margin*. Although ossification proceeds throughout the platelike portion of the bone, it remains concentrated around the orbital margin and, in particular, the lateral portion of the orbital margin. Within a week or so the center of ossification that corresponds to the frontal eminence appears. By the end of the third fetal month, the orbital region is relatively dense. The remainder of the developing bone, however, is very thin and porous (i.e. is still woven bone). During the latter part of the third fetal month, the developing frontal bone is wider than it is tall, but these proportions change by the middle of the fourth month. At this time, the presumptive *zygomatic process* can also be identified. Within a few weeks, the frontal eminences are established and the bone continues to become increasingly more arcuate posteriorly and laterally. Toward the end of the second trimester, opposing frontal bones are in close approximation inferiorly but are separated from one another superiorly by the narrowly triangular *anterior fontanelle* (Figure 2–19). The medial and superior portion of the frontal is bluntly pointed, and it remains so through term. Late in the third trimester the zygomatic process eventually makes contact with the zygomatic bone. At birth, right and left frontal bones are (normally) still separated—by the *frontal* or *metopic suture*—but they eventually begin to coalesce by the eighth year along all but the inferiormost part of the suture, becoming completely fused between the ages of 10 to 12 years. Subsequent to the closure or at least approximation of the *metopic (frontal) suture,* secondary centers of ossification, which eventually give rise to the *nasal spine,* arise at the suture's inferior end. In approximately 10% of humans, however, the metopic suture remains unfused (see Figure 9–4).

Although some sources cite the osteoclastically formed frontal sinuses (see Figure 1-5) as having begun to develop by the end of the first year, a recent study suggests that their development may occur at a later age and that there are differences in first appearance between males and females (Brown et al., 1984). The median age of first appearance of the frontal sinus was found to be 3.25 years for boys and 4.58 years for girls. The predominant increase

in size of the frontal sinuses terminated at a median age of 15.68 years for males and 13.72 years for females. Thus, frontal sinus growth begins earlier in males than in females and the period of frontal sinus growth is longer on average in males than in females, with the result that these sinuses are larger in adult males than in adult females. Brown et al. (1984) suggest further that enlargement of the frontal sinuses parallels, or occurs in tandem with, the pattern of annual growth increments (e.g. bone length) in boys and girls.

Parietal Bone

MORPHOLOGY. Externally, the parietal bone (Figure 2–20) is distinguished by (1) the temporal lines; (2) the parietal eminence (which is typically more angular and pronounced in females than males); (3) great stretches of relatively smooth, morphologically unadorned bone; and, (4) most telling, its sutures.

The temporal lines are most noticeable in the adult. They are usually more distinct in males than in females (although diet and tooth use—e.g. in hide or tool preparation—can skew this generalization the other way 'round). When discernible, the temporal lines typically are confined to the lateral wall of the parietal bone. On occasion, however, they may be located more superiorly. Although the temporal lines are identified as two separate entities—the *superior* and *inferior temporal lines*—they present themselves less as discrete lines or ridges than as the upper and lower borders of a very smooth band that arcs along the side of the parietal bone. At its widest, this band is approximately 1 cm or so thick; its arc typically parallels the curvature of the squamosal border of the parietal bone.

As reviewed earlier, the inferior or *squamosal border* of the parietal bone makes contact with the greater wing of the sphenoid for a short distance anteriorly. For most of its length, however, it articulates with the temporal bone. For the length of the short *sphenoparietal suture* and the anterior half or so of the *squamosal suture,* the squamosal border of the parietal is wedge-shaped, rather smooth or very finely ridged, and quite sharp-edged, especially anteriorly. Proceeding posteriorly from the region of the sphenoparietal suture (i.e. from the *sphenoidal angle*), the surface of the squamosal bor-

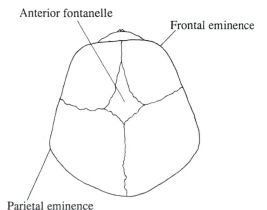

Figure 2–19 Skull of neonate *(superior view)* illustrating anterior fontanelle intervening partway between separate right and left frontal bones (the posterior fontanelle, between the parietal and occipital bones, is not visible in this view).

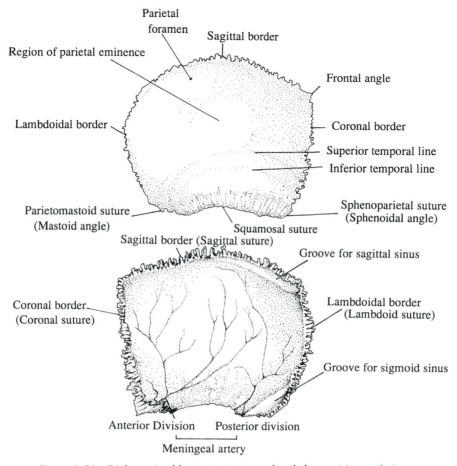

Figure 2–20   Right parietal bone: *(top)* external and *(bottom)* internal views.

der thickens and may become somewhat denticulate. These features—especially thickness—are more marked in the posterior half of the squamosal suture and remain so down to the *parietal notch*. The external surface of the thickened, wedge-shaped posterior portion of the squamosal sutural border is adorned with ridges and grooves that cut across its surface. The wedged shape of the sphenoparietal and squamosal sutural portion of the squamosal border complements the squamosal border of the temporal bone, which overrides (and thus overlies) the parietal bone.

The thickening of the squamosal border posteriorly foreshadows the noticeable change that occurs at the region of the parietal notch and persists for the length of what is then identified as the *parietomastoid suture*. Along its inferior margin and somewhat to the internal aspect of

this margin, the parietomastoid suture is distinguished by being adorned with obliquely oriented ridges and grooves that abut and interlock with the sutural border of the mastoid process below. The internally jutting corner of the parietal bone—at the juncture of the squamosal and parietomastoid sutures—is distended and actually inserts itself into the parietal notch. The posterior portion of the parietomastoid suture is called the *mastoid angle*. The short parietomastoid suture may be slightly arcuate.

The *frontal, sagittal,* and *occipital borders* of the parietal bone are all denticulate, but each has a characteristic configuration. The denticulations of the frontal border are typically the finest, while those of the sagittal suture are the thickest and longest (and the most deeply invaginated on their sides). The denticulations along the occipital border are similar in length of projection to those of the frontal border, but they are more robust. As the frontal border of the parietal bone mirrors the opposing border of the frontal bone, the denticulations of the inner table tend to become more emphasized toward the midline; laterally, the denticulations of the outer table are dominant and override the border of the frontal bone. For the 2 to 3 cm nearest the *sphenoidal angle*, the denticulations become fewer in number and more benign in expression.

For the first centimeter or so posterior to the *frontal angle* (i.e. the contribution to bregma), the sagittal border bears a series of short, closely packed denticulations, which are even finer in structure than those along the frontal border. Proceeding away from the frontal angle, the denticulations become increasingly longer and thicker and are set farther apart from one another. Approximately two-thirds along the length of the sagittal border, there is a 2-cm or so stretch along which the thick denticulations become shorter and even farther separated from one another. On either side of this portion of the sagittal border, the bone is somewhat flattened and may be perforated by a *parietal foramen*, the presence of which, either uni- or bilaterally, is considered to represent a nonmetric variant. From this short segment (which can be identified easily when the sagittal suture is articulated) to the *occipital angle* (i.e. the contribution to the anthropometric landmark lambda), the denticulations assume their characteristic length and spacing. From the occipital angle to the region of asterion (near the mastoid angle), the occipital border is characterized by the relative uniformity of its denticulations; the border's "edge" (if one can define it as such) also tends to be slightly wavy.

The internal features of the parietal bone have been adequately detailed elsewhere in this chapter. Of special note in the identification of the parietal bone are the grooves for the divisions of the *middle meningeal artery* as well as for the *sulcus for the sagittal sinus,* with its attendant *granular foveolae* (pits for arachnoid granulations) and, in older individuals, *Pacchionian depressions.* The sulcus for the sagittal sinus courses anteroposteriorly along the sagittal border and thus is situated superiorly. The divisions of the middle meningeal artery emanate from the inferior border; their course and branching pattern is posterior and superior. Parietal bone fragments usually preserve at least one of the sutural borders and enough of the meningeal branching pattern to make identification possible.

[A simple technique for determining right from left parietal bones is to imagine that your wrist corresponds to the middle meningeal artery as it arises from the squamosal border and that your fingers represent subsequent branching. By placing your hand on the side of your head, you will emulate the pattern of branching. Orient the parietal bone (or fragment thereof) to match the picture of your right or left hand.]

DEVELOPMENT AND OSSIFICATION. Each parietal bone begins to mineralize intramembranously by the end of the second fetal month via two centers of ossification that eventually coalesce during the fourth month into the presumptive *parietal eminence.* However, even before these two ossification centers fuse together, bony trabeculae begin fanning out radially from the region of the presumptive parietal eminence, creating a broad-based, cone-shaped structure. This radiating pattern of ossification continues until the sixth month, during which time the *coronal, sagittal,* and *lambdoidal borders* become recognizable and the "corners" of the coronal and sagittal, as well as of the sagittal and lambdoid, sutures become angular. Retardation in ossification of the superior angular regions, particularly of the anterior one, contributes to the formation of the *fontanelles* (or *fonticuli*), which persist for some time postnatally. The *anterior fontanelle (fonticulus)* is larger at birth than the *posterior fontanelle.*

By the middle of the third trimester the anteroinferior portion of the enlarging parietal bone has become not only more angular, but reminiscent of its final shape (and thus of the configuration of its contribution to the *pterion*). The posterior portion, however, remains rather rounded. The two inferior fontanelles at birth are, anteriorly, the *sphenoid,* and, posteriorly, the *mastoid fontanelles.* Due to the separation of the parietal bones from one another as well as from other bones at birth—especially because of the fontanelles—sutural features, including the overlapping nature of the squamosal suture, are not yet developed.

Zygoma

MORPHOLOGY. (An isolated zygomatic bone (Figure 2–21) is similar in general outline to the inverted haft of a sword. The thick vertical strut that encloses the orbit laterally and proceeds superiorly as the *frontal process* corresponds to the sword's handle. The blunt *temporal process* that extends posteriorly together with the more pointed *maxillary process* that arcs medially represent the sword's crosspiece.)

Variation is noted, for example, in the development of a temporal process that may be much shorter than the maxillary process and/or in the temporal process being distended inferiorly into a pointed slip of bone (instead of being blunt) that articulates with, and embraces from below, the zygomatic process of the temporal bone. Variation may be asymmetrically expressed in the same individual.

The articular surface of the *maxillary process* of the zygomatic bone mirrors that described earlier for its counterpart on the maxilla. On the zygoma, the edge contributing to the facial expression of the *zygomaticomaxillary suture* is variably jagged and obliquely oriented, coursing as it does inferiorly as well as laterally away from the inferior margin of the orbit. The inner surface of the maxillary process is rugose and corrugated. It thus meshes with the outwardly facing articular surface of the maxilla. The *temporal process*'s contribution to the *temporozygomatic suture* is variably denticulate, with the denticulations tending to be fine, short, and closely approximated. The temporal process is compressed laterally, and is thus much deeper than it is thick; its inner and outer surfaces are fairly smooth-boned. The *inferior margin* of the temporal process bears scars from the attachment of the masseter muscle. It is variably thin to rugose, being stouter, thicker, and more muscle-marked in males than females in populations in which females do not use their jaws and teeth as tools or vises. The zygoma is deepest inferiorly at the juncture of the temporal and maxillary processes; here, the zygoma is typically peaked or pointed. More or less directly above this point, as well as level with or slightly above the superior margin of the temporal process, one may find a small *zygomaticofacial foramen,* or, more rarely, multiple zygomaticofacial foramina. The presence of these foramina is asymmetrically variable. When present, these foramina, which communicate with the *zygomatico-orbital foramina* that perforate the floor of the orbit, are often located superior to the inferior margin of the orbit (as in the orangutan).

The morphology of the frontal process, as well as its relation medially to the orbit and posteriorly to the temporal fossa, also bears on the identification of the zygomatic bone. The orbital margin is rounded, blunt, and arcuately "L"-shaped (curved almost like a hockey stick); its smooth inner angle faces medially. The contribution of the temporal process to the lateral orbital wall is somewhat thicker and definitely deeper than the reflection of the maxillary process upon the orbital floor. Just inside the

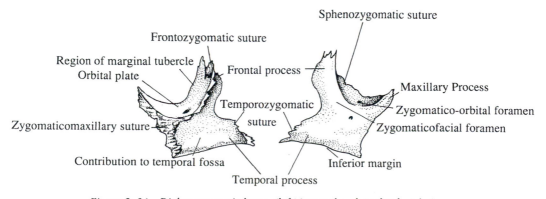

Figure 2–21 Right zygomatic bone: *(left)* internal and *(right)* facial views.

rim of the orbit and just below the *frontozygomatic suture*, the orbital border is variably thickened or swollen into the *marginal tubercle (tuberculum marginale)*. The exact shape of the orbital portion of the temporal process may differ asymmetrically within the same individual, due in part to the extent to which the bone overlaps the orbital contribution of the greater wing of the sphenoid. As a result, the edge of the *sphenozygomatic suture* is not homogeneous morphologically; in addition, the length of the thin, tapering portion of the frontozygomatic suture may vary. The surface of the more consistently triangular portion of the frontozygomatic suture is cross-hatched with a series of parallel to subparallel ridges and grooves that interdigitate with their counterparts on the zygomatic process of the frontal bone. There is either a small projection of bone, an indentation, or both (the small spit of bone lying over the indentation) at the intersection of the superior and inferior orbital flanges of the zygoma. The latter juncture marks the anteriormost extent of the inferior orbital fissure. This small stretch of bone does not bear any sutural morphology and represents a break between the orbital aspects of the sphenozygomatic and zygomaticomaxillary sutures.

The relatively thin posterior extension of the frontal process of the zygoma is oriented at approximately a right angle to the orbital projection of the process itself. The smooth surface subtended by these two flanges of bone forms the anterior wall of the *temporal fossa*. The posterior margin of the frontal process either may transcribe a relatively smoothly arc down toward the temporal process or, a centimeter or so below the frontozygomatic suture, may bulge out and then curve inward toward its juncture with the temporal process. [This bulge is often misidentified as the marginal tubercle (but see above).]

DEVELOPMENT AND OSSIFICATION. During the latter part of the second fetal month, the zygomatic bone arises intramembranously beneath and lateral to the orbital region. Mineralization begins often only in one but sometimes in as many as three centers of ossification that generally fuse into a single mass within a few weeks. Ossification then spreads out from this single center. If coalescence of multiple centers is incomplete, a horizontal suture will persist, dividing the bone unequally into a large superior and a smaller inferior moeity. The smaller, inferior moiety is identified as the *os japonicum*.

Vomer

The vomer (Figure 2–22) develops during the eighth fetal week as right and left lamellae. These lamellae arise from ossification centers that appear in the posterior and inferior portions of the membrane covering the cartilaginous septum, which bisects the nasal cavity. By the third fetal month, these two plates have begun to coalesce; complete fusion into a "single" plate does not occur until the onset of puberty. As the two lamellae become united, a groove develops between them in which the cartilaginous nasal septum rests. This groove can be seen clearly in adult specimens, in whom it can be observed that (1) the platelike "walls" of the groove are asymmetric in their height (e.g. the right lamella may be taller than the left) and (2) the groove is usually broadest at its anterior and inferiormost extent, where it flares out beyond the thin median sheet of bone of the corpus of the vomer.

The vomer increases in height and depth posteriorly and superiorly. At birth, the vomer is relatively long but not very tall; height is attained as the facial skeleton grows deeper. At the juncture of the vomer with the sphenoid, the former bone splays outward, embracing the midregion of the basisphenoid with its *alae*, which are the vestiges of its bilamellar origins. In an isolated vomer one can observe not only that the two alae do flare laterally but that they are separated by a deep cleft. (In a damaged

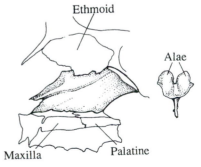

Figure 2–22 Vomer *(stippled): (left)* left side and *(right)* posterior aspect.

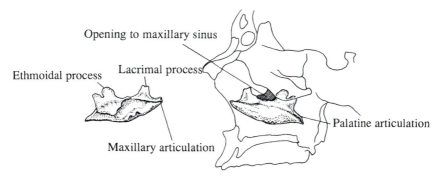

Figure 2–23   Right inferior nasal concha: *(left)* lateral and *(right)* medial views.

vomer, one can usually see that the "single" bone is composed of two lamellae that sandwich between them thin air spaces.) The contacts between the vomer and the perpendicular plate of the ethmoid above it, as well as between the vomer and the maxilla and palatine bones below, are relatively thin.

Inferior Nasal Concha

The inferior nasal concha (Figure 2–23) begins to develop during the fifth fetal month from a single center of ossification that arises endochondrally in the lateral wall of the nasal capsule. When fully formed, the inferior nasal concha protrudes medially and inferiorly into the nasal cavity. It articulates along its *superior border*, respectively and proceeding anteroposteriorly, with the maxilla, lacrimal, ethmoid, and palatine bones. It articulates thinly with the lacrimal and ethmoid via the *lacrimal* and *ethmoidal processes*. The ridgelike zones of contact (and fusion) with the maxilla and the palatine

(i.e. along the conchal crests of the maxilla and palatine) are longer and more substantial. The medial surface of the inferior nasal concha is convex and its topography rugose and variegated. In contrast, its lateral surface is concave and relatively smooth. The portion of the inferior nasal concha that is most intrusive upon the nasal cavity is expanded and spongy in texture.

Ethmoid

MORPHOLOGY. [As isolated human ethmoids are not frequently encountered in an archeological, forensic, or paleontological collection, only the bone's major features are reviewed here. Because the ethmoid (Figure 2–24) is dominated by air cells, whose walls are composed of exceedingly thin bone, ethmoidal fragments likely will come in the form of small flakes of bone, as will fragments of the thin perpendicular plate. Identifiable ethmoidal fragments usually form parts of a larger fragment, e.g. of the medial orbital wall.]

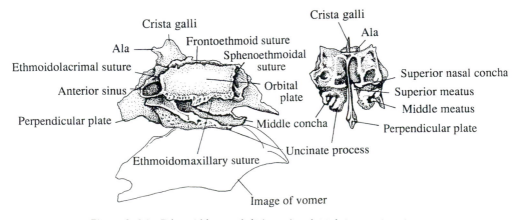

Figure 2–24   Ethmoid bone: *(left)* lateral and *(right)* posterior views.

The two air-cell-riddled labyrinths hang down like saddlebags on either side of the long, thin perpendicular plate. Their lateralmost surfaces are irregularly shaped rectangles of smooth bone whose long superior and inferior edges, and much shorter anterior and posterior edges, form thin, finely denticulate sutural contacts with neighboring bones. Since the smooth-boned portion contributes to the medial orbital wall, the sutures in question are, respectively, the *frontoethmoidal* (superior), *ethmoidomaxillary* (inferior), *ethmoidolacrimal* (anterior), and *sphenoethmoidal* (posterior) *sutures*. Medially below the labyrinthine bundle of air cells lies the somewhat inflated *superior nasal concha*, which is set off from the scrolled *middle nasal concha* by the channellike *superior meatus*. The medial nasal concha which is also medially situated and separated from the perpendicular plate, appears to hang freely. Laterally opposite the middle nasal concha and set apart from it by the relatively deep *middle meatus* is the thin, variably folded, swollen, or pointed downwardly projecting *uncinate process*.

The thin perpendicular plate descends (approximately) in the midline of the nasal cavity, and the crista galli arises more or less from the midsection of the porous cribriform plate. The upper portion of the anterior edge of the perpendicular plate articulates with the *spine of the frontal bone* and the lower portion with the *crest of the nasal bones*. From the nasal crest, the long inferior edge of the perpendicular plate courses down and back, forming a deep, anteriorly opening "V" with the vomer, which it contacts farther back in the nasal cavity. The septal cartilage of the nose lies in this "V." The perpendicular plate's articulation with the vomer angles upward as it courses posteriorly. The posterior border of the perpendicular plate articulates with the sphenoidal crest.

DEVELOPMENT AND OSSIFICATION. The ethmoid begins development endochondrally during the 16th to 18th fetal weeks, with its two labyrinths appearing as bony granules in the orbital laminae. Osteoclastic activity in the developing labyrinths results in the formation of the ethmoidal air cells, which appear before birth and continue to enlarge as the ethmoid itself increases in size. At birth, the labyrinths are small and their walls partially ossified; the remainder of

the ethmoid is still entirely cartilaginous. The single ossification center that gives rise to both the *crista galli* and the *perpendicular plate* does not appear until the first year. Only in the second year do the crista galli and perpendicular plate coalesce with the labyrinths.

Temporal Bone

MORPHOLOGY. Because it is composed of extremely dense bone, the petromastoid portion of the temporal bone (Figure 2–25) tends to be preserved with greater frequency than many other parts of the cranium, not just in archeological but in paleontological contexts as well. Here the two major features are the mastoid process and the petrous part, with its tubular external acoustic meatus. Humans are the only extant primates in which the mastoid process is so well developed inferiorly that it often protrudes noticeably beyond the base of the skull. The human mastoid process may extend as far as or even below the level of the occipital condyles. The mastoid process is usually thick anteroposteriorly at its base and its lateral surface is roughened. The tip of the mastoid process is typically narrower than the base.

Overall, the mastoid process of the male can be characterized as being stubbier and blunter than that of the female, in whom it tends to be thinner or narrower lengthwise. These characterizations are more reliable indicators of sexual differences than assuming that male mastoid processes will also be longer than those of females. Males can have short processes and females extremely long ones, but the former will often be blunter and the latter narrower and more tapering.

The medial surface of the mastoid process, which is usually smoother than the lateral surface, forms a variably steep to sloping and tall to short wall that faces directly upon an obliquely oriented, typically shallow groove called the *mastoid (digastric) notch*. The orientation of the mastoid notch tends to make the mastoid process somewhat triangular in outline (when viewed from below); that is, it is broad at its abutment with the external acoustic meatus and tapers posteriorly. Just medial to the mastoid notch and sometimes separated for some of its length from the notch by a variably thick ridge (the *occipitomastoid crest*) lies the

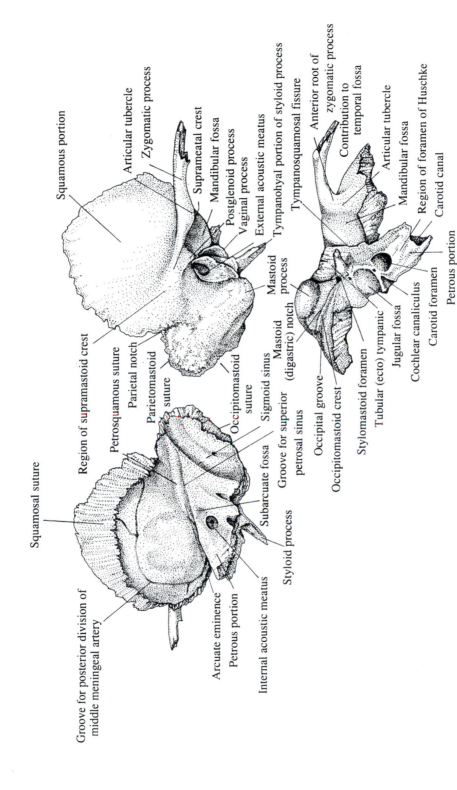

Figure 2-25   Right temporal bone: *(left)* internal, *(top right)* external, and *(bottom right)* inferior views.

occipital groove; in Neanderthals, the occipitomastoid crest equals if not exceeds in size the mastoid process (e.g. Santa Luca, 1978). The occipital groove tends to be confluent with the mastoid notch anteriorly, but the two features may be inseparable for their entire lengths. When it is not impressed upon the occipitomastoid suture itself, the occipital groove lies just on the edge of the mastoid region of the temporal bone.

Basicranially, starting at the mastoid process and proceeding medially and anteriorly along the petrosal, one encounters, respectively, (1) the mastoid (digastric) notch; (2) the *stylomastoid foramen*; (3) the styloid process (or at least its base, as this slender structure is easily broken); (4) the vacuous, posteromedially directed contribution to the *jugular fossa*; (5) the somewhat smaller but still large teardrop-shaped *carotid foramen*; and then (6) the craggy apex of the petrosal, from which the carotid canal emanates. Appressed to the anterior surface of the mastoid process is the posterior wall of the external acoustic meatus. From this juncture, and proceeding along the petrosal to or just beyond the anterior side of the carotid foramen, the external acoustic meatus appears to be creased and "thrown up" as a wall against the mastoid notch, the stylomastoid foramen, and the styloid process. On the other side of the styloid process is another crest of bone—the *vaginal process*—which appears to diverge from the crestlike edge of the external acoustic meatus.

The rather steeply inclined anterior surface of the external acoustic meatus (which faces anterolaterally) is relatively smooth-boned. It forms the posterior wall of the broad and wide mandibular fossa. At the juncture of the external acoustic meatus and the temporal bone, but not in the deepest part of the mandibular fossa, lies the *tympanosquamosal fissure*. The deepest part of the fossa, which is the true basinlike portion of the fossa, occurs anterior to the fissure. Although characteristically wide from side to side, the mandibular fossa is variably long anteroposteriorly. Thus the fossa is variably deep to shallow from one individual to another.

Laterally and posteriorly the mandibular fossa is bounded by a short, stout projection—the *postglenoid process*—that is appressed to the edge of the external acoustic meatus. Anteriorly, the fossa is constrained by the taller

articular tubercle (eminence), which courses across the entire width of the fossa. Laterally, the articular tubercle thickens somewhat and projects from the side of the cranium, forming the *anterior root of the zygomatic process.* The posterior part of the mandibular fossa also projects from the side of the cranium; its roof is a thinner strut or bridge between the postglenoid process and the articular tubercle. The degree to which the fossa and tubercle, and to some extent the process, as well, project from the side of the cranium appears to be correlated with the degree to which the *supramastoid* and *suprameatal crests* are developed. The supramastoid crest, which is a continuation of the posterior arc of the temporal lines, comes down upon the mastoid region from just above the parietal notch and curves toward the external acoustic meatus, over which, as the suprameatal crest, it courses to the postglenoid process, where it expands to become the ledge into which the mandibular fossa is impressed. The crest or thickening that proceeds posteriorly from the postglenoid process and passes above the external acoustic meatus is identified as the *posterior root of the zygomatic process.* The degree to which supramastoid/suprameatal crests are developed is a function of the demands of the temporal muscles and is also reflective, at least secondarily, of differences between males (with thicker and more marked crests) and females. A small, semitriangular, slightly raised region—the *suprameatal triangle*—is bordered superiorly by the supramastoid/suprameatal crest, which forms the "base" of the triangle.

Damage to the mastoid region will expose its characteristic internal pneumatization. These *mastoid air cells* are smaller and more profuse in the inferiormost portion as well as around the perimeter of the mastoid process. They are larger and more vacuous toward the center of the process. (In dealing with mastoid fragments, the air cells, the parietal notch, and the thick and craggy occipitomastoid suture are particularly helpful in aiding identification.)

The relatively slender zygomatic process, which projects forward as well as laterally away from the side of the cranium, is often damaged or broken off near its anterior root. Even so, vestiges of the anterior root, in conjunction with other features in the region of the mandibular fossa, provide clues toward the proper identification of fragments and determination of side. On the rare occasion that a piece of the zygomatic process is found, the clear distinctions between the anterior root and the backwardly angled temporozygomatic suture—as well as between the slightly thicker, muscle-scarred inferior surface and the finer, more edgelike superior margin—should make correct identification possible.

The relatively flat external surface of the squamous portion of the temporal bone is distinguished further by its fanlike appearance (which appears to spread out and rotate around the posterior root of the zygomatic process). Often one finds fragments of the thin squamous portion, which can be identified as such by internal features (see below) as well as by the *squamosal suture*, which (1) thins so as to overlap and (2) bears fine, radiating grooves and ridges that interdigitate with their counterparts on the parietal bone.

Internally, the anteromedially oriented, somewhat tapering petrous portion is creased superoposteriorly into an edgelike border that extends for much of its length. This edge may bear a shallow *groove for the superior petrosal sinus*, which, if present, is usually most pronounced in the midregion of the petrosal bone. In the same midregion of the petrosal the *arcuate eminence* arises from the superior surface of the bone. Farther along the superior surface of the petrosal, and still toward its edge lies the variably depressed *subarcuate fossa*, which is situated above the obliquely oriented *internal acoustic meatus*. Arcing into the middle cranial fossa and laterally around the entire petrosal is the *petrosquamous suture* (or at least traces of it), which is typically obliterated externally. The squamous portion of the middle cranial fossa is adorned with a characteristic pattern of shallow, broad grooves or depressions and low ridges that reflects the gyral and convolutional pattern of the brain; regardless of variation anteriorly, the groove for the posterior division of the middle meningeal vessel courses posteriorly and somewhat superiorly (i.e. up and back). The *sigmoidal sulcus*, which lies below the root of the petrosal, is another clue to the identification of temporal bone fragments.

Nonmetric traits commonly recorded for the temporal bone include (1) exsutural mastoid foramen (i.e. it does not lie in the occipitomastoid suture but penetrates the mastoid region instead); (2) mastoid foramen absent; (3) persistence of a foramen of Huschke; (4) development of *exostoses* in the external acoustic meatus, usually along the posterior wall or the floor; and, at the other extreme, (5) congenital absence of the entire meatus. Exostoses, which are referred to as *auditory* or *acoustic tori (tori auditivi)*, may appear as only minor thickenings of bone or be so enlarged that the struts virtually occlude the meatal openings. The development of an auditory torus may be hereditarily based, but it also may be a response to the cold and pressure experienced by habitual diving in deep coastal waters.

DEVELOPMENT AND OSSIFICATION. Developmentally, the temporal bone consists initially of three entities: the *squamous* portion ("the squama," the squamosal), the *tympanic* part, and the *petrous* portion ("the petromastoid part," the petrosal). The former two "units" ossify intramembranously, whereas the petromastoid part arises by endochondral ossification.

Between the end of the second fetal month and the middle of the third, ossification centers arise intramembranously: first, for the *zygomatic process* (at its presumptive root), and, second and third, respectively, for the anterior and posterior "halves" of the *squamous portion*. Ossification from the latter proceeds radially. These three centers quickly coalesce but a fissure delineating the anterior from the posterior squamosal moiety may be visible through term. By the end of the eighth fetal month, but perhaps at the beginning of the third trimester in (some) males, the squama fuses with the tympanic part.

The *tympanic ring* begins to ossify intramembranously during the ninth to tenth fetal weeks at both of its superior ends as well as at its inferiormost extent. Within a few weeks, these three centers of ossification coalesce. Toward the end of the third trimester, the tympanic ring begins to fuse with both the squamous and petrosal portions of the temporal bone. At birth, the still incomplete tympanic ring bears a distinct groove—the *tympanic sulcus*—in which the tympanic membrane is anchored.

Ossification of the petrous part is quite complex, with multiple centers arising endochondrally by or during the fifth fetal month. The first centers of ossification appear medially in the *tympanic cavity (otic capsule)*, which lies in the region of the presumptive *arcuate eminence*. These ossification centers contribute to the medial and posterior walls of the tympanic cavity as well as to the *cochlea*, the *vestibule*, and the *internal acoustic meatus*. The second set of ossification centers arises inferiorly, at the *promontory* on the medial wall of the tympanic cavity, and contributes to the lower portions of the tympanic cavity, the vestibule, and the internal acoustic meatus as well as to the formation of the *cochlear window* and the *carotid canal*. The third set of ossification centers emerges superiorly, over the *lateral semicircular canal*. These centers spread out so as to cap (via the tegmen tympani) the tympanic cavity and the *antrum*.

During the sixth fetal month, (1) the *superior semicircular canal ossifies*; (2) a fissure, which marks the development of the carotid canal, appears inferiorly in the petrosal; (3) and the *jugular notch* becomes distinct. By the middle of the third trimester, the "carotid fissure" has enlarged and has ossified superiorly into the carotid canal. The *mastoid region* arises from a center of ossification that emerges near the posterior semicircular canal; the primary growth of the mastoid process occurs postnatally. The *tympanohyal portion of the styloid process* arises prenatally; during the first postnatal year, it fuses with the temporal bone posterior to the tympanic ring. The petrous and squamous parts also fuse during the first postnatal year, often by the end of the first postnatal month; the persistent *petrosquamous suture* attests to the ontogenetic distinctiveness of these two bones.

Postnatally, in concert with the increasing breadth of the skull, the *mandibular fossa* and attendant *zygomatic process* become oriented more inferiorly, the mastoid region enlarges and becomes pneumaticized, the natally large subarcuate fossa becomes indistinct, the stylohyal portion of the styloid process begins to ossify (during the second year) but may not fuse with the temporal until after puberty (if at all), and the tympanic ring begins to grow outward to eventually become the external acoustic meatus. Uneven ossification of the expanding external acoustic meatus will leave a patency in its floor—the *foramen of Huschke*—which usually fills in by the fifth year but may persist uni- or bilaterally and to varying degrees of openness.

The presence in the adult of a foramen of Huschke is sometimes recorded as a nonmetric variant.

Occipital Bone

MORPHOLOGY. When viewed from behind, the isolated occipital bone (Figure 2–26) looks like a broad leaf or petal with jagged edges. Superior to the horizontal plane that passes through the external occipital protuberance (which also may be the plane that passes through asterion bilaterally) lies the *planum occipitale* (occipital plane), which is somewhat convex (swollen outward) and relatively smooth-surfaced. Technically (see above), the planum occipitale begins at the level of the *highest nuchal lines,* which, however, are not always discernible. When fully expressed, a highest nuchal line begins laterally and slightly above the level of asterion, arcs upward, and then curves gently down toward the external occipital protuberance, with which it may be confluent. (However, because development to any visible extent of the highest nuchal line is quite variable, the most distinct feature in the general region is often the external occipital protuberance.)

The densely and strongly denticulate *lambdoid border* begins at asterion and, in two stages, courses upward and toward the midsagittal plane. The lower half of the lambdoid border is more vertical than the upper portion, which angles inward more severely toward the peak (or at least narrower portion) of the occipital bone, which nestles in between the parietals at *lambda*. This "peak" (i.e. the superiormost point of the occipital bone) is called the *superior angle*. The most inferior point of the lambdoid border (i.e. that which contributes to asterion) is identified as the *lateral angle*. The lambdoid border bears two parallel rows or layers of articular denticulations. One layer protrudes from the outer table of the bone and the other from the inner table. With the exception of the 2 to 3 cm of the lambdoid border closest to asterion, the denticulations of these two rows are similar in length. Toward asterion, however, the denticulations of the inner table may become the more predominant.

The *planum nuchale* is adorned with much more surface topography than the occipital plane. The *superior nuchal lines* originate from

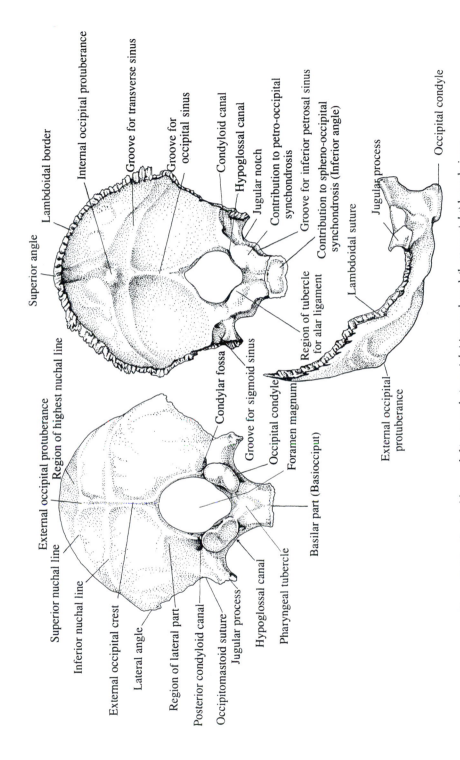

Figure 2–26 Occipital bone: *(left)* external, *(top right)* internal, and *(bottom right)* lateral views.

the region below asterion and curve up toward the external occipital protuberance, with which they may be confluent. The superior nuchal lines increase in thickness and distinctiveness as they approach the midsagittal region of the bone. At times, the external occipital protuberance appears to be a natural extension of the increasingly thickening lines. If vestiges of the (fetal) lateral occipital fissures persist (as they sometimes do) into the adult, they lie slightly below the lateral angle and delineate further the lateral portion of the superior margin of the superior nuchal lines.

The variably distinct and ridgelike *external occipital crest (median occipital crest)* emanates from the external occipital protuberance and courses down the midline of the nuchal plane to the posterior margin of the foramen magnum. In younger individuals, in particular, this crest may be more pronounced than the external occipital protuberance, which, at that time developmentally, may be nothing more than a smooth area that is "etched out" on its sides by the superior nuchal lines. As the external occipital crest proceeds away from the (region of) the external occipital protuberance toward the foramen magnum, it intervenes between two pairs of variably ovoid, roughened patches of bone: a superior pair and an inferior pair.

The superior pair of roughened areas is bordered above by the superior nuchal lines and, below, by the *inferior nuchal lines*. In some individuals, the inferior nuchal lines may be restricted to the inferior border of the roughened areas alone. In other individuals, these lines may arc craggily or as a series of scallop shapes around the foramen magnum, eventually terminating medial to the *occipitomastoid crest* and *suture*. And in yet other individuals, the most prominent features are the part of the inferior nuchal line that lies just below the semiovoid roughened area and the stretch of bone that extends for a few centimeters just in front of the occipitomastoid crest/suture. Rarely does the inferior nuchal line extend around the foramen magnum as far as *jugular process*. This process projects laterally from the lateral margin of the occipital condyle; it reaches its greatest height before or at the *occipitomastoid suture*.

The inferior pair of semiovoid, roughened depressions is delineated anteriorly by the rim of the foramen and, posteriorly, by the inferior nuchal line; these depressions constitute the thinnest portions of the entire occipital bone. These depressions are also bounded laterally by another pair of longer, arcing depressions, which correspond to the developmentally distinct lateral parts of the occipital bone. In some individuals, this region at large may bear three or more pairs of roughened depressions.

When viewed from the side, the nuchal plane may present itself in one of two general configurations: it may angle inward along a single plane, or it may it may be folded along the "horizontal axis" provided by the inferior nuchal line into a second plane of angulation. In either case, the inferiorly placed, ovoid *foramen magnum* essentially remains horizontally oriented, with its anterior margin being only slightly below the level of its posterior margin. From the foramen magnum, the basilar part of the occipital bone angles upward sharply as it extends to meet the base of the sphenoid. With the exception of the degree to which the basilar part is flexed upward, the other planes, angulations, and orientations of the different regions of the occipital bone are established by the time of birth.

In the adult, the *occipital condyles* (which arise from the fusion of contributions from the lateral and basilar parts) lie along the margins of the anterior portion of the foramen magnum. Specific details of occipital condylar morphology can be quite variable; in general, however, an occipital condyle is characteristically longer in one dimension than the other and often somewhat elliptical in outline. The long axis of an occipital condyle is oriented obliquely in two planes. In one plane, the anterior end of the condyle is more medial than the posterior end. In the other, and when viewed looking down upon it, the medial edge of the condyle is elevated far above its lateral margin. Thus the smooth articular surface, which faces away from the opening of the foramen magnum, is oriented obliquely and laterally. The medial edge of an occipital condyle may also extend slightly over and thus protrude somewhat into the space of the opening of the foramen magnum. As it is situated on the lateral rim of the foramen magnum and roughly parallels the inwardly curving arc of the rim of the foramen, an occipital condyle is also convex in the plane of its long axis, arcing upward and outward from its anterior and posterior ends.

The edges of the articular surface of an occipital condyle are usually raised and fairly well delineated. The posterior end of the condyle, however, is not always crisply delineated from the *condylar fossa* into which it points or projects. The *posterior condyloid canal* is variably located in the region of the condylar fossa and at times may lie quite close to the posterior end of the occipital condyle. The rim of the foramen magnum posterior to the condyle is irregularly and variably thickened and roughened. The posteriormost portion of the foramen's rim, which corresponds to that part of the nuchal plane which, in the fetus, intervenes between the two lateral parts, typically is the smoothest and thinnest part of the rim. The "Y" of the basilar part of the occipital bone that separates the two condyles, and which forms the anterior section of the rim of the foramen magnum, is the thickest portion of the rim.

Variation in the region of the foramen magnum is noted in the development of a patent posterior condyloid canal and in the extent to which the occipital condyles are partitioned into two (usually unequal) moieties. The partitioning may be complete, with the creation of so-called twinned, demiarticular facets, or it may be as benign as the pinching in of the (usually medial) side of the condyle. Variation in the unity versus partitioning of an occipital condyle appears to be related to the degree to which the contributions from the lateral and basilar parts of the occipital bone coalesce to form an occipital condyle.

Proceeding inferiorly from the *lateral angle* (i.e. the contribution to the asterion), the lateral borders of the occipital bone are directed inward; thus the rather straight-sided region of the occipital in which the foramen magnum sits becomes constricted and narrower. The *mastoid border* of the occipital bone bears oblique ridges that contribute to the formation of the *occipitomastoid suture*. The edge of the mastoid border may also may bear a portion of the occipital groove, which, in some individuals, may be captured between the occipital bone and the mastoid portion of the temporal. At the *jugular process*, the mastoid border of the occipital becomes variably distended inferiorly. Thus the mastoid border can contribute variably to the

lateral margin of the *jugular notch*, which forms the inferior border of the jugular foramen (the superior border of the jugular foramen is formed by the petrosal portion of the temporal). The aperture of the jugular foramen is oriented anteroposteriorly. An upwardly constricted strut of bone, through which the *hypoglossal canal (anterior condylar canal)* courses, extends between the jugular notch and the occipital condyle. This canal is oriented anteroposteriorly. Slightly anterior and medial to the hypoglossal canal (if not at the anteromedial edge of the mouth of the canal) is an unnamed, small, tuberclelike elevation of bone onto which the rectus capitis anterior muscle inserts. Medial to this small tubercle, the basilar part of the occipital becomes narrower. The *pharyngeal tubercle* lies midsagittally, between the right and left of these two small tubercles, or just anterior to a line drawn between them. The pharyngeal tubercle is an anteroposteriorly oriented, low, thin to moderately swollen bony elevation. On either side of the pharyngeal tubercle and slightly anterior to it is another (unnamed) low tubercle to which the longus capitis muscle attaches. The anteriormost portion of the basilar part, which contributes to the spheno-occipital synchondrosis, is referred to as the *inferior angle*.

(The internal morphology of the occipital bone is discussed in detail in the section on the interior of the skull, above, and thus is addressed here only briefly.)

Of note, internally, on the *squamous portion* of the occipital bone is the subdivision of this region into four quadrants by the various grooves for the meningeal sinuses. The four quadrants consist of two paired depressions into which, superiorly, the occipital lobes of the cerebrum, and, inferiorly, the cerebellar lobes sit. In the middle of the cruciate partitioning pattern lies the variably raised *internal occipital protuberance*. A midline crest descends to the internal occipital protuberance, and it is to the right of this crest that the *groove for the superior sagittal sinus* typically courses most markedly; to the right of the protuberance, the groove is identified as the *groove for the transverse sinus*. At or about the region of asterion, the groove for the transverse sinus begins to arc inferiorly. Although the general downward curvature of the groove for the sinus may have begun on the occipital bone, it is not identified as the *groove for the sigmoidal sinus* until it crosses over onto the temporal bone. Although the superior sagittal sinus bifurcates into right and left transverse sinuses, the groove for the left transverse sinus, which may be less well developed than the right, gives the impression of taking origin directly from the internal occipital protuberance. Occasionally, however, the transition between the superior sagittal sinus and the left transverse sinus is emphasized.

In addition to these grooves, the internal surface of this portion of the occipital bone may also bear a variably distinct crest that courses between the internal occipital protuberance and the midline of the posterior margin of the foramen magnum. The details of this crest, however, may be quite variable: that is, it might broaden slightly toward the rim of the foramen magnum; it might be a rather broad, shallow, groovelike depression; or it might assume any configuration in between. Whatever the configuration in any individual case, however, the "structure" that courses between the internal occipital protuberance and the rim of the foramen magnum is called the *groove for the occipital sinus.*

Internally, and proceeding anteriorly around the foramen magnum, the bone thickens and becomes elevated (due to the upward deflection of the basilar part). Parallel (approximately) to the midpoint of the length of the foramen magnum, the groove for the *sigmoidal sinus* courses across the occipitomastoid suture and onto the occipital bone. This sinus curves upward and anteriorly to terminate at the *jugular notch*, which is typically larger on the right side than on the left. The terminus of this groove is also bordered anteriorly and medially by the fairly large and swollen *jugular tubercle*, which is distended medially, toward the foramen magnum. The *hypoglossal canal*, which is oriented somewhat posteriorly and slightly inferiorly, is located below and just behind the most swollen portion of the jugular tubercle. Arising from this swollen portion of the jugular tubercle and projecting upward and slightly medially is the variably roughened and distended *tubercle for the alar ligament*, which may be barely visible on some specimens and quite prominent on others. The anterior ends of the jugular tubercles are separated from one another by a rather broad, shallow groove that traverses the length

of the basilar part. This is the *groove for the medulla oblongata*, which, following the perimeter of the anterior portion of the rim of the foramen magnum, becomes splayed inferior to the jugular tubercles.

The width of the basilar part narrows toward the inferior angle. The surface of the inferior angle—that is, the surface at the end of the basilar part that contributes to the *spheno-occipital synchondrosis*—in the precoalesced state is roughened and pitted, and its edges may be raised. The sides of the basilar part, which contribute to the *petro-occipital synchondrosis*, are also roughened and may be traversed by an inconsistently distinct *groove for the inferior petrosal sinus*, which variably reaches the jugular notch and/or groove for the sigmoidal sinus. (The *superior petrosal sinus* is located on the medial, superior margin of the petrosal portion of the temporal bone.)

DEVELOPMENT AND OSSIFICATION. The occipital bone begins to develop during the seventh to ninth fetal weeks from multiple ossification centers, most of which are endochondral (i.e. in the chondrocranium). Two intramembranous centers appear by the end of the second or the beginning of the third fetal month; they are located toward the midline but well above the large chondrocranial portion of the presumptive occipital bone. Within a week or so, two other intramembranous centers arise. Eventually, these intramembranous centers coalesce almost completely with one another (to form the presumptive *occipital plane*) and, as a "unit," unite almost completely with the ossifying lower squamous portion of the occipital bone (i.e. the presumptive *nuchal plane*). The lateral areas of the occipital, however, remain open due to the persistence of a single midline fissure superiorly and the pervasion of an inferiorly oblique fissure on each side of the squama. The superior fissure begins to close slowly after birth, whereas the inferior fissures—the *transverse occipital fissures (mendosal fissures* or *sutures)*—do not begin to close over until the third or even the fourth year.

The intramembranous portion of the occipital squama corresponds to the *occipital plane (planum occipitale)*, whose inferior boundary is indicated in the adult by the nuchal lines. The *nuchal plane (planum nuchale)* lies below the nuchal lines. Incomplete union of the large interparietal portion with the nuchal plane, or the occasional occurrence of a supernumerary center of ossification at the midline, creates the *Inca bone* (or *interparietal bone*), which occurs as a variant among populations. Incomplete union of any of the original intramembranous areas of ossification yields ossicles along the lambdoid suture.

Toward the end of the second fetal month or by the early part of the third, two centers of ossification (but occasionally one transversely elongate center of ossification) appear endochondrally in the midsagittal region of the presumptive nuchal plane. By the middle of the third month, these two centers unite and form the core from which trabeculae spread laterally and superiorly. Until the middle of the third trimester, the enlarging occipital squama is wider than it is tall (i.e. typically being widest at the lateral plates above the transverse occipital fissures). But subsequent rapid vertical growth of the squama eventually equalizes (more or less) these dimensions.

The portions of the occipital that subtend the foramen magnum laterally and anteriorly (the *lateral parts* and the *basilar part*, respectively) arise endochondrally as separate elements. Mineralization of the basilar part (which, in the adult, corresponds to the *basiocciput*), begins during the middle of the third fetal month from one or sometimes two centers of ossification. During the fourth month, the originally spindle-shaped presumptive basilar part becomes tapered at its ends and nearly doubles in size. During the fifth fetal month, the posterior end of the basilar part begins to bifurcate and assume its characteristic "Y" shape; the "arms" of this "Y" subtend the foramen magnum anteriorly. Concomitantly, the anterior end broadens and flattens to form its contribution to the *spheno-occipital synchondrosis*.

The lateral parts of the occipital begin to ossify at approximately the same time as the basilar part. Each lateral part originates from a single ossification center, which arises lateral to the presumptive foramen magnum as a thin lamina. With growth, the anterior end of the presumptive lateral part thickens and eventually bifurcates into two somewhat closely approximated "arms." One arm lies below the other, and the two arms create a "U" shape. Together, these arms contribute to the formation of the *hypoglossal canal (anterior condylar canal)*. The arm

of the lateral part that is fully exposed basicranially contributes in large part to the formation of an occipital condyle. The arm of the basilar part, which abuts and eventually fuses with the arm of the lateral part, contributes to the anterior portion of an occipital condyle. Posterior to its "U"-shaped anterior end, the lateral part of the occipital broadens, flattens, and assumes a slightly arcuate shape because the lateral side of the bone grows at a faster rate than its medial side. This differential growth causes the medial border of the lateral part, which subtends the foramen magnum, to become arcuate. Within the posterior cranial fossa is a thickened band that emanates from the arm of the lateral part that subtends the hypoglossal canal internally. The *condyloid canal* arises lateral to this thickened band.

The lateral parts do not fuse with the squama until the fourth year. The occiput does not become a unified, single bone until the sixth year (approximately). The *spheno-occipital synchondrosis* usually remains patent until about the 17th year and often closes by the 22nd year. However, this synchondrosis may remain incompletely fused until the 25th year. Closure of the spheno-occipital synchondrosis is one of the criteria commonly used to define the beginning of an individual's period of "juvenile age."

Sphenoid

MORPHOLOGY. [It is rare to find a complete, isolated sphenoid (Figure 2–27) during fieldwork or in any paleontological or archeological collections, but one comes across parts of sphenoids, either as isolated fragments or as contributions to larger cranial fragments that also include parts of adjacent bones. Because portions of a sphenoid do crop up under different and unexpected circumstances, discussion of the isolated bone is practical.]

Within the interior of the cranium, the dominant features of the sphenoid are the thick, deeply indented *sella turcica (hypophyseal fossa)* and the *greater* and *lesser wings*. The sella turcica can be oriented properly because the variably elevated, wall-like *dorsum sellae* stands alone posteriorly and its posterior surface is essentially vertical; whereas the surface that faces upon the sella turcica is concave (the *posterior clinoid processes* may not provide useful clues to identification because they project

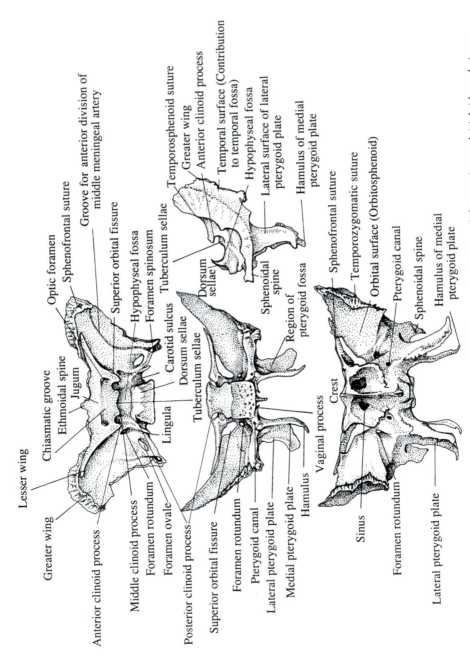

Lesser wing

Greater wing

Chiasmatic groove

Optic foramen

Ethmoidal spine

Sphenofrontal suture

Jugum

Groove for anterior division of
middle meningeal artery

Anterior clinoid process

Superior orbital fissure

Middle clinoid process

Hypophyseal fossa

Foramen rotundum

Foramen spinosum

Foramen ovale

Tuberculum sellae

Carotid sulcus

Lingula

Dorsum sellae

Posterior clinoid process

Tuberculum sellae

Temporosphenoid suture

Greater wing

Anterior clinoid process

Temporal surface (Contribution
to temporal fossa)

Hypophyseal fossa

Lateral surface of lateral
pterygoid plate

Hamulus of medial
pterygoid plate

Dorsum
sellae

Sphenoidal
spine

Region of
pterygoid fossa

Superior orbital fissure

Foramen rotundum

Pterygoid canal

Lateral pterygoid plate

Medial pterygoid plate

Hamulus

Vaginal process

Crest

Sphenofrontal suture

Temporozygomatic suture

Orbital surface (Orbitosphenoid)

Pterygoid canal

Sphenoidal spine

Hamulus of medial
pterygoid plate

Sinus

Foramen rotundum

Lateral pterygoid plate

Figure 2–27 Sphenoid bone: *(top left)* superior, *(middle left)* posterior, *(bottom left)* anterior, and *(right)* lateral views.

up or outward from the superior corners of the dorsum sellae and are easily damaged). The dorsum sellae is accentuated further by the almost vertical indentation in front of it on each side created by the *carotid sulcus*. The sulcus itself may be partially or completely enclosed laterally (thus creating more of a foramen than a sulcus) by a variably developed spit of bone, the *lingula*.

The anterior part of the sella turcica is bulkier and broader and bears various landmarks. Immediately opposite the dorsum sellae is a variably distinct, horizontal ridge that courses between the inferior margins of the right and left *optic foramina*. This ridge is the *tuberculum sellae*; it may be distended slightly into weak lateral "corners," identified as the *middle clinoid processes*. Another variably distinct horizontal ridge courses between the superior margins of the optic foramina and delineates between it and the tuberculum sellae a shallow groove for the optic chiasma called the *chiasmatic groove*. A stout, rapidly tapering, pointed extension—the *anterior clinoid process*—embraces each optic foramen laterally and projects posteriorly along each side of the sella turcica (an anterior clinoid process is thick enough at its base that damage will not destroy the entire structure). The anterior clinoid process is the "back end of the wing " of the lesser wing. The lesser wing, which tapers laterally along its rather crisp posterior edge, terminates as a laterally directed point. The *sphenofrontal suture*, which courses between the lesser wing and the frontal bone, is mildly undulating; its margin bears fine denticulations that extend from both the inner and outer tables of bone. The variably broad, thin-boned *ethmoid spine* projects anteriorly from the region of the jugum to meet the cribriform plate (this spine may survive even if the ethmoid is damaged).

Lateral and anterior to the body of the sphenoid, the *greater wing of the sphenoid* contributes, respectively, to the base and lateral wall of the cranium, as well as to the lateral and posterior walls of the orbit. Viewed from the interior of the cranium the concave surface of the greater wing has a somewhat corrugated appearance (reflecting the gyral impressions of the brain through the meninges). Superiorly, the surface of the greater wing may also bear the *groove* for an *anterior branch of the anterior division of the middle meningeal artery*. A par-

ticular aspect of the sphenoid (proceeding from top to bottom and from side to side) is the arcuate pattern created by the *superior orbital fissure*, the *foramen rotundum*, the *foramen ovale*, and the *foramen spinosum*. The relatively large, subtriangular *sphenofrontal sutural* contact (i.e. the *frontal margin)* that the greater wing makes with the frontal bone above it is distinguished further by its pitted and spiky surface. This surface is bounded laterally by the thin, almost vertical extension of the infratemporal surface of the greater wing. In turn, this thinned portion of the greater wing overlaps externally the frontal and the parietal bones along the short sphenoparietal and sphenofrontal sutures (i.e. with regard to the latter, the lateral expression of the sphenofrontal suture).

Externally and laterally, the greater wing is relatively tall and thin and, especially superiorly, its infratemporal/temporal fossa surface is concave along the vertical axis. This concavity is bounded anteriorly by the lateral portion of the flat, smooth *orbital surface*, which almost forms a right angle with the temporal surface. The relatively thin lateral extension of the orbital plate contributes to the *sphenozygomatic suture;* its sutural margin is deeply indented. The inner table of bone of the posterior and superior margins of the greater wing is extended beyond the outer table, thus mirroring the squamosal portion of the temporal, which overlaps the greater wing in the formation of the *temporozygomatic suture*. The inferior part of the greater wing's contribution to the temporozygomatic suture is thicker, and platelike extensions of inner and outer tables subtend a hollow that is pervaded by bony denticulations.

As the greater wing descends, it curves medially along its vertical axis. At about the level of the inferior margin of the orbital plate—which also corresponds to the sphenoidal margin along the inferior orbital fissure—a variably modestly to markedly developed horizontal ridge courses across the external surface of the greater wing. Inferior to this ridge, the sphenoid is markedly displaced medially and its lateral surface is concave; this constitutes the lateral surface of the *lateral pterygoid plate*. Just below the level of this ridge, the sphenoid extends posteriorly, particularly along the basicranial portion of the sphenosquamosal suture and terminates in a spikelike projection—the *sphenoidal spine*—which, in the articulated skeleton, would be sandwiched in the corner between the mandibular fossa and the petrosal bone. The *foramen spinosum* and the *foramen ovale*, respectively, lie increasingly medial to the sphenoid spine; the sometimes thin bony wall that forms the posteromedial boundaries of these foramina appears to emanate from the spine. (Even if the region is damaged, the sphenoidal spine and the indented anterior margins of the sphenoidal foramina are often left intact.)

Because they are thin and their inferiormost extents are often peaked or pulled out into spikelike, posteriorly pointing projections, the *pterygoid plates* are easily damaged. The medial plate also bears inferiorly the fragile *pterygoid hamulus*. (If, however, these structures are found relatively intact, the anteriorly invasive *pterygoid fossa,* which is subtended by the two pterygoid plates, is a useful clue to identification.) The bony strut that encloses the foramen ovale posteriorly is more often confluent with the "base," superiorly, of the lateral pterygoid plate than it is with base of the medial pterygoid plate. The margin of the medial pterygoid plate is distinguished superiorly by its termination in a flattened, posteriorly directed projection, the *pterygoid tubercle*. (Damage to the body of the sphenoid, in the region between the medial pterygoid plates and inferior to the sella turcica and the area of the jugum, will expose the vacuous, variably partitioned *sphenoidal sinuses.)*

DEVELOPMENT AND OSSIFICATION. The sphenoid arises from multiple intramembranous as well as endochondral centers of ossification. The first to appear, during the eighth to ninth intrauterine weeks and in the presumptive region of the *foramen rotundum* and *foramen ovale*, is the intramembranous center from which the *greater wing of the sphenoid* develops. These foramina, and the *foramen spinosum* as well, ossify around the structures they come to encase. The foramen rotundum is complete by the middle of the second trimester and the foramen ovale by late in the third trimester. The foramen spinosum, however, does not ossify fully until at least the first postnatal year. The *medial* and *lateral pterygoid plates* may arise intramembranously as early as the ninth to tenth weeks; but perhaps with greater frequency they appear during the 14th to 15th weeks. The medial and lateral pterygoid plates may fuse together in the sixth fetal month, and

the medial pterygoid plate, at least, joins with the greater wing about a month later. At that time, the *vaginal process* also develops from the medial and superior margin of the medial pterygoid plate. The *hamulus* arises from its own center of ossification, which appears a year or two after birth.

By 4 to 4½ fetal months, part of the *body of the sphenoid* has arisen endochondrally either from a pair of centers or (sometimes) from a single center of ossification. The depression denoting the presumptive *sella turcica (hypophyseal fossa)* is also visible at that time. At about the beginning of the fifth month, a pair of centers or sometimes a single center of ossification arises endochondrally in the posterior part of the presumptive body of the sphenoid and will give rise to the *dorsum sellae*. Within 2 months, the dorsum sellae is morphologically identifiable. Its shape as well as that of the sella turcica changes little from then on. The dorsum sellae, sella turcica (hypophyseal fossa), greater wing, and pterygoid plates constitute the *postsphenoid*. It is only during the seventh-eighth fetal months that the *posterior part of the body of the sphenoid* (composed of the dorsum sellae and sella turcica) fuses with the *anterior part of the body* (from the region of the tuberculum sellae anteriorly). The anterior part of the body of the sphenoid, together with the lesser wings, is referred to as the *presphenoid*.

The *lesser wings of the sphenoid* arise toward the end of the fourth fetal month, each from an endochondral center of ossification located just lateral to the presumptive *optic canal*. Although the lesser wings continue to grow in all directions, it is not until the sixth month that growth accelerates, the lateral ends become pointed, and the lesser wings look winglike. The anterior part of the body of the sphenoid arises endochondrally from a pair of ossification centers that appear between the end of the fifth and the beginning of the sixth fetal months. The optic canal does not become complete until (perhaps) during the sixth fetal month—but definitely during the seventh to eighth fetal months—at which time the lesser wings unite with the anterior part of the body of the sphenoid. In turn, this unit fuses with the posterior part of the body of the sphenoid. Although now surrounded by bone, the optic canal is triangular and does not assume its characteristic circular shape until after birth. Incomplete union of the presphenoid and postsphenoid results in the persistence of a *craniopharyngeal canal*, along which *craniopharyngeomas* (epithelium-lined cysts) may occur.

At birth, the lesser wings are still unconnected across the midline, although they do form a unit with the body of the sphenoid. Also at birth, the *greater wings* and *pterygoid plates* are separate right and left elements and the sphenoidal sinuses, at best, are tiny. During the first postnatal year, the lesser wings unite at the midline and the greater wing/pterygoid plate unit fuses with the rest of the sphenoid, resulting, for example, in the formation of the *pterygoid canal*. The smooth-boned medial region posterior to the *ethmoid spine* (which abuts the *cribriform plate*) and between the optic canals represents the area of union between right and left lesser wings and, although not delineated in the adult by obvious boundaries, is identified as the *jugum* or *jugum sphenoidale*. As mentioned above (in the discussion of the occipital bone), the body of the sphenoid and the inferior angle of the basilar part of the occipital bone do not coalesce across the spheno-occipital synchondrosis until the 21st or 22nd year or even as late as the 25th year.

Hyoid

[Although the hyoid bone (Figure 2–28) is not usually recovered during excavation unless overall preservation of the entire skeleton is good, it is detailed briefly in case one is encountered.]

The adult hyoid is relatively thin and is similar in general appearance to an edentulous mandible. The *body of the hyoid* arcs forward or anteriorly. Posteriorly, its right and left

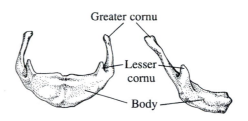

Figure 2–28 Hyoid bone: *(left)* anterior and *(right)* lateral views.

branches turn upward, each terminating in a *greater cornu*. Above and more or less in front of the region of the "angle" between the body and a cornu, a smaller projection extends superiorly; this is the *lesser cornu*. The anterior surface of the hyoid is vaguely reminiscent of the mental region of the mandible: its inferior margin is somewhat "cornered" (however, it also may be distended or swollen inferiorly) and its midline region somewhat raised. The posterior surface of the midline region of the hyoid body may be variably concave. The hyoid is derived from the cartilaginous branchial arch skeleton and each cornu (see Figure 2–13), as well as each side of the body of the hyoid, arises from a separate center of ossification. Ossification begins late in fetal development in the body and the greater cornu but not in the lesser cornu until 1 or 2 years postnatally. The hyoid is distinguished not only because it does not look like any other bone of the body but also because it bears no zones of contact with other bones.

Inner Ear Bones

[Under typical conditions of recovering skeletal remains, the three inner ear bones (Figure 2–29) are rarely encountered. These tiny bones may

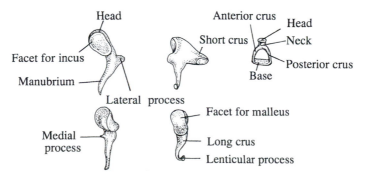

Figure 2–29 Right inner ear ossicles: malleus *(top left)*, medial and *(bottom left)* posterior views; incus *(top middle)* medial and *(bottom middle)* anterior views; stapes, superior view *(right)*.

be discovered by the careful excavator or they may "appear" during, or as a consequence of, preparation of a dirt-plugged, matrix-encased cranium that preserves the auditory region. Only extremely fine mesh (e.g. carburetor or window screen)—much finer than that commonly used archeologically in sieving the dirt from burials—will have the potential of capturing these extremely tiny bony elements.]

The inner ear bones or *auditory ossicles* develop from the cartilaginous branchial arch skeleton. The *incus* and the *malleus* arise from the first and the *stapes* from the second branchial arch (see Figure 2–13). The incus and malleus appear during the latter half of the fourth fetal month, approximately a month or so earlier than the stapes. Growth of all three ossicles continues after birth. The malleus is attached to the tympanic membrane and the stapes to the fenestra vestibuli. The incus articulates between the two other auditory ossicles.

The *malleus* consists of a long, inferiorly tapering portion, on top of which sits a semiglobular "head." (The name of the bone derives from its obvious resemblance to a hammer.) The *head of the malleus* is rounded anteriorly and concave posteriorly (the latter feature forms the *facet for the incus)* and is tilted medially at its juncture with the handle or *manubrium.* When viewed medially, the manubrium appears to be relatively straight, but when viewed posteriorly, one can see that it is oriented medially except for its tip, which curves downward. At the juncture of the manubrium with the head of the malleus, a small, variably blunt to pointed projection juts out laterally; this is the *lateral process.* (By orienting the head upward, the facet for the incus posteriorly and the lateral process laterally, one can "side" the bone.)

The *incus* is so named because it looks somewhat like a tiny anvil. Like the malleus, the incus bears inferiorly a long tapering extension (the *long crus).* This extension appears somewhat straight when viewed medially, but when viewed posteriorly, it has the shape of elongate, shallow "S," with its tip arcing tightly in a medial direction. The tip also flares out a bit into the *lenticular process,*which articulates with the stapes. The upper part of the incus is elongate and wedge-shaped, and it tapers posteriorly into the *short crus;* this is the part that resembles an anvil. The taller anterior end is concave and bears the *facet for the malleus.*

The stirrup-shaped *stapes* is composed of a narrow end (the *head* and *neck)* and a more or less flat *base.* The "U"-shaped section of the bone that bifurcates from the neck and meets the base comprises two parts, an *anterior* and a *posterior crus.* In vivo, the base of the stapes is oriented medially and slightly above the level of the laterally positioned head. When viewed from below, the base (medial surface) of the base of the stirrup is slightly convex along its superiorly margin and, concomitantly, slightly concave along its inferior margin.

The Postcranial Axial Skeleton: The Vertebral Column, Sacrum, Sternum, and Ribs

Along with the skull, the **vertebral column** (or backbone), the **sternum** (or breastbone), and the **ribs** constitute the **axial skeleton**. Together they form the **thoracic cage** (**thorax** or **chest**), which surrounds and protects the heart and lungs. The first 10 ribs are anchored anteriorly either directly or indirectly via costal cartilages to the sternum, and all 12 attach posteriorly to the thoracic vertebrae. The thorax is narrowest superiorly and broadens throughout most of its length. As in other hominoid primates (i.e. the lesser and great apes) but no others, the thorax in humans is relatively broad laterally and, concomitantly, relatively compressed anteroposteriorly (dorsoventrally). For practical reasons, the skull has been dealt with separately. The remainder of the axial skeleton will be discussed here.

Vertebral Column: Overview

Morphology

The **vertebral column** (Figure 3–1) or backbone serves the dual role of providing somewhat of a rigid support for the upper body and protecting the spinal cord, which courses within it. With the exception of the coccygeal vertebrae, all vertebrae have certain features in common, in addition to which are features specific to each type of vertebra. At birth, all elements of the vertebral column are separate entities, and each

"vertebra" consists of three components. In the adult, however, these three components are fused and form individual **vertebrae** (the singular is **vertebra**) that extend from the base of the skull to the level of the pelvis. In general among humans, five vertebrae fuse together to form a roughly triangular unit, the **sacrum**. The upper portions of the lateral sides of the sacrum—the *auricular surfaces*—articulate between the auricular surfaces of the right and left ilia posteriorly. Articulating with the inferior "tip" of the sacrum may be three to five but typically four rudimentary, sequentially tapering vertebrae, which form the **coccyx**; the coccyx may eventually fuse with the sacrum. Sacral and coccygeal vertebrae are referred to as *false* or *fixed vertebrae*.

The individual vertebrae that lie between the skull and the sacrum are identified as *true* or *movable vertebrae*. Three groups of true vertebrae are recognized. The first 7 vertebrae below the skull are called the **cervical vertebrae**; the next 12 are the **thoracic vertebrae**; and the remaining 5 constitute the **lumbar vertebrae**. These vertebrae can also be referred to by the first letter of each group's name (i.e. C, T, or L); a specific vertebra can be identified by its numerical position within a given set (e.g. C1, T6, L3). All vertebrae have a *body* or *centrum* and a *vertebral* or *neural arch*. *Intervertebral discs*, which are elastic and fibrocartilaginous, intervene between the body of the first sacral

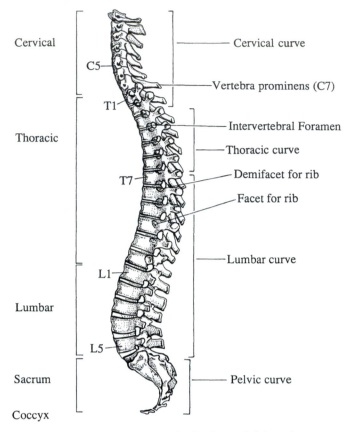

Cervical

Cervical curve

C5

Vertebra prominens (C7)

T1

Intervertebral Foramen

Thoracic

Thoracic curve

Demifacet for rib

T7

Facet for rib

Lumbar curve

L1

Lumbar

L5

Sacrum

Pelvic curve

Coccyx

Figure 3–1   Articulated vertebral column *(left lateral view)*.

segment and the body of the last lumbar vertebra as well as between the bodies of all other
neighboring vertebrae with the exception of the
first and second cervical vertebrae. These cartilaginous discs do not survive burial.

The vertebral arch projects posteriorly and
delineates between it and the body of the vertebra the *vertebral foramen*, through which the
spinal cord passes. Projecting posteriorly from
the midline of the vertebral arch is the *spinous
process*. In C1 to C6 these processes are short
with bifid tips; C2, however, may develop a
slightly longer, nonbifid spine. From C7 to T12
the spines are quite elongate. In the lumbar region, the spinous processes are shorter and
deeper superoinferiorly. From T2 to T11, the
spines become deflected increasingly downward. In contrast, the spines of the lumbar vertebrae and, on occasion, those of the cervical
region are essentially horizontal. The noticeably
protruding, virtually horizontally oriented spinous process of C7 is referred to as the *vertebra
prominens*. Spinous processes are usually ves-

tigial along the sacrum and nonexistent on coccygeal vertebrae.

In adult humans with normal vertebral articulation and positioning of intervertebral discs
(i.e. normal posture), the vertebral column naturally assumes a series of *spinal curvatures*. Proceeding down from the skull, the cervical vertebrae make a gentle, inward (anterior or
ventral) arc and then a gentle outward (posterior or dorsal) arc. The thoracic vertebrae continue to arc posteriorly but do so more vigor-
ously, peaking at about the level of the seventh
thoracic (T7), after which the vertebrae curve
inward; an exaggeration of the outward curvature of the thoracic vertebra *(kyphosis)* may
result from either degeneration of intervertebral
discs *(primary kyphosis)* or collapse of vertebra
(secondary kyphosis) due to the effects of, for
example, osteoporosis, osteomalacia, parathy-
roidism, or Paget's disease (see Chapter 1 on
bone for discussion). The lumbar vertebrae
carry the arc even farther anteriorly, until the
level of L4. At L5 the curve becomes directed

posteriorly again, reaching its peak in the mid-region of the sacrum, below which the curve is reversed, sometimes so severely that the coccyx points straight forward. The sacral-coccygeal curvature is called the *pelvic curve* and the curvature from T7 to the sacrum is identified as the *lumbar curve*. These curvatures are present in the newborn and are referred to as *primary curvatures*. An exaggeration in the lumbar curve is called *lordosis*. The curves from C1 to T2 and T2 to T7 are identified, respectively, as the *cervical* and *thoracic curves* and are referred to as *secondary* or *compensatory curves* because they become pronounced as the child develops into an increasingly proficient biped.

A vertebral body is in general columnar, with largely roughened cranial and caudal tablelike surfaces that are ringed by a variably thin, slightly raised band of smooth bone. The lateralmost borders of the cranial side of the bodies of C3 to C7 are distended upward, creating a saddle-shaped surface that cups the caudal side of the vertebral body above it. Concomitantly, the lateralmost borders of the caudal side of the bodies of C2 to C6 are truncated and the band of smooth, circumferential bone "pushed up" along the sides of the body.

Although the shapes of vertebral bodies may differ or change gradationally, the basic pattern is an increase in vertebral body size in all dimensions as one proceeds inferiorly along the vertebral column. The outlines (when viewed either cranially or caudally) of the vertebral bodies of C3 to T2 and T12 to L5 are essentially the same: the body is wider laterally than it is deep dorsoventrally; the ventral surface is arced somewhat convexly in its transverse plane but concave from top to bottom (superoinferiorly); and the dorsal surface may be relatively straight to gently concave (i.e. indented ventrally). The breadth of these vertebral bodies contributes to the formation of roughly triangular vertebral foramina (whose bases are delineated along the dorsal border of the body and whose apices are located on the insides of the bases of the spinous processes) that are wider than they are deep. From T3 to about T8 or T9, the shapes of the vertebral bodies change sequentially from one vertebra to the next such that the dorsoventral dimension becomes emphasized over width. The ventral surface also becomes more acutely convex and arced and the dorsal surface more noticeably concave or indented ventrally. Con-

comitantly, the vertebral foramen becomes narrower and more circular in outline. From T8 or T9 sequentially through the lower thoracic vertebra, the shapes of the vertebral bodies change gradationally to being wider than they are deep, and the outlines of the vertebral foramina "revert" from being circular to being broad and shallowly triangular.

The sides of a vertebral body are covered with compact bone, which may be perforated ventrally and ventrolaterally by a variable number of small nutrient foramina and dorsally by one or perhaps several typically large and oddly shaped *vascular foramina* through which the basivertebral veins course.

The thoracic vertebrae are distinguished as a set in that their bodies bear somewhat concave depressions or *facets for articulation with ribs*. These facets occur laterally on each side, at the dorsalmost extent of the body (i.e. just in front of the pedicle). A facet may be either complete (representing total contact between a rib and one vertebra) or a partial *demifacet* (indicating the contact of one rib with two adjacent vertebrae). A complete facet is variably ovoid in outline.

The body of T1 bears on each side a complete facet just below the edge of the cranial surface and, inferiorly, a demifacet that is confluent with the edge of its caudal surface (Figure 3–2). The body of T9, on the other hand, bears on

Figure 3–2 Schematic drawings of thoracic vertebrae to illustrate differences in facets/demifacets for ribs as well as in orientation and shape of spine: *(from top to bottom)* T1, T9, T10, T11, and T12.

each side only a single demifacet—but often a large one—that descends from the edge of its cranial surface; sometimes this demifacet may appear to be a complete facet separate from the cranial edge. T10 to T12 are characterized by having on each side only a single complete facet that lies just below the edge of the cranial surface. The size and definition of this facet seems to vary most in T12. The bodies of T2 to T8 bear two demifacets on each side: one looks as if it were "dripping" over the side from the edge of the cranial surface and the other, which is often smaller, appears to be "pushed up" from the edge of the caudal surface.

Development and Ossification

The vertebral column develops from the mesenchymal segments—sclerotomes—that differentiate around the notochord and neural tube (see Figure 1-7). But instead of there being a correlation between one vertebra and one sclerotome, each sclerotome eventually divides in half; it is from the coalescence of adjacent halves of sclerotomes that a vertebra develops. The myotomes—which originally matched the sclerotomes in a one-to-one relation and give rise to associated musculature—do not divide. Therefore, the segmental arrangements of myotomes and "reformed" sclerotomes are half a segment out of sync with one another, which results in a single myotome being associated with two vertebrae.

Vertebral anlagen differentiate in a craniocaudal direction, reaching the caudal end during the second intrauterine month. At this time the cartilaginous vertebrae are complete in the sense that the vertebral arch and body have fused together and the various processes can be identified. The odd upward projection from the body of the second cervical vertebra results from the coalescence of the body of the first cervical vertebra with the body of the second. Thus the first cervical vertebra lacks a body or centrum altogether. Spina bifida, which affects the lumbar region most and the cervical region least frequently, occurs when there is incomplete fusion of the right and left sides of the vertebral arch. Spondylolisthesis results from the displacement of a vertebra due to incomplete coalescence of the vertebral arch with the body.

True Vertebrae

Morphology

The true vertebrae (Figures 3–1 to 3–3), C3 to L5, are sufficiently similar in overall morphology that their common features can be discussed collectively and comparatively. Each has a body or centrum, a vertebral arch that circumscribes a vertebral foramen, and a spinous process that emanates from the midline dorsally of the vertebral arch.

Somewhat toward or level with the posterior extent of the vertebral foramen (depending on the individual vertebra) and on each side of the foramen lie the platform-like surfaces or processes about which neighboring vertebrae articulate with one another. There is thus a pair of superior articular processes and a pair of inferior articular processes, and their surfaces are aligned roughly parallel to each other. The superior articular processes of C3 are oriented slightly dorsally (i.e. they are tilted up slightly) and, concomitantly, the inferior articular processes are oriented slightly ventrally (i.e. they are tilted down slightly). The inclination of these articular processes becomes increasingly severe as one proceeds down the vertebral column, so that, perhaps by T1 and definitely by T2, the superior articular processes face directly dorsally and the inferior articular processes face directly ventrally; these processes are oriented almost at the vertical. At T12, however, the direction toward which the articular surfaces of the articular processes face changes, although the processes themselves remain vertical. With specific regard to T12, the articular surfaces of the inferior articular processes are rotated laterally almost 90°; in some cases, the configuration of the articular surface itself becomes rounded or rolled as well. To accommodate the inferior articular processes of T12, the superior articular processes of L1 are rotated medially and may also be concave. The medial rotation of the superior articular processes and the lateral rotation of the inferior articular processes (with interlocking surfaces mirroring each other's contours) are maintained in L1 to L5. On the sacrum, the articular processes that receive the inferior articular processes of L5 are also rotated medially and their inner surfaces reflect the specific configuration of the vertebra's processes. The superior articular processes of L1 to

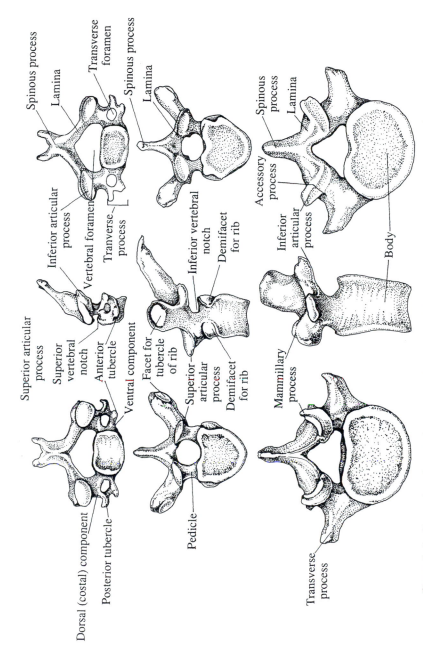

Figure 3–3   Examples of cervical *(top row)*, thoracic *(middle row)*, and lumbar *(bottom row)* vertebrae: *(left column)* superior, *(middle column)* left lateral, and *(right column)* inferior views.

L5 bear on their posterior or dorsal margins a thickening or swelling that variably distends the bone in that direction. These specifically lumbar features are called *mammillary processes*.

In C3 to L5, the part of the vertebral arch on each side that proceeds dorsally to the base of the spinous process is referred to as the *lamina*. The portion of the vertebral arch on each side that proceeds ventrally from the articular process to the body of the vertebra is called the *pedicle* or *root of the vertebral arch*. Each pedicle is constricted such that, when two adjacent vertebrae are in articulation, the inferiorly "pinched" border of one pedicle and the superiorly pinched border of the neighboring pedicle create a laterally directed *intervertebral foramen* through which spinal nerves and vessels pass. On the cervical vertebrae, the superior border of the pedicle is at least as deeply notched as the inferior border (i.e. the *superior vertebral notch* is at least as deeply excavated as the *inferior vertebral notch*). However, the inferior vertebral notch is markedly dominant from T1 to L5, creating larger intervertebral foramina than in the cervical region.

A *transverse process* projects laterally from the general region of each pedicle on C3 to C6, jutting out at the level of the vertebral body. On C7, however, and thereafter, the transverse processes take origin at the juncture of the pedicle and lamina (i.e. the root of the transverse process lies between the superior and inferior articular processes). A specific feature of not just C3 to C7 but of also of C1 and C2, which have transverse processes as well, is that a variably large, superoinferiorly and mediolaterally oriented foramen—the *transverse foramen (foramen transversarium)*—perforates each transverse process. In C1 to C6, the vertebral artery and vein as well as sympathetic nerves course through the transverse foramina. The transverse foramina of C3 to C6 bear at their lateral termini two tubercles. The *anterior tubercle of the transverse process* projects upward and slightly laterally away from the slip of bone that subtends the transverse foramen on its ventral side. This slip of bone is called the *ventral* or *costal component*, because this bony strut (plus its tubercle) is a vestige of the *costal process* or *element* that is associated with a thoracic vertebra and from which a rib does develop. The spit of bone that subtends the other side of the foramen—the *dorsal component*—actually borders only the dorsolateral aspect of the transverse foramen, taking origin from the columnar stretch of bone that connects the superior and inferior articular processes. The dorsal component is oriented laterally and ventrally and terminates in a noticeable projection, the *posterior tubercle of the transverse process*. This tubercle tends to point directly laterally and it extends farther outward than does the anterior tubercle. The seventh cervical vertebra normally possesses a ventral or costal component, which closes off the transverse foramen, but it typically lacks an anterior tubercle. However, C7 usually develops a stout dorsal component that extends prominently and laterally as a true transverse process. In summary, the dorsal component and its posterior tubercle together constitute the homologue of the transverse process of a thoracic vertebrae. *Variations* in the expression of transverse foramina are common and take various forms: that is, varying degrees of closure of the foramen by the costal component; asymmetry in foramen size between sides of the same vertebra, multiple or accessory foramina bi- or unilaterally.

The transverse processes of T1 to T10, if not T11 as well, are distinguished by their length, shape (they are thick and swell into a knoblike end), and orientation (they are directed dorsolaterally and even slightly upward). (The processes make a vertebra look like a caricature of either a stubby-armed diver preparing for take-off or an odd bird in flight.) The transverse processes of T12 and often T11, however, are not as prominent, projecting, or terminally knob-like. From T1 to T10, the swollen end of each transverse process bears (or even at times appears to "cup") on its ventral side a variably ovoid *facet for articulation with the tubercle of the rib*. The surfaces of the transverse processes of T11 and T12 tend to be knobby and lack facets for articulation with ribs. The transverse processes of T12 are short and folded backward or dorsally and are often distended into three recognizable tubercles. Of these, the *superior* and *inferior tubercles* of the transverse process of T12 are situated dorsally. The *lateral tubercle* is a variably low-peaked swelling that is located just in front of the inferior tubercle and is oriented laterally.

Lumbar transverse processes are usually

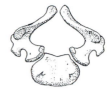

Figure 3–4 Vertebral arch components and body of typical cervical vertebra (C5) of third trimester fetus: *(left)* superior, *(middle)* left lateral, and *(right)* inferior views.

fairly horizontal but are gently angled dorsally. At the root of each transverse process inferiorly, just to the side of the inferior vertebral notch, is a roughened, variably small and elevated, *accessory process.* The transverse processes of especially L1 to L4 are typically thinner, more compressed dorsoventrally, and, overall, more gracile than those of the thoracic vertebrae, although they can project laterally quite prominently. The transverse processes of L5 are often thicker than those of the others, they may be the longest, and they may appear to be twisted so that their somewhat flat dorsal surfaces are oriented toward the sacrum. At times, one even finds evidence of articulation between the adjacent surfaces of the transverse processes of L5 and the sacrum. In those instances in which the actual fifth lumbar vertebra fuses with the sacrum, the transverse processes of the "new" last lumbar vertebra (L4) may develop some of the features of a true L5.

Development and Ossification

Ossification of the true vertebrae (Figures 3–4 to 3–6) begins in the cervical region as early as the seventh and as late as the tenth week, with a center of ossification appearing in each side of the vertebral arch, near the root or juncture between each arch and a cartilaginous vertebral body. Ossification of the neural arches then proceeds caudally with ossification of individual vertebral arches spreading out laterally and ventrally (anteriorly) into the various processes as well as dorsally (posteriorly) toward the spine. Complete ossification (and thus closure) posteriorly of the vertebral arch does not occur until the first postnatal year, at which time the process begins in the lumbar region and proceeds cranially.

Between puberty and 16 years of age, *secondary centers of ossification* appear as epiphyses on the ends of each transverse process as well as at the tip of the spinous process. Usually by 20 years of age, coalescence of the processes with the vertebral arch is complete.

Within a week of the onset of ossification in the vertebral arches, ossification of the vertebral bodies begins, with centers appearing in the lower thoracic and upper lumbar regions and then spreading cranially and caudally. Ossification of the dorsolateral "corners" of each vertebral body derives, however, not from the body itself but from the vertebral arch. There-

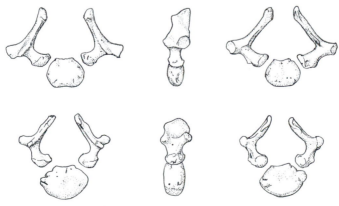

Figure 3–5 Examples of upper (T1) and lower (T11) thoracic vertebral arch components and bodies of third trimester fetus: *(left)* superior, *(middle)* left lateral, and *(right)* inferior views.

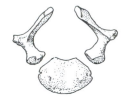

Figure 3–6 Vertebral arch components and body of typical lumbar vertebra (L2) of third trimester fetus: *(left)* superior, *(middle)* left lateral, and *(right)* inferior views.

fore, the true configuration of the vertebral body before it fuses with the vertebral arch is somewhat fan- or scallop-shaped, with the narrow end (which faces upon the vertebral foramen) gripped by the two ends of the arch. The rest of the body fans out anteriorly. The junctures between the ends of the vertebral arch and the body are cartilaginous and referred to as *neurocentral synchondroses*. Ossification of these synchondroses begins in the upper vertebrae (either cervical or thoracic) during the third year and extends to the lower lumbar region by the sixth year. Within the next 2 years, the lumbar accessory and mammillary processes ossify and the articular processes, which were originally oriented as in the thoracic vertebrae, rotate medially away from the sagittal plane (i.e. the superior articular processes come to face medially and the inferior articular processes laterally).

Ontogenetically, it appears that the transverse process of a lumbar vertebra is homologous with the costal process of a thoracic vertebra. The costal process of a thoracic vertebra thus may be conceived of as a vestigial rib fused to the body of the vertebra (see section on ribs, below). Morphologically, the thinner transverse process of a lumbar vertebra is more riblike than thick and is not terminally swollen as is the transverse process of a thoracic vertebra. However, rather than having lost or inhibited altogether the homologue of a transverse process (taking a thoracic vertebra as a standard), it may be that the "superior articular process" of a lumbar vertebra is a modified version of a thoracic vertebra's transverse process, which coalesced with the true superior articular process. Furthermore, the distinctive orientations of the inferior articular process of T12 and of all of the articular processes of the lumbar vertebrae are attained during childhood.

Until the appearance of secondary ossification centers during the 16th or 17th year, the cranial and caudal "surfaces" of a vertebral body are cartilaginous discs. Ossification of these discs produces thin bony plates that fuse to the bodies of the vertebrae between the ages of 20 and 25 years.

First and Second Cervical Vertebrae

Morphology

[The first and second cervical vertebrae (Figure 3–7) are distinctive in their morphology and thus warrant separate discussion.]

The **first cervical vertebra** or **atlas** (so named after the Greek god who held the earth on his shoulders) is distinguished by its being basically an elliptical ring of bone encompassing a vacuous *vertebral foramen*. It bears (1) small, laterally projecting *transverse processes*; (2) large, often teardrop-shaped *superior articular facets* for accommodating the occipital condyles of the skull; and (3) a reduced if not vestigial and vaguely bifid spinous process (in this case called the *posterior tubercle*). It also lacks a *vertebral body*. (Recall that, even before ossification of the vertebrae begins, the cartilaginous body of C1 becomes fused with the body of C2.) The mere strut of bone that spans the region where one would expect to find a vertebral body is referred to as the *anterior arch*, which bears in the midline of its ventral surface a variably swollen to peaked *anterior tubercle*, and, on its dorsal surface (facing the vertebral foramen), a smooth, variably ovoid facet for articulation with the vertical process or *dens* of C2 (i.e. the "lost" vertebral body of C1). The vertebral arch of C1 is referred to as the *posterior arch*. The posterior arch broadens on each side and becomes superoinferiorly flattened as it ap-

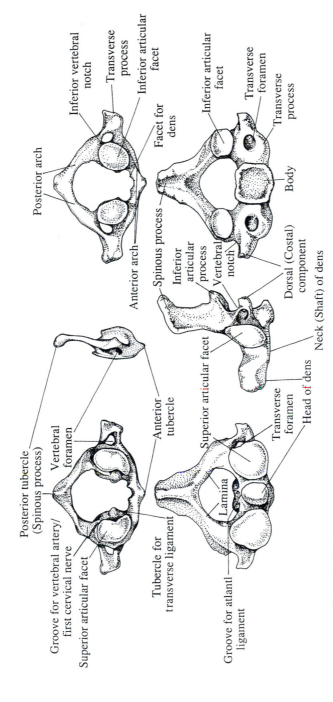

Figure 3–7 (Top row) first (C1) and (bottom row) second (C2) cervical vertebrae: (left) superior, (middle) left lateral, and (right) inferior views.

The following labels appear in the figure:

Inferior vertebral notch
Transverse process
Inferior articular facet
Facet for dens
Posterior arch
Anterior arch
Spinous process

Inferior articular facet
Transverse foramen
Transverse process
Body
Inferior articular process
Vertebral notch
Dorsal (Costal) component
Neck (Shaft) of dens

Superior articular facet
Head of dens

Posterior tubercle (Spinous process)
Vertebral foramen
Anterior tubercle
Groove for vertebral artery/ first cervical nerve
Superior articular facet
Tubercle for transverse ligament

Transverse foramen
Lamina
Groove for atlantl ligament

proaches the superior articular facets and transverse processes. It is across the expanded cranial surface of the posterior arch that one finds the *groove for the vertebral artery* and *first cervical nerve.*

The superior articular facets are somewhat concave and obliquely inclined, sloping from the ventral border toward the vertebral foramen. The typically narrower, ventral end of each facet lies more medially than the swollen dorsal end; however, the dorsal end rises more noticeably above the posterior arch. *Variation* is sometimes seen in the delineation of the facet into two subequal moieties. This may be as benign as having a crease coursing across the facet or as marked as a more severe pinching of the facet or even the delineation of two distinct facets. These variations may mirror the patterns of variation seen in the occipital condyles and may be expressed bi- or unilaterally, but they may also be differently expressed on each facet.

The transverse processes of C1 take root from below the swollen ends of the superior articular facets and each is perforated by a relatively large *transverse foramen.* Unlike the lower cervical vertebrae, the transverse processes of C1 are not bifid. On the other side of each superior articular facet, along the inner surface of the vertebral foramen and toward the ventral end of the facet, lies the small, swollen, facetlike *tubercle for the transverse ligament,* which is usually offset anteriorly and posteriorly by small depressions of variably porous bone. The shapes of the *inferior articular surfaces* vary between being roughly ovoid, elliptical, and circular. The actual articular surface is essentially planar or only slightly concave. If there is a narrower end, it faces toward the anterior tubercle. The anterior end of the articular surface is distinguished from the anterior arch by a thin rim. From here, the surface becomes increasingly elevated toward its posterior margin, which extends out over the transverse foramen. At the juncture of the posterior arch with the base of the inferior articular surface is a variably broad and shallow groove—the *inferior vertebral notch*—which courses laterally away from the vertebral foramen. The inferior articular surface, like the superior articular surface, is aligned obliquely along its long axis. The inferior articular surface is also oriented such that the side that borders the vertebral foramen is much lower than the opposite side. Since the inferior articular surfaces of C1 articulate with the superior articular surfaces of the C2, the shapes and orientations of these opposing facets are mirror images of one another. The superior and inferior articular surfaces and transverse process together are referred to as the *lateral mass.*

The **second cervical vertebra** (also **axis** or **epistropheus**) can be distinguished easily by the almost phallic projection that rises out of its vertebral *body.* Indeed, this projection can be described as having a *neck* or shaft on top of which sits a blunt-tipped, superiorly tapering head that swells out at its base beyond the width of the shaft. This process is called the *dens* and, as reviewed earlier, results from the fusion of the presumptive vertebral body of C1 with the presumptive vertebral body of the axis. Thus, when the atlas and axis are in association, the dens protrudes up into the vertebral foramen of C1—in the general region of where a body would have been on C1—and articulates against the inner surface of the anterior arch of that vertebra. As such, the dens bears a smooth, roughly ovoid articular facet on its ventral surface, just above the midpoint of the shaft. The tip of the dens protrudes above the level of the anterior arch of C1. A blunt midline ridge courses down the dorsal surface of the tip of the dens, terminating in a basal swelling, below which is the long and shallow *groove for the transverse atlantal ligament* (the transverse atlantal ligament stretches between the tubercles for the transverse ligament and essentially lashes C2 to C1).

As mentioned earlier, the large *superior articular surfaces* of C2 mirror in morphology and orientation the inferior articular surfaces of C1. Rotation of the head occurs across these articulating surfaces. The *inferior articular surfaces* of C2 are pedestalled on *inferior articular processes.* The inferior articular surfaces are much smaller than the superior articular surfaces and are steeply inclined, with the articular facets facing essentially ventrally. The inferior articular surfaces on C2, unlike those on all other vertebrae, do not lie immediately below the superior articular surfaces; rather, the inferior articular surfaces are positioned more posteriorly than the superior articular surfaces. The superior articular processes and surfaces of C3 mirror the features of the inferior articular processes of C2. The *costal* or *dorsal component* of the *transverse process* is thick and caudally deflected such that it terminates below the anterior half of the superior articular surface. The costal component of the transverse process is separated posteriorly from the inferior articular process by a variably deep *vertebral notch.* The more or less laterally directed *transverse foramen* lies directly above or directly above and slightly anterior to this notch. Caudally, the transverse foramina lie well in front of the inferior articular processes and face downward.

The vertebral arch of C2 is basically the same shape as the arches of lower cervical vertebrae, but it is thick and more rugose in all dimensions. Cranially, the *lamina* is compressed into a ridge that circumscribes most of the vertebral foramen. The sides of the lamina are deep. The *spinous process* is thickened and roughened at its end, which is quite variable in the degree to which it may be bifid. Anterior to this terminal thickening, the spine is deeply indented on its sides. Caudally, the spinous process broadens and flares out and the inferior surface of the process is somewhat grooved or roughly concave, almost as if to envelope and embrace the spine of the vertebra below it. The spine of C2 projects dorsally beyond the spine of C3.

Development and Ossification of C1 and C2

Ossification of the posterior arch of C1 (Figure 3–8) begins as early as the seventh and as late as the tenth week. At about the same time, an ossification center for each lateral mass appears. At birth, the region of the posterior tubercle is still cartilaginous and the posterior arch does not become continuously ossified until the third to fourth years; a separate center of ossification may appear in the the cartilaginous region of the posterior arch. The anterior arch, which arises from the hypochordal plate (notochord), does not begin to ossify from its one or sometimes two centers until during or as late as the end of the first natal year. Coalescence of the anterior arch with the lateral masses occurs during the fifth to ninth years.

As in other vertebrae, the body and each side of the vertebral arch of C2 ossifies from a single center; the ossification center for the body appears at about the fourth fetal month and those for the halves of the vertebral arch during the seventh or eighth fetal week. The arch fuses with the body between the third and sixth postnatal years. During the fourth to fifth (or even sixth) fetal months, two centers appear at the base of the dens and soon coalesce, leaving a cleft at the top in which the still cartilaginous tip of the dens is nestled. The ossified dens does not fuse with the body until the fourth to sixth years. Ossification of the cartilaginous tip of the dens does not occur until the second to third years, and it does not fuse with the rest of the dens until about the twelfth year. (This "tip" corresponds to the pro-atlas or last occipital vertebra of primitive vertebrates.) Noncoalescence of this part of the dens produces an "atavistic" (or "hypostotic") variant. The caudal surface of the body of C2 bears an epiphyseal plate which ossifies sometime about the 17th year.

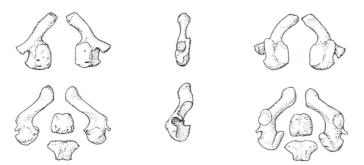

Figure 3–8 *(Top row)* first (C1) and *(bottom row)* second (C2) cervical vertebrae of third-trimester fetus: *(left)* superior, *(middle)* left lateral, and *(right)* inferior views.

Sacrum

Morphology

In the adult, the **sacrum** (Figure 3–9) normally consists of five vertebral segments that have fused together to form a solid, superoinferiorly arcuate (i.e. dorsally convex and ventrally concave), inferiorly (caudally) tapering (from side to side) and dorsoventrally thinning unit. In general, the sacrum in females is shorter and broader (adding to the vacuity of the pelvic canal when the sacrum is articulated with the ilia) and less severely curved caudally into the pelvic canal (thus reducing obstruction that might interfere with childbirth); in males, the sacrum in outline is a longer, more tapering triangular unit, whose caudal end may protrude into the pelvic canal more prominently. Vertebral morphology is suggested by the variably protrusive series of midline *spinous processes,* which diminish in prominence caudally. Collectively, these spinous processes form the *median sacral crest.* Vertebral morphology in the sacrum is particularly obvious superiorly in the large, lumbar-like *body* and medially directed *articular processes* of the first sacral segment, which articulates with the last lumbar vertebra. The extended and liplike ventral margin of the body of the first sacral segment is called the *promontory*; it protrudes into the region of the pelvic canal. The fused spinous processes and associated *lamina* of the sacral segments form a continuous space—the *sacral canal*—over the bodies of the fused segments. The sacral canal diminishes in size caudally.

Winglike extensions project from each side (laterally) of the body of the first sacral segment. Because of their appearance, these projections are called *alae* (the singular is *ala,* which means a "winglike process"). In females, the alae are typically quite large; they are markedly flared laterally and distended. Female sacral alae thus tend to appear large relative to the articular surface of the body of the first sacral segment. In males, the alae are usually much smaller; relative to the size of the alae, the articular surface of the body of the first sacral segment is quite large and dominant. The highest point of an ala is on its dorsal side; its superior (cranial) surface slopes increasingly caudally in the ventral direction. Sometimes an ala appears to bear a thickened, dorsally angled

strut that lies in front of and in parallel with the articular process. This strut represents the *transverse process,* which has coalesced with an expanded *costal process.* One cannot always distinguish one process from the other, but the region of the transverse process rather consistently seems to be represented by the more roughened portion of bone.

Caudally, the alae and the body of the first sacral segment are fused to the respective parts of the segment below it, and thus the pattern continues throughout the length of the sacrum. The fused alae on each side form the *lateral parts of the sacrum.* Pairs of large *pelvic sacral foramina (anterior sacral foramina)* occur between adjacent alae, just to the sides (laterally) of the lines (i.e. the *transverse lines)* of fusion between segmental bodies; the size of each pair of foramina diminishes caudally. Ventrally, these foramina, which may also be somewhat funnel-shaped, penetrate the bone in a lateromedial direction, becoming confluent with the sacral canal and creating at those points the *intervertebral foramina,* through which course sacral nerves, arteries, and veins. From the dorsal side, the corresponding pairs of foramina (the *posterior sacral foramina),* which are slightly smaller than their ventral counterparts, open onto the mouths of the intervertebral formina.

From the cranial edges of its alae and caudally for some part of its length, the sacrum is sandwiched between the posterior portions of the right and left ilia, with the granular auricular surfaces of the ilia abutting the respective and similarly granular *auricular surfaces* of the sacrum. The shape of a sacral auricular surface mirrors that of the adjoining ilium. However, regardless of individual details of shape, the margins of the sacral auricular surfaces are similar in being indented to some extent dorsally but protrusive ventrally [sometimes looking like an ear (hence the term "auricular") or the letter "C"]. In males, the auricular surface typically extends from the edge of the ala to the region of the third sacral segment; in females, it is usually restricted to the first and second sacral segments.

The concave, relatively smooth-boned ventral or *pelvic surface* of the sacrum contrasts markedly with the roughened, morphologically highlighted, convex *dorsal surface.* In addition to the features already mentioned, the dorsal

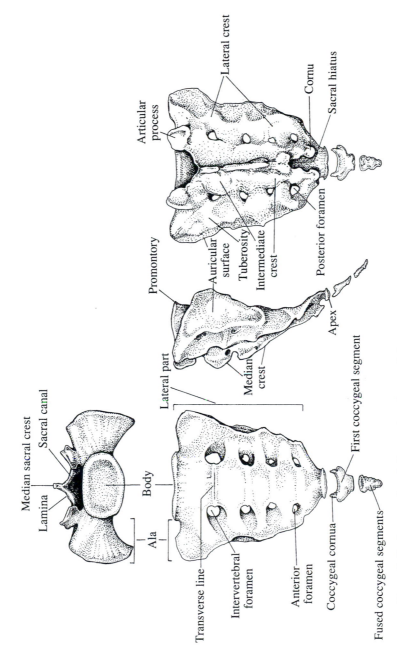

Figure 3–9 Sacrum: *(top left)* superior, *(bottom left)* anterior, *(middle)* right lateral, and *(right)* posterior views.

Median sacral crest

Lamina

Sacral canal

Body

Ala

Transverse line

Intervertebral foramen

Anterior foramen

Coccygeal cornua

Fused coccygeal segments

Lateral part

Median crest

Apex

First coccygeal segment

Promontory

Auricular surface

Tuberosity

Intermediate crest

Posterior foramen

Articular process

Lateral crest

Cornu

Sacral hiatus

surface bears on each side (and lateral to the series of posterior sacral foramina) a wavy, at times peaked crest called the *lateral sacral crest*; this pair of crests may be variably thick or compressed, rugose or smooth. The lateral crests terminate caudally in variably distended swellings that define the *inferior lateral angle* of the sacrum; this angle tends to be more pronounced in females than in males and thus adds to the breadth of the sacrum in females. The peaked elevations along each crest are identified as the *sacral tuberosities*; there may be as many as five and as few as three of these, and their expression is not always bilaterally symmetrical. The portion of the sacrum that lies between these tuberosities and the dorsal margin of the auricular surface is typically roughened and pocked with variably large, craterlike pits.

Medial to at least some of the posterior sacral foramina on each side and at the same level as those foramina is a variable number of smaller, less protrusive tuberosities (unnamed), which together constitute the *intermediate crest*. The most consistent feature of the two intermediate crests is that they terminate caudally in variably small to prominent projections, which are identified as *sacral cornua* (singular, *cornu*). The sacral cornua subtend the variably enlarged caudal opening of the sacral canal, called the *sacral hiatus*. The ventral or pelvic surface of the sacrum extends caudally beyond the mouth of the *sacral hiatus* and terminates in the *apex* of the sacrum, which articulates with the coccyx. The morphologically detailed dorsal plate of bone that encloses the sacral canal may become separated from the body of the sacrum after burial, but it is identified easily because of the smooth surface of the sacral canal, the spinous dorsal surface, and the series of sacral foramina.

Development and Ossification

There is some disparity in data on ossification of the sacrum (Figure 3–10). For example, Clemente (1984) states that ossification of the body of the first sacral vertebra begins at about the eighth to ninth fetal week, Netter and Crelin (1987) give it at 10 weeks, but Fazekas and Kósa's (1978) analyses yield an age of 6 fetal months. Netter and Crelin put the onset of ossification of the vertebral arches at 10 weeks, but Clemente's figures are 6 to 8 months and

Figure 3–10   Sacral elements of third-trimester fetus: *(left)* superior and *(right)* inferior views of each segment.

Fazekas and Kósa's 6 to 7 months. According to Netter and Crelin, ossification of the lateral part (i.e. costal element or process) begins during the sixth fetal month. Clemente cites between the sixth and eighth fetal months, but Fazekas and Kósa do not find this occurring until birth or even later.

There is more consensus with regard to the fusion of the vertebral arches with the bodies, which begins caudally during the second year and reaches the upper segments during the fifth to sixth years. Coalescence of right and left vertebral arches occurs during the seventh to fifteenth years; the sacral hiatus results from the lack of fusion of the vertebral arches of the lower segments. The costal processes fuse with the bulk of the sacrum coincident with puberty. Between puberty and age 16, the cranial and caudal epiphyseal plates ossify and fuse with the sacral vertebral bodies. The lateral surfaces of the sacrum, which have remained cartilaginous, ossify during the 18th and 20th years. At approximately the same time, ossification begins in the intervertebral discs between the caudalmost segments and proceeds cranially, reaching the uppermost disc between 25 and 30 years of age. The pelvic curve, which is a primary curvature of the vertebral column, is present at birth. The sacral vertebrae, however, do not begin to broaden and thicken until the development of bipedality.

Coccyx

Morphology

The **coccyx** (Figure 3–9) may be composed of three to five but typically four rudimentary, sequentially tapering vertebrae or segments. With the frequent exception of the first segment, these vertebrae typically coalesce into a single unit; particularly in females, the first segment may become fused to the sacrum. Only coccygeal segments 1 to 3 retain any features that can be identified as vertebral—that is, vestigial bodies, transverse processes, and articular processes. As the segments taper caudally, there is a diminution of discernible morphology, such that the last segment typically is a very rudimentary, variably pea-shaped piece of bone.

The first coccygeal segment bears the most prominent transverse processes of the series. It also bears on either side of the surface that articulates with the apex of the sacrum two hornlike projections, the *coccygeal cornua*, which are created by the fusion of the presumptive articular, transverse, and costal processes. Each cornu points up toward but is separate from the respective cornu on the sacrum.

Development and Ossification

The coccygeal vertebrae ossify from single centers that begin to appear after birth, in the first year in the first segment and variably between the fourth to tenth years in the second segment. The cornua of the first segment ossify from separate centers. The third segment ossifies between the 10th and 15th years and the fourth and frequently last segment between the 14th and 20th years (i.e. typically, the third segment ossifies prior to and the fourth after puberty). Between the ages of 25 and 30 years, coalescence of the segments begins caudally and proceeds cranially. In females, the coccyx may fuse to the sacrum.

Sternum

Morphology

The adult **sternum** (Figure 3–11), which for the most part is broader laterally than it is deep dorsoventrally, is composed of three units: the *manubrium* superiorly, the *body*, and the *xiphoid process* inferiorly. Because the sternum is composed largely of spongy bone covered with a thin layer of compact bone, it feels lighter in weight than one would expect. In general outline, the adult sternum looks spikelike, with the typically pointed xiphoid process being the sharp end and the manubrium being the broader, flatter head. The dorsal or posterior surfaces of the manubrium and body tend to be slightly concave or depressed. The ventral surface of the manubrium is typically slightly swollen or convex, whereas the ventral surface of the body can be variably flat, shallowly depressed, or a combination of both. The ventral surface of the sternal body is often elevated in the region of the *sternal angle,* which lies at the juncture of the manubrium and the body. When viewed from the side, this angle is discernible, even thought it may be very shallow. The xiphoid process is distinguished by often being narrower and rarely as thick as the inferior end of the body of the sternum, with which it articulates.

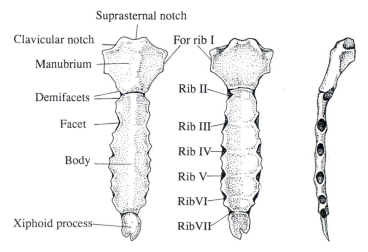

Figure 3–11 Sternum: *(left)* anterior, *(middle)* posterior, and *(right)* left lateral views.

The isolated manubrium looks like a stubby "Y." The very shallow and broad superior notch between the arms of the "Y" constitutes the *jugular* or *suprasternal notch*. The ends of the arms of "Y" are subdivided along their lateral borders into a larger superior and a smaller inferior notch. The larger notch—the *clavicular notch*—whose surface is generally composed of smooth articular bone, faces obliquely as well as superiorly and laterally; it receives the sternal end of the clavicle. The smaller notch, which is more notchlike than the one above it, is oriented essentially outward and receives the costal cartilage of the first rib. The broad stem of the "Y," which abuts the body of the sternum, is usually smooth-boned. On those rare occasions in very old individuals when the manubrium appears to have fused to the body of the sternum, coalescence typically occurs only along the perimeter of the contact and thus encases the cartilaginous disc that remains between the manubrium and body. The lateral "corners" of the base of the manubrium are truncated and indented, as are the lateral corners of the superior end of the sternal body. These partial indentations—*demifacets*— together contribute to the formation on each side of a complete notchlike facet, which receives the costal cartilage of the second rib. The line of contact between the manubrium and body delineates the midline of adjacent demifacets.

Proceeding inferiorly along the lateral borders of the sternal body, one finds—at irregular intervals—four complete indentations or *facets*, which receive the costal cartilages of the third to sixth ribs. Coursing across the ventral surface of the sternal body, between the midpoints of each right and left pair of costal cartilage facets, are variably discernible lines of union between earlier, ontogenetically separate sternal segments. The dorsal surface of the sternal body typically bears vertical lines or striations. The inferior end of the sternal body, which typically lies just below the facet for the sixth costal cartilage, is truncated and also indented by a demifacet whose sister demifacet may be visible on the xiphoid process. Together these demifacets form the facet for the seventh costal cartilage. Sometimes, however, one may find only the one demifacet on the inferior end of the sternal body. When viewed from the front, the sternal body, especially when the xiphoid is fused

to it, looks like a strange, segmented, legless insect.

Development and Ossification

At or about the sixth intrauterine week, the sternum (Figure 3–12) emerges as two separate mesenchymal bars. Shortly thereafter, a suprasternal mesenchymal mass arises above each sternal mesenchymal bar; each suprasternal mass represents that portion of the future manubrium which will articulate with the clavicle. The presumptive upper ribs (see below) begin to coalesce with the sternal bars and, as they do, the sternal bars begin to fuse together (like a zipper). By 9 weeks or so, the sternal bars have coalesced completely, the suprasternal masses have fused with this presumptive sternum, and the whole "unit," including the ribs, has become a cartilaginous cage. Incomplete union of the sternal bars anywhere along the sternum can result in a cleft or *sternal foramen* (like a gap in the zipper). If the two inferior ends of the sternal bars do not completely join, the xiphoid process will be bifid.

The ribs, which ossify earlier than the sternum (see below), cause the cartilaginous sternum to become segmented into (typically) six *sternebrae*. One corresponds to the manubrium, another to the xiphoid process, and the rest make up the sternal body. Ossification centers appear superiorly, in the manubrial sternebra, during the third to sixth fetal months. The second sternebra begins to ossify at the same time or at least by the seventh month, by which time all but the last two sternebrae have also begun to ossify. The last sternebra of the sternal body begins to ossify during the first

Figure 3–12 Sternal elements *(anterior view)* of third-trimester fetus.

postnatal year or so. The sternebra of the xiphoid process ossifies between the 5th and 18th years. Coalescence of the sternal body segments begins after puberty in the lowest portion and proceeds superiorly; the uppermost sternebrae fuse at or about the 25th year.

Ribs

Morphology

Ribs (Figures 3–13 and 3–14) constitute the most numerous elements of the thoracic cage. There are normally 12 pairs of **ribs**, all of which attach posteriorly to the thoracic vertebrae. However, only 10 pairs of ribs are also anchored, via the costal cartilages, to the sternum. Some of these ribs are anchored directly and others indirectly to the sternum. The seven pairs of facets on the sternum for receipt of costal cartilages reflects the fact that seven pairs of ribs attach directly to the sternum [the first of these pairs of facets is located on the manubrium (see

above)]. These ribs are identified as **true** or **vertebrosternal ribs**. The eighth rib attaches via its costal cartilage to the costal cartilage of the seventh rib; the ninth and tenth ribs attach via their costal cartilages to the costal cartilages of, respectively, the eighth and ninth ribs. The seventh to tenth ribs are referred to as **vertebrochondral ribs**. The eleventh and twelfth ribs are unattached at their anterior ends and are called **false, free,** or **floating ribs**. In addition to their relative slenderness, inferior declination away from their vertebral articulations (which can be easily reconstructed), and other peculiar morphologies (see below), floating ribs can be distinguished from the other ribs in that their anterior ends taper, or at least do not flare out, as they do in ribs in which thick costal cartilage is lodged.

In general, all ribs are similar in that a *head* and a *body* can be identified. Only the first through tenth ribs also develop a *neck*. The head is that portion which articulates directly with a vertebra or vertebrae. With the exception

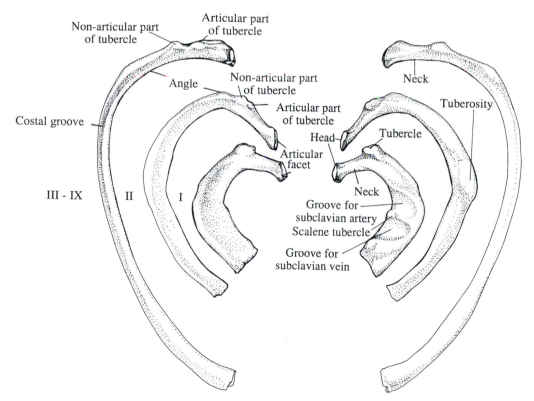

Figure 3–13 Left ribs: *(left group)* inferior and *(right group)* superior views; *(outermost)* example of ribs III to IX, *(middle)* rib II, and *(innermost)* rib I.

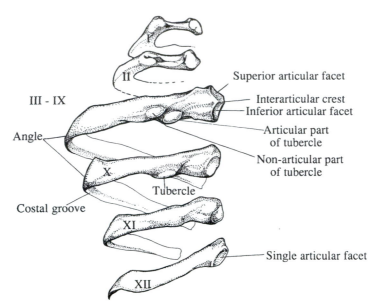

Figure 3–14 Posterior view of left ribs: *(from top to bottom)* I, II, example of III to IX, X, XI, and XII.

of being somewhat more rounded on the first rib, a rib's head typically is beveled such that the articular surface essentially faces medioventrally; it also tapers or thins toward its end. The number of *articular facets* a rib's head bears is correlated with the number of vertebrae with which it articulates: that is, the heads of the first and tenth to twelfth ribs articulate with a single vertebra and thus bear a single articular facet (as do T1 and T9 to T12); the remaining ribs articulate with two adjacent vertebrae, and thus their heads bear a somewhat cranially directed *superior articular facet* and a slightly caudally directed *inferior articular facet*, which are further delineated from one another by a peaked, horizontally oriented *interarticular crest*. The neck is slenderer than the head. It is relatively straight and flattened dorsoventrally on most ribs; on the second and third ribs, however, the flattened sides are twisted in a more craniocaudal direction. The dorsal surface of the neck of the third through twelfth ribs is variably roughened; the internal surface, however, is quite smooth, often being the smoothest stretch of bone on the rib. The caudal or inferior surface of the neck of the first two ribs is rougher-boned than the superior or cranial surface.

Laterally, at the terminus of the neck, the rib swells out noticeably into a posterior *tubercle* (this tubercle serves to delineate the terminus of the neck). On the first rib, the tubercle bears an *articular part* for articulation with the transverse process of T1. On the second through tenth ribs, an *articular part of the tubercle* lies medial to a *nonarticular part of the tubercle*. These two "parts" become increasingly separated from one another as one proceeds down through the series of ribs; the articular part articulates with the transverse process of the associated thoracic vertebra. Floating ribs typically do not develop these tubercles; if tubercles are present, they are poorly defined.

At some point, either coincident with or a centimeter or so laterally beyond the tubercle, the body of the rib begins to curve, sometimes subtly, sometimes abruptly. This point is called the *angle* of the rib. On the first few ribs, the angle occurs at the tubercle. On most other ribs, the straightness of the neck extends beyond the tubercle and the angle is indicated externally by a low mound of roughened bone, beyond which the body becomes thicker. It is also in the region medial to the angle that fractures can occur easily, isolating the sometimes amorphous tubercle/neck/head portion from the body. At best, one might be able to discern a slight angle on the eleventh rib but never on the twelfth rib.

When holding a rib in its anatomical position, one can see that its body arcs laterally. The arc typically is more severe near the vertebral end and becomes gentler toward the anterior end (the arc of a rib thus looks the like the outline of half a heart). The first and second ribs are the most tightly arced, while the floating ribs are the most gently arced of the set. When the ribs are in articulation with the vertebrae, their dorsal (posterior) ends are higher than their ventral (anterior) ends. As such, the anterior portion of the body assumes a downward twist, which is particularly noticeable on the third through twelfth ribs. All but the twelfth rib bear a blunt and relatively thickened *superior border*. For approximately half to two-thirds of its length (starting from the tubercle or angle), the *inferior border* of the body is relatively sharp-edged and impressed internally by the *costal groove*, in which the intercostal vessels and nerves course. Most rib body fragments at least can be allocated to side by determining the direction of arcing and then orienting the downward twist and inferior border and costal groove properly. As indicated above, the floating ribs, especially the twelfth rib, can be identified on the basis of their minimal body morphology; the first and second ribs can be identified individually on the basis of their peculiar body morphology.

The superior surface of the first rib is highlighted along its dorsal half by two shallow, variably broad depressions or grooves. These grooves are delineated from one another by a variably triangular, slightly raised area of bone that emanates from the inner margin of the bone. The small raised area between the two grooves is the *scalene tubercle* and is the site of attachment of the anterior scalene muscle. The groove closer to the middle of the rib's body, and the one that is often the smaller of the two, is the *subclavian groove*, across which course the subclavian artery and part of the brachial plexus. The subclavian groove may extend over and thus indent the inner margin of the rib. The more sternal and usually deeper groove is the *groove for the subclavian vein*. Almost halfway around the curve of the second rib, the outer margin of the superior or cranial surface is thickened and somewhat roughened into the *tuberosity (for the serratus anterior) of the second rib*.

Development and Ossification

As reviewed earlier in this chapter, the costal process of a thoracic vertebra, the anterior tubercle and ventral (costal) component of the transverse process of a cervical vertebra, and the transverse process of a lumbar vertebra are homologous structures. In thoracic vertebrae, the costal processes do not fuse to the vertebrae, but, instead, remain separate and develop into ribs (Figure 3–15). Mesenchyme intervenes between the chondrifying rib and adjacent vertebrae and eventually develops into an articular cavity. Cervical ribs do not result from the lack of fusion of the anterior tubercle and ventral component to the rest of the vertebra but from the appearance of a separate center of ossification.

The presumptive ribs become cartilaginous at their vertebral ends first, with chondrification continuing into the presumptive sternum, from which the ribs do not become separate until later on. As early as the seventh but certainly by the eighth or ninth intrauterine week, the cartilaginous rib cage is defined and ossification

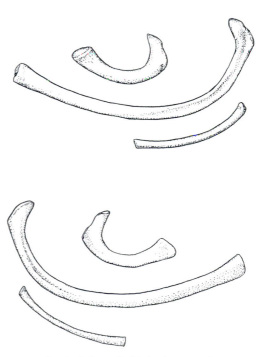

Figure 3–15 Ribs of third-trimester fetus: *(top group)* superior and *(bottom group)* inferior views of rib I *(uppermost)*, VII *(middle)*, and XII *(lowermost)*.

begins with the appearance of a center in each of the angles of the fifth through seventh ribs (onset of ossification in the ribs is slightly earlier than in the vertebrae). Ossification centers appear rapidly thereafter in the other ribs. Within each rib, ossification proceeds away from the angle in both directions but does not continue ventrally through the entire length of the costal cartilage. This truncation of ossification "creates" the cartilaginous costal cartilages one sees throughout life; in old age, calcification may encroach on these cartilages. Ossification of the head and tubercle does not begin until the 16th to 17th years or even as late as the 20th year; fusion of these elements with the rest of the rib occurs between the 20th and 25th years. In those ribs with an articular as well as a nonarticular component of the tubercle, two centers

of ossification appear. (Recall that the floating ribs lack tubercles and that there is a single tubercle on the first rib.)

Rickets may be indicated if the ventral ends of the ribs are overly enlarged and bear (at least on their inner surfaces) globular swellings of bone. *Scoliosis* (which occurs when the vertebral column is bent or deflected away from the vertical for some of its length) should be suspected if "expected" rib curvature is noticeably deformed such that the posterior and anterior ends of ribs from one side of the body are oriented more posteriorly and almost in parallel with one another, while ribs from the other side of the body are distorted on both ends in an anterior direction. The former set of ribs would be from the convex side of the lateral scoliotic curvature and the latter from the concave side.

CHAPTER FOUR

The Upper Limb

The **upper limb** is composed of the following major elements: the **scapula** or shoulder blade, which, with the **clavicle** or collar bone, forms the **shoulder girdle**; the **humerus** or upper arm bone, which articulates with the **scapula**; the **radius** and **ulna**, which together constitute the **forearm**; and the **hand**, which consists of the **carpals** (wrist bones), **metacarpals** (the bones of the palm), and the **phalanges** (the bones of the fingers or digits of the hand).

Scapula

Morphology

The **scapula** (Figure 4–1) is a thin, internally mildly concave and externally gently convex bone. It is fairly triangular in outline and is adorned externally with a spine and laterally with various bony projections. The long side of this "triangle" faces and is roughly parallel with the vertebral column. This side is referred to as the *medial* or *vertebral border* or *margin* of the scapula; it is variably rugose and thickened and can be variably straight, undulating, gently arced inward, or slightly convex. The thickened and strutlike *axial* or *lateral border* or *margin* extends from the often flattened *inferior angle* and slopes upward and laterally. Although the axial border is anything but straight, it always bears a slight inward dip approximately two-thirds along its length, which represents the *groove for the circumflex scapular vessels*. Near the lateral- and uppermost portion, the lateral border thickens into the *infraglenoid tubercle*, to which attaches the long head of the triceps

brachii muscle. The infraglenoid tubercle is so named because it lies below the *glenoid process* or *head* of the scapula, which, in turn, constitutes the terminus of the lateral border. The humerus articulates in the shallow depression or *glenoid fossa (cavity)* of the scapular head. From the thin *superior angle* of the scapula, the equally thin *superior border* or *margin* descends rather steeply to a variably acute to obtuse notch (the *scapular* or *suprascapular notch*), which lies at the base of a bony projection (the *coracoid process*). The coracoid process arises from behind and comes to overlie and project beyond the head of the scapula.

The *scapular spine* takes origin on the *dorsal* or *posterior side* approximately one-fifth of the length of the medial border from the superior angle. As it proceeds toward the scapular head, this spine increases in height and robustness laterally and somewhat superiorly. The spine eventually sends out a broadened extension that projects laterally well beyond the glenoid process itself. The scapular spine divides the dorsal surface of the bone into two greatly unequal areas: the one above the spine is referred to as the *supraspinous* or *supraspinatus fossa*; the much larger, lower region is the *infraspinous* or *infraspinatus fossa*. Particularly in the case of the infraspinous fossa, the bone is quite thin and often translucent (it is reminiscent of a membrane stretched across a frame constructed by the strut supporting the scapular spine and the thickened bone of the medial and especially the lateral borders). With increasing age, the scapula continues to thin, creating large patches of translucent bone within the two fossae.

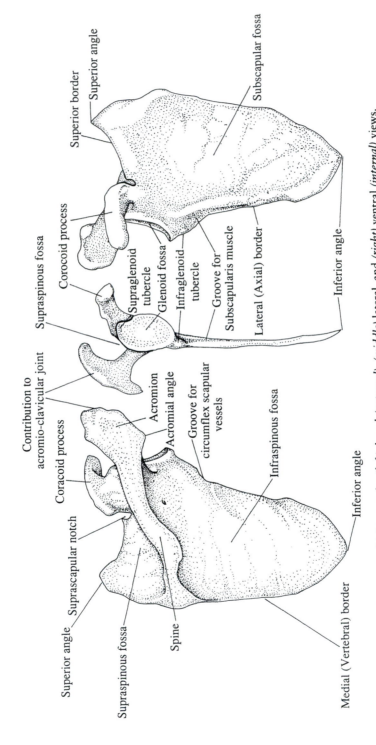

Figure 4–1 Right scapula: *(left)* dorsal *(external)*, *(middle)* lateral, and *(right)* ventral *(internal)* views.

The juncture between the spine and the medial border is flattened, relatively smooth, and somewhat triangular. As the spine becomes increasingly elevated, however, its surface becomes rougher and its course more sinuous; approximately one-third of its length away from the medial border, the scapular spine typically becomes distended inferiorly. At the point at which the spine lies just behind the head of the scapula, it is quite elevated dorsally. The spine continues over and laterally beyond the head as a spit of bone that broadens and becomes rather golf club–shaped, with the "heel" of the club inferiorly placed and the thick "toe" angled superolaterally. This spitlike projection of the spine, called the *acromion* or *acromial process*, is platelike and slightly arced, being gently concave internally; as a whole, the acromion is directed inwardly, or anteriorly, from its heel to its toe. The acromial heel is referred to as the *acromial angle*; the process's medial edge forms a joint with the clavicle, the *acromioclavicular joint*. The internal surface of the acromion, which contributes to an arch that protects the shoulder joint, is somewhat smoother than its outer surface.

The *lateral border* of the scapula bears a dorsally displaced edge that courses inferiorly from the infraglenoid tubercle; however, this edge may lose its discreteness approximately one-third to one-half the distance toward the inferior angle. The edge of this border subtends internally (ventrally) a shallow *groove for* the attachment (laterally) of *the subscapularis muscle*. The lateral border separates the subscapularis muscle from the dorsal muscles—that is, the teres major and, above it, the teres minor.

The *head* or *glenoid process* of the scapula sits as a rimmed, subovoid expansion upon the lateral border of the bone superiorly. In outline, the scapular head is somewhat teardrop-shaped: that is, it is narrow at the top, broad and round inferiorly, and arcuately expanded dorsally. The internal or ventral border of the glenoid process, however, is expanded less fully, at least superiorly. The ventral border is often gently notched approximately one-third down from the top, beyond which the surface does swell out inferiorly. The *articular surface* or *glenoid fossa* is mildly concave and, in profile, can have a slight inward curvature (from top to bottom) as well.

The largely liplike rim of the scapular head delineates behind it the thick *neck* of the scapula. Superiorly, the rim of the head is less protrusive, becoming locally thickened into the *supraglenoid tubercle*, at or just behind which the deep base of the *coracoid process* is rooted. The medial edge of the platelike base of the coracoid process contributes to the formation of the *suprascapular notch*. Atop this base the coracoid process extends well above and laterally beyond the head of the scapula as a somewhat flattened, fingerlike projection, whose superior surface is quite roughened and often irregular; in contrast, the inferior surface tends to be smooth and flexed downward. The base of the coracoid process typically arcs inward (somewhat liked a "cocked hat" on top of the scapular head) and, because it may be skewed in that direction, the fingerlike projection may carry this orientation even farther.

The *internal* or *costal surface* of the scapula is a fairly uninterrupted, slightly concave surface, the *subscapular fossa*. Emanating from the medial border and proceeding inward is a variable number of low, roughened ridges. The strutlike inner border of the groove subtended by the edge of the lateral border is the dominant feature of this side of the scapula.

Variation in the scapula is noted not only in the variable delineation of the suprascapular notch but also in the presence or absence and number of *foramina* below and above the scapular spine. A single foramen below the spine and on the infraspinous portion is typical. Care should be taken when encountering thin, platelike fragments of bone not to confuse scapula with *os coxa* (specifically ilium).

Development and Ossification

Developmentally, the scapula usually becomes recognizably scapular in shape by the end of the third or the beginning of the fourth fetal month (Figure 4–2). Mineralization up to this point is fairly rapid because the first center of ossification—near the scapular neck (lateral angle)—does not appear until the end of the second fetal month or perhaps even a few weeks later. This center gives rise to the body of the scapula. At or about this time the spine begins to differentiate and another center appears, near the base of the coracoid process. This center of ossifica-

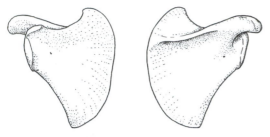

Figure 4-2 Right scapula of third-trimester fetus: *(left)* ventral (internal) and *(right)* dorsal (external) views.

tion will contribute to the formation of the superior portion of the glenoid cavity. Although the acromial end of the scapular spine is at first barely distinct from the glenoid cavity, its rate of growth is much faster than that of the glenoid and neck regions; thus it rapidly comes to extend laterally beyond the neck. The acromion and the coracoid processes are connected to the presumptive clavicle via the presumptive coracoclavicular ligament.

At birth, mineralization in the scapula is restricted to the body and spine. The glenoid cavity, the acromial and coracoid processes, and the vertebral (medial) border remain cartilaginous. Each process will ossify from two centers of ossification, whereas the other cartilaginous regions will ossify from separate centers. The first postnatal center appears in the projecting

portion (not the base) of the coracoid process. Fusion of the coracoid process to its base does not usually occur until the 15th year or so; fusion of the base of the process to the body of the scapula does not usually occur until the 17th or 18th year. The glenoid cavity ossifies and fuses to the body of the scapula during this time, as well. Ossification of the more medial acromial center occurs around the 15th year, the lateral acromial center and that of the inferior angle about a year later, and the vertebral (medial) border coincident with the base of the coracoid process. Complete union of the acromion and inferior angle occurs at approximately 22 years of age and that of the vertebral (medial) angle a year or so later. There may, however, be a great deal of variation in the ages at which various epiphyseal unions occur.

Clavicle

Morphology

The **clavicle** (Figure 4–3), which articulates between the scapula and the sternum, is easily identified by its elongate and shallow "S" shape. Viewed from above, the clavicle arcs gently outward or anteriorly as it courses laterally from its *sternal end*. Approximately one-third of the distance from its sternal end the bone begins to curve inward or posteriorly for

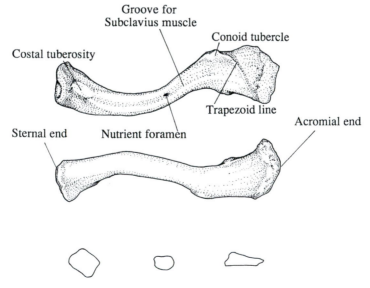

Figure 4–3 Right clavicle: *(top)* inferior and *(middle)* superior views; *(bottom)* cross sections through shaft.

slightly more than one-third of its length, at which point it swings abruptly outward again, terminating in its *acromial end*. Although muscles do attach to portions of the superior surface of the clavicle and thus leave roughened areas (particularly noticeable on the acromial end), the *inferior surface* of the bone is often the more scarred (and even grooved) surface.

Typically, one can identify on the inferior surface of the clavicle a shallow *groove for the subclavius muscle* (along the second third of the bone), the *conoid tubercle* (at the point where the acromial end begins to swing outward), and the *trapezoid line* (coursing from the conoid tubercle across the inferior surface to the lateral margin of the acromial end). Approximately halfway along the bone, and in or sometimes above the groove for the subclavius muscle lies a small, slitlike *nutrient foramen* that pierces the shaft horizontally in a mediolateral direction; sometimes there is an additional nutrient foramen, which may not be in close proximity to the primary one. Along the anterior third of the bone inferiorly and toward its anterior margin lies another typically shallow groove which bears a roughened surface for attachment of the pectoralis major muscle. Just on the inside of this groove, and more toward the sternal end of the bone, one can at times distinguish a triangular depression left by the costoclavicular ligament.

The *sternal end* of the clavicle differs from the *acromial end* in that it is bulkier, somewhat ovoid in outline, and more expanded; the acromial end is much flatter, wider anteroposteriorly, and compressed superoinferiorly. Regardless of its actual shape and outline (which can be quite variable), the sternal end appears to flare out from the shaft of the bone, particularly along its posterior side. Proceeding laterally from the sternal end, the shaft of the bone is subtriangular in cross section (with the "triangle's" base facing upward and its apex inferiorly) as far as the conoid process, after which the inferior surface flattens and widens in concert with the superior surface. The acromial end often bears on its lateral edge a flattened area of contact with the acromion of the scapula. The inferior border of the sternal end bears an area of contact with the cartilage of the first rib (i.e. the first costal cartilage); it may also be indented in the region of this contact. A raised area in the region of the contact with the cartilage of the first rib is called the *costal tuberosity*.

Development and Ossification

Developmentally, the clavicle is the first bone to begin to ossify and one of the last, if not the last, to be fully ossified (Figure 4–4). Starting at the acromial end, the presumptive mesenchymal clavicle elongates until, at about the sixth fetal week, it contacts and coalesces with the first rib. The shaft of the clavicle ossifies from two *primary centers*, which appear within the latter half of the second gestational month. By the end of the third fetal month, the body is ossified and its shape established. A secondary center of ossification does not appear in the cartilaginous sternal end until 18 to 20 years of age. The sternal end typically unites with the body of the clavicle around the 25th year, but union can occur as early as the 20th or as late as the 30th year.

Humerus

Morphology

The **humerus** (Figure 4–5), the bone of the upper arm, is much longer and more robust than either of the two long bones of the lower arm (the radius and ulna). The proximal and distal ends of the humerus are morphologically quite different—the proximal end is roughly globular whereas the distal end is wide from side to side and compressed from front to back—and they are separated by a long, relatively straight shaft.

The *proximal end* of the humerus bears on its anterior side two swellings (tuberosities or tubercles), which are separated from one an-

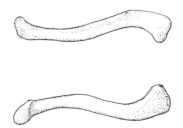

Figure 4–4   Right clavicle of third-trimester fetus: *(top)* inferior and *(bottom)* superior views.

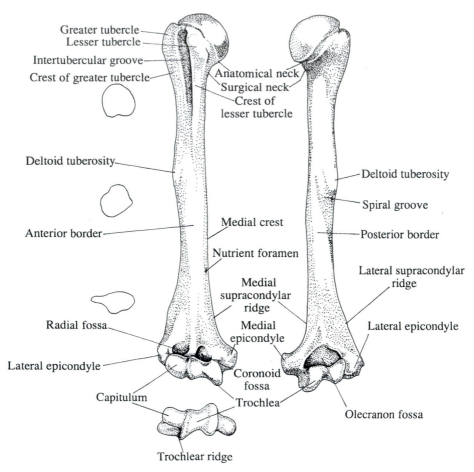

Greater tubercle
Lesser tubercle
Intertubercular groove
Crest of greater tubercle
Anatomical neck
Surgical neck
Crest of lesser tubercle
Deltoid tuberosity
Deltoid tuberosity
Spiral groove
Anterior border
Medial crest
Posterior border
Nutrient foramen
Lateral supracondylar ridge
Medial supracondylar ridge
Radial fossa
Medial epicondyle
Lateral epicondyle
Lateral epicondyle
Coronoid fossa
Capitulum
Trochlea
Olecranon fossa
Trochlear ridge

Figure 4–5   Right humerus: *(left)* cross sections through shaft; *(middle top)* anterior, *(middle bottom)* distal, and *(right)* posterior views.

other by a moderate to deep groove (the *bicipital* or *intertubercular groove*) that courses only a short distance down the shaft just lateral to the midline of the bone. The *lesser tubercle*, which lies medial to the groove, is the smaller of the two tubercles and is confined essentially to the anterior surface of the bone. The lesser tubercle is drawn out into an oblique crest, whose surface may be roughened; the face of the tubercle below this crest is longer and more vertically oriented than the shorter, more horizontal superior portion. The *greater tubercle* lies lateral to the intertubercular groove and expands out and around the lateral side of the bone proximally, encroaching upon the posterior surface of the bone and underlying to some extent the head of the humerus. It is separated from the head inferiorly by a shallow and broad depression. The greater tubercle bears a crest or

thickened edge that distinguishes its long vertical side from a much shorter and horizontal superior plane; this crest continues for a short distance the upward obliquity established by the lesser tubercle, but then it turns or corners downward as it traverses the lateral aspect of the greater tubercle. If one were to draw a line between the crests of the two tubercles, it would traverse an arc that roughly parallels the curvature of the spherical humeral head.

The relatively smooth articular *head* of the humerus is oriented posteromedially. It is large and globular, but it represents only a portion of a sphere. If one thinks of the humeral head as having been sliced (well off center) from a spherical object, one can describe the plane of this cut (which would correspond to the epiphyseal line and the *anatomical neck* it delineates) as being obliquely oriented such that its upper margin lies anterior to the midline axis, while its inferior margin juts out from the postero-medial side of the bone; this plane also parallels the orientation of the crest on the lesser tubercle. The uppermost portion of the humeral head rises slightly above the level of the greater tubercle (which itself rides higher up on the bone than does the lesser tubercle); the inferiormost portion of the head descends further than either tubercle. Just below the most inferior extent of the humeral head the shaft of the bone narrows, thereby demarcating what is referred to as the *surgical neck* of the humerus.

From each tubercle, a crest of variable length and rugosity descends along the *shaft* of the humerus; a continuation of the intertubercular groove intervenes between these two crests. As a rule, the *crest of the lesser tubercle* tends to be shorter and less pronounced than the *crest of the greater tubercle*. The crest of the lesser tubercle, which may be grooved inferiorly, presents itself as a blunt, truncated edge upon the medial surface of the shaft. Below the inferior terminus of this crest, a sharper, straighter crest (the *medial crest)* continues the rest of the way down the medial side of the shaft, coursing to if not surmounting the *medial epicondyle* (see below). Not quite halfway up the bone from the distal end, a small, slitlike, inferiorly directed *nutrient foramen* penetrates the shaft obliquely; this foramen lies on or near the medial crest.

The usually roughened crest of the greater tubercle defines a stout, thick *anterior border* of the humerus that extends almost halfway down the shaft of the bone. Toward the lower portion of this crest, which may be bounded inferiorly and laterally by a groove, the bone swells out into the *deltoid tuberosity*. This configuration of crest and tubercle gives a "twisted" effect to the shaft. The crest and tubercle also create a shallow and broad depression on the shaft that, from the posterior side, curves up and around the bone below the deltoid tuberosity. This feature is called the *spiral groove* (for the radial nerve), which may be delineated further by a thin crest proceeding down the posterior side of the shaft; on or near this short posterior crest one occasionally finds a tiny, inferiorly directed *nutrient foramen* penetrating the bone obliquely. Extending from below the region of the spiral groove laterally is a thin *posterior border*, which creates an edge to the bone that

continues inferiorly as the *lateral supracondylar ridge* to the *lateral epicondyle* (see below). Coincident with the emergence inferiorly of the lateral and medial supracondylar ridges, the humerus becomes flatter on its posterior surface and widens markedly from side to side as it approaches the distal end.

The *distal end* of the humerus bears a prominent projection medially (the *medial epicondyle*); a more truncated, flangelike lateral projection (the *lateral epicondyle*); and an unmistakable, rounded, anteriorly tripartite *articular surface* that is delineated superiorly by two fossae in front and one large fossa behind.

(A very simple approach to visualizing the distal end of the humerus is to think of it as a "hand" in which the tripartite articular surface represents the knuckles of a fist and the medial epicondyle the "thumb" sticking out; the large fossa on the posterior side of the distal end would correspond to the cupped palm. The hand, of course, would be from the same side of the body as would the bone itself.)

The large, medially projecting *medial epicondyle* is compressed from front to back and, in concert with the rest of the bone inferiorly, is flatter on its posterior side. (It is across the posterior surface of the medial epicondyle that the ulnar nerve courses and thereby lies unprotected, producing the "funny bone" when it is hit inadvertently.) The *medial supracondylar ridge*, which is a continuation of the medial crest (described above), may continue so far distally that it surmounts the medial epicondyle. In profile, the end of the medial epicondyle may be either rounded, straight with "corners," or somewhat peaked. *Variation* in this region of the humerus is noted in the sometime development of a small process—the *supracondyloid process*—situated superior to the medial epicondyle.

The *articular region* of the distal end of the humerus is asymmetrical: it is expanded into a wheellike rim medially (the *trochlea*) and is rounded and caplike laterally (forming the *capitulum*). The ulna articulates around the trochlea (in a parasagittal plane) and the radius articulates around and distally on the capitulum (parasagittally as well as rotationally or pivotally). The trochlea, which forms a rather vertical wall against which the base of the medial epicondyle abuts, is typically more expansive and inferiorly distended than the capitulum. The trochlea is fully developed on all sides of the distal end of the bone. The capitulum, however, becomes increasingly truncated lateromedially in its course around the distal end of the bone; the capitulum thus lacks a posterior component. The lateral face of the trochlea and the medial face of the capitulum slope inward, toward the midline of the articular region.

Anteriorly, a low, broad, vertical ridge wraps around the confluence of the trochlea and capitulum; this *trochlear ridge* is more smoothly continuous with the trochlea than with the capitulum, from which it is often delineated by a narrow groove. In posterior aspect, the trochlear ridge is visible only at the inferiormost margin of the epiphysis. Posteriorly, the trochlea is "spindle-shaped," being smoothly and deeply concave with raised, ridgelike lateral and medial borders; the lateral border is elongate superiorly and the medial border (the edge of the distinctively "wheellike" end of the spindle) is distended inferiorly. Posteriorly, the superior margin of the trochlea is inferiorly curved, descending from the higher lateral border and then back and up slightly to the top of the medial border. The superior margin of the trochlea bounds a large fossa—the *olecranon fossa*—in which the olecranon process of the ulna becomes nestled when the arm is extended (see below). A nonmetric *variant* is sometimes noted in the perforation of the wall of bone in the olecranon fossa. This perforation, called the *septal aperture*, may be as small as a pinhole or almost as vacuous as the fossa itself. The development of a septal aperture seems to be more prevalent in females than in males and seems to occur on the left side more frequently than on the right.

On the anterior side of the distal end of the humerus, one finds two smaller fossae, one above the trochlea and the other above the capitulum. The former is referred to as the *coronoid fossa* [because the coronoid process of the ulna encroaches upon it when the lower arm is flexed (see below)]; it is bounded on its sides by ridgelike thickenings of bone, the lateralmost of which separates the two fossae from one another. When a septal aperture is present, it communicates between the olecranon fossa and the coronoid fossa.

The fossa superior to the capitulum is called the *radial fossa* because it receives the head of the radius when the lower arm is flexed (see below). The radial fossa tends to be shallower and broader than the coronoid fossa; it is bounded by but may also expand onto the lateral epicondyle.

The *lateral epicondyle* presents itself as a truncated, flangelike adornment on the lateral side of the distal end of the humerus. It is traversed, at least in part, by the lateral border or crest (described earlier); the inferior portion of this crest is identified as the *lateral supracondylar ridge*. When viewed from the side, the lateral epicondyle appears to be bent forward, away from the lateral border of the trochlea, and to be tucked into the overlying capitulum. Posteriorly, the lateral epicondyle is relatively smooth. Laterally, nearer the capitulum, the surface of the lateral epicondyle becomes more irregular and is surmounted by at least one short, obliquely oriented crest or ridge.

Development and Ossification

The shaft or body of the humerus begins to ossify from a single center by the end of the second fetal month (Figure 4–6). (The femur also begins to ossify at this time, but initially the humerus is longer; eventually, femoral growth speeds up so that, by the middle of the third month, the two bones are of equal length, after which the femur increases more rapidly in

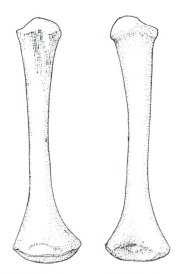

Figure 4–6 Right humerus of third-trimester fetus: *(left)* anterior and *(right)* posterior views.

length.) The shaft of the humerus is almost completely ossified by birth, at which time the only other area of ossification may be found in the appearance of a secondary center in the proximal epiphysis of the humeral head. In most individuals, ossification in the humeral head begins during the first year of life. In general, the remaining cartilaginous parts of the humeral ends begin to ossify in the following sequence: capitulum (by the end of the second year), greater tubercle (by the third year), medial epicondyle (around the fifth year), lesser tubercle (by the fifth year), trochlea (during the tenth year), and lateral epicondyle (between the twelfth and thirteenth years). The head and the tubercles begin to coalesce during the fifth year, and, within the sixth year, join to form a larger epiphysis, which, in turn, typically unites with the shaft during the twentieth year; complete union, however, may occur as late as the twenty-fifth year. Between the sixteenth and seventeenth years, the trochlea, capitulum, and lateral epicondyle begin to unite with one another as well as with the end of the shaft; union may not, however, be complete until a year later. In general, then, the proximal end of the humerus completes ossification somewhat later than the distal end. As a rule, the elbow joint (i.e. the proximal radius and ulna and distal humerus) is completely ossified earlier than the shoulder (i.e. the proximal humerus and scapula) and wrist joints (i.e. at least the distal radius and ulna).

Radius

Morphology

The **radius** (Figure 4–7) articulates superiorly with the capitulum of the distal humerus and laterally with the ulna; distally, the radius contributes to the wrist joint. The *head* of the ra-

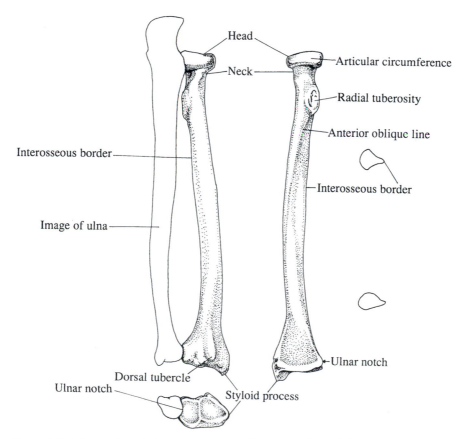

Figure 4–7 Right radius: *(left top)* posterior (with image of ulna), *(left bottom)* inferior, and *(middle)* anterior views; *(right)* cross sections through shaft.

dius is subcircular in outline and presents itself as an upwardly directed, shallow, cup-shaped structure; a moderately thick rim circumscribes the cavity. The capitulum sits in this depression in the radial head. A thick articular band—the *articular circumference*—wraps around the perimeter of the radial head; this band rotates in the radial notch of the ulna (see below). The articular circumference is thinnest laterally and posteriorly (when the radius is properly positioned) and deepens to its thickest dimension anteromedially. The radial head is broader, especially laterally, than the shaft on which it sits, and thus the *neck* of the bone is easily delineated.

A few centimeters below the neck of the radius and in the same anteromedial orientation as the thickest section of the articular circumference, a large ovoid to elliptical platform of bone swells out markedly. This is the *radial tuberosity*, onto which the biceps muscle inserts; its surface is variably granular, pitted, and grooved, and, overall, irregularly contoured. The anterior boundary of the radial tuberosity tends to be less well defined than its posterior border, which is more edgelike. A low ridge courses inferiorly from the radial tuberosity, arcs toward the lateral side of the anterior surface (for the short distance of this excursion it is called the *anterior oblique line*), and then extends for the length of the shaft, veering outward with the lateral expansion of the bone's distal end. This anterior oblique line may also become crisper in appearance distally. Approximately at the level at which this low ridge assumes a more lateral position (i.e. a few centimeters below the radial tuberosity), the otherwise rather circular radial shaft becomes severely compressed medially into a sharp, crestlike border whose upper extent is variably distended and roughened. If a radial *nutrient foramen* is present, it will be found in the region between this variably distended and roughened section of the medial crest and the oblique line opposite it; such a foramen will be minute and slitlike and will penetrate the shaft obliquely in a superior direction. From this roughened medial region, inferiorly, the shaft of the bone arcs gently lateromedially.

The medial crest represents the *interosseous border* of the bone. It extends as a sharp edge for much of the length of the shaft, bifurcating inferiorly as it approaches the *ulnar notch* (see below). For its last distal fifth or so, the radial shaft broadens markedly, from side to side, toward its end. The bone of the anterior surface of this thin, subtriangular region is relatively smooth and flat. As one approaches the epiphyseal region, this anterodistal plane arcs upward (i.e. becomes further elevated in the anterior dimension), especially in its mediodistal corner; this anterior expansion widens the articular surface of the distal epiphysis from front to back. Still on the anterior side distally, the mediodistal "corner," which is more rounded or "peaked" medially than squared up, projects medially to contribute to the side of the shallow *ulnar notch*. On the distolateral side, the thin crest described above courses down to the level of the mediodistal corner and, typically, swings or angles inward toward the medial side, sometimes continuing across the entire end of the bone. Just on the inside of this thin crest, the distally tapering *styloid process* takes origin and extends the length of the radius on its lateral side. The anterior surface of the styloid process is usually slightly concave, smooth, and covered with articular-looking bone, which, in turn, may be highlighted on its sides by thinly raised edges.

The *posterior surface* of the radius, which is more rounded and swollen than the anterior side, bears a variably low to ridgelike keel that arcs laterally as it descends partway down the shaft from its origin just above the superiorly roughened portion of the medial, interosseous border. In its most pronounced state, this keel delineates a shallow and moderately broad groove between it and the interosseous border. Otherwise, a thinner shallow groove may be found coursing just inside and along the interosseous medial edge. Sometimes the keel may extend weakly to the distal end of the bone, where it becomes confluent with the always present *dorsal tubercle*, which itself is typically a prominently raised and vertically oriented feature at the midpoint of the distal end of the bone.

The dorsal tubercle may be subtended on its medial side by a groove of variable depth, which itself is often bordered medially by a noticeable ridge; thus the dorsal tubercle has a "twinned" appearance. The area between the tubercle and its associated groove (and its associated ridge, if present) is slightly concave; this concavity eventually courses up to and terminates in the variably right-angled to rounded mediodistal corner of the bone. Lateral to the dorsal tubercle, the mildly concave distal edge of the bone becomes distended into the styloid process, whose posterior surface may be variably irregular and faintly grooved. The groove or grooves medial to the dorsal tubercle are associated with various extensor muscles for the thumb (pollex) and other digits of the hand; muscles that extend the wrist lie lateral to the dorsal tubercle.

Typically, the *distal articular surface* is smoothly concave and crudely wedge-shaped in outline. The narrower, variably pointed to blunted end of the distal articular surface corresponds to the distension of the styloid process, medial to which the surface expands to the level of the dorsal tubercle. At this point the anterior edge is indented slightly; the posterior edge (just medial to the dorsal tubercle) may be indented as well. In the latter case, the articular surface appears "pinched" or "waisted," and there may be a shallow but very faint groove or depression coursing across the surface between the two indentations, which create the impression that one large facet is subdivided into two separate and unequal portions. The lateral portion of the large facet articulates above and its associated styloid process to the side of the scaphoid bone (which belongs to the proximal-row of carpal or wrist bones). The smaller medial portion of the large facet articulates with part of the lunate bone (another proximal-row carpal). Medial to the anterior of the two indentations, the distal articular surface of the radius arcuately expands posteriorly, terminating at the corner of the variably concave medial edge. The posterior edge proceeds more directly to its respective corner of the medial edge. The articular surface, however, does not terminate at the medial edge but wraps around and up into the shallow ulnar notch, into which the distal end of the ulna nestles.

Development and Ossification

Ossification of the radius (Figure 4–8) begins during the eighth fetal week with the appearance of a center in the cartilaginous diaphysis. At birth, the shaft is well ossified, but the prox-

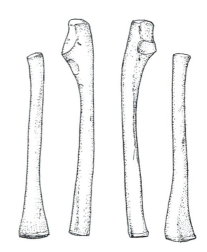

Figure 4–8   Radius and ulna of third-trimester fetus: *(far left)* anterior and *(far right)* posterior views of radius; *(middle left)* medial and *(middle right)* lateral views of ulna.

imal and distal ends are still cartilaginous. During the first but sometimes not until the second year, the distal end begins to ossify. Ossification in the proximal epiphysis does not occur until the fifth year. This epiphysis begins to coalesce with the shaft at the onset of puberty; complete fusion generally occurs between the ages of 15 and 18 but is sometimes delayed until age 19. The distal end typically fuses with the diaphysis during the 17th to 20th years (it may commence and complete union a year earlier in females than in males), although complete fusion may not occur until the 23rd year. The radial tuberosity may sometimes arise from a separate center of ossification, which appears during the 14th or 15th years.

Ulna

Morphology

Whereas the radius is narrow on top and broad at its distal end, the shape is essentially the reverse in the **ulna** (Figure 4–9). The proximal end of the ulna is enlarged and the relatively thin shaft tapers to a small, globular distal end that is adorned posteriorly by a modestly pointed process. Because the ulna lies medial to the radius, features of the ulna that correspond to this association lie on the lateral side of the bone (i.e. on the same side of the bone as the side of the body from which it came).

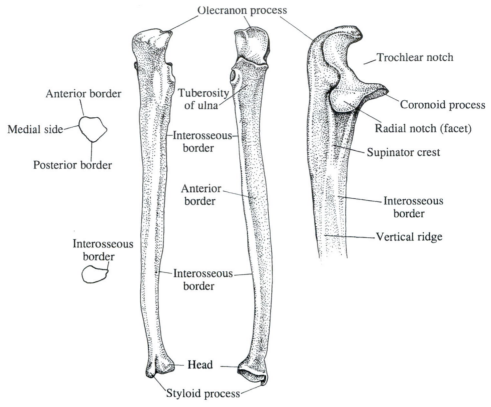

Figure 4–9 Right ulna: *(far left)* cross sections through shaft; *(middle left)* posterior and *(middle right)* anterior views; *(far right)* detail of proximal portion, lateral view.

Anteriorly, the *proximal end* of the ulna is crescentic in shape and thus creates the *trochlear notch*, which cups the trochlea of the distal humerus. The trochlear notch rotates around the trochlea of the humerus in a longitudinal or parasagittal plane. The posterior surface of the proximal end of the ulna is essentially vertical and flat. The upper "horn" of the crescentic trochlear notch, which protrudes anteriorly as a ledgelike, relatively broad structure, is called the *olecranon process*, which nestles into the olecranon fossa (on the posterior side of the distal humerus) when the lower arm is extended. The superior surface of the olecranon process is variably roughened and irregularly ovoid to subtriangular in outline. The anterior rim of the olecranon process slants downward toward its medial side. The anterior rim is variably distended by the terminus of a longitudinal, very low, ridgelike swelling that traverses the inner surface of the trochlear notch to its liplike,

markedly protruding inferior horn, called the *coronoid process*. The coronoid process comes to lie in the coronoid fossa on the anterior surface of the distal humerus when the lower arm is flexed. The coronoid process projects much farther anteriorly than does the olecranon process.

The longitudinal ridge within the trochlear notch represents a boundary on either side of which the articular surface slopes posteriorly. This longitudinal "ridge" does not, however, bisect the trochlear notch into two equal halves. Rather, the bulk of the coronoid process lies to the medial side of this ridge and extends even farther medially as a ledgelike projection. Not too far lateral to this ridge, the coronoid process is severely truncated at an oblique angle and its articular surface appears as if it has been creased and appressed to the side of the bone. This additional "facet," which is pointier anteriorly, is variably ovoid to elliptical in shape and modestly concave. This concavity constitutes the *radial notch,* in which the articular circumference of the head of the radius rotates.

Variation in the proximal ulna is noted in the morphology of the trochlear notch. Specifically, this variation is expressed in the extent to which the articular surface is indented by nonarticular bone at the point at which the coronoid process begins to expand medially; it is also from this point that a crease or groove may course across the articular surface, dividing it into upper and lower sections. Other variations in the proximal ulna can be noted, in the degree to which the posterior and inferior edges of the radial notch facet are distinct from the surrounding bone and in the presence on this facet of a secondary facet posteriorly.

Extending downward a short distance from the medial and lateral corners of the coronoid process are two ridges that subtend between them a variably excavated and roughened trough or groove; the entire roughened area is referred to as the *tuberosity of the ulna.* The medial of the two ridges is accentuated by a depression that courses behind it and also to some extent by the medial lip of the coronoid process. The lateral ridge is enhanced by a longer depression that descends from the inferior edge of the radial notch facet. The medial and lateral ridges may converge upon each other and enclose the trough and tuberosity of the ulna between them. If this is the case, the rounded medial border of the anterior surface of the shaft—identified as the *anterior margin* or *border*—proceeds inferiorly from the point of confluence of the two ridges. When, however, the lateral ridge remains fairly vertically oriented or otherwise fails to contact the medial ridge, the medial ridge alone continues as the anterior margin. In either case, the anterior margin becomes thickened and elevated approximately two-thirds to three-fourths down the length of the shaft. Often, a small, slitlike, upwardly directed, *nutrient foramen* penetrates the anterior margin or the bone just medial to it a few or more centimeters below the region of the ulnar tuberosity.

From the posterior portion of the radial notch facet, a relatively sharp crest—the *supinator crest*—descends either as a single thick elevation or as a series of thickened elevations along the *lateral side* of the shaft. At some variable point within 1 cm or more of the radial notch facet, the supinator crest appears to bifurcate into two crests or ridges; the posterior ridge is usually the more faintly developed. The inferior ridge is called the *vertical ridge* and it courses for almost the entire length of the shaft. The anterior ridge is much stouter and more pronounced and constitutes the *interosseous margin* or *border.* This border extends for much of the length of the shaft and mirrors the similarly crisp and distended interosseous border of the radius; the intervening interosseous membrane tethers the radius and ulna together. (The ulnar interosseous border, like the radial notch superior to it, is found on the side of the bone corresponding to the side of the body from which the bone comes.) The interosseous border of the ulna is more anteriorly oriented than the anterior border, and the bone between these borders is variably concave or troughlike. A much shallower and narrower groove or trough is subtended by the interosseous border and the vertical ridge posterior to it.

The raised *posterior border* of the ulna descends like a tail from the rather flattened, triangularly elongate surface that caps the olecranon process from behind. The posterior border is a distinct, compressed, crestlike feature for only two-thirds or so of the upper length of the shaft. For the distal third—all the way to the spikelike *styloid process* at the very end of the bone—the posterior border is expressed more subtly. The posterior border parallels in its course the mildly sinuous configuration of the ulna: there is a lateral arc for approximately the proximal one-fourth to one-third of the bone, followed by a long medial arc and then another lateral inclination for the last distal one-fourth or so of the bone.

The *medial side* of the ulna is smooth and gently rounded for much of its length. It is flattened to varying degrees below the depression that is located beneath the lip of the coronoid process. In cross section and taking into account the various ridges, borders, grooves, and convexities, the shaft of the ulna is, nonetheless, more or less triangular for much or all of its length.

Although the ulna tapers rather markedly toward its *distal end*—which is identified as the *head*—it does expand or flare out somewhat above the epiphyseal region. The inferiorly projecting *styloid process* is appressed to the posteromedial side of the head of the ulna. The bulk of the ulnar head, which is somewhat semicircular in outline, expands out from the "apex" created by the styloid process, from which it may be separated by a shallow groove and/or pit(s). Even though it does not directly contact the carpal bone (the triquetral) below it, the inferior surface of the ulnar head is articular in nature; an articular disc is interposed between the ulnar head and the triquetral. Most of the circumference of the ulnar head, which thickens vertically as it proceeds away from the styloid process, is, however, represented by articular bone. The shallow ulnar notch of the distal radius rotates around this articular perimeter.

Development and Ossification

Ossification begins in the ulna (Figure 4–8), as it does in the radius and humerus, with the appearance of a center in the shaft during the eighth fetal week. The shaft is well ossified by the time of birth, but the distal epiphyseal region and most of the olecranon (which is itself an epiphyseal cap atop the process) remain cartilaginous. The ossification center in the distal end appears between the ages of 5 and 6 years or even as late as the seventh year; fusion occurs between 21 and 25 years of age. This is quite a bit later than in the distal radius (the distal radius, however, does articulate directly with its neighboring carpals, whereas the distal end of the ulna is separated by an articular capsule from the underlying triquetral). Ossification of the olecranon usually begins during the tenth year but may occur as early as 7 years or as late as 14 years; fusion to the shaft typically occurs during the 16th but sometimes may be as late as the 19th or even the 23rd year.

The Hand

The **hand** is composed of eight **carpal bones** (short bones of the wrist region), which make up the **carpus**; five **metacarpal bones** (lying just distal to the carpals), which constitute the **meta-**

carpus; and fourteen **phalanges** (lying distal to the metacarpals), which are the bones of the **digits** or fingers. The general arrangement of the bones of the hand is similar to that of the foot and ankle bones. With the exception of the distal phalanges, all cartilaginous, presumptive elements are present by the second fetal month.

Carpus

The **carpus** or wrist (Figures 4–10 and 4–11) comprises eight small **carpal bones** arranged in two rows—a **proximal** and a **distal row**—each row consisting of four bones. In the proximal row, from the lateral to the medial side (as defined when the hand is in the anatomical position), are the **scaphoid** and **lunate** (which articulate with the distal radius), the **triquetral** or **triquetrum** (which is separated from the head of the ulna by an articular disc), and the **pisiform**. The distal row of carpal bones, from the lateral to the medial side, is composed of the **trapezium** (which lies between the scaphoid and the first metacarpal), the **trapezoid** (which lies between the scaphoid and the second metacarpal), the **capitate** (which articulates proximally with parts of the scaphoid and lunate and distally with the third and part of the fourth metacarpals), and the **hamate** (which articulates proximally with the triquetral and part of the lunate and, distally, with the fourth and fifth metacarpals).

Ossification of the Carpals

In addition to the normal number of hand bones, other elements are detectable by the second fetal month. One corresponds to the *os centrale* or "central carpal," which is typically a separate bone in all monkeys and prosimian primates, and the other to the hamulus or "hook" of the hamate, which eventually coalesces with the bulk of that carpal. It is only among humans and apes that a separate os centrale may not be found. There has been quite a lot of debate on the evolutionary significance and even reality of the absence of the os centrale (e.g. see Schultz, 1936), the common belief being that the cartilaginous precursor of this small bone fuses to the scaphoid (e.g. Cinák, 1972). Fazekas and

Kósa (1978), however, state that this cartilaginous element merely disappears during the third or fourth fetal month.

Ossification in the carpals—each from a separate center—occurs postnatally. During the first year, the capitate and then the hamate begin to ossify. The triquetral is next (second to third year); followed by the lunate (fourth year in females and a year later in males); the trapezium, trapezoid, and scaphoid (fifth year in females and a year or two later in males); and then the pisiform (ninth year in females and as late as the eleventh year in males). These bones continue to grow in concert with the individual's growth.

Scaphoid

Although the **scaphoid** (Figure 4–10) is named after its presumed resemblance to a boat (an upside down boat at that), it would be misleading to think of it as actually resembling anything boat-shaped other than that its superior surface is, in part or in whole, arcuate and convex, and that its inferior surface may bear a circumscribed, concave articular region.

The *proximal* or *radial surface* of the scaphoid is dominated by a roughly triangular to semicircular convex facet that articulates with the lateral portion of the distal epiphysis of the radius. This *radial facet* extends for two-thirds to three-fourths the mediolateral width of the bone. The anterior and medial margins of the scaphoid's *radial facet* are "free" (i.e. they also form the border of the bone), whereas the posterior or dorsal margin of the facet subtends a thin to moderately broad, horizontally oriented, variably pitted and grooved strip of nonarticular bone that subdivides the bone into "upper" or proximal and "lower" or distal parts; the distal component lies more or less at a right angle to the proximal part. The proximal component constitutes the radial facet and the nonarticular strip of bone extends beyond it medially and distally. When viewed from above, the narrower nonarticular strip of bone looks vaguely like the head of a snail and the radial facet like the snail's shell. The "snail's head" extends medially, or to the side of the

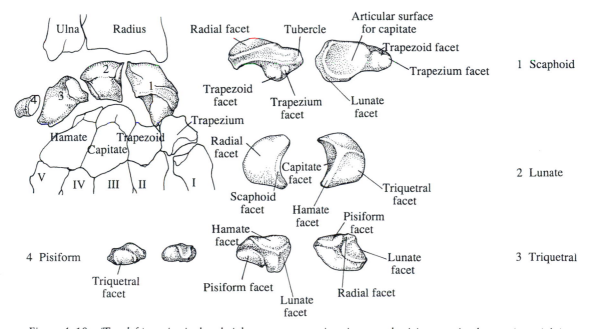

Figure 4–10 *(Top left)* semiarticulated right carpus, posterior view, emphasizing proximal row; *(top right)* scaphoid [*(right)* distal and *(left)* dorsomedial views]; *(middle right)* lunate [*(right)* dorsal and *(left)* proximal views]; *(bottom right)* triquetral [*(right)* proximal and *(left)* distal views]; *(bottom left)* pisiform [*(right)* ventral (palmar) and *(left)* dorsal (posterior) views].

body from which the scaphoid comes, and swells somewhat proximally; this swollen region is the *tubercle* of the scaphoid. The distal component is almost a mirror image of the "upper" part, albeit it is shifted medially (remember, the distal component is also at a right angle to the radial facet, so that its predominant articular surface faces distally). The facet of the distal component—the *trapezium-trapezoid facet*—articulates with both the trapezoid and trapezium. It hangs below (i.e. is distal to) the nonarticular strip of bone. The medial side of the trapezium-trapezoid facet is gently convex, whereas its lateral side is variably mildly to markedly concave. The proximal surface of this region is somewhat swollen and irregular topographically.

The *distal* or *inferior surface* of the *radial facet* is somewhat saddle-shaped, with the trapezium-trapezoid facet protruding above a larger articular region. The long axis of this vaulted, distal articular region of the scaphoid is oriented mediolaterally. Because it articulates with the head of the capitate, it is identified as the *articular surface for the capitate*. Arcing medioanteriorly around the circumference of the *articular surface for the capitate* is an obliquely offset semilunar area—the *lunate facet*—which abuts the side of the lunate laterally.

Lunate

The **lunate** (Figure 4–10) is so named because its inferior or distal articular surface, when viewed laterally, is roughly lunate or crescentic in shape. The articular surface itself is narrow mediolaterally, elongate anteroposteriorly, and concave; it broadens anteriorly. Both the *distal articular region* of the lunate and the distal articular region of the scaphoid cup the arced and convex proximal end of the capitate. The articulated proximal surfaces of the scaphoid and lunate form a large convex surface. The lateral side of the lunate bears a bandlike articular region for contact with the medial side of the scaphoid. This articular region parallels the concave lateral margin of the scaphoid's distal facet.

The *proximal surface* of the lunate is smoothly convex and nestles into the medial component of the articular surface of the distal

radius. This *radial facet* of the lunate is roughly triangular or spearhead-shaped in outline, with rounded or blunted corners; the "triangle's" apex is directed anteriorly (ventrally). Distally, the bone extends beyond the posterolateral "corner" of the articular surface (nesting a bit under the scaphoid). However, posteromedially, the bone and its corner are obliquely truncated. When the lunate is viewed from its *distal* or *posterior aspect*, the lateromedial slant of the posterolateral corner of the bone as well as its general lateral inclination are obvious. The somewhat paralleliform, nonarticular, posterior (dorsal) surface thus formed is irregular and deeply pitted.

The *lateral side* of the lunate parallels the lateromedial slant of the posteromedial corner of the bone. It is subdivided into (1) a larger, flat facet for contact with the medial side of the triquetral and (2) a narrow, sometimes slightly groovelike facet that follows the margin of the facet for the capitate and which receives the compressed proximolateral edge of the hamate below it.

The *anterior, ventral,* or *palmar side* of the lunate is narrow, rounded from side to side, convex proximodistally, and contributes to the crescentic extension of the distal articular facet.

Triquetral

The *proximal surface* of the triquetral (Figure 4–10) continues the convex *radial surface* established by the scaphoid and lunate; it is separated from the distal end of the ulna by an articular disc. The carpal's large, slightly arced *distal facet* articulates laterally with the hamate. The triquetral also has two of its articular facets at right angles to one another; a distinct "corner" intrudes between them. The larger and almost vertical facet articulates with the obliquely truncated posterolateral corner of the lunate; the facet is variably crescentic to rhomboid in outline. The *anterior, ventral,* or *palmar side* of the triquetral extends only a short distance laterally from the edge of the facet for the lunate and then the bone angles or corners at the side of the second facet (the *pisiform facet*), which is directed anteriorly; the surface of the short spit of bone that proceeds away from the *tri-*

quetral-lunate facet bears a depression which is itself deeply pitted.

An anteriorly facing facet articulates with the pisiform. This pisiform facet is generally ovoid in outline, although some irregularities along its perimeter are common. The edges of this facet are usually delineated quite sharply and often emphasized further—especially proximally and laterally—by a constriction of the bone which serves to pedestal the facet.

The proximal surface of the triquetral is adorned with a roughened and somewhat pitted groove that emanates from just behind the facet for the pisiform and courses posterolaterally. This groove parallels the posterolaterally oblique, long side of the triquetral; it may extend completely across the bone to its postero-lateral corner (which is the posterior margin of the facet for the lunate), or it may fade out anywhere along the way. In any case, proximally, two raised areas are delineated posterior to the facet for the pisiform; the extent to which these two areas remain separated from one another is a function of the length of the groove between them.

The inferior or distolateral surface of the tri-quetral bears a facet that articulates with the hamate. The anterior or palmar margin of this hamate facet is fairly straight; it courses later-ally from the edge with the facet for the lunate and continues below the facet for the pisiform. The roughly parallel posterior margin of the ha-mate facet is also straight, but it is much shorter: it is truncated by the posteromedially oblique long side of the bone. The edge of the facet for the hamate is distinguished further by a shallow groove that is especially prominent along the posteromedially oblique long side of the bone. The facet for the hamate, which is the largest of the three articular areas of the trique-tral, faces laterally and forms a crisply delin-eated corner with the facet for the lunate; it is separated completely from the facet for the pi-siform. (After delineating the facet for the ha-mate, one can identify the facet for the lunate, which faces proximally, i.e. toward the side of the body from which the triquetral comes.)

Pisiform

The pisiform ("pea-shaped" carpal; Figure 4–10) is the fourth and last bone of the proximal row of carpals. It articulates with only one other carpal, the triquetral, and thus its sole articular facet, which is mildly concave, faces postero-medially. The bulk of the pisiform rises from the articular facet like an amorphous mound that is longer proximodistally than it is wide medi-olaterally. Its anterior or palmar surface is less bulbous than its posterior surface. The articular facet for the triquetral may be offset by a nar-row groove that constricts the bone for some extent around its perimeter. A broader groove is typically present on the posterodistal side of the bone.

Trapezium

The trapezium (Figure 4–10) is the most lateral bone of the distal row of carpals. It articulates proximally with the scaphoid, distally primarily with the first metacarpal (metacarpal I), and distomedially with part of metacarpal II. A dis-tinctive feature of the trapezium is the saddle-shaped facet it bears for articulation with the first metacarpal; this first metacarpal facet faces distally and laterally (i.e. to the side of the body from which the bone comes). In outline, this saddle-shaped first metacarpal facet is subcres-centic, with its "horns" pointing posteriorly or dorsally. The anterior peak of this subcrescentic facet lies just below the terminus of a stout crest on the anterior or palmar surface—the palmar ridge—that courses proximally in a mediolat-eral direction. The palmar ridge juts out a bit proximally, at which point it is identified as the tubercle of the trapezium; when in articulation, this tubercle lies beneath the distal articular process of the scaphoid. Medial to and coursing in parallel with this thick palmar crest is a pro-nounced, troughlike groove along which the tendon of the flexor carpi radialis courses. This groove is subtended medially by a peaked ele-vation of bone that corresponds to a distinct downward bend in the large, proximal articular surface. This downward flexure subdivides the articular surface into two components; the smaller one faces essentially upward while the longer facet is oriented medially and posteriorly (ventrally).

The slightly concave proximal articular re-gion is roughly rhomboidal in outline; the scaphoid articulates here. The longer, slightly concave to undulating facet articulates with the

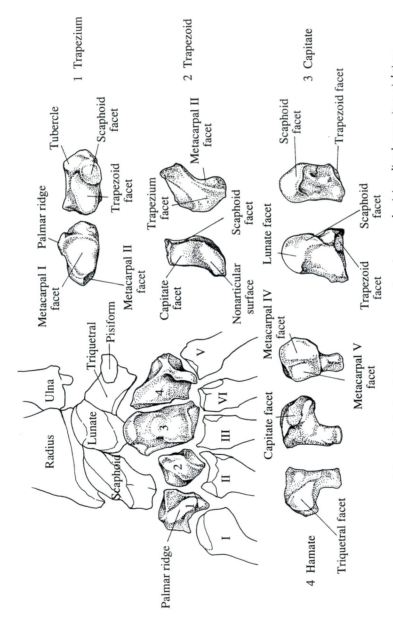

Figure 4–11 (*Top left*) semiarticulated right carpus, anterior view, emphasizing distal row; (*top right*) trapezium [(*right*) proximal and (*left*) distal views]; (*middle right*) trapezoid [(*right*) lateral and (*left*) medial views]; (*bottom right*) capitate [(*right*) lateral and (*left*) dorsal (posterior) views]; (*bottom left*) hamate [(*right*) distal, (*middle*) lateral, and (*left*) proximomedial views].

trapezoid. The articular surface of the trapezoid facet extends farther along and around the narrow distal end of the bone to contact between the trapezium and the proximolateral corner of the second metacarpal. *Variation* in the trapezium may be noted in a pinching off of the ventralmost portion of the long facet for the trapezoid, which, in turn, is reflected in the facet for the second metacarpal.

The *posterior* or *dorsal surface* of the trapezium bears a raised, heellike eminence (directly beneath the region of the tubercle) from which emanates a low, variably distinct, medially directed, moundlike ridge that courses along the bone, following the flexure of the medial surface. This low, moundlike ridge may terminate distally in a slight swelling just dorsal to the facet for metacarpal II.

Trapezoid

The **trapezoid** (Figure 4–11) nestles up against the lateral side of the trapezium and the medial side of the capitate. Proximally the trapezoid articulates with the scaphoid and distally with the second metacarpal. Whereas the dorsal side of the trapezium tapers distally, the dorsal side of the trapezoid broadens distally. The narrow end of the trapezoid is directed anteriorly (ventrally), and its broad end is oriented posteriorly.

The *lateral side* of the trapezoid mirrors the medial side of the trapezium such that the abutting facets are similar in outline although mirror images in contour. The *facet for the trapezium* is variably convex to undulating and typically expands toward the *palmar (anterior, ventral) side* of the bone (although this facet may be pinched distoanteriorly in concert with *variation* in the expression of its sister facet on the trapezium). A shallow groove of pitted, nonarticular bone lies anterior (palmar) to the facet for the trapezium. This strip of nonarticular bone may course sufficiently along the distal surface to completely separate the facet for the trapezium from the distally located *facet for the second metacarpal*. However, this nonarticular strip may terminate such that the two facets are confluent posteriorly across a bend in the bone.

The trapezoid's facet for the second metacarpal is asymmetrical as it broadens posteriorly; that is, following the shape of the bone itself, this facet expands medially. Thus, the medial margin of the facet is arcuate and concave, whereas the lateral margin is merely mildly convex. A low "keellike" ridge or narrow eminence may course down this facet, emphasizing its convexity mediolaterally. (When viewed from the side, the facet for the second metacarpal is noticeably concave.)

Distally, the trapezoid is dominated by a large *facet for the scaphoid bone*. The medial margin of this facet forms a "corner" and is confluent, with the articular surface for the capitate. The lateral margin of this facet also forms a corner and is confluent with the articular surface for the trapezium. Together with the trapezium's facet for the scaphoid, the trapezoid's facet for the scaphoid creates a slightly concave surface in which the distal articular region of the scaphoid nestles. The roughened, nonarticular, posterior or dorsal surface of the trapezoid may extend onto the medial surface posteriorly.

Capitate

The **capitate** (Figure 4–11) articulates laterally with the trapezoid, medially with the hamate, proximally with the scaphoid and lunate, and distally primarily with the third metacarpal and only slightly with the second and fourth metacarpals. The bone's name reflects the "headlike" shape of its *proximal end*, which is relatively smooth and somewhat domelike and from which (like "earflaps" along the medial and/or lateral sides) continuations of its articular surface may extend. Viewed from the palmar side, the proximal end is mildly convex superiorly (where it contacts the scaphoid) and laterally (where it meets the lunate); these two articular regions form a slight crease at their juncture. The sometimes slightly concave lateral side of the capitate is the more vertical; it forms a rather distinct corner with the superior articular prominence. The helmet-shaped appearance of the proximal end in palmar aspect is enhanced further by a groove and/or pitting along the perimeter that delineates the roughened, obliquely oriented palmar or anterior surface.

Below the capitate's head, the *palmar surface* becomes increasingly swollen distally as it comes to mirror the apex of the base of the third metacarpal. This palmar swelling is lopsided; that is, the medial half is flatter than the lateral half of the surface.

The *distal end* of the capitate can readily be distinguished from the domelike proximal end. When viewed "head-on," the articular surface of the distal end approximates a right triangle. The short base courses along the posterior (dorsal) margin of the distal end and forms a right angle with the side that courses posteroanteriorly. The second metacarpal articulates along the lateral edge of this side. The shorter side of the right angle extends the distal end of the bone medially, or away from the side of the body from which the bone comes; the fourth metacarpal overlaps this medial extension. When the bone is placed in the anatomical position (lying on the shorter, posterior edge of its distal end) and viewed from either the medial or lateral side, one sees that the distal surface is slightly concave and that the bone expands convexly from below the dome-shaped proximal end to the distal "peak" of the palmar surface. When viewed laterally, the posterior surface is pinched or indented, just below the proximal end.

The *trapezoid facet* occurs on the *lateral side* of the capitate distally. The trapezoid may articulate "high" or "low" relative to the distal surface of the capitate. Roughly midway along its length, the lateral side of the capitate is deformed outward or laterally, mirroring the concavity on the corresponding surface of the trapezoid; this "deformation" may take the form of a tiny flexure or elevation, a distinct swelling, or a markedly pronounced crest or ridge. It appears that the degree to which the lateral side of the capitate is deformed outward is correlated with the degree to which the capitate's trapezoid facet is (1) confluent with the more proximal facet for the scaphoid and (2) either a single, broadly continuous facet or divided into distinct areas of articulation. For example, when the lateral deformation is minimally expressed, the capitate's trapezoid facet is the most smoothly expansive and broadly confluent with the capitate's scaphoid facet; a broad pit lies below or posterior to (and delineates posteriorly) the confluence of these two facets. When the lateral deformation is a pronounced crest, the capitate's trapezoid facet is pinched or "waisted" just below this crest, creating two semidistinct, trapezoidal articular regions. The

facets for the trapezoid and the scaphoid are not confluent. Furthermore, it may appear as if the broad pit that otherwise lies posterior to the confluence of the capitate's scaphoid and trapezoid facets has both interposed itself between these two facets and contributed to the subdivision of the trapezoid facet.

The *posterior surface* of the capitate distal to the smooth articular head is roughened and irregular in contour. The posteromedial margin can be gently concave or variably "edgelike," depending on the degree to which the facet on the medial surface for contact with the hamate is continuous or disjunct. If the (lateral) articular region for the trapezoid is markedly subdivided, the posterolateral margin may bear a few swellings.

The *medial surface* of the capitate essentially consists of two different "zones": (1) a roughened, perhaps pitted and somewhat swollen anterior (palmar) component that is a continuation of the palmar surface and (2) a posterior articular region. This *posterior articular region* (for the hamate) is continuous with the "head." Approximately midway down the medial side, the articular facet for the hamate narrows appreciably. It is in this area of constriction that *variation* can occur—that is, in the extent to which the articular facet tapers, becomes pinched, or is even subdivided into a large proximal and a much smaller subovoid distal facet. Just anterior to the point at which the facet may be disrupted lies a swelling whose size and pervasiveness covaries with the degree to which the facet for the hamate is subdivided. The configuration of the capitate's hamate facet and accompanying swelling is reflected on the lateral surface of the hamate.

Hamate

"Hamate" means "shaped like a hook" or "bearing a hooklike process." And indeed, the hook is the most distinctive feature of this bone (Figure 4–11). Because the hook protrudes anteriorly (toward the palmar side) and its end hooks laterally (toward the side of the body from which it comes), one can always distinguish right from left hamates.

Proximal to the *hook*, the bone tapers, reflecting the fact that it is wedged between the capitate (laterally) and the triquetral (medially). At the base of the hook, the hamate widens markedly toward the distal surface, which articulates with the bases of the fourth and fifth metacarpals. Although the hamate's hook is gently concave laterally throughout its length, it is convex medially only at its anteriormost portion. Posteriorly, the hook is buttressed medially and broadened by a strut of bone that also forms the proximal border of the *facet for the fifth metacarpal*. The base of the hook expands somewhat laterally and proximally as a tongue of slightly roughened, pitted bone. This "tongue" may be circumscribed at its most proximal portion by the margin of an articular region that courses along the perimeter of the bone. This margin is formed by the confluence of the *articular facets for the capitate* (laterally) and *the triquetral* (medially). The convex and posteriorly oblique facet for the triquetral may be in one of two configurations: (1) it may continue up to and thus flare out in conjunction with the winglike extension of the distal surface (that contacts the fifth metacarpal) or (2) it may be truncated in front by a depression that pervades the region behind the medial strut of the hook.

The *lateral surface* of the hamate is relatively deep anteroposteriorly. Following the contour of the distal *facet for the fourth metacarpal*, the distolateral margin of the bone is slightly concave. The variably tapered proximal portion of the lateral side of the hamate bears the smooth *articular facet for the capitate*. A depression along the posterior border of the bone delineates the distal boundary of the large proximal portion of the facet for the capitate. Farther distally, this facet continues as a narrow articular strip. This narrow articular strip, which also contacts the capitate, may be separated completely from the larger articular region by a posterior invagination of the depression or groove described above. The degree to which the hamate's capitate facet is pinched or subdivided, and to which the vertical groove extends posteriorly reflects, respectively, the subdivision of the corresponding facet on the capitate and the development of its midbody swelling.

The *posterior side* of the hamate is roughly triangular in outline and its surface is irregular and pitted. Its *medial border* may be concave, reflecting the degrees to which (1) the winglike

extension of the articular surface for the fifth metacarpal protrudes medially and (2) its (proximal) apex is broadened by the confluence of the facets for the capitate and the triquetral.

The *distal surface* of the hamate is somewhat rectangular, but with rounded corners; one or both of the posterior "corners" may be swollen or expanded. A slight anteroposterior elevation of the distal surface divides it into two mildly concave articular planes that face slightly away from one another. The lateral plane (i.e. articular surface) receives the base of the fourth metacarpal; the slightly smaller medial surface (from which the hook "protrudes") accommodates the fifth metacarpal.

Metacarpal Bones

Morphology

The five **metacarpal bones** (metacarpals I to V; Figure 4–12) constitute the **metacarpus** and are situated between the distal row of carpals and the proximal phalanges. Similar to the metatarsals of the foot, the metacarpals have a *head* (the distal end), a *shaft*, and a *base* (the proximal end). The most lateral of the set is metacarpal I and the most medial is metacarpal V. (It is the reverse in the metatarsals: metatarsal I is the most medial and metatarsal V is the most lateral of the set.)

The metacarpals as a group are similar morphologically in that their *heads* are wrapped anteroposteriorly by articular bone. This articular bone extends farther upon the palmar surface medially and laterally and thus forms an inverted "U"-shaped border on this surface; sometimes, the lateral arm of the "U" is the more pronounced or elongate of the two. Posteriorly or dorsally, the head is narrower, bearing shallow depressions on its medial and lateral sides. These depressions emphasize the medial and lateral "peaks" just behind the head, where the distal flare of the shaft terminates. Proceeding proximally from this distal flare, the *shaft* narrows toward and expands at its juncture with the base of the bone; this tapering is minimal on metacarpal I. The posterior (dorsal) surface of the shaft is noticeably flat just behind the head of the bone. On metacarpals II to V, this flat surface tapers proximally (creating a long, flat triangular region);

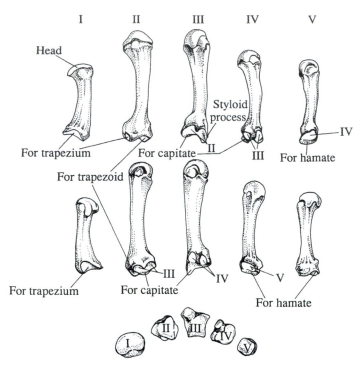

Figure 4–12   Right metacarpals: *(from left to right)* I to V; *(top row)* lateral (radial), *(middle row)* medial (ulnar), and *(bottom row)* proximal (basal) views.

on metacarpal I, the posterior surface remains broadly flat for the length of the shaft.

One can always distinguish the first metacarpal on the basis of overall size and morphology: it is the stoutest and shortest of the set. Of the remaining four metacarpals, II and III are the longest and V is the shortest and most slender. Metacarpals I and V are also distinctive in that each articulates with only one other metacarpal. Thus metacarpal I lacks a facet on the lateral side of its base and metacarpal V lacks a facet on the medial side of its base.

The *base* of each metacarpal is distinctive. On *metacarpal I*, the proximal articular surface, while being variable in outline, is consistently long and convex mediolaterally and short and gently concave anteroposteriorly. This surface, in conjunction with the trapezium, forms the *saddle joint of the thumb*.

The base of *metacarpal II* is deep anteroposteriorly at its midline; it is elevated along its medial margin. The medial side of this margin bears a moderately developed band of articular bone for contact with the third metacarpal. Distally along the shaft, a variably deep pit or depression separates this articular strip (for meta-

carpal III) from a variably rugose buildup of bone. The outline of the articular surface of the base is roughly triangular. Posteriorly (dorsally), the articular surface is indented. A groove circumscribing the shaft of the bone separates the perimeter of the base from a variably rugose buildup of bone just distal to it. Laterally, the base of this metacarpal bears a small, somewhat ovoid, variably projecting facet against which the base of metacarpal I articulates medially. This distolateral facet is oriented obliquely and thus generally faces palmad as well as laterally (i.e. to the side of the body from which the bone comes). Proximal to this facet lies the *facet for the trapezium*.

The base of the *third metacarpal* mirrors in outline the irregularly triangular to trapezoidal outline of the distal end of the capitate. The long axis of this surface is oriented anteroposteriorly. The "base" of this triangle/trapezoid lies along the posterior (dorsal) aspect of the bone; it is oriented mediolaterally. The proximolateral corner of this base is distended, thus giving a lateral twist to the articular surface (i.e. the articular surface is set obliquely, facing away from the side of the body from which the bone comes). The lateral side of the proximal articular surface of metacarpal III bears a variably undulating to subdivided articular band for contact with the medial side of the base of metacarpal II. Just distal to this articular region, the surface of the bone may be pitted or depressed; farther distally, the bone may be variably rugose and raised. The medial side of the base (i.e. the proximal articular surface) of metacarpal III is also articular; it contacts the base of metacarpal IV laterally. If this articular band is continuous rather than disjunct, it is taller on its dorsal side and tapers to the palmar side. If it is subdivided into two facets, the dorsal facet is rather ovoid in shape. The dorsal surface around the base is roughened and irregular; it is dominated proximolaterally by a spike- or stylarlike projection.

Although its palmar portion is truncated, the base of the *fourth metacarpal* is, nonetheless, a reasonable copy of the base of the third. However, the medial margin of the base of metacarpal IV is concave, due to a slight expansion of its dorsomedial "corner." The lateral side of the base of metacarpal IV bears either a single articular strip or two separate facets, thus mirroring the articular configuration of the medial side of the base of metacarpal III. The medial side of the base of metacarpal IV—which is longer and slightly concave—tends to be a continuously ovoid or elliptical facet against which a similarly shaped facet on the lateral side of the base of metacarpal V articulates. Depressions and/or pitting may delineate the lateral, anterior, and medial sides of the base of metacarpal IV from a variably raised and rugose buildup of bone farther distally along the shaft. The posterior or dorsal margin of the base of metacarpal IV may be indented or even slightly grooved. At least the medial half if not the entire base of the fourth metacarpal may be angled slightly medially, mimicking the medial twist of the base of metacarpal III. The articular surface of the base of metacarpal IV tends to be gently convex.

The base of the *fifth metacarpal* is short and concave mediolaterally and broad and convex anteroposteriorly. Laterally along the base lies a variably ovoid to elliptical facet for articulation with the base of metacarpal IV. The medial side of the base of metacarpal V, which lacks a facet, is variably swollen. This swelling contrib-

utes to a slight lateral twist of the base of the bone (i.e. the base of metacarpal V is angled toward the side of the body from which it comes). Just distal to the articular base, the posterior (dorsal) surface is variably depressed and irregular. Elsewhere, the bone may be roughened and somewhat swollen.

Development and Ossification

Metacarpals II to V (Figure 4–13) ossify individually from two centers of ossification: one in the shaft and one in the head (i.e. the distal epiphysis). Ossification begins in the shaft, typically during the ninth fetal week, but not in the head until the second or even third year. In a small percentage of individuals, a center of ossification may arise in the base (i.e. the proximal end) of metacarpal II. The first metacarpal also has an ossification center in the shaft that appears during the ninth fetal week. However, in 94% of individuals, the second center of ossification of metacarpal I arises in the base, not the head, which is the pattern characteristic of the phalanges. In 6% of individuals, the second center appears in the head of metacarpal I. Because of its pattern of development, the thumb has been interpreted as lacking a metacarpal and possessing three rather than two rows of phalanges. Regardless of the true identity of metacarpal I, its base as well as the heads of metacarpals II to V unite with their respective diaphyses at approximately the same time as the phalangeal bases unite with their respective diaphyses—that is, between the 18th and 20th years.

Figure 4–13 Bones of the right hand (there are none in the wrist) of third-trimester fetus: metacarpals and phalanges, posterior view.

Phalanges

Morphology

There are 24 **phalanges** (depending on how one interprets the bones of the pollex): 3 in each of digits II to V and 2 in the first digit (Figure 4–14). Like the metacarpals, the phalanges are seen as tiny "long bones," replete with *shafts* and *proximal* and *distal ends*; the proximal end is also referred to as the base of the bone. As a set, the *first* or *proximal row* of phalanges are morphologically similar, as are the phalanges in the *distal* or *terminal row*. The major differences between individual bones of a row are size and robustness. The phalanges of the middle or second row on digits II to V are, for the most part, similar to the proximal phalanges, from which they differ particularly in the articular morphology of their bases. As a set, the middle phalanges are smaller and slightly more gracile than the proximal phalanges. Within the set, the middle phalanges differ from one another by size and degree of gracility and/or robustness.

In general, the *shafts* of the phalanges of the *first* and *second rows* are somewhat flattened on their anterior (palmar) surfaces and rounded posteriorly (dorsally). The outline of a cross section through a phalangeal shaft would resemble a half circle. The shafts of these phalanges are gently concave on the palmar side. They flare out on their sides toward the bone's base and head; the flare is broader and more marked proximally than distally because the proximal end is broader. To some extent, the medial and lateral palmar margins of the phalangeal shafts of digits II to V tend to be crisp and sometimes even raised. These "edges" extend distally approximately two-thirds the length of the shaft on the proximal phalanges but less than half the length of the shaft of the middle phalanges. At their distal termini, these edges are even more distended. Proximally, these edges become more swollen, rounded, and expansive, creating a variably shallow depression between them but also adding to the bulk of the bone's base. The base of the proximal phalanx of digit I is similar to that of the other proximal phalanges.

The *distal end* or *head* of proximal and middle phalanges is covered largely by articular bone. This articular surface extends farther along the palmar than the dorsal side. The head bears elevated medial and lateral elevations; it is thus depressed somewhat toward its midline. These medial and lateral elevations are more moundlike on the proximal phalanges and thus create on these bones a somewhat undulating palmar surface. In contrast, on the middle phalanges, these elevations tend to be more abrupt, which makes the surface between them smoother and more broadly concave. In medial and lateral profile, the distal end of the bone is somewhat ovoid or subcircular (giving the impression of a strangely shaped hubcap); the palmar portion rises above the level of the shaft. Typically, all but the proximal portion of the perimeter of the distal end is raised. Where it is raised, the perimeter subtends a shallow depression, which, in turn, may bear either a small crest or a few small, irregular bumps.

The *proximal end* or *base* of a proximal phalanx bears a mildly depressed ovoid or elliptical articular facet for contact with the head of the metacarpal that lies distal to it. This articular facet is buttressed, at least anteriorly, by the two (medial and lateral) swellings described above; the base may be distended elsewhere around the perimeter of the articular facet. In addition, the base of a middle phalanx bears an ovoid or elliptical articular facet. However, because this facet articulates with the undulating head of a proximal phalanx and not the globular head of a metacarpal, its surface is elevated into a midline "keel," on either side of which lie two obliquely offset, shallowly concave surfaces. This midline keel nestles in the midline depres-

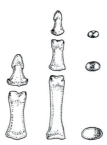

Figure 4–14 Right phalanges: *(left column)* I, posterior view, *(top)* distal and *(bottom)* proximal phalanges; *(middle column)* example of II to V, posterior views of *(from top to bottom)* distal, middle, and proximal phalanges; *(right column)* example of II to V, *(from top to bottom)* proximal (basal) views of distal, middle, and proximal phalanges.

sion, and the two surfaces on either side of the keel receive the two somewhat moundlike elevations of the head of a proximal phalanx. A middle phalanx is distinguished further from a proximal phalanx in that, posteriorly (dorsally), its base may be distended into a swelling or tuberclelike feature; this gives a somewhat beaklike appearance to this end of the bone.

Proximal and middle phalanges can be discriminated from one another by differences in the configuration of their bases. Although a middle phalanx—particularly from digit III or IV—may appear similar, at first glance, to a proximal phalanx of the first digit, the medial and lateral edges of the shaft and the configuration of the base distinguish the bones of these different phalangeal sets. In turn, the proximal phalanx of digit I can be identified as a proximal phalanx by the configuration of its base; it can also be distinguished from other proximal phalanges by its lack of medial and lateral edges on the palmar side of its shaft. Otherwise, identification as to specific digit of an isolated middle or proximal phalanx is basically impossible. In the series, however, the proximal phalanx of digit I is the shortest while that of digit V is the most gracile; the middle phalanx of digit V is usually the shortest and typically the most gracile of its set. Discrimination of right from left proximal and middle phalanges is not possible.

The *distal*, *third*, or *terminal phalanges* are quite distinctive in having very broad bases, short shafts, and somewhat harpoon-shaped heads. If one does not include the flare and expansion of the base, a terminal phalanx can be described as being essentially flat on its palmar side and somewhat arced dorsally. Proceeding distally, the bone becomes more compressed anteroposteriorly, coincident with the fanning out of the head. Terminal phalanges have only one articular end. They are also the smallest of the phalangeal sets.

In general, the *base* of a terminal phalanx is similar to that of a middle phalanx. The articular surface of a terminal phalanx does not, however, bear as distinctive a midline "keel" as does its proximal neighbor because the head of a middle phalanx (with which a terminal phalanx articulates) is more broadly and smoothly arcuate than the head of a proximal phalanx (with which a middle phalanx articulates). The

shaft of a terminal phalanx tapers inwardly quite drastically from the base. The confluence of the shaft and the base on the palmar side tends to be rather roughened.

The harpoon-shaped *head* of a terminal phalanx broadens out beyond the sides of the shaft and sometimes sends two barblike extensions proximally, each projecting away from the side of the shaft. The margin of the head is roughened and arcuate.

In contrast to the fifth pedal digit, the terminal phalanx of digit V of the hand is not diminutive and truncated in morphology, although it is sometimes the most gracile of its set. The terminal phalanx of digit I is the broadest and most robust and often also the longest bone of the set. Discriminating terminal phalanges especially of digits II to IV from one another and identifying the side of the body from which a particular terminal phalanx comes is essentially impossible.

Development and Ossification

Ossification of the phalanges (Figure 4–13) generally begins at about the same time as that of the metacarpals and well ahead the onset of ossification of the carpals. In some texts (e.g. *Gray's Anatomy*), the age of 8 fetal weeks is given for the onset of ossification in the noncarpal bones of the hand, but differences in timing do exist. The tips of the distal (third row) phalanges begin by intramembranous ossification, after which, during the seventh or eighth weeks, endochondral ossification spreads throughout the shaft. The diaphyses of the first row (proximal phalanges) begin to ossify during the ninth week, and those of the second row (middle phalanges) as early as the eleventh and as late as the seventeenth fetal week. Ossification of the bases or proximal epiphyses of the phalanges does not begin until after birth. In the proximal phalanges, the onset of ossification of the bases can occur between 1 and 3 years; in the other phalanges, it occurs between the ages of 2 and 3 years or as late as the fourth year. The proximal ends may begin to coalesce with the shafts of the phalanges as early as 14 years and may fuse completely by the age of 18 years or as late as 25 years.

CHAPTER FIVE

The Lower Limb

The **lower limb** consists of the following major elements: the **pelvic girdle** (which, in turn, is made up of a right and a left hip bone or **os coxa** (often referred to as the **innominate**; pl. **os coxae**), each of which articulates posteriorly or dorsally with the upper segments of the sacrum and which together articulate anteriorly or ventrally at the pubic symphysis; the **femur** or thigh bone; the **patella** or knee cap; the **tibia** and **fibula**, which constitute the leg proper; and the **foot** (which contains the bones of the ankle region or **tarsals**, the **metatarsals** or "long bones" of the body of the foot, and the **phalanges** or toes).

Pelvic Girdle

Morphology

[Because the sacrum has been dealt with elsewhere (Chapter 3) in conjunction with the vertebral column, only the os coxa (Figure 5–1) will be discussed here.]

The **os coxa** is a large, oddly shaped bone which, when viewed laterally, gives the appearance of a misshapen, top-heavy hourglass. Viewed from above, the superior and inferior portions of the os coxae lie at approximately right angles to one another, seemingly being rotated around the "waist" of the hourglass. Dominant in this constricted region is the socket—the *acetabulum*—in which the head of the femur articulates. In the adult, a raised and thickened anteroinferiorly incomplete (and thus horseshoe-shaped) band—the *lunate surface*—courses just within the rim of the acetabulum.

Beneath the two ends of the lunate surface lies a large foramen—the *obturator foramen*—which is characteristically ovoid in males and triangular in females. Occasionally, the continuous part of the lunate surface may be interrupted: that is, there may be a small, roughened triangular region or a more extensive disruption, which, in its extreme expression, presents itself as a distinct and superiorly elongate crease; these configurations may occur uni- or bilaterally. These disruptions betray the fact that, developmentally, the acetabulum represents a region of fusion between three ontogenetically distinct bones: the **ilium** superiorly and, below it, the **pubis** and the **ischium**.

The **ilium** is the largest of the three bones of the os coxa. It is described as variably "blade-like," which reflects the fact that it is somewhat thin, anteroposteriorly deep, and squat. The bulk of the ilium lies posteriorly; the anterior region is quite truncated. A somewhat "U"-shaped notch—the *greater sciatic notch*—is subtended on its superior side by the inferior border of the posterior portion of the ilium, and, on its anterior side, by the posterosuperior portion of the ischium. The greater sciatic notch tends to be narrower and may appear deeply invaginated in males; in females, it is characteristically more obtuse and appears shallower. The outer surface of the ilium is gently sinuous, bulging outward in the region above the acetabulum and then smoothly curving inward until, at its most posterior extent, it again swings out more boldly. Internally (medially), the ilium is continuously concave up to its area of articulation with the sacrum. The **arcuate line**,

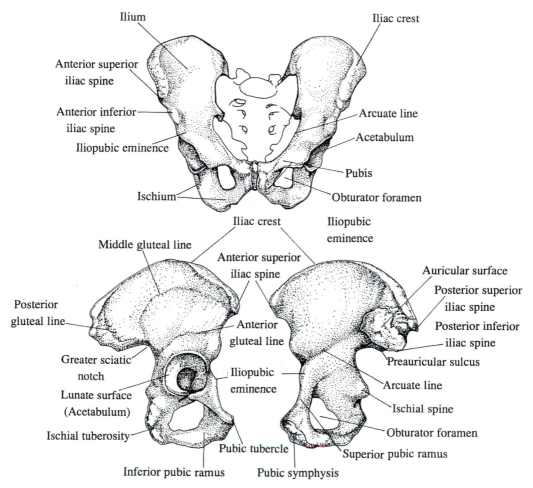

Figure 5-1 Articulated pelvis with image of sacrum, anterior view *(top); (bottom)* right os coxa [*(left)* medial and *(right)* lateral views].

which highlights the curvature of the ilium from the sacroiliac articulation and along the long axis of the superior pubic ramus, forms an inferior border to the internal aspect of the ilium. The arcuate line tends to be more rugose in males than in females.

The superior margin of the ilium is the *iliac crest*. The iliac crest is superiorly arcuate (more noticeably in males than in females) and irregularly thickened. It is thickest in the region near the highest part of the arc of the crest. This thickened region is thicker and more pointed in males than in females, in whom it is longer and less protrusive.

The iliac crest terminates anteriorly in a blunt "point," the *anterior superior iliac spine.* Posteriorly, the iliac crest thickens broadly into the *posterior superior iliac spine,* which projects

posteriorly beyond the sacrum and its vertebral spines. The bone beneath each superior iliac spine is indented to some degree. Below each indentation lies another spine—that is, respectively, the anterior and *posterior inferior iliac spines.* The anterior inferior iliac spine presents itself as a knobby projection immediately above the level of the rim of the acetabulum; its posterior counterpart, which participates in the articulation with the sacrum, is laterally more compressed and may be more spikelike. A swollen to rugose eminence—the *iliopubic eminence*—lies below the anterior inferior iliac spine. Not to be confused with the posterior inferior iliac spine (although it often is) is another spinelike projection 1 to 2 cm away that subtends the ilial portion of the greater sciatic notch. This particular unnamed bony distension may protrude into the space of the notch, thus giving the impression that the notch is narrower than it really is. If the effect of the intrusive component on the shape of the greater sciatic notch is not taken into consideration, the angle of the notch will be incorrectly assessed.

The outer surface of the ilium bears muscle scars. Sometimes more markedly expressed in males than in females, these muscle scars correspond to the attachment sites of the gluteal muscles, which insert upon the femur; all of these scars arc anteroposteriorly from top to bottom. The *posterior* or *superior gluteal line* is usually confined to the region just in front of the posterior superior iliac spine. The *middle gluteal line* courses from in front of and immediately below the midanterior thickening of the iliac crest. The *anterior* or *inferior gluteal line* originates above the anterior inferior iliac spine and fades out along the posterior rim of the acetabulum.

The inner surface of the ilium is relatively smooth, with the exception of its posterior, *auricular* (i.e. *sacral articular*) *surface*. The auricular (sacral articular) surface consists of two distinct components: one superior and the other inferior to it. The superior component is variably craggy in appearance and may bear accessory articular facets. The inferior articular region is club-shaped in outline: it is broadest where it abuts the arcuate line and tapers as it courses to the end of the posterior inferior iliac spine. The surface of the inferior component of the auricular surface is more granular than the superior component.

Immediately below the distinct inferior edge of this club-shaped inferior articular component and coursing beneath the posterior inferior iliac spine may lie a groove, called the *preauricular sulcus*. Sometimes the preauricular sulcus is quite shallow and minimally expressed; at other times, it may be well excavated and course along the entire length of the inferior edge of the auricular region. Some authorities consider the presence/absence of the preauricular sulcus to be reflective of, respectively, female/male dimorphism (e.g. St. Hoyme and İşcan, 1989); others regard the development of this feature as a non-sex-related nonmetric variant among humans (e.g. Finnegan, 1978).

Right and left os coxae articulate anteriorly at the midline. This region is called the *pubic*

symphysis, at which the two adjacent pubic surfaces are separated by a cartilaginous interpubic disc. The surface of the pubic bone contributing to the pubic symphysis is roughly lozenge-shaped. The shape, texture, and external morphology of this region change with the increasing age of the individual (see Chapter 7).

The **pubis** is composed of two branches or rami that extend as arms of a "V" away from the midline symphyseal region (i.e. the *pubic symphysis*). The *superior pubic ramus* encompasses that portion of the acetabulum lying anterior to the anterior inferior iliac spine, and it subtends the obturator foramen superiorly. A few centimeters lateral to the pubic symphysis, the superior margin of the superior pubic ramus bears a variably blunt to peaked tubercle, the *pubic tubercle.* The region between the tubercle and the pubic symphysis is roughened. The superior pubic ligament courses across the roughened region to the tubercle. The inguinal ligament stretches between the pubic tubercle and the anterior superior iliac spine.

The *inferior pubic ramus* courses inferiorly and laterally away from the symphysis. It joins with an ascending ramus of the ischium to form the medially oblique boundary of the obturator foramen. The juncture of the inferior pubic ramus and the ischium may be indicated by a slight pinching of the bone.

The *ischium* encompasses essentially the inferior half of the acetabular region. Posterior and slightly inferior to the acetabulum, the protrusive *ischial spine* delineates the inferior limit of the greater sciatic notch. Below the acetabulum, the ischium continues as a short, stout ramus, which is capped inferiorly by the roughened, subdivided, *ischial tuberosity.* The upper and broader component of this tuberosity is noticeably flatter than the lower portion, from which it is delineated by a transverse ridge. The inferior portion of the ischial tuberosity bears a longitudinal ridge. The thinner portion of the ischium, which joins the inferior pubic ramus, courses up from the region of the ischial tuberosity.

Development and Ossification

Ossification of the os coxa (Figure 5–2) begins with the appearance of three centers in the general region of what will become the acetabulum.

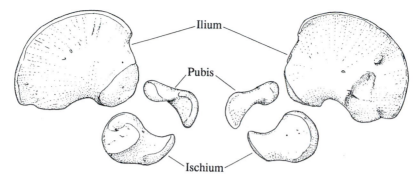

Figure 5–2 Right ilium, pubis, and ischium of third-trimester fetus: *(left)* lateral and *(right)* medial views.

The first center of ossification, which corresponds to the presumptive ilium, appears above the area of the future greater sciatic notch by the end of the second or the beginning of the third fetal month. By the middle of the fourth month, the ilial contribution to the acetabulum and posterior inferior iliac spine are discernible; thus, the greater sciatic notch is identifiable. Within a few weeks, the presumptive anterior inferior iliac spine becomes distinct. The second center of ossification appears inferiorly along the body of the ischium as early as the third or as late as the fifth fetal month. The characteristic shape of the ischium is attained prenatally. As an isolated bone, the ischium looks somewhat like a comma or hook, with its thickened end contributing to the acetabular region, its "stem" circumscribing the obturator foramen from behind, and its hooked end pointing anteriorly and superiorly. The third center of ossification arises in the presumptive superior pubic ramus sometimes as early as the fourth but more typically during the fifth or sixth fetal month. Throughout intrauterine life and until the os coxa unites as a whole, the pubis presents itself as a smaller mirror image of the ischium: Its thickened end contributes to the acetabulum, its stem subtends the obturator foramen from above, and its shorter hooked end points inferiorly and somewhat posteriorly toward the hooked end of the ischium. (If the acetabular region is thought of as a hinge, the ischium and pubis vaguely resemble the arms of a spreading caliper.)

At birth, the ilium, pubis, and ischium are separated from one another by a thick, "Y"-shaped *triradiate cartilage,* which constitutes the acetabular region. Also present are four sec-ondary centers of ossification, corresponding to the ischial tuberosity, the pubic symphysis, the anterior inferior iliac spine, and the iliac crest. Between the second and sixth postnastal months, the acetabulum, although small, has assumed the shape of a shallow cup; ossification continues such that each of the three bones extends increasingly farther into the acetabular region. Coalescence of the pubis and ischium around the obturator foramen is usually well advanced by the age of 6 years and virtually complete by the eighth year. Between the ages of 9 and 12 years, ossification in the triradiate cartilage via one or more centers commences. Ossification and union in the acetabulum occurs first between the pubis and the ilium, then between the ilium and the ischium, and, finally, between the pubis and the ischium. These three bones may become unified across the acetabulum between the ages of 14 and 16 or as late as 18 years. Onset of ossification in the remaining elements usually coincides with the onset of puberty; the union of these secondary elements to the bulk of the os coxa commences around the age of 16 or 17 years and is completed between the ages of 23 and 25 years.

Femur

Morphology

The thigh-bone or **femur** (Figure 5–3); which constitutes the upper leg, is the largest and sturdiest of the long bones. It articulates proximally with the acetabulum and distally with the proximal tibia; the patella rides anteriorly over the distal articular region of the femur. The long femoral *shaft* is essentially smooth along much of its anterior surface; its posterior surface is

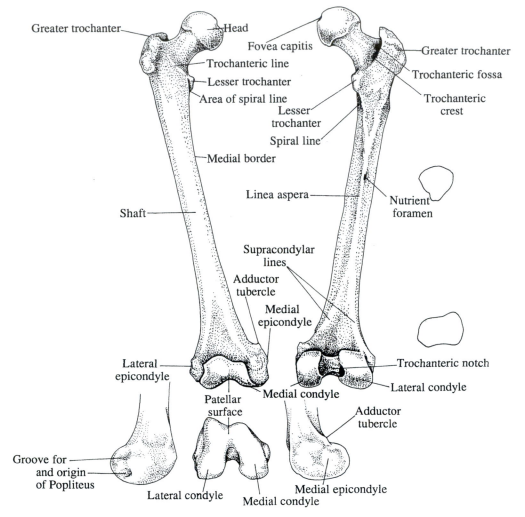

Figure 5–3 Right femur: *(top left)* anterior and *(top middle)* posterior views; *(top right)* cross sections through shaft; *(bottom)* distal end [*(left)* lateral, (middle) distal, and *(right)* medial views].

more rugose and anatomically detailed. The *greater trochanter* lies parallel to the long axis of the femoral shaft, cupping it proximally and anteroposteriorly. In lateral aspect, the greater trochanter broadens the proximal femur anteroposteriorly. Coursing across the anterior face of the proximal femur, from the raised medial aspect of the greater trochanter to the *medial border* of the shaft, is a variably rugose and thickened bony line or band called the *trochanteric line*. Posteriorly, the greater trochanter forms a vertical, liplike projection that is further accentuated medially by a moderate to large pit, the *trochanteric fossa*. Confluent with and continuing down and arcing medially away from

the thick edge of the vertically projecting greater trochanter is the expanded *trochanteric crest*, which terminates in a moderately pointed to broad *lesser trochanter*. When the femur is viewed anteriorly one can see the lesser trochanter projecting beyond the medial border of the shaft. Extending superiorly and medially from the region sandwiched between the trochanteric line and trochanteric crest is the stout, short, slightly laterally compressed *neck* of the femur, which tapers slightly and then broadens in all directions. The neck is capped by the semispherical *femoral head*. Typically posterior if not also somewhat inferior to the center of the femoral head lies a variably broadly shallow to deeply constricted pit—the *fovea capitis*—in which the ligament of the femoral head attaches.

A muscle scar descending from the inferior region of the greater trochanter eventually thickens into the *gluteal tuberosity* at a level below the lesser trochanter. The gluteal tuberosity is approximately a few centimeters in length. It is more like a raised band than a projection and constitutes the scar left by the gluteus maximus muscle. An enlarged, medially projecting gluteal tuberosity occurs in humans as a nonmetric *variant;* in these instances, it is identified as a *third trochanter*. (In prosimian primates and mammals in general, the development of a third trochanter is the rule.)

The feature identified as the *spiral line* may present itself as a continuation of the trochanteric line, or it may originate along the medial border of the femoral shaft, just inferior to the trochanteric line. The spiral line passes well below the lesser trochanter and courses to the midline of the shaft posteriorly to become confluent with the inferiormost extension of the gluteal tuberosity. It is near this confluence, which typically occurs less than halfway down the shaft, that one often encounters a moderately elongate and slitlike *nutrient foramen* penetrating the femoral shaft obliquely and in an upward direction (away from the knee). The merging of the spiral line and the gluteal tuberosity creates a single, greatly thickened and raised, squared and/or broad, muscle scar, the *linea aspera*. This prominent posterior femoral feature may continue an additional one-quarter to one-third of the way down the shaft before it begins to fade and subsequently bifurcate into *medial* and *lateral supracondylar lines*, which diverge as they course inferiorly and to their respective sides of the distally widening bone. These supracondylar lines, of which the medial tends to be the more obscure, subtend a somewhat posteriorly flattened, tall, triangular region identified as the *popliteal surface* (the anterior surface is also somewhat flattened distally). Variably near the apex of the triangular popliteal surface but more consistently closer to the medial supracondylar line, one may find a second nutrient foramen. This additional nutrient foramen, although sometimes larger than the primary nutrient foramen, is nonetheless similarly elongate and slitlike and

perforates the shaft obliquely and in an upward direction.

The supracondylar lines terminate distally in swellings called *epicondyles*—the *medial* and *lateral epicondyles*. The medial supracondylar line also thickens into a sometimes crestlike tubercle, the *adductor tubercle,* which lies atop the medial epicondyle. The bulk of the distal end of the femur consists of two large *condyles,* from the sides of which the two epicondyles bulge. The *medial* and *lateral condyles* are swollen posteriorly and separated by a deep *intercondylar notch*. Each condyle bears a characteristically smooth *articular surface* which originates just below the popliteal surface and wraps around the posteriorly swollen condyle. At about the midpoint of the inferior surface, the two articular areas merge around the intercondylar notch into one articular surface, which, in turn, proceeds to overlap the distal end anteriorly, eventually forming the *patellar surface*. The patellar surface is concave, due to the protrusion anteriorly of the medial and lateral condyles. This concave patellar surface is asymmetrical because the lateral condyle protrudes farther anteriorly than the medial condyle. The concaveness and asymmetry of the patellar surface mirrors the configuration of the posterior surface of the patella.

When the femur is viewed distally while on its posterior side, the condyles approximate, respectively, the perpendicular and long sides of an isosceles triangle: the lateral condyle is more or less vertical (and in line with the lateral side of the femoral shaft), the apex of the triangle is the farthest point anteriorly of the articular surface, and the medial condyle appears to course (albeit arcuately) from this apex to the most posterior and medial corner of the distal articular region. Also apparent when the femur is lying in this position is (1) the difference between the medial and lateral epicondyles (the medial is arcuate, longer, and more swollen, whereas the lateral appears more confined and ridgelike, even though it contributes anteriorly to much more than half of the patellar surface); and (2) the twist in the shaft of the femur (i.e. the medial border of the shaft becomes more delineated in its upper portion and the head and neck of the femur, which are oriented obliquely and anteriorly, are not in the same plane as the condyles).

In addition to being somewhat "bowed" or curved anteriorly, the femur does not assume the perpendicular while in the anatomical position. Holding the femur upright so that it is resting flat on its condyles, one can see the outward or lateral orientation of the long axis of the bone. One can also appreciate the distinctions between the medial and lateral condyles (the lateral is shorter, protrudes anteriorly, and is oriented essentially anteroposteriorly, while the medial is obliquely skewed outward and posteriorly) as well as the degree to which the femur is twisted slightly superiorly and the head and neck are oriented anteriorly.

Development and Ossification

Ossification in the shaft of the femur (Figure 5–4) usually begins by the end of the seventh fetal week. (The femur is the second bone of the body to begin to ossify, following quickly on the heels of the clavicle.) By birth, the only other sign of mineralization may be the presence of a secondary center of ossification in the middle of the distal epiphysis. In 7% of individuals, this center may arise 1 or perhaps even 2 months prior to term, whereas in 12% of individuals, this center appears after birth. Ossification in the

distal epiphysis gives rise to the condyles and the epicondyles. The head of the femur begins to ossify by the end of the first year, the greater trochanter during the fourth year, and the lesser trochanter between the thirteenth and fourteenth years. Fusion of these elements to the shaft of the femur does not occur until after puberty, starting at about 15 years with the lesser trochanter and then proceeding to the greater trochanter, the head, and finally the distal epiphysis. The proximal femoral elements unite with the shaft between the ages of 18 and 20 years, prior to fusion of the distal epiphysis (at 20 to 23 years). The femoral and pelvic contributions to the hip region solidify before those of the knee joint. The typical shape of the femur can be recognized well before birth.

Patella

In basic outline, the **patella** (Figure 5–5) looks more or less like a guitar pick. Its *base* is broadly arcuate superiorly and its *apex* points inferiorly. The *anterior* and *posterior surfaces* are distinctly different from one another. The anterior patellar surface is somewhat roughened and, to varying degrees, bears markings or even plate-like scars left by the quadriceps femoris tendon, which encapsulates the bone. The posterior surface is dominated by the large, smooth *posterior articular facet,* below which the apex of the patella extends. Since this posterior articular facet articulates with the femoral patellar facet, it mirrors the anterior configuration of the femoral condyles: it is convex, but asymmetrically so. The roundedly ridgelike, vertical "peak" of the surface separates a long, gently sloping *lateral facet* from a more steeply inclined *medial facet.* In turn, the medial facet is subdivided into an upper and an even more steeply inclined but

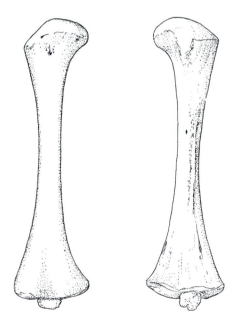

Figure 5–4 Right femur, with ossifying distal epiphysis, of third-trimester fetus: *(left)* anterior and *(right)* posterior views.

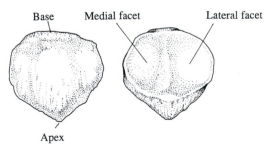

Figure 5–5 Right patella: *(left)* anterior and *(right)* posterior views.

smaller lower section. The long lateral slope corresponds to the greater contribution of the lateral condyle to the femoral patellar facet. The shorter medial slope corresponds to the lesser contribution of the medial condyle to the femoral patellar facet. The smaller, lower portion of the medial facet contacts the medial condyle of the femur when the knee joint is in extreme flexion. One can distinguish quite easily right from left patellae because the bone, when placed on its asymmetric posterior surface, always comes to lie on the longer, larger, lateral portion of the facet (i.e. lying to the side of the body from which it came). The patella ossifies from several centers that may begin to appear as early as the second year or as late as the sixth year.

Tibia

Morphology

The **tibia** (Figure 5–6) is the second longest bone of the leg as well as of the skeleton. It is easily distinguished from its smaller and slenderer partner in the lower leg, the fibula.

The *proximal end* of the tibia is broad, especially laterally. It bears two subequal condyles whose superior articular surfaces correspond to and reflect similar differences between the medial and lateral condyles of the femur, with which it articulates. Thus the *medial condyle* of the tibia tends to be longer than the *lateral condyle*. The lateral condyle is distinguished further from the medial condyle because, posterolaterally, it bears a somewhat inferiorly directed, variably ovoid or elliptical facet for articulation superiorly with the fibula. The tibial condyles protrude posteriorly beyond both the neck and shaft of the bone.

Both tibial condylar articular surfaces are somewhat lima bean–shaped, with the counterpart of the seed's scar being a raised, sometimes rather sharply delineated prominence called the *intercondylar eminence*. There are thus two intercondylar eminences. The region between these two eminences may be delineated further by a shallow depression. Two semitrapezoidally shaped depressed areas expand outward—a large one anteriorly and a smaller one posteriorly—from the region of the intercondylar eminences. Variably impressed upon these depressed regions as well as upon the area between the intercondylar eminences are the attachment sites of the (semilunar and cruciate) ligaments that secure the knee joint.

The proximal end of the tibia is expanded anteriorly by the *tibial tubercle,* to which the patellar ligament attaches superiorly. This tubercle may be delineated superiorly by a fairly horizontal groove. A variably distinct and distended crest may also lie 1 to 2 cm below this groove. The tibial tubercle is the proximal terminus of the *anterior border* of the tibial shaft.

The *anterior border* emanates from the region of the *medial malleolus* of the distal tibia (see below) as a low, rounded margin. It typically becomes sharply and crisply defined as it comes to swing laterally beyond the midshaft and then broadens as it courses toward the tibial tubercle. The lateral aspect of this border remains crisp as it arcs from the tibial tubercle to the lateralmost limit of the lateral condyle. [Thus the morphology of the anterior border of the tibia and the direction of its course along the tibial shaft are relatively consistent clues not only in identifying bone fragments as being tibial in origin but also in determining whether the fragment is from the right or left side (i.e. the more sharply delineated border of the tibial tubercle swings laterally, or to the side of the body from which the bone comes).]

Other aspects of the shaft of the tibia also are distinctive. For instance, in cross section, the shaft remains roughly triangular throughout most of its length: the anterior border is the triangle's apex; the *posterior surface*, like the triangle's base, is somewhat flat; and the posterolateral edge or *interosseous border* is angularly defined and almost cornerlike along much if not all of the length of the shaft. The upper third or so of the posterior surface of the tibial shaft bears two major landmarks that distinguish it further. These are (1) a rough muscle scar, the *soleal line* (created by the attachment of fascia associated with the soleus muscle as well as the popliteus and deep muscles of the leg), which courses obliquely from just below the lateral condyle to the medial border of the bone; and (2) a typically very long and slitlike *nutrient foramen*, which enters the bone steeply from above and is located in the region between the soleal line and the interosseous border.

The *distal end* of the tibia differs markedly in

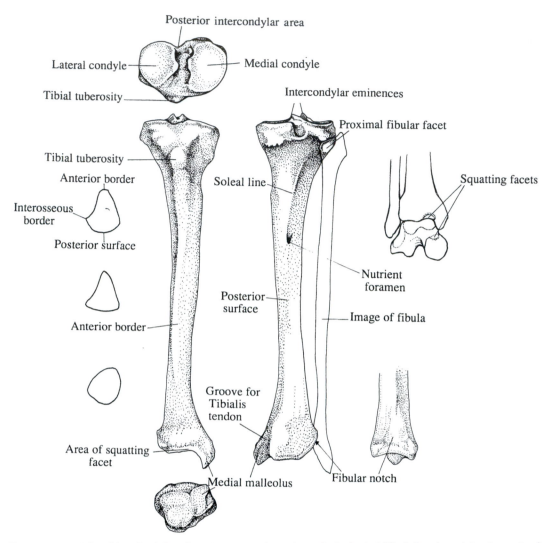

Figure 5–6   Right tibia: *(far left column)* cross sections through shaft; *(middle left column) (top)* proximal, *(middle)* anterior, and *(bottom)* distal views; *(middle right column)* posterior view with image of fibula; *(far right column) (top)* articulated distal tibia and fibula with talus, anterior view, and *(bottom)* distal end of tibia, medial view.

shape from and lies in a different plane than the proximal end. When the tibia is placed with its anterior surface facing up (and is thus lying on the posterior edges of both condyles), the medial, inferiorly distended "hook" or *malleolus* of the distal end is oriented upward approximately 45°. This *medial malleolus* ("malleolus" meaning "little hammer") also expands the distal portion of the tibia medially. When viewed from the medial side, the asymmetry of the malleolus is obvious (it is more inferiorly distended along its anterior portion), as is its narrowness

(when compared to the lateral side of the distal end of the tibia).

The *medial malleolus* is rather rugose and flat across most of its medial surface and is delineated from the distended anterior region below by an oblique and crest- or ridgelike edge; this crest is confluent with the lower extent of the anterior border of the tibia (described above). The medial malleolar surface also bears a posterior, somewhat vertical edge or crest (which extends a few centimeters superiorly along the shaft of the tibia); this crest subtends, just on the posterior surface, a *groove for the tibialis posterior tendon*. The posterior malleolar crest joints the anterior and more oblique crest described above to form an apex, which may lie to one side or the other of a variably excavated concavity. This concavity separates the anterior and inferior distension of the malleolus from the slightly swollen inferior extension of bone that bears the groove for the tibialis posterior tendon.

On the anterior side of the distal end of the tibia, the medial malleolus is delineated by a variably pronounced concavity that is also variably confluent with one or more depressions along the region of the *epiphyseal line*. At times, a continuous, thin, undulating groove may incise the epiphyseal line anteriorly; nonetheless, approximately midway along its course, this groove will be accentuated if not also briefly interrupted by a small swelling of bone. Just superior to the depression that is closest to the medial malleolus, the lower end of the tibia tends to bulge. The anterodistal margin, in conjunction with the medial malleolus, is thus particularly telling in the identification of tibial fragments and the determination of the side of the body from which a fragment comes.

The lateralmost limit of the anterior face of the distal end of the tibia often looks in profile like a corner whose point has been cut off obliquely. The surface of this region also tends to be rather rugose. The lateral edge of this "corner" is typically quite crest- or ridgelike; it extends inward as well as superiorly, often becoming confluent with the interosseous line. This lateral crest or ridge also subtends on one side a somewhat triangular depression. This lateral depression broadens as it descends to the inferior border of the distal tibia. Part of the lower portion of the shaft of the fibula nestles in this rather large triangular depression, the *fibular notch*.

The posterior surface of the distal end of the tibia is similar to the anterior surface in general outline. However, the posterior surface is distinguished, for example, by the groove for the tibialis posterior tendon and by the fact that it bears the shorter side of the medial malleolus. The lateralmost extent of the posterior surface is somewhat similar to its anterior counterpart in being a "corner without a corner." However, it is different in that it is less distended laterally

and bears a variably developed crest, which can be weakly pronounced in some individuals or sufficiently marked to become confluent with the interosseous line. This crest, which courses superiorly as well as inward, subtends the other side of the fibular notch.

The distal surface of the tibia is represented by a large articular region, which partially cups the superior portion of the talus from above as well as medially. A large, subtrapezoidal articular facet—which is broader laterally than it is medially—courses across the inferior surface of the distal end of the tibia, "kinks" at approximately a 90° angle at the base of the medial malleolus, and then proceeds to cover most of the inner surface of the malleolus. Anteriorly, at the base of the medial malleolus, the continuity of the articular surface might be disrupted either slightly by a minor "pinching" or more markedly by a definite crease or looplike invasion of nonarticular bone.

Midway along the anterior edge of the distal margin of the tibia one may find on occasion a distinctly delineated ovoid or elliptical surface. In such instances the structure is an articular facet, which develops as a result of constant contact with the head talus. Contact between the head of the talus and the anterodistal margin of the tibia is achieved when the ankle is in extreme flexion *(hyperflexion)*, as when squatting, thus creating what are referred to as *"squatting facets."* Often overlooked in looking for the squatting facet on the tibia is the squatting facet that also develops on the superior surface of the head of the talus. Although squatting facets on the anterodistal margin of the tibia are the most common examples given in osteology textbooks, there are many more that have been identified on the tibia, some of which reflect extreme flexion at the ankle, while others reflect extreme flexion at the knee joint (see review by Kennedy, 1989): for example, a rounded posterior margin of the lateral condyle, a twisting backward (retroversion) of the head, and a groove on the side of tibial tubercle created by the patellar ligament.

Development and Ossification

Ossification of the tibia (Figure 5–7) begins in the shaft during the eighth fetal week, a week or so after the femur. At birth the only other

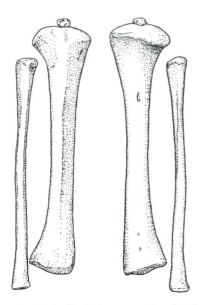

Figure 5–7 Right fibula *(outermost)* and right tibia with ossifying proximal epiphysis *(innermost)* of third-trimester fetus: *(left)* anterior and *(right)* posterior views.

tibial region to have begun to ossify is the proximal epiphysis, in which the secondary center usually arises shortly before term (this center, however, may not appear until just after birth). The shape of the tibia is recognizable early on, as is that of the proximal epiphysis (including an anterior projection that corresponds to the tibial tuberosity). Ossification of the distal epiphysis begins during the second year; fusion to the shaft commences at about the age of 16 years and complete union occurs between 18 and 20 years. Coalescence of the proximal epiphysis to the shaft also begins at about 16 years, but complete fusion does not occur until later, between the ages of 20 and 23 years. Once the distal epiphysis has begun to ossify, one can easily recognize it by its shape, which is retained into adulthood.

Fibula

Morphology

The **fibula** (Figures 5–6 and 5–8) is a long, slender bone that articulates with the lateral side of the tibia at two points: (1) proximally, on the inferior and posterolateral aspect of the lateral condyle, and (2) distally, in a relatively long, shallow, somewhat triangular depression (whose "base" is formed by the distolateral margin). The distal portion of the fibula, which extends below the level of the medial malleolus of the tibia, forms the lateral wall of the "cup" in which the superior portion of the talus nestles.

The fibula is distinguished by its sharp, crisp, longitudinal borders and edges. At first glance, its proximal and distal ends appear similar in overall shape, including being pointed. However, close inspection reveals that the *proximal end* or *head* of the fibula is much bulkier and more expanded three-dimensionally than the distal end. These features are exaggerated further by the presence of a severely constricted *neck* and a profile that approximates the shape of an equilateral triangle. In marked contrast, the *distal end* or *lateral malleolus* is broader, flatter, and compressed laterally; its outline resembles more closely that of a right-angled triangle. In addition, the pointedness of the fibular head is often more acute, forming a *styloid process,* whereas the terminus of the lateral malleolus tends to be blunter.

The styloid process of the fibular head nestles up against the tibia's lateral condyle posteriorly. Thus the styloid process of the fibula bears internally an articular facet which mirrors that on the tibia; this facet varies in size from individual to individual. Below the styloid process, the fibular head is somewhat swollen into a "heel" that embraces the tibial condyle inferiorly and laterally. This heel may receive on its internal surface the proximal terminus of the thickened and flattened *anterior surface,* which itself is created medially by the sharp *interosseous border* and laterally by the equally distinct *anterior border;* both of these borders course along the fibular shaft.

The opposite and less expanded side of the fibular head may bear a crest that courses inferiorly and may become continuous with the medial border of the fibula. The posterior surface of the fibular head (defined when the fibula is articulated with the tibia) may be rugose, but it is also the most planar part of the head. If the posterior surface is taken as reflecting the orientation of the entire fibular head, one sees that it lies in a plane that is juxtaposed approximately 90° to the plane of the distal end of the fibula. Thus, the major plane of the proximal end of the fibula faces anteroposteriorly while the major plane of the distal end is directed out-

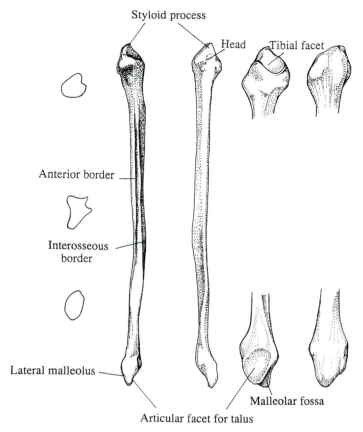

Figure 5–8 Right fibula: *(left)* cross sections through shaft; *(middle pair) (left)* anterior and *(right)* posterior views; *(right pair) (top)* detail of proximal end [*(left)* anteromedial and *(right)* lateral views] and *(bottom)* detail of distal end [*(left)* medial and *(right)* lateral views].

ward or laterally. This twist in the fibula is also reflected somewhat along the shaft of the bone: A concomitant torque in cross-sectional shape (basically, an equilateral triangle with concave sides) twists the courses of the crests and borders.

The *distal end* or *lateral malleolus* of the fibula is somewhat flattened and compressed laterally. Articulated, it nestles into the fibular notch on the distolateral surface of the distal tibia. The shape of the lateral malleolus resembles that of a right-angle triangle (if the base of this triangle is taken as an imaginary line separating the malleolus from the shaft of the fibula—in the subadult individual, the distal epiphyseal line, which tends to persist more visibly internally than externally, would delineate the base of this triangular feature). The posterior border of this bone descends to form the triangle's perpendicular side. The apex of this

right-angle triangle is the most distal and posterior extent of the fibula.

Internally, a large portion of the distal and posterior part of the fibular malleolus is demarcated by a pitted, depressed area called the *malleolar fossa*, to which attach the various tibiofibular ligaments. Superior and anterior to the malleolar fossa is the edge of a large *articular facet for the talus*, which is shaped more or less like an (upside down) equilateral triangle, whose base is usually delineated by the epiphyseal line. The posterior face of the lateral malleolus is bisected by a variably excavated and vertically pervasive groove through which traverse the tendons of the peroneus brevis and peroneus longus muscles. [The peroneus brevis inserts onto the lateral tubercle on the base of the fifth metatarsal and the peroneus longus onto (at least) the lateral sides of the base of the first metatarsal and the medial cuneiform; both muscles participate, among other actions, in eversion of the foot.]

Development and Ossification

Ossification of the fibula (Figure 5–7) begins in the shaft during the eighth fetal week, coincident with the onset of ossification in the shaft of the tibia. Initially, the fibula and tibia are the same length. From about the middle of the third fetal month through term, the tibia is noticeably longer than the fibula. Subsequently, although the tibia remains the longer of the two bones, the difference in length is not as marked. Ossification of the distal fibular epiphysis begins during the second year and that of the proximal epiphysis between the third and fourth years. Fusion of both ends to the shaft may begin at about 16 years of age, with complete union of the distal end occurring at approximately 20 years and of the proximal end between 23 and 25 years. The general shape of the fibula is recognizable early on.

The Foot

The **foot** (pes) is composed of 7 **tarsal bones** (short bones of the ankle region), which make up the **tarsus;** 5 **metatarsal bones** (lying just anterior to the tarsals), which constitute the **metatarsus;** and 14 **phalanges** (lying just anterior to the metatarsals), which are the bones of the **pedal digits** or toes. The general arrangement of the bones of the foot and ankle is similar, respectively, to that of the hand and wrist. Because of the orientation of the foot, the directional terms "inferior," "plantar," and "distal" are often used interchangeably, as are "superior" and "proximal." With regard to "anterior" and "posterior," for example, the heads of the metatarsals lie anteriorly (ventrally) and their bases posteriorly (dorsally); the phalanges lie anterior and the tarsals posterior to the metatarsals.

Tarsus

Morphology

The **tarsal bones** of the **tarsus** (Figures 5–9 and 5–10) are arranged in two rows. The **talus** and the **calcaneus** (also referred to as the *calcaneum*) constitute the **first** or **proximal row.** The talus sites on top and to the medial side of center of

the calcaneus and constitutes the primary contact between the bones of the foot and leg. The **second** or **distal row** of tarsals is composed of two subsets. The **navicular** bone (medially) and the **cuboid** (laterally) articulate with the heads of the talus and calcaneus, respectively. However, while the fourth and fifth metatarsals articulate directly with the cuboid, three other bones—the **medial, intermediate,** and **lateral cuneiforms**—intervene between the navicular bone and the first, second, and third metatarsals, respectively.

Development and Ossification

Ossification of the tarsus (Figure 5–11) variably commences with the calcaneus and the talus. A center of ossification may appear in the body of the calcaneus during the twelfth fetal week or be delayed until sometime during the seventh month. Ossification in the body of the talus often begins during the latter part of the sixth fetal month. At birth, the only other area of mineralization in the tarsus could be in the cuboid: ossification might begin late in the ninth month, but it could also be delayed until shortly after birth. After the cuboid, ossification commences sequentially in the lateral cuneiform (the first year), the medial cuneiform (second to fourth year), and then the intermediate cuneiform and navicular (third to fifth year). Ossification of the calcaneal epiphysis begins as early as the seventh or as late as the tenth year; fusion of the epiphysis with the body begins at about 12 years and complete union occurs between 20 and 22 years. Sometimes a separate center of ossification gives rise to the posterior process of the talus. If this region of ossification does not coalesce with the body of the bone, it remains as a small, sesamoidlike bone called the *os trigonum.*

Talus

The **talus** (Figure 5–9) is a stout, asymmetrical bone. (Impressionistically, a talus looks like a subtubular object that has been cut into top and bottom halves, with the bottom half then displaced anteriorly half a length.) The talus articulates (1) with the distal tibial facet above it via its trochlear surface; (2) medially, with the me-

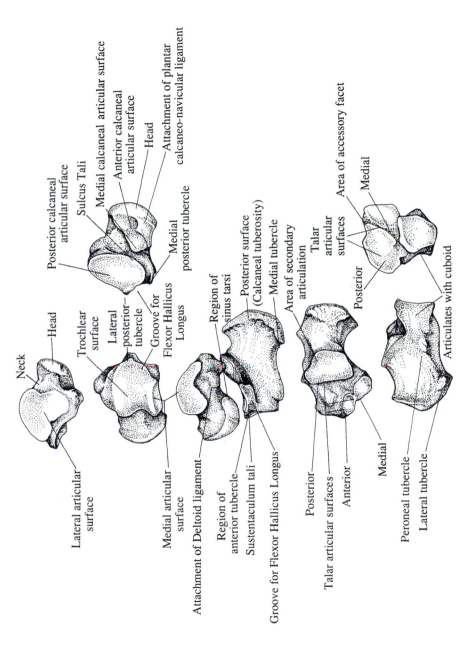

Neck

Head

Lateral articular surface

Posterior calcaneal articular surface

Sulcus Tali

Medial calcaneal articular surface

Anterior calcaneal articular surface

Head

Attachment of plantar calcaneo-navicular ligament

Medial posterior tubercle

Trochlear surface

Lateral posterior tubercle

Groove for Flexor Hallicus Longus

Medial articular surface

Attachment of Deltoid ligament

Region of anterior tubercle

Sustentaculum tali

Groove for Flexor Hallicus Longus

Region of sinus tarsi

Posterior surface (Calcaneal tuberosity)

Medial tubercle

Area of secondary articulation

Area of accessory facet

Medial

Talar articular surfaces

Posterior

Articulates with cuboid

Posterior

Talar articular surfaces

Anterior

Medial

Peroneal tubercle

Lateral tubercle

Figure 5–9 Right talus and calcaneus (proximal row of tarsus): *(left column, from top to bottom)* talus, lateral view; talus, superior view; talus and calcaneus, medial view; calcaneus, superior view; and calcaneus, lateral view; *(top right)* talus, inferior view; *(bottom right)* calcaneus, anterior view.

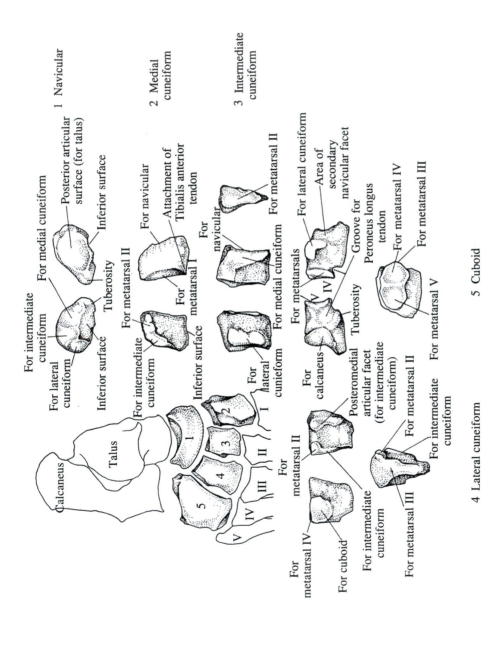

Figure 5–10 (*Top left*) semiarticulated tarsus emphasizing distal row; (*right, from top to bottom*) navicular [(*left*) anterior and (*right*) posterior views], medial cuneiform [(*left*) lateral and (*right*) medial views], intermediate cuneiform [(*left*) lateral and (*right*) medial views], cuboid [(*left*) lateral and (*right*) medial views], cuboid, anterior view; (*left, far bottom*) lateral cuneiform, anterior view; (*left, bottom*) lateral cuneiform [(*left*) lateral and (*right*) medial views].

Figure 5–11 Bones of left foot of third-trimester fetus, plantar surface.

dial malleolus of the tibia; and (3) laterally, with the lateral malleolus of the fibula. Anteriorly, the semi-ball-shaped head of the talus is received by the shallow, cup-shaped posterior articular region of the navicular bone. Inferiorly and somewhat posteriorly, the head of the talus articulates superiorly with portions of the calcaneus. Most of the inferior surface of the body of the talus articulates with the underlying calcaneus. The talus does not anchor any muscles, but many ligaments attach to it.

The superior portion of the talus—the *trochlear surface,* which articulates with the tibia distally—is composed largely of an arced, semilunate articular surface with blunt, almost parallel medial and lateral edges; the lateral edge is somewhat shorter than the medial edge. The region between these two edges is depressed slightly, giving the surface the appearance of a shallow pulley. The articular facet "drapes" over the sides of the elevated eminence, with the *lateral articular surface* (for the lateral malleolus of the fibula) being roundedly triangular in shape and the *medial articular surface* (for the medial malleolus of the tibia) being somewhat lunate. The general configurations of these medial and lateral articular areas conform to the shapes of their respective articular surfaces on the tibia and fibula. When viewed from above, the anterior border of the trochlear surface is often straighter than the posterior border, which may be more arcuate posteriorly. Occasionally, the trochlear surface may be distended by a liplike articular projection that articulates with the medial malleolus of the tibia.

In viewing the talus from above, one can make several observations: (1) The lateral articular surface may be oriented rather vertically, whereas typically the inferior articular area for the lateral malleolus of the fibula is reflected outward. (2) In the anatomical position, the *head* and *neck* of the talus are directed anteriorly relative to the long axis of the body of the talus; because the long axis of the body of the talus is oriented obliquely, it forms an obtuse angle with the long axis of the neck. And (3) the "heel" of the talus is swollen in its midline into an elongate *lateral posterior tubercle;* the lateral posterior tubercle is separated from a bulkier *medial posterior tubercle* by the obliquely inclined and variably distinct *groove for the flexor hallucis longus.*

In lateral aspect, the triangular articular extension of the trochlear surface is dominant. It is circumscribed to some extent on its sides and below by nonarticular bone. It is adorned posteriorly by the variably taillike protrusion of the posterior tubercle. Anteriorly, the neck of the talus is inset medially; its downward angulation is obvious.

In medial aspect, the lateral edge of the trochlear surface rises above the level of the medial edge; the lateral posterior tubercle projects further posteriorly than the medial posterior tubercle. The difference in the configurations of these two tubercles is obvious: the lateral posterior tubercle is inclined superiorly (it rises to a blunt end superiorly), whereas the medial posterior tubercle is truncated and comes to a blunt point inferiorly. The site of *attachment of the deltoid ligament* is marked by a swelling immediately anterior and superior to the medial tubercle; this swelling may be either confluent with the tubercle or more clearly delineated as a separate entity. The *attachment site for the plantar calcaneonavicular ligament* lies near the most inferior and posterior limit of the articular region of the head of the talus. The degree to which this attachment site is discernible is quite *variable:* that is, it may not be distinguishable from the rest of the articular surface of the head of the talus or it may be a distinct, flattened area that may be further demarcated anterosuperiorly and inferoposteriorly by creases or shallow grooves.

Inferiorly, the talus presents itself as two distinct articular regions, one corresponding to the body of the bone and the other to the neck and head. Coursing at approximately 45° relative to the long axis of the body of the talus is a large, concave surface that articulates atop the large, posterior articular surface of the calcaneus. This *posterior calcaneal articular surface (talar articular area for the calcaneus)* is bounded medially first by the thick *medial posterior tubercle* and then by the oblique *groove for the flexor hallucis longus;* the *lateral posterior tubercle* forms the posterior external corner of this groove. This articular surface descends rather drastically from the height of these tubercles but comes to arc more gently as it approaches its most anterior and lateral limit; here, it is more tapered (or at least more rounded) than at the posteromedial edge. The anterolateral portion of this articular surface contributes to the variably developed inferior projection of the facet for the lateral malleolus of the fibula.

The region of the *neck* and *head* of the talus is delineated sharply from the posterior calcaneal articular surface by a deep groove (the *sulcus tali*), which may be variably smooth to deeply pitted. The sulcus tali, which emanates from the anterior face of the medial posterior tubercle and follows its oblique orientation, becomes wider and deeper as it proceeds laterally to the anteriormost extent of the talar head. The articular area on the inferior surface of the neck and head of the talus is narrowest just below the region of the medial posterior tubercle. It expands toward the talar head and encompasses three variably distinct surfaces. The *medial calcaneal articular surface,* which lies immediately below the medial posterior tubercle, may be relatively flat and vaguely triangular in outline; it articulates with the middle articular surface of the calcaneus below it. Another relatively flat but thinner and broader articular surface lies horizontally and thus forms an obtuse angle with the middle calcaneal articular surface behind it. This *anterior calcaneal articular surface* of the talus articulates with the anterior articular surface of the calcaneus. It is variably delineated from the rest of the articular surface of the talar head, which articulates anteriorly with the navicular bone.

Nonmetric variation in the talus is quite common and takes the form of "pinching," "waisting," or even complete subdivision of articular surfaces, especially of the posterior calcaneal articular surface and of the boundary between the middle and anterior calcaneal articular surfaces. As already noted, the attachment sites for the deltoid and plantar calcaneonavicular ligaments are variably delineated. A squatting facet (corresponding to one that may develop on the anterodistal rim of the tibia) may be found on the talus superiorly, at the juncture of the neck and head.

Calcaneus

The **calcaneus** (also *calcaneum*; Figure 5–9), whose posteriormost portion constitutes the heel of the foot, is the largest and most robust tarsal bone. It is much longer and deeper than it is wide. It consists of three morphologically distinct components: (1) an *anterior component,* which provides the articular surfaces for the talus above and the cuboid bone anteriorly; (2) a *posterior element,* which receives the insertions of the calf muscles and therefore provides the lever action of the bone; and (3) an *inferior* or *plantar surface,* which extends for the entire length of the bone. (These distinct components are invaluable clues to orienting the calcaneus properly.)

The articular surfaces of the *anterior component* of the calcaneus mirror in general shape and contour their sister facets on the talus. In order to accommodate the talus, the anterior component of the calcaneus is sharply concave in its midregion, with an oblique crease (the *sulcus calcanei*) separating the *posterior talar articular facet* both from the *anterior talar articular facet* and the medially projecting *middle talar facet.* The posterior facet is more than twice as expansive as the middle facet, which, in turn, is typically much larger than the anterior articular facet. Together with the sulcus tali (on the talus), the sulcus calcanei encloses what is called the *sinus tarsi,* which houses the interosseous talocalcaneal ligament.

Recalling the general configuration of the posterior calcaneal articular facet of the talus (it is concave, obliquely oriented, and tapers laterally), one can see its image mirrored to some extent in the large *posterior talar articular surfaces*. This articular region extends posteriorly over the superior surface of the calcaneus in concert with the variable posterior extension of the talus and, in particular, its lateral posterior tubercle. The degree to which the posterior edge of the posterior talar articular surface is straight and squared up, rounded, or tapering is related to the development of the lateral posterior tubercle of the talus and the skewness of the plane created by the wall of bone that connects the lateral posterior and medial posterior tubercles of the talus. Occasionally a *secondary facet*, corresponding to the lateral posterior tubercle of the talus, develops on the calcaneus just behind the true border of its superior articular surface.

Proceeding anteriorly along the calcaneus, the *posterior talar articular surface* expands medially as it approaches the medially displaced *medial talar articular surface*. At this juncture, the posterior talar articular surface descends almost vertically. At the same time, the breadth of the posterior talar articular surface becomes truncated along its mediolateral surface. The sulcus calcanei separates the middle talar from the posterior talar articular surface. The sulcus calcanei separates the middle talar from the posterior talar articular surface. A pit, which may be either very shallow or very deeply excavated, borders the laterally positioned, inferior terminus of the posterior talar articular surface medially.

The *medial talar articular surface* is elongate and variably but crudely ovoid to elliptical in shape; it may or may not be confluent with the smaller, ovoid, anterior facet below it (the *anterior talar articular surface*). Together, the medial and anterior talar articular surfaces form a slightly concave surface that sits atop a bony strut, the *sustentaculum tali*. The sustentaculum tali projects medially from the body of the calcaneus and is most prominent below the region where the medial talar articular surface lies across from the posterior talar articular surface. The sustentaculum tali (bearing the anterior talar articular surface above it) projects anteriorly beyond the vertical facet for the cuboid (at the front of the calcaneus).

The medial and anterior talar articular surfaces articulate, respectively, with the middle and anterior calcaneal articular facets of the talus. However, there appears to be no correlation between the development of separate middle and anterior facets on the calcaneus and on the talus: these facets may occur as separate entities on one bone but be confluent on the other. The occurrence of separate medial and anterior facets on calcanei and tali is often noted in studies on *nonmetric variation*, as is the absence on the calcaneus of the anterior talar articular surface.

The remainder of the calcaneus anteriorly and superiorly is represented by a roughened hollow, which, in conjunction with the elevated concavity of the inferior surface of the talus above, creates the expanded *sinus tarsi*. This hollowed-out region of the calcaneus is typically devoid of much articular detail. However, an *accessory facet* may develop just on the inside of the medial talar articular surface as a secondary point of articulation with the medial rim of the posterior calcaneal articular surface of the talus. The pit described above (as lying just medial to the inferiormost portion of the posterior talar articular surface) may also become expanded anteriorly into a shallow basin, which, in turn, may be subtended on both sides by elevated bony struts.

When viewed from above, the *posterior component* of the calcaneus extends backward—in some individuals with fairly straight and parallel sides but in others with a medial curvature—terminating in a roughened *posterior surface*. The *lateral surface* of the calcaneus, from the posterior talar articular surface to the posterior surface or "heel," is rather flat and vertical. The lateral surface is concave superiorly between the posterior calcaneal articular surface for the talus and the posterior surface. Along its inferior border, the lateral surface is variably straight; posteriorly, it thickens into a *lateral tubercle*. Proceeding anteriorly, the lateral surface of the calcaneus decreases in height (following the descent of the posterior talar articular surface). Midway between the inferiormost extent of the posterior articular surface and the roughened inferior border of the calcaneus, the lateral surface may bear a raised area, which is identified as the *peroneal tubercle*. Development of a peroneal tubercle is considered a *nonmetric variant* in humans; often, it is minimally elevated, although it may become large enough to be palpable in the living individual.

The *medial surface* of the calcaneus is divided essentially into two components by a horizontal, thickened region extending posteriorly from just below the sustentaculum tali. This thickened area contributes to the apparent parallel-sidedness of the calcaneus when it is viewed from above. This area of thickening subtends the *groove for the flexor hallucis longus,* which lies on the underside of the sustentaculum tali. Beneath the sustentaculum tali, this thickened region arcs inferiorly, following the declivity of the bony projection, until it eventually fades out. Below this thickening, however, the calcaneus is variably concave, being more severely scooped out as one proceeds anteriorly along the bone.

Beneath the region where the medial and anterior talar articular surfaces might meet, the calcaneus swells into a modest *anterior tubercle.* Because of the increased concavity of the bone in that region, the anterior tubercle is situated quite medially. It is separated from the articular surface for the cuboid by a roughened area of bone, which, in turn, is typically accentuated by a groove delineating the medial border of this cuboid facet. A short plantar ligament attaches to both the anterior tubercle and the roughened area in front of it. Posteriorly and inferiorly, the calcaneus swells into the *medial tubercle,* which is markedly larger than the lateral tubercle. The medial tubercle creates somewhat of a "corner" at the base of the posterior surface.

The *inferior surface* of the calcaneus has the general appearance of an elongate, right-angled triangle. Its apex is represented by the anterior tubercle and its sides terminate in the medial and lateral tubercles. This triangular surface serves for the attachment of the long plantar ligament. The vertical side of the triangle, which is a variably thickened band of coarse bone, extends between the anterior and medial tubercles and roughly parallels the long axis of the calcaneus. This band of roughened bone terminates at the base of the medial tubercle, which is distended downward and usually circumscribed medially, laterally, and anteriorly by a distinct edge or lip of bone. (The distension of

the edges of the medial tubercle is associated with the attachments of the abductor hallucis, the superficial part of the flexor retinaculum, the plantar aponeurosis, the flexor digitorum brevis, and part of the abductor digiti minimi; the latter originates on the lateral tubercle.) In some individuals, a sharply excavated groove separates the lateral tubercle from the larger medial tubercle; in other individuals, the borders of the tubercles are not clearly delineated.

The *posterior surface* of the calcaneus (the *calcaneal tuberosity*), when viewed from the side, is convex. When viewed straight on, it is broader inferiorly than superiorly. Frequently, the inferior surface of the small lateral tubercle lies well above the level of the inferior surface of the medial tubercle. At other times, however, the lateral tubercle is distended inferiorly so as to create a corner and square up the base of the posterior surface. Three areas are usually distinguishable on the posterior surface of the calcaneus. The uppermost area is smooth and usually small and delineated inferiorly by a shallow, irregularly coursing, horizontally oriented groove. The middle area is bounded superiorly by this groove and, inferiorly, by another groove; the second grove is accentuated by a raised edge of rugose bone, to which attaches the calcaneal (Achilles) tendon. The third division of the posterior surface of the calcaneus lies below this roughened elevation of bone.

The entire *anterior surface* of the calcaneus serves as the area of *articulation with the cuboid.* This vertical cuboid articular facet is oriented obliquely relative to the long axis of the calcaneus. Thus the medial edge of the cuboid articular facet lies posterior to its lateral margin. The superior portion of this facet is slightly concave, whereas, inferiorly, it is gently convex. The overall shape of the anterior surface is quite variable, but it is often narrower inferiorly, even if minimally, than it is superiorly. (When the posterior end is viewed straight on, the articular region of the calcaneus, anteriorly and superiorly, looks somewhat like a mitten, with the medial talar and cuboid articular surfaces corresponding, respectively, to the thumb and ball of the hand. The posterior talar articular facet corresponds to the area of the fingers. The "thumb" points away from the side of the body from which the bone comes.)

Navicular

The **navicular** bone (Figure 5–10) articulates posteriorly primarily with the head of the talus, but there may also be a slight contact with the calcaneus posteromedially. Anteriorly, the navicular articulates with the three somewhat wedge-shaped cuneiforms. As its name reflects, the navicular is (vaguely) a boat-shaped bone: it is concave posteriorly, convex anteriorly, and bears a (presumably) rudderlike extension medioinferiorly.

The *posterior articular surface* mirrors in part the contour and configuration of the head of the talus: it is rather teardrop-shaped, with its apex pointing medioinferiorly. The rudderlike extension—the *tuberosity of the navicular*—is somewhat hooked inferiorly; it projects beyond the apex of the posterior articular surface. The perimeter of the posterior articular surface, from the apex around the superior (proximal) and lateral sides to the midpoint of the inferior (distal) side, is elevated. However, the remainder of the perimeter of the posterior articular surface is unbounded and is thus "open" inferiorly. It is also at the midpoint of the inferior side that the outline of the posterior articular surface may become slightly angular or wavy. The body of the navicular bone extends beyond the perimeter of the posterior articular surface.

The *inferior (plantar, distal) surface* of the navicular bone, like its superior surface, is roughened. This surface may bear small, irregular, elevated patches of bone, some of which may also lie in the broad groove situated lateral to the navicular tuberosity. Because the *navicular tuberosity* is thick anteriorly and tapers posteriorly, it is obliquely oriented. This groove, which is usually more deeply incised just on the inside of the tuberosity, transmits part of the tendon of the tibialis posterior (which inserts largely on the navicular tuberosity but also courses to the cuneiform bones as well as to the bases of metatarsals II to IV).

The *anterior surface,* although often described as convex, is actually composed of three vaguely triangular articular planes whose apices approach the midpoint of the inferior edge of the bone and whose bases fan out to the respective lateral and superior borders. These three articular planes correspond to the areas of contact with the three cuneiform bones. In general, the *medial articular area for the medial cuneiform* is the largest of the three. The *middle* and *lateral articular areas* are subequal in size and are associated with the *intermediate* and *lateral cuneiform bones,* respectively. The middle articular surface is actually somewhat concave, thus creating distinctly raised borders with the medial and lateral articular regions on either side of it. The "convexity" of the anterior surface of the navicular bone, therefore, results more from the declination of the medial and lateral articular regions away from the middle articular surface than from a continuous arcing of the entire anterior articular surface. The broadened base of the navicular tuberosity extends beyond the limits of the articular region for the medial cuneiform.

The lateral side of the navicular bone is quite variable in that it may be smoothly convex, rather vertical, or even angular in outline. Furthermore, although the anteroposterior depth of the navicular bone seems to be consistently between 1 and 2 cm medially, the depth on the lateral side can differ markedly from one individual to the next.

Medial Cuneiform

The relatively tall and thin **medial cuneiform** (Figure 5–10) articulates posteriorly with the medial articular region of the anterior surface of the navicular bone and anteriorly with the first metatarsal. It makes contact laterally with the medial side of the intermediate cuneiform as well as with the base of the second metatarsal. Of the three cuneiforms, the medial cuneiform is the largest in height, depth, and width. It is roughly 2.5 to 3 times higher (inferosuperiorly) and two times deeper (anteroposteriorly) than it is wide (mediolaterally). The medial cuneiform is an extremely variable bone in various details of its shape and articular surfaces, but certain characteristics are relatively constant.

In general, the medial cuneiform is broader inferiorly, at its base, than superiorly. The bone of the *inferior* or *plantar surface* is usually quite roughened. The surface itself may be relatively flat or somewhat convex; its configuration is typically rectangular or trapezoidal. Superiorly, the bone curves downward from its distinct lateral margin (its contact with the base of the second metatarsal) to its medial side. When viewed from above, the medial cuneiform is broader anteriorly than posteriorly; its lateral margin may be accentuated by a bony ridge. Medially, the superior margin is convex, sloping downward as it proceeds posteriorly.

The upper and lower halves of the *medial surface* of the medial cuneiform are gently convex. The midpoint of this surface, however, is noticeably concave. Anteriorly, this inferior portion of the medial cuneiform bears on its medial surface a slightly elevated, variably configured flattened area, which is the attachment site of the tibialis anterior tendon. Immediately posterior to this attachment site, the bone may be either depressed into a shallow pit or elevated into a small, secondary point of attachment or a minor swelling.

The *posterior articular surface* of the medial cuneiform, which mirrors the articular surface of the navicular bone behind it, is slightly concave and variably teardrop-shaped. It may also be asymmetrical in outline, with the medial margin being more concave than the lateral margin (the medial margin contributes to the medial curvature of the bone and its articulation with the intermediate cuneiform). The inferior portion of the bone swells out below the posterior articular surface, while the medially cresting superior portion rises significantly above it.

Most of the *lateral surface* of the medial cuneiform is variably straight to mildly concave. Its superiormost portion curves inward to some extent. Bandlike articular surfaces along the posterior and superior margins of the lateral surface are often connected to one another, forming an upside down "L." (In some individuals, however, the posterior and superior articular surfaces may be disjunct.) The posterior articular strip forms a corner with the lateral margin of the posterior articular surface; it and most of the *superior articular surface* contact the *intermediate cuneiform*. Immediately in front of the superior articular surface lies a variably developed surface, which articulates with the posteromedial portion of the second metatarsal. This second, anterosuperior articular surface may be either quite large and distinctly

separate from the longer articular region behind it, or diminutive and barely distinguishable from the dominant superior articular area. The anterior margin of the lateral surface of the medial cuneiform may bear a slight vertical groove just behind the edge of the anterior articular surface (the anterior articular surface may surmount the bone for its entire height). Because this vertical groove follows the contour of the anterior articular surface, it may be inwardly curved toward the midregion of the bone. In addition, the inferolateral "corner" of the bone may present itself anywhere from being unexpanded to being markedly swollen and distended.

The *anterior articular surface* of the medial cuneiform is much taller than the posterior articular surface and its morphology is much more variable. (For the most part, however, this articular surface looks like the footprint of a slipper or moccasin, with its heel inferiorly placed and the inward curvature of its arch located near the horizontal midline of the bone. The heel of this articular surface tends to be slightly concave and the ball somewhat convex.) Within this visual context, *variation* is seen in the degrees to which the different components of the foot are narrow, broad, and curved. Additional variation is seen in the anterior articular surface being noticeably "pinched" or "waisted" at its midline or even bisected into separate articular facets.

Intermediate Cuneiform

The **intermediate cuneiform** (Figure 5–10) is the smallest and most wedgelike of the three cuneiform bones. Its *anterior* and *posterior articular surfaces* are essentially triangular in outline. The medial side may be in part convex, paralleling the slightly concave configuration of the lateral side of the medial cuneiform, against which this surface lies. The posterior surface, which articulates with the middle articular region of the anterior surface of the navicular bone, is often slightly concave. In contrast, the anterior articular surface may be gently convex, relatively flat, or mildly concave. Sometimes the anterior articular surface is longer than the posterior one, but the reverse also may occur. The *superior surface* of the intermediate cuneiform is broad, variably bumpy to smooth, and relatively flat to gently convex. The *inferior* or *plantar surface* is more a thickened margin than it is a platform.

The *medial surface* of the intermediate cuneiform bears an inverted, variably "L"-shaped, articular surface. The base of the "L" courses along the superior margin; its side extends part or all of the way down the posterior margin. The configuration of this oddly shaped articular surface corresponds to the upside-down "L"-shaped articular surface on the lateral surface of the medial cuneiform. However, even if the articular "L" of the medial cuneiform is separated into distinct superior and posterior articular regions, the "L"-shaped articular surface on the medial face of the intermediate cuneiform may remain intact, and vice versa. The area circumscribed by the "L"-shaped articular surface—usually just the anteromedial corner of the bone—is a roughened surface within which secondary areas of articulation with the medial cuneiform may develop.

The *lateral surface* of the intermediate cuneiform bears an articular surface that corresponds to its zone of contact with the lateral cuneiform. Like the medial articular surface, the lateral articular surface may also extend along the superior and posterior margins of the bone. However, the superior articular portion tends to fall short of reaching the anterior margin (whereas it tends to do so on the medial side), while the thick, posterior articular portion more frequently extends for the length of the posterior margin. The lateral articular surface is, therefore, more truncated anteroposteriorly. Although forming more or less a right angle in its superoposterior corner, the lateral articular surface, internally, is not similarly indented. The rest of the lateral surface of the intermediate cuneiform is roughened, but it may develop a *secondary articulation* with the lateral cuneiform.

Lateral Cuneiform

The **lateral cuneiform** (Figure 5–10) also is wedge-shaped. It is broad superiorly and narrow along its inferior or plantar surface. The *superior surface* is variably rough to smooth and flat to undulating. Its sides are not straight, but they do parallel one another in that the medial edge bends inward and the longer lateral edge buckles outward at the midpoint of the superior surface. (The medial edge of the lateral cuneiform, therefore, appears to wrap around the smaller intermediate cuneiform.) The longer lateral edge parallels the oblique orientation of the posterior articular surface of the bone. The inferior margin of the lateral cuneiform is typically straight and truncated posteriorly; thus, it does not extend the full length of the bone.

The *anterior articular surface* primarily abuts the base of the third metatarsal, but its anteromedial corner does contact the posterolateral margin of the second metatarsal. The anterior articular surface is basically shaped like an elongate triangle, but it is swollen to some extent superolaterally and its lateral margin is indented. The surface of this triangle is variably flat to undulating.

The *posterior surface,* which contacts the lateral facet of the anterior articular surface of the navicular bone, is small, subtriangular, and consistently albeit slightly concave overall. A raised rim may course around the perimeter of the medial margin of this surface, from its superior to its inferior limits. The thickened inferior margin of the bone extends markedly below the posterior surface. (As mentioned above, the posterior articular surface of the lateral cuneiform is oriented obliquely relative to the plane of the anterior articular surface.)

The *medial side* of the lateral cuneiform (the side making contact with the intermediate cuneiform) bears a relatively large, variably ear- to inverted-boot–shaped articular facet—the *posteromedial articular facet*—which is confluent around the posteromedial edge of the bone with the small posterior articular facet. This posteromedial articular facet is somewhat convex, thus mirroring the slight concavity of the corresponding articular surface of the intermediate cuneiform. Most of the medial side of the lateral cuneiform is roughened, nonarticular bone with irregular surface topography. However, there may be as many as three small articular regions along the anteromedial border. One of these three may be located in the superior and anteromedial corner of the bone; the second will be at the inferior and anteromedial corner of the bone, where the second metatarsal may make contact posterolaterally; and the third facet will lie directly along the border, where a point of secondary articulation with the intermediate cuneiform may also develop.

A flexure or "bend" in the *lateral side* of the lateral cuneiform just anterior to its midpoint subdivides it into two planes. The posterior plane is dominated by a large *articular facet for the cuboid*. This facet is vaguely wing-shaped and primarily confined to the upper two-thirds to one-half of the posterolateral aspect of the bone. Sometimes, however, this articular region may extend as far as the inferior margin of the bone. Just in front of the inferior portion of this articular region (regardless of its length) lies a variably small, shallow pit. In addition, in the anterosuperior corner of the bone, an extremely small (sometimes barely visible) articular facet, which contacts the posteromedial edge of the fourth metatarsal, may occur with some frequency. This facet will be confluent at the margin of the bone with the anterior articular surface and connected posteriorly to the larger posterosuperior articular facet (for the cuboid) by a ridge. The region below this ridge may be partially articular as well as roughened. As with the other cuneiforms, which serve to maintain the transverse arch of the foot, ligaments attach to the nonarticular surfaces of the medial and lateral sides of the bone.

Cuboid

The **cuboid** (Figure 5–10) is the longest, deepest, and bulkiest of the distal row of tarsal bones. It articulates (1) posteriorly with the anterior articular surface of the calcaneus, (2) medially with the lateral cuneiform and the anterolateral edge of the navicular bone, and (3) anteriorly with the fourth and fifth metatarsals. Bearing in mind the position of these bones relative to one another and taking the articulation between the cuboid and the calcaneus as the point of reference, one can see that the body of the cuboid is skewed laterally while the articular surfaces for the fourth and fifth metatarsals are oriented obliquely. Viewed from above, the cuboid is broader posteriorly than anteriorly; it has a short, concave or notched lateral side and a markedly longer medial side that forms a corner near the posterior base of the bone.

The *superior surface* of the cuboid is rough-ened and variably flat to undulating. Various dorsal ligaments—which course between this tarsal and the calcaneus, navicular, lateral cuneiform, and metatarsals—attach to its superior surface. The *inferior* or *plantar surface* of the cuboid is readily distinguished from its superior surface by a shallow to moderately excavated *groove* that courses between the anterior margin of the bone and a modest to well-developed *ridge* situated approximately one-third the distance from the anterior margin of the bone. The ridge parallels the orientation of the anterior surface of the bone and the groove it subtends houses the peroneus longus tendon, which courses through the *notch* on the lateral side of the bone. Occasionally, the ridge protrudes markedly laterally. When it does, it—in conjunction with a lateral lipping of the anterior articular surface—accentuates the lateral notch further. Laterally, the ridge may remain anterior to but may also become coincident with the corner of the posterior articular surface. The lateralmost portion of the ridge is called the *tuberosity of the cuboid bone*. Its surface is variably smooth, because it articulates with either a true sesamoid bone or an inclusion of unossified cartilage in the peroneus longus tendon. Posterior to the oblique plantar ridge, the remaining two-thirds to three-quarters of the bone is more or less triangular in outline and its surface is mildly concave and roughened.

The *posterior articular surface* of the cuboid roughly mirrors the triangular outline of the anterior articular surface of the calcaneus. Its inferior margin is long and relatively straight (in the anatomical position, it would be mediolaterally angled downward), and its superolateral side is somewhat longer than the superomedial side; the corners of this "triangle" are curved, not angular. Reflecting further the anterior articular surface of the calcaneus, the posterior articular surface of the cuboid is gently concave and slightly twisted: that is, its inferomedial aspect is deflected partially upward while its superolateral border faces downward slightly.

The long *medial side* of the cuboid is dominated superiorly and somewhat centrally by a large *articular facet for the lateral cuneiform*. This facet tends to mirror the configuration (or at least the emphases) of the corresponding facet on the lateral cuneiform: that is, if the facet of the lateral cuneiform is elongate superiorly and somewhat truncated inferiorly or if it is relatively short superiorly and thickened and extended inferiorly, so is the facet on the cuboid. Regardless of the range of potential variations, the anteroinferior edge of the cuboid's articular facet is delineated further by a moderately excavated and rather extensive depression, which may extend as far as the border of the anterior articular surface of the bone. Posterior to this facet, the bone either angles toward the edge of the posterior articular surface or simply curves posteriorly. In either case, a smaller, additional *secondary articular facet* may be present at the posterior boundary of the articular facet for the lateral cuneiform. This secondary facet reflects a point of *articulation with the anteromedial margin of the navicular bone* and may be accentuated by a pit or crease along its inferior border.

The *anterior surface* of the cuboid is distinguished by a "pinching" or "waisting" just behind its rim and by its being unequally subdi-

vided into two—a medial and a lateral—somewhat concave articular planes that differ in size and orientation. The medial articular plane faces more directly forward to articulate with the base of the fourth metatarsal; the most medial extent of the rim of this surface may also contact the posterolateral edge of the third metatarsal. The lateral plane, which articulates with the base of the fifth metatarsal, is directed outward. The lateral plane thus forms a very obtuse angle with the medial plane, from which it is sometimes further delineated by a vertical ridge. The (medial) border of the medial articular area is foreshortened, whereas the lateral articular surface is more elongate.

Metatarsal Bones

Morphology

The **metatarsus** of the foot is composed of five **metatarsal** bones (I to V); (Figure 5–12) which

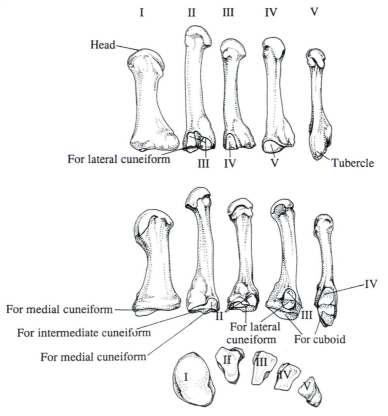

Figure 5–12 Right metatarsals: *(from left to right)* I to V; *(top row)* lateral, *(middle row)* medial, and *(bottom row)* proximal (basal) views.

are situated between the distal row of tarsal bones and the phalanges. The metatarsals are similar to long bones in that each has a *head,* a *shaft,* and a *base.* Unlike a typical long bone, however, the head of a metatarsal is located at its distal or anterior end and the base at its proximal or posterior end.

The *first* (i.e. most medial) *metatarsal (metatarsal I)* can be recognized because it is the shortest, and, in all respects, the bulkiest of the metatarsals. It is also distinctive because it bears an articular facet (for metatarsal II) only on its lateral side (i.e. the side of the body from which the bone comes).

The *base* of the first metatarsal is vertically accentuated and vaguely ear-shaped in outline; its surface mirrors in part the shape of the anterior surface of the medial cuneiform, with which it articulates. *Variation* in the *posterior surface* is manifested in a pinching or notching approximately midway along the slightly concave lateral margin, below which a small pit may develop. Some individuals also develop a notch in the noticeably convex medial margin. Less frequently, the medial and lateral notches are more invasive. This results in the segregation of two articular regions, between which a horizontal ridge may also course. The somewhat concave posterior surface is circumscribed by a shallow groove. It is composed of a broader and more concave upper portion and a narrower, less concave lower portion. The lower portion faces somewhat lateromedially.

In cross section, the *shaft* of the first metatarsal is essentially triangular, with its base oriented laterally and its apex medially. As such, the *superior surface* of the shaft is slanted downward lateromedially, the *lateral side* is basically flat, and the *medial aspect* is highlighted by a longitudinal ridge, which may swell into a small tuberclelike structure just in front of the rim of the posterior articular surface. Anteriorly, the *inferior* or *plantar margin* of the lateral surface swings laterally outward and becomes distended into a short, tonguelike projection, over which spreads the articular surface of the head of the bone. Posteriorly, the inferior margin of the lateral surface of the first metatarsal terminates in a roughened, somewhat ovoid, flattened to gently concave attachment site for the peroneus longus tendon. Superiorly on the lateral side of the rim of the posterior articular surface, there may be a variably developed *facet*

for (contact with) *the second metatarsal* (the second metatarsal bears its corresponding facet anterior to the facet on the margin of its base for contact with the edge of the medial cuneiform). The inferior margin of the lateral side of the first metatarsal is somewhat concave. As it proceeds posteriorly from the head, the inferior margin narrows slightly; it then descends more drastically as it nears the inferior limit of the base of the bone. The superior margin, however, remains relatively straight. It terminates anteriorly in a small, low to spikelike projection.

The *head* of the first metatarsal is broad. Its surface is largely articular and wraps around the head of the bone, well onto the plantar surface. Viewed head-on, the superior margin of the head of metatarsal I is slightly convex; its medial edge descends fairly vertically but, about halfway down, its lateral edge is deflected outward. The medial margin of the head is quite thick. Just off center laterally is a ridge that thickens as it proceeds downward. In concert with the inferomedial margin of the head, the medial side of this ridge bounds a relatively deep groove. The lateral side of this ridge, in tandem with the lateral margin, circumscribes a shallower groove. These two grooves are most pronounced on the plantar area of the head's articular surface, which is where the off-center ridge is most exaggerated. The off-center ridge and its attendant grooves create a "W" shape, with the lateral arm of the "W" being the more robust and elongate. Small *sesamoid bones,* which ossify between 8 and 14 years, ride in these grooves.

The **second metatarsal** is longer than but similar in overall shape to the third and fourth metatarsals. Although the shape of the *shaft* of metatarsal II is somewhat more similar to that of the first metatarsal (i.e. slanted and triangular in cross section), it is extremely thin, its inferior margin is more evenly concave, and its superior border is gently convex. When viewed from above, the superior surface of the bone broadens slightly anteriorly and terminates in two marginal swellings, which are offset from the gently convex head by a circumferential groove. Posteriorly, the superior surface becomes somewhat flattened and roughened, and it broadens dramatically toward the base.

The *posterior surface* of the second metatarsal, which articulates with the intermediate cuneiform, is mildly concave and roughly triangular in outline, with its base oriented superiorly and its blunt apex directed inferiorly. Confluent with the posterior surface is the variably developed *facet for the medial cuneiform.* This anterolaterally situated facet wraps around the medial as well as a superior portion of the posterior rim. Another facet—the *facet for the first metatarsal*—may develop anterior to this facet and lie posterolaterally along the bone. The area below and medial to the facet for the medial cuneiform is roughened. Laterally and superiorly, at the margin of the posterior surface, may lie a variably developed *facet for* (contact with the anteromedial edge of) *the lateral cuneiform.* Anterior to this facet if not also confluent with it is yet another facet, the *facet for the third metatarsal.* The *facet for the second and third metatarsals* is found laterally and in the posteroinferior corner of the bone. This facet may be ovoid and localized to that corner of the bone, or it may extend upward to some degree. A roughened, variably excavated groove separates the superior facet(s) from the inferior facet.

The *head* of the second metatarsal is taller than it is wide (the reverse of the first metatarsal head) and its medial side is taller (i.e. extends more prominently superiorly and inferiorly) than the lateral side. Thus, when viewed head-on, the superior border slopes upward and the inferior or plantar border slopes downward from the lateral to the medial side. Both the lateral and medial margins of the head continue along the plantar side of the bone, creating a somewhat "U"-shaped edge to the articular surface. The lateral arm of this "U" extends farther posteriorly than the medial arm, which is also characteristic of metatarsals III and IV. (Thus the longer arm of the "U" is on the same side of the bone as the side of the body from which the bone comes.) The swollen plantar extremity of the medial border nestles in the "crook," superiorly, of the lateral projection of the head of the first metatarsal.

In overall design as well as in specific detail, the **third metatarsal** is quite similar to the second. It is, however, variably shorter, its shaft is typically more slender, its *head* and *base* are narrower, and the disparity in height between the medial and lateral sides of the head is not as pronounced. The *posterior surface,* which articulates with the lateral cuneiform, is gently concave. The ovoid, tongue-shaped *facet for the second metatarsal* is confluent with this surface around its edge and superiorly, along the medial side of the base. The area beneath this facet is roughened and may also be slightly concave. Somewhat inferiorly, an additional *secondary facet for* (articulation with) *the second metatarsal* may develop. The typically well-developed, ovoid *facet for the fourth metatarsal,* which contacts the metatarsal at its edge, is found superiorly on the *lateral side.* Roughened areas delineate this facet in front and below. Also, inferiorly, the bone may be excavated into a shallow, horizontal groove. In contrast to the second metatarsal, the posterior part of the third metatarsal does not develop a second, inferiorly placed point of articulation on its lateral side.

The **fourth metatarsal** is somewhat similar to the third and second. The *head* of the fourth metatarsal is virtually identical morphologically to the third and second metatarsals, including the emphasis on the lateral extension onto the plantar side of the "U"-shaped articular surface. However, its head is more laterally and its base more medially deflected, and it bears a more distinct longitudinal ridge medially on its *superior surface.* This ridge, which gives the bone a longer, more slanted lateral side, terminates posteriorly in an elevated, roughened region. The *posterior surface* of the fourth metatarsal is less consistently wedgelike. Thus the medial and lateral sides of the base are more parallel to one another. The posterior surface is variably concave to concavoconvex, mirroring the variability in the corresponding articular facet of the cuboid. A *facet for* (articulation with) *the third metatarsal* lies superiorly on the *medial side* of the base. This facet (which may invade the raised and roughened area associated with the ridge of the superior surface) can be somewhat ovoid and elongate or elliptical; its distance from the edge of the base of the bone is also variable. A crease or groove just lateral to its margin delineates this facet further from above. Below and behind this facet, the bone is quite roughened and irregular. The area is circumscribed by a shallow to deep groove. A smaller *facet for* (contact with the anterolateral edge of) *the lateral cuneiform* occurs either just posterior to the facet for the third metatarsal or along the lateral edge of the base of metatarsal IV.

The *lateral side* of the base of the fourth

metatarsal bears a somewhat holster-shaped *facet for the fifth metatarsal.* This facet courses down from the superior margin of the base; its straighter side is folded along the posterior surface of the bone, sometimes forming an edge. This distinct facet may be surrounded by roughened, irregular bone or it may be set off by a sometime deeply excavated groove. Anterior and perhaps somewhat inferior to this roughened to grooved region is a slightly elevated, ovoid to subtriangular area for the attachment of an interosseous muscle.

The **fifth metatarsal** is the most easily identified of metatarsals II to V: it bears only a posterior and a medial articular facet. Viewed from above, the bone broadens posteriorly, culminating in a large *tubercle* that lies laterally adjacent to the posterior articular surface. In concert with the marked inward orientation of the *posterior surface* (which corresponds to the orientation of the surface on the cuboid), the tubercle extends metatarsal V posteriorly; in some individuals, the tubercle is a blunt, hooklike projection. The *shaft* of the bone may be relatively straight or inwardly curved. In lateral aspect, the shaft becomes increasingly compressed in a posterior direction. The *base* is thus wider than it is tall, which is the reverse of the configuration of the bases of metatarsals II to IV. The broad *superior surface* slopes downward mediolaterally, thereby elaborating further on the pattern established on the fourth metatarsal. The slightly concave to saddle-shaped posterior surface is thus taller along its relatively vertical medial border, and it tapers laterally to a blunt or rounded terminus. A variably ovoid to lunate facet—the *facet for the fourth metatarsal*—lies somewhat superiorly along the medial side of the base. It is confluent with the posterior articular surface. The facet is surrounded inferiorly and somewhat anteriorly by roughened bone. The *head* of the fifth metatarsal may be more asymmetrical than on metatarsals II to IV, particularly in the extent to which the lateral articular margin on the plantar surface is enlarged.

Development and Ossification

Mineralization of the metatarsals (Figure 5–11) begins during the eighth to tenth fetal weeks with the appearance of a center of ossification in the shaft of each bone. In metatarsals II to V,

ossification can occur in the heads (distal epiphyses) anytime between the third and eighth years. Secondary ossification begins in metatarsal I during this period in the proximal epiphysis, at the base of the bone. The pattern of ossification of metatarsal I is thus similar to that of the pedal phalanges, metacarpal I, and the phalanges of the hand. Union of the relevant epiphyses to the metatarsal shafts may begin at about 12 years of age, with complete union occurring between 18 and 22 years.

Phalanges

Morphology

Although differing in size and robustness, the **phalanges** of the foot (Figure 5–13)—also called the *phalanges digitorum pedis*—are essentially similar in overall design. Each has a *head* (distally), a *shaft,* and a *base* (proximally). Their bases are broad and sublunate to elliptical in outline. Their shafts are narrower than their heads and bases. Thus the sides of the bones have a slightly "scooped-out" appearance. Pedal digits II to V are composed of three phalanges each (a proximal or first row, a middle or second row, and a third distal or terminal row). In contrast, the first pedal digit—the *hallux*—comprises only two rows of phalanges.

The bones of the **proximal** or **first row** of phalanges are similar in that their *bases* are sublunate in outline (being flatter along the plantar or inferior edge) and uniformly concave (with a raised rim all around for articulation with the rounded heads of the metatarsals). The first proximal phalanx (the singular of phalanges) is

Figure 5–13 Right phalanges: *(left)* I, anterior view [*(top)* distal and *(bottom)* proximal phalanges]; *(middle)* example of II to V, anterior view [*(from top to bottom)* distal, middle, and proximal phalanges]; *(right)* example of II to V, proximal (basal) view, [*(from top to bottom)* distal, middle, and proximal phalanges].

the largest of the set. The *head* of a proximal **phalanx** is relatively compressed superoinferiorly. When viewed from above, the head of a proximal phalanx is somewhat concave centrally; this centrally emplaced indentation receives the central "keel" in the posterior articular surface of the phalanx in front (see below). When viewed head-on, the superior margin of the proximal phalanx is convex and its inferior margin concave. The miniature "wings" that these curvatures create on the phalangeal head may be relatively flat on their sides, or slightly concave, or they may bear swellings reminiscent of the epicondyles of the distal femur. The latter configuration is most characteristic of the first proximal phalanx. The first proximal phalanx is further distinguished in that the curvatures of its head—above, in front, and below—are also the most exaggerated.

The *superior surface* of the shaft of a proximal phalanx, which is smoothly convex along much of its length, becomes flatter just behind the head. On the first proximal phalanx in particular, the region just behind the height is slightly roughened; it may also be irregular and even surmounted by a small elevation of bone. The *plantar* or *inferior surface* of the shaft is flatter throughout most of its length. Its medial and lateral borders may bear longitudinal ridges of some distinction. On the first proximal phalanx, a pit of variable depth usually develops just behind the head of the bone. This pit delineates articular projections on either side of it.

The proximal phalanges are typically so symmetrical that clues to determining the side of the body from which a particular bone comes are virtually nonexistent. Sometimes, however, and especially on the first proximal phalanx, the head of the bone is deflected slightly laterally (i.e. to the side of the body from which it comes); thus, the lateral side of the shaft may be somewhat more concave than the medial side. Although the first phalanx can be identified with certainty, the slightly smaller and definitely more gracile second to fifth phalanges are usually indistinguishable from one another.

The **middle phalanges** of the second to fifth digits are essentially short-shafted versions of the proximal phalanges. However, their *posterior articular surfaces* are broader, sublunate in outline, and bear gently raised, vertical, central "keels" that correspond to the indentations on the heads of the proximal phalanges. The middle phalanx of the fifth pedal digit is the most likely of the set to be identified with any certainty because it quite frequently is the most asymmetrical, truncated in length, and prone to morphological alteration.

The **terminal** or **distal phalanges** have broad, flared-out *bases;* short, markedly inwardly curving *shafts;* and flattened, fanlike *heads.* The base of a distal phalanx (which looks like a pedestal on which the rest of the bone sits) is somewhat elliptical in outline. Its *articular surface* is rimmed and elevated vertically in the midline, thus mirroring the indentation in the head of the phalanx behind it. The medial and lateral "corners" of the base may be either blunt and stout or curved and winglike. The *shaft* is essentially flat on its plantar or inferior surface and convex superiorly; a longitudinal, keellike ridge may course along the shaft. The *head* of the bone is convex superiorly and very flat and roughened inferiorly; its terminal edge is quite compressed, laterally extended, and variably smoothly arcuate to spearheadlike in outline. The terminal phalanx of the first pedal digit is by far the largest, while that of the fifth is typically the smallest and most amorphous in shape. Determining the side of the body from which a terminal phalanx comes is nearly impossible, but the head of the terminal phalanx of the first pedal digit is sometimes tilted slightly medially (i.e. away from the side of the body from which it comes).

Development and Ossification

Mineralization of the phalanges (Figure 5–11) starts with the appearance during the ninth or tenth week of centers of ossification in the shafts of the distal row of phalanges. At about the same time or only slightly later, centers of ossification arise in the shafts of the phalanges of the proximal row. During the fourth month, ossification begins in the shafts of the middle row of phalanges. Centers of ossification usually appear in the bases (proximal epiphyses) between the second and third years but may be delayed until the tenth year. Union of the bases to the shafts begins at approximately 14 years and is completed between the ages of 17 and 21 years.

CHAPTER SIX

Teeth

Although teeth contribute little to the total volume of an individual's skeleton, they are extremely complex in development and morphology.

Basic Gross Dental Anatomy

A tooth (Figures 6–1 and 6–2) is composed of different tissues of different degrees of hardness. The hardest dental tissue is the **enamel,** which comes to encapsulate most if not all of that portion of the tooth that protrudes from the gum. The enamel-covered portion of a tooth is the **crown.** Depending on the species of mammal and the specific tooth under discussion, a tooth is secured to the jaw by one or more **roots;** polyphyodont animals (e.g. sharks) do not develop anything that can be called a root system. In humans, upper molars typically develop the greatest number of roots (three). Root surfaces are covered by **cementum,**which is softer than enamel. Cementum is usually deposited as a thin layer, whereas the thickness of enamel may vary from tooth to tooth and from species to species; humans are among the few extant primates in which the enamel covering the cheek teeth (the premolars and molars) is unusually thick. The junction of the enamel and the cementum is identified the **neck** or **cervix** of the tooth; this area may also be constricted or "waisted." In addition to other criteria (enumerated elsewhere in this chapter), deciduous teeth can often be distinguished from permanent teeth by having thinner and shorter and, if multiple, more splayed roots; this accentuates

the waisting of the cervical region of the tooth and adds further to the distinctiveness of crown versus root.

Underlying both the enamel and cementum is a continuous tissue layer called **(primary) dentine.** Dentine surrounds the **pulp cavity.** Nerves and arteries penetrate the tooth via openings in the apices of the roots and are channeled into the pulp cavity through the root canals. When dentine is exposed through the enamel—either by wear or breakage—it is worn away at a faster rate than the enamel around it. In time, severe abrasion can wear down the crown of the tooth to where the sensitive pulp cavity is endangered. If infection and decay do not complicate matters, the tooth at this stage of extreme attrition can generate **secondary dentine.** Secondary dentine is somewhat harder than primary dentine and serves to prolong the life of the tooth and minimize discomfort. If infection invades the pulp cavity—because of caries of the crown or abscessing around the root tip— nerve death and thus death of the tooth can occur.

Teeth are not immovably fixed in the jaw. Each root is supported variably along its length by fibers of a **periodontal ligament** (thus, actually, periodontal ligaments) that stretches between the root and the wall of the alveolus, acting as a miniature shock absorber. [Some experimental evidence indicates that the periodontal ligament develops ultimately from the proliferating cell mass that also gives rise to the tooth, its different component tissues, and the alveolar bone that supports it (Ten Cate and Mills, 1972)]. With bone in a state of constant

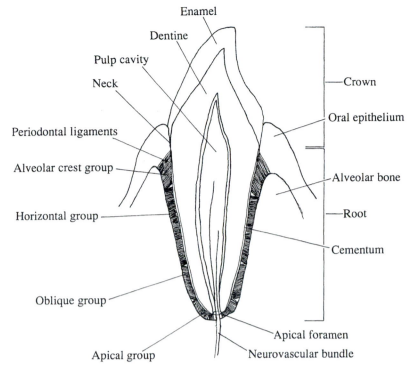

Figure 6–1 Schematic representation of gross anatomical regions of a tooth and its surrounding and supporting structures.

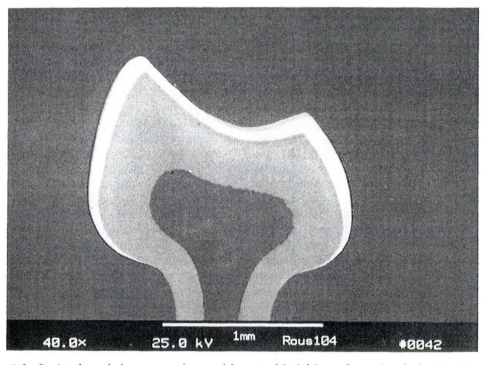

Figure 6–2 Section through the crown and some of the root of the left lower first molar of a fruit bat *(Rousettus amplexicaudatus)* illustrating (from outer layer to inner chamber) the layer of enamel *(white)*, dentine *(light gray)*, and pulp cavity *(dark gray)*. *(Courtesy of E. Dumont.)*

153

flux—due to the differential interplay of bone cells (osteoblasts and osteocytes)—movement of teeth forward in the jaws, called *mesial drift,* commonly occurs. Thus, for example, the incisors, especially the lower incisors, of older individuals tend to be crowded together or even to overlap one another. (Orthodontic prostheses to correct improper tooth position and/or orientation take advantage of the plasticity and responsiveness of bone relative to teeth.)

Differentiating Dentitions

Most mammals—humans included—typically develop and erupt into their jaws two generations of teeth. Some of the teeth of the first generation of teeth are thus shed, which has led to their being referred to as **deciduous teeth.** Also on occasion, deciduous teeth are referred to as **milk teeth,** not because of their association with an unweaned child but because their enamel often appears milky. **Permanent teeth** are not shed; they typically are thought of as synonymous with the adult dentition because they are retained throughout an individual's lifetime. Some permanent teeth replace deciduous teeth and thus represent a second generation of teeth developmentally. Other permanent teeth, however—the molar teeth of humans, for example—share with deciduous teeth the characteristic of not replacing teeth; the only difference between these permanent teeth and deciduous teeth is that they are not replaced; thus they are defined as permanent, not deciduous, teeth because of their fate. By these definitions, and with the addition of the molar teeth, humans and other mammals develop more permanent than deciduous teeth.

Animals that develop two "sets" of teeth during their lifetimes are **diphyodont** ("di" = "two," "phyo" = "families or generations," "dont" = "teeth"; the condition is *diphyodonty*). Some extant mammals (e.g. manatees) develop only a single generation of teeth and are thus **monophyodont.** Most reptiles and fish develop a lifetime of generations of successional teeth: as if on a conveyor belt, wave upon wave of maturing teeth march toward the edges of the jaws as earlier rows of teeth are shed, some of their members being lost in the process of acquiring food. These animals are referred to as being **polyphyodont** (poly = many). In addition to a brief functional life, the teeth of polyphyodont animals are typically morphologically simple (often being conical or relatively flat and triangular in outline); they are also rootless and thus poorly anchored in the jaws.

An animal whose teeth are similarly shaped has a **homodont** (= "same" toothed) **dentition.** Although seals and cetaceans, for example, possess homodont dentitions, most mammals develop morphologically distinct groups of teeth; individual tooth groups are morphologically recognizable. These nonhomodont mammals possess **heterodont** (i.e. different-toothed) **dentitions** and the morphologically relatable groups of teeth are **tooth classes.** The maximum number of tooth classes a mammal apparently can develop is three: **incisor, canine,** and **molar** (e.g. see Figures 6–12 and 6–13). Following traditional terminology, there are **deciduous** and **permanent incisors** and **canines** (e.g. see Figures 6–12 and 6–13). **Deciduous molars** (sometimes referred to as **deciduous premolars**) are replaced by **premolars;** by definition, premolars are permanent teeth and are so named because they precede the permanent **molars** in the jaws (e.g. see Figures 6–12 and 6–13). Characteristically in heterodont mammals, successional teeth, although often larger than the teeth they replace, are morphologically simpler (however, at least in glossophagine phylostomatid fruit-eating bats, the situation is reversed, i.e. the deciduous teeth are small, pointed, and morphologically simple).

When present, incisors are the anteriormost teeth in the jaws. The stereotypical incisor is a somewhat spatulate or chisellike, occlusally straight-edged, tooth; teeth that look like incisors (or the idealized incisor) are described as *incisiform.* Many mammals, including humans, develop the same number of deciduous and permanent incisors in both upper and lower jaws. It is not surprising to find an upper incisiform tooth, as one of the anteriormost teeth in the jaws, rooted in the premaxilla.

Immediately behind the last or lateralmost incisor lies the tooth identified as the canine. Mammals are supposed to develop at most only one pair of canines in the upper and one pair in the lower jaw. Stereotypically, as, for example, in carnivores, the canine—especially the upper canine—is depicted as a relatively tall, pointed, single cusped tooth; in humans, the canine (even the upper canine) is only modestly elongate and pointed. A tooth that looks like a canine, even though it might not be in the same position in the jaw as "the canine," is described as *caniniform*. Although caniniform teeth can be found in various positions in the jaws of different mammals, the upper canine itself, when present, has traditionally been identified as the first tooth behind the premaxillary-maxillary suture. The tooth traditionally identified as the lower canine is the tooth that occludes in front of the upper canine.

The teeth that lie behind the canine belong to the molar class. Molars and at least the posterior deciduous molars are consistently the most morphologically complex teeth in a mammal's mouth. In fact, the posteriormost deciduous molar of a heterodont mammal looks like a molar. Characteristically in mammals, and thus humans as well, when deciduous and permanent molars are studied together as members of the same tooth class, it is obvious that they form a size and shape gradient. It is only when the typically morphologically less complex successors to the deciduous molars, the premolars, are compared to the permanent molars series that such a gradient is not apparent; thus, with the exception of those mammals that develop a *molariform* posterior premolar (e.g. horses and the prosimian *Hapalemur*), premolars indeed do appear to constitute a set of teeth that can be contrasted morphologically with permanent molars. Although teeth identified as premolars of various mammals may be single-cusped, they are typically lower-crowned with more subsidiary morphological embellishment than canines. Human premolars are either uni- or bicuspid. Teeth that look like premolars are described as *premolariform*.

The number of kind of tooth in each jaw is often represented in shorthand notation called a **dental formula**. The *dental formula of the normal human permanent dentition* (compare with Figures 6–12 and 6–13) is:

$$\frac{2.1.2.3}{2.1.2.3}$$

The first column represents permanent incisor number; the second column is for the canine, the third for premolars, and the fourth for permanent molars. Since mammals are bilaterally symmetrical animals, a dental formula is often constructed and read as representing one-half of the upper and one-half of the lower dentition. In order to calculate the number of teeth in either the upper or lower jaw, the total number of teeth in the appropriate part of the formula is multiplied by 2 (e.g. for the human upper dentition: $2 + 1 + 2 + 3 = 8 \times 2 = 16$). One also can think of a dental formula as representing pairs of teeth in each category. Although humans are among those mammals that develop the same number of each kind of tooth in the upper as well as the lower jaw, this is not constant among mammals (thus the numerator and denominator of a dental formula will not be identical), nor is the development of a tooth in each category (e.g. ruminating artiodactyls, such as cows and deer, for example, lack permanent upper incisors altogether but develop them in the lower jaw).

The *dental formula for the normal human deciduous dentition* (compare with Figures 6–12 and 6–13) is:

$$\frac{2.1.2}{2.1.2}$$

The first column denotes deciduous incisors, the second deciduous canines, and the third deciduous molars. Although humans, as well as most other mammals, develop as many replacing teeth as deciduous predecessors, this is not universal. For example, among prosimian primates, some slow lorises (genus *Nycticebus*) erupt two pairs of upper deciduous incisors but replace them with only one pair of upper permanent incisors, and the species of the genus *Lepilemur* (the sportive lemur) erupt and eventually shed one pair of unreplaced upper deciduous incisors; some insectivores retain unreplaced "deciduous" molars into adulthood (Schwartz, 1980).

In shorthand notation, a tooth is referred to by the first letter of its name. To denote a permanent tooth using this convention, this letter is capitalized (i.e. I = incisor; C = canine; P = premolar; M = molar). Deciduous teeth are noted in various ways (e.g. dI, di, i; dc, dC, c; dm, dM, m). Just as the dental formula delineates upper from lower teeth in a straightforward manner, a notation is also used to refer to individual upper or lower teeth or a string of upper or lower teeth in the same tooth class. A common approach to identifying the individual teeth of a tooth class is to number these teeth sequentially. Using the tooth abbreviations above, upper teeth are denoted by appending the number of the tooth as a superscript and lower teeth by appending the number of the tooth as a subscript. Thus, the central or first permanent upper incisor is represented as I^1 and the second lower deciduous molar as dm_2. Upper and lower permanent and deciduous canines may be noted in one of two ways. Sometimes the C or dc is placed above (denoting upper) or below (denoting lower) a line that symbolizes the line that separates numerator from denominator in a dental formula, i.e. $\underline{C}$ or $\overline{dc}$. At other times, a super- or subscripted "1" is used (e.g. C^1 or dc_1).

Tooth Surfaces and Orientation

Teeth are anchored in a ridge of bone called the **alveolar ridge** or **process;** root sockets are referred to as **alveoli** (singular, **alveolus**) (Figure 6–1). Alveolar bone is apparently a cellular derivative of tooth development rather than being a continuation of the basilar bone of the upper or lower jaw (e.g. Ten Cate and Mills, 1972). Sometimes the teeth and the alveolar process are referred to collectively as the **dental arcade.** Mammalian dental arcades are most commonly "U"- or "V"-shaped, with the result that much if not all of one side of a jaw is straight; thus, many teeth are oriented along an anteroposterior axis. In humans, however, the dental arcade's configuration is that of a relatively squat, posteriorly broadening parabola. As such, many teeth are oriented along different axes; for example, the long axis of the central incisor forms an obtuse angle to the long axis of the third molar. In order to accommodate the different orientations teeth might have in the jaws of different mammals, a consistent set of terms has been devised to refer to the four sides of a tooth, regardless of where in the dental arcade that tooth happens to reside.

The side of the tooth that faces the tongue is called the **lingual** side. The opposite side of the tooth is called either the **buccal** (referring to the cheek) or **labial** (referring to the lip) side of the tooth. "Buccal" is used more frequently in referring to human teeth because our lips (at rest) do not extend beyond our anterior teeth. "Labial" is used more frequently in describing the teeth of animals in which the lips extend along much or all of the dentition. Here we will follow the convention for human teeth and use the terms "buccal" and "lingual". The buccal-lingual (combined as **buccolingual**) dimension describes the **width** or **breadth** of a tooth (Figure 6–3).

Mesial (or **anterior**) and **distal** (or **posterior**) refer to the other sides of a tooth. The terms "mesial" and "distal" are more accurate for describing human teeth because, strictly speaking, "anterior" means "forward-facing" and "posterior" means "backwardly directed." Given the shape of the human dental arcade, no tooth is truly oriented anteroposteriorly. "Mesial," however, denotes the side of a tooth that is closer to the midline of the jaw; "distal" refers to the side of a tooth that is farther away from the midline of the jaw. For example, the mesial side or edge of a central incisor faces directly toward the midline of the jaw and the distal side away from the midline; anterior on a human incisor is actually the buccal surface and posterior the lingual surface. The **mesiodistal** dimension describes the **length** of a tooth.

Two other tooth surfaces are identified. One is the chewing or **occlusal surface.** Chewing food, using one's teeth for processing materials for a purpose, and/or just grinding (*bruxating*) one's teeth while asleep wears down the occlusal surfaces: the higher portions (e.g. cusps, crests) are abraded so that flat surfaces—**facets**—are formed; eventually, the bulk of the enamel and even much of the crown of the tooth can become worn away, depending on various factors.

The surface between two neighboring teeth is called the **interstitial (interproximal) surface.** For example, the interstitial surfaces between the central incisors are their mesial surfaces; the interstitial surfaces between a first and second molar are the distal surface of the first molar and the mesial surface of the second molar. Since teeth can and do move in the jaws, neighboring teeth will abrade against one another. Over time, this will produce a flattened area of contact—an *interstitial (interproximal) wear facet*—on the mesial and distal surfaces of

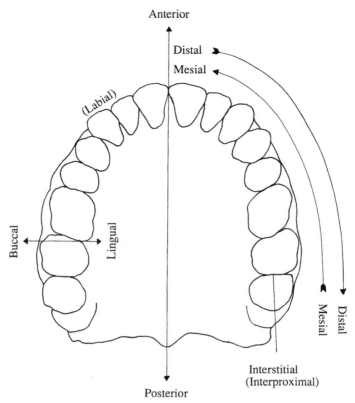

Figure 6–3 Schematic representation of an upper jaw to illustrate dental terminology for defining position and direction.

neighboring teeth. Increasing interstitial wear will eventually shorten a tooth, thereby increasing the inaccuracy of tooth length measurements. The presence or absence of interstitial wear facets on a tooth, however, can provide clues to the existence of neighboring teeth, which, in turn, can yield potentially important information: for example, noting whether a first molar had erupted behind a second deciduous molar or a second molar had erupted behind a first could affect the determination of age parameters. Identification of a tooth as a third molar could be firmed up by noting the absence of an interstitial wear facet on its distal surface. Matching up interstitial wear facets by size and shape can also provide clues to the correct association of isolated teeth.

Tooth Development

Largely through the work of such experimental embryologists as Glasstone (e.g. 1967), Kollar and Baird (e.g. 1971), and Miller (e.g. 1971), we now know that tooth development relies on the interaction of two **cell types**: neural crest–derived **ectomesenchyme** (sometimes referred to simply as **mesenchyme**) and **epithelium** (which is defined as **oral epithelium** because of its location along the presumptive embryonic jaws). **Neural crest cells,** apparently following cleavage planes and/or pathways established by pioneer nerves (see Lumsden, 1980), migrate from the embryonic *neural crest* and invade the presumptive jaws, eventually coming into close proximity with the oral epithelium. The sites into which neural crest cells migrate may have been determined by fibers of the maxillary and mandibular branches of the fifth cranial or trigeminal nerve (a sensory nerve); it may also be the case that innervation initiates the process of ectomesenchymal-epithelial interaction (Lumsden, 1980).

Until recently, debates over whether ectomesenchyme or oral epithelium actually carried the information necessary to induce tooth formation favored the role of ectomesenchyme, because in vitro experimentation indicated that tooth germs could be generated from the association of any, not just oral, epithelium and oral ectomesenchyme (e.g. Glasstone, 1967; Kollar, and Baird, 1971). Miller's studies (e.g. 1971), however, suggested that the roles were the other way round: oral epithelium induced tooth formation in the presence of ectomesenchyme. And this does indeed appear to be the case (Lumsden, 1988). Indeed, Kollar and Fisher (1980) have generated tooth germs in vitro by associating chick oral epithelium with mouse oral ectomesenchyme. Miller's colleagues had been using older mouse embryos than he had, and thus the oral ectomesenchyme of the older experimental animals had already been committed to tooth formation.

A general model of mammalian and thus human tooth formation suggests that, quite early in embryogenesis, the oral epithelium develops or acquires tooth-forming potential. Subsequently, underlying ectomesenchyme is incorporated into the process of tooth formation and becomes fully committed into the process of producing a tooth rather than some other organ. From experimental evidence, it appears that all the different tissues that eventually make up a tooth are derived from the cell mass that initiates tooth formation. For example, extirpated presumptive tooth-forming ectomesenchyme and oral epithelium, when grown in vitro but especially in vivo, produce teeth in which enamel and dentine are differentiated (e.g. Kollar and Baird, 1971). Ten Cate and Mills (1972) transplanted presumptive tooth-forming regions of fetal mice into different areas (e.g. skull, back) of host animals with the result that not only did teeth with differentiated crowns and roots form but these teeth "erupted" through the epidermis of the hosts and developed their own periodontal ligaments and surrounding alveolar bone. These latter results are particularly relevant to the observation that, when a tooth is lost from the jaw, only the alveolar bone in the affected region is resorbed, not the basilar bone of the mandible or the bone of the maxilla proper.

The onset of **tooth development** (Figure 6–4) is heralded by a condensation of ectomesenchyme in the region where tooth formation will occur and a concomitant thickening of the overlying oral epithelium. Subsequent cytological and structural changes, however, are subject to alternative interpretations. One suggestion is that the oral epithelium continues to thicken longitudinally in each jaw quadrant, resulting in what is called the **primary epithelial band;** the thickening epithelium also invades the ectomesenchyme beneath it. As the oral epithelium invades farther into the underlying ectomesenchyme, it appears to bifurcate into buccal and lingual extensions. The lingual extension, which will become associated with the developing tooth germ, is called the **dental lamina.** Eventually, the dental lamina expands into the **cap** and then the **bell** shapes associated with later phases of tooth development. The buccal division, referred to as the **vestibular lamina,** will continue to invaginate into the presumptive jaw, creating the **vestibule of the mouth** and delineating the lip.

The alternative, and perhaps more viable, interpretation of early tooth development is that there is a "tug-of-war" between the proliferating ectomesenchyme and oral epithelium, with the latter trying to contain the enlarging mass of ectomesenchymal cells. Consequently, the epithelium expands and, as it passes through the cap and bell stages, eventually encapsulates most of the ectomesenchymal mass. Within the framework of this model, there is no primary epithelial band and the vestibular and dental laminae develop as independent structures.

As the epithelial "cap" enlarges, its cells change their morphology and association from polygon-shaped cells that maintain contact along all sides to star-shaped cells that are connected to one another only at their "points." The **intercellular spaces** that separate the star-shaped cells are swollen by water that is attracted to the region by macromolecules called *hydrophilic acidic mucopolysaccharides.* This transformation results in a cellular layer, identified as the **stellate reticulum** (i.e. starlike network), whose functions may include protection of the developing tooth germ and maintenance of an environment around the dental organ that provides the space necessary for tooth formation to proceed unimpeded. The outer layer of the stellate reticulum is bounded by the **external (outer) dental (enamel) epithelium,** which is essentially a continuation of the oral epithelium. The external dental epithelium is also confluent with an **internal (inner) dental (enamel) epithelium** that is cytologically distinguished by its

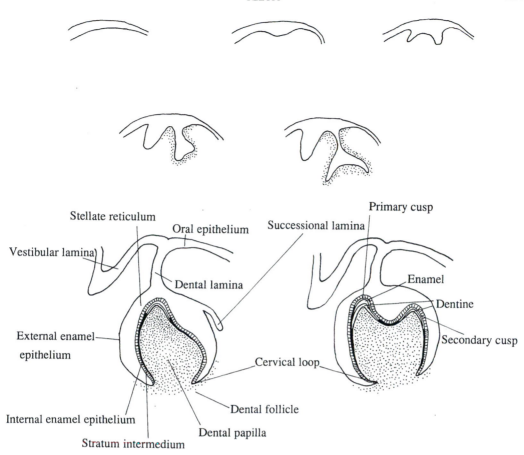

Figure 6–4 Schematic representation of major aspects of tooth development (as seen in the lower jaw, lingual is to the right): *(from top left to bottom right)*: the oral epithelium thickening and eventually producing two projections, a vestibular lamina *(on the left)* and dental lamina *(on the right)*; the dental lamina eventually expands into cap and then bell stages as it "captures" ectomesenchyme *(stippled)*; *(bottom row)* *(left)* example of a single-cusped tooth, *(right)* example of a multicusped tooth (see text for further elaboration).

low, cuboidally shaped columnar cells. Eventually, another layer of cells—the **stratum intermedium**—differentiates and interdigitates with the cells of the internal dental epithelium. At the bell stage, the internal and external dental epithelial juncture creates the **rim** or **cervical loop** of the **enamel organ,** which, in turn, surrounds the **dental papilla** (Figure 6–4). The cervical loop constrains expansion of the tooth germ. The entire tooth germ then becomes surrounded by the **dental follicle,** which is derived from ectomesenchymal cells that had become displaced from the dental papilla. Nerves and arteries pass through the "base" of the dental papilla and pervade the dental follicle. Upon eruption of the tooth, the dental follicle gives rise to the periodontal ligament.

A tooth that develops in association with the dental lamina—that is, is connected directly to the oral epithelium via the dental lamina—is a **primary tooth.** Developmentally, in humans and all other mammals, the "permanent molars" are primary teeth because they arise sequentially from the posteriorly elongating lamina that gave rise to the "deciduous molars" (Ooë, 1979). The *dental formula for the human primary dentition* (compare with Figures 6–12 and 6–13) is:

$$\frac{2.1.5}{2.1.5}$$

A **successional tooth** arises *lingually* from the external dental epithelium of the tooth it will eventually replace (Ooë, 1965; cf. Osborn, 1971; Tonge, 1976) (Figure 6–4). Therefore, a successional tooth is not connected directly to the oral epithelium. In a diphyodont animal, a successional tooth is referred to as a **secondary tooth**. The lingual extension from the external dental epithelium of a primary tooth that gives rise to a secondary tooth is the **successional lamina** (Figure 6–4) [thus a tertiary tooth (see Figure 6–10), for example, would arise from the successional lamina of a secondary tooth]. In polyphyodont animals, such as sharks, each tooth of each generation develops via a successional lamina that is a lingual outgrowth of the external dental epithelium of the tooth it will replace.

Since erupted secondary teeth in humans and other diphyodont mammals are normally not shed, they can also be referred to as *permanent teeth*. In humans, these teeth are the successional incisors, canines, and premolars. As mentioned above, the permanent molars are developmentally primary teeth. Obviously, not all permanent teeth are the same developmentally. Thus, while there might be historical reasons for referring collectively to the teeth of an adult individual as permanent teeth, these teeth may not be serially homologous structures. The *dental formula for the human secondary dentition* (compare with Figures 6–12 and 6–13) is:

$$\frac{2.1.2}{2.1.2}$$

Crown shape is initiated during the bell stage (Figure 6–4). It results from a flexing or folding of the internal dental epithelium as it continues to increase in surface area—due to ongoing mitotic processes of cell division and proliferation—while, at the same time, it also is being restricted in its outward growth by the cervical loop. The fold or flexure in the internal dental epithelium occurs at a quiescent, nondividing region, which gets pushed into the stellate reticulum. This creates the peak or elevation of a **primary cusp**; in humans and apes, for example, the protoconid is the first lower molar cusp to develop. The region of the primary cusp is also the region at which **odontoblasts** differentiate and begin depositing dentine (Ten Cate and Osborn, 1976).

Roughly coincident with the differentiation of odontoblasts, the cells of the internal dental epithelium elongate, alter their cytoplasmic constitution, and become capable of producing enamel. Enamel-producing cells are called **ameloblasts.** They deposit enamel on top of the dentine, first at the apex of the newly forming cusp and then down the sides of the presumptive cusp, following in the wake of dentine deposition. The border between enamel and dentine is called the **dentinoenamel juncture. Cusp height** is achieved as the internal dental epithelium continues both to expand into the dental papilla and to elongate the sides of the developing cusp.

Additional cusps arise in the same way that a primary cusp does: cell division stops in a particular region of the internal dental epithelium, the region becomes flexed and pushed into the stellate reticulum, odontoblasts differentiate and deposit dentine, and then newly formed ameloblasts deposit enamel on top of the dentine. (It would be of potential significance if the sequences in which cusps are initiated were in any way taxonomically relevant.) The degree to which cusps end up being separated from one another is a function of the extent to which the internal dental epithelium continues to proliferate and enlarge cusp size. Eventually, dentine fills in the basins between cusps and the final shape of the tooth is established. Deposition of enamel follows on the heels of dentine deposition, sometimes reflecting in detail the surface topography of the dentine, sometimes obscuring details that might be in the dentine, or at other times adding features to the crown's surface.

Enamel

Like bone, enamel is the product of **mineralization,** a process by which **hydroxyapatite** is deposited within a **cellular matrix.** The major differences between bone and enamel formation are that (1) the cells that produce teeth and their components are derivatives of neural crest–derived ectomesenchyme, whereas bone is mesodermal in origin, and (2) in contrast to bone, enamel does not have a definitive organic precursor. During the early phase of enamel deposition, the ameloblast begins to move away from the dentine surface and the secretory end of the ameloblast begins laying down a layer of **enamel matrix** between it and the dentine. Enamel matrix is a combination of organic and inorganic—**enamel crystallite**—material. Subsequent to laying down the enamel matrix, the secretory end of the ameloblast changes shape, becoming conical with an extended pointed end; it invades the enamel matrix and begins to lay down enamel. At this point the secretory end of the ameloblast is identified as **Tomes's process.** (Additionally, an ameloblast may be functionally analogous to an osteoclast in the sense that it appears to be involved in the removal of material from the enamel matrix.) The last phase of mineralization occurs very rapidly, producing the hard, final enamel product. Rates of enamel deposition and the length of time over which enamel is deposited vary among mammals. Thus, enamel thickness can be different in different mammals; for example, humans and pigs have a thick layer of enamel, especially on the molars, whereas lemurs do not.

A fundamental difference in microstructure between mammalian and reptilian teeth is the development in mammalian enamel of crystallite patterns called **enamel prisms.** But although one can observe that the enamel crystallites in mammalian teeth are laid down in particular orientations such that prisms are created (as opposied to the *aprismatic* enamel of reptiles), the underlying process of prism formation is not yet completely understood. Nevertheless, it does seem, from circumstantial evidence, that enamel prism patterns exist in mammals because the movement of the ameloblast away from the dentine layer is restricted by the stellate reticulum, which, in turn, leads to a compression of and change in the parallel flow lines the enamel matrix otherwise would follow if ameloblast movement were unimpeded. In mammals, enamel crystallites become oriented along the *nonparallel flow lines* of the secreted enamel matrix. Prisms become defined as a consequence of the development of **interprismatic regions,** which arise as a result of resorption of enamel matrix in areas that lie opposite the secretory sides of the Tomes's processes. With the advent of more sophisticated approaches to scanning electron microscopy, it has become increasingly popular to investigate the patterns of crystallites in different mammalian groups. Among mammals, two **enamel prism patterns** are commonly identified on the basis of a rough interpretation of a cross section of prism shape within an interprismatic space. One is a *"circular" pattern (pattern 1)* and the other is the *"keyhole" pattern (pattern 2)* (e.g. Boyd, 1971; Figure 6–5).

Sometimes it appears that more than one

5 μm

Figure 6–5   Confocal images of cross-sectioned enamel prisms (illustrating the "keyhole" pattern) in two fossil (Eocene) primates: *(left) Cantius mckennai* and *(right) Notharctus* sp. *(Courtesy of E. Dumont.)*

enamel prism pattern can be identified on the same tooth. But this illusion is probably due to the degree to which the ameloblasts (or their course of movement) bend or *decussate* (Figure 6–6). For after all, a single ameloblast is responsible for the enamel laid down along a single pathway from the dentinoenamel juncture to the surface of the crown, regardless of the number of different prism patterns that might appear to be identifiable under scanning electron microscopy. The undulating path that an ameloblast follows also creates patterns of cross striations—the so-called **Hunter-Schreger bands**—that are observable under reflected light (Figure 6–7).

Interference with the process of amelogenesis is referred to generally as **hypocalcification.** Among the various defects that can occur during amelogenesis and that may disrupt it, the most commonly noted can be grouped together as **gross enamel hypoplasias** (e.g. Goodman and Armelagos, 1985; Goodman and Rose, 1991; Lukacs, 1989; Skinner and Goodman, 1992). In general, enamel hypoplasias are recognized as regions on a tooth crown in which the enamel is thinner than surrounding, "normal" regions of enamel; interestingly, enamel hypoplasias are most often noted on the buccal surfaces of teeth. Total lack of enamel in a region of a crown occurs with extraordinary infrequency.

Inasmuch as it appears that hereditary causes of such defects are rare, the major factors affecting amelogenesis are stresses that interfere with proper growth: for example, nutrional imbalances, vitamin D deficiency, hypoparathyroidism, and such serious childhood illnesses as rheumatic fever. Given the chronology of tooth crown formation, the actual time period over which such stresses could widely affect amelogenesis is approximately until the onset of puberty. Enamel hypoplasias may reflect a stress or trauma whose effect is **localized** to one or a few (not necessarily neighboring) teeth throughout the jaw *(localized enamel hypoplasia),* or they may be more **systemic,** affecting the majority of tooth *(systemic enamel hypoplasia).* Such assaults can also be (or at least appear to have been) recurrent.

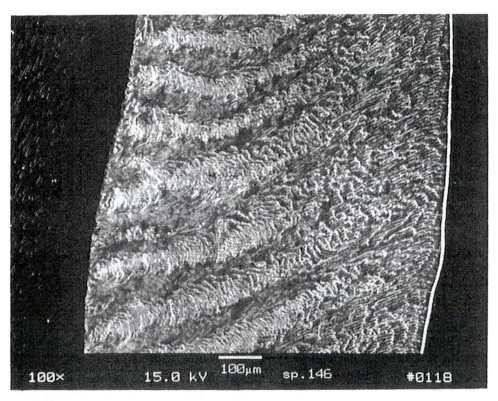

100×   15.0 kV   100µm   sp.146   #0118

Figure 6–6 Photomicrograph illustrating prism decussation: cross section through a right lower first molar of an Old World monkey *(Cercocebus torquatus). (Courtesy of E. Dumont.)*

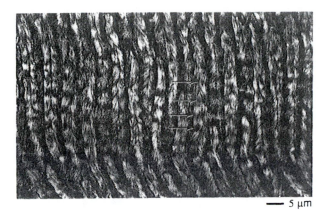

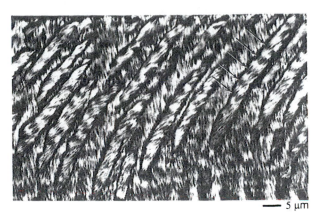

Figure 6–7 Backscattered electron microscopy images of prism cross striations (Hunter-Schreger bands) *(indicated by arrows): (top)* a prosimian primate *(Galago alleni)* and *(bottom)* a sac-winged bat *(Taphozous mauritianus). (Courtesy of E. Dumont.)*

The most common expression of hypoplasia is the development of horizontal grooves running across the enamel surface, giving the appearance of constricting the crown at these regions (Figure 6–8). In extreme cases, some or all of these grooves may entirely encircle the crown (Figure 6–9; also Figure 9–11). Such hypoplasia is sometimes referred to as **chronologic** or **linear hypoplasia.** These grooves occur most frequently in the middle and cervical thirds of the crown and are more often noted on the anterior rather than posterior permanent teeth. Although there has yet to be developed a universally accepted chronology of tooth formation (see Chapter 7), there have been various attempts at estimating the age(s) at which an individual suffered the stresses recorded permanently in teeth as linear enamel hypoplasia (e.g. see Goodman and Rose, 1991; Murray and

Murray, 1989; Skinner and Goodman, 1992). Assuming constant rates of crown growth—and that the same tooth takes the same amount of time to form regardless of whether it is much larger or smaller in one individual compared to another—the age at which an insult occurred is calculated by measuring the distance of the hypoplastic groove from the dentinoenamel juncture and either matching this measurement with a standardized chart or entering the data into a readily available computer program.

Another form of hypoplasia, most frequently expressed in lower molars as a deep, conical pit at the base of the crease between the protoconid and hypoconid, is called a **foramen caecum** (Figure 6–8). A foramen caecum may be localized to only one or two teeth or may be found throughout a molar series, either uni- or bilaterally. The osteologist should take care not to

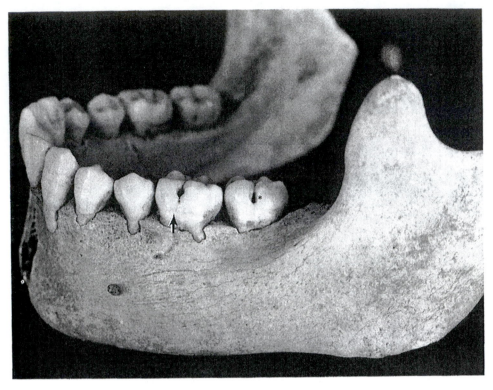

Figure 6–8   Hypodontia (lack of M$_3$) and examples of hypoplasia: grooves indicative of linear hypoplasia are noted on all teeth *(e.g. see arrow)* and a foramen caecum *(e.g. asterisk)* is present buccally on each lower molar; also note on M$_1$ *(just distal to the arrow)* an enamel extension coursing down between the buccal roots (prehistoric, Pennsylvania).

confuse such a hypoplastic pit with a carious lesion (see Chapter 8). Broadly shallow hypoplastic pits may develop on the buccal surfaces of anterior teeth. Although technically these forms of abnormal enamel deposition can be classified as hypoplasias, it is unclear that they should be regarded in the same category etiologically as (systemic) linear enamel hypoplasias.

Determination of Tooth Shape

Although one can describe the course by which a tooth develops into the shape it will eventually have, the underlying mechanism by which tooth shape is actually determined is still a matter of debate. Usually the argument is presented in the context of an explanation of the differences in tooth shape among mammals. A few of the competing alternative theories are presented here.

The longest standing explanation of differences in heterodonty among mammals is Butler's (e.g. 1939, 1978) **Field Theory**. The emphasis here is on the constancy between *tooth type* (i.e. incisor, canine, premolar, molar) and *tooth position* in the jaw. The guide to the identity of teeth is the premaxillary-maxillary suture, which must be delineated first, because only then can the upper canine—and thus all other teeth—be identified. The focus of this theory is the adult dentition, in which incisors, canines, molars, and premolars are potentially identifiable. Given these foci, two types of questions emerge: (1) "Why in some mammals (e.g. shrews or hedgehogs) is, for example, the shape of the anteriormost incisor caniniform rather than incisiform and that of the second incisor premolariform rather than caniniform?" And (2) "How, for example, can some mammals (e.g. horses) have premolars that are as large and complex morphologically as their molars?"

The second kind of question is seemingly the

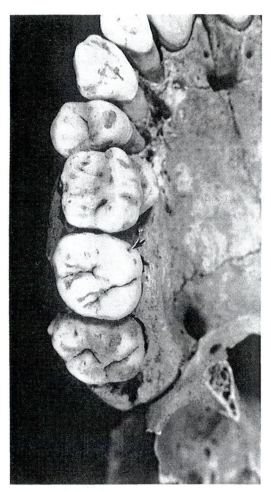

Figure 6–9 Upper jaw illustrating how premolar number could be reduced while still maintaining three molariform teeth: the second deciduous molar is retained as the first molariform tooth, the third molar is inhibited, and the first and second molars then become the second and third molariform teeth in the series [in reality, the second premolar of this individual (visible under the crown of dm²) had started to erupt]; also note, for example, that the canine crown is circumscribed by a deep linear hypoplastic groove and the M¹ bears a small Carabelli's pit *(arrow)* (prehistoric, Pennsylvania).

easier to answer and thus to incorporate into the formulation of the Field Theory. If the position of type of tooth is constant in all mammals, there must be some influence external to the developing tooth germ that determines its ultimate shape. In the case of horses developing molariform premolars, it is postulated that the same external source that influences the shape

of the molars expanded with similar intensity into the region of the developing premolars. In other mammals, such as humans, the intensity of this *molar field* would taper off anteriorly, thereby resulting in the development of teeth that are less complex morphologically than molars but more complex (because of their being under the same field as the molars) that canines and incisors. In addition to a molar field, Butler hypothesized the existence of *incisor and canine fields* [Patterson (1956) suggested that there might be a premolar field as well]. As such, it can be postulated that the extent to which neighboring **morphogenetic fields** overlap one another or to which one field excludes another from a dental region can explain all of the permutations in heterodonty observed among mammals. For instance, in shrews and hedgehogs, the first incisor is caniniform because the canine field shifted to the front of the jaw and overwhelmed the incisor field; the remaining incisors as well as the canine are premolariform because the molar field expanded forward. The explanation for why the anterior premolars of these mammals are not bicuspid is that there is a slight overlap of the canine field with the molar field.

In terms of our current understanding of developmental processes, the essence of the Field Theory is that tooth-forming ectomesenchymal and oral epithelial cells in the presumptive jaws are uncommitted to producing a tooth of any particular shape. It is only under the influence of an extrinsic source of "information"—such as a morphogenetic field—that these cells will produce a tooth of a certain shape. The Field Theory thus rests upon a model (a "**source-sink**" or **gradient model**) derived from study of embryonic differentiation in various amphibians, such as newts and salamanders, in which it has been postulated that a chemical "source" of information travels along a presumptive limb or axial skeleton towards a "sink," creating a meristic (merismatic) patterning or gradient of structure as it proceeds (e.g. see Melton, 1991).

Osborn (1978) proposed the **Clone Model** as an alternative to the Field Theory. This model differs from its predecessor in that it posits that the determination of *tooth shape* is an intrinsic property of the tooth-forming cells themselves. Concomitantly, *tooth classes* (i.e. incisor, canine, molar) are established by initial cell masses *(stem progenitors)* that subsequently proliferate and expand horizontally along the jaws to produce the specific number of teeth that will represent any given tooth class. Thus teeth within a particular tooth class will have the characteristics of that tooth class because the gradient of morphological complexity within it is determined by the shape-producing potential of the cells as they continue to divide and proliferate. Since the cells that could be identified as stem progenitors are those in the embryonic stage of development, the focus of the Clone Model, at least initially, is the primary dentition.

Underlying much of the Clone Model is Lumsden's (1979) experimental research on the mouse dentition, in which he demonstrated that not only the first, but the second and third molars develop in sequence as a result of cellular proliferation from the presumptive cell mass that gives rise initially to the first molar. The experimentally "grown" molars mirrored the size and shape gradient of the normal mouse molar dentition. Osborn chose to characterize the process by which the molar series enlarged into three discrete units as *cloning*.

A logical extension of the Clone Model not completely developed by Osborn is that the shape of a tooth, rather than its position in the jaw, is the clue to the identity of that tooth (see Schwartz, 1980). However, because he adhered to the assumption that the anteriormost tooth in the jaw is probably an incisor, Osborn was obliged to identify the anterior caniniform tooth of a shrew or hedgehog as an incisor. If, however, the canine class can be lost in mammals—and, regardless of one's preferred model of mammalian heterodonty, it is generally agreed upon that various mammals (e.g. rodents, many artiodactyls) do not develop the canine—it can also be hypothesized that any tooth class or classes can be lost (or, more properly, inhibited from developing). Thus, the caniniform tooth at the front of the jaw in, for example, shrews and hedgehogs would be a canine; the incisor tooth class would have been inhibited in these mammals.

Under the constraints of the Clone Model, the explanation for the development of molariform premolars (e.g. as in the horse) is another matter altogether, precisely because premolars are secondary, not primary teeth. As such, one

has to consider first the characteristics of the primary teeth from which the secondary teeth bud. With regard to the horse, the primary teeth that precede and then are replaced by the premolars are themselves molariform; these primary teeth thus conform to the morphological gradient that includes the molars. [As discussed earlier, deciduous molars are part of the same developmental/morphological gradient that includes the posteriorly developing permanent molars; this continuity between dm2 and M1 results in the posteriormost deciduous molars of virtually all heterodont mammals being molariform (e.g. Figure 6–9) and thus often misidentified as permanent molars.] The explanation invoked by the Clone Model for why the horse has a molar class in which morphological complexity is maintained throughout the series of teeth is that the developmental potential and competence of the proliferating cell mass did not diminish. But since each secondary tooth derives from the cell mass of the primary tooth that precedes it, one must expand the concepts of the Clone Model to embrace the vertical nature of primary-secondary tooth development (Schwartz and Langdon, 1991). Thus, in terms of the molariform premolars of the horse, tooth size- and shape-forming potential of the ecto-mesenchymal/epithelial cells that will give rise to the individual secondary teeth does not diminish. In most mammals, however—humans included—premolars are often simpler morphologically and smaller in crown dimensions than their primary predecessors, which suggests that tooth size-and shape-forming potential of epithelium/ectomesenchyme in these animals does diminish with the origin of secondary teeth.

To summarize, the Field Theory (Butler, 1939, 1978) relates to the acquisition of shape by the permanent teeth that erupt into an adult individual's jaws, whereas the Clone Model (Osborn, 1978) and its modifications (Schwartz, 1980) begin with the initiation of the primary dentition. Of course, one can push the Field Theory back into the early stages of primary tooth development and suggest that primary teeth arise from separate clumps of cells upon which incisor, canine, and molar fields impose themselves. Since we know that each successor buds directly from an individual predecessor, the logical extension of the Field Theory is that each successional tooth germ lacks the competence to induce its own shape. Thus each successive tooth germ must be captured by a morphogenetic field that remains in the region in question beyond the phase of primary tooth development or by a field that enters the region anew, displacing or replacing the field that had earlier acted upon the predecessor teeth.

Supernumerary Teeth and Tooth Agenesis

Although most mammals develop an expected number of teeth, an occasional individual may develop more or fewer teeth than is typical of the individual's species. Additional teeth—which may present themselves as either rudimentary structures or fully formed, recognizable teeth—are referred to as **supernumerary teeth.** The suggested mechanisms behind supernumerary tooth development are summarized below; the result is called **hyperdontia.** The process of tooth loss is called **tooth agenesis;** the result is **hypodontia** (Figure 6–8).

If teeth are viewed as individually independent, developmentally discrete units, then the development of supernumerary structures as well as the loss of teeth must always be interpreted as resulting from isolated, usually de novo developmental events. If, however, tooth classes are seen as the products of proliferation of an initial stem progenitor cell mass, a model that can account for both tooth loss and the development of supernumeraries becomes available.

The simplest examples of supernumerary teeth are seen in the posterior addition of tooth structures to the molar tooth class. Even humans occasionally develop fourth molars. When such a supernumerary tooth is fully formed, it is complementary in morphology and size to the gradient already established along the normal molar tooth series. When only part of the crown of a supernumerary molar forms, the cusps present correspond to the cusps that calcify first during normal development of that tooth—that is, the anterior cusps (Schwartz, 1984). Although such a rudimentary or morphologically incomplete molar is usually interpreted as having split off from the tooth germ developing in front of it, there is an alternative explanation: since the molar class teeth appear to "clone" posteriorly, a supernumerary tooth,

or at least a truncated supernumerary tooth, will develop if the developmental potential of the posteriorly proliferating cell mass is maintained and there is sufficient space in the jaw for a tooth to form (Schwartz, 1984). In mammals such as the phalangeroid marsupial *Peradorcas,* which normally develops seven or eight supernumerary molars in each quadrant of each jaw, and the manatee, which grows a lifetime of molars by adding new molars posteriorly as the worn teeth are shed anteriorly, one can hypothesize that competence for tooth formation is maintained in the posteriorly proliferating cell mass; in each case, those teeth that might be thought of as supernumerary molars complement in size and morphology the molar teeth that developed and erupted before them. In the case of the incomplete supernumerary structure, the albeit truncated "tooth" also complements the molar size and shape gradient morphologically.

Dental agenesis or tooth "loss" also can be explained in terms of the potential and competence for tooth formation in the proliferating cell mass of a tooth class. In this case, however, it is the contraction or inhibition of this potential. Third molar agenesis—which, for example, occurs with relatively high frequency among Alaskan Eskimos (Davies, 1972; Moorrees, 1957)—would thus result from the truncation of a posteriorly enlarging molar tooth class. Such truncation would result from the restriction of developmental space and/or the loss of tooth-forming potential in the molar-class cell mass posteriorly. In the case of marmosets (a group of New World monkeys distinguished from others, for instance, by third-molar agenesis), radiographic analysis reveals that third molars do begin to develop but are resorbed prior to reaching a stage of formation beyond which complete development and eruption necessarily would result (Hershkovitz, 1977). Thus it would seem that the molar-class cells of marmosets are sufficiently competent to initiate third-molar development but not to sustain development to the critical threshold beyond which the tooth would be committed to erupting into the jaw. As has been suggested elsewhere (Lumsden, 1979; Osborn, 1970, 1973; Schwartz, 1984), both expression (normal or supernumerary) and reduction in number of teeth (i.e. inhibition of tooth development) appear to be related to degrees of inhibition imposed upon an established developmental system rather than being distinctly unique phenomena.

Ooë's (e.g. 1965, 1969, 1971) embryological work on human tooth development is compatible with the suggestion that truncation/inhibition of developmental competence and cellular proliferation, rather than a de facto loss of structure, can lead to a reduction in tooth number within a tooth class.

In this seminal series of articles, Ooë demonstrated the existence in humans of potential successors to the premolars as well as to the first and second molars (he did not study the third molar); these potential successional teeth are resorbed at a rudimentary stage of development.

Importantly, these resorbed tooth germs—whether associated with premolars or molars—conformed to the "textbook picture" of successional tooth development: each arose lingually from the external dental epithelium of a predecessor tooth germ. In addition, they can be identified easily as developing tooth germs and distinguished from extraneous mesodermal condensations. Yet we know, as a rule among humans and mammals in general, that premolars and molars are not replaced by other teeth. Although more than two sets of teeth may be initiated, only two sets of teeth normally develop and erupt into the jaws—but there are some individuals in whom a "third" dentition does develop (e.g. Figure 6–10). Thus, it would appear that a viable interpretation of Ooë's dis-

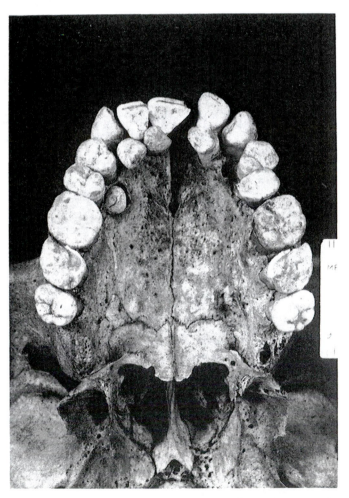

Figure 6–10 Upper jaw of individual with supernumerary antemolar teeth representing a "third" dentition (erupting lingual to the normally present permanent or secondary teeth) (prehistoric, Alaska).

coveries is that diphyodonty in humans (and, presumably, other mammals) results from the truncation/inhibition of tooth development to two *functional* sets of teeth.

Basic Nomenclature of Crown Anatomy

There is a specific nomenclature for identifying the various cusps, crests, depressions, and other structures that can make up the crown of a tooth (Figure 6–11). Regardless of the tooth under investigation, there are certain consistencies in the system of identifying the morphological components of a tooth's crown. **Primary cusps** are represented by the word root *con;* cusps of an upper tooth are *cones* and those of a lower tooth *conids* (in general, the suffix *-id* refers to a feature on a lower tooth). Subsidiary or **secondary cusps** on upper teeth are identified on upper teeth as *conules* and, on lowers, as *conulids*. **Crests** or **ridges** on upper teeth are *cristae* (the Latin feminine plural—*crista* is the singular) and those on lower teeth are *cristids*. A three-dimensional band or ledge of enamel on the side (not occlusal surface) of a tooth is referred to either as a *cingulum* or a *cingulid,* depending on whether it is an upper or lower tooth; the plural of "cingulum" is "cingula." A cingulum/cingulid may surround a tooth completely or it may be restricted to one or some of its sides; cingular development in humans is rare and minimal when it does occur. A small and topographically restricted swelling or distension of enamel on the side of a tooth (usually the buccal and/or lingual side) is called either a *style* or a *stylid*. Prefixes (e.g. **proto-, para-, meta-**) are used in conjunction with *cone/conid, conule/conulid, style/stylid, crista/cristid* to refer to specific structures in specific locations on a tooth.

Although it is more accurate in terms of ontogenetic context to describe first the primary tooth classes and then the secondary teeth within each tooth class, the following discussion follows convention by describing the "adult" or permanent teeth as a "set" and then the deciduous teeth. Since the molar teeth are morphologically the most complex of an individual's dentition and certain conventions used in the identification of molar structures are applied to morphologically less complex teeth, the

discussion begins with these posterior molar class teeth. In order to minimize confusion on upper versus lower tooth terminology, we focus first on the upper dentition.

Molars: An Overview

Certain generalizations can be applied to upper and lower human molars alike (see Figures 6–11 to 6–16):

1. Human upper and lower molar teeth characteristically decrease in size and morphological complexity in the sequence M1 → M2 → M3.
2. Correlated with this general size-shape gradient is a morphological gradient. Occlusally, M1 is typically the most while M3 is the least complex molar morphologically. For example, a cusp (or any other feature) may be fully expressed on M1, less so on M2, and absent on M3.
3. Molar roots also tend to conform to a gradient. Typically, the roots of M1 are the most splayed and separated, while the roots of M3 are the most closely approximated. A gradient from M1 to M3 can also exist where the M1 roots are separate only toward their tips while those of M3 are totally undivided. In the latter extreme case, longitudinal grooves or furrows delineate these ontogenetically undivided structures.
4. Molar roots tend to arc posteriorly toward their tips (which provides a secondary clue to the identification of a tooth); this is a function of the coincidence of the path along which any given molar erupts and the fact that the jaws are still expanding at the time of molar eruption. The intensity of this root deflection posteriorly increases from the first to the third molar.

Upper Molars

M^1 is typically square (or the most square of the three), M^2 is more rectangular (its mesiodistal length is shorter than its buccolingual breadth/width), and M^3 tends to be more triangular in shape (Figures 6–11, 6–12, and 6–14 to 6–16).

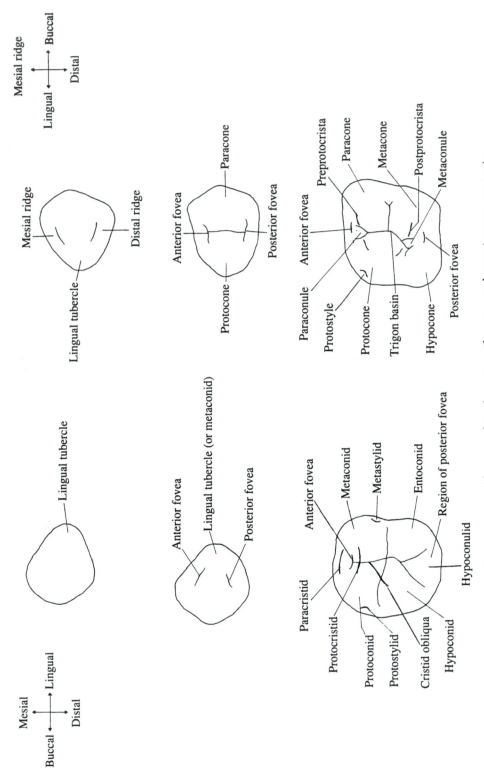

Figure 6–11 Some basic anatomical features of tooth crowns: *(from top to bottom)* permanent canines, premolars, and molars; *(left column)* lower and *(right column)* upper teeth.

170

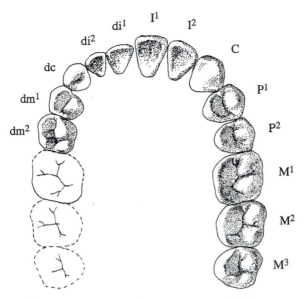

Figure 6–12   Occlusal view of upper permanent *(right)* and deciduous *(left)* dentitions; images of the permanent molars are drawn distal to dm² to illustrate the morphological continuity within the primary molar class.

Upper molars characteristically develop three roots. When the gradient of root coalescence is such that M³ roots are undivided (forming a pyramidal configuration), the delineation of the potential roots is often realized by the presence of three longitudinal grooves as well as three distinct root canal openings.

On M¹, M², and M³ alike, one can delineate

a triangular arrangement of low, bulbous cusps, with two cusps positioned buccally and the third—the apex of the triangle—located lingually and somewhat mesially. These three cusps form the *trigon;* the center of the trigon is a shallow basin, the *trigon basin.* The mesiobuccal cusp of the trigon is the *paracone,* the distobuccal cusp the *metacone,* and the mesio-

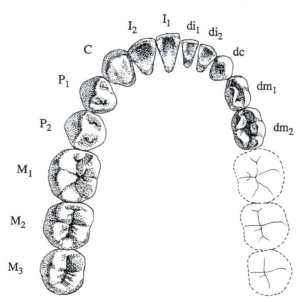

Figure 6–13   Occlusal view of lower permanent *(left)* and deciduous *(right)* dentitions; images of the permanent molars are drawn distal to dm₂ to illustrate the morphological continuity within the primary molar class.

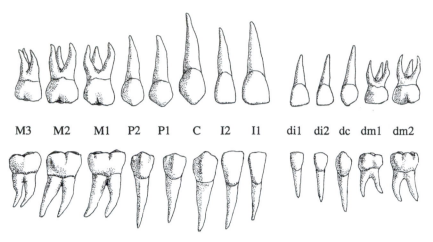

Figure 6–14 Buccal view of *(top)* upper and *(bottom)* lower dentitions; *(right)* left deciduous teeth; *(left)* right permanent teeth.

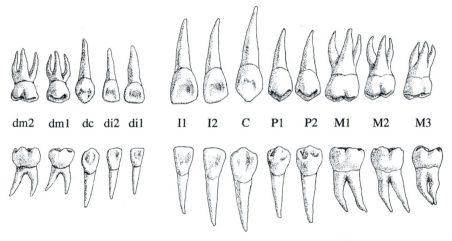

Figure 6–15 Lingual view of *(top)* upper and *(bottom)* lower dentitions; *(left)* left deciduous teeth; *(right)* right permanent teeth.

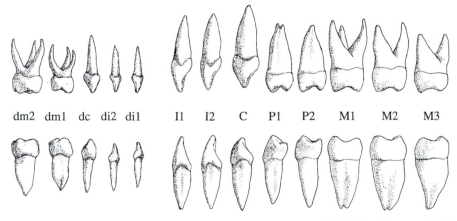

Figure 6–16 Mesial view of *(top)* upper and *(bottom)* lower dentitions; *(left)* left deciduous teeth; *(right)* right permanent teeth.

lingual cusp the *protocone*. A root is associated ontogenetically (and thus spatially) with each trigon cusp; thus an upper molar possesses one lingual and two buccal roots. A fourth cusp, the *hypocone*, may develop in the distolingual corner of an upper molar. The hypocone can be delineated by an oblique groove or crease that demarcates the distal side of the trigon. Technically, the hypocone or any observable swelling in the distolingual region of the tooth is referred to as the *talon* (= "heel" in Greek). If an individual develops upper molar hypocones, they will be most fully expressed on M^1 and least developed or even absent on M^3. If the upper molar size/shape gradient is quite severe, metacone size reduction may accompany hypocone absence. Although human molar cusps are much lower and more bulbous than those of many other mammals—which is in large part due to deposition of a thick layer of enamel over the more detailed surface of the dentine—human upper molars nonetheless retain the typical mammalian characteristic wherein buccal cusps are taller than lingual cusps.

To the extent that additional morphological features are discernible, one can usually delineate two stout, thick crests or cristae emanating from the protocone. One crest, the *preprotocrista* ("pre-" because it courses in front of, or "before," the protocone), connects the protocone with the paracone. The second crest, the *postprotocrista* ("post-" because it courses behind or posteriorly away from the protocone), connects the protocone with the metacone. Collectively, the pre- and postprotocristae are referred to as the *protocristae*. In humans, the preprotocrista is frequently the more observable and dominant protocone crest.

Sometimes there is a swelling midway along the preprotocrista that may even be emphasized by thin longitudinal creases. This small, cusp-like structure is the *paraconule*. A *metaconule* is much less frequently present, but when it is, it is associated with the postprotocrista. As with other features, conules tend to be most expressed on the first molar and least on the third.

Mesial to the preprotocrista and distal to the postprotocrista (if one is present) are variably developed depressions, called *foveae*; the singular is fovea. The fovea in front of the preprotocrista is the *anterior fovea*, which is typically more markedly excavated than the other fovea, the *distal* or *posterior fovea*.

Upper molar cingula are rare in humans (e.g. see Swindler and Olshan, 1988), but when they do occur, they usually develop along the lingual sides of the molars. More commonly but still in rather low percentages (e.g. see Swindler, 1976), a localized swelling of enamel may develop on the lingual face of the protocone, which, if found in a nonhuman mammal, is identified as the *protostyle*. In humans, it is referred to as *Carabelli's cusp*. Variations may include a pit *(Carabelli's pit)* distally alongside Carabelli's cusp or just a pit alone (e.g. Figure 6–9). Carabelli's cusp/pit expression conforms to the molar size/shape gradient.

Upper Premolars

Upper **anterior (first)** and posterior (**second**) **premolars** are morphologically quite similar to one another (Figures 6–11, 6–12, and 6–14 to 6–16). They develop two cusps—one buccally and the other lingually opposite it—and two roots, each in the region of a cusp. Premolar cusp identity is based on the invalid assumption that molars are premolars with additional cusps. As such, the buccal cusp is referred to as the *paracone* and the lingual cusp as the *protocone*. The paracone is somewhat larger than the protocone in height as well as mass (the disparity is more obvious on the first premolar). Buccolingually oriented *anterior* and *posterior foveae* bound the bases and thus add to the delineation of the paracone and protocone. A plane passing through the apices of the paracone and protocone divides the crown asymmetrically. The portion of the crown in front of this axis is slightly smaller than the portion posterior to it. This asymmetry is also noted in viewing the outline of the paracone from the buccal side: the sloped edge from the cusp's apex to the most mesial extension of the crown is shorter than the posterior edge.

The apices of the cusps of the first premolar are positioned slightly more internally on the crown than they are on the second premolar. As such, the angle between the opposing faces of these cusps is steeper and more acute on the first premolar than on the second; when viewed from the mesial or distal side, the opposing faces of the paracone and protocone on the first premolar form a narrower and more acute "V" than on the second premolar. This difference in cusp position is noted further in viewing the premolars from the mesial or distal side: the buccal and lingual surfaces of the first premolar are slightly more bulbous or arced than those on the second premolar.

In comparison to a lower premolar, the root complex of an upper premolar is characteristically bulkier and buccolingually deep (and is thus less delineated at the neck from the crown); rather than being conical, upper premolar roots are typically flattened along the mesial and distal surfaces. The stereotype about upper premolars is that they have two roots while lower premolars have one. In practical terms, two roots are more frequently seen as distinct entities on the first upper premolar than on the second premolar, where they are more often less fully divided. The ontogenetic potential for two roots is demonstrated on an upper premolar by longitudinal grooves that course, respectively, along the mesial and distal sides of the undivided root complex. Although root deflection as a clue to tooth identity is less obvious in premolars than in molars, the root tips may arc or bend distally.

Upper Canine

The upper canine is a stout, single-cusped, roughly conical single-rooted tooth (Figures 6–11, 6–12, and 6–14 to 6–16). The mesial edge of the crown (as measured from the cusp apex to the most mesial extent of the crown) is shorter than the distal edge; thus, in buccal outline, the crown is subtriangular in shape. The upper canine's root is quite robust and long; the tip may be deflected distally.

Aside from its prominent primary cusp (which may or may not be a *protocone*), an upper canine usually lacks major additional morphological adornment. A *lingual swelling* (*lingual tubercle* or *tuberculum dentale*) may develop near the base of the crown; it may be delineated further by being slightly elevated. Low, rounded lingual marginal ridges of enamel may emanate from the lingual tubercle, with one ridge proceeding mesially and the other distally; these ridges are sometimes identified as the *mesial* and *distal ridges*. When surface topography is lost through wear and attrition, the existence of a ridge can sometimes be established by the presence of a thin groove, which

would have bound the inner margin of the ridge.

Upper Incisors

Human upper incisors (Figures 6–12 and 6–14 to 6–16) are typically morphologically simple teeth with only one root. Although upper incisors are frequently described as being spatulate, it is perhaps more accurate to characterize them as being spade-shaped: the buccal surface is only gently concave and the lingual surface minimally convex with, on occasion, some lingual swelling near the base. When viewed buccally, the mesial edge of an upper incisor emerges as the more vertical, whereas the distal edge is the more arcuate or flared; there is individual variation in the degree to which these features are expressed. However, even if the differences are subtle, the mesial edge can be distinguished from the distal edge.

Typically, the **lateral (second) incisor** is smaller than the **central (first) incisor,** although the size difference may be subtle in some individuals. Lateral incisors also tend to be more variable in shape than central incisors: they may be somewhat conical, narrow, and/or even more markedly curved along the distal edge.

An adornment of the lingual surface of the upper incisors most frequently attributed to Asian peoples and those of Asian origin (especially Native North Americans) (e.g. Turner, 1984) consists of the buildup of thickened marginal ridges lingually on the mesial and distal edges that are confluent with an enlarged lingual tubercle. In cross section, such an incisor looks like a small scoop and is referred to as *shovel-shaped*. Sometimes the thickening of the marginal ridges is so severe, particularly as they converge upon the lingual swelling, that they create a tubular configuration with a pitted bottom; this most frequently seen on the lateral incisor, which may be described as *barrel-shaped*. *Double-shovelling* refers to the development of mesial and distal marginal ridges on the lingual as well as the buccal surfaces of the incisor crown.

Lower Molars

Although they decrease in size and morphological complexity in the sequence $M_1 \rightarrow M_2 \rightarrow$

M₃, all lower molars (Figures 6–11 and 6–13 to 6–16) tend to be rectangular in shape, being longer mesiodistally than they are buccolingually wide or broad. Lower molars typically develop two roots. These roots are broad buccolingually and somewhat compressed mesiodistally, and they become increasingly appressed to each other and even less completely divided in the sequence $M_1 \rightarrow M_2 \rightarrow M_3$. Each root corresponds to roughly half of the tooth (a mesial half and a distal half). A third root, which is distinctively spindly, may be found emanating from the region of the cleft between the two primary roots on the lingual side and near the neck and can occur as an isolated developmental phenomenon on any lower molar (e.g. Schwartz, unpublished data; Turner, 1984).

The human lower molar crown characteristically bears four major cusps that are relatively subequal in general size and shape. The *metaconid* lies in the mesiolingual corner of the crown; the *protoconid* lies opposite the metaconid in the mesiobuccal corner; the *entoconid* (whose prefix is the only one that provides a clue as to the name of a cusp) sits behind the metaconid and occupies the distolingual corner; and the *hypoconid* lies opposite the entoconid in the distobuccal corner. The lingual cusps of a lower molar are taller than the buccal cusps, but the bases of the buccal cusps are more swollen. The mesial root lies under the metaconid-protoconid pair and the distal root underlies the region of entoconid and hypoconid.

A fifth cusp, the *hypoconulid,* may also be present. When it is, it usually appears as a small pie-shaped wedge squeezed between the entoconid and hypoconid near the midline of the tooth [a centrally emplaced hypoconulid is characteristic of the larger taxonomic group of catarrhine (Old World monkey, ape, hominid) primates (Kay, 1977)]. If a hypoconulid is present in the lower molar series, it will be most fully expressed on M_1 and decrease in size in the sequence $M_1 \rightarrow M_2 \rightarrow M_3$. The presence of a hypoconulid on M_1 does not imply its presence on M_2. If this cusp is not developed on M_2, it will not be present on M_3.

Of the other features that might occur occlusally on a primate's lower molar, the most common and consistent in humans is a relatively well-defined fovea that lies in front of the metaconid-protoconid pair. This is the *anterior fovea;* mesially, it delineates a thickened ledge of enamel that may be referred to as a *paraconid shelf* or *paracristid.* The low ridge delineated behind the anterior fovea and between the metaconid and protoconid is variably identified as the *distal trigonid ridge,* the *distal trigonid crest,* or the *protocristid.* On lower molars lacking a hypoconulid, a shorter *posterior fovea* may occur just behind the entoconid-hypoconid pair of cusps. The ledge of enamel delineated distally by a posterior fovea is not usually identified nomenclaturally in humans; in other primates, it is the *hypocristid.*

In common with other primates, humans retain a crest that courses between the hypoconid and the metaconid. It is called the *cristid obliqua,* or oblique crest, and is one of the features paleontologists have long used to distinguish primates, especially early fossil primates, from other mammals. In contrast to most other primates, in which this crest is longer and more clearly defined, it is stout and truncated in humans.

Lower molar *cingulid* development in humans is uncommon. However, when it does occur, it is most frequently expressed on the buccal side of the tooth, usually as a truncated structure (e.g. Swindler and Olshan, 1988). Infrequently, human lower molars may be adorned by a stylid on the buccal face of the protoconid, the *protostylid.* In general, however, protostylids are rare among primates. Protostylid development is characteristic only of the slender loris *(Loris tardigradus)* of Sri Lanka and *Indraloris,* its potential fossil relative from the Miocene of Indopakistan; it is also noted in some species of the Plio-Pleistocene hominid *Australopithecus* (e.g. Schwartz, 1986, and personal observations).

A feature often identified as a *metastylid* (cf. Scott and Dahlberg, 1980; Turner, 1984) may present itself as a small conulid wedged in between the metaconid and hypoconid. In nonhuman primates, a feature identified as a metastylid is more stylidlike in position (buccal and on the posterior face of the metaconid) as well as morphology (elevated and peaked).

Lower Premolars

Contrary to received wisdom (e.g. Clark, 1966), human lower premolars (Figures 6–11 and 6–13 to 6–16) are not, as a set, *bicuspid* teeth.

Each lower premolar is dominated by a buccal cusp—identified by convention as the protoconid—lingual to which there is some degree of swelling or distension. In neither lower premolar is the buccal cusp as tall or well defined as the buccal cusp of an upper premolar. In the lower **anterior (first) premolar**, lingual "cusp" development is often constrained to the level of what in other primates—the orangutan, for instance—would be identified as a *lingual tubercle,* on either side of which is a small fovea (*anterior* and *posterior foveae,* respectively) and from which a crest may course along the lingual face of the protoconid toward its apex. The lower anterior premolar of humans is, therefore, essentially *unicuspid*—as it is in all anthropoid primates with the exception of the Plio-Pleistocene *Australopithecus africanus, A. (Paranthropus) robustus,* and *A. (P.) boisei,* but not *A. afarensis*—and cannot be characterized in the species as a bicuspid tooth, even though variants with a greater amount of lingual expansion are on occasion encountered. Indeed, the singularity in morphology of the human lower anterior premolar makes it one of the easiest teeth to identify when found isolated from the jaw.

Superficially convergent on what might otherwise be identified as a metaconid is the sometime development on the Eskimo lower anterior premolar of a feature called an *odontome.* This cusplike elevation of enamel lies closer to the protoconid than a metaconid would and results from the deposition of enamel directly atop an anomalous extension of the pulp cavity (e.g. Cruwys, 1988); thus, the enamel on an (Eskimo) odontome covers the pulpal extension and does not overlie dentine.

The human lower **posterior (second) premolar** does bear a cusplike structure lingually that is often of sufficient size to be identified as a *metaconid.* But this metaconid rivals the protoconid neither in size nor in height, as the upper premolar protocone does the paracone. Typically, the metaconid of the lower posterior premolar remains lower than and broad relative to the base of the protoconid; it may also be delineated in front and behind by weak grooves or creases. This tooth also typically bears *anterior* and *posterior foveae.*

When viewed buccally, the anterior and posterior lower premolar protoconid outline is characteristically asymmetrical: the mesial edge of the cusp (as measured from the apex of the cusp to its most mesial extent) is shorter than the distal edge of the tooth (as measured from the apex of the cusp to its most distal extent). This asymmetry reflects the fact that each premolar is somewhat expanded distally.

A lower premolar typically bears a single somewhat conical root. The root of the lower anterior premolar is quite slender and acutely tapered toward its apex. The root of the lower posterior premolar is somewhat thicker but does not approach the robustness or shape of a fused upper posterior premolar root. Occasionally, a supernumerary root may appear on a lower premolar; like that of the "third" root of a lower molar, its anomalous nature is obvious.

Lower Canine

The lower canine (Figures 6–11 and 6–13 to 6–16) is a semiconical, single-cusped, single-rooted tooth that can be distinguished from the upper canine by being smaller and less robust. The lower canine crown is narrower, more straight-sided, and, in cross section, less circular or ovoid at its base. The lingual surface of the lower canine is also less swollen basally and less frequently adorned with even slight tubercle development. The root is shorter and less massive. However, like the upper canine, the crown of the lower canine is asymmetrical in buccal outline: when it is viewed in buccal outline, the mesial edge is shorter than the distal edge.

Lower Incisors

Like lower canines and premolars, lower **central (first)** and **lateral (second) incisors** (Figures 6–13 to 6–16) are simpler morphologically than their upper counterparts. In general, lower incisors are narrower, more straight-sided, and less buccolingually thick at their bases than upper incisors. Their mesiodistally compressed roots are also thinner and shorter. The size relationship of the lower incisors is $I_1 < I_2$, which is the reverse of that of the upper incisors. Lower incisors are, however, similar to upper incisors in that the distal edge of the crown differs in orientation from the mesial edge: the distal edge is slanted more laterally away from the vertical than the mesial edge, although this distinction may be subtly expressed. Newly erupted lower incisors characteristically bear more developed *mamelons* (small mounds along the occlusal edge) than do the uppers. *Shoveling* of lower incisors may occur on occasion (e.g. Figure 9–15).

Summary of Permanent Tooth Identification

Incisors: Spatulate (somewhat buccolingually flattened, occlusally broadening) crown; more or less straight occlusal edge; single-rooted.

> **Upper:** Crown broader; distal edge arcuate and somewhat laterally flared; some lingual swelling; root thicker, longer, and more ovoid/circular in cross section; $I^1 > I^2$.

>> **Side:** Mesial edge straighter and more vertically oriented than arcuately flaring lateral edge; root tip may point mesially.

>> I^1: Overall, larger and more robust than lateral incisor; crown broader; lingual swelling more pronounced; lateral flare more markedly arcuate; stouter root.

>> I^2: Crown narrower; shape more variable (sometimes approaching conical); lateral flare less pronounced, sometimes negligible; root slenderer.

> **Lower:** Crown narrower than upper; sides straighter and divergent laterally; root slenderer and somewhat laterally (mesiodistally) compressed; mamelons (visible on unworn teeth) more developed; $I_1 < I_2$.

>> **Side:** Distal edge more divergent laterally from vertical; root tip may point mesially.

>> I_1: Crown narrower; slenderer root.

>> I_2: Crown broader; lateral edge more noticeably divergent from the vertical; root slightly stouter.

Canines: Crown roughly (sub)conical; strong, single cusp; some lingual development, possibly with mesial and distal (accessory) ridges; relatively stout single root, ovoid to circular in cross section.

> **Upper:** Crown stouter and more circular near base in cross section; single cusp higher with more widely divergent mesial and distal edges; lingual swelling/tubercle development more marked; mesial and distal (accessory) ridges more distinct; root stouter, longer, and more circular in cross section.

>> **Side:** Distal edge longer than mesial edge; buccal surface characteristically smooth and convex, with lingual surface being flatter and bearing topographic relief; root may curve gently mesially along most of its length (root tip direction unreliable).

> **Lower:** Crown narrower, shorter, and generally more gracile; mesial and distal edges shorter and less divergent from apex; lingual side flatter and less swollen at base; root more slender and variably more compressed laterally.

>> **Side:** Distal edge longer than mesial edge; buccal surface characteristically smooth and convex, with lingual surface being flatter and bearing topographic relief; root orientation uninformative.

Premolars: Two- or one-cusped; if two-cusped, lingual cusp not taller than buccal cusp; if one-cusped, lower-crowned and more gracile than any canine; double- or single-rooted; if two roots undivided, distinguishable from large single root; if one root, noticeably gracile and slender.

> **Upper:** Demonstrably double-cusped, with lingual cusp mirroring buccal cusp in shape and approaching (but not exceeding) it in height; demonstrably double-rooted, with roots being variably separate along their length or at least bifid at their tips, especially on P^1; when fused, mesial and distal longitudinal grooves present; root complex deep buccolingually.

>> **Side:** Buccal cusp taller than lingual cusp; distal edge of buccal cusp longer than mesial edge; buccolingual axis

through cusp apices divides occlusal surface asymmetrically (i.e. the distal portion is larger/bulkier than the mesial portion); root complex deep buccolingually; roots may arc distally toward apices.

P¹: Buccal and lingual cusps more subequal in size and height; buccal and lingual cusp apices closer together, forming more acute valley between cusps; double-rootedness more distinct.

P²: Buccal and lingual cusp apices farther apart, forming more obtuse and less "V"-shaped valley between cusps; roots less divided and thus more tapered toward apex/apices.

Lower: Low buccal cusp and even lower or nonexistent lingual cusp; root single and slender, with marked taper.

Side: Buccal cusp taller than lingual cusp; distal edge of buccal cusp longer than mesial edge; buccolingual axis through buccal cusp apex subdivides crown in larger distal and smaller mesial portions; root may be curved distally toward tip.

P₁: Buccal cusp dominates crown; lingual development typically no larger than a tubercular swelling; lingual surface may bear low central ridge coursing to swelling; root slender and conspicuously narrow compared to crown.

P₂: Lingual cusp more developed but still lower than buccal cusp; root variably stouter.

Molars: More than two cusps; two buccolingually broad or three somewhat more conical roots.

Upper: Three cusps arranged in a triangular configuration, with a somewhat conical root emanating from region of each cusp; a fourth cusp (hypocone) may be present in the distolingual corner of the tooth.

Side: Buccal cusps higher than lingual cusps; lingual face of tooth more bulbous than buccal face; preprotocrista stouter than postprotocrista (if present); anterior fovea (in front of preprotocrista); hypocone, if present, in distolingual corner of tooth; two roots buccal and the third lingual and somewhat mesial; Carabelli's cusp/pit, if present, on the lingual face of the protocone (which is lingual and somewhat mesial); roots may curve distally toward their tips.

M¹: The largest with the most marked features (if present, hypocone, cristae, Carabelli's cusp/pit); roots distinctly separate and most splayed, such that one or more roots may protrude beyond the margins of the crown.

M²: Slightly to somewhat smaller overall and occlusal features of detail less pronounced than on M¹; roots, although possibly distinctly separate for much of their lengths, more closely appressed toward their tips (i.e. becoming noticeably narrower than the crown).

M³: Slightly to somewhat smaller overall and occlusal features of detail less developed than on M²; hypocone often absent; metacone may be reduced relative to paracone; roots typically shorter and undivided along much of their lengths, with root apices converging into a pointed configuration; in the adult, only one interstitial wear facet (on the mesial surface).

Lower: Four cusps arranged in a rectangular configuration; a pair of buccolingually broad, somewhat mesiodistally compressed roots, one aligned under the protoconid-metaconid pair and the other under the entoconid-hypoconid pair; a small fifth cusp (hypoconulid) may be present distally.

Side: Lingual cusps higher than buccal cusps and more expanded at their bases; buccal face of tooth more bulbous than lingual face; anterior fovea more pronounced than posterior fovea (if present); hypoconulid (if present) distal or slightly buccal to midline, sandwiched between entoconid and hypoconid; roots may curve distally toward their tips.

M₁: The largest with the most pronounced hypoconulid (if present); roots distinctly separate and most splayed.

M₂: Slightly to somewhat smaller (at least shorter) than M₁, with smaller hypoconulid (if present); foveae smaller; roots closer or even partially undivided.

M₃: Slightly to somewhat smaller (at least shorter) than M₂, with even smaller hypoconulid (if present); foveae even smaller; roots may be shorter and probably partially or even completely undivided along their lengths (root tips may be separate); in adult, only one interstitial wear facet (on mesial surface).

Deciduous Teeth

Since permanent incisors, canines, and premolars develop from and then replace deciduous, predecessor teeth, it is not surprising that pairs of ontogenetically related teeth will share some of the same qualities or features. In general, though, the smaller-crowned deciduous teeth (Figures 6–12 to 6–16) have more detailed and clearly detailed feature than their successors. The enamel of deciduous teeth tends to be creamier or milkier in color rather than bright white, as in normal, newly erupted permanent teeth, probably because these teeth develop rapidly and in utero.

The roots of deciduous teeth tend to be much shorter relative to crown height, have relatively larger root canal openings, and typically taper much more drastically toward their apices than in permanent teeth. In general, the roots of deciduous teeth often look too small for the crowns with which they are associated. This incongruous association is accentuated further by the fact that the neck of a deciduous tooth, especially a multicusped, multirooted tooth, is distinctly constricted (and is usually described as "pinched" or "waisted"). In the case of the single-rooted deciduous incisors and canines, the root is narrow and the crown appears to flare outward from the neck. The peculiarities of deciduous tooth roots are in some way related to the facts that (1) the jaws in which deciduous teeth develop and erupt are small and crowded (with the developing crowns of successional teeth beneath and often between the roots), (2) the deciduous teeth have less bone in which to anchor themselves, and (3) the useful life of a deciduous tooth is much shorter than that of a permanent tooth. As such, it is not surprising that the roots of a deciduous tooth tend to be wavy or deflected in ways that make root direction an unreliable clue in siding teeth.

As mentioned above, the crowns of deciduous incisors and canines essentially look like miniature versions of their successors, but with more detail or characteristic morphology. Thus the lateral flare of the distal edge of the crowns of **upper deciduous incisors** tends to be more exaggerated. The buccal face is more noticeably convex and the lingual surface is more concave or excavated, with a more pronounced swelling near its base. If *shoveling* occurs, it will typically be marked and more often be present on both central and lateral upper deciduous incisors.

Lower deciduous incisors may be more dramatically straight along their sides than their permanent successors, but they may also veer morphologically in the opposite direction and develop a lateral flare to their distal edges. In spite of the possibility of the latter configuration developing, lower deciduous incisors can consistently be distinguished from upper deciduous incisors: they are less bulbous buccally and less convex or excavated lingually and their roots are more disproportionately smaller. Newly erupted lower deciduous incisors are even more distinctive in that their occlusal edges often bear a greater number of pronounced mamelons; sometimes mamelon development may be so marked that the occlusal edge will appear to be partially segmented into lobes. Discrimination of central from lateral and right from left upper as well as lower incisors is based on the same characteristics used in analyzing permanent incisors.

Although markedly smaller than their successors, **deciduous canines** tend to exaggerate features seen in permanent canines: for example, they have more bulbous buccal surfaces; more swelling in general around the base (especially in the upper deciduous canine); more delineation of lingual surface features (particularly on the upper canine) such as lingual tubercles, marginal ridges, and central "keels." Nevertheless, deciduous canines are sufficiently similar to permanent canines in general characteristics of shape that the same criteria can be used to identify the tooth as a canine and to determine from which jaw and from which side of the jaw a given tooth came.

Upper deciduous molars typically develop three roots. Otherwise, however, they are truly heteromorphic teeth.

The **anterior (first) deciduous molar** is a somewhat triangularly shaped tooth, being much broader buccally than mesially. The crown is dominated by the buccal cusp *(paracone);* a variably smaller lingual cusp *(protocone)* usually lies directly opposite it. These two cusps tend to be broadly separated from one another. Two blunt cristae—the *pre-* and *postparacristae*—course along the buccal edge of the tooth; each terminates in a stylar-like swelling. The preparacrista typically terminates in a more pointed or distinctly style-like structure than the postparacrista. The postparacrista is slightly if not more markedly longer than the preparacrista.

A low ridge or blunt crest that courses down the face of the paracone and up the opposing face of the protocone often reaches the apices of these cusps. Distinct foveae—a *distal* or *posterior fovea* and an *anterior fovea*—bound this central "keel" on either side. These foveae are often wider than mere creases or depressions and accentuate the raised mesial and distal margins of the crown. The posterior fovea is slightly to noticeably larger than the anterior fovea. This disparity in size between the two foveae corresponds to the overall pattern of anterior deciduous molars: the distal margin tends to be more swollen or arcuately distended than the mesial margin, which courses more directly to the style-like terminus of the preparacrista. As such, the greater bulk of the tooth lies on the distal side of an imaginary line drawn between the apices of the paracone and the protocone.

Clues to identifying dm^1 include the following: paracone larger than protocone; posterior fovea larger than anterior fovea; distal margin distended and arcuate; mesial margin straighter; terminus of preparacrista more style-like than that of postparacrista; two of the three

roots lie on the buccal side of the tooth. Even though it is basically a two-cusped tooth, dm^1 is easily distinguished from its bicuspid successor by, for example, its smaller size, greater number of roots, and slightly more detailed occlusal morphology. When viewed in conjunction with the rest of the molar tooth class, it is clear that this tooth conforms to the size/shape gradient (e.g. Figure 6–9).

Not surprisingly, given its ontogenetic relationship to the first permanent premolar and the molar class in general, the **upper posterior** (in humans, **second**) **deciduous molar** of all heterodont mammals is a distinctly *molariform* tooth. As such, and although it is often a smaller tooth with a pinched neck and a root complex characteristic of deciduous teeth, it is often misidentified as a permanent molar.

In addition to general differences in size, neck, and root, the human dm^2 differs from the first (permanent) molar in other ways. In particular, the crown is more trapezoidal than it is square and its features are more exaggerated. For example, the trigon and its basin are more pronounced and delineated, and the cusps and broadly divergent protocristae are more crisply defined; when present, the paraconule and metaconule are more distinct. The hypocone is usually quite large relative to the overall size of the crown; it is markedly swollen or distended distally, thereby elongating the tooth (particularly along its lingual side) and enlarging the talon basin. The crown's mesial margin (which can easily be confused with the preprotocrista) often swings anteriorly away from the protocone, creating a variably large anterior fovea between it and the preprotocrista. A small style- or conulelike swelling may occur midway along the mesial margin. If a Carabelli's cusp and/or pit is present, it will usually appear disproportionately large relative to the size of the crown.

Identification of an isolated dm^2 can be abetted by focusing on features of the trigon as well as on the hypocone. In addition, clues are provided by the roots: since, as in permanent molars, a root develops under each trigon cusp, two will be located on the buccal side of the tooth. Other criteria that apply to permanent molars can also be used to identify jaw and side of origin.

Similarity between the human **anterior (first)** and **posterior (second) lower deciduous molars** goes no further than the development of two mesiodistally compressed, buccolingually broad roots, one positioned mesially and the other distally. Although it is obvious that the anterior deciduous molar is part of a morphological gradient with the molariform deciduous molar behind it and the molar class in general, in crown morphology, it is arguably the most distinctive tooth of the entire dentition. It is a double-basined tooth; the anterior (trigonid) basin is somewhat triangular and smaller than the ovoid or teardrop-shaped posterior (talonid) basin. In its simplest form, a dm_1 presents itself as a bottom-heavy figure eight; in its most complex form, it is submolariform. The posterior lower deciduous molar is morphologically more similar to the first permanent lower molar.

Dm_1 is dominated by two cusps, a protoconid and a variably smaller metaconid. The apex of the metaconid is generally located slightly distal to the apex of the protoconid. The bases of these two cusps are typically confluent; sometimes the two cusps are so closely melded that only their tips are emergent. A distinct paracristid (paraconid shelf) descends from the apex of the protoconid and usually courses directly forward slightly before it "kinks" (sometimes quite sharply) and swings back to contact the base of—if it does not continue up toward the apex of—the metaconid. The first deciduous molar thus has a very large, enclosed, asymmetrical trigonid basin that is characterized by a long buccal margin and a lingually and distally directed mesial margin.

The dm_1 talonid basin extends from behind the melded protoconid and metaconid. It is much larger and elongate, as well as more rounded, symmetrical, and uniformly enclosed than the trigonid basin; its breadth or narrowness buccolingually does, however, vary somewhat from individual to individual. In contrast to the trigonid basin, the crest that circumscribes the talonid basin—that emanates from the protoconid and eventually terminates at the metaconid—is generally not punctuated with distinct, well-developed cusps. Rather, this continuous margin is often unadorned throughout; at most, it may bear three variably developed cusplike swellings that could, perhaps, be identified as *entoconid, hypoconid,* and *hypoconulid.* In Native North American populations in particular, a distinctive crest courses from the

protoconid down into the talonid basin (e.g. Dahlberg, 1949).

The lower **posterior** (in humans, **second**) **deciduous molar** may be mistaken for a permanent molar. However, its true identity is revealed by its smaller size, more distinctly constricted neck, more flared sides of the crown, markedly splayed short roots, and exaggeration of various occlusal features. For example, if present, the hypoconulid and the grooves that delineate it are more crisply defined than on a permanent molar. A hypoconulid on a dm_2 is also larger relative to the other cusps than it would be on a first permanent molar (which is consistent with a molar-class size/shape gradient), and it is typically more buccally emplaced than it is on the first permanent molar. The anterior fovea, too, is often more crisply delineated and relatively larger compared to the overall size of the crown than on M_1. In addition to **clues** used in the analysis of permanent lower molars, the position of the hypoconulid and the easily identified anterior fovea are important features in identifying a dm_2.

Tooth Eruption and Root Formation

The most frequently used primary criteria for determining the age of preadult individuals are stages of crown and root formation, eruption of the primary dentition, and replacement of the primary by the secondary dentition. Usually the data—whether in chart and/or diagram form—are presented without consideration of the developmental background. Both are provided here.

Although there have been and continue to be numerous studies detailing the eruption sequences of mammalian dentitions, the actual process of tooth eruption is not entirely known, although its potential elements seem to have been isolated (e.g. Ten Cate, 1989; Ten Cate and Osborn, 1976). Until recently, opinion was that tooth eruption was caused by forces that built up during root formation as the elongating root pushed against a so-called cushion hammock ligament that was supposed to stretch across the alveolus under the root. Such a structure does not, however, exist. Root formation (without this ligament) still remains a possible cause of tooth eruption. There was the theory—

which is still maintained in some quarters—that bone remodeling during growth of the upper and lower jaws is the proximate cause of tooth eruption. However, it appears instead that maxillary and mandibular bone resorption, deposition, and redeposition in the regions of erupting teeth are consequences, not causes of tooth eruption. The buildup of hydrostatic pressure as the force behind tooth eruption has had its share of proponents. However, experimental studies do not provide convincing evidence of this as a single factor.

It appears that, although other factors may come into play, the periodontal ligament, which arises coincident with the onset of root formation, is primarily responsible for tooth eruption. It is not exactly clear how the ligament, or some set of its cell types, does this (possibly by contraction), but experimental evidence suggests that the periodontal ligament must be present for tooth eruption to occur. In addition, continued tooth movement after eruption (such as compensatory eruption as tooth crowns are worn down) appears to be maintained by the periodontal ligament. Conservatively and in descending order of contribution, it appears that tooth eruption results from contraction of the periodontal ligament, proliferation of periapical tissues associated with root growth—either individually or collectively—and, perhaps, fluid pressures from vascular tissues.

In most instances, resorption of alveolar bone is sufficient to allow the crown to pass through it. As the tooth is erupting, alveolar bone redevelops around it. A successional tooth causes the hard and soft tissue of the tooth it will replace to be resorbed. The cells responsible for the resorption of tooth-related structures are sometimes identified as *odontoclasts* (which are essentially identical to osteoclasts) (Ten Cate, 1989). Although odontoclasts can resorb all dental tissues, including enamel, the portion of a deciduous tooth that is affected is that with which the successional tooth comes into contact. In general, however, the periodontal ligament (and thus support) of the tooth that will be shed is rapidly lost.

The onset of **root development** is associated with the appearance of *Hertwig's root sheath,* which develops as an outgrowth of the cervical loop during the late bell stage of tooth formation (see above, this chapter). The "edge" of the cervical loop circumscribes the perimeter or *di-*

aphragm, which, at the onset of root formation, lies at the presumptive neck of the crown. During root development, Hertwig's root sheath grows down between the tooth follicle and the dental papilla; it comes to encase the dental papilla and the neurovascular supply to the pulp. As the root grows, the diaphragm becomes separated from the region of the tooth neck; the diaphragm then corresponds to the aperture at the end of the elongating root. In a single-rooted tooth, the diaphragm persists as the opening in the root tip through which pulpal nerves and arteries course. This single opening is identified as the *primary apical foramen.* In a multicusped, multirooted tooth, the once-single diaphragm becomes subdivided (see below), with pulpal innervation and vascularization coursing through two or more *secondary apical foramina.*

Root multiplication begins with the development of projections—*diaphragmatic processes* or *interradicular tongues*—from the edge of the single diaphragm that comes to delineate the circumference of the neck of the crown. These interradicular tongues extend toward and converge upon one another in the center of the pulp cavity. Elongating interradicular tongues delineate "bays," and as the "bays" differentiate, blood vessels (and possibly nerves) segregate into groups. With the coalescence of these interradicular tongues in the center of the pulp cavity, the bays become fully enclosed and form individual diaphragms called *radicular rings.* Each radicular ring corresponds to a presumptive root and each "captures" its own neurovascular bundle. Thus, in the same way that foramina elsewhere in the skeleton form around and are not "burrowed into" by nerves and arteries, roots form around the nerves and arteries that serve a tooth. If the process of interradicular tongue development occurs rapidly, the roots will be short; the longer the process takes, the longer the roots will become. From an evolutionary perspective, reduction in root number is a consequence, therefore, not of root fusion but of a decrease in the number of developing interradicular tongues. In the context of dental anthropological studies that focus on root number, teeth (such as upper premolars and upper and lower molars) with "partially fused roots with separate apices" are examples not of root fusion but of delayed interradicular tongue development.

Junction lines form between abutting inter-radicular tongues. At times, however, the juncture may be incomplete; this disjuncture creates *pulpoperiodontal canals* that transmit vascularization and nerves. Pulpoperiodontal canals occur most frequently in deciduous molars. Since the primary plexus of blood vessels (and possibly nerves) segregates into smaller bundles as the "bays" are forming, it is obvious how perturbations or irregularities in interradicular tongue expansion could isolate and "capture" a vascular branch or two.

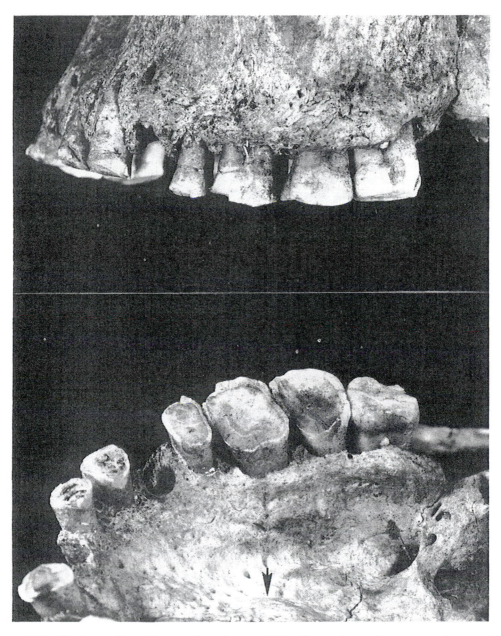

Figure 6–17   *(Top)* enamel pearl between buccal roots of M³ and enamel extensions coursing between buccal roots of M¹⁻² *(e.g. small arrow); (bottom)* enamel pearl on lingual root of same M³; also note, for example, severe attrition encroaching on pulp cavities of M¹⁻², varying degrees of pulp cavity exposure on P², the canine, and I², remodeling buccally of the alveolar crest in the region of the premolars and molars (probably due to apical inflammation [see Chapter 8]), and the presence of a palatal torus *(large arrow)* (prehistoric, Alaska).

Extraneous enamel deposits may be laid down on the interradicular tongues in the region of root arborization; such apparent hyperamelogenesis is presumably the result of an enamel-producing potential of the root sheath. The extraneous deposit may be either raised and three-dimensional and take the form of a small, semi-isolated sphere—called an *enamel pearl* (Figure 6–17)—or it may be low, thinly tapering, and smoothly continuous with the enamel of the crown. The latter configuration—identified as an *enamel extension* (Figures 6–8 and 6–17)—most frequently occurs on the buccal sides of upper and lower permanent molars alike (with the thin spit of enamel coursing between the cleft of the roots); a somewhat truncated enamel extension may develop on the upper molars above the cleft between the lingual and mesiobuccal roots as well as between the lingual and distobuccal roots (D. Stone, personal communication). Interradicular enamel can interfere with proper attachment of the interradicular group of fibers of the periodontal ligament as well as more broadly with the attachment of the oral epithelium. These weaknesses can be aggravated by pulpal inflammation and can also lead to pocketing.

Preliminary observations on a sample of 500 human crania (Schwartz, unpublished data) indicate that enamel extensions tend to occur on molar teeth that are also high-crowned (i.e. the enamel extends further down the tooth all around). In addition, in the same individual, fully or essentially single-rooted tooth (which do not develop cervical interradicular tongues and thus cannot form enamel extensions) also appear to be high-crowned.

Other anomalies include *fossacoronoradicular* and *syndesmocoronoradicular teeth*. A fossacoronoradicular tooth is characterized by a hollow in the junction line between the enamel and cementum which invaginates into the crown and may also extend for the entire length of the root; this hollow occurs more frequently buccally than lingually. A syndesmocoronoradicular tooth is affected on its lingual side by a drastic invagination of the cementoenamel junction into the crown of the tooth, such that enamel continuity is disrupted; a groove may also extend from the hollow either partially or for the entire length of the root.

Root elongation results from the induction by Hertwig's sheath of the proliferation of odontoblasts, which, in turn, produce the dentine of the root. There are two phases of root development and elongation: the **eruptive phase** and the **penetrative phase**. During the eruptive phase, the root elongates such that its tip remains at a constant level (relative to the alveolar bone) and the crown of the tooth is "pushed" toward the occlusal plane. The eruptive phase continues until the tooth comes come into occlusion with its "mate." At this point, the root may be approximately two-thirds developed. The penetrative phase is heralded when the root tip begins extending into the basilar bone of the jaw. The two phases leave telltale signs on the root: the portion of the root formed during the eruptive phase is smooth, whereas that formed during the penetrative phase is roughened and corrugated. Sometimes a line or crease around the circumference of the root delineates the two phases. Premature or abnormal contact with another tooth or bony surface can initiate the penetrative phase, causing impacted or imbedded teeth. If there is subsequent loss of periodontal tissue, *ankylosis* or fusion of the root to the surrounding bone can occur.

Kovacs (1971) has devised a formula to express the relative length of the root: *length of root × 100/length of tooth = index of relative length of root*. Among his results is the suggestion that the deciduous rather than the permanent teeth are the more securely anchored in the jaws.

Aging

Overview

In approaching the determination of age at death from the skeletal remains of postnatal individuals, the life history of an individual can be subdivided into two or three phases, with developmental and morphological changes generally characterizing each.

Acsádi and Nemeskéri (1970) distinguished three phases. The more common delineation in the literature of two phases perhaps too restrictively compresses Acsádi and Nemeskéri's "juvenile" and "adult" into a single "adult" phase. I list Acsádi and Nemeskéri's three phases together with other potentially useful criteria.

1. **Childhood:** Growth and eruption of deciduous and permanent teeth; appearance of centers of ossification; growth of cranial bones—for example, the petrosal (petromastoid region) and temporal bones and the elements of the occipital bone.
2. **Juvenile age:** Union of epiphyses to diaphyses; unification of the os coxa; closure of the spheno-occipital synchondrosis.
3. **Adulthood:** Closure of cranial sutures; changes in the surface of the pubic symphysis, the auricular surface, and the sternal end of the rib; structural changes in the spongy substance of the proximal epiphysis of the humerus and of the femur; patterns and degrees of tooth wear.

As in the determination of the sex of an individual from the skeleton (see Chapter 9), variability rather than consistency is the rule in determining an individual's age at death. Even under "normal" and developmentally uneventful conditions, the rates at which various components of one individual may grow and take shape, erupt or fuse, or become obliterated and incorporated into a larger whole may vary conspicuously from individual to individual of the same sex as well as between individuals of different sexes. Furthermore, and again paralleling the state of the art of determining sex from skeletal remains, the generalizations concerning the determination of age at death that have come to dominate texts and review articles on human skeletal analysis are based on region- or site-specific rather than worldwide populational samples. Thus one must use caution when applying aging criteria and standards to one's particular study group. Finally, one must always bear in mind that individual life histories complicate the task of determining age at death. Hormonal imbalances, socioeconomic factors (e.g. diet and some disease or other assaults to the body's systems), as well as the relative onset and pace of aging may interfere to some degree with the processes as well as the timing of tooth formation and may be quite disruptive to normal growth patterns of the nondental skeleton. At best, the assessment of age at death is an approximation, which is usually most accurate in the younger phases of development. Inaccuracy, due to the inevitabilities of individual life histories, increases with age.

Dividing an individual's life history into phases is, of course, somewhat artificial, due to the fact that patterns of ontogenetic and post-ontogenetic transformation of any given skeletal "unit"—teeth, skull, elements of the postcranium—do not themselves form a neat sequence of events (i.e. first teeth, then skull, then postcranial features). There can be and is overlap of various events. However, since certain criteria do lend themselves to compartmentalization into rough age phases, I shall try to adhere to Acsádi and Nemeskéri's divisions whenever possible.

Prenatal development and ossification of bony elements and teeth are dealt with in the appropriate morphological sections on individual bone and teeth, to which the reader is referred for in-depth discussion. The age-related essentials are summarized here in Tables 7–4 and 7–6.

Childhood

Tooth Formation

Subsequent to the fetal phase, the postnatal phases of tooth growth and eruption can be broken down as follows:

1. The toothless phase of infancy (0 to 7 months).
2. The teething phase: that is, the eruption of the deciduous teeth (7 months to 2 years).
3. The (use) phase of the deciduous teeth (2 to 6 years).
4. The phase of eruption of the permanent teeth and replacement of deciduous teeth: that is, the phase of the mixed dentition (6 to 12 years).
5. The (use) phase of the permanent teeth (12+ years).

The phases that are most helpful in determining age are those of teething and the mixed dentition because these phases show activity with easily identifiable changes in relative states of crown and root formation as well as of tooth position within the jaw and/or above the alveolar margin. The latter part of phase 4 (particularly with regard to the third molar) and the fifth phase are relevant to the determination, respectively, of juvenile and adult ages but are listed here for completeness.

Visual assessment of phases of tooth activity is essentially limited to the evaluation of the emergence of the crown above the alveolar margin. This is particularly true of a secondary tooth, of which, at best, the cusp tip or tips are barely visible through a preeruption perforation of the alveolar margin (a foramen through which the gubernaculum of a successional tooth courses) that lies lingual to the already emplaced primary tooth. In the case of primary teeth (including, of course, the "permanent" molars) crown development can be assessed with varied success directly through the incomplete alveolar margin. The most effective manner (especially in cost and time) in which to analyze relative states of crown and root formation and of tooth eruption is by radiography. Often, the type of x-ray unit available (e.g., dental, "oven," hospital) and the limitations on settings of kilovolts (kv), milliamps (ma), and length of exposure time will affect the degree with which one can control the crispness (high contrast) or softness (greater spectrum of grays) of the radiograph. Also, the type of x-ray film used and the recommended developing chemicals can influence the contrast; for example, Kodak x-ray film tends to produce a crisper image than Agfa film. High kilovolt and milliamp settings with short exposure times, depending on bone and tooth density, often produce crisper radiographs than those with longer exposure times but lower kilovolt and milliamp settings.

Various authors' data on the timing of dental growth and eruption are presented in Tables 7–1 to 7–3; (see Chapter 6 for tooth notation). The common order of eruption of the deciduous teeth is $di_1 \rightarrow di^1 \rightarrow di^2 \rightarrow di_2 \rightarrow dm1 \rightarrow dc \rightarrow dm2$, although variations do occur. There are no apparent sexual differences in the order, but in general the timing of deciduous tooth eruption is earlier in boys than in girls. The reverse applies to the timing of eruption of the permanent teeth—that is, typically, these teeth erupt earlier in girls than in boys. The data compiled by Olivier (1960) provide more detailed information on deciduous and permanent teeth than just basic times of eruption of individual teeth. They thus offer the possibility of a more precise reconstruction of the age of a pre- or postnatal individual, even if all of the dental elements are not present (e.g. having been lost postmortem, for example, during secondary burial or excavation).

Table 7-1 Chronology of Tooth Eruption

Tooth	Females		Males	
	Upper	Lower	Upper	Lower
Deciduous dentition				
di1	9 m 0 d ± 2 m	7 m 9 d ± 2 m	8 m 14 d ± 2 m	7 m 6 d ± 2 m
di2	10 m 23 d ± 2 m	11 m 23 d ± 2 m	10 m 23 d ± 2 m	11 m 9 d ± 3 m
dc	18 m 5 d ± 2 m	13 m 6 d ± 3 m	17 m 18 d ± 3 m	18 m 0 d ± 3 m
dm1	14 m 23 d ± 2 m	14 m 27 d ± 2 m	14 m 24 d ± 2 m	16 m 3 d ± 2 m
dm2	24 m 24 d ± 6 m	24 m 18 d ± 3 m	24 m 7 d ± 6 m	23 m 28 d ± 3 m
Permanent dentition				
I1	7 y 0 m 0 d ± 0 y 9 m	6 y 1 m 23 d ± 0 y 8 m	7 y 2 m 13 d ± 0 y 11 m	6 y 3 m 23 d ± 0 y 8 m
I2	7 y 11 m 14 d ± 0 y 11 m	7 y 1 m 8 d ± 0 y 9 m	8 y 4 m 12 d ± 0 y 0 m	7 y 4 m 20 d ± 0 y 9 m
C	10 y 6 m 1 d ± 1 y 1 m	9 y 8 m 10 d ± 1 y 2 m	11 y 1 m 23 d ± 1 y 2 m	10 y 8 m 28 d ± 1 y 2 m
P1	10 y 1 m 8 d ± 1 y 3 m	10 y 0 m 3 d ± 1 y 4 m	10 y 7 m 6 d ± 1 y 4 m	11 y 6 m 8 d ± 1 y 3 m
P2	10 y 8 m 7 d ± 1 y 5 m	10 y 1 m 27 d ± 1 y 4 m	11 y 4 m 12 d ± 1 y 4 m	11 y 6 m 8 d ± 1 y 3 m
M1	6 y 3 m 15 d ± 0 y 10 m	6 y 2 m 22 d ± 0 y 11 m	6 y 4 m 1 d ± 0 y 10 m	6 y 2 m 26 d ± 0 y 9 m
M2	11 y 11 m 26 d ± 1 y 2 m	11 y 6 m 10 d ± 1 y 4 m	12 y 6 m 1 d ± 1 y 3 m	12 y 0 m 7 d ± 1 y 3 m

Source: Modified from Moyers (1959).

Abbreviations: d = day; m = month; y = year.

Table 7–2 Chronology of Tooth Eruption

| Tooth | Deciduous | | Permanent | |
	Average Age (months)	Normal Range (months)	Tooth	Normal Range (years)
Upper dentition				
di1	7	8–11	I1	7–8
di2	9	8–11	I2	8–10
dc	18	16–24	C	11–12
dm1	14	9–21	P1	10–11
dm2	24	20–36	P2	10–12
			M1	6–7
			M2	12–13
			M3	17–30
Lower dentition				
di1	6	4–8	I1	6–7
di2	8	7–12	I2	7–10
dc	18	16–25	C	9–10
dm1	12	9–21	P1	10–12
dm2	22	20–36	P2	11–12
			M1	6–7
			M2	11–13
			M3	16–30

Source: Modified from Vallois (1960).

Although Moorrees et al. (1963a, b) discriminated deciduous tooth formation/age stages more finely than Olivier (1960), they studied only the mandibular deciduous canines and molars, the successors of these teeth, and the permanent molars. Moorrees et al. also collected data on the timing of the resorption of the roots of the deciduous teeth. From their sample of modern white children from Ohio, Moorrees et al. found most tooth variability to occur during the phase of root formation; they also found differences between girls and boys.

Demirjian (e.g. 1980), whose studies have focused on the permanent dentition, argued that it is unnecessary, as is traditionally done, to radiographically analyze the teeth on both sides of the upper and lower jaws in order to achieve an accurate assessment of an individual's age. He based this conclusion on the conclusions of others that differences in timing between teeth in the upper versus the lower jaw follow essentially the same pattern of growth and eruption. Thus, because it is much easier to radiograph

mandibular than maxillary teeth, one need only concern oneself with the former. In addition, Demirjian points to an apparently high degree of correlation in the development of right and left lower teeth as the rationale for using only one side of the mandibular dentition as representative of the entire dentition.

Demirjian (1980) developed a method of assessing relative states of tooth formation of the left mandibular permanent teeth that divides the process for each tooth into eight stages. Rather than provide exact ages for each stage of tooth formation, he constructed tables for girls and boys of maturity scores correlated with stages of tooth formation. Maturity scores can be used comparatively among individuals without assuming accurate dental ages. Precise dental ages, however, can be reconstructed by applying the sum total of the maturity scores to the (50th centile or median) age curves produced by the study. Demirjian rightly points out the difficulty in assessing absolute values of growth—of crown as well as of root length—

Table 7–3   Chronology of Tooth Formation and Eruption

			Deciduous Dentition			
Tooth	Appearance of Tooth Germ (fetal months)	Percent Crown Formation at Birth	Crown Fully Formed (months)	Root Fully Formed (years)	Reabsorption of Root (years)	Exfoliation (years)
di1	4–4.5	upper: 83 lower: 60	upper: 1.5 lower: 2.5	1.5 1.5–2	4–5	6–7
di2	4.5	upper: 66 lower: 60	upper: 2.5 lower: 3	1.5–2	4–5	7–8
dc	5	33	9	3.25	6–7	10–12
dm1	5	cusps continuous	5.5–6	2.5	4–5	9–11
dm2	6	cusps still distinct	10–11	3	4–5	10–12

		Permanent Dentition	
Tooth	Appearance of Tooth Germ	Crown Fully Formed (years)	Root Fully Formed (years)
M1	At birth	2.5–3	9–10
I1	3–5 months	4–5	9–10
I2	Upper 10–12 months Lower 3–4 months	4–5	10–11
C	4–5 months	6–7	12–15
P1	1.5–2 years	5–6	12–13
P2	2–2.5 years	6–7	12–14

Source: Modified from Olivier (1960).

which can vary considerably among individuals, and recommends assessing the relationship between crown and root size whenever possible. Evaluating relative states of tooth formation also increases the age range within which the analysis can take place. If age determination were based solely on tooth emergence, the analysis would be restricted, at least with boys, to the periods of approximately 6 to 7 years (for the incisors and first molar) and approximately 10.5 to 11.5 years (for the canine, premolars, and second molar). Variability in timing of crown and root formation of the third molar make this tooth unreliable as a potential indicator of age.

Although certainly time-saving in terms of reaching a general assessment of maturational age, the compression into one quadrant of one jaw, or even only one jaw, of the entire picture

of an individual's history of dental growth and eruption might also result in loss of potentially significant information—with regard, for example, to intra- as well as interpopulational differences when standards of known age are lacking for comparison. Furthermore, as more studies on variations in patterns of dental growth and eruption emerge (see, e.g. Winkler et al., 1991, and references therein), it is becoming ever more apparent that differences in timing between upper and lower teeth are indeed real, as had been pointed out in earlier studies on the human dentition (e.g. Kronfeld, 1954; Moyers, 1959; Olivier, 1960; Schranz, 1959; Vallois, 1960).

Often reprinted in osteology textbooks is Ubelaker's (1989) diagramatic representation of tooth formation/eruption at various ages. The part illustrating eruption of the permanent

Molar   Premolar   Canine   Incisor

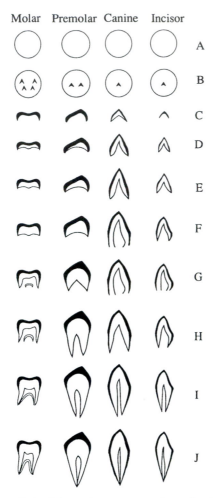

Figure 7–1 Schematic representation of relative "stages" of tooth crown and root formation (after Winkler et al., 1991): A = tooth crypt present; B = initial calcification; C = crown one-quarter formed; C = crown one-half formed; E = crown three-quarters formed; F = crown fully formed; G = onset of root formation (whether single- or multirooted); H = apical foramen/foramina broad, walls of root canals funnel-shaped, root outline more definitive, with root length equal to or slightly greater than crown height; I = apical foramen/foramina still somewhat open, walls of root canals parallel; J = apical foramen/foramina "closed."

teeth is based on Native North Americans and various other "nonwhite" groups, while the information on earlier phases is derived primarily from studies on white North American groups.

Although, as with the field of osteology in general, there is a long history of studies on cor-

relating tooth formation/eruption with an individual's age, many studies are not comparable and, as Smith (1991) points out in her valuable summary of the state of the art, there is still much work to be done. I heartily recommend Smith's (1991) article to the interested student. As a key to deciphering relative tooth/root formation for those who will be encountering relevant skeletal material, Figure 7–1 presents Winkler et al's (1991) elaboration on Demirjian's (e.g. 1980) eight phases. Inasmuch as any attempt to delineate stages in what is essentially a developmental continuum is arbitrary, the osteologist will probably have to extrapolate between phases in order to evaluate relative states of formation/eruption more accurately. In order to assess an individual's potential age at death using dental criteria, Table 7–4 provides some details of crown/root formation correlated with approximate ages; differences between females and males are provided for the permanent dentition.

Cranium

Two regions of the skull present themselves as potential indicators of the age of young individuals.

Weaver (1979) divided the growth of the *petrosal* (petromastoid region) and *tympanic plate* of the temporal bone into six stages, the first four of which he felt could be associated with ages. The sample he used, derived from the Grasshopper Pueblo skeletal series, consisted of 179 temporal bones from individuals for whom dental age could be estimated. As such, Weaver used one set of estimates (dental age) to establish yet another set of estimates (tympanic plate age). In and of itself, this should cause the casual user to be cautious, regardless of whether one is applying these criteria to skeletal remains from nonsouthwest Native North Americans.

The stages and ages Weaver (1979, pp. 264–266) delineated are as follows:

1. Petromastoid portion present but tympanic ring undeveloped: fetal or newborn.
2. "U"-shaped, incomplete tympanic ring partially coalesced with lateral margin of petromastoid: newborn to 0.5 years.
3. Tympanic ring well coalesced inferiorly

with petromastoid, which markedly extends laterally beyond the ring anteriorly and posteriorly (i.e. forming a "U"-shaped and incomplete tympanic plate): 1.0 to 2.5 years.

4. Tympanic plate more fully realized laterally and anteroposteriorly through the closure of the "U" into an "O," which leaves a patency (presumptive foramen of Huschke) in the middle of the "O," and its lateral edge remains medially jagged and indented ("U"-shaped): 1.0 to 2.5 years.

5. The lateral edge of the tympanic plate is more laterally extended, its margin more smoothly defined, and the patency is more completely ossified: no age determined.

6. The tympanic plate now forms a well-defined external acoustic meatus and its floor is typically completely ossified: no age determined.

Although the illustration of and the morphological criteria for this sequence are repeated in textbooks and other publications, some emendations are in order. Particularly important is the fact that the *tympanic ring* is an ossified structure prior to birth. But because the tympanic ring in the neonate is secured by soft connective tissue to the basicranium and typically does not fuse with the basicranium until the end of the first postnatal year, this element is often missing not only in prepared specimens but especially in specimens that have endured burial and subsequent excavation. Nevertheless, the groovelike impression left by the tympanic ring along the lateral margin of the expanding bulla (i.e. the "petromastoid" portion) is a clue to this bone's pre- and neonatal existence. It is with fusion of the tympanic ring to the lateral margin of the bulla that, in archeological and other potentially destructive conditions, one more frequently finds the tympanic ring in place. It is also with fusion of the ring to the bulla that the ring begins its ossification laterally as a bony tube; this process of ossification and extension is most aggressive in the regions along the ring's anterior and posterior cornua.

Other aspects of petrosal (petromastoid) and temporal bone development should be taken into consideration, as well. For example, in the neonate, the *arcuate eminence* is not low and rounded, as in the adult, but is a prominent elevation created by the underlying and somewhat laterally aligned superior semicircular canal. In the neonate, the anterior face of the eminence descends more or less vertically from the elevation of the semicircular canal; at this time, the posterior face of the eminence is more gently sloping. Also in contrast to the adult, the neonatal *subarcuate fossa* is quite large; that is, it is a vast opening subtended by the *superior semicircular canal*. The *internal acoustic meatus* is more anteriorly displaced away from the subarcuate fossa in the neonate than it is in the adult, and the entire *petrosal bone* is unfused to the *squamous portion of the temporal bone*. This fusion does not usually occur until later during the first postnatal year.

The components of petrosal and temporal bone development that thus present themselves as potentially useful in assessing young ages are as follows: (1) changes in the shape and relative size of the arcuate eminence; (2) changes in the shape, relative position, and relative size of the subarcuate fossa and of the internal acoustic meatus; (3) fusion of the petrosal to the squamosal portion and the cornua of the tympanic ring with the basicranium (by the end of the first year); (4) fusion of the tympanic ring to the lateral edge of the bulla and its growth laterally as well as inferiorly, with the latter being correlated with the diminution of a presumptive *foramen of Huschke* (by the end of the fifth year). Because the mastoid process becomes an extension of the petrosal region once the latter has coalesced with the squamous portion of the temporal (ergo, the petromastoid portion), it should be pointed out that the development of any elevation that could be identified as a mastoid process does not usually occur until toward the end of the second year. It thus would seem that, if dental ages from a given sample could be correlated with morphological changes in the petrosal/temporal bone, additional criteria for assessing age in the absence of preserved dental remains would be available.

Redfield (1970) developed a scheme of *occipital bone* formation based on samples he had analyzed as well as on his review of the literature. Collectively, these sources demonstrated considerable variability in time of fusion of (1)

Table 7–4   Chronology of Tooth Formation and Eruption

Tooth	Mineralization Onset	Crown at Birth	Crown Complete	Crown Complete: F	Crown Complete: M	Emergence
Upper di1	14 weeks iu	83%	1.5 months			7.5 months
Lower di1	18 weeks iu	60%	2.5 months			6 months
Upper di2	16 weeks iu	66%	2.5 months			9 months
Lower di2	18 weeks iu	60%	3 months			7 months
Upper dc	17 weeks iu	33%	9 months			18 months
Lower dc	20 weeks iu	33%	9 months			16 months
Upper dm1	12.5–15.5 weeks iu	cusps united	6 months			14 months
Lower dm1	12.5–15.5 weeks iu	cusps united	5.5 months			12 months
Upper dm2	12.5–19 weeks iu	cusps separate	11 months			24 months
Lower dm2	12.5–18 weeks iu	cusps separate	10 months			20 months
Upper M1	at birth			2.6 years	2.7 years	
Lower M1	at birth			2.6 years	2.7 years	
Upper M2	2.5–3 years			6.3 years	6.7 years	
Lower M2	2.5–3 years			6.3 years	6.7 years	
Upper M3	7–9 years			12.7 years	13.3 years	
Lower M3	8–10 years			12.8 years	13.3 years	
Upper I1	3–4 months			3.3 years	3.7 years	
Lower I1	3–4 months			3.3 years	3.6 years	
Upper I2	10–12 months			3.8 years	4.0 years	
Lower I2	3–4 months			3.7 years	4.0 years	
Upper C	4–5 months			4.1 years	4.8 years	
Lower C	4–5 months			4.1 years	4.9 years	
Upper P1	1.5–1.75 years			5.1 years	5.8 years	
Lower P1	1.75–2 years			5.0 years	5.6 years	
Upper P2	2.2–2.5 years			5.9 years	6.3 years	
Lower P2	2.2–2.5 years			5.9 years	6.3 years	

Source: Modified from Ten Cate (1989). Abbreviations: iu = in utero; F = female; M = male.

the mendosal fissures (the remnants of the different developmental origins of the occipital and nuchal planes) and (2) the lateral and basilar parts with one another as well as with the rest of the occipital bone. Perhaps the most valuable piece of data from Redfield's effort is the indication that all occipital elements fuse into a single "unit" by the age of 7 years. Prior to the age of 7 years, according to Fazekas and Kósa (1978), the mendosal fissures usually close by the third year. However, this closure may be delayed until the fourth year, at which time the lateral parts typically fuse with the squamous portion of the occipital.

Postcranium

Postcranially, there are changes of importance that occur in the *os coxa*. In the neonate, the pubis, ischium, and ilium converge within the presumptive *acetabulum* and are separated from one another by the thick *triradiate cartilage*. By the sixth postnatal month, the acetabulum has been transformed into a shallow cuplike structure, into which the three bones extend farther. Prior to ossification in the acetabulum, the pubis and ischium join around the obturator foramen; this union is marked by the sixth year and essentially complete by the ninth. Between 9 and 14 years, ossification occurs across the

Emergence: F	Emergence: M	Root Complete	Root Complete: F	Root Complete: M	Eruption Sequence
		1.5 years			3
		1.5 years			1
		2 years			4
		1.5 years			2
		3.25 years			8
		3.25 years			7
		2.5 years			6
		2.25 years			5
		3 years			10
		3 years			9
7.2 years	7.8 years		9.2 years	10.1 years	13 (3)
7.2 years	7.8 years		9.2 years	10.0 years	12 (2)
11.8 years	12.4 years		13.6 years	14.6 years	23 (13)
11.8 years	12.5 years		13.8 years	14.8 years	24 (14)
17.8 years	17.4 years		18.8 years	18.2 years	26 (16)
17.7 years	17.4 years		18.3 years	18.5 years	25 (15)
7.4 years	8.3 years		9.3 years	10.6 years	15 (5)
7.3 years	7.3 years		8.1 years	9.2 years	11 (1)
8.1 years	9.1 years		9.7 years	11.1 years	16 (6)
7.3 years	8.1 years		8.8 years	9.9 years	14 (4)
9.4 years	11.0 years		11.9 years	13.7 years	18 (8)
9.2 years	10.9 years		11.4 years	13.5 years	17 (7)
9.7 years	11.1 years		11.8 years	13.5 years	19 (9)
9.9 years	11.2 years		11.9 years	13.3 years	20 (10)
10.6 years	11.6 years		12.6 years	13.8 years	21 (11)
10.6 years	11.9 years		12.8 years	14.0 years	22 (12)

triradiate cartilage, first between the pubis and ilium, then between the ilium and ischium, and then, finally, between the pubis and ischium.

Juvenile Age

Overview

Juvenile age is generally thought of as beginning at about 15 years, well *after* the *eruption of the second molar* (12 years). Sometimes the completed eruption of M3 is used as a marker of this period, but this criterion is of limited value, since the third molar can be found completely erupted in individuals ranging in age from 17 to 30 years. A somewhat more reliable criterion for assessing this age period is the closure of the *spheno-occipital synchondrosis,* which begins at approximately 17 years and may be complete between the ages of 22 and 25 years (see Figure 9–15). Krogman (Krogman and İşcan, 1986) found that the central tendency for closure of the spheno-occipital synchondrosis is 23 years.

Epiphyseal Fusion

The most accurate source of information for determining ages within the juvenile period is the sequence of *fusion of epiphyses with long bones* and the *unification of the three bones of the os coxa and its epiphyses* into one solid bone. Vallois (1960) modified Martin's scale, as it was originally used to record cranial suture closure, for use in assessing stages epiphyseal fusion.

1. Stage 0: Open; no fusion; the metaphyseal region, between the epiphysis and diaphysis, is cartilaginous.
2. Stage 1: Ossification between epiphysis and diaphysis extends approximately one-fourth along circumference.
3. Stage 2: Ossification extends approximately one-half along circumference.
4. Stage 3: Ossification extends approximately three-fourths along circumference.
5. Stage 4: Metaphyseal line present only in traces along circumference.

Vallois's (1960) data on recent Europeans are presented in Table 7-5. Unfortunately, the data are analyzed collectively and not by sex. The lower age for each element corresponds to stage 1 and the higher age to stage 4. In scrutinizing the sequence of fusion reported for this sample, one notices, for example, that the distal humeral epiphysis is the first to completely unite with a disphysis while the last three to fuse are the humeral head, the distal radial epiphysis, and then the sternal end of the clavicle. In some contrast, Stewart's (1934) data on Eskimos and other Native North Americans as well as Johnston's (1961) on an archeological collection from the site of Indian Knoll indicate the reverse sequence of fusion for the humeral head and the distal radial epiphysis. Although it was based on a large sample ($N = 375$), the often-cited study by McKern and Stewart (1957) was based solely on American male soldiers who fought in the Korean War; in addition, McKern and Stewart only analyzed one end of each long bone.

As a general rule of thumb, it appears that complete union of epiphysis and diaphysis usually occurs 1 to 2 years earlier in females than

Table 7-5   Chronology of Ossification and Fusion of Some Epiphyses in a European Sample

Bone	Epiphysis	Appearance of Ossification Center (years)	Union Completed (years)
Clavicle	sternal	16–20	21–25
Humerus	proximal	1	18–22
	distal	1–2	14–15
Radius	proximal	4–7	14–18
	distal	1–2	21–23
Ulna	proximal (olecranon)	10–12	15–17
	distal	4–6	18–20
Femur	distal	1	17–20
	greater trochanter	—	17–20
	lesser trochanter	—	16–20
Patella	—	3–5	—
Tibia	proximal	—	17–20
	distal	2	16–19
Fibula	proximal	3–5	17–20
	distal	2	16–19

Source: Modified from Vallois (1960).

in males (Krogman, 1962; Stewart, 1979). The unfortunate aspect of extant epiphyseal union studies, however, is that a global sampling, with distinctions consistently made between males and females, is lacking. Thus, until this lacuna is filled, the osteologist will be forced to apply age estimates of epiphyseal union (which themselves may have been derived from the application first of other sets of age estimates) from one population to another, perhaps totally inappropriate, population.

According to various authors (e.g. Flecker, 1942; Johnston, 1961; Todd, 1930), *ossification of the pubis, ischium, and ilium within the acetabulum* may be fairly well along at least as early as, if not even slightly earlier than, similar states of union of the first long bone epiphyses. The apparent age of complete union within the acetabulum in males is 14 years; in females, however, complete union can occur between 11.5 and 13 years and may even be retarded until the 18th year. Ossification in the *iliac crest, the ischial tuberosity, the anteroinferior iliac spine,* and the *pubic symphysis* coincides with the onset of puberty. Coalescence of these epiphyses with the *os coxa* begins at approximately 16 to 17 years and is completed between 23 and 25 years, slightly after the union of the *head of the humerus,* and more or less in synchrony with the *spheno-occipital synchondrosis,* the *distal end of the radius* (in some populations), and the *sternal end of the clavicle.* The onset of puberty in different populations—whether from the distant past, recent past, or present—is not, of course, a constant, although the relationship of relative times of ossification and union of bony elements may be more consistent across human groups. Thus, one should exercise some caution in assigning definitive ages, especially if there is any concern about developmental timing differing from "the expected."

Stewart (1979) suggests that the common sequence among joints of epiphyseal union proceeds from elbow to hip, ankle, knee, wrist, and, finally, shoulder. For purposes of aging, an attempt at summarizing ossification center appearance/epiphyseal union data for elements of each bone is presented in Table 7–6. More information on development for each bone is provided in the appropriate section of the appropriate chapter.

Adulthood

Pubic Symphysis

In 1920, Todd introduced a method for determining adult age which assessed changes in the morphology of the pubic symphysis. These changes involve a breakdown or deterioration of the horizontally *wavy* or *ridged pubic symphyseal surface,* which is characteristic of *young adults,* into the *pitted* or *granular surface* of *old individuals.* Concurrent with the transformation to granularity is the development of a *lipped rim* along the *dorsal margin* (i.e., dorsal "plateau") of the symphysis and a beveling of the *ventral border* that eventually is transformed into a *rampartlike* feature via bony extensions from the superior and/or inferior extremity/ies of the symphysis. The sample Todd used was entirely male and spanned the ages 18 to 50+ years; he subdivided this span of years into 10 age-related phases. Todd's (1920, see pp. 301–314) method involved an overall evaluation of the symphyseal region. Todd's phases and correlated ages are presented in Figure 7–2 and Table 7–7.

In an attempt to refine Todd's method, McKern and Stewart (1957) subdivided the pubic symphysis into *three components:* the *symphyseal rim* and *dorsal* and *ventral demifacets.* In reality, the component "symphyseal rim" is an overall assessment of symphyseal change, which includes details not only about rim formation and its deterioration but about surface transformation as well. Furthermore, one should not expect to find a symphyseal rim, or even any sign of a symphyseal rim, in very young or very old adults, because this feature becomes expressed and then broken down with increasing age. The dorsal and ventral demifacets are delineated by a longitudinal elevation or disruption of the horizontal ridging (of varying definition and straightness) that courses more or less down the center of the symphyseal face. In the McKern and Stewart method, aspects of the breakdown of the horizontal ridging and of the development of a dorsal plateau are evaluated at the same time. Similarly, aspects of the breakdown of the horizontal ridging and the development of a ventral rampart are considered together. McKern and Stewart introduced the term *billowing* to refer to the horizontal ridges on the symphyseal surface.

Table 7–6   Chronology of Postcranial Bone Formation

Bone Element	Ossification Begins	Fusion Begins	Fusion Complete
First cervical vertebra			
Posterior arch	7–10 f/wk		3–4 yr
Lateral mass	7–10 f/wk		
Anterior arch	≤1 yr		5–9 yr
Second cervical vertebra			
Body	4 f/mo		
Arches	7–8 f/wk		3–6 yr
Dens (base)	4–6 f/mo		4–6 yr
Dens (tip)	2–3 yr		12 yr
Epiphyseal plate	17 yr		
True vertebrae			
Arches	7–9 f/wk (beginning in cervicals)		≥1 yr (beginning in lumbars)
Transverse process	puberty–16 yr		≤20 yr
Spinous process	puberty–16 yr		≤20 yr
Body	8–10 f/wk (beginning in lower thoracics—upper lumbars)		3–6 yr (beginning in cervicals and/or thoracics)
Epiphyseal plate	16–17 yr		20–25 yr
Sacrum			
Vertebrae	6–9 f/wk (beginning superiorly)		
Arches	6–10 f/mo		7–15 yr
Arch/body			6–9 yr (beginning caudally)
Lateral part (coastal process)	6 f/mo–≥birth		puberty
Epiphyseal plates	puberty–16 yr		puberty–16 yr
Auricular surface	18–20 yr		
Intervertebral disc	18–30 yr (beginning caudally)		
Coccyx			25–20 yr (beginning caudally)
First segment	≤1 yr		
Second segment	4–10 yr		
Third segment	10–15 yr		
Fourth segment	14–20 yr		
Ribs			
V–VII	7–9 f/wk		
Other ribs	≥9 f/wk (rapidly)		
Head	(14)16–20 yr	≥17 yr	20–25 yr
Tubercle	(14)16–20 yr	≥17 yr	20–25 yr

196

Table 7–6 *(continued)*

Bone Element	Ossification Begins	Fusion Begins	Fusion Complete
Sternum			≤puberty (beginning inferiorly)
Manubrial stenebra	3–6 f/mo		≥25 yr
2nd–4th sternebrae	3–7 f/mo		
5th sternebra	≤1 yr		
6th (xiphoid) sternebra	5–18 yr		
Scapula			
Body	<birth		
Spine	<birth		
Glenoid cavity	c. 10 yr	10 yr	puberty
Head of coracoid process	1–2 yr	10 yr	puberty
Base of coracoid process	puberty		20 yr
Lateral center of acromion	16 yr	10–14 yr	22–23 yr
Medial center of acromion	15 yr	10–14 yr	22–23 yr
Vertebral border	puberty	puberty	20–23 yr
Medial angle	16–18 yr	19–20	22–23 yr
Inferior angle	16–18 yr	19–20	22–23 yr
Clavicle			
Diaphysis	6–8 f/wk		
Acromial end	c. 20 yr		c. 20 yr
Sternal end	16–20 yr	21–22	25–30 yr
Humerus			
Diaphysis	2 f/mo		
Head	c. birth	20 yr	25 yr
Greater tubercle	7 mo(f)/1 yr(m)–3 yr	20 yr	25 yr
Lesser tubercle	7 mo(f)/1 yr(m)–5 yr	20 yr	25 yr
Medial epicondyle	5–7 yr	12 yr	19–20 yr
Lateral epicondyle	12–13 yr	16–17 yr	18 yr
Trochlea	10 yr	16–17 yr	18 yr
Capitulum	5 mos(f)/7 mo(m)–2 yr	16–17 yr	18 yr
Radius			
Diaphysis	8 f/wk		
Proximal epiphysis	5 yr	puberty	15–18 yr
Distal epiphysis	1–2 yr	17–20 yr	20–23 yr
Radial tuberosity (if present)	14–15 yr		
Ulna			
Diaphysis	8 f/wk		
Olecranon	7–14 yr	≥16 yr	≤23 yr
Distal epiphysis	5–7 yr	≥21 yr	≤25 yr

(continued)

Table 7–6   Chronology of Postcranial Bone Formation (continued)

Bone Element	Ossification Begins	Fusion Begins	Fusion Complete
Scaphoid (body)	5–7 yr		
Lunate (body)	4–5 yr		
Triquetrum (body)	2–3 yr		
Pisiform (body)	9–11 yr		
Trapezium (body)	5–7 yr		
Trapezoid (body)	5–7 yr		
Capitate (body)	birth–1 yr		
Hamate (body)	birth–1 yr		
Metacarpals (I–V)			
Diaphysis (I)	9 f/wk		
Proximal epiphysis (I)(94%)	2–3 yr		18–20 yr
Distal epiphysis (I)(6%)	2–3 yr		18–20 yr
Diaphysis (II–V)	9 f/wk		
Distal epiphysis (II–V)	2–3 yr		18–20 yr
Proximal epiphysis (II)(rare)			18–20 yr
Proximal manual phalanges (I–V)			
Diaphysis (I–V)	9 f/wk		
Proximal epiphysis (I–V)	1–3 yr	14 yr	18–25 yr
Middle manual phalanges (I–V)			
Diaphysis (I–V)	11–17 f/wk		
Proximal epiphysis (I–V)	2–4 yr	14 yr	18–25 yr
Distal manual phalanges (I–V)			
Diaphysis (I–V)	7–8 f/wk		
Proximal epiphysis (I–V)	2–4 yr	14 yr	18–25 yr
Os coxa (innominate)			
Ilium	2–3 f/mo		
Ischium	3–5 f/mo		
Pubis	4–6 f/mo		
Acetabulum		9–12 yr	13 yr (f), 14–18 yr (m)
Ischiopubic ramus		≤6 yr	8 yr
Ischioiliac ramus			17 yr
Ischial tuberosity	13 yr (f), 15 yr (m)	16–17 yr	23–25 yr
Pubic symphysis	puberty	16–17 yr	23–25 yr
Anterior inferior iliac spine	puberty	16–17 yr	23–25 yr
Iliac crest	12 yr (f), 13 yr (m)	16–17 yr	23–25 yr

Table 7–6   (continued)

Bone Element	Ossification Begins	Fusion Begins	Fusion Complete
Femur			
Diaphysis	7 f/wk		
Lesser trochanter	(9)13–14 yr	15 yr	18–20 yr
Greater trochanter	(1–)4 yr	≥15 yr	18–20 yr
Head	≤1 yr	≥ 15 yr	18–20 yr
Distal epiphysis	7 f/mo–birth	≥15 yr	(18)20–23 yr
Patella	2–6 yr		
Tibia			
Diaphysis	8 f/wk		
Distal epiphysis	2 yr	16 yr	18–20 yr
Proximal epiphysis	9 f/mo	16 yr	20–23 yr
Tuberosity	≤39f/wk–birth	8–12 yr (f), 10–13 yr (m)	19 yr
Fibula			
Diaphysis	8 f/wk		
Proximal epiphysis	3–4 yr	16 yr	23–25 yr
Distal epiphysis	9 mo (f), 1 yr (m)–2 yr	16 yr	20 yr
Talus			
Body	6 f/mo		
Posterior process (os trigonum if unfused)	8–11 yr		
Calcaneus			
Body	12 f/wk–7 f/mo		
Calcaneal epiphysis	(4)7–10 yr	12 yr	(16)20–22 yr
Cuboid (body)	9 f/mo–birth		
Lateral cuneiform (body)	1 yr		
Medial cuneiform (body)	2–4 yr		
Intermediate cuneiform (body)	3–5 yr		
Navicular (body)	3–5 yr		
Metatarsals (I–V)			
Diaphysis (I–V)	8–10 f/wk		
Proximal epiphysis (I)	3–8 yr	12 yr	18–22 yr
Distal epiphysis (II–V)	3–8 yr	12 yr	18–22 yr
Proximal pedal phalanges (I–V)			
Diaphysis (I–V)	9–10 wk		
Proximal epiphysis (I–V)	2–10 yr	14 yr	17–21 yr

(continued)

Table 7–6   Chronology of Postcranial Bone Formation (continued)

Bone Element	Ossification Begins	Fusion Begins	Fusion Complete
Middle pedal phalanges (I–V)			
Diaphysis (I–V)	4 mos		
Proximal epiphysis (I–V)	2–10 yr	14 yr	17–21 yr
Distal pedal phalanges (I–V)			
Diaphysis (I–V)	9–10 wks		
Proximal epiphysis (I–V)	2–10 yr	14 yr	17–21 yr

Abbreviations: f/wk = fetal week; f/mo = fetal month; yr = year; (f) = female; (m) = male.

In determining the age of an individual using McKern and Stewart's method, each symphyseal component is analyzed separately and assigned a stage from 0 to 5; the stages are then summed. The total thus achieved is converted to an age or age range by comparison with a table calculated from the sample of individuals of known age. The *dorsal demifacet* is defined as *component I,* the *ventral demifacet* is *component II,* and the *symphyseal rim* is *component III.* As change in the dorsal demifacet typically precedes any noticeable change in the ventral demifacet, and the ventral demifacet be-gins to change before the onset of change in the symphyseal rim, component scoring typically proceeds in the sequence component I to II to III.

Sixteen years after this latter study, Gilbert and McKern (1973) produced yet another refinement in the analysis of age-related pubic symphyseal morphology. The attempt was to provide more accurate criteria by which one could assess the age of females. The reason for this effort was that, after applying Todd's method to a collection with females of known age, Gilbert and McKern concluded that the se-

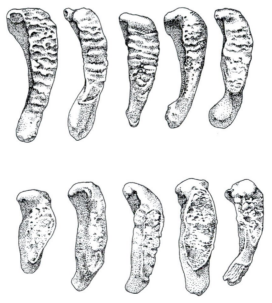

Figure 7–2   Examples of right pubic symphyses illustrating Todd's 10 age-related stages of change (adapted from Todd, 1920): *(top row, left to right)* stages 1 to 5, *(bottom row, left to right)* stages 6 to 10; see Table 7-7 for description and associated ages of each stage.

Table 7–7   Todd's 10 Stages of Pubic Symphyseal Age-Related Change

1. *18–19 years (first postadolescent phase):* Clearly defined horizontal ridges and furrows; margin and ventral beveling as well as ossific nodules lacking.
2. *20–21 years (second postadolescent phase):* Dorsal furrows filling in with finely textured bone and dorsal margin becoming defined; occasional development of ossific nodules; hints of ventral beveling.
3. *22–24 years (third postadolescent phase):* Destruction and filling-in of horizontal ridge-furrow pattern; dorsal margin more clearly delineated; onset of ventral beveling and rarefaction (porous beveled strip of bone along ventral border) obvious; ossific nodules present.
4. *25–26 years [24–26 years as emended by Brooks (1955)] (fourth phase):* Continued destruction of ridge-furrow pattern; dorsal margin complete; ventral beveling more pronounced (increased rarefaction); lower extremity of symphyseal surface becoming delineated.
5. *27–30 (26–27) years (fifth phase):* Lower extremity of symphyseal surface more clearly defined and upper extremity becoming delineated; continued ventral beveling.
6. *30–35 (27–34) years (sixth phase):* Symphyseal surface granular; upper and lower extremities even more clearly delimited with partial (central) or complete development of ventral rampart.
7. *35–39 (34–38) years (seventh phase):* Rarefaction of symphyseal surface and ventral border decreasingly active; mineralization into attendant tendons and ligaments (hyperostotic activity).
8. *39–44 (38–42) years (eighth phase):* Symphyseal surface and ventral border smooth; extremities clearly defined, adding to definition of ovoid perimeter of modified symphyseal surface.
9. *45–50 (42–51) years (ninth phase):* Ovoid perimeter modified into thin rim (similar to rim around glenoid fossa of scapula) (dorsal and ventral margins thus lipped).
10. *50+ (51+) years (tenth phase):* Erosion with possible osteophytic outgrowth of symphyseal surface; breakdown of ventral, lipped margin.

Source: From Todd (1920).

quence of transformation of overall symphyseal morphology as well as of a symphysis's components were sufficiently distinct in females that age estimates using Todd's criteria would be inaccurate by ±10 years. To compensate for this apparent error, Gilbert and McKern devised a set of criteria for analyzing the female symphyseal region that followed the three-component system of McKern and Stewart (1957). As in the McKern and Stewart method, each component was broken down into six stages (0 to 5) of age-related morphological change. The calculation of average age also was done the same way. The total score obtained was converted to age by comparison with a table of female-specific age brackets.

In more recent years, there has been continued questioning of the accuracy and applicability of these landmark studies. The most obvious general criticism is that age ranges can be exceedingly broad (as can be seen easily in the tables presented above). More specifically, there was the problem of replicability in applying McKern and Stewart's and particularly Gilbert

and McKern's standards to other large samples derived from individuals of known age at death. Meindl et al. (1985) tested these criteria against a sample of African American and American white females and males of known age at death and concluded that Todd's method could be applied with confidence to individuals of either sex and of either group. These authors suggested that Todd's 10 phases could be compressed into 5 stages (Table 7–8). [Angel et al. (1986) also suggested that Todd's 10 phases could be collapsed into 5. They further concluded that the most accurate component of McKern and Stewart's analysis was component III (overall symphyseal change, which, of course, is the focus of Todd's system), which could be collapsed into fewer age categories.] It would appear, therefore, that a reorganized version of Todd's criteria for determining the age at death of adults on the basis of changes in the pubic symphysis remains the best currently available. It would be interesting to see if the applicability of these criteria would hold up against samples from other regions. If so, one

Table 7–8   Summary of the Revision by Meindl et al. of Todd's Stages of Pubic Symphyseal Age-Related Changes

1. *Todd's stages 1–5 = preepiphyseal phase:* Modal phase, 20–29 years, crisply defined billowing without ventral rampart formation (age range in sample 18–37 years); 20–25, crisply defined billowing without ventral bevel and defined lower extremity; 26–29, reduced billowing with little ventral rampart formation or definition of lower extremity (overall 18–25, marked billowing; 24–37, reduction in billowing; 24–37, ventral rampart formation; ≥25, appearance of distinct lower extremity; ≤29, indistinct lower extremity; 21–30, ossific nodules without ventral rampart formation clearly defined horizontal ridges and furrows; margin and ventral beveling as well as ossific nodules lacking).

2. *Todd's stage 6 = active epiphyseal phase:* Modal phase 30–35 years, active onset and completion of ventral rampart formation.

3. *Todd's stage 7 = immediate postepiphyseal phase:* Modal phase, 36–40, symphyseal surface and ventral margin become fine-grained and dense.

4. *Todd's stage 8 = predegenerative (maturing) phase:* 40–44, quiescent period with no change in symphyseal surface.

5. *Todd's stages 9–10 = degenerative phase:* 45–50, formation of thin rim around perimeter of symphyseal surface with lipping of dorsal margin and mineralization in ligamentous/tendonous attachment sites (also in females, further erosion of symphyseal surface, possibly due to postmenopausal osteoporosis); the broader the symphyseal surface (e.g. as in males), the less the change that may occur with age (and thus less correct information forthcoming about age above 40 years).

Source: Meindl et al. (1985)

could then apply them with a certain degree of confidence to skeletal material derived from archeological or even more obscure contexts.

Auricular Region (Ilium)

In the same volume of the *American Journal of Physical Anthropology* in which Meindl et al. (1985) published their critique of the pubic symphysis in age determination, Lovejoy et al. (1985b) introduced a new method by which one could assess an individual's age. This method is based on changes in the *auricular* and contiguous *area of the posterior portion of the ilium*. Although Lovejoy et al. (p. 15) admit that age changes in the auricular surface "are somewhat more difficult to interpret than those used in pubic symphyseal aging," they rightly point out that "the rewards are well worth the effort" in light of the fact that the auricular region is more frequently preserved intact than the pubic symphysis in archeological, and, I would add, in similar forensic contexts.

The features of the auricular region of interest are the *apex* as well as the *superior* and *inferior demifaces* of the auricular surface, the *preauricular sulcus*, and the *retroauricular area*. The *apex* is often somewhat peaked or bluntly pointed and is the most anterior extension of the auricular surface. Essentially, the apex represents the posterior terminus of the arcuate line. If you were to imagine a continuation of the arcuate line across the auricular surface, you would delineate above this imaginary line the *superior demiface* and, below it, the *inferior demiface*. The *preauricular sulcus*, if present, will be located lateral to the anterior margin of the auricular surface, facing into the space of the greater sciatic notch. The *retroauricular area* is the expanse of roughened bone that lies between the auricular surface and the iliac crest.

The changes that occur in the auricular surface—that is, the ilial contribution to the sacroiliac joint—are those that accumulate with age and must not be confused with those changes in the same general region that may result from degenerative osteoarthritis and/or the onset of osteophytic growth. True age-related changes of the subchondral bone of the ilial auricular surface result from an increase over time in the amount of fibroid cartilage that covers the surface regardless of the occurrence of osteoarthritic or osteophytic change.

Lovejoy et al (1985, pp. 18) offered the following terms to refer to aspects of auricular surface change: *porosity* (with *microporosity* referring to fine, barely visible perforations and *macroporosity* to large, oval, irregular perforations ranging in diameter from 1 to 10 mm); *grain* (e.g. with "markedly grainy" having the appearance of fine sandpaper); *billowing* (adopted from pubic symphyseal analyses and used to refer to the *transverse ridges* across the auricular surface, which can range from being topographically large or finely grained to barely visible); and *density* (e.g. "dense" meaning that the subchondral bone is compact, smooth, and lacking "grain").

Figure 7–3 illustrates a sampling of auricular surfaces at various ages for males and females separately; in practice, the assessment of age is independent of the sex of the individual. (As in using illustrations of the pubic symphyseal region for assessing age, illustrated examples of the auricular surface are just that, illustrative, and not meant to serve as "type specimens" for each age bracket.) Lovejoy et al. (p. 26) recommend that aspects of the auricular surface itself (not including surrounding features) should be relied upon most heavily when assessing age. Common sense will dictate which end of the age bracket the assessment should favor; for example, "[i]n the case of a coarsely grained surface, but one that still retains some billowing, the former indicator is paramount, but the latter should be used to reduce the age

estimate slightly (within the mode)" (Lovejoy et al., p. 27). Further modifications of the assessment of age, slightly up or down, also may be indicated by features of the apex and retroauricular area. Finally, and although these criteria in general are applicable to individuals of either sex, one should be aware of the degree to which the preauricular sulcus is excavated (being typically more so in females), because a well-developed preauricular sulcus can skew estimates. The age ranges (in years) and associated changes as determined by Lovejoy et al. are summarized below:

1. Ages 20 to 24: "Youthful appearance"; that is, well-defined, broad transverse billows covering most of surface, which is finely granular with no porosity; absence of retroauricular and apical activity.
2. Ages 25 to 29: Still rather "youthful" looking (i.e. distinct transverse pattern) but with some loss of billowing and concomitant increase in *striae* (i.e. striations) as well as an increase of coarseness in grain; absence of retroauricular and apical activity.
3. Ages 30 to 34: More in the inferior than the superior demiface, there is noticeable replacement of billowing by striae and continued loss of the transverse pattern,

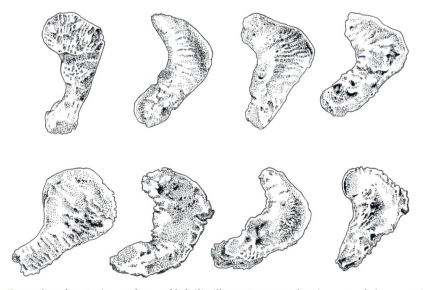

Figure 7–3 Examples of auricular surfaces of left ilia illustrating age-related stages of change (adapted from Lovejoy et al., 1985): *(top row, from left to right)* stages 1-5, *(bottom row, left to right)* stages 6-10; see text for description and associated ages of each stage.

resulting in a smoother appearance; there is also an increase in the coarseness of grain of the surface with the possible development of patches of microporosity; activity is more likely to occur in the retroauricular region than at the apex.

4. Ages 35 to 39: Breakdown of transverse patterning, almost complete obliteration of striae and especially of billowing, and a fairly uniform increase in the coarseness of granularity across the entire surface; minimal activity still in the retroauricular region and even less at the apex.

5. Ages 40 to 44: Billowing absent and remaining striae obscure; continued breakdown of transverse patterning; patches of denser texture, with possible microporosity, appear within the coarsely granular surface; activity at the apex more frequent but more evident in the retroauricular region.

6. Ages 45 to 49: Absence of billowing, striae, and transverse patterning; the surface (and its margins) are distinctly irregular due to an almost complete transformation of granularity and microporosity to a denser texture; activity at the apex is slight to moderate but, again, more prevalent in the retroauricular region.

7. Ages 50 to 59: More extensive irregularity of the surface and its margins, with transformation from granular to dense texture and occasional development of macroporosity; lipping of the inferior margin of auricular facet is common and often extends below the body of ilium; activity in the retroauricular region, and sometimes even in the apical region, is moderate to marked.

8. Age 60+: Extensive topographic and marginal irregularity with marginal lipping and macroporosity; overall deterioration of subchondral bone prevalent; activity at the apex is often marked but is even more marked in the retroauricular region, the surface of which is largely osteophytic.

Rib (Sternal End)

The age-estimating potential of the sternal end of the rib had been pointed out as early as 1957 by McKern and Stewart and reemphasized 13 years later by Kerley (1970). However, more exact studies on the specific criteria involved were still not forthcoming for some time thereafter (İşcan et al., 1984a, b; 1985; 1987; İşcan and Loth, 1986, 1989; Loth and İşcan, 1987). Although this avenue of investigation is still in its youth, İşcan and colleagues have made some interesting observations: there are differences in the timing of changes between American white females and males and apparently between samples of African Americans and American whites. In the sample of American whites and in apparent correlation with the different ages of the onset of puberty, age changes in the sternal end of the rib were noted earlier in females (beginning at approximately 14 years) than in males (approximately 17 years). İşcan et al. (1984a, b) also suggested that ossification in the sternal end of the rib is more extensive at an earlier age in African Americans than in American whites, even though the bones in general, including the ribs, of African Americans do not become thinner and more fragile with age as they do in their American white counterparts. Although corroborating the results of İşcan et al. in aging individuals using the sternal end of the fourth rib, Russell et al. (1993, p. 53) found that African Americans showed not an acceleration in rib end changes but "a non-significant trend for the rib changes to be delayed compared to" American whites. Until work in progress on criteria for assessing the ribs of African Americans is completed and additional studies involving a global sampling of human populations become available, the only unquestionable standards are those on American white females and males. Although the original studies were carried out on the right fourth rib, İşcan and colleagues state that the analysis is not compromised by right/left differences and that they also have obtained accurate age assessments on the third and fifth ribs using the criteria established for the fourth rib.

The sternal end of a rib can be thought of as a billowy surface that, with age, becomes cuplike and thus comes to embrace the costal cartilage that spans it and the sternum (see Figure 7–4). The elements of this "cup" that are subject to change are its depth, floor, walls, and rim or margin. The specific criteria that İşcan and colleagues look for in assessing the sternal end

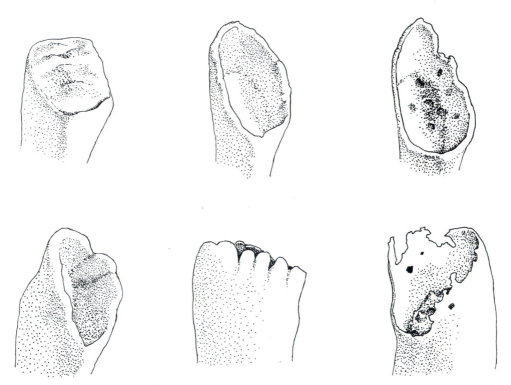

Figure 7–4   Examples of age-related features of the sternal end of rib (typical of ribs III-V) (after İşcan and Loth, 1986): *(top left)* showing features of phase 0, *(bottom left)* phases 2-3, *(top middle)* phase 4, *(bottom middle)* phase 5, *(top right)* phases 6-7, and *(bottom right)* phase 8; see text for descriptions and associated ages.

of the rib are (1) *smoothness versus sharpness* of the rim (2) *scalloping* along the *rim;* (3) *projections* from the *rim;* (4) the formation of a *pit* in or *indentation* of the *floor;* (5) the *shape* of the *pit* or indentation ("V" or "U"); and (6) thickness and *solidness versus brittleness* and fragility of the *walls* of the pit.

The age-related changes of the sternal end of the rib (at least of ribs 3, 4, and 5) of American white females and males are summarized below. The age ranges for females are listed in the parentheses first, followed by those for males. It will be noted that females reach phases 0 to 4 at earlier ages than do males, whereas males pass through phases 5 to 8 at earlier ages than do females. In general, it also appears that the description of a "V"-shaped pit more frequently applies to females than to males, although individuals of either sex could end up being described as having a "U"-shaped pit. Males are described by İşcan et al. as having a narrow "U"-shaped pit, whereas females are described as having a "V"-shaped pit (the reader should

bear this distinction in mind in reading the descriptions). More specific differences between females and males are noted as necessary within the discussion of each phase.

1. Phase 0 (≤13 years; ≤16 years): Sternal surface unexcavated, billowy, or ridged and seemingly "wrapped" in an extra layer of bone; rim continuous and smooth; bone generally solid and smooth.
2. Phase 1 (14 to 15; 17 to 19): Onset of change in regularity or evenness of rim as well as in sternal surface, with some indentation possible.
3. Phase 2 (16 to 19; 20 to 23): Development of "V"- (or narrow "U"-) shaped pit in sternal end, with the "V" being created between what are now thick anterior and posterior "walls"; rim still smooth and rounded with scalloping possible; floor may retain some billowing.
4. Phase 3 (20 to 24; 24 to 28): "V"-shaped indentation wider and becoming "U"-

shaped as walls thin (still fairly thick in males); the floor of the indentation or pit begins to assume an inwardly arced configuration along its superoinferior (long) axis; rim still smooth and rounded but scalloping prevalent (perhaps more irregular in males).

5. Phase 4 (24 to 32; 26 to 32): Depth of pit, broad "V"- or "U"-shape, and superoinferior arc further accentuated; walls thinner and edges possibly flared; rim still smooth but scalloping deteriorating in definition; bone begins to show change in solidness.

6. Phase 5 (33 to 46; 33 to 42): Broad "V"- or "U"-shape further accentuated as walls continue to thin; rim now more sharp than smooth and rounded with loss of scalloping; floor of pit at least partially covered with dense layer; bone continues to lose solidness and become brittle (but perhaps less so in males).

7. Phase 6 (43 to 58; 43 to 55): Progressive deepening of pit and widening and flaring of "V" or "U" as walls thin; rim increasingly irregular and sharp and possibly adorned with sharp, pointed projections; floor of pit may show signs of porosity (especially in males); bone overall continues to deteriorate.

8. Phase 7 (59 to 71; 54 to 64): Pit typically flared and "U"-shaped with markedly thin walls and often bearing irregular bony projections internally; pit decreasing in depth in females but remaining deep in males; rim irregular, sharp, and bearing bony projections, particularly at its superior and inferior margins; there is a prevailing deterioration of bone solidness and an increase in porosity, including in floor of pit.

9. Phase 8 (70+; 65+): Bone deterioration extremely marked, in general as well as in the floor of the pit; bony projections prevalent in floor of "U"-shaped pit (obliterating central arc) as well as on markedly thinned, irregular rim, especially at its superior and inferior margins; the pits of males that lack bony projections are very deep; perforations ("windows") may occur in the walls.

Other Postcranial Elements

Age-related changes in the *vertebral column* have received much less attention than in other parts of the skeleton. The most useful aspect of age-related vertebral change is the development of bony spicules or spurs *(osteophytes)* around the perimeter of the superior and inferior margins of the lumbar vertebrae. The process is called *osteophytosis,* commonly referred to as the development of *lipping* (see Chapter 8). In fully expressed cases of osteophytosis, osteophytes form a projecting rim or lip around the margin that goes from the pedicle on one side all the way around to the pedicle on the other.

Stewart (1958) devised a scale of "0" to "+++" to reflect a gradient of "lipping absent" to "maximum lipping." The degree of osteophyte development is assessed separately for the superior and inferior margins and the two scores are averaged; this could yield, at times, total average scores of "something and one-half" (e.g., ++½). Stewart's sample of known age and sex was heavily white-and-male-biased (368 Korean War dead and 87 males, but only 17 females from the Terry Collection). Stewart suggested cautiously that the most one could say was that, in the case of American whites, individuals below age 30 typically yield an average score of less than ++, while individuals above age 40 would yield average scores higher than ++.

Weisl's (1954) study of the articular (auricular) surface of the sacrum [the sister facet of the auricular surface of the ilium studied by Lovejoy et al. (1985)] provided only broad, general clues to determining an individual's age; that is, young individuals have topographic elevations of the sacral auricular surface confined to the superior and inferior portions, whereas in older individuals the size and number of such elevations increase.

Skull

The historically oldest approach to determining age in adults relies on degrees of cranial suture closure. As will be seen, this approach does have its shortcomings, but if a skull is all that one has to work with, this is probably more consistently reliable than using relative degrees of tooth wear.

As Meindl and Lovejoy (1985) point out, the use of cranial suture closure as an estimate of an individual's age—which Todd and Lyon (1924; 1925a, b, c) believed they had perfected—fell out of favor during the 1950s largely because it became increasingly apparent that this approach could not provide easy and accurate results. For instance, Singer (1953, p. 59) adamantly concluded from his attempt to replicate Todd and Lyon's accuracy of age determination that, "with techniques available at present, an assessment regarding the precise age at death of any individual, gauged only on the degree of closure of the vault sutures of the skull, is a hazardous and unreliable procedure." In more recent years, however, it has become overwhelmingly apparent that no one method of assessing an individual's age can be considered eminently and consistently "the most reliable," and that as many aspects as possible should be analyzed in order to achieve a desirable level of accuracy (e.g. see Acsádi and Nemeskéri, 1970). As such, cranial suture closure is once again being used to aid in the determination of age.

Using Todd and Lyon's (1924; 1925a, b, c) approach, endocranial closure was considered more reliable in the assessment of the earlier adult years because closure endocranially tends to precede closure ectocranially; the latter seemed to be excessively variable in timing. Endocranial suture closure still tends to be favored over ectocranial closure, but the criteria now used are appreciably more sensitive than as originally formulated by Todd and Lyon (e.g. see Acsádi and Nemeskéri, 1970; Krogman and İşcan, 1986).

Acsádi and Nemeskéri (1970, pp. 115–121) determined age on the basis of the average assessment of different components of the coronal, sagittal, and lambdoid sutures endocranially. In order to use their technique, the coronal suture on either side of bregma is divided into three segments (C_1, C_2, C_3, proceeding laterally from bregma), the sagittal suture into four segments (S_1, S_2, S_3, S_4, proceeding posteriorly from bregma), and the lambdoid suture on either side of lambda into three segments (L_1, L_2, L_3, proceeding laterally from the lambda); each segment corresponds to a naturally occurring (and easily identified) portion of a suture that is distinguished by its own particular configuration and degree and tightness of interdigitation. Martin's scale is used for scoring closure: 0 = open; 1 = incipient closure; 2 = closure in progress; 3 = advanced closure; and 4 = obliterated. Each sutural segment is scored for degree of closure. All segments are averaged to achieve a score closure for each suture, then these average scores are averaged, which yields "the mean of closure stage." Age can then be estimated by either referring to Table 7–9 or using the following regression equation:

$$y = 1.1627 + 0.4212x - 0.0171x^2$$

where y = the mean of closure stage, and x = the age rank [from which the associated age can then be determined (Table 7–10)].

Meindl and Lovejoy (1985) developed a method for assessing age (based on a sample of 236 crania of known age and sex from the Hamann-Todd Collection) using degrees of ectocranial closure of cranial vault and lateral anterior sutures. They chose to concentrate on ectocranial suture closure because such synostotic events are "far more closely associated

Table 7–9   *Age at Death (in Years) Based on Suture Closure*

Mean Closure Stage	Mean Age	Mean Deviation	Range
0.4–1.5	28.6	13.08	15–40 (juvenile-young adult)
1.6–2.5	43.7	14.46	30–60 (young-middle adult)
2.6–2.9	49.1	16.40	35–65 (young-middle adult)
3.0–3.9	60.0	13.23	45–75 (middle-old adult)
4.0	65.4	14.05	50–80 (middle-old adult)

Source: Based on Acsádi and Nemeskéri (1970).

Table 7–10   *Age Ranks and Associated Age Ranges (in Years)*

Age Rank	Age Range
1	15–19
2	20–24
3	25–29
4	30–34
5	35–39
6	40–44
7	45–49
8	50–54
9	55–59
10	60–64
11	65–69
12	70–74
13	75–79
14	80–84
15	85–89

Source: Based on Acsádi and Nemeskéri (1970).

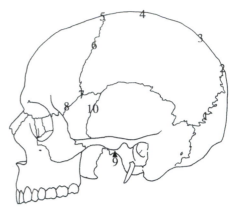

Figure 7–5 Ectocranial landmarks of the lateral and vault systems used by Meindl and Lovejoy (1985) in estimating age at death: 1 = midlambdoid, 2 = lambda, 3 = obelion, 4 = anterior sagittal, 5 = bregma, 6 = midcoronal, 7 = pterion, 8 = sphenofrontal, 9 = inferior sphenotemporal, and 10 = superior sphenotemporal; see text and Appendix F for descriptions.

with extreme age (for which new forensic standards are most needed)" (Meindl and Lovejoy, 1985, p. 58). After investigating the accuracy in age determination of 17 ectocranial sites (each defined as a 1-cm circle whose center is the specific landmark or point), Meindl and Lovejoy (pp. 59–60) concluded that the following were viable (Figure 7–5):

1. Midlambdoid: Centered at the midpoint of each half of the lambdoid suture—that is, in the pars intermedia of the lambdoid suture.
2. Lambda: Centered at the lambda—that is, in the pars lambdica of the sagittal and of the lambdoid sutures.
3. Obelion: Centered at obelion—that is, in the pars obelica of the sagittal suture.
4. Anterior sagittal: Centered at a "point on the sagittal suture at the juncture of the anterior one-third and posterior two-thirds of its length (usually near the juncture of the 'pars bregmatic' and 'pars verticis' of the sagittal suture)".
5. Bregma: Centered at bregma—that is, in the pars bregmatica of the coronal and of the sagittal sutures.

6. Midcoronal: Centered at the midpoint of each half of the coronal suture—that is, in the pars complicata of the coronal suture.
7. Pterion: Centered at pterion—that is, "the region of the upper portion of the greater wing of the sphenoid, usually the point at which the parietosphenoid suture meets the frontal bone" (see Appendix F for alternative definitions of "pterion").
8. Sphenofrontal: Centered at the midpoint of the sphenofrontal suture (alternatively identified as the region of pterion, see Appendix F).
9. Inferior sphenotemporal: Centered at a "point of the sphenotemporal suture lying at its intersection with a line connecting both articular tubercles of the temporomandibular joint."
10. Superior sphenotemporal: centered at a "point on the sphenotemporal suture lying 2 cm below its juncture with the parietal bone."

Meindl and Lovejoy identified ectocranial sites 1 to 7 as belonging to the "vault system" and sites 8 to 9, when taken in conjunction with sites 6 and 7, as the "lateral system." A scale of 0 to 3 is used to score each site within each sys-

Table 7–11   Age at Death (in Years) Based on Ectocranial Lateral-Anterior Suture Closure

Composite Score	Mean Age	Mean Deviation	Range
0 (open)			−50
1	32.0	6.7	19–48
2	36.2	4.8	25–49
3, 4, 5	41.1	8.3	23–68
6	43.4	8.5	23–63
7, 8	45.5	7.4	32–65
9, 10	51.9	10.2	33–76
11, 12, 13, 14	56.2	6.3	34–68
15 (closed)			

Source: Based on Meindl and Lovejoy (1985).

tem: 0 = open, no evidence of incipient synostosis; 1 = minimal to moderate (≤50%) closure or synostosis across the site; 2 = significant (≥50%) but not complete closure across the site; and 3 = complete closure. A composite score of suture closure is calculated by adding up the individual scores for each site within each system. Thus a separate composite score is obtained for the vault system and another for the lateral system. Composite scores (based on seven sites) for the vault system can range from 0 to 21; composite scores (based on five sites) for the lateral anterior system can range from 0 to 15. A composite score thus obtained is translated into an approximate age by comparison with the appropriate table (Table 7–11 for the

Table 7–12   Age at Death (in Years) Based on Ectocranial Vault Suture Closure

Composite Score	Mean Age	Mean Deviation	Range
0 (open)			−49
1, 2	30.5	7.4	18–45
3, 4, 5, 6	34.7	6.4	22–48
7, 8, 9, 10, 11	39.4	7.2	24–60
12, 13, 14, 15	45.2	10.3	24–75
16, 17, 18	48.8	8.3	30–71
19, 20	51.5	9.8	23–76
21 (closed)			40–

Source: Based on Meindl and Lovejoy (1985).

lateral anterior system and Table 7–12 for the vault system). Because the age, sex, and population (i.e. African American and American white) of each individual in their sample were known, Meindl and Lovejoy tested the possibility of error of age prediction due to sex and population and found that neither variable contributed "any measurable bias" (p. 64). One would hope that follow-up studies of such precision on other populations would yield similarly accurate results.

Age-Related Changes in Teeth

Because the morphology of a tooth is determined—and produced—prior to the tooth's eruption into the jaw, one cannot study tooth alteration with age in the same manner as alteration of other skeletal elements. However, teeth do erupt in the jaws at different times; as they do, their occlusal and interstitial surfaces will suffer differing amounts of attrition. The "ideal" dentition, therefore, will display a pattern of differential wear reflecting the different lengths of time teeth have been subjected to attrition. As such, and assuming a constant rate of wear on teeth throughout one's life, the degree to which teeth are worn down should reflect the age of the individual at death, because the approximate times at which teeth erupt are known.

Of course, theory and reality do not always coincide. Different diets, extraneous inclusions in food substances (e.g. grit from utensils used for food preparation and/or as found naturally in food), tooth loss/survivorship (e.g. through periodontal disease or carious infection), the use of teeth as tools (e.g. in the preparation of hides or the stripping and softening of bark), the modification of teeth (e.g. anterior upper and/or lower tooth ablation, or holding a pipe stem), the introduction of dentistry, and differences between the sexes within any of these categories can cause subtle to extreme differences between populations. And this, in turn, would obviate any possibility of being able to develop globally or temporally useful age-related scales of tooth wear patterns. In some instances, however, one might be able delineate a pattern of tooth wear that persists over time and from one population to the next; for instance, Brothwell (1972) has suggested that age-related rates and patterns of wear on upper and lower molars were relatively constant among British populations from the Neolithic to the Middle Ages.

As Brothwell (1972), for example, points out, the larger the study population and the more ages represented in it, the better able one will be to develop an age-wear chronology for the population. It is hoped that one would at least be able to establish a chronological seriation (cf. Lovejoy et al., 1985a) reflecting relative ages within the population.

A chronology of dental wear with absolute ages—or at least estimates of absolute age—can be achieved by linking defined stages of wear with stages of change in other parts of the skeleton for which ages can be determined. If one is fortunate to have in the sample under study individuals in whom teeth are still erupting or growing in the jaws and these individuals can be seriated by dental age, one can construct a tooth-wear chronology by noting how much tooth wear accumulates during the time between the eruption of one tooth, and then another, and so on.

Studies of age-related stages of tooth wear have concentrated on attrition as it affects the "adult" dentition (e.g. Lovejoy, 1985; Molnar, 1971) and have sometimes been restricted to the permanent molars alone (e.g. Brothwell, 1972; Miles, 1963). It would seem, though, that analysis of the entire set of teeth—or as many as are typically preserved—would provide the more complete and more interesting picture of tooth wear. Furthermore, and although children might not be as well-represented in any given sample as adults, it would seem that these younger age groups should be included in the overall chronology of tooth wear whenever possible—not only for the purposes of establishing an additional criterion for assessing individuals of young age but also for investigating potential differences in rates of attrition which might, for example, reflect shifts in diet or tooth use activities. In any case, when one is attempting to construct a chronology of tooth wear, it should not be forgotten that occlusal surfaces begin to show attrition when they are sufficiently erupted to come into contact with the substances being chewed, which occurs prior to the tooth's occlusal surface becoming level with the occlusal surfaces of neighboring teeth. This

point gains further relevance in light of an increasingly common complaint about studies of tooth growth and eruption patterns—that is the incomparability of "alveolar eruption" with "gingival eruption," the latter being the criterion used on living individuals or cadavers. Careful attention to the identification of incipient tooth wear—through polarized light or scanning electron microscopy—can provide evidence of an incompletely erupted tooth having emerged occlusally through the gum.

The first rigorous and systematic approach to the determination of age based on aspects of the dentition was developed by Gustafson (1950). He advocated investigating changes associated with attrition, periodontosis (i.e., recession of the gums leading to exposure of the root), the formation of secondary dentine in the pulp cavity, the deposition of cementum on the root, atrophy of the root or roots, and thinning of the root with a concomitant increase in its translucency. Each category is evaluated on a scale of 0 (absent or incipient) to 3 (most marked), and the scores are summed. This total is taken as x in the equation

$$y = 11.43 + 4.56x$$

where y represents age; S.D. $= \pm 3.6$ years.

There are problems, however, in applying these criteria to skeletal material. The most obvious one is that alveolar resorption, which can easily be evaluated on skeletal material, does not necessarily mirror the extent to which recession of the gums had proceeded; as with correlating alveolar with gingival eruption, data relevant to translating alveolar into gingival resorption are still lacking. More generally, Miles (1963) found that application of Gustafson's method (38% accuracy ± 3 years) did not significantly improve upon his own more intuitive estimates of individuals' ages (34% accuracy ± 3 years).

Miles did suggest, however, that the criterion of "root translucency" was a potentially viable feature—that is, there is a general tendency for the root, beginning with the apex, to become thinner and, in longitudinal section, to become more translucent with increasing age. In a pilot study of upper central incisors of individuals of known age ($N = 118$), Miles (1963) plotted length in millimeters of the translucent part of root (x) against individual age (y) and found that the data could be characterized roughly ($p \le .05$, correlation coefficient $= .73$) by the regression equation

$$y = 21.857 + 4.6169x$$

When this equation was applied to another sample, Miles achieved a 32% (± 3 years) rate of accuracy in assessing age. This is hardly an impressive result, but Miles did suggest that if this body of data were increased (and I would include in this the analysis of additional teeth), the technique could be applied "by those with virtually no previous experience of either root translucency or age determination" (p. 197). The implications would seem to be particularly relevant to forensic investigations, in which skeletal remains are typically very recent in origin, leeching and possible redeposition of minerals are less likely to obscure results, and evaluation could be done efficiently.

Molnar (1971) presented a very complete and also very complex approach toward evaluating attritional effects on the "adult" dentition, which he organized into the groups "incisor + canine," "premolar," and "molar." He subdivided the category of tooth wear into eight components, which can be described roughly as the development of wear facets, the exposure of dentine (minimal, maximum), the presence of secondary dentine (moderate to extensive), loss of crown enamel (at least one side) and the development of extensive secondary dentine, and the involvement of the roots in occlusion. He also proposed categories of direction of tooth wear and of occlusal surface form. Unfortunately, Molnar did not correlate stages or states of tooth wear with age, and an attempt to apply his approach to another sample failed (Lunt, 1978).

Lovejoy (1985) did develop a seriated sequence of stages or patterns of tooth wear on the Libben population. Fortunately, he found that these stages of tooth wear could not only be correlated with age but were an excellent reflection of age (Lovejoy et al., 1985a). A major reason for Lovejoy's success was the presence in his sample of individuals ($N = 132$) who were young enough (6 to 18 years) to allow him to define functional rates of wear on the anterior teeth (incisors + canines), premolars, and

molars. Overall, "dental wear was found to be sufficiently regular to allow the designation of modal wear groups (with attendant age estimations)" (Lovejoy, 1985, p. 54). Upper and lower dentitions were analyzed separately and modal age-related wear patterns derived for each jaw (9 for the maxilla and 10 for the mandible). When the sexes were analyzed separately, Lovejoy found that females had a slightly higher rate of dental attrition. However, one should be prepared to find such differences in other samples. For example, Campbell (e.g. 1939) did find sex-related differences in tooth wear among Australian aborigines, with females, who are the major food collectors, having higher rates of attrition because they test the different types of food they seek to collect.

Clearly, if the necessary elements are present, study of age-related changes in patterns of dental attrition can be a fruitful component of the analysis of a skeletal population, for not only will another age criterion be available but details of tooth use among age groups and between the sexes can be reconstructed.

The Complex Method of Determining Adult Age (after Acsádi and Nemeskéri, 1970)

Although the history of the study of age-related skeletal changes reveals an overwhelming desire to isolate one accurate method for any given phase of life, the reality of the situation is that the use of only one approach is often riddled with unreliability. This, of course, is especially unsatisfactory in dealing with forensic and medicolegal cases and makes viable paleodemographic reconstructions impossible. In order to overcome this problem, Acsádi and Nemeskéri (1970, p. 122 et seq) introduced "the complex method of determining the age of adults," which is based on the combined age-related characteristics of different skeletal regions. After evaluating the relative accuracy of the various analyses and methods reported in the literature, Acsádi and Nemeskéri concluded that the four most reliable indicators of age-related change are the endocranial sutures (see above), the proximal humerus, the proximal femur, and the pubic symphysis (a modification of Todd's stages). Changes in the proximal humerus and femur are primarily internal and involve a decrease in trabeculation and pervasiveness of spongy bone that is correlated with an expansion upward of the medullary cavity and a general increase in cavitation. Externally, the proximal epiphyses atrophy, with concomitant alteration of topographic features, and the cortical bone thins. Acsádi and Nemeskéri identified six phases of age-related change for the proximal region of each bone, which must be

determined either radiographically (or fluoroscopically) or by longitudinal sectioning.

The Proximal Humerus: Phases of Age-Related Change

The examples of each phase are illustrated in Figure 7–6. A description of each phase and the ages (mean age ± standard deviation and actual

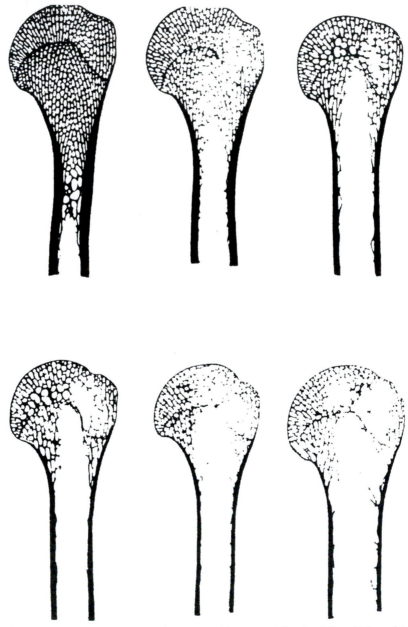

Figure 7–6 Phases of age-related change in the proximal humerus (after Acsádi and Nemeskéri, 1970): *(top row, left to right)* phases 1 to 3 and *(bottom row, left to right)* phased 4 to 6; see text for description and associated ages.

range in years) associated with it are listed below.

1. 41.1 ± 6.60 (18 to 68): The apex of the medullary cavity terminates well below the surgical neck and the trabeculae are arranged primarily in a radial pattern.
2. 52.3 ± 2.51 (24 to 76): The apex of the medullary cavity extends to or above the level of the surgical neck and is subtended by a more fragile trabecular system that assumes the overall appearance of a pointed arch (e.g. ogival).
3. 59.8 ± 3.59 (37 to 86): The apex of the medullary cavity may reach the epiphyseal (metaphyseal) line; the trabecular system subtending the medullary cavity assumes the distinct shape of a pointed arch, while the trabeculae along the metaphyseal line become more vacuous, with thicker walls.
4. 56.0 ± 1.84 (19 to 79): The apex of the medullary cavity extends to or above the level of the metaphyseal line; the trabeculae subtending the medullary cavity are in the process of breaking down, as is the spongy bone within the greater tuberosity.
5. 61.0 ± 2.05 (40 to 84): The apex of the medullary cavity extends variably but noticeably above the level of the metaphyseal line and is subtended only by fragments of trabeculae; distinct large spaces (2 to 5 mm) develop within the greater tuberosity.
6. 61.1 ± 3.39 (38 to 84): The process of deterioration within the greater tuberosity forms a large cavity (≥5 mm) and may reach the cortex; the apex of the medullary cavity often merges with the cavity formed within the greater tuberosity; trabeculae within the epiphysis are thin-walled, and spongy bone is sparsely distributed; externally, the features of the proximal humerus are atrophied and the cortex is thin and transparent.

The Proximal Femur: Phases of Age-Related Change

The examples of each phase are illustrated in Figure 7–7. A description of each phase and the ages (mean age ± standard deviation and actual range in years, when available) associated with

it are listed below. Age changes in the proximal femur begin earlier than they do in the proximal humerus (mean ages being, respectively, 31.4 and 41.1 years). Change in the proximal femur is slow until the third phase, when the rate of deterioration parallels that of the proximal humerus.

1. 31.4 (18 to 52): The apex of the medullary cavity lies well below the level of the lesser trochanter; the trabeculae are densely packed, obscuring individual trabecular detail.
2. 44.0 ± 2.6 (19 to 61): The apex of the medullary cavity extends to or above the inferior portion of the lesser trochanter; the details of trabecular morphology and patterning are more clearly defined, with most loss of density occurring in the medial region of the femoral neck.
3. 52.6 ± 1.86 (23 to 72): The apex of the medullary cavity extends to the top of the lesser trochanter; the trabeculae continue to deteriorate and become thinner, especially in the medial region of the neck, as does the spongy bone within the greater trochanter.
4. 56.0 ± 2.32 (32 to 86): The apex of the medullary cavity extends above the top of the lesser trochanter; continued deterioration of trabeculae and spongy bone is pervasive within the greater trochanter, along the metaphyseal line, and in the region just internal to the fovea of the femoral head; such deterioration also creates a large cavity (5 to 10 mm) in the medial portion of the neck.
5. 63.3 ± 2.17 (38 to 84): The apex of the medullary cavity extends well above the top of the lesser trochanter; the walls of the medullary cavity bear only vestiges of trabeculae; continued deterioration of trabeculae and spongy bone enlarges the cavities within the greater trochanter (3 to 5 mm), beneath the fovea, along the metaphyseal line, and within the neck.
6. 67.8 ± 3.64 (25 to 85): The medullary cavity, which is subtended at best by fragments of trabeculae, may merge with the large cavity in the neck (typically ≥ 10 mm); the other cavities are also larger, with the cavity within the greater trochanter often being ≥5 mm; externally, the

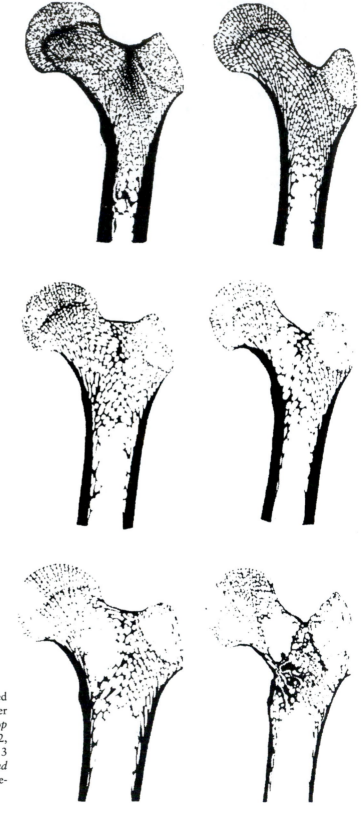

Figure 7–7 Phases of age-related change in the proximal femur (after Acsádi and Nemeskéri, 1970): *(top row, left and right)* phases 1 and 2, *(middle row, left and right)* phases 3 and 4, and *(bottom row, left and right)* phases 5 and 6; see text for description and associated ages.

features of the proximal femur have atrophied and the layer of cortical bone is thin and transparent.

The Pubic Symphysis: Phases of Age-Related Change

Although Acsádi and Nemeskéri present their own set of illustrations of the pubic symphysis—which is often reprinted along with all of the others in other texts—this will not be done here, especially since any set of illustrations, like any list of phase/stage descriptions, constitutes a compilation of modal summaries that should be used as guides and not taken as universally applicable examples. The reader can refer to the illutrations of the pubic symphysis provided above (Figure 7–2) but is advised to gain experience through study of actual specimens. A description of each phase and the ages (mean age ± standard deviation and actual range in years, when available) associated with it are listed below.

1. 26.3 (18 to 45): The symphyseal surface is convex and transversely billowy (i.e. with horizontal ridges and furrows); the transition from the symphyseal margins (lower and upper extremities) into the inferior and superior pubic rami is smoothly arcuate.

2. 46.5 ± 1.76 (23 to 69): Deterioration of the symphyseal surface begins to break down ridges and furrows; the dorsal and ventral margins are becoming rimmed, as are the upper and lower extremities.

3. 51.1 ± 1.62 (25 to 76): The symphyseal surface is primarily granular, with only vestiges of billowing visible; the dorsal and ventral margins are almost completely rimmed and the upper and lower extremities bear distinct edges.

4. 58.1 ± 2.16 (24 to 81): The symphyseal surface is flat and granular in texture; the dorsal and ventral margins bear sharp rims and the lower extremity terminates in a distinct ridge.

5. 68.5 ± 2.53 (41 to 86): The symphyseal surface is porous and appears to have collapsed inward; the "sunkenness" of this surface is accentuated by the essentially continuous, raised rim around it; this rim

is continuous with the inferiorly extending, ridgelike lower extremity.

Calculation of Age

Upon comparing these four sources of age-related data, Acsádi and Nemeskéri found that endocranial suture closure begins earlier and advances rather rapidly in earlier ages than do changes in the proximal humerus and femur and in the pubic symphysis. Table 7–13 lists the mean ages for each of the four skeletal regions examined as well as the lower and upper limits of the age ranges for each of these four skeletal regions.

Acsádi and Nemeskéri recommend assessing the pubic symphysis first. If the age determined from this region is less than 50 years (i.e. phases I and II), they suggest using the age values listed for the lower limit of the age range of each skeletal component. If the age estimate from the pubic symphysis is approximately 50 years (i.e. phase III), the mean age values for each skeletal component should be used. And, if pubic symphysis morphology reflects an apparent age of 50+ years (i.e. phases IV and V), one should use the age values listed for the upper limit of the age range of each skeletal component. The age values obtained for each skeletal component are then averaged in order to eliminate bias from any one source. Thus, for individuals who, on the basis of pubic symphyseal morphology, appear to be younger than 50 years, the lower limits of the age ranges will be averaged (i.e. the sum of the four lower age limits ÷ 4); for individuals who appear to be approximately 50 years of age according to symphyseal morphology, the means of the age ranges will be averaged; and, for individuals who appear to be older than 50 years on the basis of pubic symphyseal morphology, the means of the upper limits of the age ranges will be averaged. As Acsádi and Nemeskéri (p. 131) point out, this approach results in the " 'most probable' age at death of an individual" and reflects an 80% to 85% degree of accuracy with a ±2.5-year margin of error. The average age determined for any individual should be represented with this margin of error.

In an example of their method, Acsádi and Nemeskéri presented an analysis of the skeleton of a young individual in whom endocranial su-

Table 7-13 *Ranges (in Years) Predicted by Four Age Indicators*

Phase	Lower Limit				Mean				Upper Limit			
	Suture	Symphysis	Femur	Humerus	Suture	Symphysis	Femur	Humerus	Suture	Symphysis	Femur	Humerus
I	23	23	23	23	30	32	33	41	39	40	43	57
II	35	37	35	41	44	44	44	51	52	49	53	61
III	45	46	44	48	53	52	52	57	60	58	59	65
IV	53	54	50	52	60	60	58	59	66	68	56	67
V	58	61	54	54	63	67	63	61	72	75	71	69
VI	—	—	58	55	—	—	67	62	—	—	76	70

Source: From Acsádi and Nemeskéri (1970).

ture closure was evaluated as being phase II while the proximal humerus, pubic symphysis, and proximal femur were phase I. The lower limits for the age ranges of these phases are 35, 23, 23, and 23, respectively. The total of these figures summed is 104. As 104 ÷ 4 = 26.0, the estimated age is 26.0 ± 2.5 years. The actual age of this individual was 23 years.

The Multifactorial Method of Determining Summary Age (after Lovejoy et al., 1985a)

Lovejoy et al. (1985a) proposed a multiple-skeletal-component system for estimating what they refer to as a "summary" age at death of individuals. In order to develop and test this method, they used a sample of 512 individuals from the Hamann-Todd collection for whom reliable documentation as to age, etc., was available. Of the potential skeletal sources from which age at death can be calculated, Lovejoy et al. delineated five that appeared to be the most appropriate indicators of age for this particular sample: the pubic symphyseal surface, the auricular surface, the internal structure of the proximal femur, degrees of dental wear, and ectocranial suture closure. These age indicators were used according to the modifications Lovejoy and colleagues suggested in the companion articles of this issue of the *American Journal of Physical Anthropology* (see above). Upon applying this method to the Libben site skeletal population, Lovejoy et al. found that they could also include age-related data on the radius, which raised to six the number of age indicators that could be used in assessing this population.

In practical terms, the number of usable age indicators, as well as the specific age indicators employed in a study, is determined on a case-by-case basis for each skeletal population analyzed. Thus, this approach is distinguished, among other things, by its flexibility of applicability to different skeletal populations, each of which would be distinguished by specific populational norms as well as by differing preservational histories of deposition and preservation. For example, assessment of degrees of dental wear may yield valuable comparative information for some populations (e.g. because teeth are retained longer) whereas for others

such data may not even be attainable (e.g. because teeth are lost early on due to periodontal disease).

In order to achieve complete objectivity in data collection, each skeletal age indicator should be analyzed independently of all others. For example, Lovejoy et al. masked the pubic symphyseal regions (with tinfoil) when they were assessing age on the basis of ilial auricular morphology, and vice versa. Lovejoy et al. also advocate seriation of the skeletal material to be analyzed—that is, to arrange the material serially in an internally consistent sequence of morphological and thus age-related change for the population. They argue convincingly that seriation of skeletal material reduces observer error in the assessment of age.

The general procedure in calculating an individual's *summary age* begins with the determination of age based on each skeletal age indicator (e.g. pubic symphysis, cranial suture closure) used in the study for each individual in the study population. Such data can easily be entered into any number of readily available spreadsheet programs. All age indicators for all individuals are then used in the generation of an *intercorrelation matrix* (spreadsheet data can be imported into various statistical programs, such as the powerful SPSS, BMDP, and SYSTAT, or such smaller statistical packages such as STATVIEW and FASTAT). The intercorrelation matrix thus obtained is subjected to *principal components analysis*, which also is referred to as *unrotated factor matrix analysis* (principal components analysis is packaged in a number of statistics software programs). The *first component factor* score is taken as representing *true chronological age*. The weight of an indicator is represented by the correlation of that indicator with the first component factor determined for that age indicator—that is, the weight is represented by the *correlation coefficient*. The *summary age* of an individual is calculated by (1) multiplying each age indicator by its weight (i.e. its correlation coefficient), (2) summing all of these products, and then (3) dividing this total by the sum of the weights (i.e. the sum of the correlation coefficients). In order to improve accuracy in the calculation of summary age, Lovejoy et al. (1985a, p. 10) suggest the following corrections: for individuals for whom a summary age of 45 to 55 years is obtained, one should recalculate summary age with the lowest age indicator excluded from the calculation; for individuals for whom a summary age of 55+ years is obtained, one should recalculate summary age with the two lowest age indicators excluded from the calculation.

Of particular note with regard to the accuracy with which Lovejoy et al. calculated summary age for the individuals in their Hamann-Todd sample (when these ages were compared to recorded ages) is that this sample was more diverse in its composition (i.e. broadly geographically, ethnically, and socioeconomically) than one would expect to be the case in any archeologically derived skeletal population. Lovejoy et al. (1985a, p. 12) suggest that "[a]ge determination in archaeological populations is generally more accurate than in modern anatomical collection samples because both environmental and genetic variables are more uniform in the former" and that "[w]hen such age determinations are made by composite methods . . . they may provide more accurate mortality profiles than those derived from living 'primitive' populations."

More recently, Bedford et al. (1993) tested this aging method using a skeletal collection of known ages at death. They found that "[m]ultifactorial age estimates correlated better with real age than did those from any single indicator used" (p. 287) and that "[t]he method produces estimated age distributions which are statistically indistinguishable from those of real age" (p. 297).

Histological Age-Related Changes in Bone

Two of the attributes that Acsádi and Nemeskéri (1970) evaluated in their "complex method of determining adult age" involved age-related changes in trabecular and cortical bone in the humerus and femur. Such changes are also characteristic of other skeletal elements so far studied. However, the only studies to date that have attempted to correlate structural change in bones with age are those summarized above for the proximal humerus and femur. Other aspects of bone resorption and remodeling will be discussed here as they relate to the estimation of an individual's age from the skeleton.

Specimen Preparation

Although the study of internal structural change in the proximal humerus and femur can be accomplished radiographically, other aspects of bone change can be assessed histologically—that is, only after a cross section of bone has been prepared for microscopy. This entails access to certain equipment, which may limit the widespread use of these histological analyses. Unfortunately, only the long bones of the leg have been analyzed in terms of correlating changes with age—although cranial bones (Frost, 1987a) as well as ribs, vertebrae, and the iliac crest (Stout and Teitelbaum, 1976) should be amenable to the same analyses and yield equally informative information. As such, the discussion here focuses on the preparation of undecalcified thin sections limited primarily to the long bones (following procedures suggested in Blumberg and Kerley, 1966; Putschar, 1966; Stout, 1989; Stout and Teitelbaum, 1976; and Ubelaker, 1989, in which the prodecure is also illustrated).

Commonly, a midshaft cross-sectional slice of approximately 1 cm is removed using a fine-toothed saw. If the material is judged as being too friable to undergo direct mounting to the specimen stage of a thin-section cutoff saw and/ or to be thin-sectioned without crumbling, it should be embedded first in synthetic resin, varieties of which are readily available from major biological supply companies. Prior to embedding, it is advisable to dehydrate the specimen in a series of 8-hour alcohol baths (70%, 95%, and then two baths in absolute alcohol). A thin section can then be cut, ground, and polished (see below) to the required thickness. Unfortunately, a specimen prepared in this manner may retain foreign particles derived from the soil penetrating the specimen prior to excavation or being incorporated into the preservative applied during excavation.

An unembedded bone section that is sufficiently solidified to be mounted on the specimen stage of a thin-section saw and sectioned could be reduced to an approximately 5-mm thin section. With a thinner piece of bone to work with, one can attempt to remove foreign particles and/or preservatives. Because the polymeric plastic preservatives used in the field are typically dissolved and the resultant solution diluted to the necessary consistency in the organic solvent toluene, a series of toluene baths, with ultrasonic agitation to speed up the process, should redissolve the preservative (small ultrasonic cleaners can be purchased through major biological and chemical supply companies or at the jewelry counters of large—and often discount—department stores). Ubelaker recommends cleaning thin sections for approximately 50 minutes in a solution of Decal (a product commercially available from Scientific Products), with the beaker of Decal suspended in a water bath in the well of an ultrasonic cleaner. The Decal solution is removed from the cleaned specimen by immersing it in the water bath in the well of the ultrasonic cleaner, after which it is dried overnight. The specimen is then embedded in synthetic resin in preparation for the next phase. The specimen may be immersed in a bath of synthetic resin, or embedding may be accelerated by placing the container (with specimen and resin) in a vacuum chamber.

The next step is to grind and polish the specimen on both sides, reducing it, in the process, to a thickness of approximately 75 μ (50 to 90 μ). Electric grinding and polishing wheels are commercially available from biological supply companies, but both tasks may be accomplished by hand (and with a bit of elbow grease). W. von Koenigswald (personal communication, 1980) uses a series of graded sandpapers to grind and then polish teeth he embeds for scanning electron microscopic analysis of enamel prism patterns. Kits for polishing plastic-embedded specimens are available from biological supply companies.

The finished thin section is mounted on a slide and protected with a cover slip. The slide should be labeled with information not only about the specimen's origin (e.g. skeletal catalogue or field number) but also about its orientation (i.e. which side is anterior, posterior, medial, or lateral, which can be denoted as the directions on a weathervane).

An infrequently cited approach to obtaining a sample of bone that also captures cortical thickness is bone core analysis (Thompson, 1978; also Laughlin et al., 1979). In this case, a 0.4-cm diameter core is obtained using a hollow bone-core drill bit. A major advantage to this method is that it leaves the target bone intact and relatively unreduced in size, which is particularly important if the specimen from which a sample must be taken is unique or fragmentary. The small piece of bone thus obtained can be cleaned, embedded, and thin-sectioned as summarized above. As only four loci [at 12, 3, 6 (or linea aspera), and 9 o'clock] of a femoral cross section are analyzed in order to estimate age [i.e. on the basis of secondary osteons, osteon fragments, nonhaversian canals, and circumferential lamellar bone (Kerley, 1965; see below)] and the recommended field size for a locus is less than 2.0 mm (Kerley and Ubelaker, 1978), the study of small bone cores taken from these loci can yield results with minimal destruction of bone.

Gross Histological Changes in Cortical Bone

Changes in the cortex of the femur, tibia, and fibula in areas of resorption have been correlated with age (Kerley, 1965; 1970). In general, different areas of the cortex undergo resorption at different ages. Early in life, when bone size (especially girth) is increasing, resorption is most active in the endosteal region or medullary cavity. As growth ceases and osteoclastic and osteoblastic activity are more or less in equilibrium, resorption can be detected throughout the entire cortex and, eventually, in the periosteal portion as well. After a period of inactivity and with increasing age, resorption in the endosteal region becomes accelerated. As will be noted, the age brackets thus delineated are quite broad but can be of assistance in sorting bones into age groups if one is confronted with bones from ossuaries, multi-individual graves, or the unintentional mixing of skeletal elements during long-term use and reuse of burial plots.

The cortex can be subdivided roughly for this analysis into an inner third and an outer third. From birth through the third year, resorption is most active in the inner third. From 4 years into the tenth year, evidence of intense resorption is distributed fairly evenly throughout the depth of the cortex. During the next 7 years (until almost 17 years of age), resorption tends to be restricted to the outer third, and, in particular, the region close to the periosteal surface. After 17 years of age, osteoblastic and osteoclastic activity are normally more or less in equilibrium. Thus, areas of intense resorption are not noted until later in life. In females, marked resorption in the inner third of the cortex may begin as early as age 40 but also may be delayed until as late as age 60. Although there is some variation in timing, intense resorptive activity in the inner third of the cortex in males tends to begin at age 40. In both sexes, this osteoclastic activity results in a thinning of the cortex because of the diminished activity of bone-replacing osteoblasts.

Detailed Histological Changes in Cortical Bone

In an attempt to refine age estimates on the basis of histologically recognizable changes in cortical bone, Kerley (e.g. 1965) compiled data from midshaft cross sections of the femur, tibia, and fibula of 126 individuals; the sample ranged in age from birth to 95 years, with a median age of 35. The sample sampled female and male African Americans, Asian Americans, and American whites. Only sections free of pathology were deemed suitable for analysis. In order to record with as much accuracy as possible the cellular life history of the bone under study, Kerley chose to focus on the outer third of the cortex. This is the portion of the cortex that is least affected by intense resorption and therefore retains a more uniform texture throughout an individual's life. As mentioned above, four loci on each section were studied microscopically; these loci correspond to the anterior, posterior, medial, and lateral "borders" of the bone (or, as described above, the positions corresponding to 12, 3, 6, and 9 o'clock). At first, Kerley suggested using a circular microscopic field 1.25 mm in diameter (formed by 10× ocular wide-field lenses in conjunction with a 10× objective lens). Subsequently, however, Kerley and Ubelaker (1978) found that intermicroscope error could lead to an underestimation of age. In order to correct for this potential error, they suggested using a field of 1.62 mm in diameter [and introduced a modified set of regression equations by which to calculate age (see below)]. The components of the cortex that are analyzed are the separate totals across all four fields of the number of (1) whole osteons, (2) fragments of osteons, and (3) nonhaversian canals (see Figure 1–8). In addition, the average percent to which all four fields contain circumferential lamellar bone is calculated.

In carrying out osteon analysis, one counts the number of whole osteons, osteon fragments, and/or nonhaversian canals present in all four loci of a section. The total count thus achieved is regressed, using the appropriate equation. Average percent of circumferential lamellar bone is estimated. Given the problems in intermicroscope calibration mentioned above, Kerley and Ubelaker (1978, p. 546) recommend the following corrections for adjusting the data to a field diameter of 1.62 mm:

> The area (πr^2) of the 100× field of the microscope used must be calculated using a stage micrometer and that field size divided into 2.06 mm² (area of a field diameter of 1.62 mm) to determine the relationship between the original field size and the field size of the individual microscope being used. All counts of osteons, fragments or nonhaversian canals should then be multiplied by that factor. The estimate of percentage of lamellar bone is not affected.

In his original paper, Kerley (1965) presented graphs and regression equations that would translate the counts and averages into age estimates for each bone studied—that is, femur, tibia, and fibula. This study was criticized by Ahlqvist and Damsten (1969), but Bouvier and Ubelaker (1977) subsequently demonstrated the greater reliability of Kerley's method. The generally preferred regression equations are those that were modified by Kerley and Ubelaker (1978) (Table 7–14), which, according to Stout (1989, p. 45), are the most accurate and reliable of available histological aging methods when the ages obtained from these equations are averaged together.

Stout (1989) also refers to studies in his laboratory that have attempted to use osteon data from the rib and clavicle to estimate age. The advantage of using these bones, in contrast to the long bones of the leg, is that they are not weight-bearing. This appears to be significant, because a problem that does arise when using weight-bearing bones is that mechanical influences can greatly affect bone remodeling (e.g. Frost, 1987a). With regard to the rib, at least two cross sections should be prepared from the middle third of the sixth rib. All osteons and osteon fragments are counted together to achieve "total visible osteon density." If more than one cross section can be prepared for analysis, an average "total visible osteon density"

Table 7–14   Predicting (Regression) Equations for Estimating Age at Death

Bone Elements	Predicting Equation	Mean Square Residual
Femur		
Whole osteons	$Y = 2.278 + 0.187X + 0.00226X^2$	9.19
Osteon fragments	$Y = 5.241 + 0.509 + 0.017X^2 - 0.00015X^3$	6.98
Lamellar bone	$Y = 75.017 - 1.79X + 0.0114X^2$	12.52
Nonhaversian canals	$Y = 58.390 - 3.184X + 0.0628X^2 - 0.00036X^3$	12.12
Tibia		
Whole osteons	$Y = 13.4218 + 0.660X$	10.53
Osteon fragments	$Y = -26.997 + 2.501X - 0.014X^3$	8.42
Lamellar bone	$Y = 80.934 - 2.281X + 0.019X^2$	14.28
Nonhaversian canals	$Y = 67.872 - 9.0870X + 0.440X^2 - 0.0062X^3$	10.19
Fibula		
Whole osteons	$Y = -23.59 + 0.74511X$	8.33
Osteon fragments	$Y = -9.89 + 1.064X$	3.66
Lamellar bone	$Y = 124.09 - 10.92X + 0.3723X^2 - 0.00412X^3$	10.74
Nonhaversian canals	$Y = 62.33 - 9.776X + 0.5502X - 0.00704X^3$	14.62

Source: Modified from Kerley and Ubelaker (1978).

can be obtained. Stout (1989, p. 47) proposed using the following regression equation to predict age:

$$y = 2.87351x - 12.3490$$

where y = age in years, x = total visible osteon density, $r = 0.68244$.

Most recently, Stout and Paine (1992, p. 112) introduced a different equation for predicting age based on the rib as well as equations for predicting age based on the clavicle and the rib and clavicle together: "The data were made linear by using natural log (L^n) age as the dependent variable." The sample size was 40 individuals and the age range 13 to 62 years; $s = 12.9$ and $t_{0.05} = 2.0244$. For the rib, the predicting equation is:

$$L_n Y = 2.343 \pm 0.050877X_r$$

where $s_{yx} = L_n 0.231$, $\bar{x} = 18.03$, $s_x^2 = 51.696$, $r^2 = 0.7211$.

For the clavicle:

$$L_n Y = 2.216 + 0.070280X_c$$

where $s_{yx} = L_n 0.239$, $\bar{x} = 14.86$, $s_x^2 = 26.256$, $r^2 = 0.6989$.

For the rib and clavicle together:

$$L_n Y = 2.195 + 0.029904X_r + 0.035430X_c$$

where $s_{yx} = L_n 0.209$, $r^2 = 0.7762$. If both bones are available, Stout and Paine suggest that the latter regression equation is the most accurate predictor of age.

Frost (1987b) also developed an algorithm for estimating missing osteons in fields of sec-

Table 7–15   Examples of Elements That Could Affect Osteon Formation, Number, etc.

Actual age, mean tissue age, life span, sex, taxon
Anemias, Paget's disease
Bone growth, modeling patterns, hormones, skeletal maturation, regional acceleration
Diet, nutrition, vitamins, electrolyte imbalance
Drugs, toxic agents, radiation
Genetic (structural) disorders
Infectious/systemic disease, tumors
Metabolic disorders, alkalosis, acidosis
Mechanical strain, usage, disuse (acute), paralysis
Regional trauma, microdamage

Source: Modified from Frost (1987a).

ondary osteon populations. The impetus was to try to deal with the fact that "as the number of secondary osteons increases in a given diaphyseal cross section, new ones can begin to remove all microscopic evidence of older ones. . . . [Thus] increasing numbers of observed osteons tend to become progressively smaller fractions of all osteons created in that domain" (Frost, 1987b, p. 239). Most recently, Stout and Paine (1994, p. 123) tested Frost's algorithm on an autopsy sample ($N = 44$ ribs) and found that "[e]stimates of activation frequency . . . and bone remodeling rate . . . using the new algorithm are in reasonable agreement with age-matched tetracycline-based values." Therefore, Stout and Paine concluded, Frost's algorithm can be applied to archeologically derived osteological material. Inasmuch as application of this algorithm requires determining mean osteonal cross-sectional area, mean cross-sectional diameter of intact osteons, intact and fragmentary osteon density (from which osteon population density can then be calculated), and accumulated osteon creations, the pursuit of this analysis would be limited to labs geared to such tasks. I thus refer the interested student to these two publications for explication of the algorithm and procedure.

Clearly, the application of histological analyses to the determination of age at death of individuals is a potentially viable pursuit. As Frost (1987a) points out, however, many factors are known and suspected of affecting osteon creation (Table 7–15). But, as Frost (1987a, p. 237) elaborates further, before one can even deal adequately with these sources of potential error in estimation, one must know

> . . . the normal drift patterns, rates, and durations at the diaphyseal level(s) the section(s) came from and for the bone involved. That means atlases are needed for those properties in standard normal bones, but such atlases do not exist yet because there has been little apparent need or usefulness for this kind of information. Certainly there has been little incentive for expending the labor and time needed to obtain such information. The bones studied could be the tibia, femur, rib, a vertebra, humerus, parietal bone, radius, and/or pelvis, and in such work an accounting should be made for the effects of chronological age, mechanical usage, species, and locations in the bone itself. . . . A future task consists of constructing such atlases.

It is hoped that this will be recognized by potential osteologists as a task worth undertaking.

CHAPTER EIGHT

Pathology: Disease, Trauma, and Stress

Overview

The topics covered in this chapter—disease, trauma, and stress—can be characterized as assaults on an individual's body, in contrast to those "pathologies" (discussed elsewhere) that result from developmental, endocrine, or nutritional disturbances or imbalances (see Chapter 1, on bone, and chapters on individual bones). Of course, while one can discuss disease apart from trauma, and both apart from stress, it is equally obvious that one can affect or lead to another—for example, infectious disease can arise secondarily from a traumatic or stress-related assault on the body. The problem, however, with identifying any of these potential "pathological" agents is that they may not leave their marks on bone, even if (and perhaps especially because) they are lethal. Unfortunately, the ability of the forensic osteologist or pathologist to identify any particular assault on bone is dependent on the injured individual's ability to survive the assault (e.g. Wood et al, 1992).

Of course, this note of negativism can be partially modified. Certain types of trauma will leave instantaneous signs on bone and teeth—for example, intentional mutilation, complete/compound fracture, weapon wounds. However, because the effects of other kinds of trauma—such as stress or fatigue fractures—as well as those of occupational stress and various infectious diseases accumulate over years, they may not be detectable at the time of the individual's death; had the individual survived longer, however, they would have had an impact on bone. Thus the number of potential as-

saults on an individual's body is greater than the number that *might* leave telltale signs on bone or tooth. And, in turn, the latter is greater than the number of assaults that actually *do* leave their imprints on hard tissue.

Compounding potential difficulties in correctly assessing or even being able to assess certain kinds of assaults on the skeleton is the taphonomic history of the skeleton itself. For example, was it intentionally buried or had it lain exposed to the elements? If buried, was burial primary or secondary? What climatic/environmental conditions confronted it? What were the pH and other characteristics (e.g. wet, saline, peaty) of the attendant soil? If excavated, washed, or cleaned, what techniques and implements were employed? Any of these could cause at least alteration if not obliteration of surface detail. In more severe cases, bone could become fragmentary or even destroyed.

Care must be taken to distinguish postmortem damage from antemortem assaults. On a very gross level, postmortem breakage or puncturing of excavated bone, as well as of enamel and dentine, is often indicated by a difference in color between the edge created by the break and the rest of the bone or tooth structure. The broken surface (i.e. newly exposed bone or tooth surfaces) will usually be lighter in color. Postmortem breakage or impact also tends to produce fragments with edges that are unnaturally angular or serrated. Weathering (e.g. exposure to freezing and thawing, wetness and aridity) as well as acidic conditions can lead to loss of outer layers of cortical bone; teeth can also split and enamel flake off. Weathering can

Table 8–1   *Summary of Major Diseases that Impact the Skeleton (Not Including Osteomyelitis or Tumors). (See Text for Fuller Description.)*

Disease	Features	Skull	Mandible	Ribs	Vertebrae
Fungal					
Actinomycosis	min. reactive new bone; many small resorptive foci		1° "lumpy jaw"	3° resorbed	2° neural arches, centra (thoracic, lumbar)
Blastomycosis	lytic lesions; soil-borne; inhaled; N. America	3°		2°	1° centra; 2° neural arch
Coccidioidomycosis (San Jaoquin fever; Valley fever)	inhaled/abrasions; 1° males; resorptive lesions bony prominences; Meso- and S. America			x	centra, neural arches, spines 1° C1/2
Cryptococcosis	lytic lesions; bony prominences; 1° Europe	1°			
Histoplasmosis	murky lytic lesions; <1 yr or adult; Mississippi/Ohio valleys				
Sporotrichosis	thorn punctures; 1° males; hematogenous; periosteal lesions; latitudes 50° N, S	4° cranium, face		5° (including clavicle)	5°
Bacterial (other than osteomyelitis)					
Brucellosis (Mediterranean, goat's milk fever)	multifocal lytic lesions; min. reactive bone formation; dog, goat, pig, cow; 2° leads to osteomyelitis, suppurative arthritis				1° centra, resorptive lesions
Viral					
Smallpox	1° infants, children (bone); destruction of metaphyses; separation of epiphyses; no sequestrae; primary periostitis				
Parasitic					
Echinococcosis	tapeworm; dog, pig, sheep, cow; erosive, expansive lesions; monostotic; calcified sacs				centra (may lead to gibbus)
Granulomatous (*unknown etiology*)					
Sarcoidosis	youth/young adult; lesions multiple, lytic, round, 1° distal epiphysis, 1° bilateral; no reactive bone formation; similar to lepromatous leprosy	2° cranium, especially nasal bones			2° centra (not disc or pedicle), ≥ 1 involved (not necessarily contiguous)

Pelvis	Leg	Arm	Hand	Foot
	3° tibia		3°	3°
	long bones	long bones	diaphyses	diaphyses
	1° diaphyses, cortical thickening, rarified areas	same as leg		
	1° knee and tibia	3° ulna, radius	2°	2°
1° sacroiliac joint, resorptive lesions	2° diaphyses, periostitis	same as leg		
	3° knee joint	1° elbow joint, including radius, bilaterally	2° wrist joint	2° ankle joint
x	long bone metaphyses	same as leg		
2°	2° tubular bones	same as leg	1° fingers	1° toes

(continued)

Table 8–1   (continued)

Disease	Features	Skull	Mandible	Ribs	Vertebrae
Joint					
Ankylosing spondylitis (spondylarthropathy)	syndesmophyte formation at vertebral margin, symmetrical; few peripheral joints (pauciarticular); ankylosis; young individuals; 3 males: 1 female			costovertebral joints	zygoapophyseal joints; centra squared-up
Osteoarthritis	1° diarthrodial and weight-bearing joints				zygoapophyses
Spondylosis deformans	perpendicular osteophytes; diarthrodial joints do not ankylose				lipping of centra
Rheumatoid arthritis	symmetrical; polyarticular (virtually all peripheral diarthrodial joints, no ankylosis); periarticular loss of trabecular bone				1° juncture of C1/2 (when spine involved)
DISH (diffuse idiopathic skeletal hyperostosis)	typically males > 50 yrs; no reactive sclerosis or erosion; ossification at sites of insertion of ligaments, tendons, joint capsules	x	x	x	1° anterior spinal ligament (distinct from centrum)
CPDD (calcium pyrophosphate deposition disease) (crystalline arthritis)	often precedes osteoarthritis; primary CPDD correlated with aging (30–75 yrs); pauciarticular, subchondral erosions not crisp; trabecular bone remains dense; no reactive bone formation; zygoapophyseal, costovertebral joints spared				calcification of nucleus pulposus or annulus fibrosus

x = common site of disease; 1°, 2°, 3°, etc. = typical frequency/order of sites of disease.

Pelvis	Leg	Arm	Hand	Foot
	x	x	especially carpal-metacarpal, PIP, DIP	x
	1° ulnar styloid	1° carpal, metacarpal-phalangeal, and PIP joints	1° metatarsal-phalangeal, PIP and ankle joints	
x	x	x	x	x
joints at cartilage margin	joints at cartilage margin (shoulder, radiocarpal, elbow)	sclerotic margins, cysts communicating with surface, MP, PIP, DIP joints; subchondral erosion 1° MP, PIP, DIP	subchondral erosion 1° PIP, DIP; ankle, midtarsal	

create a multilayered, terraced effect on diaph-yseal cortical bone and expose spongy bone beneath the thinner compact bone of epiphyseal regions; in addition to breakage, weathering can also lead to exposure of tooth roots through thin alveolar bone, producing an artifact that might be mistaken for abscessing. Conditions that lead to rapid demineralization but slow remineralization of bone (e.g. acidic clays and sandy soils) produce light, friable bone. Until the osteologist gains experience in detecting postmortem effects on bone and tooth, suspicion should be aroused by such attributes as "lack of symmetry," "irregularity," "angularity," "sharpness" (of edges, corners). Even root marks etched on the surfaces of bones tend to look "unnatural."

The discrimination of one infectious disease from another—or any malady from an array of maladies that might leave seemingly similar clues—is referred to as *differential diagnosis.* The process of differential diagnosis requires a systematic elimination of the least and then less likely infections or other possible causes of the features observed. But while the clinical diagnosis of disease can claim a high degree of certainty (e.g. from early, observable signs to pre-cise laboratory tests), the diagnosis of disease from bone can be highly inaccurate and often seemingly subjective. Ultimately, and for whatever reason (e.g. state of preservation of the skeletal material, the parts of the skeleton preserved, the age and/or sex of the individual, how far advanced the disease was at time of death), even a careful differential diagnosis might not be able to whittle down the choices to fewer than two or three alternative diseases or conditions. A choice between alternatives might then be suggested by such criteria as age, sex, and/or geography as well as cultural, behavioral, or other inferred and reconstructed aspects of the population [e.g. populational density (tuberculosis is associated with crowding), agriculturalism (certain fungal infections, such as blastomycosis, are soil-borne), types of domesticates maintained (certain bacteria, such as *Brucella,* can be transmitted across species)].

It is frequently difficult (not just for the beginner, but even for the weathered osteologist) to decipher and apply with confidence the terminology, descriptions, and even illustrations in available reference works. Insofar as this is not a textbook on paleopathology, no attempt is

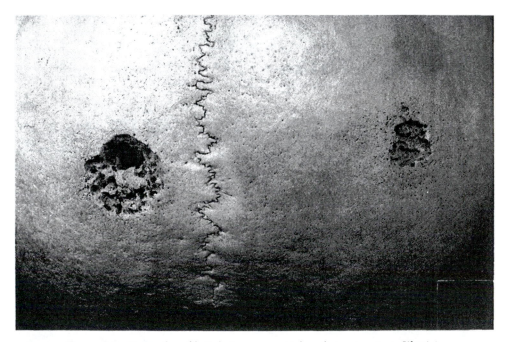

Figure 8–1   Examples of lytic lesions on cranial vault (postcontact, Siberia).

made here to be all-inclusive in the description or illustration of disease. As in other chapters of this text, the information provided here is meant to be introductory. The discussion is also meant to be helpful in focusing thought on approach and method and in potentially provoking future research or refinement of work in this field of study. Details of most of the diseases and conditions discussed below are summarized in Table 8–1. The accompanying figures show examples of types of lesions central to the diagnosis of diseases: lytic (Figure 8–1), resorptive (Figure 8–2), proliferative (Figure 8–2), and erosive (Figure 8–3).

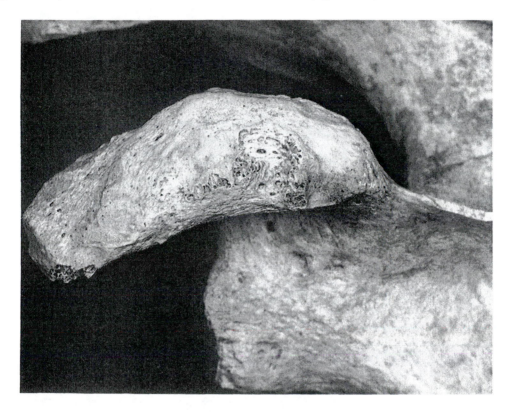

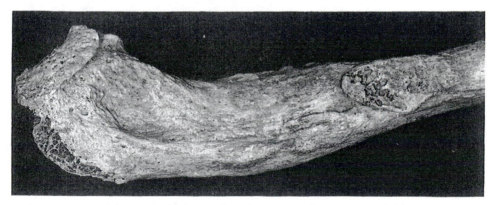

Figure 8–2 *(Top)* coracoid process of left scapula with resorptive lesion surrounded by sclerotic, remodeled bone; *(bottom)* inferior view of right clavicle displaying proliferative lesion of sternal end, lateral to which is a healed, resorptive lesion, and then reactive bone (prehistoric, Pennsylvania).

Figure 8–3 Right proximal tibial fragment with erosive lesion and eburnation on lateral condylar surface *(arrow)* (prehistoric, Pennsylvania).

Infectious Diseases of Bone

Although an infection may lead to death, it may not cause any detectable alteration of the bone. As summarized by Kelley (1989), the following infectious diseases can potentially produce telltale lesions on bone: actinomycosis, blastomycosis, brucellosis, coccidioidomycosis, cryptococcosis, echinococcosis, histoplasmosis, leprosy, osteomyelitis (suppurative/pyogenic and nonsuppurative/nonpyogenic), periostitis, poliomyelitis, smallpox, sporotrichosis, treponemal infections [syphilis (endemic/nonvenereal and venereal) and yaws], tuberculosis, and typhoid spine. Of course, since our diagnosis of disease derives from studying the effects of known, identified diseases, it is always possible that lesions on the skeletons of past populations represent a now extinct or unknown infectious disease.

More importantly, as recognized by Kelley (1989) and others (e.g. Mensforth et al., 1978), what is still lacking in the field of paleopathology is a precise terminology shared even by those who are considered to be the experts in

the field. Mensforth et al. (1978) suggest describing lesions as "active," "healed," "unremodeled," or "remodeled." Kelley (1989) distinguishes lesions as being "resorptive," "lytic," "proliferative," "periostitic," "fused," "healed," or "unhealed." Clearly, there is more information in delineating, for example, resorptive from lytic lesions, and less in distinguishing only between remodeled and unremodeled states. But there is also information to be had in describing the characteristics of the bone that surrounds a lesion (e.g. see Buikstra, 1976; Rothschild and Martin, 1993).

Infection leads to inflammation of tissues. Specifically, **osteitis** refers to inflammation of bone, which can result from various insults to the skeleton. Acute bacterial infections are generally indicated by pus formation, and in bone are reflected in the development of *abscesses* (lacunae or pockets caused by bone death or necrosis) and drainage holes *(cloacae).* Viral infections, which usually do not lead to pus formation, typically do not leave such bony clues.

Inflammation of the periosteum leads to **peri-**

ostitis (Figure 8–4). The normal surface morphology of cortical bone is disturbed with the reactive, unhealed bone having a more porous and lamellar appearance. Healed periosteal lesions are denser, less porous, and more sclerotic (i.e. thicker, denser) but often retain their distinctiveness from surrounding, undisturbed cortical bone. Inflammation of the periosteum from either infection or trauma may produce **primary periostitis**. Primary periostitis typically does not affect a bone in its entirety and is thus localized or unevenly distributed. Often, the affected regions are thickened or appear to have an additional layer applied or adherent to them. **Secondary periostitis** arises in conjunction with

or as a result of some other disease (such as osteomyelitis), which can spread to or otherwise affect the periosteum. Thus, for example, **secondary periostitis** in concert with osteomyelitis is distinguished from **primary periostitis** by its association with the features that go along with osteomyelitis—that is, abscesses, involucra, sequestra, and cloacae (see below). The osteologist should attempt to distinguish between primary and secondary periostitis.

Infection of bone (**osteomyelitis**) can be caused by the introduction of bacteria locally (i.e. from an adjacent wound or infected soft tissue) or via the bloodstream *(hematogenously)* from a site of infection elsewhere in the

Figure 8–4 Left and right tibiae *(left and right)* with (apparently primary) periostitis (see text for discussion) (prehistoric, Pennsylvania).

body. *Hematogenous osteomyelitis* typically affects one (and much less frequently two or more) of the long bones, especially the femur and tibia (Ortner and Putschar, 1981). Being transported by the vascular system, hematogenous osteomyelitis arises in the medullary cavity of a bone; in young individuals, it tends to localize in the metaphyseal regions of growth. Infection spreads through the medullary cavity, destroying spongy bone. Cortical bone death eventually occurs because pus and other exudates expand within marrow spaces and eventually cut off the blood supply. Loss of blood supply eventually leads to bone death *(necrosis)*, which, in turn, can produce islands of dead cortical bone (called *sequestra;* singular = *sequestrum)*. Often, a sequestrum is surrounded by thickened, hard *(sclerotic),* heavily vascularized bone (identified as *involucrum;* plural = *involucra),* which is produced by the periosteum in response to the infection. Ultimately the expanding pus may erupt to the surface of the bone through an opening or *cloaca* in the involucrum (Figure 8–5; see also Figure 9–4). Often, a sequestrum is found in the aperture of the cloaca. In extreme cases, the entire diaphysis may become a sequestrum, which, in turn, is surrounded by a sheathlike involucrum that is perforated by one or more cloacae.

Descriptively, osteomyelitis can be suspected in tubular bones in which the diaphysis appears to be unnaturally and asymmetrically swollen or expanded along its length. This would constitute the site of the involucrum. In addition, one metaphyseal region may appear unusually swollen and the other unusually thinned. The external surface of the bone can, at the same time, be reactive and variably textured (e.g. nodular, stringy, fibrous, layered—rather than relatively smooth as in normal cortical bone) as well as thickened and even harder and more compact than usual.

It may be difficult, however, to diagnose osteomyelitis arising from infection spreading to underlying bone from soft tissue because the infection may not spread to the medullary cavity of the bone. Such osteomyelitis, therefore, would be more localized and not necessarily accompanied by the typical telltale signs of the infection (abscess, involucrum, sequestrum, cloaca). Furthermore, whatever sclerosing may have occurred during the life of the infection

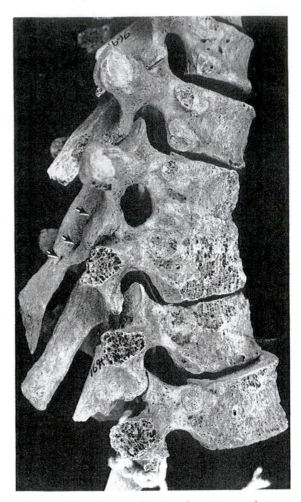

Figure 8–5 Osteomyelitis in thoracic vertebrae; note small cloacae *(arrows)* in the spine of the upper of the two ankylosed vertebrae (prehistoric, Pennsylvania). (Tuberculosis would be distinguished by the development of abscesses anteriorly in thoracic vertebrae.)

might eventually become obliterated. It is also possible that such localized osteomyelitis may not be distinguishable from primary periostitis.

Osteomyelitis can also be caused by various chronic infections that are neither pyogenic nor even bacterial in origin. These nonpyogenic infections are called **granulomas** because their mechanism of healing often involves an overgrowth of tissue by granulation, which causes a general swollen appearance or a series of swellings (e.g. Figure 8–6); ("oma" refers to "tumor," which means "swelling"). Typical granulomas are *tuberculosis (tubercular osteo-myelitis), leprosy, syphilis (syphilitic osteomy-elitis), yaws,* and *fungal (mycotic) infection.* The most common overall similarities between granulomatous infections and pyogenic bacterial infections leading to osteomyelitis are the development of lesions, abscesslike lesions *(gumma),* and even abscesses. When abscesses are present, however, they often lack the large sequestra typical of pyogenic osteomyelitis. Sometimes the drainage material itself may become calcified. Although there may be alteration of cortical bone (e.g. through the healing of lesions or various avenues of cortical thickening, or through cortical erosion and destruc-

tion), osteitic and/or periostitic reactive bone is not always associated with the disease.

Tuberculosis, which is caused by a bacterium, most frequently affects children and subadults (Kelley, 1989; Rothschild and Martin, 1993). In its skeletal manifestation, tuberculosis is typically thought of as affecting the vertebral column. The reason for this is that, as difficult as it is to diagnose spinal tuberculosis incontrovertibly, the effects of tuberculosis elsewhere in the skeleton are much more difficult to discriminate from other possible causes. Even the diagnosis of spinal tuberculosis is not necessarily a simple matter. For example, Morse (1978, p. 45) lists the following diseases as having to be

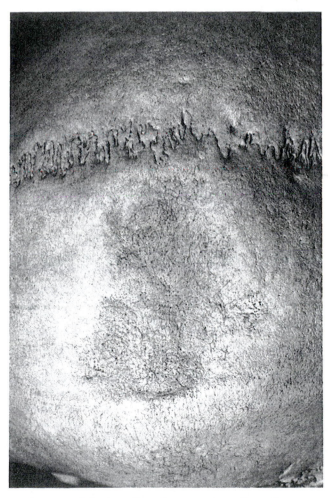

Figure 8–6 Healed granulomatous infection of cranium; note overall swollen appearance as well as more localized swellings (postcontact, Siberia).

eliminated from consideration prior to arriving at a diagnosis of tuberculosis: chronic pyogenic osteomyelitis, traumatic arthritis, rheumatoid arthritis, malignancy, typhoid spine, sarcoidosis, actinomycosis, blastomycosis, coccidioidomycosis, Paget's disease (osteitis deformans), osteochondritis, and neuroarthropathies. Compression or crush fractures can also create what might appear to be tuberculosis-affected vertebrae.

Features specific to tuberculosis are erosion of bone (i.e. destruction of cortical as well as spongy bone, leading sometimes to the excavation of cavities in the trabecular bone of articular regions) and absence of bone regeneration. The stereotypic picture of spinal tuberculosis is that of unabated destruction and erosion of vertebral bodies, leading to their eventual collapse. Typically, the maximum number of vertebrae involved is four. Only rarely does tuberculosis affect the transverse processes, neural arches, or vertebral spines. Again, typically bone does not regenerate, nor do affected adjacent vertebrae fuse (ankylose) to one another. Visually as well as radiographically, collapsed vertebral bodies, in lateral view, are wedge-shaped, tapering toward their ventral (anterior) sides (see Figure 8–13 for an example of a collapsed vertebra). In severe cases of vertebral body collapse, the vertebral column can become kyphotic, with the deflection anteriorly in the sagittal plane being angular, not curved. (Sharply angular kyphosis is referred to as gibbus.) Thus, although tuberculosis may result in kyphosis, kyphosis is not associated exclusively with tuberculosis. As summarized by Morse (1978), gross similarities between tuberculosis and pyogenic osteomyelitis can be found in the development of cold abscesses (with cloacae) posteriorly in the cervical region and anteriorly in the lower thoracic and lumbar regions. These tuberculotic abscesses are characterized by their large surface apertures and a route of erosive penetration into the bone that often courses downward.

After spinal involvement, the area next most frequently affected by tuberculosis is the the hip joint (the acetabulum, the femoral head, or both), followed by involvement of the knee, foot, and elbow joints. Much less frequently affected by tuberculosis are, in the adult, the sternum, ribs, shoulder joint, and pelvic (sacroiliac)

joint, and, in children, the tubular bones of the hands and feet. Cold abscesses in the pelvic region may develop as a result of tubercular infection. In general, the affected region is characterized by erosion and perforation of cortical bone and destruction of subchondral/subarticular as well as trabecular bone (sometimes with development of cavities) but without noticeable development of reactive bone.

Brucellosis is a bacterial (bacillary) infection that secondarily produces osteomyelitis and suppurative arthritis (spondylitis). Also known as undulant, Mediterranean, or goat's milk fever, brucellosis can be transmitted to humans from dogs, goats, pigs, and cattle. Lumbar vertebral bodies and the sacroiliac joint are the most frequently affected parts of the skeleton. Typically, lesions are multiple and produce cavities; in vertebrae, the lesion may extend the length of an entire centrum and even pass through an intervertebral space and on into an adjacent vertebral body. Lesions have been described as either lytic or resorptive. Infection may secondarily affect the diaphyses of leg and arm bones and may be associated with periostitis. One might suspect that the spread of brucellosis would be correlated with the domestication of herding animals and the use of the dog in herding.

Syphilis (both endemic and venereal) and **yaws** are caused by a treponemal spirochete that invades the host either through the skin or the superficial mucous membranes. Syphilis and yaws are similar in that both can lead to periostitis and osteitis of the long bones (often involving the tibia) as well as of the skull, with the frontal and parietal bones often being the first cranial bones to be affected. In long bones, cortical thickening and diminution of the medullary cavity may occur. However, in contrast to pyogenic osteomyelitis, sequestra usually do not form. Periostitic layering on the tibia can create the so-called saber shin, which is characteristically bowed anteroposteriorly because bone remodeling thins the anterior margin and thickens the posterior surface (i.e. the anterior margin become convex, the posterior surface concave). Saber shin is often thought of as characteristic of syphilis, but it can also develop in cases of tertiary yaws.

Syphilis is more readily distinguished from yaws by the frequency and morphology of its effects on the skull. Although there can be destruction of the bone surrounding the nasal cavity in both diseases, in syphilis, such destruction also typically subsumes the nasal septum, spreading down and throughout the hard palate or up and into the nasal bones. Lesions of the tabular cranial bones—the frontal and parietal, in particular—are more characteristic of syphilis. These lesions take the form of a central zone of destruction surrounded by an often irregular perimeter of reactive bone. Over time, with the healing of lesions and the eruption of new lesions and their subsequent healing, the sclerotic surface of the cranium takes on a mottled, sculpted appearance. This produces the "worm-eaten" look so characteristic of crania displaying advanced cases of syphilis (e.g. Ortner and Putschar, 1981; Figure 8–7).

Although venereal syphilis can be transmitted across the placenta from mother to fetus, it and endemic syphilis are most frequently seen in postpubescent individuals. In contrast, yaws is typically contracted and expressed in young individuals. However, yaws may go undiagnosed, because the early lesions produced by this disease may heal without leaving clues. In terms of biogeography, the preantibiotic distributions of yaws and endemic syphilis also differ. Yaws was prevalent in populations throughout the tropics, whereas endemic syphilis was restricted to temperate and subtropical regions of the non-European Old World. The spread of venereal syphilis is correlated with European colonization.

Leprosy is caused by a bacterium that primarily infects nonosseous tissues but which may spread to the skeleton. Ortner and Putschar (1981) suggest that, although the distribution of leprosy used to be all but global (exclusive of the Arctic), it was probably introduced into the New World after European contact and in conjunction with European colonization. Its spread was slow because, in spite of the fact that it is an infectious disease, it is not very contagious.

Ortner and Putschar (1981) delineate two skeletal manifestations of leprosy: (1) *lepromatous osteomyelitis and subperiosteal periostitis* and (2) *neurotrophic bone* as well as *lesions* to and *degenerative arthritis* of the *weight-bear-*

Figure 8–7 "Worm-eaten" appearance of cranial bone characteristic of advanced syphilis (postcontact, Siberia).

ing joints of the foot and ankle. The effect of lepromatous osteomyelitis on the lower face and nasal region is quite similar to that of syphilis and yaws. This relatively rare form of leprosy can, however, lead to characteristic widening of the nasal aperture and destruction of the nasal conchae, in addition to destruction of the nasal septum, hard palate, and nasal bones seen in syphilitic individuals. In contrast to syphilis, in leprosy, the flat bones of the cranium are not involved. If subperiosteal periostitis develops on the long bones, it is characterized by thin, longitudinally oriented striations.

Neurotrophic bone changes, caused by loss of sensory nerve function, result in the disfigurement most commonly thought of as representing leprosy: loss of fingers and toes. The process typically begins in the hand: segments are slowly resorbed in a distoproximal direction, and the metacarpals may also be affected in some individuals. Involvement of foot bones proceeds in the opposite direction, from the metatarsal-proximal phalangeal region to the terminal phalanges. Although these changes may resemble those brought about by rheumatoid arthritis, which affects the hands and feet (see below), characteristic arthritic changes are lacking. Because of sensory nerve death, the affected individual is also vulnerable to injury, which can lead to infection, which, in turn, can result in ordinary osteomyelitis and septic arthritis.

Fungal infections that may ultimately affect the skeleton include *actinomycosis, blastomycosis, coccidioidomycosis, cryptococcosis, histoplasmosis,* and *sporotrichosis.* [For the purposes of discussion here, actinomycosis, which Ortner and Putschar (1981) attribute to a higher bacterium rather than a fungus, and sporotrichosis, which Kelley (1989) does not include with fungal infections, but Ortner and Putschar (1981) and Rothschild and Martin (1993) do, will be grouped as fungal infections.] All but sporotrichosis, which is introduced via thorn punctures and spreads hematogenously (i.e. through the bloodstream), are inhaled, often resulting first in infection of the lungs. With regard to the effect of fungal infection on joints, Rothschild and Martin (1993, p. 73) identify the focus of infection as the articular surface of a bone, which is typically undercut by marginal

erosion. Ortner and Putschar (1981) suggest that, because the bony lesions produced by these fungal infections are indistinguishable from one another morphologically, biogeographic distribution is primary in arriving at a diagnosis. Rothschild and Martin (1993; see also Buikstra, 1976) do, however, itemize some morphological characteristics that appear to be distinctive of each kind of fungal infection. Because of the potential ambiguities in diagnosing fungal infections as well as possible confusion with the diagnosis of tuberculosis and other infections, the student is advised to consult Table 8–1 in addition to the brief descriptions provided below.

As a class, fungal infections affect the skeleton in relatively low frequencies. In this context, the incidence of bony lesions due to **actinomycosis,** which is global in its distribution, is quite low. Nonetheless, clues to diagnosing actinomycosis are (1) and especially, the development of the condition referred to as "lumpy jaw" and (2) the presence of many small lesions emanating from the periosteum, which often creates a "worm-eaten" look due not only to bone resorption but also to an increase in vascularization of the affected region. [The literature appears to be contradictory with regard to the incidence of reactive new bone formation: e.g. Ortner and Putschar (1981) illustrate and describe significant periosteal reactive bone deposition in specimens diagnosed as having actinomycosis, whereas Buikstra (1976) states that bone proliferation in association with actinomycosis occurs infrequently. The difference here, however, seems to be a matter of identifying periostitis versus endostitis (i.e. sclerotic bone proliferation originating in the endosteum, as seen in pyogenic osteomyelitis). Clearly, in the case of the mandible, periosteal inflammation leading to periostitis would produce a "lumpy jaw."] After the mandible, the next most frequently affected regions of the skeleton are the thoracic and lumber vertebrae (neural arches and centra alike) and then the ribs, which may show areas of resorption. Vertebral collapse rarely occurs.

A relatively common fungal infection, **blastomycosis,** is found primarily in North America (especially the Ohio and Mississippi Valleys) and affects males five times more frequently than females. Because it is soil-borne, its representation skeletally is thought to be associated with the development of agriculturalism (e.g. Kelley, 1989). Blastomycosis typically produces lytic lesions (with crisp perimeters) and most frequently affects the vertebral bodies. Ribs adjacent to affected vertebrae may also become involved, as may the neural arches. Subsequently, bones of the skull, hands, and feet as well as the tibia may be affected. Contradictory diagnoses suggest that destruction of vertebral bodies and intervertebral discs, with subsequent collapse and kyphosis, is either characteristic of blastomycosis or rarely associated with the infection.

Coccidioidomycosis (often referred to as San Joaquin or Valley fever) is found in the North American Southwest and areas of Meso- and South America. The disease may be contracted either by inhalation or through an abrasion and is seen more frequently in males than in females. Lesions typical of coccidioidomycosis have been described as either lytic or resorptive. The vertebral column is most frequently involved, with centra and neural arches being affected (in contrast to tuberculosis, in which the neural arches are not involved). (If collapse of vertebrae and intervertebral discs, leading to kyphosis, does occur, the specifics of vertebral involvement are important criteria in discriminating coccidioidomycosis from tuberculosis.) Infection often spreads from the vertebral column to the ribs. After the vertebral column, virtually every bone of the skeleton appears to be vulnerable to the infection. This is because cocciodomycosis characteristically attacks bony prominences and protuberances. Thus, in addition to obvious parts of the skull, articular and other epiphyseal regions of the long bones can be affected. In the hands and feet, however, the diaphyses of bones are typically infected.

Another fungal infection that tends to lodge in bony prominences is **cryptococcosis**. This infection, however, occurs primarily in Europe and is not sex- or age-specific. Cryptococcosis typically produces lytic lesions, and although any bone in the body is potentially vulnerable, it frequently affects the cranium and those vertebrae closest to the skull.

A common fungal infection that only rarely shows up skeletally is **histoplasmosis**. This infection, which occurs most frequently in the Ohio and Mississippi Valleys, is typically found in either adults or infants less than 1 year of age. Primarily affected are the diaphyses of the arm and leg bones as well as bones of the skull. Multiple lytic lesions may be associated with cortical thickening as well as areas of rarified bone.

Sporotrichosis is another fungal infection that may, on rare occasion, affect the skeleton. Primarily found in individuals living in regions between latitudes 50° north and south and predominantly affecting males, the infection is usually introduced by way of thorn punctures. It spreads hematogenously. Lesions are typically periosteal and occur most frequently in the tibia, followed by the bones of the hands and feet, the bones of the face and skull, and then the ribs, clavicle, and vertebrae.

The only parasitic disease in humans that produces significant bony changes is **echinococcosis**. The disease results from infestation by the larvae of a tapeworm that can be transmitted to humans from dogs, cattle, sheep, or pigs. It can manifest itself in the ossification of cysts and/or the development of expansive, erosive lesions. Commonly affected areas are the pelvis, vertebral centra [possibly leading to collapse and gibbus (compare with tuberculosis)], and, because the larvae are blood-borne, the metaphyseal regions of the long bones of the arm and leg. Europe is the primary geographic locus of echinococcosis, which appears to have arisen regionally in conjunction with the domestication of herding animals and the use of dogs in herding.

A viral disease that can affect the skeleton (of infants and small children but not adults) is **smallpox**, which used to be global in its distribution. Diagnostic clues include the settling of the infection in joints and the destruction of metaphyses, leading at times to the separation of epiphyses. Particularly telling is that (1) the elbow (the primary locus of the infection) is affected bilaterally and (2) in addition to the humerus and ulna, the radius (which usually is not involved in other infectious diseases) is affected. After the elbow joint, the wrist and then the ankle and knee are most frequently involved. Periostitis is commonly associated with smallpox. If abscessing occurs, sequestra typically are not formed.

Sarcoidosis is a granulomatous collagen-vascular disease whose cause remains unknown. It is characterized by multiple round, lytic lesions that typically occur bilaterally and are not accompanied by reactive bone formation. Primarily affected are the finger and toes and thereafter the tubular bones of the leg and arm, vertebral centra (multiple but not necessarily contiguous), and the bones of the pelvis and skull (especially the nasal bones). Children and young adults are most frequently affected. Sarcoidosis is most similar to lepromatous leprosy.

Joint Diseases

In discussing diseases of the joints, the one term that probably comes to mind most frequently is "arthritis." And as a cursory review of archeologically derived skeletal analyses reveals, *osteoarthritis* (i.e. arthritis impacting bone) is arguably the most frequently diagnosed malady affecting the nondental parts of the skeleton. But although there indeed may be changes of joint surface topography associated with osteoarthritis, not all joint surface changes are the result of osteoarthritis.

In spite of the fact that the suffix "itis" is part of "arthritis," arthritis (or, in reference to its effect on the skeleton, osteoarthritis) is not an inflammatory disease (e.g. Ortner and Putschar, 1981). Inflammation of joints may be a complication of osteoarthritis, but it is not an attribute of osteoarthritis. For this reason, the term "osteoarthrosis" has at times been suggested as being a more accurate referent (see Rothschild and Martin, 1993). Another misconception about the nature of osteoarthritis is that although it may not be an inflammatory disease, it is a degenerative disease. Hence the term "degenerative osteoarthritis" has enjoyed widespread use in the literature, either as a misnomer for an array of joint diseases or as a descriptive attempt at trying to distinguish among various kinds of joint disease.

But if osteoarthritis is not what it has typically been assumed to be, what is it?

An apparently obvious reason why osteoarthritis has been thought of as being either inflammatory or degenerative in nature is that it is associated with morphological changes in joint surfaces: normal joint surface topography is noticeably altered or destroyed, and these abnormal-looking joint surfaces often bear spike- or sheetlike outgrowths along their perimeters. And seemingly similar changes in joint surface morphology with seemingly similar attendant growths also appear to characterize other diseases that are indeed inflammatory or degenerative in nature. But differences within these apparent similarities do exist.

Osteoarthritis develops as a result of interruption of or interference with normal joint function and stability, which is brought about primarily by injury to the joint cartilage and the bone beneath the cartilage. The more stabilized the joint (e.g. the ankle), the less likely it is to be disrupted. Thus, for example, the ankle is typically exempt from osteoarthritic changes. The less stabilized the joint (e.g. the knee), the more likely it is that osteoarthritis will develop in it. And as it turns out, the knee is the joint most frequently affected by osteoarthritis.

Osteoarthritis occurs because the rate at which the articular cartilage and attendant subchondral bone is destroyed is faster than the rate of repair (Rothschild and Martin, 1993). Subchondral bone modification results in (1) sclerosis in the area of injury (often because of healing of minute fractures caused by the injury) and (2) the outgrowth of bony spicules or spurs (called *osteophytes)* around the perimeter of the joint cartilage. These bony outgrowths are thus not the result of ossification of soft connective tissue. In fact, the attachment areas of tendons, ligaments, and joints capsules remain unaffected in osteoarthritis. (Mineralization of soft tissue does, however, characterize other forms of "arthritis.") Over time, remodeling of the subchondral bone can lead to its becoming not only denser but also polished [*eburnated* (Figure 8–3)] and even grooved, due to the contact of bone on bone that results when the intervening joint cartilage is totally destroyed. (In advanced cases of osteoarthritis, for example, areas of the knee joint often show signs of eburnation and grooving.) Although cysts may develop in the subchondral bone, erosion or resorption of subchondral bone does not occur. The development of sclerotic subchondral bone, perhaps containing cysts, and of osteophytes thus constitute primary clues to the diagnosis of osteoarthritis. Furthermore, and in contrast to other joint diseases, fusion or *an-*

kylosis of adjacent bony elements is not a feature of osteoarthritis (Ortner and Putschar, 1981).

The development of osteophytes (i.e. *osteophytosis*) may occur on vertebrae (creating the often described condition of vertebral "lipping"); strictly speaking, however, the term "osteoarthritis" should be used only in reference to diarthrodial joints exhibiting subchondral bone remodeling and osteophytosis (Rothschild and Martin, 1993). Technically, lipping of vertebral bodies should be identified as **spondylosis deformans** (Figure 8–8). Only if the zygoapophyseal joints (which are diarthrodial joints between articulating superior and inferior articular surfaces of vertebrae) bear osteophytes can one identify osteoarthritis as

being present in the vertebral column. Thus, the diagnosis of osteoarthritis rests almost entirely on identifying changes in diarthrodial joints in the skeleton other than in the vertebral column.

In **spondylosis deformans**, osteophytes grow from the superior and/or inferior margins of a vertebral body and extend across the intervertebral space toward an adjacent vertebra (Figures 8–8 and 8–9). An important diagnostic feature of spondylosis deformans is that osteophytes grow somewhat parallel to the vertebral end plate and project out from (often at a right angle to) the vertebral body; then they curve toward neighboring vertebrae (Rothschild and Martin, 1993, p. 121). In advanced cases of spondylosis deformans, adjacent osteophytes often ankylose. Thus, spondylosis de-

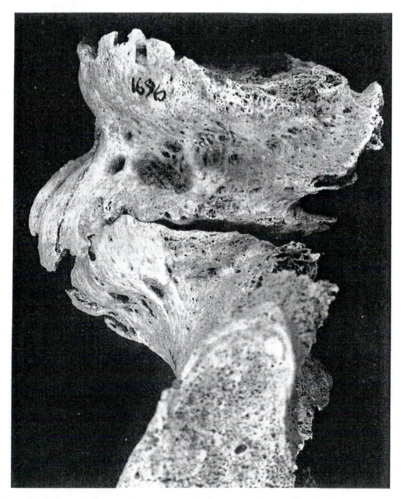

Figure 8–8 Last lumber vertebra and sacrum with horizontal osteophytes characteristic of spondylosis deformans (prehistoric, Pennsylvania).

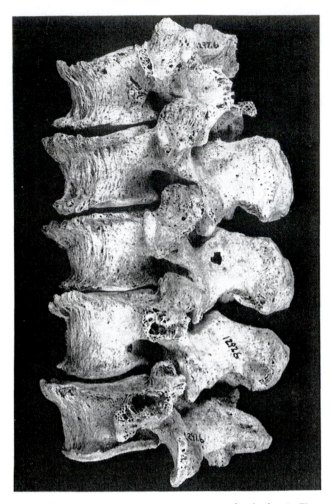

Figure 8–9 Horizontal osteophytic growths on T12 to L4 (same individual as in Figure 8–8 with spondylosis deformans), illustrating lack of involvement/ankylosis of zygoapophyseal joints (which would be involved in arthritis).

formans is characterized by ankylosing of vertebral bodies alone and not concurrently in zygoapophyseal or costovertebral joints (Figure 8–9), in contrast to *ankylosing spondylitis* (see below). In spondylosis deformans, the cervical and lumbar vertebrae are more frequently affected than are the thoracic vertebrae. [In *DISH* (diffuse idiopathic skeletal hyperostosis; see below)—another disease that can affect the spine and which has often been mistakenly identified as spondylosis deformans—the thoracic vertebrae are most frequently affected.] Also, in spondylosis deformans, the intervertebral disc cartilage may be extruded *(herniated)* either through a portion of the perimeter of the ver-

tebral body (through the annulus fibrosus, the fibrous ring that bounds the pulpy center of an intervertebral disc), or, as can be observed on bone, into the vertebral body's end plate, often near its center. The herniated nodule of cartilage is called a *Schmorl's node,* and the depression it leaves in the end plate can look like an erosive (lytic) lesion. The size of such a depression can vary, depending on how large the Schmorl's node becomes. The disc cartilage may herniate superiorly and inferiorly into the end plates of adjacent vertebrae.

Ankylosing spondylitis is probably the best-known (and most frequently diagnosed) example of the class of inflammatory *arthritides* (the plural of arthritis) known as **spondyloarthro-pathies**. In spondyloarthropathy, there is a tendency for erosion, reactive bone growth, and fusion of adjacent bones as well as for mineralization of attachment areas of soft connective tissue (Rothschild and Martin, 1993). Osteophytelike spurs that arise as a result of ossification of soft connective tissue (e.g. ligaments, tendons, annulus fibrosus) are identified as *syndesmophytes*.

Ankylosing spondylitis is characterized by involvement of the vertebral column and sacroiliac joints. Diagnostic changes include erosion followed by fusion of the zygapophyseal joints; erosion of the superior and inferior anterior margins of vertebral bodies, which eventually causes the typically concave surface to become straighter, thus squaring up the vertebral body; vertically oriented syndesmophytes [rather than horizontal osteophytes (see spondylosis deformans above)] that arise from the margins of vertebral bodies (because they originate in the annulus fibrosus between vertebrae) and which form bony links connecting adjacent vertebral bodies; uniform or symmetrical formation of syndesmophytes around the perimeters of the vertebral bodies; erosion and/or fusion of the sacroiliac joint; and erosion and fusion of zygapophyseal (costovertebral) joints (Figure 8–10) (Rothschild and Martin, 1993).

Syndesmophyte formation typically proceeds along the vertebral column in an inferosuperior direction (i.e. from the lumbar region, through the thoracic vertebrae, and eventually up through the cervical vertebrae). Inasmuch as syndesmophyte formation is continuous around the margins of adjacent vertebrae, the bridged intervertebral space becomes thickened and reminiscent of the segmental ring of a stalk of bamboo. In advanced ankylosing spondylitis, wherein a number of vertebral bodies are bridged by marginal syndesmophytes, the configuration is often described as *bamboo spine*. Ankylosing spondylitis occurs in males three times more frequently than in females.

Whereas ankylosing spondylitis is the best-known variety of spondylarthropathy, **rheumatoid arthritis** is the best-known example of a class of arthritides called **polyarticular erosive arthritis**. Aside from affecting many joints (i.e.

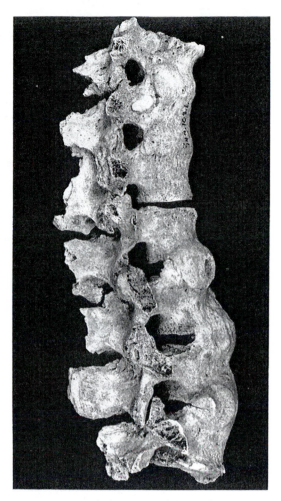

Figure 8–10 Ankylosing spondylitis in lower spine; note squared-off appearance of vertebral bodies, regular spacing of vertebrae, and uniform formation of vertically oriented syndesmophytes bridging various vertebrae (prehistoric, Pennsylvania).

being poly- rather than pauciarticular), rheumatoid arthritis is characteristically expressed bilaterally and symmetrically and is found three times more frequently in females than in males. It is most commonly expressed during adulthood (although a juvenile form of the disease is known). Because it is an erosive form of arthritis, lesions expose trabecular bone as smoothly remodeled fields within cortical bone (Figure 8–11). A field of trabecular bone produced by rheumatoid arthritis will be at the same level as and appear to be continuous with the surrounding cortical bone. In contrast, a field of trabec-

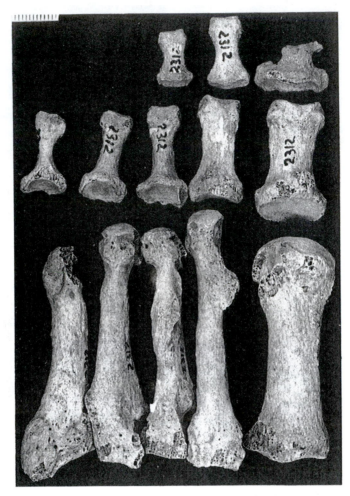

Figure 8–11 Rheumatoid arthritis of left foot bones; note, for example, characteristic exposure of cancellous bone (see text for discussion) (prehistoric, Pennsylvania).

ular bone exposed by postmortem damage or weathering will be situated below the level of the cortical bone, creating a terraced effect.

Typical of rheumatoid arthritis, lesions begin to resorb bone "at the 'bare area' or cartilage margin [which is] the region . . . between the subchondral bone (that covered with cartilage) and the point of insertion of the joint capsule into the bone" (Rothschild and Martin, 1993, p. 93). Diagnostically, these lesions are not associated with sclerotic bone or reactive bone formation. Over time, the joint is destroyed and the surrounding bone becomes markedly porotic (on the surface as well as subchondrally). Bone remodeling across the joint space can lead to ankylosis. Often occurring in the hand, re-

modeled articular surfaces cause a deviation of the bones medially (i.e. toward the ulnar side).

Most frequently affected in rheumatoid arthritis are the carpal, metacarpophalangeal, metatarsophalangeal, proximal interphalangeal (PIP, on both hands and feet), and ankle joints (Ortner and Putschar, 1981; Rothschild and Martin, 1993). Joints of the hand tend to be involved first and more often than those of the feet. Also frequently affected is the ulnar styloid process, but distal interphalangeal (DIP) joints are not affected as often as proximal interphalangeal (PIP) joints. Essentially, though, any peripheral joint (e.g. shoulder, hip, elbow, knee) can be affected by rheumatoid arthritis. Also diagnostic of rheumatoid arthritis is the typical lack of involvement of most of the vertebral column and the sacroiliac joint. If the vertebral column is involved, the first and second cervical vertebrae are the most frequently affected.

A form of crystalline arthritis with characteristics that can variably be misinterpreted as having been caused by osteoarthritis, rheumatoid arthritis, or ankylosing spondylitis is **calcium pyrophosphate deposition disease (CPPD)** (Resnick and Niwayama, 1988; Rothschild and Martin, 1993). This condition is the result of both mechanical problems and inflammation. There are also primary and secondary expressions of CPPD; the latter is associated with aging, its onset typically being in individuals above age 30. Although certain details differ between "varieties" of CPPD, one thing that is common to most of them is some form of bone formation—that is, as subchondral bone, as wall-like extrusions around the perimeter of articular surfaces, or as calcification across joint spaces.

Calcification of the annulus fibrosus and squaring up of the anterior faces of vertebral bodies can be confused with ankylosing spondylitis. However, in CPPD, the zygoapophyseal and costovertebral joints are unaffected. Calcification of the pulpy center (nucleus pulposus) of intervertebral discs can also occur in CPPD. Although there may be erosion in some forms of CPPD, these lesions can be distinguished from the lytic and well-defined lesions of ankylosing spondylitis and rheumatoid arthritis in that they are less crisply delineated around their perimeters. Lesions associated with CPPD are also distinguished from those resulting from rheumatoid arthritis in that they do not affect the trabecular bone. Erosion typically affects only a few joints (i.e. is pauciarticular) and is not accompanied by reactive bone formation. Erosion may also simply take the form of destruction of an articular surface. If cysts form, they are huge, in contrast to the small cysts typical of osteoarthritis. Cysts resulting from CPPD are further distinctive in that they communicate with (i.e. open upon) the articular surface and have sclerotic margins. Some individuals with CPPD also develop "holes" in bones, particularly in bones of the metacarpophalangeal and wrist joints. In general, a differential diagnosis of CPPD should also include an as-

sessment of the number and distribution of joints involved, inasmuch as such attributes do distinguish it from osteoarthritis, ankylosing spondylitis, and rheumatoid arthritis (see Table 8–1).

Diffuse Idiopathic Skeletal Hyperostosis (DISH)

Diffuse idiopathic skeletal hyperostosis (DISH) is easily mistaken for spondylitis deformans. However, once its characteristics are understood, DISH can be distinguished from the latter (see Rothschild and Martin, 1993).

DISH is typically found in old individuals. As the word "hyperostosis" indicates, a major feature of DISH is aggressive ossification of soft tissue. In particular, in DISH, the ligaments that run alongside and in parallel with the vertebral column mineralize (coming to look like dripping wax). Thus, zygoapophyseal and sacroiliac joints are not affected. Most frequently, the anterior longitudinal spinal ligaments and the region of the thoracic vertebrae are involved. When expressed in the thoracic region, ossification is asymmetrical, affecting the side not in association with the aorta—that is, in most individuals, ossification in the region of the thoracic vertebrae will occur in the right anterior longitudinal spinal ligament. If DISH involves the lumbar vertebrae, both anterior ligaments will become ossified and motion will be impeded. Because vertebrae become linked as a result of mineralization of the ligament that courses alongside them, there is an observable (either visually or radiographically) space between the ossified ligamentous band and the vertebral bodies. In contrast, the osteophytes and syndesmophytes that form, respectively, in spondylitis deformans and ankylosing spondylitis are confluent with the vertebral bodies.

Although most frequently observed in the vertebral column, DISH can affect any site of soft connective tissue attachment (tendon, ligament, joint capsule). In these cases, DISH is often noted as a spur at the locus of tendon or ligament insertion, or, in the case of the iliac crest and ischial tuberosity, "pelvic whiskering" along these expansive surfaces.

In light of the fact that many "nonmetric

variations" are hyperostotic in nature, a cautionary note—on not conflating these "features" with those of DISH (if one can indeed always distinguish between them)—would seem to be in order.

Tumors

A tumor arises as a result of cellular proliferation. If the growth of this cell mass is confined in location and/or limited in size, the tumor is probably **benign**. If its growth is unlimited—in size as well as location—the tumor is most likely **malignant** (cancerous). Tumors that are specific to bone are called **primary (skeletal) tumors**. Tumors that are *metastatic* (i.e. that develop as a result of the spread of cells from a tumor that began in soft tissue) are **secondary (skeletal) tumors**. Whether benign or malignant, primary skeletal tumors typically arise in individuals still in the active phase of growth. Primary skeletal tumors do not occur as frequently as secondary skeletal tumors (Ortner and Putschar, 1981).

The term for a benign bony (osteoblastic) tumor is **osteoma**. A common osteoma is typically expressed as a small, dense, buttonlike, low mound growing on the surface of one of the flat cranial bones. The perimeter of the base of this kind of osteoma is incised; thus the tumor looks as though it had been "stuck" onto the bone. An individual may develop more than one of these osteomata (the plural of osteoma). On occasion, an osteoma may grow to about 2 cm in diameter. Ortner and Putschar (1981) also cite exostoses of the external auditory (acoustic) meatus (meatal tori)—which are otherwise considered to represent hyperostotic nonmetric variants (Saunders, 1989)—as examples of osteomata. Osteomata may proliferate within the paranasal sinuses as well. If an osteoma develops intraosseously, it is identified as an **osteoid osteoma** and is characterized by an unossified center. An osteoid osteoma would be suspected within or underlying a localized area of markedly thickened cortical bone. Its existence would have to be confirmed radiographically.

Tumors associated with bone may also be cartilaginous in origin. A common benign, cartilage-derived (chondroblastic) tumor is a **chondroma**, which typically develops from (exogenous) epiphyseal plate cartilage in the metaphyseal region of tubular bones. The most common chondroma—an **enchondroma** (i.e. singular as well as plural, although "enchondromata" is also a plural form)—occurs intraosseously and most frequently affects the small tubular bones of the hand (Rothschild and Martin, 1993). Enchondromata can arise in females and males alike and often occur in older children through middle-aged adults (Ortner and Putschar, 1981). **Ollier's disease** is the development in early childhood of multiple enchondromata. The presence of an enchondroma is detected radiographically.

Another common benign chondroblastic tumor is an **osteochondroma**, which, like a chondroma, is an outgrowth of epiphyseal plate cartilage. Like the cartilage-derived bone from which it is an outgrowth, an osteochondroma ossifies endochondrally. An osteochondroma stops enlarging when the epiphysis fuses to the diaphysis. Any postcranial bone can be affected, but osteochondromata most frequently involve the distal femur and proximal tibia. Also referred to as a *cartilaginous exostosis* (Ortner and Putschar, 1981), an osteochondroma is distinguished from a "true" exostosis by the persistence of a cartilaginous cap (Rothschild and Martin, 1993)—which is reflected osteologically in irregular surface of the "tip" of the osteochondroma (like the surface on a diaphysis for an unfused epiphysis).

In addition to originating from epiphyseal plate cartilage, tumors can arise from the periosteum. The most common of these is a **fibroma** (fibrous cortical defect), which can affect the alveolar margins of the jaws as well as the tubular bones of the postcranium (Resnick and Niwayama, 1988). A fibroma may be a single- or multichambered lesion lying just beneath the cortex. Its inner surface is lined with sclerotic bone. Although a fibroma may be suspected beneath a thin cortex, its presence must be verified radiographically. Although typically benign, a fibroma can become malignant. Rather than being cut off from the medullary cavity of the affected bone by its sclerotic lining, it may penetrate and produce an expansive lesion.

Malignant tumors affecting bone are relatively rare. The two most common forms are **osteosarcomata** and **chondrosarcomata**. Like benign tumors, osteo- and chondrosarcomata are typically associated with metaphyseal regions of actively growing bones. Osteosarcomata are typically intraosseous (most frequently arising in the knee joint and in twice as many males as females) and may be evidenced as destructive lytic lesions or growths of sclerotic, internally amorphous bone with exotic surface patterns. In response to the destruction of bone, the periosteum may produce new bone around the area of the lesion. Sometimes an osteosarcoma may develop on the cortex of the bone. Benign chondroblastic tumors as well as, potentially, any cartilage can give rise to chondrosarcomata. Although it may be difficult to differentiate on skeletal material between an osteosarcoma and an ossified chondrosarcoma, the latter tends to produce a more nodular tumor with a more structured, trabeculated interior.

Cancer can also spread and metastasize to bone from soft tissue. Tumor cells migrate through the bloodstream to the bone marrow. There they multiply, eventually replacing bone marrow and then destroying spongy and eventually cortical bone. The axial skeleton is the most frequently affected, but the femur, ribs, sternum, and humerus are often involved as well. As characterized by Ortner and Putschar (1981, p. 393), "fast growing tumors are mainly osteolytic, while slow growing ones elicit an osteoblastic response." Lytic lesions are the more common; they are often circular or ovoid in outline and may look "punched out." Osteoblastic response may result in sclerotic lesions or various forms of hyperostotic bone growth (e.g. nodular or radiant). Breast and prostate cancer are the most common carcinomas metastasizing to bone. Metastatic breast cancer produces lytic lesions, while metastatic prostate cancer produces an osteoblastic response.

Bone Necrosis

Bone death or necrosis (Figure 8–12) results ultimately from the loss of blood supply to a bone or region of bone. As discussed above with regard to pyogenic osteomyelitis and the formation of sequestra, infection can also lead to bone death. So too, for example, can trauma (such as dislocation) or fracture, vitamin D–deficient rickets, rheumatoid arthritis, and some forms of metastatic carcinoma (Rothschild and Martin, 1993). The hip joint, especially the femoral head, which is a site of stress and potential trauma, is a frequent locus of bone necrosis. As bone necrosis sets in, the affected bone or portion thereof can become diminished in size and robustness, especially of cortical thickness, which can also lead to fracture as well as articular epiphyseal displacement.

Fractures and Trauma

Undue or unusual stress on bone can cause it to fracture. A bone fractures because the force of the assault outpaces the rate at which the bone can respond to the stress (i.e. by remodeling and forming a callus to strengthen the bone in the region of stress). Unfortunately, since bone remodeling entails osteoclastic action prior to bone deposition, stressed bone becomes even more vulnerable to fracture.

Stress can result from injury (caused, for example, by a fall or wound), the carrying or lifting of a heavy load, assuming an awkward movement or position, and even undergoing an invasive medical procedure. As in the case of an injury or a medical procedure, the effect of the assault can cause an immediate response in the bone or bones involved. Types of stress that might be produced in a traumatic injury would be *compression, twisting* or *torsion, bending,* and *shearing*; in surgery, sawing and drilling, for example, would leave their marks.

Collapsed vertebrae are often the result of *compression* (Figure 8–13). A blow to the head will also compress bone and create a depression fracture (Figure 8–14). Sometimes the blow is sufficiently severe that it causes the bone of the inner table to become detached (Figure 8–15). Because the force of the blow radiates outward from the point of impact—creating a conical field (similar to that caused by a pellet hitting plate glass)—the affected surface area of the inner table will often be larger than the affected surface area of the outer table. In long bones, compression along the long axis of the bone—as would be produced by the impact from a fall from a great height—can cause a bulging of the diaphysis with potential cracking of cortical bone.

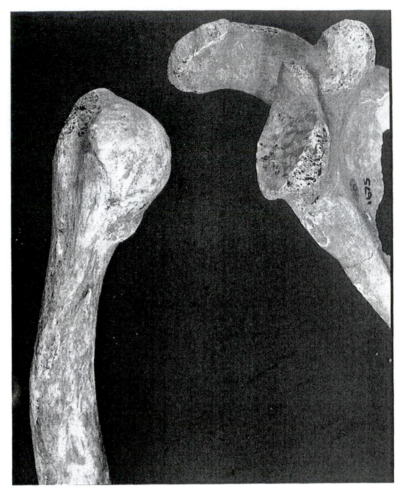

Figure 8–12 Necrosis of right shoulder joint; note, for example, alteration of scapular glenoid fossa and diminution in size and robustness of humerus (prehistoric, Pennsylvania).

Twisting or *torsion* fractures—also called *spiral* fractures—are typically noted in long bones. The twist or unnatural rotation of part of a bone around its long axis can cause a break that, characteristically, is obliquely oriented— that is, one side of the break will be longer than the side opposite it. Thus, a common feature of a spiral fracture is that one end of each part of the severed bone looks pointed, and the plane of the break along the thickness of the cortical bone has an "edgelike" appearance. The osteologist, however, must be cautious in identifying a spiral fracture as being pre- rather than postmortem in origin: for example, sometimes factors of preservation and deposition can cause a break that looks like a spiral. Such caution is particularly germane to animal bone analyses when human (at least, hominid) activity is suspected as the cause of the spiral fracture (e.g. twisting a bone in order to break it to gain access to the marrow).

While falling from a great height can cause a compression fracture, it can also lead to a bending fracture. Inasmuch as any premortem fracture affects green rather than dry bone, bone will "give" until the point at which it finally snaps. The more "give" a bone has—as in younger individuals—the more likely it is that a break will go only partway through the side that is being stretched; the break then often courses up and down the shaft of the bone. This produces a *greenstick fracture*. With increasing

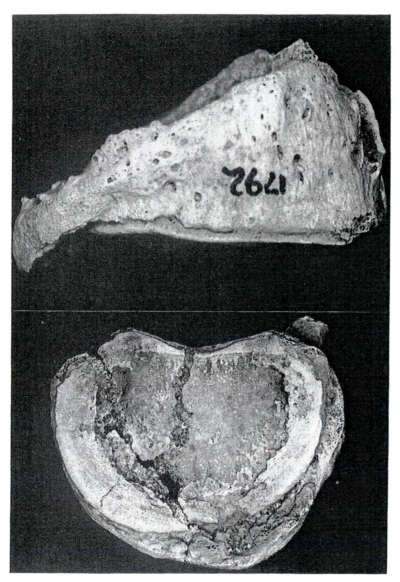

Figure 8–13 Collapsed, wedge-shaped vertebral body, probably caused by compression (as opposed to tuberculosis); *(top)* left lateral and *(bottom)* inferior views (prehistoric, Pennsylvania).

age, bone becomes more rigid and brittle; thus a bending fracture is more likely to "pop out" a wedge-shaped piece of bone. Reminiscent of the spread of impact of a compression fracture, the wedge of bone that is displaced is narrowest on the side of the bone being flexed and broadest on the side of the bone being stretched. *Shearing fractures*—which result from opposing forces across a bone—may not be distinguishable from bending fractures.

The effects of various kinds of stress (e.g. opposing muscle action) can accumulate or increase over time, eventually leading to microfractures and then, perhaps, complete fractures [an incomplete fracture is sometimes called an *infraction,* while a complete break is referred to as a *fracture* (Merbs, 1989; Ortner and Putschar, 1981)]. The fracture of a neural arch from a vertebral body is referred to as *spondylolysis,* but the degree of separation can range

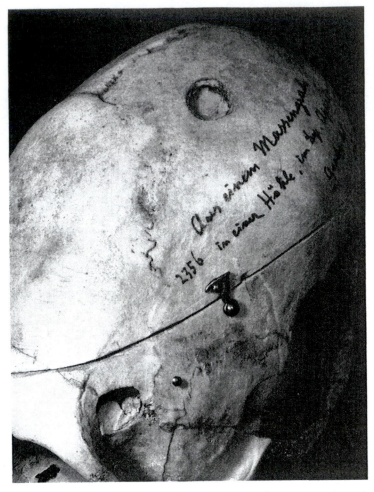

Figure 8–14   Deformed (elongate) skull with perforating compression fractures (one in parietal bone, the other near pterion); note possible healed compression fracture in coronal suture (prehistoric?, Peru).

from a minor severing to a marked chiasm and can be manifested either uni- or bilaterally. [Stress fractures leading to separation of the superior and inferior articular processes are particularly common in the fifth lumbar vertebra and have been of special interest in archeologically derived Eskimo populations (e.g. Lester and Shapiro, 1968; Merbs, 1989).] Fractures resulting from the accumulation of stress rather than from a single stressful event are often referred to as *fatigue fractures*.

If bone is already weakened because of some preexisting condition (e.g. rheumatoid arthritis, leprosy, necrosis), the amount and kind of stress that can lead to fracture will be appreciably less than for healthy bone. Fractures occurring in bones already affected by some pathology are *pathological fractures* (Merbs, 1989).

A characteristic shared by all fractures is that the edges of the break become necrotic due to disruption of the blood supply. Therefore, the bone of these edges does not participate in the healing process. In fact, if the edges of the broken bone are not separated from one another even slightly, reestablishment of blood supply and eventual union of the fracture may be impeded, leaving an *ununited fracture*. Sometimes the ends of an ununited fracture will develop articular surfaces against one another. If the broken ends have become too separated for healing to set in, a *displaced fracture* develops (Merbs, 1989). For proper healing to occur, the

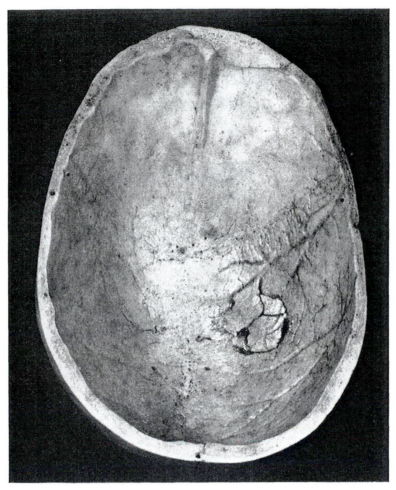

Figure 8–15   Interior of calvaria of individual in Figure 8–14 illustrating large area of bone dislodged (larger than area of impact).

break must be "filled by a highly vascular fibrous callus containing focal avascular regions of fibrocartilage" (Rothschild and Martin, 1993, p. 57). Although new bone deposition occurs endosteally, ossification of the fibrocartilaginous "plug" is also necessary for complete union of the ends of the broken bone to occur. Eventually, the normal cellular activities and features of osteogenesis characterize the region of the break. If the periosteum is also torn as a result of the fracture, its osteogenic potential will be activated and an external bony callus will form. If the fracture is profound enough to expose the break (to the outside)—constituting a *compound fracture*—secondary infection can set in, leaving evidence of both the break and

the infection (Figure 8–16). [A fracture that is not exposed to the outside is a *simple* or *closed fracture* (Merbs, 1989).] Sometimes one finds evidence of *multiple fractures*. If healed fractures are not identifiable visually (e.g. because of obvious displacement or angulation or by the presence of an external callus), they can often be diagnosed radiographically on the basis of localized cortical bone thickening.

Wounds caused by projectiles or other weapons as well as by surgical procedures (such as trephination) can also be classified as fractures (Ortner and Putschar, 1981). The extent to which such wounds may have led to the death of the individual can be inferred from the degree of healing of the wound. In the case of *trephi-*

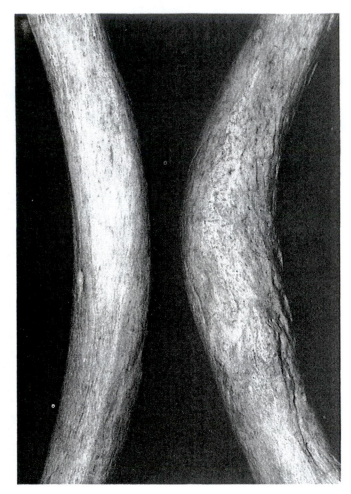

Figure 8–16 Left and right clavicles *(left and right)* of same individual; the right clavicle shows evidence of healing [with sclerosis and secondary periostitis (from localized osteomyelitis?)] of compound fracture (prehistoric, Pennsylvania).

nation—the excising of pieces of bone from the flat cranial bones (Figure 8–17)—the archeological record is replete with examples of individuals who survived multiple such surgeries, often with much in-filling of the trephined region or regions.

The surgical extraction or blow-induced exfoliation (shedding) of teeth would constitute trauma to the jaws, and, as pointed out by Merbs (1989), would produce a "compound fracture" in the sense that the wound is exposed to the outside.

The term "trauma" has also been extended to embrace the results of surgerylike or other body-altering behaviors (e.g. Merbs, 1989). Dental examples—collectively referred to as *dental mutilation*—abound, from both the ar-

cheological record and recent history. The teeth most frequently affected are the upper incisors and canines and common expressions are seen, for example, in the filing of teeth into different shapes, the incising of patterns on the buccal (labial) surfaces, and the encrusting of teeth in semiprecious stones, gold, and/or silver (the latter accomplished by drilling the buccal surfaces to receive the implants) (Carter et al, 1987; Merbs, 1989; Romero, 1970). Nondental examples of body-altering trauma reflected in skeletal remains include the recently banned practice of *foot binding* in China and the numerous examples of artificial *cranial deformation*. Some types of cranial deformation—such as head binding in pre-Columbian Andean and Mesoamerican populations (Romero, 1970)—

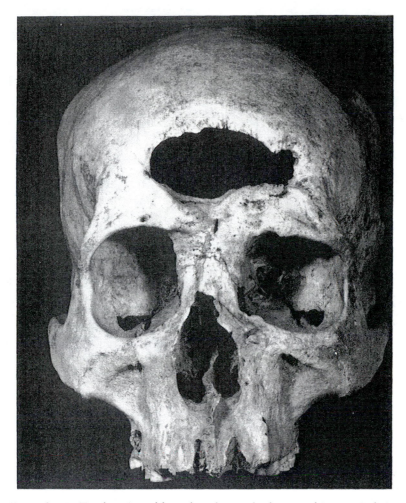

Figure 8–17 Trephination of frontal (with some healing) (prehistoric?, Bolivia).

were purposeful in that specific devices were employed on the very young to determine a specific head shape [often somewhat conical (e.g. Figure 8–18)]. Occipital flattening, however, which is quite commonly observed in archeological populations of the North American Southwest [and has also been recorded for the Neolithic of Cyprus (Angel, 1953; Schwartz, 1974)], may be considered secondary if it arises as a result of the primary activity of binding an infant to a swaddling board.

Infectious and Degenerative Diseases of the Jaws and Teeth

Inasmuch as developmental (e.g. hypoplasia) and genetic (e.g. hypo- and hyperdontia) aspects of tooth "pathology" have been dealt with

in Chapter 6, on teeth (and in keeping with the format employed for addressing the nondental skeleton), only infectious and degenerative diseases are discussed here.

With regard to infectious and degenerative diseases, Lukacs (1989; p. 264) cites the following as representative of each category: (1) infectious—dental caries, dental caries–induced pulp chamber exposure, dental abscess, abscess- or caries-induced antemortem tooth loss, periodontal disease, and (2) degenerative—attrition-induced antemortem tooth loss, attrition-induced pulp chamber exposure, periodontal disease, calculus (tartar) accumulation [calculus/tartar accumulation results from the mineralization of plaque (Hillson, 1986)]. The listing of periodontal disease as a type of infectious as well as degenerative disease may seem confusing in that, in both cases, the disease is

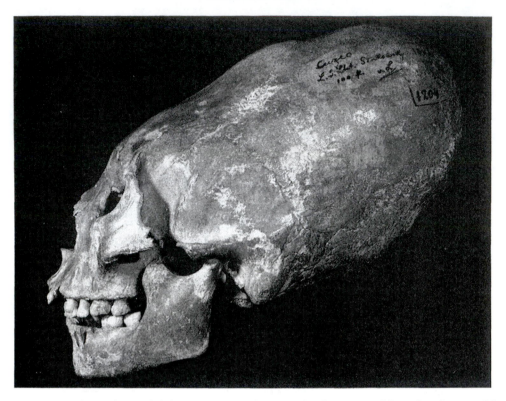

Figure 8–18 One form of cranial deformation; note, for example, elongation of frontal and occipital bones and consequent displacement of coronal and lambdoidal sutures (prehistoric, Peru).

often referred to broadly as "periodontitis." But, as will be reviewed below, the study and identification of periodontal disease are not free of problems (cf. Clarke and Hirsch, 1991).

Unlike the antiseptic, enclosed environment in which bone is normally found, teeth are exposed upon eruption to a host of microorganisms inhabiting the moist and warm oral cavity (which is a corridor to the outside environment). Bacteria, viruses, yeasts, and even protozoa may exist in the oral cavity. However, it is most commonly a variety of bacterium that causes infections of the teeth and associated tissues. It is bacteria, plus a matrix they produce, in addition to salivary proteins, that make up what is called **plaque**. The plaque adherent to the smooth coronal and root surfaces, coronal crevices and grooves, and even the periodontal/alveolar region is populated, respectively, by different bacteria (see review by Hillson, 1986). Except for a brief period after extensive cleaning, an individual's dental surfaces are never entirely free of plaque. (For archeological or fo-

rensic analyses, it is imperative that care be taken *not* to clean plaque from teeth.)

Under normal circumstances and when the person is not consuming food [especially sugar (in particular sucrose)], the pH of the saliva is neutral. When pH levels become high, mineral crystals tend to form in the plaque matrix. This mineral deposit is referred to as **dental calculus** or **tartar** (see Figures 9–4 and 9–10). First as isolated specks and then as three-dimensional flakes, these deposits can eventually become continuous bands around the lower perimeters of the crowns. If left unimpeded, these deposits can expand down and up the crown as well as outward. Various ways of scoring degree and amount of calculus buildup on individual teeth have been developed by osteologists who categorize such buildup as, for example, isolated patches, continuous, three-dimensional, slight, medium, heavy).

When carbohydrates and in particular sucrose are ingested, plaque bacteria immediately begin to ferment them. Such fermentation results in the production of acids, which lower the pH of the saliva; more injuriously for teeth, it also lowers the pH of the plaque matrix adherent to a region of a tooth, an entire tooth, or a number of teeth. Over time, an acidic environment can lead to the demineralization not only of tooth enamel but of cementum and dentine as well (e.g. Hillson, 1986; Lukacs, 1989). Such demineralization results in the development of **dental caries** or **carious lesions.**

A carious lesion can develop anywhere on a crown *(coronal caries)* or exposed root surface *(root caries)*. Typically in analyses, the location of the carious lesion is noted—for example, occlusal, interstitial (interproximal), buccal pit (foramen caecum), cervical, root (see Figure 8–19). (Certain analyses might demand greater specificity about location of caries on crown and root.) In enamel, the onset of caries is noted by the development of a spot of opacity (often white but sometimes dark, which characterizes more mature carious lesions); on roots, caries usually is indicated by spots that are somewhat yellow or light brown (Hillson, 1986). As demineralization proceeds, a cavity forms. A carious lesion is typically shallow on roots, whereas on crowns, the depth and breadth of the cavity are more variable, often being narrow and deep if in crown fissures. (Care should be taken not to identify as a carious lesion the concavity that normally develops when the enamel that caps a cusp or crest is worn away and the softer, more darkly colored dentine is exposed.)

In root lesions, the cavity becomes narrower as it penetrates the dentine. In coronal caries, however, the lesion spreads out along the

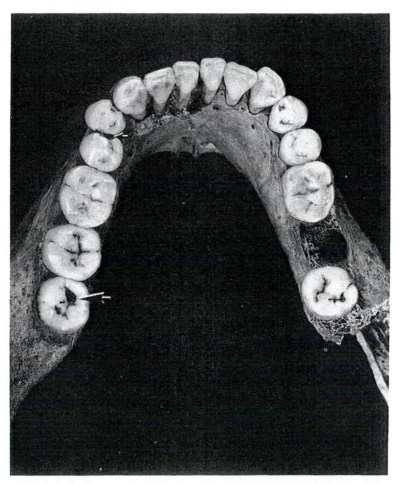

Figure 8–19 Examples of occlusal *(large arrow)* and interstitial *(small arrow)* caries (prehistoric, Pennsylvania).

enamel-dentine junction, eventually thinning the enamel and causing it to collapse, thereby enlarging the cavity. If the infection proceeds into the dentine, acidogenic (acid producing) bacteria first demineralize the dentine, leaving a matrix that will subsequently be attacked by proteolytic (protein destroying) bacteria. In response to this bacterial assault, secondary dentine may be deposited (see Chapter 6, on teeth). If the process of dentine caries is halted, the secondary dentine will appear darker than the primary dentine around it. If the infection spreads into the pulp cavity (or infection is introduced into the pulp cavity of a tooth that is severely worn), it can travel through the root tip and into the surrounding bone.

As occurs in bacterial infection in bone, bacterial infection in teeth leads to necrosis of living tissue (e.g. dentine tubules, nerves, blood supply) and often to the production of pus. If the infection spreads through the root apex, the surrounding alveolar bone can become necrotic and a balloonlike, pus-filled cavity—a *periapical* or *apical abscess*—will form; at this stage it can only be recognized radiographically. With unimpeded infection, the periapical abscess will enlarge (filling with pus), bone will continue to become necrotic, and a drainage hole may erupt through the alveolar surface (most frequently on the buccal side); in dried specimens, the root tip or tips will be visible through this hole, which can itself become quite spacious (Figure 8–20). In contrast to the jagged edges of broken bone or the developmental thinning of bone that exposes underlying roots [either as a *dehiscence* (see Figure 6–8), which is a deficiency that begins at the alveolar margin and can course much of the length of a root, or a *fenestration* (Figure 8–20), which exposes a portion of the root], the drainage hole of an abscess

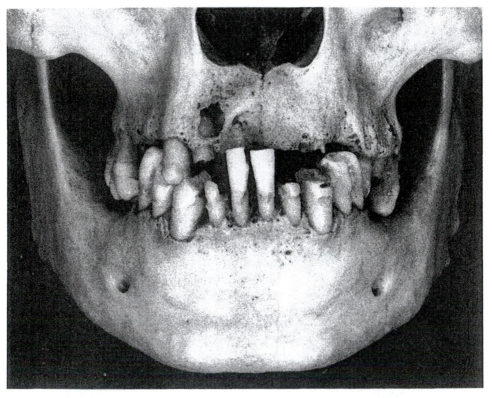

Figure 8–20 Loss of upper anterior teeth probably due to periapical inflammation (note severe attrition of various lower anterior teeth); also note, for example, periapical abscess exposing root of right upper canine, fenestration in left maxilla (exposing root of second premolar), and continued growth of various upper and lower teeth in the absence of occlusal counterparts (provenience unknown, University of Pittsburgh Dental School collection).

will typically be ovoid to circular in shape, with thin but crisply defined edges. The abscess itself will be three-dimensionally symmetrical (typically circular). Continued enlargement of the abscess can progress to the alveolar margin, leaving the tooth sitting precariously in soft tissue. Inasmuch as such infections also affect the periodontal ligaments, antemortem exfoliation or evulsion of the involved tooth or teeth may occur. In the upper jaw, infection can spread into the maxillary sinuses as well as the nasal cavity. (Sometimes teeth which in life would have had little to tether them in place will be shed postmortem and should not be overlooked in excavating around the skull.)

Infection and inflammation not related to coronal caries can also affect the periodontal ligaments and surrounding alveolar bone, resulting in eventual tooth loss. For example, severe attrition exposes pulp cavities, which can then become inflamed. Such inflammation can spread through the root canals and affect the periodontal ligaments, not just apically but anywhere along the length of the root. Eventually, inflammation turns to infection, resulting in lesion and abscess formation within the periodontium. These abscesses thus originate away from the alveolar margin. As with the more stereotypical periapical abscess, these nonapical periodontal abscesses (of pulpal origin) can expand three-dimensionally, destroying bone toward and away from the alveolar margin as well as toward the exterior. Because, like periapical abscesses, these periodontal abscesses are tooth- rather than region-specific, the alveolar bone on either side of the affected tooth/alveolar bone will present normal (nonpathological) morphology—unless, of course, adjacent teeth had suffered pulpal inflammation and subsequent periodontal abscessing. Nevertheless, and even in the case of multiple adjacent teeth being lost due to periodontal abscesses, the restrictiveness rather than the pervasiveness of alveolar marginal destruction will be discernible.

Along with caries, the most frequently diagnosed pathological condition involving the jaws and teeth is **periodontal disease** or **periodontitis**. Technically, as the word implies, periodontitis is an inflammatory disease. It is generally thought of among osteologists as being characterized by a destruction of the alveolar margin, sometimes leading to destruction of tooth

attachment and subsequent tooth loss. However, as summarized by Clarke and Hirsch (1991, p. 241), the effects of periodontitis are less extensive: "In periodontitis, the crestal [alveolar] margin of bone undergoes loss of the surface cortical bone, exposing the porous cancellous structure of the supporting bone, usually with an accompanying change of the contour of the crest."

Historically, periodontitis has been thought of as the end of a sequence that begins with the accumulation of plaque, which then causes inflammation of the gums (gingivitis), which, in turn, leads to inflammation of periodontal tissues and destruction of the alveolar margin. This, however, may be the less frequent sequence of events. Rather, periodontitis often appears to be its own malady (Clarke and Hirsch, 1991). Osteologically, periodontitis typically has been diagnosed on the basis of increased distance (greater than 2 mm) between the alveolar margin and cervix or enamel-cementum juncture of a tooth. This criterion is evident in the classification Lukacs (1989, p. 271) provides for scoring degrees of alveolar resorption: "(0) absent—no resorption; (1) slight—less than one-half of the root exposed; (2) moderate—more than one-half [of] the root exposed; (3) severe—evulsion of the tooth, remnants of the alveolus discernible; and (4) complete—tooth avulsed, alveoli completely obliterated." Factors other than periodontitis, however, can achieve the same results: root exposure and eventual tooth loss.

Recently, Clarke and Hirsch (1991) have reviewed the field and literature and, in addition to providing new data, have pointed out that continued facial growth (particularly of the lower face) throughout adult life as well as progressive dental attrition can lead to a distancing between the enamel-cementum juncture of a tooth and the alveolar margin. That is, in the absence of other factors, the result of either continued growth of the lower face or dental attrition (and especially if both occur) would be the "disarticulation" between upper and lower teeth that otherwise should be in occlusion with one another. The reason that an individual's upper and lower teeth remain in occlusion is that they continue to erupt. And it is the continual albeit incremental eruption of teeth throughout much of an individual's life—rather than periodontitis—that can (and often does) lead to the distancing between enamel-cementum juncture and alveolar margin (Figure 8–20). Thus, if one uses, for example, the inferior dental canal (through which the mandibular nerve courses within the body of the mandible) as a stable landmark, one would find that the distance between it and the alveolar margin changes little over the life of an individual in whom an increasing amount of tooth root has become exposed. Critical to a diagnosis of periodontitis, therefore, is not a measurement of amount of root exposure but an inspection of the condition of an individual's alveolar margin in order to determine if the crestal bone is still healthy and crisply defined or if it does indeed appear pathological (e.g. being resorbed and/or lacking contour) (see Figure 8–20 as well as Figures 6–17 and 9–4).

One might think that nontraumatic loss of a tooth, if not the result of unabated abscessing, would otherwise have to be due to some infectious disease, such as periodontitis. However, again as pointed out by Clarke and Hirsch (1991), continued tooth eruption can lead to tooth loss merely through the diminution of root available within the alveolus for adequate anchoring via the periodontal ligaments. Although the tooth may generate additional root cementum, the rate at which it is deposited (and the rate at which compensatory root lengthening would occur) is not equal to the rate of compensatory tooth eruption. The cautionary note here is that the osteologist must be careful "to separate physiological attachment loss resulting from continuous tooth eruption from pathological bone loss" (Clarke and Hirsch, 1991, p. 247). Indeed, Clarke and Hirsch find that, in contrast to pulpal infections (leading to alveolar bone destruction), periodontitis plays and has played a minimal role (if any) in causing tooth loss.

Differentially Expressed Morphological Character States: Nonmetric Variation, Race, and Sex Determination

Overview

The study of nonmetric variation, or the delineation of nonmetric traits, is the descriptive counterpart to the analysis of measurements of teeth and bones. Thus, studies on nonmetric variation tend to focus on recording differences and similarities between individuals in details of skeletal morphology. The impetus for such studies is twofold: first, to try to describe groups or populations by the relative frequencies of expression of the traits recorded and, second, to try determine how closely or distantly related to one another groups thus defined are. The rationale behind these endeavors is that if there is a genetic basis for morphology, the more similar groups are to one another morphologically, the more closely related they must be. Conversely, the less similar groups are to one another, the less closely related they must be. In order to calculate the relative frequencies of expression of traits in a group or population, that group or population must be defined or delineated on the basis of other information, which usually derives from a cultural, linguistic, archeological, or some other nonmorphological source. Degrees of closeness, based upon the comparative relative frequencies of traits in different groups, are calculated using various statistical approaches, among which The Mahalanobis D^2 distance is most popular (see van Vark and Schaafsma, 1992, for a general dis-

cussion of quantitative analyses). Although the trait lists that are brought to bear on these analyses have been augmented over the years, the features scrutinized and recorded—dental as well as non-dental—tend to be the same from one study to the next. An important criterion in the choice of "good" nonmetric traits is that they should be "resistant to environmental stress" (Saunders, 1989, p. 96).

During the nineteenth century, most studies on what we would now call nonmetric variation dealt with one of two subjects. Some studies sought to delineate distinguishing features of "races." More ambitious studies sought to interpret features in which non-European populations differed from the European ideal. These studies, however, tended to be cloaked in the guise of a purported evolutionary perspective, in which at least some group or groups among our own species were seen as the pinnacle of morphological change. For those individuals or groups of individuals who were found to differ from this "ideal," the variant features of the former were interpreted as being either retained primitive features or *atavisms* (evolutionary reversals to more primitive states).

Early-twentieth-century studies began to concentrate on the developmental aspects of nonmetric traits. By the 1950s, interest shifted to the genetic basis of nonmetric variation (e.g. summarized in Grüneberg, 1963). In the 1960s, the focus was on the general applicability of the

257

study of nonmetric variation and the delineation of the differential distribution of nonmetrically variable traits to the problem of distinguishing populations from one another (e.g. Berry, 1968). The debate continues as to which, or whether any, study of nonmetric traits reveals more population-specific information than the metric analysis of skeletal variation (Saunders, 1989).

Nonmetrically variable traits are often identified as those features of the skeleton whose representation from one individual to the next may differ. Such character states are recorded, for instance, as present/absent, open/closed, more /fewer (than expected number), or within/outside of suture. Typical examples of categories of nonmetric variation are (1) "foramen spinosum: open or closed" or "third trochanter on femur: present or absent"; (2) "frontal (metopic) suture: fully persistent, partially expressed, or totally obliterated" or "talar calcaneal facet: single, pinched, double, or anterior facet absent"; (3) "infraorbital foramen: single or multiple"; (4) "mastoid foramen: sutural or exsutural (i.e. lying on the mastoid region)." Most frequently in textbooks, the topic of nonmetric variation is discussed in its own chapter or section and thus is set apart from what in reality constitute other expressions of nonmetric morphological variation. As one hopes will be appreciated here, features whose expression may differ between the sexes (i.e. features related to sexual dimorphism)—which, in turn, are often presented in a separate chapter—also constitute nonmetric morphological variation.

It is still a matter for debate which is the best way in which to record and evaluate nonmetric variables (as traditionally identified). For example, there is the question of how to take into account a trait that, in one individual, might be expressed only on one side of the body (unilaterally), but, in another individual, may be expressed bilaterally. Some osteologists advocate recording a trait as present for an individual regardless of whether it is unilaterally or bilaterally expressed. In this case, the frequency of representation of the feature is a ratio based on the number of individuals with the trait relative to the total number of individuals in the study population. Other osteologists insist on counting the number of variant traits on each side of the body. In the latter instance, the frequency

of a feature is a ratio based on the number of individuals with the trait on a given side of the body relative to the total number of individuals for which data on that side of the body can be collected. There remains lack of agreement as to which approach is "better" or more accurate, primarily because it is still not known whether trait expression is truly side-dependent (i.e. genetically based and correlated with a specific side of the body) or essentially random (see Saunders, 1978, 1989). Further complicating such analyses is the suggestion that changes in frequency of trait expression—specifically, a shift from unilateral to bilateral—may increase with age (e.g. Saunders, 1978). But even if this is true for some traits (e.g. "accessory facets"), it would seem unlikely to be true for all traits (e.g. multiple foramina) that have been classified as "nonmetric variants" (see discussion below).

Considering the Bases of Nondental, Nonmetric Variation

On a very general level, there is a well-established tradition of how nonmetric traits are categorized and recorded (see Table 9–1). With regard to the nondental skeleton (teeth are dealt with separately below), one kind or category of nonmetric trait that has been recognized in the literature is characterized by the proliferation of bone into or in response to the action of soft tissue structures. Such a trait is often referred to as **hyperostotic**. Examples include the following: (1) a **trochlear spur** (a small spit of bone in the medial orbital wall above and behind the posterior lacrimal crest), which may result from either mineralization of a ligament that is ultimately associated with the superior oblique muscle (one of the muscles that move the eye) or pulling on the bone by the muscle via its ligament; (2) a **third trochanter** on the femur, which represents an enlargement of the gluteal tuberosity, onto which the lower part of the gluteus maximus muscle inserts; (3) **bridging of cranial canals** (e.g. the **optic** and **hypoglossal canals**); (4) **doubling of cranial** and **vertebral foramina** [e.g. **accessory frontal** or **infraorbital foramina** (Figure 9–1) and **accessory cervical transverse process foramen**, respectively]; and (5) **excessive ossification** along the "roof" of the

Table 9–1 Examples of Nonmetric, Nondental, Non-Sex-Related Traits

Hyperostotic (i.e. increased/extended bone growth)

Division/bridging of foramina/canals

Optic canal

Hypoglossal (anterior condylar) canal

Infraorbital foramen

Jugular foramen

Transverse foramen (vertebral)

Bridging of neural canal of first cervical vertebra (lateral or posterior)

Mineralization of connective tissue/deep fascia

Complete supraorbital foramen

Extension of lacrimal hamulus across inferior border of lacrimal fossa (in greatest degree of expression, excludes maxilla from inferior border of lacrimal fossa)

Pterygospinous bridge (between lateral pterygoid plate and sphenoid spine; lies medial to foramen ovale)

Pterygobasal spur/bridge (spur lies lateral to foramen spinosum and ovale; bridge is enlarged spur-to-lateral pterygoid plate)

Clinoid bridge (between anterior and middle clinoid processes; or between anterior and posterior clinoid processes)

Mylohyoid bridge (internal, mandible; spans mylohyoid groove; variable in expanse)

Enlargement of posterior lacrimal crest

Infraorbital canal length > infraorbital groove length

Response to soft tissue

Trochlear spur (medial orbital wall)

Extension of vaginal process (postglenoid plate/sheath of styloid process)

Highest nuchal line

Distension of maxillary tuberosity

Enlarged hamulus (medial pterygoid plate)

Shape/size of posterior nasal spine

Shape/size of genial tubercles (mandible)

Precondylar tubercle

Third trochanter (femur)

Peroneal tubercle (calcaneus)

Accelerated closure/union

Craniostenosis/cranial synostosis [e.g. of squamous portion of temporal and adjacent parietal bones (i.e. squamoparietal synostosis), sagittal suture (i.e. scaphocephaly), coronal (with/without sphenoparietal synostosis)]

Reduction in lumbar vertebrae via incorporation into sacrum

Excessive bone deposition of unknown origin/etiology

Palatal torus

Mandibular torus

Excessive bone deposition of apparent (non–soft tissue) known origin/etiology

Exostoses—for example auditory torus (induced by cold/hydrostatic pressure)[1]

Osteomas

Osteochondromas

(continued)

Table 9–1 (continued)

Supernumerary elements: additional centers of ossification

Ossicles [at lambda, bregma, asterion, parietal notch, pterion (i.e. epipteric bone); in coronal, sagittal, lambdoid sutures; not including Inca bone]

Os japonicum (inferior portion of zygoma, delineated superiorly by transversozygomatic suture)

Supernumerary elements: aggressive preossification differentiation

Vertebrae

Digits

Cervical ribs

Hypostotic (i.e. less extended/truncated bone growth)

Incomplete coalescence of elements: cranial sutures

Frontal (metopic) suture (resulting in metopism)

Transverse occipital (mendosal) sutures/fissures (complete patency yields transverse occipital suture, delineating Inca bone inferiorly)

Infraorbital suture

Squamomastoid suture (extending from parietal notch, temporal bone)

Transversozygomatic suture (yielding os japonicum)

Incomplete coalescence of elements: postcranial

Pinched/doubled occipital condyle

Spina bifida (lumbosacral; occulta or severe)

Sacral segments (separate)

Incomplete mineralization of soft tissue precursor

Foramen of Huschke (dehiscence in floor of tympanic plate)

Septal aperture (olecranon fossa of humerus)

Infraorbital groove length > infraorbital canal length

Enlarged foramen lacerum

Incomplete carotid canal (petrosal, internally and/or externally)

Emarginate/(vastus) notched patella

Incomplete preossification development

Sternal aperture (incomplete coalescence of cartilaginous sternal bars)

Pharyngeal fossa (midline depression/pit in basiocciput externally; possible vestige of pharyngeal pouch)

Anterior facial cleft (lip/palate)

Foramina

Absent

Posterior ethmoid

Mastoid

Foramen spinosum (?)

Zygomaticofacial (?)

Atypically present

Parietal

Zygomaticofacial (?)

Supraspinous (scapula)

Foramen in clavicle (for supraclavicular nerve)

Table 9–1   (continued)

Multiple

Infraorbital

Anterior ethmoid

Posterior ethmoid

Supraorbital/frontal

Frontal process

Nasal bone (superior or inferior/marginal)

Zygomaticofacial

Mastoid

Palatine

Position

Infraorbital high on frontal (i.e. frontal foramen)

Mastoid (exsutural; high on mastoid region)

Anterior ethmoid (exsutural)

Posterior ethmoid (exsutural)

Groove for middle temporal artery (restricted to external surface of parietal bone)

Articular facet—configuration and number

Calcaneus (talar): single, pinched (symmetrically, asymmetrically), subdivided (anterior, middle), anterior absent

Talus (calcaneal): single, pinched (symmetrically, asymmetrically), subdivided (anterior, middle), anterior absent

Trochlear surface (olecranon process of ulna): single, pinched (asymmetrically, from medial margin), subdivided (superior, inferior)

Intermetatarsal (proximal end; single, subdivided, truncated)

Intermetacarpal (proximal end; single, subdivided, truncated)

Accessory occipital condyle (uni-, bilateral)

"Squatting facets" (midline, anterodistal margin of tibia; midline, anterodistal edge of articular surface of head of talus)[1]

Other

Bifid anterior nasal spine

Coincidence/separation of dacryon and lacrimale (i.e. degree of approximation of superior extents of posterior and anterior lacrimal crests, reflecting openness/closedness of lacrimal fossa superiorly)

Position of base of medial pterygoid plate relative to width/sides of basisphenoid

Position of base/alae of vomer relative to spheno-occipital synchondrosis

Degree of extension of maxilla medially beyond superior margin of infrorbital foramen

Distension/reflection of inferior orbital margin

Degree of depression of region at/below infraorbital foramen (general region of canine fossa)

Course/configuration of zygomaticomaxillary suture (e.g. arced, straight on the diagonal, "cornered" or "reclining checkmark")

Course/configuration of zygomaticotemporal suture [e.g. arced, straight on the diagonal, stepped (short, long)]

Palate/dental arcade shape (e.g. "V," "U")

Degree of alveolar prognathism

(continued)

Table 9–1   (continued)

Degree of anterior projection/curving back of zygoma (extreme anterior projection increases relative zygomatic arch length and produces angularity or "cornering" of zygomatic arch at region of maxillary tuberosity)

Degree of lateral flaring of zygomatic arch (produces large, triangular, or small, narrow temporal fossa)

Orientation of articular fossa (directly lateral or diagonally forward)

Jugular foramen right/left asymmetry (size, configuration, degree of "pocketing")

Jugular foramen orientation (anteriorly, vertically, posteriorly angled)

Carotid foramen orientation (anteriorly, vertically, posteriorly angled)

Angularity/"filling out" of parietal notch

---

[1] Although these features are traditionally included in lists of nonmetric traits, it must be borne in mind that they result from culturally emphasized behaviors. As such, this kind of feature, while perhaps providing insights into cultural activities, does not contribute to a systematic analysis of relationships.

infraorbital groove (which leads to a relative lengthening of the infraorbital canal). It also seems reasonable to suggest that **muscle scars** or markings, including those of less frequent appearance (e.g. **highest nuchal line**) as well as well-delineated, thickened bands or tori of bone [e.g. **palatal torus** (Figure 6–17) **auditory torus** (Figure 9–2)], should be regarded as hyperostotic characters (even if their precise etiology is,

at present, unknown, as in the case of palatal tori; auditory tori, however, may be induced by regular bouts of aquatic activity, such as diving (e.g. Katayama, 1988).

Ossenberg (1976) has suggested that early and complete closure or **synostosis** of the squamoparietal suture between the squamous portion of the temporal bone and the parietal bone—as especially noted in the posterior

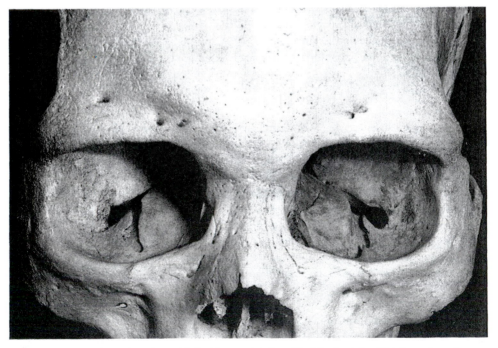

Figure 9–1   Accessory frontal (right and left sides) and infraorbital (only right side) foramina; also note, for example, differences in length of infraorbital groove (longer on the left) and development of sharp, ledgelike posterior lacrimal crests (postcontact?, Alaska).

Figure 9–2 Auditory torus (exostosis) occluding acoustic meatus; (postcontact?, Chile).

extent of the squamoparietal suture—should be categorized as a nonmetric variant. If synostosis is recognized as a nonmetric variant, it could be thought of as a hyperostotic trait because premature or accelerated closure represents atypical ossification into the connective tissue of the sutural zone. But if one particular example of premature or accelerated closure of a cranial suture (i.e. **cranial synostosis** or **craniostenosis**) constitutes a nonmetric variant, then so do all other forms or expressions of cranial synostoses.

Squamoparietal synostosis is neither associated with nor does it cause noticeable alteration of cranial shape or detail. However, other synostoses are or do—for example, premature closure of the sagittal suture appears to be correlated with the development of an atypically elongate cranium as well as, perhaps, with deflection of the frontal forward and/or of the occipital inferiorly and the development of an elevation along the posterior portion of the synostosed suture (this produces **scaphocephaly**); and premature synostosis of the coronal and sphenoparietal sutures is associated with a **postbregmatic depression**. Since the latter forms of cranial synostosis result in changes in skull shape, it might be impossible for the osteologist

encountering one or the other to distinguish between a group that had a "preferred" skull shape (which would have been caused by a particular craniostenosis) and a group in which cranial synostosis was simply one of its distinguishing developmental features (one would predict, however, that the development of the feature preceded its being maintained in the group).

Supernumerary or extra **structures** constitute another potential source of variation or deviation from the typical skeletal pattern. Often listed in this category are the variably small to medium-size islands of bone—called **ossicles** or **wormian bones** (Figure 9–3)—that may develop within the territories of sutures—that is, along the sagittal, lambdoidal, coronal, and sphenoparietal sutures, at *asterion* (i.e. the juncture of the occipital bone, petromastoid region of the temporal bone, and parietal bone), and at the parietal notch (i.e. the region of transition between the squamosal and mastoid sutural regions of the temporal bone, into which the "corner" of the parietal nestles). Details of ossicles are presented elsewhere in this text as part of the descriptions of individual cranial bones. It should be noted here, however, that, although the presence and frequencies of sutural ossicles

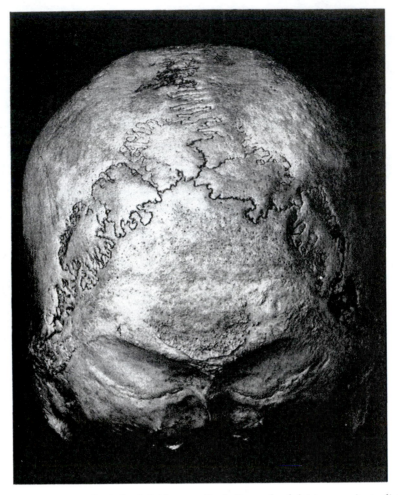

Figure 9–3 Ossicles in lambdoid suture (including at lambda) (recent, Australia).

within skeletal populations have long been recorded, the etiology of these supernumerary structures is still debated (e.g. see Ossenberg, 1970). Perhaps confounding an understanding of the subject is the sometime identification of the sutures that delineate these islands of bone as *supernumerary sutures* (e.g. Ossenberg, 1970; Saunders, 1989). To be sure, the presence of extra "pieces" of cranial vault bone necessitates the presence of additional sutural joints. However, since the existence of sutural contacts depends first on the growth of membranous bones from their initial centers of ossification, it would seem that focus should be on the ontogeny of the ossicle itself, not on the suture that may come to surround it.

Ossenberg (1969) found in the 22 Native North American populations she studied that,

although frequency of posterior and lateral cranial vault ossicles differed among groups, there was a correlation within each population between the frequencies of posterior and lateral ossicle expression (Pearson's r_s = .609, $p <$ .01). In undeformed crania, posterior and lateral cranial vault ossicles were found to occur with equal frequency. However, in skulls that were deformed posteriorly (as a result of infants having been swaddled to a cradleboard) compared to undeformed skulls from the same population, Ossenberg (1970) found a higher incidence of posterior ossicles but a decrease in the frequency of lateral ossicles; specifically, posterior ossicles were found more frequently than lateral ossicles by a ratio of 3:1. She (1970, p. 366) interpreted these data as indicating "that inhibition of the normal growth rate produces stress which either encourages the formation of supernumerary sutures, or delays their closure (or both); while acceleration of the normal growth rate either inhibits their formation or speeds up their obliteration (or both)." However, as suggested above, it might be more fruitful to investigate ossicle formation in terms of factors that would lead to the development of supernumerary centers of ossification along the margins of expanding cranial vault bones. For instance, one might ask the question, "Do differential rates of cranial vault bone expansion create regions that would be depauperate of (presumptive) bone if additional centers of ossification did not arise?"

A totally different kind of supernumerary bony element has been noted in the zygomatic region. This extra element is the so-called **os japonicum** of the zygoma and it presumably develops as a result of the appearance of an additional center of ossification; a "normal" zygoma otherwise develops from a single center of ossification. In its full-blown state, the os japonicum is identified as the inferior portion of a zygoma in which a transverse suture (i.e. the **transversozygomatic suture**) subdivides a typically single zygomatic bone into upper and lower moieties. Sometimes this suture is complete in its horizontal course across the zygomatic bone; at other times, it may extend only a centimeter or so from a juncture with the zygomaticotemporal suture. In the literature, the expression of a truncated transversozygomatic suture is often identified as an incomplete suture, which, in some individuals, may come to extend fully across the zygomatic bone (e.g. Ossenberg, 1976). I would suggest, however, that it is the other way 'round: the truncated transverse suture results from the partial obliteration of a suture whose presence was dictated by the appearance of a supernumerary center of ossification in the presumptive zygoma.

I suggest that the development of supernumerary elements in general should be thought of as hyperostotic in nature. Included in this category, therefore, would be sutural ossicles [but not including the special case of the Inca bone (see below)] as well as an os japonicum with a complete transversozygomatic suture. The variable obliteration of the transversozygomatic suture would result from the imposition of yet another kind of hyperostotic event—that is, the

premature ossification of sutural connective tissue. **Supernumerary digits (polydactyly), supernumerary vertebrae,** and **supernumerary cervical ribs,** for example, arise not from the development of excessive ossification of (or into) a normally extant structure but by way of the ossification of precursors that had arisen via hyperdifferentiation. Such supernumerary skeletal elements (which result from aggressive preossification differentiation), for the sake of simplicity, are included in Table 9–1 as a subset of the hyperostotic nonmetric traits listed. [**Supernumerary molars** may be likened to supernumerary vertebrae (in that they arise via hyperdifferentiation of premineralized precursors; see discussion below and Table 9–2).]

If one also takes into consideration features attributed to sexual dimorphism (see below, Table 9–6), the number of traits that emerge as potential variants of hyperostotic origin increases. For example, consider such stereotypically male features as a pronounced external occipital protuberance, enlarged malar and maxillary tuberosities, an elongate and stout mastoid process, a marked occipitomastoid crest, and a projecting ischial spine; flare and/or eversion of the margin of the goneal region of the mandible; robustness and/or rugosity of the linea aspera, temporal and nuchal lines, and the inferior surface of zygomatic arch; or even protrusion of the anterior nasal spines (which grow either because of traction from the septopremaxillary ligament or as an infilling of bony matrix in the wake of an anteriorly expanding nasal capsule).

In contradistinction to hyperostotic features are **hypostotic** features. Hypostotic features result from an incomplete or arrested ossification of a structure or from an incomplete or arrested union of structures. Representative of hypostotic traits are, for example, the following: (1) the **persistence** of certain **cranial sutures** or contacts that would otherwise close [e.g. the **frontal** or **metopic** suture (i.e. **metopism**; Figure 9–4), the **infraorbital suture** (Figure 9–4), **transverse occipital (mendosal) fissures;** a complete transverse occipital suture, which isolates from below the large occipital ossicle identified as the **Inca bone** (which looks like a large, equilateral triangle, with its apex at lambda, its sides delineated by the right and left arms of the lambdoid suture that course down and away from

Table 9–2 Examples of Nonmetric Dental Traits

Elaboration/proliferation of enamel

Shovel-shaped upper central incisors [e.g. marked with lingual tubercle, faint margocristae (marginal crests)]

Shovel-shaped upper lateral incisors [e.g. marked with lingual tubercle, faint margocristae (marginal crests)]

"Distal accessory ridge" on upper/lower canines

Enamel extends beyond neck [possible on all teeth; on molars, enamel "tongue" may also develop between buccal roots (i.e. enamel extension)]

Enamel pearl (isolated enamel nodule below neck, often in cleft of roots)

Cusp, etc., elaboration/proliferation

"Carabelli's cusp" (the protostyle of other mammals)

Metastylid on lower molars (especially on M_1 = so-called cusp 7)

Protostylid on lower molars (especially on M_1)

Enlargement of lingual tubercle on P_1 (large—could be identified as a metaconid)

"Twinning" of P_2 metaconid

"Twinning" of lower molar hypoconulid (especially on M_1, entoconulid, so-called cusp 6)

Supernumerary structures (i.e. polydontia/polygenesis)

Teeth

Post-M3 "peglike" tooth (i.e. portoconid; uni- or bilaterally, upper or lower)

Post-M3 "partial" tooth (protoconid + metaconid + talonid basin; uni- or bilaterally, upper or lower)

Post-M3 tooth (complete; uni- or bilaterally, upper or lower)

Post-M4 structures (repeat above)

"Twinned" tooth (usually antemolar secondary teeth; twinned I^2 often in association with anterior facial cleft/cleft lip-palate)

Roots

"Third" root on lower molars (may be thin or stout, but conical/tapering)

"Fourth" root on upper molars (beneath hypocone)

"Split"/bifid tip of buccal root on upper premolars (especially on first)

Reduction in tooth number (i.e. agenesis/hypodontia)

M3 absence (uni- or bilaterally, upper or lower)

P2 absence (uni- or bilaterally, upper or lower; often associated with retention of dm2)

I2 absence (uni- or bilaterally, upper or lower; in upper jaw, sometimes associated with anterior facial cleft)

Reduction in root number (i.e. "coalescence"/lack of separation)

Upper premolars (partial, bifid tip, complete)

Upper molars (mesiobuccal and lingual roots spanned by lamina; roots appressed to one another; coalescence partial, tips separate, complete)

Lower molars [mesial and distal root coalesced buccally (forming "C" or reversed "C"); roots appressed to one another; coalescence partial, tips separate, complete]

Other

"Carabelli's pit" on upper molars (may be in association with "Carabelli's cusp")

Groove on internal surface of buccal root of upper premolar

Winging of I^1 (uni-/bilaterally)

Counterwinging of I^1 (uni-/bilaterally)

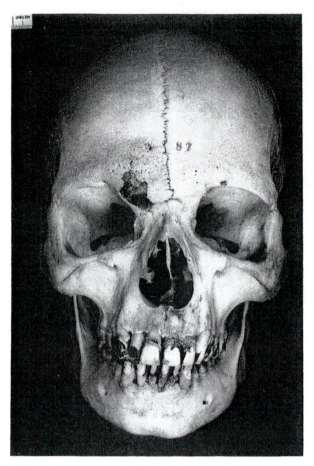

Figure 9–4 Persistence of frontal (metopic) and infraorbital sutures; also note, for example, abscessing of right frontal sinus, somewhat deviated vomer, three-dimensional calculus around exposed tooth roots, and betel nut staining on crowns of various teeth; (recent, Indo-Pakistan).

lambda, and its base delineated by the transverse occipital suture; Figure 9–5)]; (2) the **persistence** of separate **sacral segments**; (3) **arrested ossification**, for example, of the floor of the auditory meatus (leaving a **foramen of Huschke**), of the medial border of the **foramen ovale**, of the "roof" of the infraorbital canal [which increases the relative length of the **infraorbital groove** (e.g. Figure 9–1)], and of the petrosal bone along the length of the **carotid canal** (which can lead to truncation of the petrosal bone and thus increase in size of the foramen lacerum as well as to patencies along the internal and external walls of the petrosal bone; Figure 9–6); (4) and the **lack** or **incomplete fusion** of vertebral spinous processes [**lumbosacral spina bifida** *(occulta* or *severe)*]. Incomplete or arrested ossification would also result in the

persistence of the patency identified in the olecranon fossa of the humerus as a **septal aperture**.

Inasmuch as there appear to be different levels to be considered in the development of hyperostotic traits, so, too, there may be different etiologies for hypostotic traits. For example, a **sternal aperture**, which is a patency in the body of the sternum (Figure 9–7), is sometimes identified as an hypostotic trait (Saunders, 1989). However, a sternal aperture does not arise as does, for example, a septal aperture or a foramen of Huschke. Rather, a sternal aperture will arise when, during fetal development, the right and left cartilaginous bars that contribute to the formation of the presumptive sternum do not coalesce completely along the midline (see discussion of development of the sternum, Chapter 3). Because separate centers of ossification

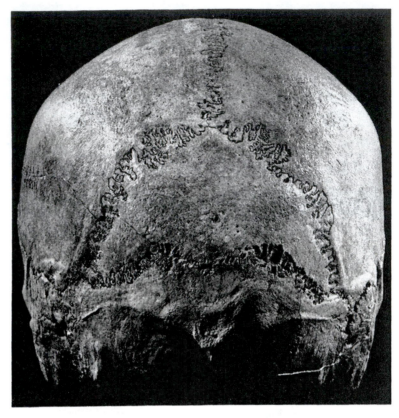

Figure 9–5 "Inca" bone; also note, for example, development of highest nuchal line (especially visible on left side) and ossicle near parietal notch (right side) (prehistoric, Pennsylvania).

within the cartilaginous precursor of the sternum give rise to its various segments, ossification of a cartilaginous precursor in which the sternal bars have left a patency results in the development of a sternal aperture. Thus, a sternal aperture exists because of disturbances in preossification development. Similarly, the persistence of a small centrally emplaced pit or **pharyngeal fossa** in the basiocciput appears to be a hypostotic trait that results from incomplete preossification development (see Chapter 1).

Anterior facial cleft (lip) and **cleft palate** are often discussed exclusively under the categories of congenital abnormalities and skeletal malformations. However, it might not be unreasonable to identify anterior facial cleft and cleft palate as hypostotic in nature, being analogous to a sternal aperture in the sense that these conditions arise as a result of disruption of or interference with proper development of a preossification precursor. In the case of **anterior facial cleft,** the embryonic maxillary isthmus, which normally maintains mesenchymal continuity between the maxillary and median nasal prominences, becomes severed (Andersen and Matthiessen, 1967). During proper development, separate centers of ossification—one appearing in the median nasal prominence and the other in the maxillary prominence—give rise, respectively, to the premaxilla and maxilla; premaxilla and maxilla eventually ossify across the maxillary isthmus, which then forms the roof of the infraorbital foramen (Andersen and Matthiessen, 1967). If, however, connection between the median nasal and maxillary prominences is lost, the ossifying facial elements will be separated from one another, leading, in this case, to anterior facial cleft. **Cleft palate** results from failure of the embryonically vertical and separate palatal shelves to hydrate sufficiently for them to elevate and meet at the midline to form the presumptive palate. Ossification of the separated palatal shelves yields the gap

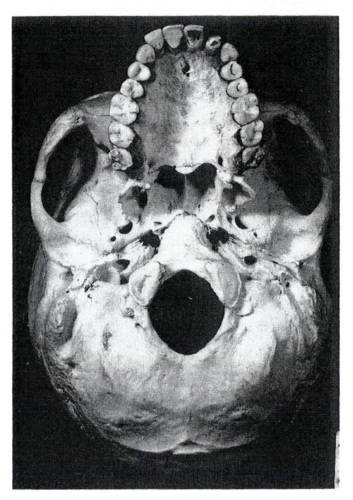

Figure 9–6 Examples of various "nonmetric" features: for example, bony spur across incisive foramen, incomplete ossification of carotid canals, large foramina lacera, slight foramen of Huschke (left side), incompletely ossified styloid processes, notably asymmetrical jugular foramina, obliterated posterior condyloid canals, exsutural mastoid foramina (multiple on left side) (recent, India).

along the midline of the bony palate. The occurrence together of anterior facial cleft and cleft palate involves the expression of two different, developmentally disruptive phenomena, both of which occur prior to the onset of ossification. Thus, these two varieties of clefting would represent hypostotic traits that arise as a result of incomplete preossification development.

Sometimes cited as an example of an hypostotic variant is the so-called **supraorbital notch**, which results from lack of ossification of the soft tissue that bounds the inferior border of the **supraorbital foramen**. However, the presence of a supraorbital foramen is also frequently cited

as a nonmetric variant, one that would then be categorized as a hyperostotic trait. Regardless of which character state—notch or foramen— is the true variant, one can usually find in a series of skulls examples spanning the gamut of variation from "broad, shallow notch," to "deeper and more narrowly constrained notch," to "partial closure of notch," to "complete foramen." The particular variant of notch/ foramen may be expressed either bilaterally or asymmetrically (see Figure 9–10). In the broader comparison, however, even a cursory study of supraorbital notch versus foramen expression among primates reveals that, if there is any feature of note in the region of the supra-

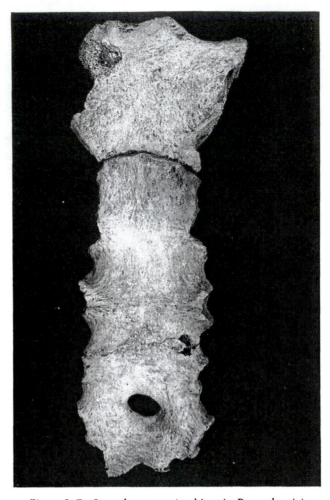

Figure 9–7   Sternal aperture (prehistoric, Pennsylvania).

orbital margin, the most prevalent one is a notch (Schwartz, unpublished data). As such, I would suggest that the supraorbital foramen in *Homo sapiens* represents the variant trait, and I have so listed it in Table 9–1.

Variations in articular facet number and/or morphology have typically been thought of as representing a unified category of nonmetric traits. However, it would appear to be more appropriate to break this category up into ontogenetically meaningful sets. For example, one should single out the development on the occiput of **doubled** (or **twinned**) **condylar facets** and deal with this "variant" separately, identifying it as a potential hypostotic feature. The reason for this is that, while various postcranial articular facets (e.g. the talar calcaneal facet) may be expressed in a doubled (twinned) form, the development of a doubled condylar facet can be attributed to a disruption of the coalescence of two ontogenetically discrete elements. That is (as is detailed in Chapter 2 on the cranium), the anterior part of an occipital condyle arises on the basiocciput while the posterior portion arises on the lateral part of the occipital. During growth, the lateral parts of the occipital coalesce medially with one another. Anteriorly, each lateral part unites with an arm of the basilar portion of the occipital, which, in most individuals, results in the formation of a pair of single, unified occipital condyles. Incomplete coalescence of the parts that contribute to the formation of a single condylar facet would yield a disrupted facet. In contrast, disjunctions in the surfaces of postcranial articular facets have different origins. A more complete list of nonmetric variants of possible hypostotic origin is presented in Table 9–1.

Additional or **supernumerary** articular **facets** as well as variations in **number** and/or **morphology** of postcranial articular **facets** do appear to represent other kinds of nonmetric traits: the former arise as a result of unusual or exaggerated contact between bones; the latter, although between articulating bones, are of unknown origin (e.g. Figure 9–8). Common examples of the former are the **"squatting facets"** that develop from contact between the anterodistal margin of the tibia (in the midline) and the head of the talus when the ankle is frequently hyperflexed (see Figure 5-6); these squatting facets are typically ovoid or elliptical in shape. Uni- or bilateral development of ac-

cessory occipital condyles also results from unusual contact, in this case between the first cervical vertebra and the base of the skull lateral to the occipital condyle itself.

Although variation in number and morphology of postcranial articular facets is often illustrated in texts, their etiology and ontogeny are still unknown, even though one can make a case for their heritability (Saunders, 1978). An additional and curious aspect of such variation in articular facet morphology is that expression of a facet variant on one bone does not appear to be a correlated with expression of an analogous (mirror-image) variant on the opposing articular facet—for example a talar calcaneal facet may be subdivided into anterior and middle moieties, but the sister facet on the talus may be smoothly single and not even pinched or otherwise modified; this point is highlighted by those cases in which an occipital condylar facet is single but its sister facet on the first cervical vertebra is pinched or even more completely divided (Schwartz, personal observations). Table 9–1 lists the general regions in which one typically finds variation in facet number and/or configuration. Specific details of facet variation on a particular bone are discussed in the descriptive section for that bone.

Distinguishing foramina that are "doubled" or otherwise subdivided by virtue of the development of a thin bony septum within their walls (mentioned above in the context of hyperostotic traits) from other kinds of **secondary** or **accessory foramina** would appear to depend on the focus of the observer: Is it the foramen or the soft tissue structure around which the foramen has formed? It is true, as Fazekas and Kósa (1978) point out, that bone forms around soft tissue structures (e.g. neurovascular bundles). Thus, in the case, for example, of the infraorbital foramen, the difference between a foramen that is subdivided internally by a septum and a typically large and single infraorbital foramen in the vicinity of which are one or more smaller foramina reflects ossification around infraorbital neurovascular bundles at different points of arborization. As such, one can suggest the following explanation for "typical variations" in infraorbital foramen number: a single infraorbital foramen formed around an undivided neurovascular bundle; a septum within a fora-

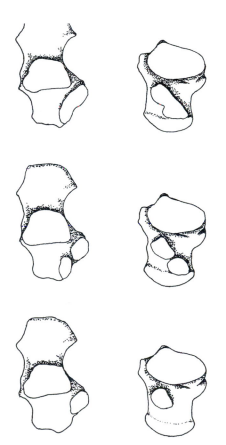

Figure 9–8 Examples of articular facet variation in talus *(right column)* and calcaneus *(left column)*.

men formed near the base of a furcation in a neurovascular bundle or at least prior to extensive separation between branches; a primary foramen and one or more separate accessory foramina ossified around a more fully arborized neurovascular bundle. The problem that remains, however, is determining on a case-by-case basis whether the plane of the foramen remained constant relative to the point of arborization of the neurovascular bundle or whether it shifted relative to the point of arborization. That is, differences between individuals with a large, single infraorbital foramen, those with a subdivided infraorbital foramen, and those with separate secondary foramina would seem to arise because either (1) the trunk was arborizing at different points along its length or (2) facial growth differed such that the neurovascular bundle was captured at different points along its length. In a broader context, therefore, the study of foraminal variation might serve as a potential window into differential rates of growth of parts of the skeleton among different populations.

Other oft-cited osteological nonmetric variants may be explained in terms of ossification around soft tissue structures and the relative location and/or course of these soft tissue structures. Let us consider, for the moment, the cases of **foraminal position/location/trajectory** as well the **presence** or **absence** of **grooves** or **foramina.** Typical examples of variants in location of cranial foramina are a foramen's being either *sutural* (i.e. created in a sutural joint between bones as a result of a nerve and/or blood vessel being captured there) or *exsutural* (the result of the same nerve and/or blood vessel coursing the membranous or cartilaginous precursor of a particular bone—for example, mastoid foramen, anterior ethmoid foramen). Displacement of nerve or vascular course/trajectory within the preossification matrix would explain the occasional appearance of a *clavicular foramen* (the clavicle ossifies around the supraclavicular nerve), the **presence** or **absence** of **grooves** (e.g. a groove made by the middle temporal artery), as well as the **presence** or **absence** of **foramina** (e.g. zygomaticofacial foramen, posterior ethmoid foramen). In the case of absence of the posterior ethmoid foramen, and although the posterior ethmoid nerve may be ab-

sent in some individuals, the posterior ethmoid artery persists but takes a different course into the anterior cranial fossa.

Taking note of and recording these kinds of traits is straightforward (see Table 9–1), but it is still unclear for many traits which character state actually represents the variant. For example, agreement is lacking on the interpretation of polarity of presence versus absence of the zygomaticofacial foramen. But a cursory survey of primates (Schwartz, unpublished data) reveals that the presence of this foramen is widespread, with foraminal size, number, and position (e.g. below/level with/above the infraorbital margin) being the variables of interest. It would seem, therefore, that "absence of a zygomaticofacial foramen" and "more than one zygomaticofacial foramen" represent variants (or, more precisely, different character states) in primates, including humans; they are listed as such in Table 9–1. In a study of 500 human crania representing a global sampling of populations, two foramina were often present and their position was typically above the level of the infraorbital margin (Schwartz, unpublished data).

In addition to the features discussed above, which represent a variety of categories of non-sex-attributed nonmetric traits, I have included under the section "Other" in Table 9–1 a series of different kinds of features that have either been studied as "racially revealing features" or have not been studied at all. This section is not meant to be exhaustive by any means, but, like the traits listed in other sections of Table 9–1, these features are offered with the intention of provoking new approaches to the study of nonmetric skeletal variation.

The features discussed above are listed in Table 9–1; additional examples are included within trait categories.

Dental Nonmetric Traits

In general, categories of dental trait variation (Table 9–2) appear to parallel those of the nondental skeleton. That is, there seems to be an analogue of excessive growth leading to hyperostoticlike traits as well as a dental counterpart of interrupted or diminished growth leading to hypostoticlike traits. With teeth, however, one must distinguish the different levels of tooth differentiation and development.

As summarized in Chapter 6, tooth development must be appreciated on its different levels: primary versus secondary. There is the level of cellular proliferation that leads to the differentiation of tooth classes and the number of primary teeth within a tooth class, with a secondary tooth being derived from the external dental epithelium of the tooth it eventually replaces.

A reduction in tooth number—the lack of development of a tooth being referred to either as **agenesis** or **hypodontia**—can occur among the primary teeth or among the secondary teeth. If a primary tooth that is normally replaced by a secondary tooth does not develop, the secondary tooth will not develop either. What we see ultimately as agenesis of a primary tooth can be affected in more than one way, however: by inhibition of cellular proliferation, by the resorption of a tooth germ, or by the obliteration of the presumptive tooth by some disruptive or traumatic assault on the region in question. "Permanent" molar agenesis, which occurs at the end of the primary molar class (resulting in "loss of M3"), may result from inhibition of cellular proliferation posteriorly ("truncation of the dental lamina") or resorption of a presumptive tooth germ (e.g. as occurs in marmosets, which are distinguished among primates by the *eruption* of only two instead of three molars in each quadrant of the jaw). Reduction in secondary tooth number would be affected by inhibition of cellular proliferation from the predecessor primary tooth or resorption of the presumptive tooth germ. An interesting phenomenon, but one which occurs infrequently in humans, is "loss" of M3, the retention of dm2, and the inhibition or resorption of P2. This reduces premolar number but maintains three functional, molariform teeth (see Figure 6–9).

It has been suggested that fusion of (primary) tooth germs may be another way in which tooth number is reduced absolutely (e.g. see Berkovitz and Thomson, 1971, on fetal ferrets). However, because one cannot pursue a longitudinal study of the process, it is equally possible that presumptive tooth germs that appear to have coalesced may, instead, be presumptive tooth germs that failed to separate [i.e. their cell

masses did not migrate sufficiently apart from one another for a zone of inhibition to intervene and thus lead to the separation of dental entities (e.g. see Lumsden, 1979)].

The development of extra or **supernumerary teeth** produces the condition called **polydontia** or **polygenesis**. There appear to be two ways in which supernumerary teeth can arise. One is related to process—excessive cellular proliferation within a tooth class—while the other is more mechanistic—the splitting of a tooth germ. Although "extra teeth" are, indeed, produced in each case, the bases of supernumerary tooth development are very different from one another.

Supernumerary structures at the end of the molar series are by far the most commonly noted supernumerary dental features (see review by Schwartz, 1984). They range from being conical-crowned, single-rooted structures; to being two-cusped, one- or two-rooted teeth (with variable talon/talonid development); to being full-blown teeth. These possible developmental states of a supernumerary tooth actually conform to a morphocline of tooth formation, culminating in a morphologically full-blown supernumerary tooth (a "fourth" molar) which looks as though it belonged in the size/shape gradient of the molar series. Also, a second supernumerary molar (i.e. "fifth" molar or part thereof) will not be more morphologically complex than the supernumerary molar anterior to it, but again will conform to a gradient of size, shape, and complexity. Although, of course, these examples constitute only indirect evidence, it does appear that such a gradient of size and morphological complexity of supernumerary structures is a consequence of a maintenance of tooth-forming competence of a posteriorly expanding molar tooth class (Schwartz, 1984). [Truncation of the molar tooth class, with, for example, third-molar agenesis can be appreciated as the converse of supernumerary molar development (see Figure 6–8)].

Supernumerary teeth can also arise in the middle of a tooth class, apparently by interstitial budding between two tooth germs that migrate apart from one another (see Schwartz, 1982; 1984). The latter explanation accommodates the supernumerary primary tooth

Table 9-3 The Skull and Mandible: Determining Sex via Discriminant Function Analysis of Measurements

Cranial Measurements	Based on American Whites						Based on African Americans						Based on Japanese	
	Function						Function						Function	
	1	2	3	4	5	6	7	8	9	10	11	12	13	14
Maximum cranial length	3.107	3.400	1.800		1.236	9.875	9.222	3.895	3.533		2.111	2.867	1.000	1.000
Maximum cranial breadth	−4.643	−3.833	−1.783		−1.000		7.000	3.632	1.667		1.000		−0.062	0.221
Maximum cranial height	5.786	5.433	2.767				1.000	1.000	0.867				1.865	
Basion-nasion length		−0.167	−0.100	10.714		7.062		−2.053	0.100	1.000		−0.100		
Bizygomatic breadth	14.821	12.200	6.300	16.381	3.291	19.062	31.111	12.947	8.700	19.389	4.963	12.367	1.257	1.095
Basion-prosthion length	1.000	−0.100	−1.000	−1.000		−1.000	5.889	1.368		2.778		−0.233		
Alveolare-nasion length	2.714	2.200		4.333		4.375	20.222	8.158		11.778		6.900		0.504
Maxilloalveolar breadth	−5.179		−6.571				−30.556		−14.333					
Porion-mastoidale	6.071	5.367	2.833	14.810	1.528		47.111	19.947	14.367	23.667	8.037			
Sectioning point (> = male)	2676.39	2592.32	1296.20	3348.27	536.93	5066.69	8171.53	4079.12	2515.91	3461.46	1387.72	2568.97	579.96	380.84
Percent of sample correctly identified	86.6	86.4	86.4	84.5	85.5	84.9	87.6	86.6	86.5	87.5	85.3	85.0	86.4	83.1

Mandibular Measurements

	Based on American Whites			Based on African Americans			Based on Japanese
	Function			Function			Function
Mandibular Measurements	1	2	3	4	5	6	7
Symphyseal height	1.390	22.206	2.862	1.065	2.020	3.892	2.235
Mandibular body height		-30.265			-2.292		
Maximum projective length		1.000	2.540		2.606	10.568	
Mandibular body breadth			-1.000			-9.027	
Minimum ramus breadth			-5.954			-3.270	1.673
Maximum ramus breadth			1.483			1.000	
Coronoid process height	2.304	19.708	5.172	2.105	3.076	10.486	2.949
Bigonial breadth	1.000	7.360		1.000	1.000		1.000
Sectioning point (> = male)	287.43	1960.05	524.79	265.74	549.82	1628.79	388.53
Percent of sample correctly identified	83.2	85.9	84.1	84.8	86.9	86.5	85.6

Cranial and Mandibular Measurements Combined

	Based on Japanese			Based on African Americans		
	Function			Function		
Cranial and Mandibular Measurements Combined	1	2	3	4	5	6
Maximum cranial length	1.000	1.000	1.000	1.000	1.000	1.289
Maximum cranial height	2.614	2.519		2.560	2.271	-0.100
Bizygomatic breadth	0.996	0.586	0.785	1.084	1.391	
Alveolar-nasion length						1.489
Porion-mastoidale						4.289
Symphyseal height	2.364				2.708	-0.987
Maximum projective length						-0.544
Coronoid process height	2.055	2.713	1.981	2.604		3.478
Bigonial breadth		0.661	0.404			1.400
Sectioning point (> = male)	850.66	807.40	428.05	809.72	748.34	718.23
Percent of sample correctly identified	89.7	89.4	86.4	88.9	88.8	88.3

Sources: After Giles (1970) and Hanihara (1959).

germs that Ooë (1971) found in humans: in one specimen, a presumptive germ had begun to differentiate between the growing dm_1 and dm_2, and, in two other specimens, a supernumerary primary tooth germ had begun to differentiate between the growing di_1 and di_2. It is important to point out that these examples of interstitial supernumerary teeth are of teeth that are primary in origin. A secondary supernumerary tooth can arise only if it is preceded by a primary supernumerary tooth.

The most common example of an extra tooth structure that can be explained by an externally induced splitting of a tooth germ is the "twinned" di^2 that sometimes accompanies anterior facial clefting (see review by Schwartz, 1984). Developmentally, the epithelial thickening of the presumptive di^2 arises in the maxillary prominence (i.e. presumptive maxilla) and migrates into the median nasal prominence (i.e. presumptive premaxilla) (Ooë, 1956, 1957). As the tooth germ migrates, it crosses the maxillary isthmus, which maintains mesenchymal continuity between these two prominences (cf. Andersen and Matthiessen, 1967). Inasmuch as anterior facial clefting results from a severing of the maxillary isthmus, causing separation of the median nasal prominence (Andersen and Matthiessen, 1967), a migrating di^2 germ would be affected as well if it were in the region of the maxillary isthmus (Schwartz, 1982). Since another dental feature associated with anterior facial clefting is the absence of a lateral incisor, and this phenomenon can be explained as the ablation of a tooth germ in the wake of the destruction of the maxillary isthmus, it seems reasonable to suggest that another consequence of the severing of the maxillary isthmus could be the splitting of a tooth germ (Schwartz, 1982). In general, it would appear that more instances of "extra" teeth can be explained as resulting from excessive cellular proliferation within or at the end of a tooth class than from an external source or assault.

Given the above, I suggest, therefore, that the term "supernumerary" should be used to refer to teeth which, like supernumerary digits (producing polydactyly), arise because of something intrinsic to the process of development and differentiation: in this case, excessive cellular proliferation. "Supernumerary" would then be re-

stricted to those situations in which the extra tooth or teeth—first, and at least, at the level of the primary tooth class—either fits into the normally present morphological/size gradient of the tooth class in which it occurs or adds another successional generation of teeth (e.g. a "third" dentition) (see Figure 6–10). The mechanical disruption of a developing tooth germ leading to its being cleaved in some way might better be referred to as "twinning" (i.e. "twinned" structures are produced).

The Assessment of Skeletal Sexual Dimorphism

Although *Homo sapiens* is only weakly sexually dimorphic—in size and some morphology—compared to other large-bodied hominoids, males tend to be somewhat larger than females and there are a few skeletal features that seem to consistently distinguish one sex from the other (Tables 9–3 to 9–7).

Because there is often a size difference between females and males, various studies have attempted to distinguish between the two sexes on the basis of measurement of skull and mandible (Table 9–3), skull and postcranial elements (Table 9–4), and postcranial elements alone (Table 9–5). With males being on average somewhat larger that females, a generalization that is commonly employed in approaching the determination of sex on the basis of skeletal morphology is that the cortical bone of males will be thicker and, overall, individual bones will be more massive and heavier. Because of the latter, the muscle markings on a male's bones will be more pronounced and rugose. For example, in males, as the generalization goes, such features as the linea aspera, the gluteal lines on the ilium, the deltoid crest on the humerus, the inferior margin of the zygomatic arch, the nuchal region, the mastoid process, the temporal lines, and the goneal angle of the mandible will tend to more clearly delineated, marked, and/or distended (see Tables 9–6 and 9–7). Obviously, physical activity or its lack can affect the robustness of bone and its attendant muscle markings. Therefore females can display supposedly male attributes, and vice versa.

Stereotypes also exist for analyzing sex-re-

Table 9–4   The Skull and Postcranium: Determining Sex via Discriminant Function Analysis of Measurements Based on Japanese

Measurement	Function						
	1	2	3	4	5	6	7
Maximum cranial length	1.000			1.000	1.000	1.000	1.000
Maximum cranial height		1.000	1.000				
Femur: physiological length	0.107	0.031	0.176	0.138		0.220	
Scapula: length of glenoid cavity	6.644	4.390		8.117	−5.586	−3.816	
Ishiopubic index	−5.050	−2.654	−3.281	−5.156			
Atlas: maximum breadth	2.678		2.090		2.152	2.491	2.124
Sectioning point (> = male)	299.18	117.11	142.12	157.76	233.09	194.55	494.36
Percent of sample correctly identified	99.0	98.8	96.4	98.6	98.8	97.4	92.5

Source: Based on Giles (1970).

lated differences between females and males in cranial, mandibular, and especially pelvic (including sacral) morphology. In the skull and mandible, for instance (see Figures 9–9 to 9–12), the female is supposed to have a more vertical frontal bone, higher and more rounded orbits lacking attendant supraorbital or glabellar thickening or distension, thinner zygomatic arches, a more obtuse goneal (mandibular) angle, and a less pronounced mental trigon (see Table 9–6). Because females may bear children, features of the articulated pelvis and its separate elements are supposed to reflect this aspect of reproduction. As such, the female pelvis (including sacrum) is thought of as being broader; having a more vacuous pelvic inlet with less protrusion into its realm of, for instance, the ischial spine and distal sacrum and coccyx; having an obtuse subpubic angle; and having relatively longer pubic bones, deeper and more laterally flared ilia, and more obtuse and open greater sciatic notches (see Figures 9–13 and 9–14 and Table 9–7).

Inasmuch as these generalizations of female/male differences are based largely on European material, it is not surprising that they do not hold up uniformly across all groups of humans, present and past. The sex or degree of sexualization (Acsádi and Nemeskéri, 1970) of an individual is therefore often determined as an average of features coded as female, male, or indeterminate. In order to try to take into con-

sideration different factors that could produce female versus male features, Acsádi and Nemeskéri (1970) introduced a weighted scheme of sex determination. Here, features are scored +2 = hypermasculine, +1 = masculine, 0 = indeterminate, -1 = feminine, -2 = hyperfeminine. (There are stereotypes, imaginary or real, of what constitutes "hyper" versus "regular" versus "who knows?" However, it is perhaps more meaningful to try to determine these relative states of sexualization for each sample studied.) Some features are weighted twice as heavily as others (see Tables 9–6 and 9–7 for details of features). Characters that Acsádi and Nemeskéri (1970; p. 89) weight more heavily ($w = 2$) include the relative states of development of: glabella, supraorbital region, mastoid process, external occipital protuberance, orbital shape, supraorbital margin, mental trigon, subpubic angle, greater sciatic notch, ischiopubic index, and diameter of femoral head. Other features ($w = 1$) include the frontal and parietal eminences, nuchal region, zygomatic arch, malar surface, body of mandible, goneal (mandibular) angle, mandibular head, articulated pelvis os coxa, sacrum, linea aspera, obturator foramen, and cranial bone thickness. Degree of sexualization is calculated using the formula:

$$M = \frac{\Sigma wx}{\Sigma w}$$

Table 9-5 The Postcranium: Determining Sex via Discriminant Function Analysis of Measurements

Measurement	Based on American Whites				Based on African Americans				Based on Japanese			
	Function				Function				Function			
	1 (Right)	2 (Left)	3	4	5	6	7	8	9 (Right)	10 (Left)	11 (Right)	12 (Left)
Femur: physiological length	1.000	1.000			0.070	1.000	1.000	1.980			1.000	1.000
Femoral head: maximum diameter	30.234	30.716			58.140	31.400	16.530				9.854	9.351
Femur: least transverse diameter	−3.535	−12.643									11.988	8.369
Femur: max. bicondylar breadth	20.004	17.565									4.127	3.575
Ischial length				0.607	16.250	11.120	6.100	1.000				
Pubic length				−0.054	−63.640	−34.470	−13.800	−1.390				
Sciatic notch width			−0.115	−0.099								
Acetabulosciatic breadth			−0.182	−0.134								
Acetabulum-innominate line length			0.828	0.451	16.090							
Anterior iliac spine-auricular surface			0.517	0.325								
Humerus: maximum length					2.680	2.450			1.000	1.000		
Humerus: biepicondylar width					27.680	16.240			8.726	6.198		
Clavicle: maximum length												
Humerus: midshaft circumference									7.394	3.221		
Sectioning point (> = male)	3040.32	2656.51	9.20	7.00	4099.00	1953.00	665.00	68.00	3040.32	2656.51	9.20	7.00
Percent of sample correctly identified	94.4	94.3	93.1	96.5	98.5	97.5	96.9	93.5	94.4	94.3	93.1	96.5

Measurement	Based on Japanese Function		Based on Japanese Function		Based on Japanese Function		Based on Japanese Function		Based on Japanese Function			
	13 (Right)	14 (Left)	15 (Right)	16 (Left)	17 (Right)	18 (Left)	19 (Right)	20 (Right)	21 (Right)	22 (Left)	23 (Left)	24 (Left)
Radius: maximum length	1.000	1.000										
Radius: midshaft circumference	1.917	1.273										
Radius: head circumference	2.991	3.163										
Radius: maximum distal breadth	9.126	7.711										
Ulna: maximum length			1.000	1.000								
Ulna: transverse shaft diameter			8.068	6.501								
Ulna: maximum capitulum diameter			5.551	2.881								
Tibia: length					1.000	1.000						
Tibia: maximum midshaft A-P diameter					4.264	2.954						
Tibia: minimum shaft circumference					7.544	5.605						
Tibia: distal epiphyseal breadth					12.213	10.212						
Scapular height							1.000	1.000	1.000	1.000	1.000	1.000
Scapular spine: length							6.335	1.899		1.929	1.846	
Scapula: length of glenoid cavity							12.664	11.922	10.940	6.949	7.107	6.800
Scapula: breadth of glenoid cavity							10.991			2.120		
Scapular breadth									1.350			1.494
Sectioning point (> = male)	763.92	696.97	441.54	370.25	1802.10	1494.54	1660.16	782.10	634.75	669.79	611.03	508.35
Percent of sample correctly identified	96.7	97.0	88.9	90.5	95.7	95.3	96.8	96.0	95.6	94.8	94.7	94.1

Source: Based on Giles (1970).

Table 9–6   Features of the Skull and Mandible That May Differ between Females and Males (Based on the Stereotype)

Feature	Female	Male
Overall	Anatomical details, muscle marking, and lines less marked and smoother; bone thinner	Details more marked; bone thicker
Skull	More gracile and rounded, smaller, lighter (avg. 595 g)	Frontal more sloping, larger, heavier (avg. 795 g)
Frontal eminences	Moderate to marked; raised to rounded	Weak to undistinguished; low to absent
Parietal eminences	Moderate to marked; rounded to pointed	Weak to undistinguished; low to absent
Facial skeleton	Narrower, smaller	Especially zygoma, more rugose and massive; broader
Zygoma	Surface low, smaller, more arced, contours less defined	Surface higher and thicker; tubercle and marginal process marked
Zygomatic arch	Typically thin, moderate; weakly scarred inferiorly	Heavy, thick; muscle scarred inferiorly
Supraciliary arch	Trace to moderate	Moderate to extraordinary (toral)
Glabellar region	Flat to moderately swollen	Moderate to prominent swelling
Orbits	Large relative to face; rounded to circular; sit high on face; sharp, thin superior edge	Smaller relative to face; square to rectangular; sit low on face; blunt, thick superior edge
Nasal margin	Less clearly delineated	More crisply demarcated
Nasal bones	Relatively smaller; less protrusive	Relatively larger; more protrusive
Anerior nasal spine	Smaller, thinner	Larger, bulkier
Alveolar margin (facial aspect)	Impressions of roots faint	Impressions of roots more marked
Palate	Shorter, rounder, flatter	Broader, longer, more vaulted
Cranial base	Flatter, less marked	More rounded, marked
Occipital bone (squamous part)	Smooth to traces of nuchal lines	Marked to roughened nuchal lines and occipital crest
Mastoid process	Generally narrower, pointier; (low/narrow to high/pointed)	Generally more massive, broader, stubbier; (high/massive to broad/stubby/low)
External occipital protuberance	Smooth to weak	Marked to massive (studlike)
Mandible	Short, narrow, low, gracile, lightweight	Long, broad, high, robust, heavy
Mandibular (goneal) angle	Obtuse ($>125°$), rounded	More acute ($<125°$), rectangular
Goneal region	Surface smoother	Edge and surface of masseteric tuberosity more marked
Mental trigon	Rounded, smooth to somewhat delineated	Pronounced protuberances; protruding triangle or inverted "T"
Depth between incisors and mental trigon	Relatively short	Relatively long
Mandibular condyle	Smaller	Larger

Table 9–7 Features of the Articulated Pelvis, Os Coxa, and Sacrum That May Differ between Females and Males (Based on the Stereotype)

Feature	Female	Male
Complete pelvis	More lightly built; less muscle scarring	More robust with more muscle scarring
Pelvic aperture	Broader, more "lima bean"- to ellipse-shaped	Narrower, more "heart-shaped"
Subpubic angle	More obtuse (80–85°), rounded, more "U" shaped	More acute (50–60°), narrow, more "V" shaped
Ischiopubic ramus	More gracile; tapers toward pubic symphysis; roughened; edge everted	Deeper; flatter anterior surface
Sacrum (shape)	Broad, triangle (broader superiorly more severe taper inferiorly); appears shorter	Narrow triangle (narrower superiorly, long taper inferiorly); appears more elongate
Sacrum (curvature)	Less pronounced and intrusive into pelvic aperture	More pronounced and intrusive into aperture
Lumbosacral articular facet	<⅓ of superior width; alae appear relatively large	>⅓ of superior width; alae appear relatively small
Sacroiliac articulation (auricular facet)	Extends to second segment	Extends to third segment
Ilium (blade)	More flared laterally; wide; low	More vertical; higher; narrower
Ilium (crest)	Less rugose; less sinuous path; anteriorly curve medially directed	More rugose, more pronounced outer lip, more sinuouis path
Iliac auricular surface	Raised, narrow	Depressed, wide
Preauricular sulcus	Wider, deeper and shallow	Absent or more narrow
Postauricular area	Thin, smooth	Thick, rough
Postauricular center	Delineated (e.g. knob, bar)	Undistinguished, thick, rough
Postauricular groove	Common	Rare
Postauricular space	Wide, "loose"	Narrow, tight
Greater sciatic notch	"U" shaped, broader, shallower, more open, more obtuse angle	"V" shaped, narrower, deeper, more closed, more acute angle
Ischial spines	Shorter; less intrusive into pelvic aperture	More prominent and intrusive into pelvic aperture
Acetabulum	Smaller; oriented anterolaterally; diameter < distance from anterior edge to pubic symphysis	Larger; laterally oriented; diameter = approx. distance from anterior edge to symphysis
Obturator foramen	Edges sharp; triangular; low; wide	Blunter edges; longer vertical axis; oval
Pubic tubercle	Blunter; thicker; farther from pubic symphysis	Pointier; closer to symphysis

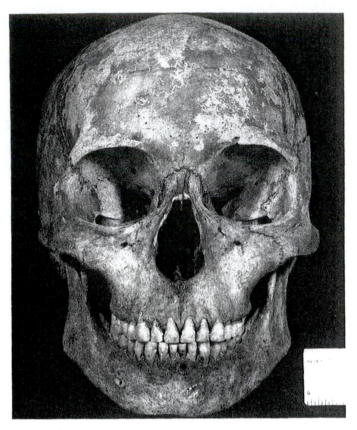

Figure 9–9   Skull exhibiting "mostly female" features (see text for discussion); also note apical abscess below left I_1 (prehistoric, Alaska).

where M = the mean value of the degree of sexualization, x = the score given a feature, and w = the weight of that feature.

Interestingly, as far as archeologically and often forensically derived skeletal material is concerned, the only features of sexual dimorphism noted for the adult skeleton that appear to distinguish female from male neonates and children include degree of protrusion of the mental trigon, greater sciatic notch angle, and degree of sigmoidal curvature of the iliac crest (Schutkowksi, 1993; see Table 9–7). [Of these, the only feature that appears to be distinctive of our own species, among those species allocated to the genus *Homo,* is the development of a chin (cf. Stringer et al., 1984).] Thus it is not surprising that an Indo-European standard for distinguishing females from males would not necessarily be applicable across all groups of humans.

Nonmetric Variation, Sexual Dimorphism, and Populations

The expression of nonmetrically variable traits has been linked to sex, size, and developmental differences between individuals. The situation is complicated further by the fact that, in some instances, sex and size may be correlated, as indeed size and robustness often are. For example, with males being on average (even slightly) larger and more robust skeletally than females, males might be expected to exhibit higher frequencies of hyperostotic traits. Females, on the other hand, might be expected to exhibit hypostotic variants. A realization of this generalization is dependent on the degree to which sex and skeletal robustness are really correlated within a given population.

Ultimately, however, all so-called nonmetric features represent differentially expressed as-

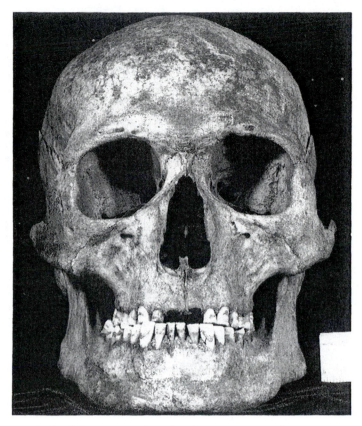

Figure 9–10 Skull exhibiting "mostly male" features (see text for discussion); also note varying degrees of calculus buildup on teeth (prehistoric, Alaska).

pects of an individual's skeletal and dental morphology—regardless of whether these features are significant at the level of the species, a population within a species, a sex within a population, or a specific individual. In some cases, it may not even be possible to determine (or at least hypothesize) anything significant about a "variant" feature: it is just there; it is noise. Not every feature is significant, nor is every feature significant at the same level—for example, species, population, or subset of population.

Perhaps we have been guided too long by the history of a discipline in which, for example, comparative anatomists and phrenologists sought to find in teeth and bone features that might be correlated with external differences between the sexes or "races." But in reality, it is still a matter of debate just how many of the features that have been catalogued over the decades as being distinctive of one "race" or population or one or the other sex really are distinctive and not merely descriptive. All too often, our analyses are formulated and channeled by our inherited history, received wisdom, and expectations. We bring into our supposedly objective analysis a partially answered question. We might not think that this is the case. But even just knowing where a particular skeleton or skeletal population came from—temporally and/or geographically—or with what external trappings it may have been associated (e.g. burial goods, grave construction, type of house), or just calling a collection of skeletons representatives of a population, can provide an unconscious bias: certain people are supposed to be characterized by certain features or traits, or at least by different frequencies of different traits.

If, however, an osteologist were presented with a skeletal collection of unknown origin

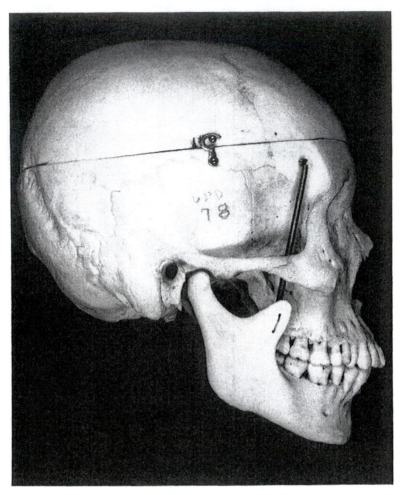

Figure 9–11   Skull exhibiting "mostly female" features (see text for discussion); also note linear enamel hypoplasia (especially visible on lower teeth) (provenience unknown, University of Pittsburgh Dental School collection).

(and, thus, of unknown "racial" and sexual composition), she or he would have to start from scratch. Is this collection a collection of individuals from the same species? (This might appear to be an unnecessary question, but it is one that has to be broached, even if unconsciously.) If so, are all individuals from the same population? And are differences between females and males discernible?

In order to deal with this nested set of questions, the osteologist must first sort out the differential representation of morphological character states in the sample: Which features are shared by all individuals? Which by only some individuals? Then would come the task of trying to determine whether any features were truly distinctive of a group or subgroups and, if so, whether within this or these hypothesized groups there were character states that could be attributed to sexual dimorphism.

By "features that might be distinctive of a group," I do not mean "features that are merely descriptive of a group" or "features other than those potentially due to sexual dimorphism that are expressed only in some individuals of a group." The former—"features that are merely descriptive of a group"—if typical of *Homo sapiens* (such as the development of a chin), could not be distinctive of any subset of *Homo sapiens*. The latter—"features other than those potentially due to sexual dimorphism that are expressed only in some individuals of a group"—

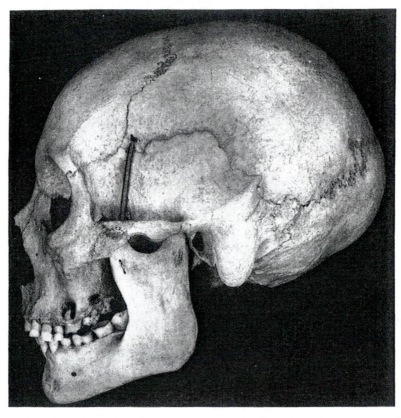

Figure 9–12 Skull exhibiting "mostly male" features (see text for discussion); also note severe dental attrition, alveolar remodeling, and apical abscesses in upper jaw (provenience unknown, University of Pittsburgh Dental School collection).

would not be distinctive of any subset of *Homo sapiens* precisely because they are not present in all individuals. Furthermore, because these latter features would not be present in all members of a group, and therefore would not be distinctive of that group, their frequencies could not be determined until a group had been defined (on the basis of other characters or attributes, whether biological, cultural, linguistic, or material). In practice, therefore, a population is presumed on nonmorphological criteria and then supposedly defined on the basis of the relative frequencies or expressions of certain morphological traits—morphological traits which, in turn, have already been decided as being reflective of populational differences.

But this is circular. How can one know beforehand what features will be distinctive of any group? Furthermore, how can one claim to have delineated a group if, for example, only 80 percent of its presumed members have a certain

feature? This question applies to members of any group, whether the group is a population or one of the sexes.

That so-called racial features fall under the aegis of nonmetric variation is self-evident. Referring to these features as population markers, or by some similar phrase, does not alter the possibility that subsets of *Homo sapiens,* may, indeed, have been and/or are distinguishable from one another by certain traits unique to each. If we were discussing the systematics of some nonhuman animal—the Malagasy primate *Lemur (Prosimia) fulvus,* for instance— we would not be constrained by social or political overtones were we to find (as is the case) that subspecies could be distinguished on the basis of very discrete, unique morphologies (Tattersall and Schwartz, 1991).

Problems arise in discussing the delineation of subsets of *Homo sapiens,* in part because of the potential racist implications and in part be-

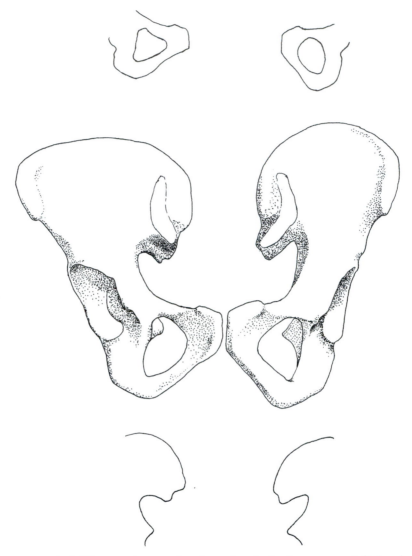

Figure 9-13 Stereotypical differences between females and males in the os coxa; *(left)* female, *(right)* male; *(top)* note especially differences in shape of obturator foramen; *(middle)* note, for example, differences in iliac shape and orientation, expression of preauricular sulcus, relative pubic length, orientation and relative size of acetabulum, location and configuration of pubic tubercle, and subpubic angle; *(bottom)* note especially differences in angle of greater sciatic notch and ischial spine. See Table 9-7 for further details.

cause of the history behind the study of "races." In the course of forensic investigations involving personal identifications, "racial identity" becomes a matter of legal importance—which, then, gives a certain (although perhaps unreasonable) credibility to the assumption that skeletally expressed "racial" or populational differences will coincide with our individual and personal visual perceptions of how "we" differ

from other humans and how "they" differ from "us."

Stereotypes of different groups of humans give the appearance of portraying significant distinguishing features. For example, Eskimos have been characterized as having narrow and unprojecting nasal bridges as well as flat, vertical, and very broad faces, while native Africans are seen as having wide and moderately

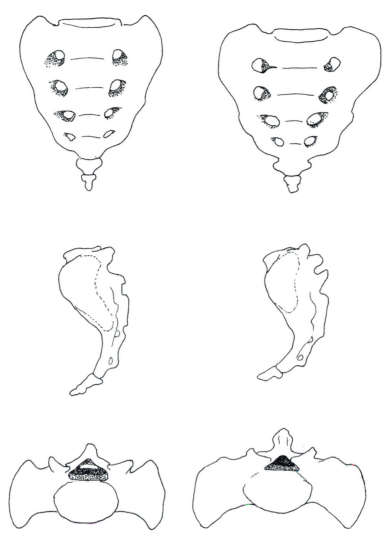

Figure 9–14   Stereotypical differences between females *(right column)* and males *(left column)* in the sacrum (e.g. overall shape, degree of curvature, extent of auricular surface, relative size of alae); see Table 9–7 for details.

projecting nasal bridges as well as slender, narrow faces with rounded foreheads and alveolar prognathism (e.g. see review by St. Hoyme and İşcan, 1989; also Table 9–8). But the broader comparison reveals, for example, that Eskimos and other Native Americans as well as Europeans develop narrow nasal bridges, and that southern Asians and Melanesians as well as Africans possess narrow faces (Table 9–8). Clearly, nasal bridge width and facial width, respectively, define by uniqueness neither an Eskimo nor an African. In addition, it would re-

quire broader comparisons among hominids, and, preferably, among hominoids, to provide the perspective necessary to judge whether the feature of "narrow nasal bridge" described for Eskimos, Native Americans, and Europeans would uniquely characterize them as a group among *Homo sapiens*, or if "narrow face" delineates Africans, southern Asians, and Melanesians as a potential group within the species.

The question that must be raised about research into the delineation of subsets of *Homo sapiens* is: "What is the purpose of such an in-

Table 9–8 Distribution of Cranial Features among Various Humans

Population	Nasal Bones	Nasal Bridge (W)	Nasal Bridge (Proj)	Prognathism	Subnasal Margin	Anterior Nasal Spine	Nasal Aperture (H/W)	Zygoma (W/ Shape)	Bizygomatic/ Bifrontal W	Chin
S. Pacific	reduced			alveolar/ dental	deep pits					rounded
Eskimo	narrow	least		face vert/ very flat	?distinct	prominent	high/average	br/lg malar tubercle	greatest/widest face	?projecting
Amerindian	narrow	?least		face vertical	?distinct	prominent	?high/average	br/lg malar tubercle	≤greatest	?projecting
European	narrow	greatest		upper face/ mid-face	distinct	prominent	high/average	slender/ triangular	medium	projecting
African	wide/flat	medium		alveolar/ dental	dep/smooth/ round	short/blunt	low/average	slender/ triangular	smallest	intermediate
Melanesian	wide/flat	?least		?face vertical	?distinct	?prominent	low/average	br/lg malar tubercle	smallest	rounded
Asia: North		least		face vertical	distinct	prominent	high/average	br/lg malar tubercle	smallest	projecting
Asia: South		least		face vertical	distinct	prominent	low/average	br/lg malar tubercle	≤indistinct	rounded

Source: Based on St. Hoyme and Iscan (1989). Abbreviations: W = width; Proj = projection; H = height; dep = depressed; br = broad; lg = large.

288

quiry?" Surely, if one is attempting to deal with questions regarding the issue of "the peopling of the New World" or "the origin of modern human populational diversity," one is dealing with a phylogenetic and systematic problem—albeit one that is below the species level—that should be dealt with in the same way and with the same rigor and objectivity as one would approach the phylogeny and systematics of, for example, a group of potentially related species.

Consider, for the moment, the often-cited trait category of "number of cusps on the first lower molar." Some apparently "natural" groups of humans have been characterized as having five cusps and other groups as having four cusps on the first lower molar (e.g. Turner, 1984). And indeed, these characterizations may be descriptively accurate. However, are these features really of equal significance in delineating each group uniquely? A cursory survey of fossil hominids and extant and fossil apes reveals that the common condition among hominoids is represented by the development of five cusps on the first lower molar. Thus, while it is true that some human groups possess five-cusped first lower molars, this particular feature is not unique to any group. In contrast, it is among that subset of *Homo sapiens* with four-cusped first lower molars that we find the distinctive—and potentially systematically significant—variant (or character state) of the category "first lower molar cusp number."

A similar questioning is warranted of the widespread claim that Native Americans are derived from an Asian group by virtue of their having in common shovel-shaped upper incisors (e.g. Carbonell, 1963). While it is true that one finds a relatively high frequency of shovel-shaped upper incisors in Asians and Native Americans, Africans and Indians have relatively high frequencies of this feature as well (e.g. see Figure 9–15). European upper incisors, on the other hand, are relatively shovel-free (cf. Carbonell, 1963; Schwartz, unpublished data; Scott, 1972). More broadly, the upper incisors of most fossil hominids are shoveled, as are the upper incisors of chimpanzees and orangutans. Thus, it would seem that the presence of shovel-shaped upper incisors among hominids, at least, is rather ubiquitous and not necessarily distinctive of any subset of *Homo sapiens*. To the contrary, it seems that the lack of shoveled upper incisors (as is characteristic of Europeans) represents the potentially significant character state.

On a broader level of inquiry, any feature of bone or tooth can be of potential significance in delineating a subset or group of *Homo sapiens*. But the degree of inclusiveness of that group—from the smallest possible subset to a group comprising many small groups defined on the basis of other features unique to them—will depend on the degree to which the potentially significant variant is distributed within the species.

Rather than reiterating or seeking additional features to corroborate established stereotypes, it might be more productive to approach the topic of human populational diversity in a different way. That is, instead of first deciding what the groups are—on the basis, for example, of biogeography or linguistic or cultural attributes or such "morphological" features as "skin color"—and then trying to find skeletal morphologies that appear to distinguish some individuals of one "group" from some individuals of another, it might be of interest to analyze an array of different morphologies whose relatively unique distributions within the species might suggest a nested hierarchy of potential groupings. Ultimately, uniquenesses will be recognized that distinguish the smallest subsets (whatever or no matter how inclusive they are) from one another. If the investigator chooses to identify these distinctive features as features of "race" or "population," that is the prerogative of the investigator. In the end, some "groups" might conform to "expectation," but other emergent groupings might be totally unexpected. At the level of inquiry into the potential subspecific systematics of our own species, however, the issue is—or should be—devoid of negative connotations.

The same theoretical and practical concerns should be brought to bear on the determination of sex of an individual from osteological remains. For although stereotypes of skeletally expressed traits of "maleness" and "femaleness" abound in the literature, operationally the determination of an individual's sex is achieved as an average or a weighted average of the total number of traits over the range of their degree of development (see above). In some groups (e.g. among northern Asian and Arctic Native American groups), females exhibit more fea-

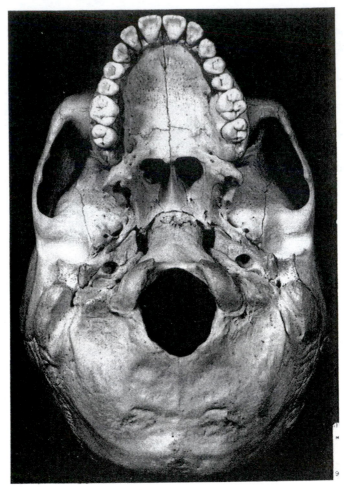

Figure 9–15 Example of shovel-shaped upper incisors; also note, for example, lack of definitive hypocones on both M2s, shape of palate, arc of zygomatic arch, bilateral expression of foramen of Vesalius, bridging of right foramen ovale, size of foramen lacerum, patent right and occluded left posterior condyloid canals; M3s are still unerupted and the spheno-occipital synchondrosis is not fully closed (recent, India).

tures of "maleness" (e.g. supraorbital, glabellar, zygomatic, and mandibular thickening or distension) than would be expected given the Indo-European standard of comparison. [St. Hoyme and İşcan (1989) give other examples of the problem of separating the analysis of sexual dimorphism from that of populational differences (e.g. chin shape).] Obviously, in such cases the total number of sexually diagnostic or revealing features would be diminished noticeably. On the other hand, a few pelvic and mandibular features attributable to sexual dimorphism appear reliable in distinguishing females from males in any population of *Homo sapiens*.

Although the obscuring of cranial clues to the sexual identity of females in such populations as Arctic Native Americans may be viewed as a hindrance to the analysis—when the goal of the analysis is to discriminate females from males—what this actually reflects is that certain nonmetric traits are expressed more equally in both sexes of some populations than they are in females and males of other groups. Since all potentially sexually dimorphic traits will not be expressed similarly—with equal intensity, clarity, or frequency—among different populations, it might be more profitable to deal with the determination of sex as a subset of the overall study of the differential expression of skeletal features (i.e. of nonmetric variation). Thus if skewed representations of certain morphologies do indeed reflect populational differences within our species, then sexual differences within each population (each population being defined by its own uniqueness or set of uniquenesses) would be delineated by other sets of morphologies. It is the responsibility of the investigator to approach each sample without preconceptions about what she or he will delineate as being diagnostic at either the populational or sexually dimorphic level of the analysis.

Recording nonmetric traits for their own sake or only within the confines of a site report does not go beyond the level of isolated description. Description is only the beginning of a meaningful analysis of nonmetric variation.

Bone Synonymy

Bone	Latin Name (Nomina Anatomica)	Synonyms
Calcaneus	calcaneus	calcaneal bone, calcaneum, heel bone, os calcis, os tarsi
	fibulare	
Capitate	os capitatum	os magnum
Clavicle	clavicula	collarbone
Coccyx	os coccygis	tailbone
Coxa	os coxae	coxal bone, os pelvicum, innominate, os innominatum, hipbone, pelvic bone
Cuboid	os cuboideum	os tarsale distale quartum
Cuneiform, medial	os cuneiforme mediale	os cuneiforme primum, first cuneiform, os tarsale distale primum
Cuneiform, intermediate	os cuneiforme intermedium	os cuneiforme secundum, mesocuneiform, middle cuneiform, second cuneiform, os tarsale distale secundum
Cuneiform, lateral	os cuneiforme laterale	os cuneiforme tertium, third cuneiform, os tarsale distale tertium
Ethmoid	os ethmoidale	
Femur	femur	thighbone, femoral bone, os femorale, os femoris
Fibula	fibula	splint bone
Frontal	os frontale	
Hamate	os hamatum	unciform, cuneiform
Humerus	humerus	(upper) arm bone
Hyoid	os hyoideum	
Incus	incus	anvil, ambos
Inferior nasal concha	concha nasalis inferior	inferior spongy bone, inferior turbinate, maxilloturbinal
Lacrimal	os lacrimale	os unguis
Lunate	os lunatum	lunare, os intermedium, semilunar bone
Malleus	malleus	hammer

Bone	Latin Name (Nomina Anatomica)	Synonyms
Mandible	mandibula	mandibulum, jawbone, lower jaw, submaxilla, inferior maxilla
Manual phalanges	ossa digitorum manus	phalanges digitorum manus, phalanges of fingers
Maxilla	maxilla	upper jawbone
Metacarpals	ossa metacarpi	ossa metacarpalia
Metatarsals	ossa metatarsi	ossa metatarsalia
Nasal	os nasale	
Navicular	os naviculare	os naviculare pedis, os centrale tarsi
Occipital	os occipitale	
Palatine	os palatinum	
Parietal	os parietale	
Pedal phalanges	ossa digitorum pedis	phalanges digitorum pedis, phalanges of toes
Pisiform	os pisiforme	subrotundum, obiculare, lentiform bone
Radius	radius	(lower) arm bone
Rib	os costale	costa, os costae
Sacrum	os sacrum	os sacrale, vertebra magna, sacred bone
Scaphoid	os scaphoideum	os naviculare manus, navicular, cotyloid, os radiale
Scapula	scapula	shoulder blade, blade bone
Sphenoid	os sphenoidale	
Stapes	stapes	stirrup
Sternum	sternum	breastbone
Talus	talus	ankle, astragalus, astragaloid bone, os tarsi tibiale, os tarsi tibialis
Temporal	os temporale	
Tibia	tibia	shinbone, shank bone
Trapezium	os trapezium	greater multangular bone, os multangulum majus, rhomboides
Trapezoid	os trapezoideum	lesser multangular bone, os multangulum minus, pyramidale
Triquetrum	os triquetrum	triquetral, triangular bone, os triangulare, cuboid, cubital bone, cuneiform bone, os pyramidale, pyramidal bone
Ulna	ulna	elbow bone
Vertebrae, cervical	vertebrae cervicales	
Vertebrae, thoracic	vertebrae thoracicae	vertebrae thoracales
Vertebrae, lumbar	vertebrae lumbales	
Vomer	vomer	
Zygomaticos	zygomaticum	cheekbone, yoke bone, jugal bone, malar bone, os malare, os mala, zygoma, os zygoma

Regions and Bones of the Adult Skeleton

Region	Bone Singular	Bone Plural	Number[a]
I. Axial Skeleton			(80)
A. Skull			(28)
1. Braincase			(8)
	frontal	frontals	1 (2 fused halves)
	parietal	parietals	2
	occipital	occipitals	1
	temporal	temporals	2
	sphenoid	sphenoids	1
	ethmoid	ethmoids	1
2. Face			(14)
	zygomatic	zygomatics	2
	maxilla	maxillae	2
	nasal	nasals	2
	lacrimal	lacrimals	2
	vomer	vomers·	1 (2 fused halves)
	palatine	palatines	2
	inferior concha	inferior conchae	2
	mandible	mandibles	1 (2 fused halves)
3. Auditory ossicles			(6)
	malleus	mallei	2
	incus	incudes	2
	stapes	stapedes	2
B. Throat			(1)
	hyoid	hyoids	1
C. Vertebral column			(26)
	cervical vertebra	cervical vertebrae	7
	thoracic vertebra	thoracic vertebrae	12
	lumbar vertebra	lumbar vertebrae	5
	sacrum	sacra	1 (5 fused elements)
	coccyx	coccyges	1 (4 fused elements)
D. Thorax			(25)
	sternum	sterna	1 (3 fused elements)
	rib	ribs	24

Region	Bone		Number[a]
	Singular	Plural	
II. Appendicular skeleton			(126)
A. Upper extremity or limb			(64)
1. Pectoral girdle			(4)
	clavicle	clavicles	2
	scapula	scapulae	2
2. Arm (brachium)			(2)
	humerus	humeri	2
3. Forearm (antebrachium)			(4)
	ulna	ulnae	2
	radius	radii	2
4. Hand (manus)			(54)
a. Wrist (carpus)			(16)
	scaphoid	scaphoids	2
	lunate	lunates	2
	triquetrum	triquetrums	2
	pisiform	pisiforms	2
	trapezium	trapeziums	2
	trapezoid	trapezoids	2
	capitate	capitates	2
	hamate	hamates	2
b. Metacarpus			(10)
	metacarpal	metacarpals	10
c. Manual digits (digitorum manus)			(28)
	proximal phalanx	proximal phalanges	10
	middle phalanx	middle phalanges	8
	terminal phalanx	terminal phalanges	10
B. Lower extremity or limb			(62)
1. Pelvic girdle			(2)
	coxa	coxae	2 (3 fused elements)
2. Thigh			(2)
	femur	femora	2
3. Knee (genu)			(2)
	patella	patellae	2
4. Leg (crus)			(4)
	tibia	tibae	2
	fibula	fibulae	2
5. Foot (pes)			(52)
a. Ankle (tarsus)			(14)
	talus	tali	2
	calcaneus	calcanei	2
	navicular	naviculars	2
	cuboid	cuboids	2

(continued)

| Region | Bone | | Number[a] |
	Singular	Plural	
	medial cuneiform	medial cuneiforms	2
	intermediate cuneiform	intermediate cuneiforms	2
	lateral cuneiform	lateral cuneiforms	2
b. Metatarsus			(10)
	metatarsal	metatarsals	10
c. Pedal digits (digitorum pedis)			(28)
	proximal phalanx	proximal phalanges	10
	middle phalanx	middle phalanges	8
	terminal phalanx	terminal phalanges	10
Total number of bones			**206**

[a]Numbers in boldface refer to the number of each bone normally present in the human adult, not to the number of centers of ossification or elements that may eventually contribute to the formation of a particular bone. The latter is provided in the text. A number in parentheses corresponds to the total number of individual bones in a particular skeletal region or subregion.

Glossary of Terms of Position, Orientation, and Movement

Directions and Positions

ANTERIOR (also *frontal*, and *ventral*): Toward the front; opposite of **posterior**.

APICAL: Pertaining to (1) the apex or highest part of a structure (opposite of **basilar**), or (2) (dental) the tip of a tooth's root (opposite of **occlusal**).

BASILAR: Pertaining to the base or lowest part of a structure; opposite of **apical**.

BUCCAL: (Teeth) Toward the cheek [also *labial* (toward the lips)]; opposite of **lingual**.

CONTRALATERAL: Refers to a structure, feature (even motion), etc., on the side of the body opposite that on which a structure, etc., of interest occurs; opposite of **ipsilateral**.

DISTAL: 1. (Limbs) Away from the trunk; opposite of **proximal**. 2. (Teeth) Away from the median plane of the dental arcade; opposite of **mesial**.

DORSAL (see also *posterior*): Pertaining to (1) the back (i.e. posterior surface) of the hand, or (2) the superior surface of the foot; opposite, respectively, of **palmar** and **plantar**.

EXTERNAL (also *exterior*, but sometimes incorrectly referred to as *lateral*): Toward the outside; opposite of **internal**.

INFERIOR [also *caudal* (toward the tail)]: Toward the feet; opposite of **superior**.

INTERNAL (also *interior*, but sometimes incorrectly referred to as *medial*): Toward the inside; opposite of **external**.

INTERSTITIAL (also *interproximal*): (Teeth) The surface of a tooth that abuts an adjacent tooth in its tooth row.

IPSILATERAL: Referring to a structure, feature (even motion), etc., occurring on the same side of the body as the structure, etc., of interest; opposite of **contralateral**.

LATERAL: Away from the median plane; opposite of **medial**.

LINGUAL [also *palatal* (toward to the palate)]: (Dental) Toward the tongue; opposite of **buccal**.

MEDIAL: Toward the median plane; opposite of **lateral**.

MESIAL: (Dental) Toward the median plane of the dental arcade; opposite of **distal**.

OCCLUSAL: (Dental) Toward the chewing surface of the tooth; opposite of **apical**.

PALMAR (also *volar*): The anterior surface or palm of the hand; opposite of **dorsal**.

PLANTAR (also *volar*): The inferior surface or sole of the foot; opposite of **dorsal**.

POSTERIOR (also *dorsal*): Toward the back; opposite of **anterior**.

PROFUNDUS: Pertaining to a structure that is farther in from the surface of the body than than another structure; opposite of **superficial**.

PRONE: Facing downward; opposite of **supine**.

PROXIMAL: (Limbs) Toward the trunk; opposite of **distal**.

SUPERFICIAL: Referring to a structure that is closer to the surface of the body than another structure; opposite of **profundus**.

SUPERIOR (also *cephalic, cranial,* and *rostral*):
Toward the head; opposite of **inferior**.

SUPINE: Facing upward with the back down;
opposite of **prone**.

Planes

ANTEROPOSTERIOR (AP) PLANE: see **median
plane**.

CORONAL PLANE: A vertical plane that passes
through the body (or structure, e.g. skull)
from side to side (i.e. parallel to the coronal suture) and divides the body (or structure) into anterior and posterior portions.
It lies perpendicular to the **median plane**.

FRANKFORT HORIZONTAL (FH) PLANE
(also the *plane of Virchow*): A horizontal
plane on which the anthropometric landmarks called porion (i.e. the midpoint of
the superior margin of the external auditory meatus) and orbitale (i.e. the inferiormost point on the inferior margin of the
orbit) are positioned, thereby providing a
standard orientation of the skull for measuring, describing, and illustrating it.

FRONTAL PLANE: see **coronal plane**.

HORIZONTAL PLANE: see **transverse plane**.

MEDIAN (SAGITTAL) PLANE: A vertical plane
that passes through the midline of the
body, parallel to the sagittal suture, from
front to back and that divides it into symmetrical left and right halves. It lies perpendicular to the **coronal plane**.

MIDSAGITTAL PLANE: see **median plane**.

OBLIQUE PLANE: Any plane not parallel to the
coronal, median, or **transverse planes**.

PARAMEDIAN (OR PARASAGITTAL) PLANE:
Any vertical plane parallel to the **median
plane**.

SAGITTAL PLANE: see **paramedian plane**.

TRANSVERSE PLANE: A horizontal plane that
passes through the body (or structure) at
right angles to both the **median** and **coronal planes,** dividing it into superior and inferior portions and creating a cross section
of the body (or structure).

Movement

ABDUCTION: A laterally directed movement in
the coronal plane that goes away from the
median sagittal plane; opposite of **adduction**.

ADDUCTION: A medially directed movement
in the coronal plane that is goes toward the
median sagittal plane; opposite of **abduction**.

CIRCUMDUCTION: A circular movement created by the sequential combination of **abduction, flexion, adduction,** and **extension**.

DEPRESSION: An inferiorly or inwardly directed movement; opposite of **elevation**.

DORSIFLEXION[a]: A bending of the foot in the
direction of the dorsum such that the angle
between the dorsum of the foot and the
anterior surface of the leg is decreased (e.g.
as in squatting); opposite of **plantar flexion**.

ELEVATION: A superiorly or outwardly directed movement; opposite of **depression**.

EVERSION: A movement of the foot that causes
the plantar surface of the foot to face laterally; opposite of **inversion**.

EXTENSION: A movement in the sagittal plane
around a transverse axis that separates two
structures (e.g. as in straightening the leg
or arm); opposite of **flexion**.

FLEXION: A bending movement in the sagittal
plane and around a transverse axis that
draws two structures toward each other;
opposite of **extension**.

INFRADUCTION: A downward rotation of the
eye around its transverse axis; opposite of
supraduction.

INVERSION: A movement of the foot that
causes the plantar surface of the foot to
face medially; opposite of **eversion**.

OPPOSITION: A movement of the thumb
across the palm such that its distoanterior
surface or pad contacts the distoanterior
surface or pad of another digit. This move-

---

[a]Because of the orientation of the foot, the terms
"dorsiflexion" and "plantar flexion," rather than the
more general terms "extension" and "flexion" are
used. Developmentally defined postaxial muscles are
responsible for extension. On the adult leg, these
muscles face anteriorly because, during embryological development, the lower limb rotates medially.
Thus these muscles flex, or dorsiflex (i.e. they cause
a decrease in the angle between the foot and the leg,
as when squatting). "Plantar flexion" is synonymous
with "extension."

ment involves **abduction** with **flexion** and **medial rotation** at the carpometacarpal joint of the thumb.

PLANTAR FLEXION[a]: A bending of the foot in the direction of the plantar surface such that the dorsum of the foot comes to lie in the same plane as the anterior surface of the leg (e.g. as in standing on tiptoe); opposite of **dorsiflexion.**

PRONATION: A medial rotation of the forearm, causing the palm of the hand to face posteriorly and the radius to cross over the ulna: opposite of **supination.**

PROTRACTION (also *protrusion*): An anteriorly directed movement, usually used to describe the forward movement of the mandible at the temporomandibular joint; opposite of **retraction.**

RETRACTION: A posteriorly directed movement, usually used to describe the back-ward movement of the mandible at the temporomandibular joint; opposite of **protraction.**

ROTATION LATERAL: Movement of a structure around its longitudinal axis, causing its anterior surface to face laterally; opposite of **medial rotation.**

ROTATION MEDIAL: Movement of a structure around its longitudinal axis, causing its anterior surface to face medially; opposite of **lateral rotation.**

SUPINATION: A lateral rotation of the forearm that causes the palm of the hand to face anteriorly and the ulna and radius to lie parallel to one another; opposite of **pronation.**

SUPRADUCTION: An upward rotation of the eye around its transverse axis; opposite of **infraduction.**

Bone Topography and Landmarks

The topography, or surface contour, of a bone is highly irregular and often replete with a variety features and structures that are delineated by size and form. For example, a particular landmark might be large and linear (the linea aspera of the femur) or small and circular (the foramen rotundum of the sphenoid). In general, such features or structures are classified as either *elevations*, *depressions*, or *openings*.

Elevations are localized areas of bone that project or extend above the surrounding region. They are often roughened as a result of the attachment of tendons, aponeuroses, muscles, ligaments, and fasciae. The pull of these fibrous structures raises the periosteum, resulting in the deposition of new bone underneath it. Thus, while the overall shape of a bone is recognizable at or even well before birth, elevations do not usually begin to develop their characteristic morphology until puberty; they become increasingly roughened during adulthood. Since the size and robustness of these landmarks are reflective of the muscularity or specific muscular activities of an individual, study of their relative degrees of expression can yield clues as to aspects of the possible way of life or occupation of an individual (e.g. Kennedy, 1989).

Confined areas that are indented below adjacent surfaces of the bone are called *depressions*. Depressions may bear the imprint of or serve as receptacles for various soft tissue organs or portions of these organs. Depressions may also serve to increase the surface area available for the attachment of fibrous structures such as muscles and ligaments.

Openings are holes or passages in bone through which nerves, arteries, and veins may course. Some openings (e.g. the foramen lacerum) do not transmit any neurovascular structure.

The technical terminology used to identify elevations, depressions, and openings is based on the size and configuration of the feature. Although other descriptive terms (e.g. "orifice," "frenulum," "furrow") may also be found in the anatomical literature, those listed here are those that refer specifically to osteological features.

Elevations

APEX (also *tip*): The top of a pointed structure (e.g. of the patella, the head of the fibula, or the petrous portion of the temporal bone).

CONDYLE: A rounded, knucklelike projection often associated with articular eminences (e.g. the lateral and medial condyles of the femur, the left and right condyles of the mandible, and the occipital condyles).

CORNU (pl. *cornua*): A hornlike projection (e.g. the complementary, articulating cornua of the sacrum and coccyx or the greater and lesser horns of the hyoid bone).

CREST (also *crista, line,* or *ridge*): A raised, linear structure that surmounts the surface of a bone or forms its border, and which is typically more prominent than a ridge (e.g. the iliac crest of the ilium, the supinator crest of the ulna, and the intertrochanteric crest of the femur).

CRISTA (pl. *cristae*): Synonymous with "crest" but sometimes used interchangeably with "ridge" (e.g. the crista galli of the ethmoid bone).

EMINENCE: A variably swollen, projecting area of bone (e.g. the parietal eminence, the canine eminence of the maxilla, and the iliopubic eminence).

HAMULUS (pl. *hamuli*): A hooklike projection (e.g. the hamulus of the hamate or the lacrimal hamulus).

LINE: In general, the least marked of the linear elevations (e.g. the temporal line, the pectineal line of the pubis, and the soleal line of the tibia).

MALLEOLUS (pl. *malleoli*): A rounded projection. The only examples are the medial malleolus of the tibia and the lateral malleolus of the fibula.

PROCESS: A general term for a projection (e.g. the anterior clinoid process of the sphenoid, the frontal process of the maxilla, and the coracoid process of the scapula).

PROMINENCE: Another term for a projection (e.g. the styloid prominence at the base of the styloid process of the temporal bone and the mental prominence of the mandible).

PROMONTORY: Usually refers to a smooth elevation (e.g. the promontory of the sacrum).

PROTUBERANCE: A small to medium elevation that may be rounded and smooth (e.g. the internal occipital protuberance and the "hyperfeminine" expression of the external occipital protuberance) or distended and peaked (e.g. the "hypermasculine" expression of the external occipital protuberance).

RIDGE: A flaring linear elevation, intermediate in development between a line and a crest, which commonly results from the confluence of two adjacent surfaces (e.g. the lateral and medial supracondylar ridges of the humerus, the longitudinal ridge of the ischium, and the vertical ridge of the patella).

SPINE (also *spinous process*): A narrowly elongated projection that is typically broad at its base and blunter than a stylus (e.g. the anterior superior iliac spine, the ischial spine, and the anterior nasal spine of the maxilla).

STYLUS (also *styloid process*): A long, pointed projection (e.g. the styloid process of the temporal bone, the styloid process of the ulna, and the styloid process of the fibula).

TORUS (pl. *tori*): A swollen or bulging projection in the shape of a bar or strut (e.g. a supraorbital torus of the frontal bone, an occipital torus, a mandibular torus, and a palatine torus).

TROCHANTER: A expansive, roughened area of bone that is much larger than a *tuberosity*. The sole examples are the greater and lesser trochanters of the femur.

TUBERCLE: A small, variably rounded, roughened elevation that is smaller than a *tuberosity* (e.g. the infraglenoid tubercle of the scapula, the dorsal tubercle of the radius, and the pubic tubercle of the pubis).

TUBEROSITY: A medium-sized, variably rounded and roughened elevation that is often larger than a *tubercle* (e.g. the tibial tuberosity, the gluteal tuberosity of the femur, and the deltoid tuberosity of the humerus).

Depressions

ALVEOLUS (pl. *alveoli*): A small saclike dilatation or socket in which the root of a tooth is nestled.

CAVITY (also *fossa* and *sinus*): A hollow space or depression [e.g. the glenoid cavity (also fossa) of the scapula, the cranial cavity (composed of numerous bones), and the pulp cavity of teeth].

FISSURE: A cleft or slit (e.g. the superior and inferior orbital fissures, the petrotympanic fissure, and the pterygoid fissure).

FOSSA (pl. *fossae*) (also *cavity* and *sinus*): A general term for a hollowed out area (e.g. the mandibular fossa of the temporal bone, the acetabular fossa, and the coronoid fossa of the humerus).

FOVEA (pl. *foveae*): A small pit (e.g. the fovea capitis of the femur, the pterygoid fovea of the mandible, and the dental fovea of the atlas).

GROOVE: A trench or channel (e.g. the lacrimal groove, the groove on the clavicle for the subclavius muscle, and the intertubercular groove of the humerus).

INCISURA (pl. *incisurae*) (also *notch*): An indentation or notch on the edge of a bone [e.g. the costal incisurae of the sternum (costal notches), the incisura of the mandible (the mandibular notch), and the parietal incisura (notch) of the temporal bone].

NOTCH (also *incisura*): A cleft or indentation, particularly on the edge of a bone (e.g. the mastoid notch of the temporal bone, the trochlear notch of the ulna, and the greater sciatic notch of the ilium).

SINUS (pl. *sinuses*) (also *cavity*): A cavity or (less frequently) a channel [e.g. the (venous) sigmoid sinus of the temporal bone, the maxillary sinus, and the frontal sinus].

SULCUS (pl. *sulci*) (also *groove* or *sinus*): A trench or channel [e.g. the preauricular sulcus of the ilium (variably present), the calcaneal sulcus, and the costal sulcus (groove) of the ribs].

Openings

APERTURE: In general, a medium to large opening (e.g. the nasal aperture or a septal aperture in the humerus).

CANAL (also *duct*): A narrow tubular channel (e.g. the hypoglossal canal of the occipital bone, the semicircular canals of the bony labyrinth of the ear, and the haversian canals of compact bone).

DUCT (also *canal*): A tubelike passage [e.g. the frontonasal duct and the acoustic duct (the external auditory meatus)].

FENESTRA (pl. *fenestrae*): A windowlike opening; not present in the human skeleton, but most mammals develop anterior palatine fenestrae.

FORAMEN (pl. *foramina*): A circular to ovoid hole or opening through a bone (e.g. the infraorbital foramen of the maxilla, the foramen ovale of the sphenoid, and the foramen magnum of the occipital bone).

HIATUS (pl. *hiatus, hiatuses*): A gap or gashlike opening [e.g. the sacral hiatus, the maxillary hiatus, and the hiatus of the canal for the greater petrosal nerve (temporal bone)].

INFUNDIBULUM (pl. *infundibula*): A funnel-shaped passage. The sole example is the infundibulum of the ethmoid bone.

MEATUS (pl. *meatus, meatuses*): A passage or opening, especially the external opening of a duct or canal (e.g. the external and internal auditory meatus and the three nasal meatuses).

OSTIUM (pl. *ostia*): An opening into a tubular structure or between two distinct cavities (e.g. the sphenoidal ostium and the tympanic ostium of the auditory tube).

Identifying Fragments: Determining Anatomical Position and Side

There are normally 86 paired bones (11 cranial, 75 postcranial) in the adult human skeleton. Determining the "side" of the body to which a bone belongs is an important part of skeletal analysis and requires a working knowledge of the anatomical position of skeletal elements—that is, the spatial relationships of structures to one another. *Anatomical position* is defined as the position of the human body (or parts of the human body) when an individual is standing erect, with the arms at the side of the body and the palms of the hands turned forward. Terms of direction, location, and movement are predicated on the body or element being in the anatomical position. Paired bones of the axial skeleton possess six surfaces: medial, lateral, anterior, posterior, superior, and inferior. The terms "proximal" and "distal" are used instead of "superior" and "inferior," respectively, in referring to the appendicular long bones.

Reference to surface markings permits orientation of a bone in three-dimensional space and in the correct anatomical position. The "side" of a bone (i.e. the side of the the body from which the bone came) can often be determined by referring specifically to those markings on the lateral and medial surfaces. Laterally oriented features "point" to the side of the body from which the bone comes. Features on the medial side of a bone are directed away from the side of the body from which the bone comes. For example, if, after being oriented in the anatomical position, the head of the humerus (which faces medioposteriorly) lies toward the right and the greater tubercle (which lies laterally) is on the left, the bone must have come from the left side of the body.

Additional (parenthetical) notes are provided when further assistance in identification appears necessary. Notes appended to nutrient foramina refer to the orientation of each foramen as it courses from the outside of the bone to the inside.

Bone/Feature	Position of Feature
CRANIAL	
Parietal	
Parietal eminence	Lateral
Superior temporal line	Lateroinferior (external)
Inferior temporal line	Lateroinferior (external)
Frontal angle	Anterosuperior

(continued)

Bone/Feature	Position of Feature
Sagittal border	Superior
Occipital angle	Posterosuperior
Occipital border	Posterior
Mastoid angle	Posteroinferior
Temporal border	Inferior
Sphenoidal angle	Anteroinferior
Frontal border	Anterior
Sigmoid sinus	Posteroinferior (internal)
Grooves for middle meningeal vessels	Medial (internal; arborize superoposteriorly)

Temporal

Zygomatic process	Lateroanterior
Articular tubercle	Inferoanterior
Mandibular fossa	Inferolateral
Postglenoid tubercle	Inferolateral
Styloid process	Inferior
External acoustic meatus	Lateroinferior
Suprameatal triangle	Lateral
Groove for middle temporal artery	Lateral
Parietal border (beveled suture)	Superior
Parietal notch	Superoposterior
Mastoid process	Lateroposterior
Mastoid notch	Inferoposterior
Occipital groove	Posteroinferior
Stylomastoid foramen	Inferior
Carotid canal	Inferomedial
Sigmoid sinus	Medioposterior (internal)
Internal acoustic meatus	Medioinferior (internal)
Groove for middle meningeal vessel	Mediosuperior (internal)

Zygomatic

Frontal process	Superior
Temporal process	Posterolateral
Maxillary process	Anteromedial
Maxillary border (craggy surface)	Medioinferior
Zygomaticofacial foramen	Anterior
Zygomatico-orbital foramen	Medial
Zygomaticotemporal foramen	Posterior
Orbital surface	Mediosuperior
Malar tubercle	Inferior

Bone/Feature	Position of Feature
Maxilla	
Anterior nasal spine	Anteromedial
Nasal crest	Medial
Nasal notch	Medial
Palatine process	Inferomedial
Incisive canal	Medioanterior
Frontal process	Superior
Anterior lacrimal crest	Laterosuperior
Lacrimal groove	Laterosuperior
Ethmoidal crest	Mediosuperior
Conchal crest	Medioanterior
Orbital surface	Superolateral
Infraorbital foramen	Anterolateral
Zygomatic process	Lateral
Maxillary tuberosity	Posteroinferior
Greater palatine canal	Posteromedial
Maxillary sinus	Medioposterior
Alveolar process	Inferior
Canine fossa	Lateroanterior
Nasal	
Nasofrontal suture (deeply serrated)	Superior
Internasal suture	Medial
Nasal crest	Posteromedial (internal)
Nasomaxillary suture (longest border)	Lateral
Inferior border (thin, sharp)	Inferior
Internal surface (concave)	Medioposterior
External surface (convex)	Lateroanterior
Groove for anterior ethmoidal nerve	Posterior (internal)
Vascular foramen	Anterior (external)
Lacrimal (smallest bone of the face)	
Lacrimal groove	Lateroanterior
Posterior lacrimal crest	Lateral
Lacrimal hamulus	Inferoanterior
Orbital surface	Lateroposterior (external)
Nasal surface	Medial (internal)
Palatine	
Horizontal plate	Inferior
Nasal crest	Inferomedial

(continued)

Bone/Feature	Position of Feature
Posterior nasal spine	Medioposterior
Greater palatine foramen	Inferolateral
Lesser palatine foramen	Inferolateral
Pyramidal process	Lateral
Perpendicular plate	Laterosuperior
Maxillary process	Anterior
Greater palatine groove	Lateroposterior
Ethmoidal crest	Mediosuperior
Conchal crest	Medial
Sphenoidal process	Posterosuperior
Sphenopalatine notch	Posterosuperior
Orbital process	Superior

Inferior Concha

Maxillary process	Lateral
Ethmoidal process	Superoanterior
Lacrimal process	Superoposterior
Posterior end (elongate)	Posterior
Anterior end (stubby)	Anterior

Malleus (hammer) (largest of the auditory ossicles)

Head (club-shaped)	Superior
Facet for incus (saddle-shaped)	Posteromedial
Lateral process	Lateral
Anterior process	Anterior
Manubrium or handle	Inferior

Incus (anvil)

Facet for malleus (saddle-shaped)	Anterior
Short crus (thick and conical)	Posterior
Long crus (S-shaped)	Inferior
Lenticular process	Medioinferior

Stapes (stirrup) (smallest of the auditory ossicles)

Head	Lateral
Anterior crus (shorter and straight)	Anterior
Posterior crus (longer and curved)	Posterior
Base or footplate (footprint-shaped)	Medial

POSTCRANIAL

Ribs I–XII

Head	Medioposterior
Tubercle (I–X)	Posterosuperior(I–II), posterior(III), posteroinferior(IV–X)

306

Bone/Feature	Position of Feature
Angle (I–X)	Posterior
Subclavian groove (I)	Superior
Scalene tubercle (I)	Superomedial
Groove for subclavian vein (I)	Superoanterior
Tuberosity for serratus anterior (II)	Superolateral
Superior border (blunt) (II–XII)	Superior
Inferior border (sharp) (II–XII)	Inferior
Costal groove or sulcus (II–XI)	Inferior and internal
Scapula	
Glenoid fossa	Laterosuperior
Supraglenoid tubercle	Laterosuperior
Infraglenoid tubercle	Lateral
Suprascapular notch	Superior
Coracoid process	Superolateral
Acromion or acromial process	Laterosuperior
Acromial angle	Posterolateral
Supraspinous fossa	Posterosuperior
Scapular spine	Posterior
Infraspinous fossa	Posteroinferior
Clavicle	
Sternal end (rounded)	Medial
Costal tuberosity	Inferoposterior
Groove for subclavius muscle	Inferior
Nutrient foramen (mediolateral)	Posteroinferior
Conoid tubercle	Inferoposterior
Trapezoid line	Inferior (lateral)
Acromial end (flattened)	Lateral
Humerus	
Head	Medioposterior
Anatomical neck	Circumferential
Greater tubercle	Lateral (proximal)
Lesser tubercle	Anterior
Intertubercular (bicipital) groove	Anterolateral
Surgical neck	Circumferential
Crest of lesser tubercle	Medial
Crest of greater tubercle	Anterior
Deltoid tuberosity	Lateral (shaft)
Spiral or radial groove	Posterolateral
Nutrient foramen (superoinferior)	Medial

(continued)

Bone/Feature	Position of Feature
Medial supracondylar ridge	Medial
Lateral supracondylar ridge	Lateral
Medial epicondyle (larger)	Medial
Lateral epicondyle (smaller)	Lateral
Capitulum	Lateral (distal)
Trochlea	Anterior and posterior
Olecranon fossa	Posterior
Coronoid fossa	Anterior
Radial fossa	Anterolateral
Ulnar groove	Medial
Ulna	
Olecranon process	Posterior
Trochlear notch	Anterior
Coronoid process	Anterior (proximal)
Radial notch	Lateral
Ulnar or brachialis tuberosity	Anteromedial
Supinator crest	Lateral
Interosseous border	Lateral (shaft)
Nutrient foramen (inferosuperior)	Anterior
Pronator ridge	Anteromedial
Groove for extensor carpi ulnaris	Posterolateral (distal)
Styloid process	Posteromedial
Articular surface of head	Anterolateral
Radius	
Radial or bicipital tuberosity	Anteromedial (proximal)
Anterior oblique line	Anterior
Nutrient foramen (inferosuperior)	Anterior
Rough area for pronator teres	Lateral (shaft)
Interosseous border	Medial
Ulnar notch	Medial
Styloid process	Lateral (distal)
Dorsal tubercle	Posterior
Scaphoid	
Radial facet	Proximal
Trapezium-trapezoid facet	Dorsal
Capitate articular surface (concave)	Medial
Tubercle of scaphoid	Palmar-lateral
Lunate	
Radial facet	Proximal
Capitate articular surface (concave)	Distolateral
Triquetral facet	Distomedial

Bone/Feature	Position of Feature
Triquetrum	
Lunar facet	Proximal
Facet for hamate (largest)	Lateral
Facet for pisiform (ovoid)	Palmar
Pisiform (difficult to side)	
Facet for triquetrum	Dorsal
Hamate	
Hamulus (points laterally)	Palmar
Facet for capitate	Lateral
Facet for triquetrum	Medial
Facet for metacarpal V	Distomedial
Facet for metacarpal IV	Distolateral
Capitate	
Facet for trapezoid	Laterodistal
Facet for scaphoid	Lateroproximal
Facet for lunate (domelike)	Proximal
Facet for hamate	Mediodorsal
Facet for metacarpal III	Distal
Trapezoid	
Facet for trapezium	Lateral
Facet for scaphoid	Proximal
Facet for capitate	Medial
Facet for metacarpal II (crescentic and concave)	Distomedial
Trapezium	
Facet for metacarpal I (saddle-shaped)	Distolateral
Facet for metacarpal II	Distal
Tubercle of trapezium	Palmar–proximal
Groove for flexor carpi radialis	Palmar–medial
Facet for scaphoid	Medioproximal
Facet for trapezoid	Mediodistal
Metacarpal I (shortest of the metacarpals)	
Base (proximomedially distended)	Proximal
Facet for trapezium (saddle-shaped)	Proximal
Nutrient foramen (proximodistal)	Medial (shaft; palmar concave)
Facet for proximal phalange (convex)	Distal
Head (palmar–medially distended)	Distal
Metacarpal II (longest of the metacarpals)	
Base (proximomedially distended)	Proximal
Facet for trapezoid	Proximal

(continued)

Bone/Feature	Position of Feature
Facet for trapezium	Palmar—lateral (proximal)
Facet for capitate	Proximomedial
Facet for metacarpal III	Medial
Nutrient foramen (distoproximal)	Medial (shaft; palmar concave)
Facet for proximal phalange (convex)	Distal
Head (palmar—laterally distended)	Distal
Metacarpal III	
Base (dorsolaterally distended)	Proximal
Facet for capitate	Proximal
Facet for metacarpal II	Lateral (proximal)
Facet for metacarpal IV	Medial
Styloid process	Dorsolateral
Nutrient foramen (distoproximal)	Medial or lateral (variable; shaft; palmar concave)
Facet for proximal phalange (convex)	Distal
Head	Distal
Metacarpal IV	
Base (medially distended)	Proximal
Facet for hamate (flattened)	Proximal
Facet for metacarpal III (double)	Lateral
Facet for metacarpal V	Medial
Nutrient foramen (distoproximal)	Medial or lateral (variable; shaft; palmar concave)
Facet for proximal phalange (convex)	Distal
Head	Distal
Metacarpal V	
Base (medially distended)	Proximal
Facet for hamate	Proximal
Facet for metacarpal IV	Lateral
Medial tubercle	Medial
Nutrient foramen (distoproximal)	Lateral (shaft; palmar concave)
Facet for proximal phalange (convex)	Distal
Head	Distal
Proximal phalanges I–V (impossible to side)	
Middle phalanges II–V (impossible to side)	
Terminal phalanges I–V (impossible to side)	
Os coxa	
Ilium	Posterior
Iliac crest	Superior
Iliac tuberosity	Medioposterior

Bone/Feature	Position of Feature
Tubercle of iliac crest	Laterosuperior
Arcuate line	Medial
Auricular surface	Medial
Anterior superior iliac spine	Anterior
Posterior superior iliac spine	Posterior
Greater sciatic notch	Posteroinferior
Iliopubic eminence	Anterolateral
Acetabulum	Lateral
Acetabular notch	Anteroinferior
Pubis	Anterior
Pectineal line	Superoanterior
Obturator crest	Anterosuperior
Obturator groove	Inferoanterior
Pubic tubercle	Anterosuperior
Pubic symphysis	Anteromedial
Ischium	Inferior
Ischial tuberosity	Inferior
Lesser sciatic notch	Posteroinferior
Ischial spine	Posteroinferior
Femur	
Head	Medial
Greater trochanter	Lateral
Intertrochanteric line	Anterior
Trochanteric fossa	Posterior (proximal)
Intertrochanteric crest	Posterior
Lesser trochanter	Medial
Gluteal tuberosity	Posterolateral
Spiral line	Posteromedial
Linea aspera	Posterior (shaft)
Nutrient foramen (inferosuperior)	Posteromedial
Lateral supracondylar line	Posterolateral
Medial supracondylar line	Posteromedial
Popliteal surface	Posterior
Lateral epicondyle	Lateral
Medial epicondyle	Medial (distal)
Adducter tubercle	Medial
Lateral condyle (smaller)	Lateral
Medial condyle (larger)	Medial
Intercondylar notch	Posterior
Patellar surface	Anterolateral

(continued)

Bone/Feature	Position of Feature
Patella	
Lateral articular surface (larger)	Posterolateral
Medial articular surface (smaller)	Posteromedial
Vertical ridge	Posterior
Base	Superior
Apex	Inferior
Tibia	
Medial condyle	Medial
Lateral condyle	Lateral (proximal)
Tibial tuberosity	Anterolateral
Fibular articular facet	Posterolateral
Anterior border	Anterolateral
Soleal line	Posterior (shaft)
Nutrient foramen (superoinferior)	Posterior
Interosseous border	Posterolateral
Fibular notch	Posterolateral
Medial malleolus	Medioanterior (distal)
Malleolar groove (for tibialis posterior)	Posteromedial
Groove for flexor hallucis longus	Posterior
Fibula	
Articular facet of head	Anteromedial (proximal)
Styloid process	Posterolateral
Interosseous border	Medial (shaft)
Nutrient foramen (superoinferior)	Posterior
Lateral malleolus	Lateroposterior
Groove for peroneus brevis	Posterolateral (distal)
Malleolar fossa	Posteromedial
Talus	
Posterior tubercle	Posterior
Groove for flexor hallucis longus	Posteromedial
Medial tubercle	Medioposterior
Posterior calcaneal articular surface	Inferoposterior (proximal)
Trochlear surface	Superior
Lateral articular surface	Lateral
Medial articular surface	Medial
Sulcus tali	Inferior
Middle calcaneal articular surface	Inferomedial (distal)
Anterior calcaneal articular surface	Inferoanterior
Navicular articular surface	Anterior

Bone/Feature	Position of Feature
Calcaneus	
Calcaneus tuberosity	Posterior
Medial tubercle	Inferomedial (proximal)
Lateral tubercle	Inferolateral
Peroneal tubercle	Lateroanterior
Posterior talar articular surface	Superior
Calcaneal sulcus	Superomedial
Sustentaculum tali	Mediosuperior
Groove for flexor hallucis longus	Mediosuperior (distal)
Middle talar articular surface	Superomedial
Anterior talar articular surface	Superoanterior
Anterior tubercle	Medioanterior
Cuboidal articular surface	Anterior
Navicular	
Tuberosity of navicular	Medioinferior
Groove for tibialis posterior	Inferomedial
Facet for talus (concave)	Posterior
Facet for medial cuneiform	Anteromedial
Facet for intermediate cuneiform	Anterior
Facet for lateral cuneiform	Anterolateral
Medial (first) cuneiform (largest of the cuneiforms)	
Facet for navicular (concave)	Posteroplantar
Facet for intermediate cuneiform	Lateroposterior and laterodorsal
Facet for metatarsal II	Lateroanterior
Facet for metatarsal I (footprint-shaped)	Anterior
Intermediate (second) cuneiform (smallest of the cuneiforms)	
Facet for navicular	Posterior
Facet for medial cuneiform (L-shaped)	Medioposterior and mediodorsal
Facet for lateral cuneiform	Lateroposterior
Facet for metatarsal II	Anterior
Lateral (third) cuneiform	
Facet for navicular	Posterior
Facet for intermediate cuneiform	Medioposterior
Facet for cuboid	Lateroposterior
Facet for metatarsal IV	Lateroanterior
Facet for metatarsal III	Anterior

(continued)

Bone/Feature	Position of Feature
Cuboid	
Facet for lateral cuneiform	Mediodorsal
Facet for calcaneus	Posterolateral
Facet for metatarsal V	Anterolateral
Facet for metatarsal IV	Anterior
Cuboid tuberosity	Plantar–lateral
Groove for peroneus longus	Plantar–anterior and lateroanterior
Metatarsal I	
Base (proximolaterally distended)	Proximal
Facet for first cuneiform (concave)	Proximal
Tuberosity for peroneus longus	Plantar–lateral
Facet for metatarsal II (if present)	Laterodorsal
Nutrient foramen (proximodistal)	Laterodorsal (shaft; plantar concave)
Facet for proximal phalange (convex)	Distal
Grooves for flexor hallucis brevis	Plantar (distal)
Head (plantar–laterally distended)	Distal
Metatarsal II *(longest of the metatarsals)*	
Base (proximolaterally distended)	Proximal
Facet for second cuneiform (concave)	Proximal
Facet for medial cuneiform	Mediodorsal (proximal)
Facet for metatarsal I (if present)	Mediodorsal
Facet for lateral cuneiform (if present)	Laterodorsal and lateroplantar
Facet for metatarsal III	Laterodorsal and lateroplantar
Nutrient foramen (distoproximal)	Lateral (shaft; plantar concave)
Facet for proximal phalange (convex)	Distal
Head (plantar–laterally distended)	Distal
Metatarsal III	
Base (proximolaterally distended)	Proximal
Facet for third cuneiform (flattened)	Proximal
Facet for metatarsal II	Mediodorsal and medioplantar
Facet for metatarsal IV	Laterodorsal
Nutrient foramen (distoproximal)	Lateral (shaft; plantar concave)
Facet for proximal phalange (convex)	Distal
Head (plantar–laterally distended)	Distal
Metatarsal IV	
Base	Proximal
Facet for cuboid	Proximal
Facet for metatarsal III	Mediodorsal (proximal)
Facet for lateral cuneiform	Mediodorsal

Bone/Feature	Position of Feature
Facet for metatarsal V	Laterodorsal
Nutrient foramen (distoproximal)	Lateral (shaft; plantar concave)
Facet for proximal phalange (convex)	Distal
Head (plantar–laterally distended)	Distal
Metatarsal V	
Base (proximolaterally distended)	Proximal
Facet for cuboid	Proximomedial (proximal)
Facet for metatarsal IV	Medial
Tuberosity	Lateral
Nutrient foramen (distoproximal)	Plantar–medial (shaft)
Facet for proximal phalange (convex)	Distal
Head (plantar–laterally distended)	Distal
Proximal phalanges I–V (impossible to side)	
Middle phalanges II–V (impossible to side)	
Terminal phalanges I–V (impossible to side)	

Glossary of Osteometric Landmarks and Anatomical Regions

Midsagittal Landmarks of the Skull

ACANTHION: The point at the base of the anterior nasal spine.

ALVEOLARE (abbreviation = *ids;* also *infradentale superius* or *hypoprosthion*): The inferiormost point of the alveolar margin between the maxillary central incisors; often confused with **prosthion.** Compare with **infradentale** and **prosthion.**

ALVEOLON (*alv*): The point on the hard palate at which a line drawn through the distal margin of the maxillary alveolar processes intersects the median sagittal plane.

APEX (*ap*): The highest point on the skull, which also lies in the same vertical plane as **porion;** the skull must be in the Frankfort Horizontal.

BASION (*ba*): 1. (General) A point at the midline of the anterior border of the foramen magnum. 2. A point at the position pointed to by the apex of the triangular surface at the base of either condyle (i.e. the average position from the crests bordering this area), about halfway between the inner border directly facing the posterior border (the **opisthion**) and the lowermost point on the border (i.e. between **endobasion** and **hypobasion**); it is the same as **endobasion** if the anterior border of the foramen magnum is thin and sharp (Howells, 1973).

BREGMA (*b*): The juncture of the coronal and sagittal sutures in the median sagittal plane; should an ossicle be present, the landmark can be located by drawing in pencil a continuation of the sutures until these lines intersect.

ENDOBASION (*endoba*): The most posterior point on the midline of the anterior margin of the foramen magnum; it is usually behind and below **basion,** but coincident with it when the margin is thin and sharp.

GLABELLA (*g*; also *metopion*): The anteriormost region (not a point) of the frontal bone above the frontonasal suture and between the superciliary arches. This region generally protrudes anteriorly, but in certain skulls this region may be flat ("hyperfeminine" skulls, infants, and juveniles) or even depressed. When it is not protrusive, glabella may be identified by a change in the direction of the frontal bone.

GNATHION (*gn*; also *menton*): The "lowest" (anterior- and inferiormost) point on the chin.

INCISION (*inc*): The point of contact [identified on the buccal (labial) side] between the mesial occlusal edges of the upper central incisors.

INFRADENTALE (*idi*; also *infradentale inferius* and *symphysion*): The superiormost point of the alveolar margin (identified on the anterior surface) between the mandibular central incisors.

INION (*i*): A point at the midline of the superior nuchal lines, which often coincides but should not be identified with the base of the external occipital protuberance. Measurement should not be taken from the protuberance.

LAMBDA [*l*; sometimes abbreviated as *la* (but see lacrimale)]: The juncture in the median sagittal plane of the lambdoid and sagittal sutures; should an ossicle be present, the landmark is located by drawing in pencil a continuation of the sutures until these lines intersect.

MENTON: see **gnathion**.

METOPION: see **glabella**.

NASION (*n*): The juncture in the median (sagittal) plane of the frontonasal and (inter)nasal sutures.

NASOSPINALE (*ns*): A midline point on a line drawn through the inferiormost margins of the nasal aperture; it may coincide but is not synonymous with **acanthion**.

OBELION (obsolete): The point of intersection between a line drawn through the two parietal foramina and the sagittal suture.

OPHRYON (obsolete): A midline point on a line drawn across the forehead and which lies on a plane that passes through right and left **frontotemporale**.

OPISTHION (*o*): A point in the midline of the posterior margin of the foramen magnum.

OPISTHOCRANION (*op*): The most posterior point on midline of the skull when the skull is oriented in the Frankfort horizontal.

ORALE (*ol*) The point of intersection of a line drawn through the lingualmost surfaces of the upper central incisors and the midline of the premaxillary region of the hard palate.

POGONION (*pg*) The anteriormost midline point of the chin; it lies anterior to and above **gnathion**.

PROSTHION (*pr*; also *exoprosthion*): The anteriormost midline point on the premaxillary alveolar process in the median (sagittal) plane; it is located slightly above **alveolare**, with which it is often confused.

RHINION (*rhi*): The inferiormost point on the (inter)nasal suture.

STAPHYLION (*sta*): The midline point of a line drawn through the anteriormost invaginations of the posterior margins of the right and left palatine bones; it typically falls anterior to the posterior nasal spine.

SUBSPINALE (*ss*): The deepest midline point in the concavity between the anterior nasal spine and the premaxillary alveolar; it is located on the crest of the midline suture.

SUPRADENTALE: see **prosthion**.

SYMPHYSION: see **infradentale**.

VERTEX (*v*): The highest midline point on the skull when the skull is in the Frankfort horizontal; it may coincide with **apex**.

Bilateral (Paired) Landmarks of the Skull

ALARE (*al*): The lateralmost point on the margin of the nasal aperture.

ASTERION (*as*): The juncture of the temporal, parietal, and occipital bones (also of the lambdoid, temporoparietal, and occipitomastoid sutures).

CONDYLION LATERALE (*cdl*): The most lateral point on the mandibular condyle.

CORONALE (obsolete): The most lateral point on the coronal suture.

DACRYON (*d*; may also be abbreviated as *dk*): 1. (Traditional; considered obsolete by Vallois, 1965) The juncture of the frontolacrimal, frontomaxillary, and lacrimomaxillary sutures; lies between **lacrimale** and **maxillofrontale**. 2. "The apex of the lacrimal fossa, as it impinges on the frontal bone" (Howells, 1973, p. 167); considered to be more easily located and useful in anteroposterior measurements.

ECTOCONCHION (*ec*; may also be abbreviated *ek*): The anteriormost point on the lateral rim of the orbit that contributes to the determination of maximum orbital breadth (as measured from **dacryon** or **maxillofrontale**); this point is also used in the measurement of facial flatness.

ECTOMOLARE (*ecm*): The most lateral extent of the alveolar process in the region of the second maxillary molar on its buccal side.

ENDOMOLARE (*enm*; may also be abbreviated as *endo*): The most medial extent of the alveolar process in the region of the second maxillary molar on its lingual.

EURYON (*eu*): The point which, on a parietal, contributes to the determination of maximum (biparietal) cranial breadth.

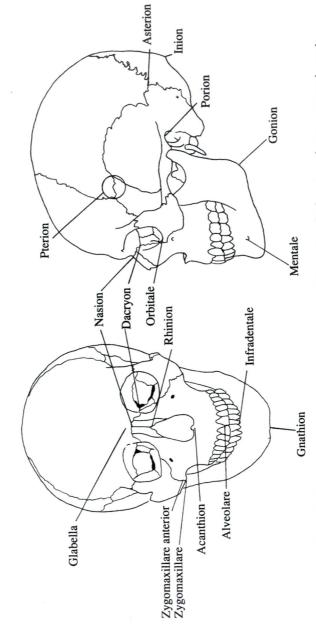

Figure F–1 (*Left*) anterior and (*right*) lateral views of skull illustrating the location of some commonly used anthropometric landmarks.

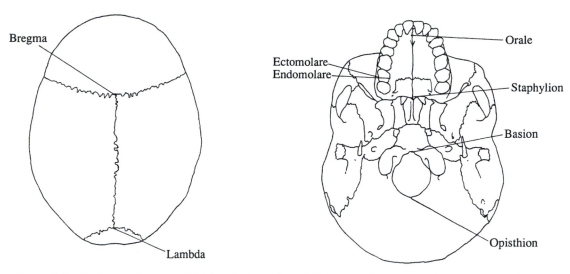

Figure F–2 (Left) superior and *(right)* basal views of skull illustrating the location of some commonly used anthropometric landmarks.

FRONTOMALARE ANTERIOR *(fm:a)*: The most anteriorly prominent point on the zygomaticofrontal suture.

FRONTOTEMPORALE *(ft)*: The point at which the temporal ridge is most inwardly or medially curved; also, the point which contributes to the determination of minimum frontal breadth.

GONION *(go;* may also be abbreviated as *g* or *gn)*: The intersection of a line tangent to the posterior margin of the ascending ramus and a line tangent to the inferior margin of the body of the mandible; also, the most marked point of transition in the upward curvature of the posteroinferior margin of the mandible.

JUGALE *(ju)*: The juncture on the posterior margin of the zygomatic bone of the horizontal and vertical portions (i.e. temporal and frontal processes, respectively) of this bone.

KROTAPHION *(k)*: The juncture of the sphenoparietal, sphenotemporal, and squamosal sutures; the location of this landmark must be estimated on those individuals in whom there is frontotemporal articulation.

LACRIMALE *(la)*: The juncture of the posterior lacrimal crest and the frontolacrimal suture; lies posterior to **dacryon.**

MASTOIDALE *(ms)*: The inferiormost point on the mastoid process when the skull is in the Frankfort horizontal.

MAXILLOFRONTALE *(mf)*: The juncture of the anterior lacrimal crest and the frontomaxillary suture; lies anterior to **dacryon.**

MENTALE *(z)*: The anteriormost point on the margin of the mental foramen (mandible).

NARIALE: The most inferior extent of the anterior margin of the nasal aperture on one side or the other of the anterior nasal spine.

ORBITALE *(or;* may also be abbreviated as *orb)*: The most inferior point on the orbital rim; used with **porion** to orient the skull in the Frankfort horizontal.

PORION *(po;* may also be abbreviated as *p)*: The most lateral point on the superior margin of the external auditory (acoustic) meatus; it is located vertically over the center and thus at the middle of the superior margin of the meatus.

PTERION *(pt)*: A region (not a point) delineated by the frontal bone anteriorly, the squamous portion of the temporal bone posteriorly, and by the area along the sphenoparietal suture; the landmark would not be recognized in those individuals with frontotemporal articulation (see **sphenion**).

SPHENION (*sphn*): The juncture of the frontal bone with the parietal bone, the greater wing of the sphenoid, and the squamous portion of the temporal bone.

STEPHANION (*st*): The point at which the inferior temporal line crosses the coronal suture.

ZYGION (*zy*): The most lateral point on the zygomatic arch.

ZYGOMAXILLARE ANTERIOR (*zm:a*): The point on the facial (anterior) surface where the zygomaticomaxillary suture intersects the attachment scar of the masseter muscle; considered more appropriate than **zygomaxillare (inferior)** for measuring flatness/protrusion of the face.

ZYGOMAXILLARE (INFERIOR) (*zm*): The most inferior point on the zygomaticomaxillary suture.

ZYGOORBITALE (*zo*): The juncture of the zygomaticomaxillary suture with the inferior orbital rim.

Postcranial Landmarks

ACROMION: The most lateral and superior point on the acromial process.

ILIOSPINALE: The peak of the anterior superior iliac spine.

MALLEOLARE: The distalmost extension of the medial malleolus.

MESOSTERNALE: A point in the midline of the anterior surface of the sternum taken at the level of the facet for the fourth costal cartilage (i.e. the fourth chondrosternal joint).

PUBES: A point in the midline of the the the superior border of the pubic symphysis.

RADIALE: A point on the proximal and posterior margin of the head of the radius.

STYLION: The distalmost extension of the styloid process of the radius.

SUPRASTERNALE: The most inferior point in the midline of the jugular notch of the sternum.

TIBIALE: The most proximal and medial point on the edge of the medial condyle of the tibia.

Anatomical Regions

ANTEBRACHIUM (pl. *antebrachia*): The forearm; the distal half of the upper limb, which lies between the elbow and the wrist and encompasses the radius and the ulna.

APPENDICULAR SKELETON: Consists of the 63 paired bones of the upper and lower limbs (appendages) and the pectoral and pelvic girdles; does not include the sacrum.

AXIAL SKELETON: The skeleton of the axis of the body, which consists of 80 bones and includes the skull, hyoid, sternum, ribs, vertebrae, sacrum, and coccyx.

BRACHIUM (pl. *brachia*): The arm or upper arm; the proximal half of the upper limb, which lies between the shoulder and the elbow and encompasses the humerus.

BRAINCASE (also the *cranium*; not including the facial skeleton): The bony cavity that houses the brain; formed by the occipital, parietal, temporal, frontal, ethmoid, and sphenoid bones.

CALVARIA (pl. *calvariae*; also *calotte, concha of cranium*, and *skullcap*, and, incorrectly, *calvarium*): The superior portion of the **braincase** or the roof of the cranial vault; formed by portions of the frontal, parietal, and occipital bones.

CAPUT (pl. *capita*; also *skull*): The head; includes the **cranium** and the **mandible**.

CARPUS (pl. *carpi*): The wrist; the region between the forearm and the hand containing eight irregular carpal bones (the scaphoid, lunate, triquetrum, pisiform, hamate, capitate, trapezoid, and trapezium).

CERVIX (pl. *cervices*): The neck; the region between the **thorax** and the **skull** formed by the cervical vertebrae and the hyoid bone.

CRANIUM (pl. *crania*): All of the bones of the head with the exception of the mandible.

CRUS (pl. *crura*): The leg or lower leg; the region, between the knee and the foot, of the two long bones, the tibia and the fibula.

CUBITUS (pl. *cubiti*): The elbow; the complex synovial joint formed by the humerus, ulna, and radius.

DIGIT: A finger (manual digit) or toe (pedal digit) formed by either two (first digit) or three (digits II to V) articulating phalanges.

FACIAL SKELETON: The skeleton of the face, which is composed of two single bones (the vomer and the mandible) and six paired bones (the zygomatics, maxillae, nasals, lacrimals, palatines, and inferior nasal conchae).

GENU (pl. *genua*): The knee; the complex synovial joint formed by the distal femur, patella, and proximal tibia.

HALLUX (pl. *halluces*): The major or great toe; the first digit of the foot.

LUMBUS (pl. *lumbi*): The lower back or loin; the region of the back, between the **thorax** and the **pelvis**, consisting of the five lumbar vertebrae.

MANUS (pl. *manus*): The hand (including the **carpus**, **metacarpus**, and manual **digits**), which is formed by 54 bones (including the scaphoid, lunate, triquetrum, pisiform, hamate, capitate, trapezoid, trapezium, metacarpals, and phalanges).

METACARPUS (pl. *metacarpi*): The palm of the hand; the region of the hand between the **carpus** and the **digits**, containing the five metacarpal bones.

METATARSUS (pl. *metatarsi*): The portion of the foot, between the **tarsus** and the pedal **digits**, which includes the five metatarsal bones.

OCCIPUT: The back of the head.

ORBIT: The bony eye socket, the walls of which are formed by portions of the frontal, ethmoid, sphenoid, lacrimal, maxillary, and zygomatic bones.

PECTORAL GIRDLE: The incomplete ring of bone, composed of the scapulae and the clavicles, that provides for the attachment of the upper limb to the **thorax**.

PELVIS (pl. *pelves*; also *pelvic girdle)*: The bowl-shaped ring of bone, formed by the two os coxae laterally and the sacrum and coccyx posteriorly, that supports the trunk of the body and transmits the weight of the upper body to the legs.

PES (pl. *pedes*): The foot, which consists of 52 bones, including the talus, calcaneus, navicular, cuboid, cuneiforms, metatarsals, and phalanges.

POLLEX (pl. *pollices*): The thumb or first digit of the hand.

SKULL (also *caput*; [incorrectly] *cranium*): The skeleton of the head, which includes the bones of the **braincase** and those of the **facial skeleton**.

TARSUS (pl. *tarsi*): The ankle; the articular region between the foot and the leg, which is formed by seven irregular bones (i.e. the talus, calcaneus, navicular, cuboid, and three cuneiforms).

THORAX (pl. *thoraces*): The chest or upper trunk; the region between the **cervix** and the abdomen, which is formed by the thoracic vertebrae, ribs, and sternum.

VERTEBRAL COLUMN: The column of bony segments which encapsulates the spinal cord; it is normally composed of 33 vertebrae [7 cervical, 12 thoracic, 5 lumbar, 5 sacral (fused into one bone, the sacrum), and 4 coccygeal (fused into one bone, the coccyx)].

Osteometry

Osteometry is the measurement of bones. Historically, such measurement has often been focused on the skull, the metric analysis of which is specifically referred to as *craniometry*. Although compiling long lists of measurements for its own sake is of little value, the quantification (or at least the attempted quantification) of morphological features is necessary in order to make accurate comparisons between and within skeletal populations. Osteometric measurements and the use of statistical techniques (such as multivariate analysis) allow the researcher to make such comparisons. However, in making these skeletal comparisons, one should never lose sight of the fact that the bone (and parts thereof) being measured was once a living and dynamic tissue, and thus the size and development of particular features may have been modified by surrounding musculature and other extraosseous tissues.

Skeletal measurements include linear dimensions between two osteometric landmarks (e.g. length, breadth, and height), circumferential dimensions around a bone or structure, arc dimensions (partial circumference) from one point to another on the margin of a rounded structure, and angles between two planes of bone. All measurements should be taken and recorded in millimeters or centimeters. Measurements that can be taken on either the right or left side (e.g. orbital height, mastoid length, minimum breadth of ascending ramus of mandible) should, as a rule, be taken on the left side, so that measurements from one study to the next will be comparable. The instruments used to take these measurements include the spreading caliper, sliding caliper, coordinate caliper, head spanner, tape, and osteometric board. The measurement of angles often requires more sophisticated and specialized instruments.

Skeletal indices are ratios that attempt to describe mathematically the shape or configuration of bones. Specifically, an index considers two traits simultaneously and is defined as a ratio of one measurement to another expressed as a percentage. Indices provide a quick and simple technique for the comparison and delineation of differences between individuals with regard, for example, to race and sex.

Cranial and Mandibular Measurements

Braincase

1. *Maximum cranial length (g-op; GOL):* Glabella to opisthocranion (spreading caliper).
2. *Maximum cranial breadth (eu-eu; XCB):* Right euryon to left euryon (spreading caliper).
3. *Maximum cranial height (ba-b; BBH):* Basion to bregma (spreading caliper).
4. *Porion-bregma height (po-b):* Porion to bregma (head spanner).
5. *Basion-porion height (ba-po):* Basion to porion (coordinate caliper).
6. *Auricular height (po-ap):* Porion to apex (head spanner).
7. *Minimum frontal breadth (ft-ft):* Right frontotemporale to left frontotemporale (spreading or sliding caliper).

8. *Biasterionic breadth (as-as):* Right asterion to left asterion (sliding caliper).
9. *Foramen magnum (foraminal) length (ba-o; FOL):* Basion to opisthion (sliding caliper).
10. *Foramen magnum (foraminal) breadth (FOB):* Maximum (sliding caliper).
11. *Frontal (nasion-bregma) chord (n-b; FRC):* Nasion to bregma (sliding caliper).
12. *Parietal (bregma-lambda) chord (b-l; PAC):* Bregma to lambda (sliding caliper).
13. *Occipital (lambda-opisthion) chord (l-b; OCC):* Lambda to opisthion (sliding caliper).
14. *Frontal arc (n-b):* Nasion to bregma (tape).
15. *Parietal arc (b-l):* Bregma to lambda (tape).
16. *Occipital arc (l-o):* Lambda to opisthion (tape).
17. *Transverse biporial arc (po-po):* Right porion to left porion (tape).

Facial Skeleton

18. *Basion-nasion length (b-n; BNL):* Basion to nasion (spreading or sliding caliper).
19. *Basion-alveolare length (b-ids):* Basion to alveolare (sliding caliper).
20. *Total facial height (n-gn):* Nasion to gnathion (spreading or sliding caliper).
21. *Upper facial height (n-ids):* Nasion to alveolare (spreading or sliding caliper).
22. *Bizygomatic breadth or facial width (zy-zy; ZYB):* Right zygion to left zygion (spreading or sliding caliper).
23. *Bimaxillary breadth (zm:-zm:a; ZMB):* Right zygomaxillare to left zygomaxillare (spreading or coordinate caliper).

Nasal Region

24. *Nasal height (n-ns; NLH):* Nasion to nasospinale (sliding caliper).
25. *Nasal breadth (al-al; NLB):* Right alare to left alare (sliding caliper).
26. *Simotic chord or least nasal breadth (WNB):* Shortest distance between right and left nasomaxillary sutures (sliding or coordinate caliper).

Orbit

27. *Orbital height (orb. h.; OBH):* Maximum vertical (i.e. perpendicular to the horizontal plane of the orbit) distance between superior and inferior orbital margins (sliding caliper).
28. *Orbital breadth (width) (OBB):* Variously defined as the distance from ectoconchion *(ec)* to either maxillofrontale *(mf)*, dacryon *(d)*, or lacrimale *(la)* (sliding caliper).
29. *Biorbital breadth (ec-ec; EKB):* Right ectoconchion to left ectoconchion (sliding or coordinate caliper).
30. *Interorbital, bidacryonic (chord) or maxillofrontal breadth:* Right maxillofrontale to left maxillofrontale *(mf-mf)* or dacryon to dacryon *(d-d)* (sliding or coordinate caliper).
31. *Midorbital breadth (zo-zo):* Right zygoorbitale to left zygoorbitale (sliding caliper).
32. *Bidacryonic arc (d-d):* Right dacryon to left dacryon (tape).

Palate

33. *Maxilloalveolar (external palatal) length (pr-alv):* Prosthion to alveolon (sliding caliper with reflexed arm).
34. *Maxilloalveolar (external palatal) breadth (MAB):* Right ectomolare to left ectomolare *(ecm-ecm)* or maximum wherever found (sliding caliper).
35. *Palatal (internal) length (ol-sta):* Orale to staphylion (sliding caliper).
36. *Palatal (internal) breadth:* Right endomolare to left endomolare *(enm-enm)* or maximum wherever found (sliding caliper).

Mandible

37. *Bicondylar (intercondylar) breadth (cdl-cdl):* Right condylion laterale to left condylion laterale (sliding caliper).
38. *Bigonial breadth (go-go):* Right gonion to left gonion (sliding caliper).
39. *Foramen mentalia breadth (z-z):* Right mentale to left mentale (sliding caliper).
40. *Ascending ramus height (go-cdl):* Go-

nion to condylion laterale parallel to the vertical axis of the ramus (sliding caliper).

41. *Coronoid process height (CrH):* Maximum vertical height of coronoid process from planar surface on which body of mandible is placed (sliding caliper).

42. *Maximum ramus breadth:* Greatest distance between a line connecting the posteriormost point on a condyle with the angle and the anteriormost point on the ramus, taken at a right angle to the imaginary line (osteometric board).

43. *Minimum ramus breadth (RB):* Minimum distance wherever found between anterior and posterior border of ascending ramus (sliding caliper).

44. *Symphyseal height (gn-idi):* Gnathion (or tangent to lowest point on either side of gnathion) to infradentale (sliding caliper).

45. *Mandibular body (corpus) height:* Maximum height at the position of the second molar taken to the alveolar margin from the surface on which the mandible is placed; also sometimes taken at the position between the second premolar and the first molar (sliding caliper).

46. *Mandibular body (corpus) breadth:* Maximum thickness at the position of the second molar taken perpendicular to the long axis of the body; also sometimes taken at the position between the second premolar and the first molar (sliding caliper).

47. *Maximum projective mandibular length:* Distance between the posteriormost extension of the mandibular condyles and gnathion; taken when mandibular body is placed on a horizontal surface (osteometric board).

48. *Mandibular body (corpus) length (gn-go):* Gnathion to gonion (sliding caliper or mandibulometer).

Cranial and Mandibular Indices

1. Cranial index (CI) = maximum cranial breadth × 100/maximum cranial length

Dolichocranic (narrow or long headed)	= <75.0
Mesocranic (average or medium)	= 75.0–79.9
Brachycranic (broad or round headed)	= 80.0–84.9
Hyperbrachycranic (very broad headed)	= >84.9

2. Cranial module = (max. cranial length + max. breadth + max. height)/3 (Reflects, numerically, the general size of the skull; classification lacking.)

3. Cranial height-length index = height (to basion or porion) × 100/max. cranial length

	To Basion	To Porion
Chamaecranic (low skull)	= <70.0	= <57.9
Orthocranic (medium height)	= 70.0–74.9	= 58–62.9
Hypsicranic (high skull)	= >74.9	= >63

4. Cranial breadth-height index = Max. cranial height × 100/max. cranial breadth

Tapeinocranic (low skull)	= <92.0
Metriocranic (medium height)	= 92.0–97.9
Acrocranic (high skull)	= >97.9

5. Mean height index = max. cranial height × 100/[(max. cranial length + max. cranial breadth)/2]

	Vallois, 1965	Stewart, 1940	Stewart, 1965
Microsemic (low skull)	= <79.0	= <80.49	= <78.99
Mesosemic (medium height)	= 79.0–85.9	= 80.50–83.49	= 79.00–85.99
Megasemic (high skull)	= >85.9	= >83.50	= >86.00

6. Mean porion-height index = porion-bregma height × 100/[(max. cranial length + max. cranial breadth)/2]

Low skull	= <67.0
Medium-high, average	= 67.0–71.9
High skull	= >71.9

7. Frontoparietal (frontal) index = min. frontal breadth × 100/Max. cranial breadth

Stenometopic (narrow frontal)	= <66.0
Metriometopic (medium frontal)	= 66.0–68.9
Eurymetopic (broad frontal)	= >68.9

8. Craniofacial transverse index = bizygomatic breadth × 100/max. cranial breadth
(Reflects the width of the cranial vault relative to that of the face; classification lacking.)

9. Prognathic (gnathic) index = basion-prosthion length × 100/basion-nasion length

Orthognathous (flat/straight face/profile)	= <98.0
Mesognathous (average, moderately projecting)	= 98.0–102.9
Prognathous (projecting face/profile)	= >102.9

10. Total facial index = total facial height × 100/bizygomatic breadth

Hypereuryprosopic (very broad, wide face)	= <80.0
Euryprosopic (broad face)	= 80.0–84.9
Mesoprosopic (medium face)	= 85.0–89.9
Leptoprosopic (narrow, slender face)	= 90.0–94.9
Hyperleptoprosopic (very narrow face)	= >94.9

11. Upper facial index = upper facial height × 100/bizygomatic breadth

Hypereuryene (very broad, wide face)	= <45.0
Euryene (broad face)	= 45.0–49.9
Mesene (medium face)	= 50.0–54.9
Leptene (narrow, slender face)	= 55.0–59.9
Hyperleptene (very narrow face)	= >59.9

12. Jugofrontal index = min. frontal breadth × 100/bizygomatic breadth
(Reflects the narrowness of the forehead relative to facial breadth.)

13. Orbital index = max. orbital height × 100/max. orbital breadth

Chamaeconchic (low, wide orbit)	=<76.0
Mesochonchic (medium, square orbit)	= 76.0–84.9
Hypsiconchic (tall, narrow orbit)	=>84.9

14. Nasal index = nasal breadth × 100/nasal height
(Broca's classification may be more relevant in assessing populational affinity.)

	Broca	Martin
Leptorrhine (narrow nose, nasal aperture)	= <48.0	= <47.0
Mesorrhine (average, medium–broad)	= 48.0–52.9	= 47–50.9
Platyrrhine (broad, wide)	= >52.9	
Chamaerrhine (broad, wide)		= 51.0–57.9
Hyperchamaerrhine (very broad, wide)		= >57.9

15. Maxilloalveolar (external palatal) index = maxilloalveolar breadth × 100/maxilloalveolar length

Dolichuranic (narrow/long upper jaw/palate)	= <110.0
Mesuranic (average, medium)	= 110.0–114.9
Brachyuranic (broad, wide)	= >114.9

16. Palatal/palatine (Internal palatal/palatine) index = palatal breadth × 100/palatal length

        Leptostaphyline (narrow palate)   = <80.0
        Mesostaphyline (average, medium–broad)   = 80.0–84.9
        Brachystaphyline (broad, wide)   = >84.9

17. Cranial base flatness index = basion-porion height × 100/basion-bregma height
[Devised by Neumann (1942) to demonstrate possible correlation between lowering of cranial vault height and cranial base flattening (i.e. the latter reflected in a decrease in the distance between basion and porion); general classification lacking, but Aleuts and Apaches sampled were found to have low (c. 13.7) and Ohio Valley Amerindians high (c. 18.4) cranial vaults.]

18. Foramen magnum index = max. foramen breadth × 100/max. foramen length

        Microsemic (narrow foramen)   = <82.0
        Megosemic (medium foramen)   = 82.0–85.9
        Megasemic (broad foramen)   = >85.9

19. Mandibular index = max. projective mandibular length × 100/bicondylar breadth
(Reflects the length of the mandible relative to its maximum width.)

20. Mandibular body breadth index = mandibular body breadth × 100/mandibular body height
(Reflects the thickness of the body of the mandible relative to the height of the mandibular body.)

Postcranial Measurements

Length measurements on long bones (see individual bones below) can be of one of two basic kinds: *morphological* and *physiological (functional, oblique, bicondylar, or anatomical)*. Morphological length is the *maximum* length that can be measured from anywhere on one end of the bone to anywhere on the opposite end; morphological length lies parallel to the long axis of the bone. When maximum length is specified below for a particular long bone, morphological length is to be taken. Physiological (functional, oblique, bicondylar, or anatomical) length measures the length of the bone as it would be oriented when articulated and in the anatomical position. When physiological length is specified for a particular bone, it will be identified as such. Transverse measurements (e.g. widths, diameters) are taken perpendicular to the long axis of the bone.

Sternum (all are maximums)

1. *Manubrium length (midsagittal):* Distance from the jugular notch to the facet of articulation with the body of the sternum (sliding or spreading caliper).

2. *Manubrium width:* Distance between midpoints of the right and left facet for the first costal cartilage taken perpendicular to the long axis (sliding or spreading caliper).

3. *Maximum length of sternal body (mesosternal) (midsagittal):* Distance from facet for articulation with the manubrium to facet for articulation with the xiphoid process (sliding or spreading caliper or osteometric board).

4. *Sternal body (mesosternal) width at first sternebra:* Minimum distance from side to side across first sternebra (lowest point between the facet for the second and third costal cartilage one each side) (sliding caliper).

5. *Sternal body (mesosternal) width at third sternebra:* Minimum distance from side to side across first sternebra (lowest point between the facet for the fourth and fifth costal cartilage one each side; sliding caliper).

6. *Maximum sternal (manubrium + mesosternum) length (midsagittal):* Distance from the jugular notch (i.e. lowest midline point superiorly) of the manubrium to the facet for the xiphoid process; Stewart and McCormick (1983) added the lengths taken separately on the manubrium and mesosternum (sliding caliper or osteometric board).

Clavicle

7. *Maximum length* (as if measuring a straight bone): Maximum distance from sternal to scapular articular end (sliding caliper or osteometric board).
8. *Maximum breadth:* widest distance taken perpendicular to the "midline" (sliding caliper).
9. *Maximum breadth of sternal end:* Widest distance taken perpendicular to the midline of the segment (sliding caliper).
10. *Midshaft circumference:* Taken midway between the articular ends (tape).

Scapula

11. *Scapular (total) height (maximum length):* Maximum distance from the superior to the inferior angle (sliding caliper of osteometric board).
12. *Scapular (maximum) breadth:* Maximum distance (following the long axis of the spine) from the middle of the posterior (dorsal) margin of the glenoid cavity to the vertebral border (sliding caliper).
13. *Length of scapular spine:* Maximum distance from the lateralmost extent of the acromion to the vertebral border; this point on the vertebral border will be the same as that determined for scapular (maximum) breadth (sliding caliper).
14. *Length of supraspinous line:* Distance between the confluence of the spine and vertebral border (i.e. the point used for maximum scapular breadth and scapular spine length) and the most superior extent of the superior angle (sliding caliper).
15. *Length of infraspinous line:* Distance between the confluence of the spine and vertebral border (see measurements 11 to 13 above) and most inferior extent of the inferior angle (sliding caliper).
16. *Length of glenoid cavity:* Maximum distance across glenoid cavity perpendicular to the anteroposterior axis (sliding caliper).
17. *Breadth of glenoid cavity:* Maximum distance acroos glenoid cavity mea-

sured at a right angle to the axis of the length of the glenoid cavity (sliding caliper).

Humerus

18. *Maximum length:* (osteometric board).
19. *(Maximum) vertical diameter of the head:* Taken parallel to the coronal plane on the margin of the articular surface of the head to obtain the maximum distance between one point and a point on the opposite side (sliding caliper).
20. *(Maximum) transverse diameter of the head:* Maximum anteroposterior distance measured between one point on the margin of the articular surface and a point on the opposite side (sliding caliper).
21. *Maximum diameter of the head:* Taken anywhere along the margin of the articular surface to obtain the maximum distance from one point to a point on the opposite side (sliding caliper).
22. *Minimum circumference of shaft:* Taken inferior to the deltoid tuberosity (tape).
23. *Midshaft circumference:* Taken on the shaft perpendicular to the midline axis at the true midpoint of maximum length (tape).
24. *Maximum midshaft diameter:* Maximum distance measured perpendicular to the midline axis at the true midpoint of maximum length (sliding caliper).
25. *Minimum midshaft diameter:* Taken as above but for minimum measurement (sliding caliper).
26. *Biepicondylar (bicondylar, distal epiphyseal) width (breadth):* Taken from the medial to the lateral epicondyle (sliding caliper).
27. *(Distal) articular width:* Distance from the most medial extent of the trochlea to the most lateral extent of the capitulum (sliding caliper).
28. *Maximum diameter (width) of capitulum:* (sliding caliper).

Radius

29. *Maximum length:* (osteometric board).
30. *Minumum shaft circumference:* Taken

perpendicular to the midline axis wherever necessary to obtain minumum (tape).

31. *Midshaft circumference:* Taken perpendicular to the midline axis at the true midpoint of maximum length (tape).

32. *Minimum shaft diameter:* Taken perpendicular to the midline axis at the true midpoint of maximum length (sliding caliper).

33. *Head circumference:* (tape).

34. *Maximum (mediolateral) distal (epiphyseal) breadth (width):* Maximum distance from the most medial extension (beyond the ulnar notch) to the lateral side (sliding caliper or osteometric board).

Ulna

35. *Maximum length:* (osteometric board).

36. *Physiological length:* (osteometric board).

37. *Minumum shaft circumference:* Taken perpendicular to the midline axis wherever necessary to obtain minimum (tape).

38. *Midshaft circumference:* Taken perpendicular to the midline axis at the true midpoint of maximum length (tape).

39. *Transverse diameter (width) of shaft:* Maximum mediolateral width taken at the point of greatest development of the interosseous crest (sliding caliper).

Metacarpals and Phalanges

40. *Physiological length:* In general, measured from the midpoint of the proximal epiphysis to the most distal point of the distal end (head); the proximal point specifically with regard to metacarpal II is the midpoint of the notch, to metacarpal III is the midpoint of the longitudinal ridge, and to metacarpal V is the deepest point in the concavity (sliding caliper).

41. *Transverse diameter:* Width measured at the proximal end (sliding caliper).

Vertebrae

42. *Anterior vertebral body (centrum) height:* Taken in the midline [median (midsagittal) plane], from the upper (cranial or superior) to the lower (caudal or inferior) margin of the anterior (ventral) side of the centrum (sliding caliper).

43. *Posterior vertebral body (centrum) height:* Same as above but taken on the posterior (dorsal) side of the centrum (sliding or spreading caliper).

44. *Maximum breadth (width):* Maximum distance between apices of transverse processes (sliding caliper).

Sacrum

45. *Sacral length (maximum anterior height):* Vertical median (midsagittal) distance from the anterior (ventral) rim of the promontory to most caudal (inferior) extent of the last vertebra; only five-segmented sacra should be compared (sliding caliper).

46. *Sacral breadth (maximum anterior breadth):* Greatest distance from the anterolateral border of right to left alae (lateral masses; sliding caliper).

47. *Midventral (curved) length:* Distance in the median (midsagittal) plane along the anterior (ventral) surface from the rim of the promontory to most caudal (inferior) extent of the last vertebra; only five-segmented sacra should be compared (tape).

48. *Maximum depth of curvature:* Greatest distance from the cord representing sacral length to the anterior (ventral) surface (coordinate caliper).

49. *Transverse diameter (external):* Maximum bilateral distance perpendicular to the median (midsagittal) plane of the body of the first sacral vertebra taken to the outside of the epiphyseal ring (sliding caliper).

50. *Transverse diameter (internal):* Maximum bilateral distance perpendicular to the median (midsagittal) plane of the body of the first sacral vertebra taken

to the inside of the epiphyseal ring (sliding caliper).

51. *Anteroposterior diameter (external):* Distance in the median (midsagittal) plane between the anterior (ventral) and posterior (dorsal) outer margins of the epiphyseal ring (sliding caliper).

52. *Anteroposterior diameter (internal):* Distance in the median (midsagittal) plane between the anterior (ventral) and posterior (dorsal) inner margins of the epiphyseal ring (sliding caliper).

53. *Length of ala (lateral part, lateral mass, transverse process element):* Maximum distance on one side from the point that yields the maximum transverse diameter of the first sacral vertebra to the lateral margin of the ala (sliding caliper).

Os Coxa and Pelvis

54. *Maximum (os coxa) height:* Greatest distance obtainable between the ischium and the iliac crest of an os coxa (osteometric board).

55. *Anteroposterior height of (articulated) pelvis (sagittal, or anteroposterior, or true conjugate diameter):* Average of measurements taken from the midpoint of the promontory (sacrum) to the right and left pubic crests (i.e. anterior border between the pubic tubercle and symphysis) (sliding caliper).

56. *Acetabular diameter:* Variably measured parallel to the superior pubic ramus, the iliac pillar, and the ascending ramus of the ischium (sliding caliper).

57. *Bi-iliac (articulated pelvic) breadth:* Greatest distance obtainable between right and left iliac crests (sliding caliper).

58. *Transverse breadth (diameter) of (articulated) pelvis:* Greatest distance obtainable between right and left arcuate lines (sliding caliper).

59. *Iliac breadth:* Taken from the anterior to the posterior superior iliac spine (sliding caliper).

60. *(Maximum) iliac height:* Greatest distance obtainable between the point of confluence in the acetabulum of the il-

ium, pubis, and ischium and the iliac crest (sliding caliper).

61. *(Maximum) ischial length:* Greatest distance obtainable between the point of confluence in the acetabulum of the ilium, pubis, and ischium and the ischial tuberosity (sliding caliper).

62. *(Maximum) pubic length:* Greatest distance obtainable between the point of confluence in the acetabulum of the ilium, pubis, and ischium and the anterior (ventral) face of the superior pubic ramus (sliding caliper).

63. *(Greater) sciatic notch position:* Taken from the point at which the line of greatest sciatic notch width and greatest depth measured from this line meet to the ischial spine (sliding caliper).

64. *(Greater) sciatic notch width or height:* Variably measured from the pyramidal spine to the base or tip of the ischial spine (sliding caliper).

65. *Acetabulosciatic breadth:* The distance from a point on the anterior border of the greater sciatic notch that is midway between the apex of the notch and the ischial spine to the acetabular border, all the while trying to stay at right angles to both borders.

66. *Acetabulum-innominate line length:* The distance from the lateralmost point on the pubic portion of the acetabular border to the innominate line, taken at a right angle to the plane of the obturator foramen.

67. *Anterior superior iliac spine "measure":* The shortest distance from the anterior iliac spine to the edge of the sciatic notch less the shortest distance from the anterior iliac spine to the auricular surface.

Femur

68. *Maximum length:* (osteometric board).

69. *Physiological (trochanteric oblique) length:* (osteometric board).

70. *Trochanteric oblique length:* Taken in the same position as physiological length but from the level of the condyles to the most proximal extent of the greater trochanter (osteometric board).

71. *Maximum vertical diameter of head:* Greatest distance obtainable from a point on the inferior edge of the margin of the articular surface of the head to a point opposite it on the superior edge of the margin (sliding caliper).

72. *Maximum subtrochanteric anteroposterior (sagittal) diameter:* Taken in the median (sagittal) plane at a right angle to the long axis of the femur immediately below the lesser trochanter (sliding caliper).

73. *Maximum subtrochanteric transverse (mediolateral) diameter:* Taken in the same plane as above but perpendicular to the maximum subtrochanteric anteroposterior diameter above (sliding caliper).

74. *Midshaft circumference:* Taken at the true midpoint of morphological length, perpendicular to the long axis of the bone, following the topography of the shaft (tape).

75. *Maximum anteroposterior midshaft diameter:* Taken at the true midpoint of morphological length, perpendicular to the long axis of the bone (sliding caliper).

76. *Maximum transverse (mediolateral) midshaft diameter:* Taken at the true midpoint of morphological length, perpendicular to the long axis of the bone (sliding caliper).

77. *Maximum bicondylar (epicondylar, distal epiphyseal) breadth (width):* Greatest distance obtainable between medial and lateral epicondyles (sliding caliper or osteometric board).

78. *Popliteal length:* Taken on the posterior (dorsal) surface from the midpoint of the intercondylar margin of the popliteal surface to the point of confluence of the medial and lateral supracondylar lines (sliding caliper).

Tibia

79. *Maximum length:* (osteometric board).
80. *Length:* Taken from the highest elevation of the lateral condyle to the distalmost extension of the medial malleolus (osteometric board).

81. *Physiological length:* Taken from the distal articular surface (just lateral to the malleolus) to the lowest point on the medial condylar surface (large sliding caliper or osteometric board).

82. *Maximum proximal (bicondylar, epiphyseal) breadth (width):* Greatest mediolateral measurement across the condyles obtainable (sliding caliper).

83. *Midshaft circumference:* Taken at the true midpoint of maximum length, following the topography of the bone (tape).

84. *Maximum midshaft (anteroposterior) diameter:* Taken at the true midpoint of maximum length (sliding caliper).

85. *Circumference at nutrient foramen:* Maximum circumference obtained following the topography of the bone (tape).

86. *Anteroposterior (sagittal cnemic) diameter at the nutrient foramen:* Maximum anteroposterior measurement obtainable taken at the level of the nutrient foramen, perpendicular to the long axis of the bone (sliding caliper).

87. *Mediolateral (transverse cnemic) diameter at the nutrient foramen:* Maximum mediolateral measurement obtainable taken at the level of the nutrient foramen, perpendicular to the long axis of the bone and in the same plane as the previous measurement (sliding caliper).

88. *Minimum shaft circumference:* Usually found toward the distal portion of the shaft and taken following the topography of the bone (tape).

89. *Distal (epiphyseal) breadth (width):* Maximum distance obtainable from the fibular notch to a point on the medial surface of the malleolus (sliding caliper).

Fibula

90. *Maximum length:* (osteometric board).
91. *Midshaft circumference:* Taken at the true midpoint of maximum length, following the topography of the bone (tape).

92. *Anteroposterior diameter:* Taken at the true midpoint of maximum length and perpendicular to the long axis of the bone, the maximum anteroposterior measurement obtainable (sliding caliper).

93. *Transverse diameter:* Taken at the true midpoint of maximum length, perpendicular to the long axis of the bone and in the same plane as the previous measurement, the maximum anteroposterior measurement obtainable (sliding caliper).

94. *Maximum distal (epiphyseal) breadth (width):* (sliding caliper).

Calcaneus

95. *Maximum length:* Maximum measurement obtainable between the posterior surface of the tuberosity and the anterosuperior margin of the cuboidal facet (sliding caliper or osteometric board).

96. *Minimum (mediolateral) width:* Taken perpendicular to the long axis of the bone and found between the tuberosity and the posterior facet for the talus (sliding caliper).

97. *Body height:* Maximum measurement obtainable between the inferior (plantar) surface of the tuberosity and the superiormost elevation of the posterior facet for the talus (osteometric board).

98. *Height of cuboidal facet:* Maximum vertical measurement, from the inferiormost to the superiormost margins of the articular surface (sliding caliper).

99. *Length posterior to the posterior facet for the talus:* With the bone oriented as for maximum length, the maximum measurement obtainable from the highest elevation of the posterior facet for the talus to the posterior surface of the tuberosity (sliding caliper).

100. *Load arm length:* With the bone oriented as for maximum length, the maximum measurement obtainable from the posterior maring of the posterior facet for the talus to the anterosuperior margin of the cuboidal facet (sliding caliper).

101. *Load arm width:* The maximum measurement obtainable between the lateral margin of the posterior facet for the talus and the medial extension of the sustentaculum tali (osteometric board).

Talus

102. *Maximum length:* The maximum measurement obtainable from the sulcus for the hallucis longus muscle posteriorly to the anterior surface of the head (i.e. the facet for the navicular) (sliding caliper).

103. *Width:* The greatest distance between the lateralmost projection of the surface that articulates with the (lateral) malleolus of the fibula to a point opposite on the surface that articulates with the tibia; the latter point is often found just anterior to the midpoint of the articular surface for the tibia (sliding caliper).

104. *Body height:* With the inferior surface of the bone lying on a flat surface (e.g. the vertical, permanent end of an osteometric board), the maximum measurement obtainable between the inferior and the highest elevation on the superior surface; the latter is often the medial rim of the facet for the tibia (osteometric board).

105. *Maximum length of the trochlea for the tibia:* Taken in the anteroposterior plane (sliding caliper).

106. *Maximum width of the trochlea for the tibia:* Taken at a right angle to the previous measurement (sliding caliper).

Metatarsals and Phalanges

107. *Maximum length:* (sliding caliper or osteometric board).

108. *Maximum width of proximal end:* (sliding caliper).

109. *Minimum dorsal-plantar width:* (sliding caliper).

110. *Minimum mediolateral width:* (sliding caliper).

Postcranial Indices

1. Scapular index = maximum breadth × 100/maximum length
   (Reflects relative squatness or narrowness of scapula; the higher the index, the broader the bone.)
2. Claviculohumeral index = max. clavicular length × 100/max. humeral length
   (Reflects breadth superiorly of the thorax relative to the length of the upper arm; the higher the index, the broader the thorax.)
3. Clavicular robustness (Robusticity, circumference:length) index = midclavicular circumference × 100/max. clavicular length
   (Reflects relative size of the shaft; the higher the index, the more robust the bone; (poor) indicator of sex.)
4. Robusticity index (humerus) = min. shaft circumference × 100/max. length
   (Reflects the relative size of the humeral shaft; the higher the index, the more robust the bone.)
5. Diaphyseal (shaft) index (humerus) = min. shaft diameter × 100/max. length
   (Reflects the relative size of the humeral shaft; the higher the index, the more robust the bone.)
6. Brachial (radiohumeral) index = max. radius length × 100/max. humerus length
   (Reflects the length of the forearm relative to the upper arm.)
7. Caliber index (ulna) = min. shaft circumference × 100/physiological length
   (Reflects the relative size of the shaft; the higher the index, the more robust the bone.)
8. Platymeric index (femur) = subtrochanteric sagittal diameter × 100/subtrochanteric transverse diameter
   (Reflects the degree to which the most proximal part of the femoral shaft is flattened or compressed anteroposteriorly.)

Platymeria (platymeric, flattened)	= <85.0
Eurymeria (eurymeric, moderate)	= 85.0–99.9
Stenomeria (stenomeric, rounded)	= >99.9

9. Robusticity index (femur) = (Mediolateral + anteroposterior diameters) × 100/bicondylar length
   (Reflects the relative size of the shaft; the higher the index, the more robust the bone.)
10. Pilastric index (femur) = anteroposterior diameter × 100/mediolateral diameter
    (Reflects relative development of the linea aspera; useful in determining sex.)
11. Intermembral index = (max. humeral + max. radial lengths) × 100/(max. femoral + max. tibial lengths)
    (Reflects the length of the upper limb relative to the lower limb; the higher the index, the longer the upper limb.)
12. Crural index = max. tibial length × 100/max. femoral length
    (Reflects the length of the lower leg relative to the thigh; the higher the index, the longer the lower leg.)
13. Humerofemoral index = max. humeral length × 100/max. femoral length
    (Reflects the length of the upper arm relative to the thigh; the higher the index, the longer the length of the upper arm.)
14. Platycnemic index (tibia) = mediolateral diameter × 100/anteroposterior diameter
    (Reflects the degree to which the most proximal part of the tibial shaft is flattened in an anteroposterior direction.)

    | Hyperplatycnemia (hyperplatycnemic, extremely flat) | = <55.0 |
    | Platycnemia (platycnemic, very flat) | = 55.0–62.9 |
    | Mesocnemia (mesocnemic, moderately flat) | = 63.0–69.9 |
    | Eurycnemia (eurycnemic, broad, wide) | = >69.9 |

15. Vertebral index = posterior body height × 100/anterior body height
    (Reflects the relative uniform thickness of a vertebra; the higher the index, the more compressed the body is anteriorly.)

16. Sacral (breadth) index = sacral breadth × 100/sacral length
    [Reflects the breadth (maximum anterior breadth) of the sacrum relative to its length (maximum anterior height); the higher the index, the broader the sacrum; historically, used in analyzing "race" (see below, from Wilder and Wentworth, 1918) and sex.]

	Female (Average)	Male (Average)
Egyptian	99.1	94.3
Andaman	103.4	94.8
African	103.6	91.4
Japanese	107.1	101.5
Australian	110.0	100.2
European	112.4	102.9

17. Ischiopubic index = pubic length × 100/ischial length
    (Reflects the length of the pubis relative to the ischium; used in determining sex, with female indices being on average 15% higher than those of males.)

American Whites		African Americans	
Male	= <90.0	Male	= <84.0
Indeterminate	= 90.0–95.0	Indeterminate	= 84.0–88.0
Female	= >95.0	Female	= >88.0

18. Pelvic brim index = anteroposterior height × 100/transverse diameter
    (Reflects the relative size of the pelvic cavity.) Classification according to Turner (1886):

Platypellic (transversely flattened pelvic cavity)	= <90.0
Mesatipellic (intermediate)	= 90.0–94.9
Dolichopellic (long anteroposteriorly)	= >94.9

According to Clyne (1963, cited in Clemente, 1984):

	Average
Platypelloid (platypellic)	59.2
Android (brachypellic)	78.1
Gynaecoid (mesatipellic)	78.9
Anthropoid (dolichopellic)	90.8

19. Acetabulum-pubic index = acetabular diameter × 100/pubic length
    (Used in determining sex.)

American Whites	
Males	= >71
Females	= <70

20. Sciatic notch–acetabular index = sciatic notch width × 100/acetabular diameter
    (Used in determining sex.)

American Whites		African Americans		Native Americans	
Males	= <87.0	Males	= <87.6	Males	= <87.0
Females	= >87.0	Females	= >87.6	Females	= >87.0

21. Calcaneal load index = load arm width × 100/load arm length
    (Reflects the relative bulk of the anterior segment of the calcaneus.)

22. Calcaneal length index = load arm length $\times$ 100/max. length
(Reflects the length of the anterior element relative to the total length of the bone; used most often in studies on locomotory differences among different species.)

23. Stature: Given the pitfalls of such reconstructions, the reader is referred to Krogman and İşcan (1986, pp. 302–351).

Comparative Osteology: Human, Deer, Bear, Pig

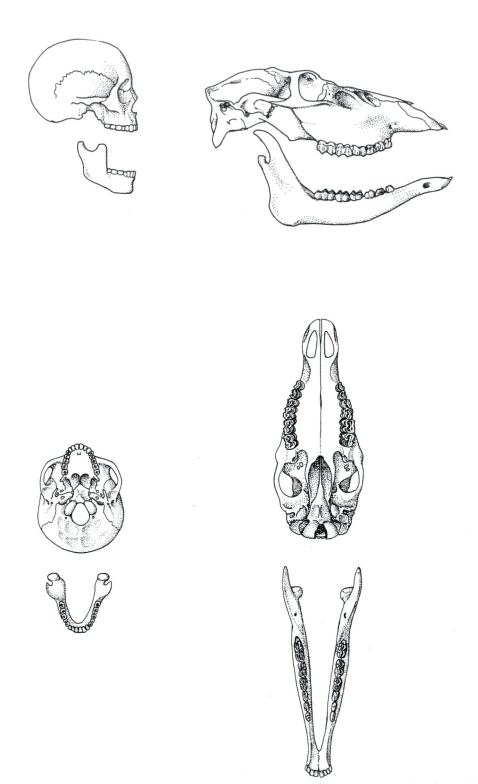

Figure H–1 Comparison of skulls of *(from left to right)* a human, a caribou [representative of a cervid (deer), which is a ruminating, "cloven-hooved" artiodactyl], a bear (representative of a carnivore), and a pig (a suid, which is a nonruminating, non-"cloven-hooved" artiodactyl): *(top row)* lateral view, *(bottom row)* occlusal view.

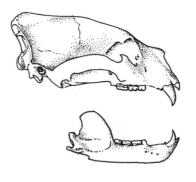

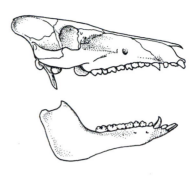

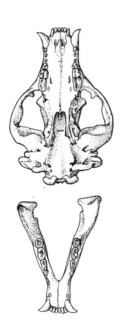

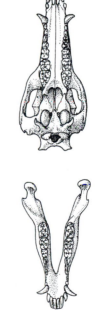

Figure H–1 (continued)

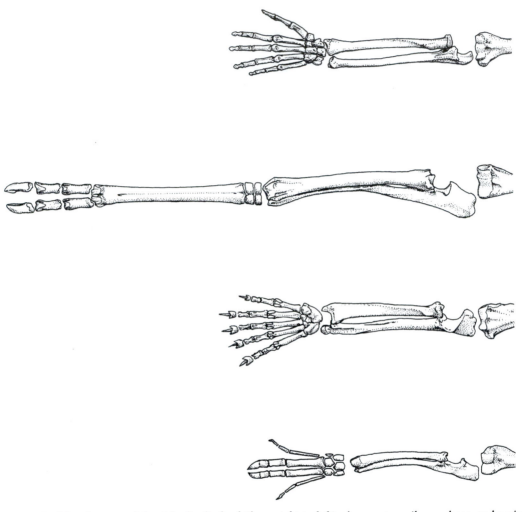

Figure H–2 The elements of the right forelimb of *(from right to left)* a human, a caribou, a bear, and a pig.

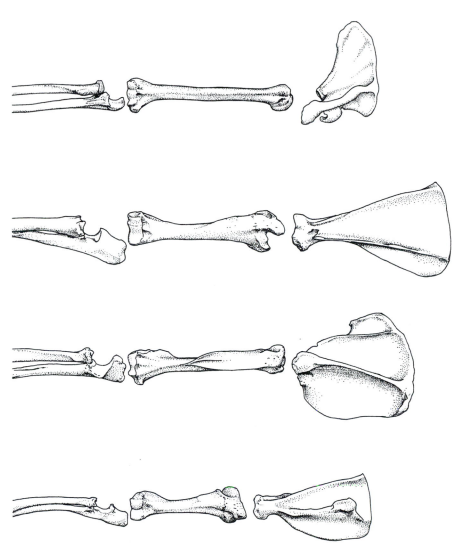

Figure H–2 (continued)

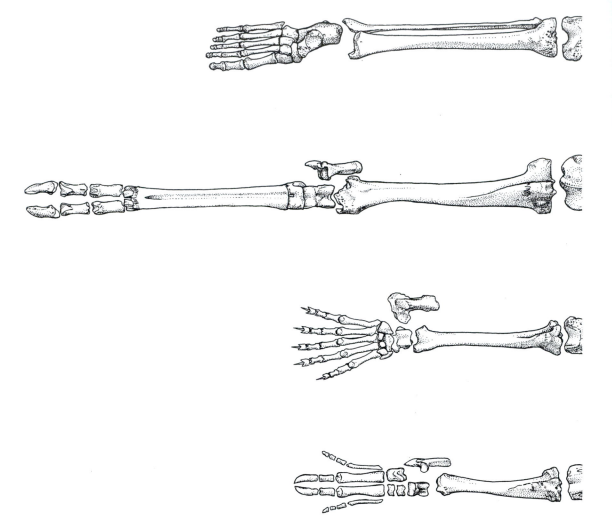

Figure H–3 The sacrum, right os coxa, and elements of the right hindlimb of *(from right to left)* a human, a caribou, a bear, and a pig.

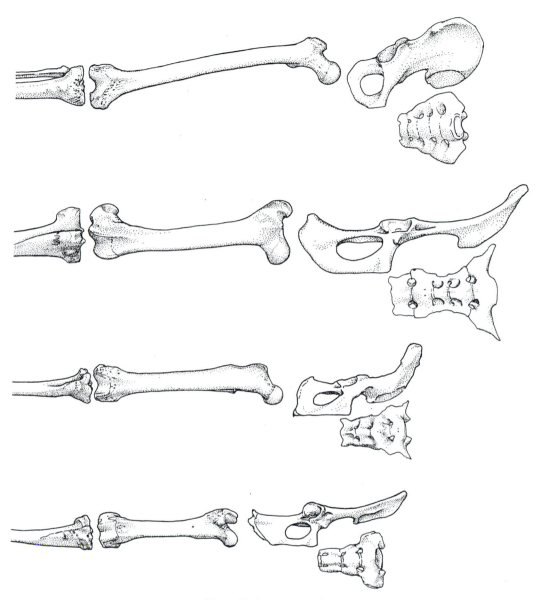

Figure H–3 (continued)

References

Acsádi, Gy., and Nemeskéri, J. 1970. *History of Human Life Span and Mortality.* Budapest: Akademiai Kiado.

Ahlqvist, J., and Damsten, O. 1969. Modification of Kerley's method for the microscopic determination of age in human bone. *J Forensic Sci* 14:205–212.

Andersen, H., and Matthiessen, M. 1967. Histochemistry of the early development of the human central face and nasal cavity with special reference to the movements and fusion of the palatine processes. *Acta Anat* 68:483–508.

Angel, J. L. 1953. The human remains from Khirokitia, in P. Dikaios (ed.): *Khirokitia, Final Report.* Nicosia: Cyrpus Department of Antiquities, pp. 416–430.

Angel, J. L., Suchey, J. M., İşcan, M.Y., and Zimmerman, M. R. 1986. Age at death from the skeleton and viscera, in M. R. Zimmerman and J. L. Angel (eds.): *Dating and Age Determination in Biological Materials.* London: Croom Helm, pp. 179–220.

Bedford, M. E., Russell, K. F., Lovejoy, C. O., Meindl, R. S., Simpson, S. W., and Stuart-Macadam, P. L. 1993. Test of the multifactorial aging method using skeletons with known ages-at-death from the Grant Collection. *Am J Phys Anthropol* 91:287–297.

Berkovitz, B. K. B., and Thomson, P. 1973. Observations on the aetiology of supernumerary upper incisors in the albino ferret *(Mustela putorious). Arch Oral Biol* 18:457–463.

Berry, R. J. 1968. The biology of non-metrical variation in mice and men, in D. R. Brothwell (ed.): *The Skeletal Biology of Earlier Human Populations.* Oxford: Pergamon, pp. 103–133.

Blumberg, J. M., and Kerley, E. R. 1966. Discussion: A critical consideration of roentgenology and microscopy in palaeopathology, in S. Jarcho (ed.): *Human Palaeopathology.* New Haven, CT: Yale University Press, pp. 150–170.

Bouvier, M., and Ubelaker, D. 1977. A comparison of two methods for the microscopic determination of age at death. *Am J Phys Anthropol* 46:391–394.

Boyd, A. 1971. Comparative histology of mammalian teeth, in A. A. Dahlberg (ed.): *Dental Morphology and Evolution.* Chicago: University of Chicago Press, pp. 81–94.

Brooks, S. T. 1955. Skeletal age at death: The reliability of cranial and pubic age indicators. Am J Phys Anthropol *13:567–597.*

Brothwell, D. R. 1972. *Digging Up Bones,* 2nd ed. London: British Museum (Natural History).

Brown, W. A. B., Molleson, T. I., and Chinn, S. 1984. Enlargement of the frontal sinus. *Ann Hum Biol* 11:221–226.

Buikstra, J. E. 1976. The Caribou Eskimo: general and specific disease. American Journal of Physical Anthropology, *45:* 351-368.

Butler, P. M. 1939. Studies of the mammalian dentition: Differentiation of the postcanine dentition. *Proc Zool Soc Lond* 109:1–36.

Butler, P. M. 1978. The ontogeny of mammalian heterodonty. *J Biol Buccale* 6:217–227.

Campbell, T. B. 1939. Food, food values and food habits of the Australian aborigines in relation to their dental conditions: Part V. *Aust J Dent* 43:177–199.

Carbonell, V. M. 1963. Variations in the frequency of shovel-shaped incisors in different populations, in D. R. Brothwell (ed.): *Dental Anthropology.* New York: Macmillan, pp. 211–234.

Carter, W., Butterworth, B., Carter, J., and Carter, J. 1987. *Ethnodentistry and Dental Folklore.* Kansas City: Dental Folklore Books.

Cinák, R. 1972. *Ontogenesis of the Skeleton and Intrinsic Muscles of the Human Hand and Foot.* New York: Springer-Verlag.

Clark, W. E. LeGros. 1966. *The Fossil Evidence for Human Evolution,* 2nd ed. Chicago: University of Chicago Press.

Clarke, N. G., and Hirsch, R. S. 1991. Physiological, pulpal, and periodontal factors influencing alveolar bone, in M. A. Kelley and C. S. Larsen (eds.): *Advances in Dental Anthropology.* New York: Wiley-Liss, pp. 241–266.

Clemente, C. D. 1984. *Gray's Anatomy,* 30th American ed. Philadelphia: Lea & Febiger.

Cruwys, E. 1988. Morphological variation and wear in teeth of Canadian and Greenland Inuit. *Polar Rec* 24:293–298.

Dahlberg, A. A. 1949. The dentition of the American Indian, in W. S. Laughlin (ed.): *Papers on the Physical Anthropology of the American Indian.* New York: Viking Fund, pp. 138–176.

Davies, D. M. 1972. *The Influence of Teeth, Diet, and Habits on the Human Face.* London: William Heinemann.

Demirjian, A. 1980. Dental development: a measure of physical maturity, in F. E. Johnston and A. F. Roche (eds.): *Human Physical Growth and Maturation: Methodologies and Factors.* New York: Plenum Press, pp. 83–100.

Falk, D., and Conroy, G. C. 1983. The cranial venous sinus system in *Australopithecus afarensis. Nature* 306:779–781.

Fazekas, I. Gy., and Kósa, F. 1979. *Forensic Fetal Osteology.* Budapest: Akademiai Kiado.

Finnegan, M. 1978. Non-metric variation of the infracranial skeleton. *J Anat* 125:23–37.

Flecker, H. 1942. Time of appearance and fusion of ossification centers as observed by roentgenographic methods. *J Roentgenol Radium Ther* 47:97–157.

Frost, H. M. 1987a. Secondary osteon populations: An algorithm for determining mean bone tissue age. *Yearbook Phys Anthropol* 30:221–238.

Frost, H. M. 1987b. Secondary osteon population densities: An algorithm for estimating the missing osteons. *Yearbook Phys Anthropol* 30:239–254.

Gans, C., and Northcutt, R. G. 1983. Neural crest and the origin of vertebrates: A new head. *Science* 220:268–274.

Garn, S. M., Silverman, F. N., Hertzog, K. P., and Rohmann, C. G. 1968. Lines and bands of increased density: Their implications to growth and development. *Med Radiogr Photogr* 44:58–88.

Gilbert, B. M., and McKern, T. W. 1973. A method of aging the female os pubis. *Am J Phys Anthropol* 38:31–38.

Giles, E. 1970. Discriminant function sexing of the human skeleton, in T. D. Stewart (ed.): *Personal Identification in Mass Disasters.* Washington, DC: National Museum of Natural History, Smithsonian Institution, pp. 99–107.

Glasstone, S. 1967. Morphodifferentiation of teeth in embryonic mandibular segments in tissue culture. *J Dent Res* 46:611–614.

Goodman, A. H., and Armelagos, G. J. 1985. Factors affecting the distribution of enamel hypoplasias within the human permanent dentition. *Am J Phys Anthropol* 68:479–493.

Goodman, A. H., and Rose, J. C. 1991. Dental enamel hypoplasias as indicators of nutritional status, in M. A. Kelley and C. S. Larlsen (eds.): *Advances in Dental Anthropology.* New York: Wiley-Liss, pp. 279–293.

Grüneberg, H. 1963. *The Pathology of Development.* New York: Wiley.

Gustafson, G. 1950. Age determination on teeth. *J Am Dent Assoc* 41:45–54.

Hall, B. K. 1988. The embryonic development of bone. *Am Sci* 76:174–181.

Hancock, R. G. V., Grynpas, M. D., and Pritzker, K. P. H. 1989. The abuse of bone analyses for achaeological dietary studies. *Archaeometry, 31:*169–179.

Hanihara, K. 1959 (Sex diagnosis of Japanese skulls and scapulae by means of discriminant function [in Japanese with English summary].) *Zinruigaku Zassi (J Anthropol Soc,* Nippon) 67:191–197.

Harris, H. A. 1926. The growth of the long bones in childhood, with special reference to certain bony striations of the metaphysis and the role of vitamins. *Arch Intern Med* 38:785–806.

Harris, H. A. 1931. Lines of arrested growth in the long bones in childhood: Correlation of histological and radiographic appearances. *Br J Radiol* 4:561–588.

Hershkovitz, P. 1977. *Living New World Monkeys (Platyrrhini) with an Introduction to the Primates.* Vol. 1. Chicago: University of Chicago Press.

Hillson, S. 1986. *Teeth.* Cambridge: Cambridge University Press.

Howells, W. W. 1973. *Evolution of the Genus* Homo. Reading, MA: Addison-Wesley.

Hunt, E. H., Jr., and Hatch, J. W. 1981. The estimation of age at death and ages of formation of transverse lines from measurements of human long bones. *Am J Phys Anthropol* 54:461–469.

İşcan, M. Y. and Helmer, R. P. (eds.) 1993. *Forensic Analysis of the Skull: Caniofacial analysis, reconstruction, and identification.* New York: Wiley-Liss.

İşcan, M. Y., and Loth, S. R. 1986. Estimation of age and determination of sex from the sternal rib, in K. J. Reichs (ed.): *Forensic Osteology.* Springfield, IL: Charles C Thomas, pp. 68–89.

İşcan, M. Y., and Loth, S. R. 1989. Osteological manifestations of age in the adult, in M. Y. İşcan and K. A. R. Kennedy (eds.): *Reconstruction of Life from the Skeleton.* New York: Alan R. Liss, pp. 23–40.

İşcan, M. Y., Loth, S. R., and Wright, R. K. 1984a. Metamorphosis at the sternal rib end: A new method to estimate age at death in white males. *Am J Phys Anthropol* 65:147–156.

İşcan, M. Y., Loth, S. R., and Wright, R. K. 1984b. Age estimation from the rib by phase analysis: White males. *J Forensic Sci* 29:1094–1104.

İşcan, M. Y., Loth, S. R., and Wright, R. K. 1985. Age estimation from the rib by phase analysis: White females. *J Forensic Sci* 30:853–863.

İşcan, M. Y., Loth, S. R., and Wright, R. K.1987. Racial variation in the sternal extremity of the rib and its effect on age determination. *J Forensic Sci* 32:452–466.

Johnston, F. E. 1961. Sequence of epiphyseal union in a prehistoric Kentucky population from Indian Knoll. *Hum Biol 33*:66–81.

Katayama, K. 1988. Geographic distribution of auditory exostoses in South Pacific human populations. *Man and Culture in Oceania 4*:63–74.

Katzenberg, M. A. 1992. Advances in stable isotope analysis of prehistoric bones, in S. R. Saunders and M. A. Katzenberg (eds.): *Skeletal Biology of Past Peoples: Research Methods* New York: Wiley-Liss, pp. 105–119.

Kay, R. F. 1977. The evolution of molar occlusion in the Cercopithecidae and early catarrhines. *Am J Phys Anthropol 46*:327–352.

Kelley, M. A. 1989. Infectious disease, in M. Y. İşcan and K. A. R. Kennedy (eds.): *Reconstruction of Life from the Skeleton*. New York: Alan R. Liss, pp. 191–199.

Kennedy, K. A. R. 1989. Skeletal markers of occupational stress, in M. Y. İşcan and K. A. R. Kennedy (eds.): *Reconstruction of Life from the Skeleton*. New York: Alan R. Liss, pp. 129–160.

Kerley, E. R. 1965. The microscopic determination of age in human bone. *Am J Phys Anthropol 23*:149–163.

Kerley, E. R. 1970. Estimation of skeletal age: After about age 30, in T. D. Stewart (ed.): *Personal Identification in Mass Disasters*. Washington, D.C.: National Museum of Natural History, Smithsonian Institution, pp. 57–70.

Kerley, E. R., and Ubelaker, D. H. 1978. Revisions in the microscopic method of estimating age at death in human cortical bone. *Am J Phys Anthropol 49*:545–546.

Klepinger, L. L. 1992. Innovative approaches to the study of past human health and subsistence strategies, in S. R. Saunders and M. A. Katzenberg (eds.): *Skeletal Biology of Past Peoples: research Methods*. New York: Wiley-Liss, pp. 121–130.

Kollar, E. J., and Baird, G. R. 1971. Tissue interactions in developing mouse tooth germs, in A. A. Dahlberg (ed.): *Dental Morphology and Evolution*. Chicago: University of Chicago Press, pp. 15–29.

Kollar, E. J., and Fisher, C. 1980. Tooth induction in chick epithelium: Expression of quiescent genes for enamel synthesis. *Science 207*:993–995.

Kovacs, I. 1971. A systematic descripton of dental roots, in A. A. Dahlberg (ed.): *Dental Morphology and Evolution*. Chicago: University of Chicago Press, pp. 211–256.

Krogman, W. M. 1962. The *Human Skeleton in Forensic Medicine*. Springfield, IL: Charles C Thomas.

Krogman, W. M., and İşcan, M. Y. 1986. *The Human Skeleton in Forensic Medicine,* 2nd ed. Springfield, IL: Charles C Thomas.

Kronfeld, R. 1954. Development and calcification of the human deciduous and permanent dentition, in *Basic Reading on the Identification of Human Skeletons*. New York: Wenner-Gren Foundation, pp. 3–11.

Laughlin, W. S., Harper, A. B., and Thompson, D. D. 1979. New approaches to the pre- and post-contact history of Arctic peoples. *Am J Phys Anthropol 51*:579–588.

Lester, C., and Shapiro, H. 1968. Vertebral defects in the lumbar vertebrae of prehistoric American Eskimos. *Am J Phys Anthropol 28*:43–48.

Loth, S. R., and İşcan, M. Y. 1987. The effect of racial variation on sex determination from the sternal rib (abstract). *Am J Phys Anthropol 72*:227.

Lovejoy, C. O. 1985. Dental wear in the Libben population: Its functional pattern and role in the determination of adult skeletal age at death. *Am J Phys Anthropol 68*:47–56.

Lovejoy, C. O., Meindl, R. S., Mensforth, R. P. and Barton, T. J. 1985a. Multifactorial determination of skeletal age at death: A method and blind tests of its accuracy. *Am J Phys Anthropol 68*:1–14.

Lovejoy, C. O., Meindl, R. S., Pryzbeck, T. R., and Mensforth, R. P. 1985b. Chronological metamorphosis of the auricular surface of the ilium: A new method for the determination of adult skeletal age at death. *Am J Phys Anthropol 68*:15–28.

Lukacs, J. R. 1989. Dental paleopathology: Methods for reconstructing dietary patterns, in M. Y. İşcan and K. A. R. Kennedy (eds.): *Reconstruction of Life from the Skeleton*. New York: Alan R. Liss, pp. 261–286.

Lumsden, A. G. S. 1979. Pattern formation in the molar dentition of the mouse. *J Biol Buccale 7*:77–103.

Lumsden, A. G. S. 1980. The developing innervation of the lower jaw and its relation to the formation of tooth germs in mouse embryos, in B. Kurtén (ed.): *Teeth: Form, Function, and Evolution*. New York: Columbia University Press, pp. 32–43.

Lumsden, A. G. S. 1988. Spatial organization of the epithelium and the role of neural crest cells in the initiation of the mammalian tooth germ. *Development 103* (Suppl):155–169.

Lunt, D. A. 1978. Molar Attrition in Medieval Danes, in P. M. Butler and K. A. Joysey (eds.): *Development, Function, and Evolution of Teeth*. New York: Academic Press, pp. 465–482.

McHenry, H., and Schulz, P. 1976. The association between Harris lines and enamel hypoplasias in prehistoric California Indians. *Am J Phys Anthropol 44*:507–512.

McKern, T. W., and Stewart, T. D. 1957. Skeletal age changes in young American males. Natick, MA: Quartermaster Research and Development Command, Technical Report EP-45.

McLean, F. C., and Urist, M. R. 1964. *Bone:* An introduction to the physiology of skeletal tissue, 2nd ed. Chicago: The University of Chicago Press.

Meindl, R. S., and Lovejoy, C. O. 1985. Ectocranial suture closure: A revised method for the determination of skeletal age at death based on the lateral-anterior sutures. *Am J Phys Anthropol 68*:57–66.

Meindl, R. S., Lovejoy, C. O., Mensforth, R. P., and Walker, R. A. 1985. A revised method of age determination using the os pubis, with a review and tests of accuracy of other current methods of pubic symphyseal aging. *Am J Phys Anthropol* 68:29–45.

Melton, D. A. 1991. Pattern formation during animal development. *Science* 252:234–241.

Mensforth, R. P., Lovejoy, C. O., Lallo, J. W., and Armelagos, G. J. 1978. The role of constitutional factors, diet, and infectious disease in the etiology of porotic hyperostosis and periosteal reactions in prehistoric infants and children. *Med Anthropol* 2:1–59.

Merbs, C. F. 1989. Trauma, in M. Y. İşcan and K. A. R. Kennedy (eds.): *Reconstruction of Life from the Skeleton*. New York: Alan R. Liss, pp. 161–189.

Miles, A. E. W. 1963. Dentition in the assessment of individual age, in D. Brothwell (ed.): *Dental Anthropology*. New York: Macmillan, pp. 191–209.

Miller, W. A. 1971. Early dental development in mice, in A. A. Dahlberg (ed.): *Dental Morphology and Evolution*. Chicago: University of Chicago Press, pp. 31–43.

Molnar, S. 1971. Human tooth wear, tooth function and cultural variability. *Am J Phys Anthropol* 34:175–190.

Moore, K. L. 1974. The Developing Human: Clinically Oriented Embryology. Philadelphia: W. B. Saunders.

Moorrees, C. F. A. 1957. *The Aleut Dentition: A Correlative Study of Dental Characteristics in an Eskimoid People*. Cambridge, MA: Harvard University Press.

Moorrees, C. F. A., Fanning, E. A., and Hunt, E. E., Jr. 1963a. Formation and resorption of three deciduous teeth in children. *Am J Phys Anthropol* 21:205–213.

Moorrees, C. F. A., Fanning, E. A., and Hunt, E. E., Jr. 1963b. Age variation of formation stages for ten permanent teeth. *J Dent Res* 42:1490–1502.

Morse, D. 1978. *Ancient Disease in the Midwest*. Springfield, IL: Illinois State Museum.

Moyers, R. E. 1959. Le stade moyen de calcification est indique pour chaque dent selon les 10 stades de calcification de la table de Nolla. *Rev. Odontostomat (Bordeaux)* 9:1424–1433.

Murray, K. A., and Murray, S. A. 1989. Computer software for hypoplasia analysis. *Am J Phys Anthropol* 78:277–278.

Nery, E. B., Kraus, B. S., and Croup, M. 1970. Timing and topography of early human tooth development. *Arch Oral Biol* 15:1315–1326.

Netter, F. H. and Crelin, E. S. 1987. *The CIBA Collection of Medical Illustrations*. Vol. 8: *Musculoskeletal System*, Part I, *Anatomy, Physiology and Metabolic Disorders*, Section II, *Embryology*. Summit, NJ: CIBA-GEIGY Corp.

Nomina Anatomica 5th ed. 1983. Baltimore: Williams & Wilkins.

Neumann, G. K. 1942. Types of artificial cranial deformation in the Eastern United States. *Am Antiq* 7:306–310.

Olivier, G. 1960. *Pratique Anthropologique*. Paris: Vigot.

Ooë, T. 1956. On the development of position of the tooth germs in the human deciduous front teeth. *Okajimas Folia Anat Jpn* 28:317–340.

Ooë, T. 1957. On the early development of human dental lamina. *Okajimas Folia Anat Jpn* 30:197–211.

Ooë, T. 1965. A study of the ontogenetic origin of human permanent tooth germs. *Okajimas Folia Anat Jpn* 40:429–437.

Ooë, T. 1969. Epithelial anlagen of human third dentition and their migrations in the mandible and maxilla. *Okajimas Folia Anat Jpn* 46:243–251.

Ooë, T. 1971. Three instances of supernumerary tooth germs observed with serial sections of human foetal jaws. *Z Anat Entw Gesch* 135:202–209.

Ooë, T. 1979. Development of the human first and second permanent molar, with special reference to the distal portion of the dental lamina. *Anat Embryol* 155:221–240.

Ortner, D. J., and Putschar, W. G. J. 1981. *Identification of Pathological Conditions in Human Skeletal Remains*. Washington, D.C.: Smithsonian Institution Press.

Osborn, J. W. 1971. New approach to Zahnreihen. *Nature* 225:343–346.

Osborn, J. W. 1971. The ontogeny of tooth succession in *Lacerta vivipara* Jacquin (1787). *Proc R Soc Lond B*179:261–289.

Osborn, J. W. 1973. The evolution of dentitions. *Am Sci* 61:548–559.

Osborn, J. W. 1978. Morphologenetic gradients: Fields versus clones, in P. M. Butler and K. A. Joysey (eds.): *Development, Function, and Evolution of Teeth*. New York: Academic Press, pp. 171–201.

Ossenberg, N. S. 1969. Discontinuous morphological variation in the human cranium. University of Toronto, Ph.D. thesis.

Ossenberg, N. S. 1970. The influence of artificial cranial deformation on discontinuous morphological traits. *Am J Phys Anthropol* 33:357–372.

Ossenberg, N. S. 1976. Within and between race distances in population studies based on discrete traits of the human skull. *Am J Phys Anthropol* 45:701–716.

Parfitt, A. M. 1983. The physiologic and clinical significance of bone histomorphometric data, in R. R. Recker (ed.): *Bone Histomorphometry: Techniques and Interpretation*. Boca Raton, FL: CRC Press, pp. 143–223.

Patterson, B. 1956. Early Cretaceous mammals and the evolution of mammalian molar teeth. *Fieldiana* 3:1–105.

Price, T. D. (ed.) 1989. *The Chemistry of Prehistoric Human Bone*. Cambridge: Cambridge University Press.

Putschar, W. G. J. 1966. Problems in the pathology and palaeopathology of bone, in S. Jarcho (ed.): *Human Palaeopathology*. New Haven, CT: Yale University Press, pp. 57–63.

Redfield, A. 1970. A new aid to aging immature skeletons: Development of the occipital bone. *Am J Phys Anthropol* 33:207–220.

Resnick, D., and Niwayama, G. 1988. *Diagnosis of Bone and Joint Disorders*. Philadelphia: W. B. Saunders.

Romero, J. 1970. Dental mutilation, trephination, and cranial deformation, in T. D. Stewart (ed.): *Handbook of Middle American Indians*, Vol. 9. Austin: University of Texas Press, pp. 50–67.

Rothschild, B. M., and Martin, L. D. 1993. *Paleopathology: disease in the fossil record*. Boca Raton, FL: CRC Press.

Russell, K. F., Simpson, S. W., Genovese, J., Kinkel, M. D., Meindl, R. S., and Lovejoy, C. O. 1993. Independent test of the fourth rib aging technique. *Am J Phys Anthropol* 92:53–62.

St. Hoyme, L. E., and İşcan, M. Y. 1989. Determination of sex and race: Accuracy and assumptions, in M. Y. Iscan and K. A. R. Kennedy (eds.): *Reconstruction of Life from the Skeleton*. New York: Alan R. Liss, pp. 53–93.

Sandford, M. K. 1992. A reconsideration of trace element analysis in prehistoric bone, in S. R. Saunders and M. A. Katzenberg (eds.): *Skeletal Biology of Past Peoples: Research Methods*. New York: Wiley-Liss, pp. 79–103.

Santa Luca, A. P. 1978. A re-examination of presumed Neandertal-like fossils. *J Hum Evol* 7:619–636.

Saunders, S. R. 1978. *The Development and Distribution of Discontinuous Morphological Variation of the Human Infracranial Skeleton*. Ottowa: National Museums of Canada, Archaeological Survey of Canada, Paper No. 81.

Saunders, S. R. 1989. Nonmetric skeletal variation, in M. Y. İşcan and K. A. R. Kennedy (eds.): *Reconstruction of Life from the Skeleton*. New York: Alan R. Liss, pp. 95–108.

Schranz, D. 1959. Kritik der Auswertung der Altersbestimmungsmerkmale van Zähnen und Knochen. *Dtsch Z Ges Gerichtl Med* 48:562–575.

Schultz, A. H. 1936. Characters common to higher primates and characters specific for man. *Quart Rev Biol* 11:259–283, 425–455.

Schutkowski, H. 1993. Sex determination of infant and juvenile skeletons: I. Morphognostic features. *Am J Phys Anthropol* 90:199–205.

Schwartz, J. H. 1974. The human remains from Kition and Hala Sultan Tekke: a cultural interpretation, in V. Karageorghis (ed.): *Excavations at Kition*. Vol. I *The Tombs*. Nicosia: Cyprus Department of Antiquities, pp. 151–162.

Schwartz, J. H. 1980. Morphological approach to heterodonty and homology, in B. Kurtén (ed.): *Teeth: Form, Function, and Evolution*. New York: Columbia University Press, pp. 123–144.

Schwartz, J. H. 1982. Dentofacial growth and development in *Homo sapiens*: Evidence from perinatal individuals from Punic Carthage. *Anat Anz Jena* 152:1–26.

Schwartz, J. H. 1984. Supernumerary teeth in anthropoid primates and models of tooth development. *Arch Oral Biol* 29:833–842.

Schwartz, J 1986. Primate systematics and a classification of the order, in D. R. Swindler and J. Erwin (eds.): *Comparative Primate Biology*. Vol. 1. *Systematics, Evolution, and Anatomy*. New York: Alan R. Liss, pp. 1–41.

Schwartz, J. H., and Langdon, H. 1991. Innervation of the human upper primary dentition: Implications for understanding tooth initiation and rethinking growth and eruption patterns. *Am J Phys Anthropol* 86:273–286.

Scott, G. R. 1972. An analysis of population and family data on Carabelli's trait and shovel-shaped incisors (abstract). *Am J Phys Anthropol* 37:449.

Scott, G. R., and Dahlberg, A. A. 1980. Microdifferentiation in tooth crown morphology among Indians of the American Southwest, in B. Kurtén (ed.): *Teeth: Form, Function, and Evolution*. New York: Columbia University Press, pp. 259–291.

Singer, R. 1953. Estimation of age from cranial suture closure. *J Forensic Med* 1:52–59.

Skinner, M., and Goodman, A. H. 1992. Anthropological uses of developmental defects of enamel, in S. R. Saunders and M. A. Katzenberg (eds.): *Skeletal Biology of Past Peoples: Research Methods*. New York: Wiley-Liss, pp. 153–174.

Smith, B. H. 1991. Standards of human tooth formation and dental age assessment, in M. A. Kelley and C. S. Larsen (eds.): *Advances in Dental Anthropology*. New York: Wiley-Liss, pp. 143–168.

Steinberg, E. F. 1994. Ancón, Peru: The enigma of porotic hyperostosis. Paper presented at the 13th annual Northeast Andean Conference, Ithaca, N.Y.

Stewart, T. D. 1934. Sequence of epiphyseal union, third molar eruption and suture closure in Eskimos and American Indians. *Am of J Phys Anthropol* 19:433–452.

Stewart, T. D. 1958. The rate of development of vertebral osteoarthritis in American whites and its significance in skeletal age identification. *Leech* 28:114–151.

Stewart, T. D. 1940. Some historical implications of physical anthropology in North America. Smith Inst, Misc Coll 100:15–50.

Stewart, T. D. 1965. The problem of analyzing the height of the cranial vault. Homenaje a Juan Comas en su 65 Aniversario 2:359–366.

Stewart, T. D. 1979. *Essential of Forensic Anthropology: Especially as Developed in the United States*. Springfield, IL: Charles C Thomas.

Stewart, T. D., and McCormick, W. F. 1983. The gender predictive value of sternal length. *Am J Forensic Med Pathol* 4:217–220.

Stout, S. D. 1989. Histomorphometric analysis of human skeletal remains, in M. Y. İşcan and K. A. R. Kennedy (eds.): *Reconstruction of Life from the Skeleton*. New York: Alan R. Liss, pp. 41–52.

Stout, S. D. and Paine, R. R. 1992. Histological age estimation using rib and clavicle. *Am J Phys Anthropol* 87:111–115.

Stout, S. D., and Paine, R. R. 1994. Bone remodeling rates: A test of an algorithm for estimating missing osteons. *Am J Phys Anthropol* 93:123–129.

Stout, S. D., and Teitelbaum, S. L. 1976. Histological analysis of undecalcified thin sections of archeological bone. *Am J Phys Anthropol* 44:263–267.

Stringer, C. B., Hublin, J. J., and Vandermeersch, B. 1984. The origin of anatomically modern humans in western Europe, in F. H. Smith and F. Spencer (eds.): *The Origins of Modern Humans: A World Survey of the Fossil Evidence.* New York: Alan R. Liss, pp. 51–135.

Stuart-Macadam, P. 1989. Porotic hyperostosis: relationship between orbital and vault lesions. *Am J Phys Anthropol* 80:187–193.

Swindler, D. R. 1976. *Dentition of Living Primates.* New York: Academic Press.

Swindler, D. R., and Olshan, A. F. 1988. Comparative and evolutionary aspects of the permanent dentition, in J. H. Schwartz (ed.): *Orang-utan Biology.* New York: Oxford University Press, pp. 271–282.

Tattersall, I. and Schwartz, J. H. 1991. Phylogeny and nomenclature in the "*Lemur*-group" of Malagasy strepsirhine primates. *Anthropol Papers Am Mus Nat Hist* no. 69: 1–18.

Ten Cate, A. R. 1989. Physiological tooth movement: Eruption, and shedding, in A. R. Ten Cate (ed.): *Oral Histology: Development, Structure, and Function.* St. Louis: C. V. Mosby, pp. 275–298.

Ten Cate, A. R., and Mills, C. 1972. The development of the periodontium: The origin of alveolar bone. *Anat Rec* 173:69.

Ten Cate, A. R., and Osborn, J. W. 1976. *Advanced Dental Histology,* 3rd ed. Bristol: John Wright & Sons Ltd.

Tobias, P. V. T. 1967. *Olduvai Gorge: Vol. 2. The Cranium and Maxillary Dentition of* Australopithecus (Zinjanthropus) boisei. Cambridge: Cambridge University Press.

Thompson, D. D. 1978. Age-related changes in osteon remodelling and bone mineralization. University of Connecticut, Ph.D. thesis.

Todd, T. W. 1920. Age changes in the pubic bone: I. The white male pubis. *Am J Phys Anthropol* 3:285–334.

Todd, T. W. 1930. Age changes in the pubic bone: VIII. Roentgenographic differentiation. *Am J Phys Anthropol* 14:255–271.

Todd, T. W., and Lyon, D. W., Jr. 1924. Endocranial suture closure: Its progress and age relationship. Part I. Adult males of white stock. *Am J Phys Anthropol* 7:324–384.

Todd, T. W., and Lyon, D. W., Jr. 1925a. Cranial suture closure: Its progress and age relationship. Part II. Ectocranial closure of adult males of white stock. *Am J Phys Anthropol* 8:23–43.

Todd, T. W., and Lyon, D. W., Jr. 1925b. Cranial suture closure: Its progress and age relationship. Part III. Endocranial suture closure of adult males of Negro stock. *Am J Phys Anthropol* 8:47–71.

Todd, T. W., and Lyon, D. W., Jr. 1925c. Cranial suture closure. Its progress and age relationship: Part IV. Ectocranial suture closure of adult males of Negro stock. *Am J Phys Anthropol* 8:149–168.

Tonge, C. H. 1976. Morphogenesis and development of teeth, in B. Cohen and I. R. H. Kramer (eds.): *Scientific Foundations of Dentistry.* London: William Heinemann Medical Books, pp. 325–334.

Turner, C. G. II. 1984. Advances in the dental search for Native American origins. *Acta Anthropol* 8:23–78.

Turner, W. 1886. The index of the pelvic brim as a basis of classification. *J Anat* 20:125–143.

Ubelaker, D. H. 1989. *Human Skeletal Remains,* 2nd ed. Washington, D.C.: Taraxacum.

Vallois, H. V. 1960. Vital statistics in prehistoric populations as determined from archaeological data, in R. F. Heizer and S. F. Cook (eds.): *The Application of Quantitative Methods in Archaeology.* Chicago: Quadrangle Books, pp. 186–204.

Vallois, H. V. 1965. Anthropometric techniques. *Curr Anthropol* 6:127–143.

Van Vark, G. N., and Schaafsma, W. 1992. Advances in the quantitative analysis of skeletal morphology, in S. R. Saunders and M. A. Katzenberg (eds.): *Skeletal Biology of Past Peoples: Research Methods.* New York: Wiley-Liss, pp. 225–257.

Weaver, D. S. 1979. Application of the likelihood ratio test to age estimation using the infant and child temporal bone. *Am J Phys Anthropol* 50:263–269.

Weisl, H. 1954. The articular surfaces of the sacro-iliac joint and their relation to movements of the sacrum. *Acta Anat* 22:1—14.

Wilder, H. H., and Wentworth, B. 1918. *Personal Identification: Methods for the Identification of Individuals, Living or Dead.* Boston: Gorham.

Winkler, L. A., Schwartz, J. H., and Swindler, D. R. 1991. Aspects of dental development in the orangutan prior to eruption of the permanent dentition. *Am J Phys Anthropol* 86:255–271.

Wood, J. W., Milner, G. R., Harpending, H. C., and Weiss, K. M. 1992. The osteological paradox: Problems in inferring prehistoric health from skeletal samples. *Curr Anthropol* 33:343–370.

Index